SOCIAL POLICY AND SOCIAL CHANGE

For Dan Jimenez

SOCIAL POLICY AND SOCIAL CHANGE
TOWARD THE CREATION OF SOCIAL AND ECONOMIC JUSTICE

JILLIAN JIMENEZ

California State University, Long Beach

Los Angeles | London | New Delhi
Singapore | Washington DC

For information:

SAGE Publications, Inc.
2455 Teller Road
Thousand Oaks, California 91320
E-mail: order@sagepub.com

SAGE Publications Ltd.
1 Oliver's Yard
55 City Road
London EC1Y 1SP
United Kingdom

SAGE Publications India Pvt. Ltd.
B 1/I 1 Mohan Cooperative Industrial Area
Mathura Road, New Delhi 110 044
India

SAGE Publications Asia-Pacific Pte. Ltd.
33 Pekin Street #02-01
Far East Square
Singapore 048763

Printed in the United States of America

Library of Congress Cataloging-in-Publication Data

Jimenez, Jillian.
Social policy and social change: Toward the creation of social and economic justice / Jillian Jimenez.
   p. cm.
Includes bibliographical references and index.
ISBN 978-1-4129-6048-9 (pbk.)
  1. United States—Social policy. 2. United States—Social conditions. 3. Social problems—United States. 4. Social service—United States. I. Title.

HN65.J56 2010
320.6—dc22

2009010778

Printed on acid-free paper.

10   11   12   13   10   9   8   7   6   5   4   3   2

Acquiring Editor:	Kassie Graves
Assistant Editor:	Leah Mori
Editorial Assistant:	Veronica Novak
Production Editor:	Sarah K. Quesenberry
Copy Editor:	Melinda Masson
Proofreader:	Theresa Kay
Indexer:	Will Ragsdale
Typesetter:	C&M Digitals (P) Ltd.
Cover Designer:	Candice Harman
Marketing Manager:	Stephanie Adams

Brief Contents

Detailed Contents

Acknowledgments

I would like to first thank David Gil, Professor of Social Policy at the Brandeis University Heller School, for his deep influence on my understanding of social problems and social policies. The vision of this book is directly due to his influence as a professor, dissertation advisor, and lifelong friend. He graciously allowed me to use an adapted version of his policy framework in the book.

I also owe a profound debt to my friend and colleague, Jo Ann Regan, University of South Carolina, who constructed all the graphs and charts in this textbook, utilizing her keen understanding of social policy issues along with her enormous talent in research and ability to conceptualize the complex issues in graphic forms.

John Oliver, Director of the Department of Social Work, secured time for me to complete the book and offered encouragement throughout. As another of David Gil's students, he shares my vision of a just society.

Marilyn Potts read parts of the manuscript and provided much support, as did Catherine Goodman, Natasha Elliot, and Susan Sragow. All encouraged me to write the book and stood by me through the various stages of excitement and frustration.

Dan Jimenez researched the vignettes and spent many hours writing them. He also read every chapter and gave me a great deal of very useful feedback. His commitment to social justice was forged at the Heller School, where we were both graduate students. I want to thank him for his contribution to this book as well as his significant contribution to my happiness and well-being over the years.

Kassie Graves was an outstanding editor at SAGE, offering intellectual guidance and support throughout the process of writing the book. The book was her idea, and I thank her for the faith she showed in me. Leah Mori found the photos for the book and did all the legwork to secure permission to use them. Sarah Quesenberry oversaw the production of the book with thoughtfulness and acumen. Melinda Masson did an outstanding job of copyediting, especially in refining the Internet citations.

I would like to thank the following reviewers who offered trenchant critiques and helpful additions to the book:

Tricia Bent-Goodley, Howard University

Linda Plitt Donaldson, Catholic University of America

Emma Gross, University of Utah

Robert Hudson, Boston University

Helen Morrow, Texas Tech University

Dianne Oakes, Binghamton University

Laurie E. Powers, Portland State University

Michael Reisch, University of Maryland

Steven R. Rose, George Mason University

Dorothy Van Soest, University of Washington

Robert Vernon, Indiana University School of Social Work

Finally I want to thank Nova Science, which allowed me to reprint part of my chapter (written with Ruth Chambers), "Children of Color in the Child Welfare System" (from *Child Welfare Issues and Perspectives,* ed. Steven J. Quintero, 2009), in Chapter 8 of this textbook.

CHAPTER

1

Introduction

This textbook analyzes key social problems and the social policies designed to address them in the United States. It focuses on the social problems and policies that have resonance for social work professionals who carry the commitment to social justice to neighborhoods, state legislatures, and national policy arenas across the country. Why do social workers need to know about social policy? Social policies are the frameworks that inform, limit, or advance social work practice and the goal of social justice. The goal of the book is to analyze the limitations of the social policies we have developed to solve social problems in the United States as well as to suggest new ideas for more socially just and equitable policies. Contemporary social policies will be linked to the historical values, the economic structure, and the legacy of discrimination in the United States, with the goal of promoting policy change that enhances our professional commitment to social and economic justice.

SOCIAL CONSTRUCTION OF SOCIAL PROBLEMS AND SOCIAL POLICIES ●

All social problems in the United States, along with our policy responses to them, are socially constructed; that is, they have been created by human beings in previous generations and continue to be held in place by our consent and our failure to act to change them. We are engaged in the social construction of reality throughout our lives, although most people do not recognize this process because they take the reality around them for granted. While all our reality, with the exception of a few biological and geographic imperatives, has been created by human beings who came before us, we may not recognize the human origin of our social and economic arrangements because they have been reified, or treated as though they exist outside of human creation. Instead they may seem necessary and even inevitable. For example, the educational system in the United States, depending as it does on lectures, absorption of material by students, and reflection back to instructors who will judge performance and offer certification, is a thoroughly socially constructed arrangement that evolved through historical contingency and may or may not be related to real learning. Does traditional academic education prepare social workers, for example, to work effectively with a wide variety of persons toward goals of social justice? Students, professors, and administrators in social work schools and departments across the country rarely ask such questions; instead they operate within the academic structure with little question and with ready compliance. All institutionalized education, not just social work, suffers from this same lack of critical thinking about the utility of our educational practices. Other social institutions, such as marriage, are also socially constructed by law and custom. While it is evident to all who approach marriage in the United States that it need not be a permanent arrangement, many brides and grooms still approach their weddings with what Berger and Luckman called the "reifying shudder of metaphysical dread" that suggests they believe that marriage is a permanent institution existing outside human creation from which they cannot escape.[1] Some of our reifications are seen as not only immutable but sacred, so suggesting revision in them elicits angry opposition. Witness the reaction to the prospect of gay and lesbian marriage in some quarters. Other socially created arrangements, including democracy and the market economy, are not only defended in the United States but thought to be far superior to other arrangements, a belief that has legitimized their exportation, sometimes under military force, to other areas of the world.

Socially constructed attitudes toward some groups have historically worked to their serious disadvantage in the United States; these social constructions include false narratives about African Americans, Latino immigrants, lesbians, gays, bisexuals, and transsexuals, as well as women. These reified beliefs about group differences were historically fashioned for reasons of social control; for many generations their ongoing viability was supported by the continual process of re-creation resting on the continued assent of many Americans. Only over the past 50 years has the socially constructed nature of these beliefs been revealed and subsequently rejected by others.

Even social problems that seem intractable are socially created arrangements that can be changed through collective will. Poverty and inequality are taken-for-granted conditions in the United States today. Few public policy movers or politicians pay any attention to the obstacles and suffering experienced by persons living in poverty. Yet poverty and much pernicious inequality could clearly be substantially reduced if not eliminated in the United States, if enough persons agreed that it should be. Just as poverty is socially constructed, so too are the problems of homelessness, marginalized housing, food insecurity, and inadequate health care and every problem social workers and their clients experience. Social policies such as welfare reform, the Social Security system, and the child welfare system are likewise socially constructed. What this means for social workers is that social problems can be reduced or eliminated and social policies can be changed. This is true even though these social policies have been reified and legitimized so thoroughly that few real alternatives are ever considered by policymakers. The recognition of the socially constructed nature of social problems and of social policies offers an empowering message to social workers, because with this insight we can see the possibility of new policies that would bring us closer to the goal of achieving social justice for our clients and for all members of society.

A THEORY OF SOCIAL PROBLEMS AND SOCIAL POLICIES ●

How are social problems created in the United States? The perspective of this — *culture* book is that in the United States social problems are created by the interaction of our *unique historical values and ideologies,* our *economic structure,* and our *legacy of discrimination against certain ethnic groups and women.* These three factors also inform and limit our policy solutions to these social problems. Without conscious awareness of the powerful role of these factors, we will find ourselves repeatedly replicating the same inequities and failures of previous social policies. Many other countries have an economic system that can be characterized as a market economy, where the government control of the forces of production, labor, capital, and credit is minimal and where private economic transactions are more or less freely made and express the will of individual economic actors. The U.S. economic system has produced great abundance at some times, as well as an unparalleled diversity of consumer goods, opportunities for great wealth accumulation, and technological innovation. Yet, as we have seen recently, our *economic system* has also led to economic insecurity, unemployment, and economic marginalization and suffering for many persons, whose number expands with the cycles of recession and depression. The natural cycles of the market economy and its negative byproducts of unemployment and poverty have been mitigated in many other industrialized countries through the creation of social welfare policies that seek to soften its negative impact. In the United States, a distinct set of *historical values and ideologies* has limited the number and impact of social welfare policies and served to delay their emergence. In this respect the United States is unique among industrialized countries in subjecting some of its citizens to unnecessary inequality and deprivation. The third factor that operates to create unique social problems and limit social policies in this country is our *legacy of discrimination* against certain ethnic groups and women as well as other marginalized groups. As a result of this discrimination, those suffering the worst effects of the inequities of the economic system are disproportionately ethnic groups and women.

These three factors—*our historical ideologies, our economic system,* and *our legacy of discrimination*—also inform and limit the *social policies* we have created to address our social problems. Each policy discussed in this book has limitations based on the interaction of these three factors. Each policy demonstrates the power of our historical ideologies and values, each policy reflects the inequities of the market economy, and each policy fails to meet the needs of groups who have been discriminated against.

The purpose of the analysis offered in this book is to liberate social workers from constricted ways of thinking that constrain us from seeing beyond the current realities when searching for policy solutions. New policy solutions will be offered, and students will be encouraged to develop their own policy models to reduce the disparities of our current ones.

● ORGANIZATION OF THE BOOK

This book has been designed for students of social work and related human services. This book will show how the interaction of historical ideologies, market capitalism, and forces of ethnic and gender oppression have operated together to cause many social problems in the United States and to limit the social policies designed to address them.

Chapters 1 and **2** will serve to introduce social workers to the study of social policies. In **Chapter 1** the premise of the book is laid out and its organization outlined. The assumption that reality is socially constructed is advanced, and the concept of social justice is discussed.

Chapter 2 examines the definition and meaning of social policy in the United States and discusses how social problems are identified and achieve the salience necessary to lead political actors to construct social policies. Broadly conceived, social policies include tax policy, farm policy, defense policy, and educational policy. Social welfare policy is a subset of the broader category of social policies. The dominant political ideologies in the United States—liberal, conservative, radical, and libertarian—are discussed in terms of their views about the relationship of government to individual liberty. Social policies emerge out of the struggle among various political ideologies about the proper role of government in individual life. The importance of policy analysis to social policy change and advocacy is discussed, and a framework for policy analysis is presented. The chapter concludes with a description of all the major social welfare policies in the United States.

The next four chapters are organized around the idea of *social justice.* **Chapters 3, 4,** and **5** will present the theoretical framework outlined in Chapter 1.

Chapter 3 will examine the most important historical values and ideologies contributing to social problems and informing social policies in the United States today. The historical origins of the belief in the value of hard work and wealth, self-reliance, and individualism are discussed, along with the belief in upward mobility, equal opportunity, and Social Darwinism. The salience of these ideologies for contemporary social policies in the United States is examined. The commitment to civil liberties outlined in the Bill of Rights is discussed as the basis for movements for equality and social justice. The idea of U.S. exceptionalism is explored: How and why are we different from other industrialized nations, and what impact does that difference have on our social policies?

Chapter 4 examines the ways the market economy has contributed to the creation of social problems, as well as to the limitations of current social policies designed to solve these problems. The philosophical foundations of the market economy are explored, along with the relationship of the market economy to poverty. The ideal operations of the market economy are contrasted with the actual workings of the market economy in the United States. Labor market theory is presented, with an emphasis on dual labor market theory and the importance of the secondary labor market. Income and wealth inequality in the United States is described, with special attention paid to economic inequality experienced by certain ethnic groups and women. The concept of poverty is explored, with a discussion of the official definition of poverty in this country. The role of tax policy and tax cuts under the Bush administration in the distribution of wealth and the promotion of inequality is examined, along with the Earned Income Tax Credit policy of the federal government. Supply side economics and its impact on inequality and the federal deficit over the past 30 years are detailed. Tax expenditures, as federal interventions into the economic system that largely benefit corporations, are described. The question of who should bear the social costs and externalities associated with market capitalism is explored, and the positions of conservatives and liberals are contrasted. Social policies designed to deal with some of the social costs or externalities that accompany the operation of the market economy in the United States are described.

Chapter 5 examines both the history and the legacy of discrimination in the United States and elaborates on the ways that discrimination has operated to limit resources and rights of ethnic groups; women; lesbian, gay, bisexual, and transgender (LGBT) persons; and persons with disabilities. The chapter utilizes critical race theory to examine the meaning of race and racism in the United States. The concepts of aversive racism and White privilege are explored as subtle but powerful variations on overt discrimination, along with the dangers of essentialism in describing oppressed groups. The history of institutional racism experienced by four ethnic groups in the United States is described—Native Americans, African Americans, Latinos, and Asian Americans—and the implications of this history are explored. The history of immigration from Mexico and Central America, the discrimination encountered by both documented and undocumented immigrants, and the strengths and resources these groups bring to the United States are described. The relationship between poverty and membership in certain ethnic groups is examined.

The economic and social discrimination experienced by women in the home, in the workplace, as parents, and in political life is described and linked to the socially constructed ideas about gender that emerged in the United States in the 19th century and the contemporary oppression of women in public and private life. Oppression of LGBT persons is described, and the consequences of institutional discrimination against these groups are explored. Discrimination against persons with disabilities is discussed and linked to other forms of discrimination. Finally, social movements begun by oppressed groups over the past 50 years that have challenged the status quo are examined, and their impact is discussed.

Chapter 6 looks at the history and philosophy of the social work profession and examines how our profession has advanced social justice in the United States. The gendered nature of the social work profession is explored, along with the role of Christianity in the early formation of the profession. The role of social workers in the creation of major social policies in the United States is included in this chapter. The commitment to social policy change evident in the early days of the profession is traced throughout its history, and the contemporary commitment to social advocacy is explored. The unique role of the social work profession in the United States as the only one whose self-defined mission is the pursuit of social justice is discussed.

Chapters 7, 8, 9, and **10** integrate the theoretical framework—*the interaction of historical ideologies, the economic structure, and the legacy of discrimination*—in the discussion of five specific social policies and the social problems that they are designed to address. These social policies are the ones most directly affecting social work clients and oppressed groups. In **Chapter 7** the major income maintenance policies in the United States—welfare for women and children

(Temporary Assistance for Needy Families, or TANF) and Social Security for older Americans—are described and examined for their impact on women and children and elderly. In **Chapter 8** policies designed to address child maltreatment in the child welfare system are examined. In **Chapter 9** health care policies are described, and the consequences of not having a national health care policy are explored. In **Chapter 10** the problems of homelessness, the lack of affordable housing, and the collapse of the housing market are examined. Housing policies in the United States are described, and their impact on the national housing problems is explored.

Each policy chapter (7, 8, 9, and 10) reviews the history of the social problems and the policies designed to address them. The policy analysis framework offered in Chapter 2 is utilized throughout these policy chapters to offer readers examples of the ways policy analysis can illuminate the real goals and objectives of policies and determine their actual outcomes.

Finally, **Chapter 11** explores the impact of the global economy on social problems and social policies in the United States and elsewhere across the globe. The impact of the attacks of 9/11 on social policies in the United States is examined, with special attention given to the Homeland Security Act. Chapter 11 also looks forward to the Obama administration's exploration of the implications of both the economic crisis and the resurgence of faith in the power of government for social policy change in the United States.

Alternatives to current policies are offered in each chapter to solve the social problems analyzed in each chapter. Each chapter begins with chapter questions, which serve to guide the student through the discussion of the social problem and social policies. The chapters end with open-ended questions designed to stimulate discussion about the themes raised in each chapter. Each chapter features tables and figures to bring the information to life visually. Vignettes focusing on persons who have challenged oppression and demonstrated moral courage in working for social change accompany each chapter.

TABLE 1.1   Infusion of Content Regarding Oppressed Groups and Location in Book

Oppressed Group	Chapter Location
Women	Chapters 5 and 6
LGBT	Chapter 5
Disabled	Chapter 5
Elderly	Chapters 6 and 9

● SOCIAL WORKERS AND SOCIAL POLICY CHANGE

[handwritten margin note: we use social policy in everything]

Many social workers think they live in a world far apart from social policies. Social workers think of themselves as professionals and expect to function in a professional environment that maximizes their autonomy and professional practice, not in a context where their work is limited by external policies. As a result, they may not appreciate the need to understand and transform the social policies that inevitably underlie their professional roles.[2] Whether working as practitioners, educators, administrators, community change agents, or researchers, all social workers will act within a social policy field, empowered and constrained by the channels for action determined by others. Funding sources, client characteristics, content and amount of services offered—all these variables are found in policies designed by federal, state, or local policymakers. Yet far more important than recognizing the constraints inherent in policies is the fact that policies are of human origin and can be changed through collective political will. It is commonplace to say that policies drive practice; it is equally important to say that practice can reveal the problems with policies, and this insight can lead to the desire to change unjust policies. The relationship between policy and practice is reciprocal. Practice should guide policy change; social workers operating in the world know which policies are constraining to their clients and which policies fail to solve the social problems that limit the full potential of their clients.

● SOCIAL JUSTICE

Social workers have had a hand in many significant policy changes thus far in American history, and the future is wide open for the struggle to refashion social welfare policy in the United States. Social workers have a professional commitment to engage in actions that will promote social justice. The National Association of Social Workers (NASW) *Code of Ethics* for social workers identifies as a core principle of the social work profession the mandate to "challenge social injustice."[3] The *Code of Ethics* defines social justice partly by its absence: social injustice, which includes "issues of poverty, unemployment, discrimination and other forms of social injustice."[4] Traditionally the social work profession has been concerned with access to economic resources and has taken up the struggle against various forms of discrimination. According to the *Code of Ethics,* social work professionals must do more than pay lip service to the concept of social justice; they should "engage in social and political action that seeks to ensure that all people have equal access to the resources, employment, services and opportunities they require to meet their basic human needs and to develop fully."[5]

What is social justice? Social justice describes the fair distribution of goods, services, rights, and duties. A socially just society is one where all, not just a privileged few, would have a say in how these fundamental necessities and freedoms are shared. Social justice does not imply absolute equality but demands that each person receive the same basic rights and unobstructed access to economic and political resources, not mediated by gender, ethnicity, level of education, economic status, or other demographic characteristics. In a socially just society, for example, all would have the same access to the same quality health care, regardless of other factors. Similarly, everyone would have access to quality education, political participation, and freedom of association and speech. Finally, in a socially just society economic resources would not be concentrated in the hands of a few but would be shared more equitably. Globally, we are far from approaching the ideal of social justice, but even within the United States, there are serious problems with access to economic resources, health care, housing, education, and political power, as this book will demonstrate. Some refer to social and economic justice as though they are two separate entities; in this book the concept of social justice will include economic justice. Clearly a society that embraces historically based values that form obstacles to social justice, supports an economic system that thwarts social justice, or fosters systematic discrimination that prevents access to economic and political resources should be unacceptable to social workers. On the one hand, social justice in the United States can be viewed as an elusive, ever-receding goal or a socially constructed concept about which few would agree. On the other hand, there are clear impediments to social justice in the United States that many could agree upon and that could be transformed through collective understanding and political action. This book will suggest new social policies that would bring the United States far closer to the ideal of social justice.

CONSTITUENCIES FOR SOCIAL CHANGE ●

How does the failure to pursue socially just policies hurt middle-class Americans? Many of the historical values described in Chapter 2 are oppressive to middle-class persons who do not live in poverty, especially as they experience economic downturns inherent in the market economy. These historical values, including self-reliance, individualism, and the Protestant work ethic, are punishing in times of economic recession, unemployment, housing market collapse, and lack of health care—all problems affecting the middle class in 2008. As the latest economic crisis has taught us, virtually no one is impervious to the actions of an unregulated market economy. Even those who considered themselves economically stable slid into economic insecurity during the recession of 2008. Economic realities trump the belief in self-reliance, and the commitment to hard work means little in the face of rising unemployment. As this book will show, many of our social problems are shared by all ethnic groups and people from all economic levels; the survival of Social Security and the viability of our health care system affect all Americans, as does the stability of the housing market and the welfare and safety of children at risk for maltreatment. Social justice is not just a concern for oppressed groups but is a concern for all Americans. It is at these times that deep social policy change is the most possible, when the common interests in socially just policies are recognized and discontent with accepted ways of organizing social and economic reality grows and is expressed through social movements and political action. Social workers can seize these moments to work with others to fashion socially just policies that move beyond the exigencies of our most punishing historical values, the worst effects of the market economy, and our historical patterns of discrimination. Such policies can be liberating for all Americans.

CONCLUSION

At the core of the social work profession is an insight about the socially constructed nature of our economic and social arrangements, as well as a deep commitment to embrace the struggle to change unjust policies. By understanding the historical origins of our policies, their relationship to our economic well-being, and their complicity with *our legacy of discrimination,* social workers can begin to transform unjust policies into ones that hold the promise of social justice for everyone.

DISCUSSION QUESTIONS

1. What are some examples of socially constructed values, institutions, or everyday practices that you can identify in your own life? In the larger society?

2. Why is the socially constructed nature of our social arrangements and beliefs difficult to perceive?

3. What do you think are the most deeply held socially constructed values or beliefs in the United States?

4. How would you define social justice?

5. What do you believe is a fair distribution of resources and rights?

NOTES

1. Peter Berger and Thomas Luckman, *The Social Construction of Reality: A Treatise on the Sociology of Knowledge* (New York: Anchor Books, 1967), 90.

2. Philip Poole and Leslie Leighninger, *The Policy Based Profession* (Boston: Pearson, 2005), 17.

3. National Association of Social Workers (NASW), *Code of Ethics of the National Association of Social Workers* (Washington, DC: Author, 2008), 5.

4. NASW, *Code of Ethics*, 5.

5. NASW, *Code of Ethics*, 27.

2

The Nature of Social Policy

CHAPTER QUESTIONS

1. How are social problems identified?

2. What are some examples of social policies that are not social welfare policies?

3. What is the difference between conservatives and liberals as far as the relationship of government to individual liberty is concerned?

4. What are the common ideologies shared by conservatives and liberals?

5. How does radical ideology differ from conservative and liberal ideology?

6. What is policy analysis, and what is an example of a policy analysis framework?

7. What are the major social welfare policies in the United States?

● ● ●

THE IDENTIFICATION OF SOCIAL PROBLEMS ●

How is a social problem identified and seen as demanding a policy solution? There are many conditions of disequilibrium, suffering, and oppression in the United States that deserve to be called social problems. Only some of these conditions of human suffering are selected from the background and given foreground status as social problems. In the United States, private issues become social problems and candidates for social policies only when they draw the attention of the media and other opinion makers and, ultimately, political actors. Various factors influence whether a private issue becomes a social problem, including how many people are affected by the problem and how intense it is perceived to be.[1] Usually there is a "policy window" during which a social problem comes to public attention and a policy solution may be attempted. When a social problem reaches critical mass in terms of public attention, there is only a brief period of time during which a public policy can be enacted, since public attention waxes and wanes about social issues. As John Kingdon noted, "Once the window opens, it does not stay open for long. An idea's time comes, but it also passes . . . if the window passes without action, it may not be open again for a long time."[2] One of the most obvious examples of a social condition being perceived as a social problem occurred in the Great Depression, when a great number of Americans were out of work and struggling with poverty. The scope and intensity of the problem raised this private suffering to the level of social problem and ultimately led to the social policies of the New Deal.

Another example of the rise of a social problem in U.S. history is the emergence of the "drug problem" and the resulting federal drug policy in the United States. The evolution of federal drug policy was a reaction against immigrant groups who were using the same drugs, although in different forms, as citizens of the United States. During the 19th century, the use of narcotics in this country was widespread, especially opium-based drugs, morphine, and to a lesser extent cocaine. After the Civil War when addiction to morphine among physicians was recognized as a problem, the solution was thought to be the development of heroin by a pharmaceutical company. Heroin was then sold as a possible cure for morphine and alcohol addiction. Opium, an ingredient in many patent medicines, was widely used as a medicinal cure throughout the 19th century. None of these drugs were illegal. When these drugs began to be identified with African Americans in the South and Chinese immigrants (who smoked rather than ingested opium) in the West, a movement to outlaw these and other narcotics as dangerous emerged.[3] Its proponents were successful in passing a federal law, the Harrison Narcotics Act, in 1914, making possession or use of all these drugs (now called narcotics) a federal crime.

While the prohibition of alcohol was lifted by the repeal of the Eighteenth Amendment to the Constitution in 1933, federal drug policy has become more stringent since the passage of the Harrison Act. Drug and alcohol policies are excellent examples of the social construction of social problems and expose the arbitrary nature of the development of social policies. Examples of social problems fading out of public attention and dissolving into virtual nonproblems include homelessness and the AIDS crisis. In the late 1980s and early 1990s, homelessness was recognized as a major social problem in states and localities across the country.[4] The federal government passed the Stewart B. McKinney Homeless Assistance Act in 1987, which focused on proving grant monies to states to build homeless shelters, a limited solution to the problem, at best. While many were concerned with the humanitarian aspects of having so many Americans live on the streets or in their cars, media outlets began to focus on the difficulties local businesses and residents were having coping with the homeless, and policies to "contain" the problem were discussed at local and state levels. Many of these ideas were draconian measures of social control, involving relocation and/or incarceration. Currently there is little interest or concern at the state or national level about homelessness. Although the number of homeless children and families has grown substantially since the 1980s, the interest in the issue has declined so that it is a nonproblem in terms of public attention and political interest.[5] (See Chapter 10.)

In the 1980s, the AIDS crisis made headlines and became a major social problem demanding a solution. The "search for a cure" summoned national interest as activist groups stormed public meetings at the state and federal levels. Interest in prevention was also high, as condom use was encouraged even at junior high school levels. Once the protease inhibitors, an effective drug treatment that prolongs the life of many persons with HIV, were widely available, the crisis atmosphere died down, and AIDS receded from the social problem agenda. Another perhaps more important reason for the turn away from HIV/AIDS was the change in demographics of those living with HIV. Ethnic minority women and their children replaced gay men as the group most at risk. Many who had donated time and money to the campaign for the cure lost interest as the HIV infection rates shifted. There is little talk of AIDS on the national or state level, although economically marginalized women and children have less access to early treatment with these powerful drugs as well as having overwhelming needs for support, health care, and child care as a result of their health status.[6]

SOCIAL POLICIES IN THE UNITED STATES ●

Clearly, as discussed above, not all social problems are viewed as candidates for social policy solutions by political actors and decision makers. Formalized, institutionalized responses to perceived social problems are what are commonly thought of as social policies, but social policies do not have to be formally institutionalized. Since social policies channel our responses to social problems, the *absence* of a decision to address a social problem with a government response (such as the lack of a national health care policy) can itself be considered a social policy. Social policies then can be thought of as collective responses to perceived social problems. Sometimes they consist of efforts to solve the problem (as in Social Security), sometimes they are efforts to ameliorate the problem without solving it (such as child welfare policies and welfare policies), and sometimes they consist of efforts to avoid the problem (as in the lack of national health insurance).

Within this definition, military policy can be considered social policy since it meets the perceived need to defend the country from foreign threat. This broad definition of military policy may not take into account military operations in other lands, which have little to do with threats to our country, in which case an argument must be made that incorporates these military operations as the result of a perceived threat to the homeland. In recent years this argument has been advanced under the theme of the war on terror. Likewise, tax policy in the United States can be considered social policy because it is a response to the need to fund government activities, including defense policies, as well as a mechanism for allocating and redistributing wealth, as we will see later in Chapter 4. All economic policies are social policies, in that they are collective responses to perceived social problems (how to regulate the interest rate, for example, or how to protect inventions through patents). Other social policies include price support policies for farmers, which are designed to protect larger farmers from the vagaries of the market economy, and immigration policy, which determines who will enter the country and contributes to the supply of inexpensive labor for businesses and corporations. The criminal justice system is made of many separate social policies addressing the nature of crime and punishment, as well as the rehabilitation of those who have committed what we define as crimes. The educational system in the United States is similarly a complex system of social policies that rest on one key assumption: Education in grades K through 12 should be provided by public funds.

All these policies have been accepted as the normal—or even the only—way to solve the problem they address. The criminal justice system is generally viewed as a necessity to protect the public from crime, both property crime and violent crime, although many question its ethnic disparities.[7] The necessity for the tax-supported public educational system is left unquestioned, but only the issue of student and teacher performance (rather than, say, unequal funding of local schools) has risen to national policy attention. As Gil points out, social policies in any society are interdependent and interact with each other, although they may not be internally consistent, since they represent the interests of different groups and the political power they can summon.[8] Tax policy makes military policy and agricultural and welfare policies possible. The specific configurations of tax policy determine which groups in society will be most burdened by support of these programs. Since the tax cuts passed under the

Bush administration beginning in 2001, this burden has been disproportionately borne by middle-class voters.[9]

All these social policies have a great impact on the well-being of individuals and families. Military spending detracts from social welfare spending, a truism that became clear under Lyndon Johnson's administration in the 1960s and has been reiterated in the funding pressure on social welfare policies caused by military spending under the Bush administration's war in Iraq.[10] Families are impacted by military deployments, and returning veterans suffer from severe stress and mental disorders, problems that should be considered social welfare problems but have not as yet emerged from the background of taken-for-granted life in the military to become social problems that many Americans want to address. Criminal justice system policies often punish family members left behind with loss of income and stability. The educational system has failed many of its students, especially at the high school level, where high dropout rates for some ethnic groups undermine its central mission.[11] School violence, disconnection from the communities schools are designed to serve, and teachers who are mired in bureaucratic demands all reduce the quality of public education. Each of these problems with public education could have emerged as a separate issue to be solved by social policies, but only one has: poor student performance. This is the issue that has been foregrounded by the legislation passed by Congress in 2001, No Child Left Behind, leaving all the other problems with public education uncharted and unnoticed by social policy actors.

Tax policy is one of the most important and broad-reaching social policies in the United States. Through the mechanism of taxes, government can redistribute income and consequently wealth, can penalize certain kinds of spending by raising taxes, and can reward other spending by lowering taxes or giving tax breaks. Income is taxed more often and, depending on one's tax bracket, at a higher rate than wealth. Whereas Americans pay taxes on their income each year that they earn income, wealth, in the form of capital gains, is taxed only at the time it is acquired. Afterwards, wealth remains untaxed except for interest rates on investment of wealth. This system privileges holders of capital (wealth) at the expense of workers dependent on income. Again these are inequities that might be viewed as social problems but thus far have not been, at least by a critical mass of Americans. The consequences of our tax policy for individuals and families are obvious. Less income and wealth equals less economic and political power.

SOCIAL WELFARE POLICIES ●

Those policies traditionally considered social welfare policies are a much smaller subset of social policies. Social welfare policies have been described as those policies that deal with regulation of benefits to those in need[12] or, more elaborately, "principles, activities or frameworks" that seek to optimize individual and family well-being.[13] Gerston defines social welfare policy as "anything government chooses to do, or not to do, that affects the quality of life of its people."[14] This is a particularly broad definition of social welfare policies that might include educational policies and criminal justice policies as discussed above. In this text, social welfare policies will be defined as public policies that affect personal and family well-being. Clearly, social welfare policies are often far more controversial than the policies discussed earlier. Welfare as a mechanism for delivering income support to poor women and children, for example, is hardly a taken-for-granted or reified solution to the problem of poverty, but then many do not see welfare as a solution to the problem of poverty but rather view it as the solution to another problem: lack of personal character or moral failures. The nature of the social problem, in other words, has not been agreed upon. In general, the less agreement that exists about the nature of a problem, the more controversial the social policy solution will be. Other social welfare policies, such as housing policy, hover at the perimeter of public attention. Recurrent efforts to shut down federal participation in providing housing for those without adequate housing have failed, but the remaining policies are marginal and contribute little to the needs of poorer persons.

● POLITICAL PHILOSOPHIES IN THE UNITED STATES

While the struggle of social workers and others to work for socially just policies may seem political in nature, underlying this political effort will be ideological struggles about the nature of U.S. society and the role of government. A strong belief that government power corrupts and destroys individual liberty has existed in the United States since the 18th century, when reaction to Britain's rule led to the American Revolution and the establishment of a separate nation. Based on their experience with what the Revolutionary generation perceived as the unjust nature of British rule (taxation without representation), leaders of the early republic feared the power of a central government. They did not want a strong central government, fearing that it would resemble a monarchy; they instead sought to design a Constitution that would divide this central power (checks and balances) and share the governing authority with the states. Thomas Jefferson was a leader of this belief in a very limited federal government (he thought the federal government should only deliver the mail) as a means of protecting individual liberties.[15] The U.S. Constitution was written so that most enumerated powers of government belong to the state, with the exception of regulation of interstate commerce. While precedence for enacting broader social policies could be found in a clause that gave the federal government the right to enact laws that would "promote the general welfare," the Constitution was silent on the specific social problems to which the federal government might respond.[16] The Constitution as it stands, therefore, does not encourage federal intervention in a host of social issues—such as civil rights, poverty, and abortion, for example—that are hallmarks of government intervention today.[17] This view of the power of the federal government as a possible threat to individual freedom dominated political discourse in the 19th century. Known as laissez faire (hands off), a strong belief that a powerful federal government would destroy individual liberty limited the federal response to social problems. This belief in the dangers of government, particularly federal power, continues to characterize *conservatives* today, who subscribe to similar views about the dangers of government power to individual liberty.

During the New Deal, this idea of government's relationship to individual liberty was turned on its head, when the federal response to social crises, such as mass unemployment and widespread unrest, took a far more aggressive form and the New Deal social policies were enacted. Under this newer view, a belief that the federal government needed to step in to defend individual liberty in the face of widespread forces, such as big business, that would crush it replaced the older laissez-faire conception of the federal government's role.[18] Those who assumed these beliefs called themselves *liberals* and continue to promote some kind of federal response to social problems, such as national health care. These two political strains, liberal and conservative, continue to dominate political ideology in the United States.

Conservatives continue to believe that all social welfare policies are compromises with the need for self-reliance and independence, which are hallmarks of the American character. They tend to see the 20th century as one of social welfare policy excess, where failed programs served to increase dependence of poor groups and sap individual initiative. Conservatives often feel that even the limited numbers of social welfare policies that exist in the United States in comparison with other industrialized countries are too extensive, and they do not wish to see more social policy interference on the part of any government body. Instead they believe that the natural workings of the market economy will serve the interests of Americans best.[19]

Liberals, sometimes called *progressives,* feel that there need to be more federal and state policies protecting individuals. They generally favor more generous welfare benefits, for example, or a broad system of national health coverage. Liberals generally support an increase in social welfare policies because they hold the principle that social welfare policies are based on compassion and fair play and serve to substantially improve the condition of Americans they benefit. Liberals tend to see the history of the United States as a progressive arc leading to the social programs of the New Deal and the War on Poverty in the 1960s, whose policies they view as necessary to meet the needs of Americans left out of the climb to upward mobility. It is these policies, liberals feel, that we must protect and, in some cases, revive if we are going to live up to the American dream. They may see a downward trend in American history since the 1960s and 1970s as far as social welfare policies are concerned; they are likely to want to return to a golden era of government-sponsored programs to help marginalized populations.

In the 1990s under the Clinton administration, *neoliberalism* supplanted New Deal liberalism in American party politics as the mainstream liberal ideology. Neoliberals are less enthusiastic about government programs to effect social change and are more committed to the role of the market economy in sustaining growth and protecting marginalized populations. They believe that investment in human capital in the form of education should replace direct government involvement in social programs like the War on Poverty. They see personal responsibility as more important than entitlement to government programs such as Social Security or welfare. In sum, neoliberals are more friendly to business interests and wary of using the federal government to solve social problems.[20] Yet their underlying message is similar to that of classic New Deal liberals: Advancing the public good is the most important goal of social policy.

In 2008 with the collapse of the housing market, the ensuing severe economic recession, and the election of Barack Obama to the presidency, the conviction that government was a necessary force for economic stability and growth reemerged in the United States. The intervention of the federal government in the financial markets (see Chapter 10), the sharp increase in unemployment, and the failure of many corporations led even conservatives at the national, state, and local levels to demand similar federal financial help. Not since the New Deal has there been such a strong consensus that action by the federal government is essential to the economic health of the country. This demand for a return to a proactive federal government has at least temporarily muted the conservative ideology discussed earlier.

Both *liberals and conservatives* share common beliefs or ideologies about the nature of the social order in the United States: its essential fairness, its open social and economic structure that allows all individuals to move up the economic ladder. These beliefs about the nature of American society emerged in the 18th and 19th centuries in this country for specific reasons not related to the validity of their assumptions. The historical origins of the ideologies that support these values have been lost over the centuries, and they appear as givens within which most political and ideological debate takes place. Few question the reality of these beliefs since they have been reified and are now taken for granted as truths. Only *radicals and libertarians* move outside the ideological consensus that has characterized American political debate.

Those who identify as *radicals* align themselves with neither the conservative nor the liberal ideology. Instead, radicals question the ability of the market economy to deliver social justice to marginalized groups; they generally want more federal policies to ensure redistribution of income and provision of necessary services such as health care and day care. Some radical groups believe that the federal government should control the economic processes of the market economy; these groups advocate price and wage controls. Radicals move outside the ideological consensus that has characterized American political debate.

Social protest in front of White House, circa 1922

SOURCE: From the Library of Congress, from the National Photo Company Collection.

They argue that social welfare policies have had largely conservative functions of shoring up the capitalist economy and conserving and protecting an unjust system that promotes inequality. They see social welfare policies as examples of social control rather than social welfare, allowing businesses and corporations to exploit workers, maintain their wealth, and avoid social unrest. This palliative aspect of social welfare policies, they argue, prevents the deep social unrest that would emerge without these policies and serves another important function by allowing us to continue to believe that we are a compassionate and altruistic society.[21]

Radicals have deep roots in American history. Members of the Socialist and, to a lesser extent, Communist parties enjoyed some political success early in the 20th century and during the Great Depression.

Libertarians, on the other hand, believe that government destroys liberty and see government as antithetical to democratic principles. Libertarians oppose government intervention into the economic sphere as well as all social welfare programs. The rise of the Libertarian Party is a relatively recent phenomenon; it was founded in 1971. In their commitment to a laissez-faire government and strong civil liberties, members of this party are part of a tradition that goes back to Thomas Jefferson. These last two groups are not part of the mainstream of American politics, currently control few political offices, and have much less impact on national and state policies than do conservatives and liberals (see Table 2.1).

All social policies including social welfare policies are contested; their successful institutionalization depends on the outcome of political struggles inside and outside legislative forums. Much of this debate takes place within the ideological consensus discussed above. In this text we will acknowledge this consensus as a reified set of beliefs about how this country operates. The discussion will make room for those who question these received truths and see them as an arbitrary and therefore relative set of values that emerged in American history at specific times and may not serve us well in the struggle for social justice.

Function of Social Policies

Do social policies allow people to fulfill their basic needs? According to Gil, this is the main criterion for evaluating social policies. Of course the question is not as simple as it seems at first glance, as there may be differing viewpoints as to what are the basic human needs. Some things are not in dispute; as Gil notes, all human beings have biological-material needs for survival, which include "life-sustaining and enhancing goods and services."[22] Gil adds many other

TABLE 2.1 **Summary of Political Ideologies in the United States and Views on Government, Social Policies, and Market Economy**

Political Ideology	View on Role of Government	View on Social Policies	View on Market Economy
Conservatives	Less government	• Compromises to self-reliance independence valued in American character • 20th-century excess of social policy and interference	Will always serve the best interests of America naturally
Liberals	More government	More social policies to protect individuals based on fair play and compassion	Social order allows individuals to move up economic ladder
Neoliberals	Less government	Wary of government to solve social problems but see role of social policies to advance public good	See market economy as way to sustain growth and protect marginalized individuals
Radicals	More government	More federal policies to ensure redistribution of income and provision of necessary services, such as health care and day care	• Question the ability of the market economy to deliver social justice to marginalized groups • Want government to control economy
Libertarians	• Laissez-faire government and strong civil liberties • Government destroys liberty and is antithetical to democratic principles	No social policies	No government involvement in economy

needs to the list of those necessary for "healthy growth and development" of humans, but in this book we will focus on those policies that directly intersect with the biological-material needs for survival. This textbook defines these needs to include access to food and housing resources throughout the life cycle, access to health care, access to a safe environment for dependent children, access to education, and the opportunity to participate in meaningful work to achieve these resources. Social policies developed to meet these needs are the subject of this book. A second tier of needs includes those that involve the free expression of beliefs and free speech, both of which have been recognized and institutionalized in the United States through the Bill of Rights and are not the subject of social welfare policies.

Conception of Human Nature and Social Policies

One's view of human nature will inevitably factor into how problems and policies are constructed. Those who view human nature as essentially plastic or malleable, responsive to environmental and cultural factors with capacities for cooperation and social altruism, will have different ideas about what is possible in social policies than those who believe that people are fundamentally aggressive and competitive and that these qualities are biologically based. Social workers should examine their own views of human nature to discover the hidden assumptions from which they are operating. The social work profession's mission to promote social justice in social policies rests on an assumption of human plasticity—the belief that people have the potential to become human in various ways depending on the cultural and family input they receive and that human potential is wide and varied. Those who believe that human nature is fixed and immutable may have a narrower scope within which to design social policies.[23]

● POLICY ANALYSIS AS A TOOL FOR SOCIAL JUSTICE

Most social policies are confusing at best at first glance. Reading a policy enacted by federal or state legislation may leave most of us in the dark about what the real intent of the policymakers was, who the target group addressed by the policy is, and what the authors intended to be consequences or effects of the policy. A policy analysis framework offers the opportunity to understand a policy in depth; uncover its objectives, both stated and unstated; link the policy to historical values and ideologies; and estimate its consequences in terms of economic gains and losses as well as gains and losses of rights and privileges. Who conducts policy analysis? The most obvious group is those working for legislative bodies or lobbyists. In order to determine whether to support or oppose any federal or state bill, legislative and lobbyist staff will use a systematic framework to analyze policy objectives and their potential effects on the target population and others. Policy analysis is also used by groups designed to advance social justice as an advocacy tool to promote or oppose a policy they assess would advance or impede their goals. Of course, policy analysis can be utilized as an advocacy tool by any group with a stake in policy outcomes, including interest groups not traditionally associated with the goals of the social work profession. Whatever the purpose, anyone conducting a policy analysis is utilizing a specific framework that guides research on the policy and is designed to produce some kind of evaluative outcome. The most important outcome that social workers are usually interested in is whether this policy advances social justice. Policies also can be compared by using a policy analysis—for example, comparing income support policies for children in various European countries and the United States. A comparative analysis reveals which policies are most effective in addressing the social problem as well as which are most consonant with the goal of social justice.

The policy analysis framework offered in this chapter asks the analyst to explore both the overt and the covert objectives. While overt objectives are clearly stated in the policy, covert objectives are sometimes only clear after the policy has been enacted and been in effect for a period of time. These objectives are not stated or obvious but may reflect values or beliefs of the policymakers that they do not wish to acknowledge publicly. When Congress passed the welfare reform legislation in 1996 (see Chapter 7), the stated objectives were to reduce the welfare rolls and move women into the job market. A close analysis of the congressional hearings conducted on the bill reveals a disdain for women on welfare, a belief that most women on welfare were there because of promiscuity and other perceived moral failures, and a desire to discipline welfare mothers, who were blamed for gang violence among urban adolescents, adolescent drug use, and other problems legislators associated with ethnic minorities in inner cities. The covert objectives were revealed by the testimony at the hearings and the fact that statistics about birth rate and single parenthood among African American women were presented separately from those among other women on welfare.[24] Covert objectives cannot be proved, but they can be inferred from the hearings and often by looking at the effects of the legislation.

One of the most powerful tools of policy analysis is the ability to foresee (if it is a proposed policy) or measure (if the policy has already been enacted) *unintended consequences*. All policies have them, for lawmakers cannot imagine or project all the possible consequences of their policies as they come to life in the real world. Persons elected to legislative offices may be uninformed about the context of the problem they attempt to solve or ameliorate through legislation.

A good example of unintended consequences of a policy can be seen in one of the effects of the "three strikes" law passed in California in 1994 by a ballot proposition. Under this law a person convicted of a third felony can be sentenced to 25 years to life in prison. The goal was to deter crime and protect the public from criminals, but one unintended consequence was that few persons arrested after the law was enacted were willing to plead guilty to felonies, since a guilty plea counted as a strike. Instead persons charged with crimes exercised their right to a trial, clogging the courts with a large increase in the number of criminal cases. Additionally, since the third strike does not have to be classified as a violent felony, some have been given a sentence of 25 years to life for relatively minor crimes, such as stealing a pizza or a video.[25]

Similarly, the federal "war on drugs" resulted in harsh penalties for persons using drugs but did not stop drug traffic to the United States; instead the law helped create the largest prison population in the world, in terms of both absolute number of prisoners and percentage of the population in prison.[26] In spite of the $50 billion a year spent by federal and state governments on the war on drugs for the past 10 years, approximately 2 million people were arrested for drug offenses in 2007; those numbers are expected to rise over the next several years. Law enforcement makes more arrests for drug offenses than for any other crime.[27] The unintended consequence of all this money and effort is the increase in costs of long prison terms and the abrogation of human rights represented by the huge increase in the prison population of the country. Without a systematic policy analysis, these unintended effects were not predicted. Both policies were the result of moral judgments, rather than systematic rational analysis about what would work to address the problem.

Policy Analysis Framework

The following policy analysis framework is a powerful tool for analyzing how social policies advance or detract from the goal of social justice.[28]

Policy Analysis Framework

The Social Problem Addressed by the Policy

1. What is/are the problem/s to be solved in the most fundamental terms?
2. What is the history of the problem/s in the United States?
3. What are the various theories about the causes of the problem/s? Based on this, what do you think is/are the most important cause/s of the problem/s?

The Policy Objectives, Value Premises, Expectations, and Target Populations

1. Policy objectives: overt and covert objectives. What are the stated objectives of the policy? In your judgment, what are the covert objectives of the policy?
2. What are values underlying the policy objectives? What values are revealed by the overt and covert objectives?
3. What did the policymakers expect would be the result of the policy?
4. Target segments of the population at whom policy is aimed. Discuss the direct target of the policy in terms of size and other demographic characteristics. Who are the indirect targets of the policy?

Effects of the Policy

1. Intended effects. What are the effects that lawmakers intended?
2. Unintended effects. What are the effects that the lawmakers did not foresee?
3. Distinguish between short-range (under 5 years) and long-range (over 5 years) effects of the policy.

Implications of the Policy

1. Changes in the distribution of material *resources*. Are there any changes to the distribution of material resources, including income and other tangible benefits, as a result of the policy for direct or indirect target groups?
2. Changes in distribution of services, rights, and statuses. Are there any changes in services, rights, or statuses as a result of the policy?

Alternative Policies

1. What alternative policy/ies would address the social problem discussed in the policy analysis more effectively while advancing social justice?

Discussion of the Framework

Social Problem Underlying the Policy

The Problem in the Most Fundamental Terms

In this section the deepest description of the social problem underlying the policy to be analyzed should be given. For example, with a welfare policy, the social problem is not how to reform the welfare system but how to ensure adequate material resources for children whose caretakers cannot provide adequately for them on their own. The deepest reading of the problem

(Continued)

(Continued)

will be the most fruitful for the analysis, because this will reveal whether the policy actually addresses the real problem. The history of the problem should trace the changes in the manifestation of the problem and the perception of it. For example, poor children and their mothers were seen as worthy of relief in the colonial period but were not the targets of large-scale federal policies until the New Deal. Understanding the historical evolution of the problem will help the analyst place the current policy in a broader context. A review of research related to the problem should be undertaken in this first section, giving the analyst a sense of what causes of the problem have been identified in the literature. For example, the poverty of women and children has been explained variously as a moral failure on the part of the parents, a lack of social and family support, and a function of the labor market and the availability of low-wage jobs.

The Policy

The Policy Objectives, Value Premises, Expectations, and Target Populations

In this section the policy itself is analyzed. The overt policy objectives are found stated in the policy; the covert objectives must be drawn from literature about the policy and are subject to various interpretations as discussed above. Here the analyst makes a reasoned judgment based on available research and his or her own reading of the policy. The section on value premises underlying both the overt and the covert objectives asks the analyst to deconstruct the policies to determine which values they embody. What values about poverty and women does welfare policy reflect? This task will be easier after reading Chapter 3. Extrapolating from the policy objectives and research related to the policy, the analyst discusses what the policymakers were thinking when they enacted the policy. What was their expectation about the outcome? Did they expect that women would stay on welfare or leave it and become self-sufficient and provide for their families? Target segments are those who are directly affected by the policy. In this section the analyst should look broadly to ascertain which other groups might be affected by the policy, not just immediate targets. In the case of welfare fathers, social workers, welfare administrators, and shop owners in low-income neighborhoods are all affected by whatever welfare policy is enacted.

Effects of the Policy

The section on effects of the policy asks the analyst to do research to find out the actual effects in both the short range and the long range. Many of the effects of the policy fall into the category of expected effects—those the policymakers hoped would occur—but others are unintended effects as discussed above. Unintended effects may be contested among analysts and may depend as much on the judgment of the analyst as on the research.

Implications

In the section on implications, the analyst looks more deeply at the effects of the policy to see which ones affect the material resources available to the target group and the indirect target groups. For example, in welfare policy children and their caretakers (usually women) receive economic resources, Medicaid, and food stamps. Others may gain employment or customers as a result of the policy. Policies usually distribute or limit rights and obligations along with material resources. Under the welfare policy passed in 1996, clients were forced to work or participate in training for a specified number of hours every week to keep their welfare checks. Some clients receive the services of a case manager while on welfare. The right to continue on welfare is greatly limited by welfare reform, and the right to have an increased grant when another child is born is eliminated. Finally, policies often distribute or reduce services or change statuses of clients and others. The status of welfare recipients may expand to include more women and children or narrow to exclude others. The services of domestic violence counselors and mental health counselors are available to some women on welfare who have identified problems in these areas. See Chapter 7 for a full discussion of welfare policy.

Alternative Policies

The analyst is asked to offer an alternative policy or alternative policies that would meet the most fundamental needs of the target population and advance social justice. These policies may or may not be based on research. Creative thinking is encouraged.

The policy analysis model offered above will be illustrated in Chapters 7, 8, 9, and 10 to offer students the opportunity to see its usefulness as it relates to specific policies.

OVERVIEW OF SOCIAL WELFARE POLICIES IN THE UNITED STATES ●

Social workers will work in a variety of systems guided by a diverse number of social welfare policies designed to address (not necessarily solve) a wide variety of social problems. The following is an overview of the most important social welfare policies in the United States (see Table 2.2).

Programs Providing Income or Tangible Goods

Social Security

Social Security is the biggest social welfare program in the United States, although strictly speaking Social Security (full name Old-Age, Survivors, and

TABLE 2.2   Summary of Social Welfare Policies/Programs in the United States

Programs Providing Income or Tangible Goods			
Program	**Year Established**	**Program Description**	**Target Population(s)**
Social Security	• 1935 • Largest social welfare program in United States, established as cornerstone of New Deal	• Mandatory insurance system that levies a tax on payrolls (FICA) • Matched funds with employer contributions that are kept in a trust fund that pays retirement pensions based on prior earnings in the labor market	• For workers when they reach retirement age (currently 66 for those born after 1942) • 90% of retired workers receive a pension through this program, but it is designed to supplement private savings and pensions
Supplemental Security Income (SSI)	• 1974	• Cash grants that replaced Old Age Assistance and Aid to Blind and Totally Disabled • Benefits not designed to bring individuals or families out of poverty but provide support	• For persons over 65 with low income and persons with disabilities • Also for children under 18 who meet income and disability criteria
Temporary Assistance for Needy Families (TANF)	• 1996 • Replaced AFDC program	• Federal income maintenance program • Receive a cash grant and Medicaid eligibility for no more than 2 years • Must participate in training or work mandated by the states • Success at reducing welfare is widely debated	• For children under 18 and adult caretakers
General Assistance	• State by state	• Provided through states (only 40 states provide this) with no direct federal funds involved • Varies from state to state in that some provide grants, assistance • Most have time limits and requirements to ensure that assistance is not a lifetime stipend	• For persons who are not caretakers of dependent children, not aged or disabled

Programs Providing Income or Tangible Goods			
Program	**Year Established**	**Program Description**	**Target Population(s)**
Veterans' Benefits	• 1862	• Pensions, disability payments, medical care	• For persons who have served in the U.S. armed forces and have suffered injury or disability as a result of their service • Survivors are also eligible for pensions
Food Stamps	• Originally created in the late 1930s • Revived in 1974 • Modified in 1977 • Name changed to Supplemental Nutrition Assistance Program (SNAP) in October 2008	• Monthly benefits through EBT to purchase some food items • Average amount of food stamps received was $300/month in 2005	• For households (without an elderly person) that have gross incomes below 130% of the poverty line • All other households must have total income less than 100% of poverty line • Mainly children receive benefit (almost 1 in 5)
Special Supplemental Nutrition Program for Women, Infants, and Children (WIC)	• 1974	• Administered by the Department of Agriculture with state health agencies • Federal program providing nutrition supplements to reduce the incidence of low birth weight and other problems for infants • Also provides coupons for use in grocery stores and formula for infants	• For low-income women and children • Pregnant women
Housing subsidies	• 1950s	• Provides subsidized rental housing through federal Department of Housing and Urban Development (HUD) • Main programs are Section 8 rental housing and public housing	• Public housing for families on public assistance • Section 8 housing provides vouchers for working persons with low incomes

(Continued)

TABLE 2.2 (Continued)

Programs Providing Health Care			
Program	**Year Established**	**Program Description**	**Target Population(s)**
Medicare	• 1965 • Added prescription coverage in 2003	• Covers most health care costs through three programs: Part A, Part B, and Prescription Drug Coverage • Financed through a payroll tax on wages, premiums paid by recipients, and general tax revenues	• For persons 65 and older and disabled Social Security beneficiaries
Medicaid	• 1965 • Modified in 1996	• Run by states but funded through a federal-state partnership • Provides health insurance and nursing homes for income-eligible elderly	• For some persons and families with low incomes • Children and caretakers receiving TANF • Low-income persons determined "medically needy" • Pregnant women and children under age 6 whose income is below 133% of the poverty line • SSI recipients and children from low-income families may qualify • Legal residents who entered the country after August 1996 must wait 5 years
Programs Providing Services			
Program	**Year Established**	**Program Description**	**Target Population(s)**
Child Welfare System	• 1974	• Complex set of federal and state policies related to mandatory reporting, investigation of child maltreatment, removal of children from families, placement of children in foster care, and oversight of foster care and placement of children in adoptive homes	• Protect the well-being of dependent children

Programs Providing Services			
Program	**Year Established**	**Program Description**	**Target Population(s)**
		• Varies widely from promoting family preservation to foster care and adoption	
The Older Americans Act	• 1965 • Reauthorized in 2000	• Grants to support community planning and service programs, research, demonstration, and training projects related to aging • Elder abuse prevention	• Homebound elders • Family members caring for resident elders

Disability Insurance, or OASDI) is not welfare. Rather the main part of Social Security is a mandatory insurance system that levies a tax on pay-rolls (known as FICA, or the Federal Insurance Contributions Act) of workers, matches these funds with employer contributions, and keeps the money in a trust fund to be paid out in the form of monthly pensions when each worker reaches retirement age (currently 66 for those born after 1942). The system is designed to draw revenue from current workers to pay retirement pensions of current retirees, so it is technically not a savings plan. Currently over 90% of retired workers in the United States receive some form of retirement pension under this policy. Social Security, like its sister program, Unemployment Insurance Benefits (UIB), distributes funds based on prior earnings in the labor market. Both were established in 1935 by the Social Security Act, the cornerstone of the New Deal. Since 1956, Social Security has also insured and thus paid workers who have lost wages due to disability. Social Security is the most important of all social welfare policies in terms of scope and coverage. In 2000, approximately 45 million persons received cash payments through OASDI, 31.8 million of whom were retirees and their dependents; 6.7 million were disabled workers and their dependents, and 7 million were children and surviving spouses of diseased workers.[29]

There are many issues surrounding the Social Security program; these include its solvency or lack thereof, ethnic and gender disparities in terms of payouts, the income cap on taxable wages, the use of the Social Security trust fund to pay current debts of the federal government, and the potential privatization of Social Security funds. These issues will be explored fully in Chapter 7.

SSI

Social Security was not intended to be the sole source of support for retired persons but rather was designed to supplement private savings and pensions. Those who receive only Social Security benefits often live at or below the poverty level. Those whose benefits level falls below the poverty line or who are ineligible for Social Security receive cash grants through the Supplemental Security Income (SSI) program. Created by Congress in 1974 to replace the previously existing programs known as Old Age Assistance and Aid to the Blind and Totally Disabled, SSI is targeted for persons over 65 with low income and persons with disabilities not otherwise eligible for grants under OASDI. Children under age 18 who are unmarried and who meet the income and disability criteria are also eligible. As a means-tested program funded largely by general revenue funds of the federal government and supplemented by some states, there is a reluctance by public officials to spend adequately for those covered by SSI. In the year 2000, approximately 20% of SSI recipients received benefits on the basis of age, 1% were blind, and 79% were disabled persons.[30] Fewer persons over 65 and increasing numbers of disabled persons have characterized the pool of recipients since 1988. Noncitizens entering the country after August 1996 and persons disabled as the result of alcohol or drug abuse are generally ineligible for SSI, regardless of age, disability, or income, as a provision of the Personal Responsibility and Work Opportunity Reconciliation Act.

The federal standard for SSI benefits is not geared to bringing individuals or families out of poverty. In 2000, approximately 50% of SSI recipients belonged to families whose income fell below the poverty line.[31] While the benefits of SSI are low, they exceed those of TANF, the federal program designed to meet the income needs of poor women and children.[32]

TANF

Temporary Assistance for Needy Families is the means-tested federal income maintenance program for dependent children under 18 and their adult caretakers. It replaced the previous welfare policy, Aid to Families With Dependent Children (AFDC), in 1996 when Congress passed the Personal Responsibility and Work Opportunity Reconciliation Act. Under this legislation, welfare was no longer an entitlement but was controlled by individual states that received a set of federal monies in the form of block grants. Each state has designed its own version of TANF to comply with the federal requirements. Federal guidelines include time limits for recipients of welfare, who are overwhelmingly women and children. Those who qualify for welfare can receive a cash grant, along with Medicaid eligibility, for no more than 2 consecutive years, provided that they participate in training or work mandated by the states. Recipients can only receive TANF for 5 years in their lifetime. States have options to pass laws excluding parents who have been convicted of drug felonies from participation in TANF. States can also sanction participants who are not complying with state-sponsored work or training programs. TANF was reauthorized in 2006 with stricter work requirements. The program is controversial as it represents a marked shift in federal policy toward low-income women and children. Its ongoing success in reducing welfare rolls has been widely debated. TANF will be discussed thoroughly in Chapter 7.

General Assistance

For those who are not caretakers of dependent children, not aged, and not disabled, there is virtually no direct federal income assistance. Forty states provide minimum income support for these persons. Of these states, five make it a county option to offer General Assistance. Eligibility for General Assistance varies widely from state to state. Some states offer small grants to employable adults provided they enter work or training programs; others provide some assistance to adults with a variety of barriers to employment. The overwhelming majority of states that offer General Assistance require recipients to be citizens or legal residents. Most states have time limits and other requirements to ensure that General Assistance does not become a lifetime stipend. Not surprisingly, given that no federal funds are involved and that able-bodied nonparents are eligible, the benefit levels of General Assistance are the lowest of all income support measures.

Veterans' Benefits

Persons who have served in the armed forces of the United States and have suffered injury or disability as a result of their service are eligible for pensions, disability payments, and medical care; their survivors are also eligible for pensions. Over 2 million veterans received some compensation in 1999 for service-related disability, at a cost of $14 million. Since 1979, benefits have taken family income into account, which has reduced the level of benefits to veterans and their families.

Food Stamps

The Supplemental Nutrition Assistance Program, known as the Food Stamp Program until October 1, 2008, is part of the federally funded safety net for economically marginalized persons. Originally created in the late 1930s, it was revived in 1974 as a nationwide program. In 1977 the current program structure was established, with a goal of alleviating hunger and malnutrition by allowing low-income households to purchase some food items from retail food purveyors.[33] Under the program, monthly benefits are given to eligible households through Electronic Benefit Transfer (EBT) systems, rather than the older "coupons," which were more stigmatizing. A household is defined as a group of people living together, not necessarily related, who prepare and eat food together. This requirement gives the program much more flexibility than other means-tested programs, which have more rigid categorical requirements for eligibility. A household without an elderly or disabled person must have a gross income below 130% of the poverty line to qualify. All other households must have a total income that is less than 100% of the poverty line to be eligible for food stamps.

The majority of persons helped by the food stamp program (SNAP) are children. Almost 1 in 5 children in the United States, or 13 million, received food stamps in 2006. In 2006, food stamps provided $23 billion in benefits to families with children. The average amount of food stamps received in 2005 was $300 a month. SNAP has been very successful in raising children out of poverty; estimates are that more than 1 million children were lifted over the poverty line in 2005 through their families' receipt of food stamps. Another 1.1 million were protected from extreme poverty (living with family income more than 50% below the poverty line).[34]

Special Supplemental Nutrition Program
for Women, Infants, and Children

This federal program was designed to provide nutrition supplements for low-income women and children and pregnant women. Established in 1974, WIC also provides coupons for use in grocery stores and formula for infants. Limited health checks for infants are offered at WIC centers. The program is administered by the Department of Agriculture in cooperation with state health agencies. The premise of the program is that nutritional supplementation will reduce the incidence of low birth weight and other problems that can lead to serious health consequences for infants. In 2006, there were more than 6 million children aided by WIC, including 2 million infants, in 10,000 clinics.[35]

Housing Subsidies

The federal government through the Department of Housing and Urban Development (HUD) administers several programs to provide subsidized rental housing. The two main programs are Section 8 rental housing and public housing.

Both programs will be discussed in Chapter 10. Public housing is less popular than it was during the early years of the program's existence in the 1950s. Locating much public housing in poor neighborhoods in the inner city resulted in deteriorating conditions for many public housing units, many of which were built as high-rise apartments. Very low-income requirements for eligibility turned away many working families and left the units for families on public assistance, which increased public opposition to the units and to their expansion.[36]

Section 8 housing programs aim to use the housing market to provide low-income housing by providing those eligible for the program with vouchers to rent housing in the community. The assumption was that the existence of vouchers would spur the construction of low-cost housing. To further encourage this, federal monies were given to states to encourage construction and rehabilitation of low-cost housing in the private sector. The supply of housing under Section 8 has always been far below demand. In the past 5 years, federal funds for Section 8 have been cut, with more cuts expected.

Programs Providing Health Care

Medicare

Medicare, along with Medicaid (see below), was passed in 1965. It covers most health care costs for persons 65 and older, as well as disabled Social Security beneficiaries. It is financed through a payroll tax on wages, premiums paid by recipients, and general tax revenues. In 2006, 43.2 million beneficiaries were enrolled in Medicare. Total expenditures for that year were $408 billion. Medicare is divided into three programs, each with its own costs, premiums, and coverage. These are the Hospital Insurance Program (Medicare Part A), the Supplementary Medical Insurance Program (Medicare Part B), and the Prescription Drug Coverage Program, added in 2003. While the Medicare fund is projected to be adequate for the projected expenditures until 2017, after that the picture is less clear.[37] Medicare is an important social policy because it prevents many near-poor elderly from falling into poverty by meeting the majority of their medical costs. There are various problems with Medicare, including the need for supplementary insurance, which must be purchased from the private insurance sector; the increasing premiums for Medicare; and the high cost of the supplementary drug benefit. Medicare works through the private health care system, reimbursing existing health care providers at prevailing rates for a large portion of the treatment of beneficiaries. Medicare utilizes the current system of high-cost health care, thus contributing to the inflation of health care costs. (See Chapter 9.)

Medicaid

Medicaid benefits the poor more directly than Medicare. Unlike Medicare, which is a federal program, Medicaid is run by the states but is funded through a federal-state partnership. Medicaid is a means-tested program that provides health insurance for some low-income individuals and families. Children and caretakers receiving TANF receive Medicaid, as do some low-income persons who are determined "medically needy" by the states administering the program. Pregnant women and children under age 6 whose income is 133% below the poverty line, SSI recipients, and children from low-income families may also qualify. The welfare reform legislation of August 1996 eliminated Medicaid eligibility for legal residents entering the country after that date. These legal residents now have to wait 5 years to apply for Medicaid. Medicaid also pays for nursing homes for income-eligible elderly. Health care under Medicaid is about 10% less expensive than private health insurance for children and about 30% less expensive for adults. This is partly because reimbursement rates to providers are generally lower under Medicaid than they are under private insurance.[38] Some states have established premiums and cost sharing at the point of service, known as copays, for Medicaid recipients, although the amount is regulated by the federal government. Very stringent income requirements mean that many families from the working poor are not covered by Medicaid. It is estimated that 40% of persons living under the poverty line are covered by Medicaid.[39] As of July 1, 2007, persons applying for Medicaid must present their birth certificates to document citizenship, which many feel is a hardship on families who cannot produce such documents.[40] Medicaid has many gaps in its coverage of the poor, and its low reimbursement rate makes many providers reluctant to accept Medicaid recipients.[41] Nonetheless, it has done a great deal to help those who do receive it obtain adequate health care.

Programs Providing Services

Child Welfare System

The child welfare system consists of a complex set of federal and state policies designed to protect the well-being of dependent children. A series of federal policies beginning in 1974 has varied widely between policies promoting family preservation and those reducing parental rights over children and promoting foster care and adoption. State policies must be in compliance with federal policies, and regular shifts in policy directions have led to a series of substantial changes in provision of child welfare services to children and families. The child welfare system is composed of policies related to mandatory reporting, investigation of child maltreatment, removal of children from families, placement of children in foster care, oversight of foster care, and placement of children in adoptive homes. These policies will be discussed in depth in Chapter 8.

The Older Americans Act

The Older Americans Act was signed into law by President Lyndon Johnson in 1965. In addition to creating the federal Administration on Aging, it authorized grants to states for community planning and service programs, along with research, demonstration, and training projects related to aging. Services are coordinated and delivered through regional agencies on aging. Services include meals for homebound elders (Meals on Wheels), information and referrals, transportation, and elder abuse prevention. The act was reauthorized in 2000, adding a new program, the National Family Caregiver Support Program, designed to help family members caring for resident elders. Services to caregivers are coordinated by state agencies and should include counseling support groups and respite care. Lack of funding has hampered the ability of agencies to meet all the needs of elders and their caretakers in local communities.[42]

Helps to take care of the elderly

How Does the Government Work With the Market Economy to Deliver Services?

Not all social welfare policies are delivered through the public or government sector of the economy. Under the Title XX Amendments to the Social Security Act in 1973, states can utilize public funds to purchase services from private agencies. These private agencies act as part of the nonprofit private sector, but they are increasingly relying on federal funds to operate.[43] While it is true that the private sector is involved in delivery of services, the overwhelming majority of social welfare services and benefits are delivered through public funding. Many social welfare policies operate in the private market economy, with government funds reimbursing eligible persons for their purchase of services, such as Medicare and Medicaid. Food stamps offer eligible persons the opportunity to purchase some food goods from local sellers in the market economy at a lower price by using government coupons. Section 8 vouchers allow recipients to rent housing in the private housing market. Both these programs offer a sort of benefits in kind rather than direct cash grants.

Sectors of the market economy also benefit from these social welfare policies: The health care sector benefits from Medicaid and especially Medicare, the agricultural sector benefits from food stamps, and the housing sector benefits from the Section 8 housing program. Social welfare policies also benefit businesses and corporations by ensuring the well-being of the workforce without raising wages (through extramarket provisions of food, shelter, and health care), and they soften the burden of unemployment, an inevitable feature of market capitalism.[44] The benefits of social welfare policies to the operation of the market economy will be discussed more fully in Chapter 4.

CONCLUSION

In this chapter we have seen how social policies are formulated to solve some social problems that are seen as important by a critical mass of voters, media, and political actors. Social policies are only one solution to a perceived social problem, *not* necessarily the most rational, effective, or socially just solution. Since social policies are human creations, they can be changed. Social workers have a professional commitment to work to achieve more just social policies. Ideas for innovative social policies that advance social justice will be presented throughout this book.

DISCUSSION QUESTIONS

1. What is your view of human nature? Do you view human beings as essentially plastic with potential to develop differently according to the culture in which they are born, or do you think human nature is fixed? If the latter, how would you describe the immutable qualities of human beings?

2. What do conservatives and liberals have in common ideologically? What divides them?

3. How has Jefferson's view of the role of the federal government changed? Which political group's philosophy most resembles his ideas about government and liberty?

4. Why have the problems of homelessness and HIV/AIDS receded from public attention and failed to inspire new social policy initiatives over the past 10 years? Which social problems have taken center stage in the national policy agenda?

NOTES

1. Larry Gerston, *Public Policy Making: Process and Principles* (New York: M. E. Sharpe, 1997), 22–49.

2. John W. Kingdon, *Agendas, Alternatives and Public Policies* (Boston: Little, Brown, 1994), 177–178.

3. David Musto, *The American Disease: Origins of Narcotic Control* (New York: Oxford University Press, 1999).

4. Bruce Jansson, *The Reluctant Welfare State* (Belmont, CA: Wadsworth, Thompson, 2001), 342–343.

5. The Urban Institute, "Preventing Homelessness," February 2, 2002, http://www.urbaninstitute.org, accessed June 25, 2007.

6. Lorece Edwards, "Perceived Social Support and HIV/AIDS Medication Adherence Among African American Women," *Qualitative Health Research* 16 (May 2006): 679–691; Gwen Van Servellen and Emilia Lombard, "Supportive Relationships and Medication Adherence in HIV-Infected Low-Income Latinos," *Journal of Nursing Research* 27 (December 2005): 1–23.

7. Robert J. Sampson and Janet L. Lauritsen, "Racial and Ethnic Disparities in Crime and Criminal Justice in the United States," in Michael Tonry, ed., *Crime and Justice: A Review of Research,* Vol. 21: Special volume titled "Ethnicity, Crime, and Immigration: Comparative and Cross-National Perspectives" (Chicago: University of Chicago Press, 1997), pp. 311–374; Robert J. Sampson, Jeffrey D. Morenoff, and Stephen Raudenbush, "Social Anatomy of Racial and Ethnic Disparities in Violence," *American Journal of Public Health* 95 (2005): 224–232.

8. David Gil, *Unravelling Social Policy: Theory, Analysis and Political Action Towards Social Equality,* 5th ed. (Rochester, VT: Schenkman, 1992), 20.

9. Mimi Abramovitz, "Definitions and Functions of Social Welfare Policy," in Joel Blau, ed., *The Dynamics of Social Welfare Policy* (New York: Oxford University Press, 2007), 505.

10. Frances Fox Piven, *War at Home: The Domestic Costs of Bush's Militarism* (New York: The New Press, 2004).

11. Child Trends Data Bank, "High School Dropout Rates," Summer 2008, http://www.childtrendsdatabank.org/indicators/1HighSchoolDropout.cfm, accessed December 12, 2008.

12. Howard Karger and David Stoesz, *American Social Welfare Policy: A Pluralist Approach* (Boston: Pearson, 2006), 2.

13. Abramovitz, "Definitions and Functions of Social Welfare Policy," 20.

14. Gerston, *Public Policy Making,* 6.

15. James Read, *Power Versus Liberty* (Charlottesville: University of Virginia Press, 2000), 119–157; A. W. Griswold, "Jefferson's Republic: The Rediscovery of Democratic Philosophy," in Jeffery Taylor, ed., *Thomas Jefferson and the Education of a Citizen* (Washington, DC: Library of Congress, 1999), 3–39.

16. Gordon Wood, *The Creation of the American Republic, 1776–1787* (Chapel Hill: University of North Carolina Press, 1969).

17. Jansson, *The Reluctant Welfare State,* 43.

18. Eric Goldman, *Rendezvous With Destiny* (New York: Vintage, 1963); Seymour Martin Lipset, *American Exceptionalism* (New York: Norton, 1996), 37–38.

19. Melvin Thorne, *American Conservative Thought Since World War II* (New York: Greenwood Press, 1999).

20. See especially Anthony Giddens, *The Third Way* (Cambridge, England: Polity Press, 1999).

21. Frances Fox Piven and Richard Cloward, *Regulating the Poor* (New York: Vintage, 1993), 3–4.

22. Gil, *Unravelling Social Policy,* 17.

23. Peter Berger and Thomas Luckman, *The Social Construction of Reality: A Treatise on the Sociology of Knowledge* (New York: Anchor Books, 1967), 90–110.

24. Mary Ann Jimenez, "A Feminist Analysis of Welfare Reform," *Affilia* 14 (Fall 1999): 278–293.

25. U.S. Department of Justice, "Three Strikes and You're Out," July 1999, http://www.ncjrs.gov/txtfiles/165369.txt, accessed December 7, 2008.

26. Susan Urahn, "U.S. Prison Population Sets New Record," Pew Center on the States, *Washington Post,* February 29, 2008, http://www.washingtonpost.com/wp-dyn/content/discussion/2008/02/28/DI2008022802960.html, accessed December 7, 2008.

27. Office of National Drug Control Policy, "Drug War Clock," http://www.drugsense.org/wodclock.htm, accessed December 7, 2008.

28. Adapted from Gil, *Unravelling Social Policy,* 69–101. Used with permission of the author.

29. Sar Levitan, Garth Magnum, Stephen Magnum, and Andrew Sum, *Programs in Aid of the Poor* (Baltimore: Johns Hopkins University Press, 2003), 43–57.

30. Levitan et al., *Programs in Aid of the Poor,* 74.

31. Levitan et al., *Programs in Aid of the Poor,* 76.

32. Abramovitz, "Definitions and Functions of Social Welfare Policy," 46.

33. Food Research and Action Center, "Federal Food Programs: Food Stamp Program," http://www.frac.org/html/federal_food_programs/programs/fsp.html, accessed June 30, 2007.

34. Center on Budget and Policy Priorities, "The Food Stamp Program's Critical Role in Helping Children," http://www.cbpp.org/4-26-07fa-fact.htm, accessed June 30, 2007.

35. Food Research and Action Center, "Child Nutrition Fact Sheet," http://www.frac.org/pdf/WICfactsheet07.pdf, accessed June 29, 2007.

36. Levitan et al., *Programs in Aid of the Poor,* 105–108.

37. U.S. Department of Health and Human Services, Centers for Medicare and Medicaid Services, "Overview," http://www.cms.hhs.gov/ReportsTrustFunds/, accessed June 30, 2007.

38. Jack Hadley and John Holahan, "Is Health Care Spending Higher Under Medicaid or Private Insurance?" *Inquiry* 40 (Winter, 2003/2004): 323–342.

39. Levitan et al., *Programs in Aid of the Poor,* 91–99.

40. Families, USA, "Medicaid and Children's Health: Federal Issues," http://familiesusa.org/issues/childrens-health/, accessed June 30, 2007.

41. Levitan et al., *Programs in Aid of the Poor,* 93.

42. Administration on Aging, "Older Americans Act," http://www.aoa.gov/about/legbudg/oaa/legbudg_oaa.aspx, accessed July 1, 2007; Center for Social Gerontology, "Reauthorization of the Older Americans Act," http://www.tcsg.org/law/oaa/reauth.htm, accessed July 1, 2007.

43. Neil Gilbert, *Capitalism and the Welfare State: Dilemmas of Social Benevolence* (New Haven, CT: Yale University Press, 1983), 7–12.

44. Abramovitz, "Definitions and Functions of Social Welfare Policy," 34–36.

CHAPTER

3

Historical Values Influencing Social Problems and Social Policies

CHAPTER QUESTIONS

1. In what ways is the United States different from other industrialized countries?
2. Why are individualism and self-reliance emphasized in the United States?
3. Why are the ideas of work, wealth, and material prosperity so deeply valued in the United States? ~ education
4. What are the consequences of these beliefs for economically marginalized persons?
5. Why do few people criticize the economic system in this country?
6. Why do most people, including the poor, believe in upward mobility and equal opportunity?
7. How important was Social Darwinism in explaining differences between ethnic groups?
8. How have benevolence and altruism been forces for positive reform in American history?
9. How can the First Amendment to the Constitution be used to promote social justice?

● ● ●

The United States is different from other industrialized countries in many ways. This country has fewer social welfare policies than other similarly developed countries and is the only developed country without national health insurance. The United States has not developed adequate social policies to address our most serious social problems, such as poverty, homelessness, health

43

care, child care, inadequate wages, poor working conditions, and the myriad of other social problems we have created. Why is this? Certain ideologies or values have emerged at various times in U.S. history that work against the construction of equitable policies and instead contribute to the emergence of social problems. Some of these ideologies are the belief in the primacy of the individual or what many call individualism, a strong commitment to work ethic, a belief that government interference is undesirable, and other beliefs that have characterized the United States since its founding. This chapter will explore the reasons for the comparative lack of social policies in the United States by exploring some historical values, beliefs, and ideologies that are distinctly American.

 ## IDEOLOGIES

The concept of ideology may seem politically freighted, as though it refers to extreme positions taken in political debate. Ideologies are really socially constructed beliefs and values that have been made into explanatory systems to make disparate events meaningful. They are explanations of why things happen and what they mean. If I explain poverty as a function of individual laziness or failure, then my ideological stance toward poverty is that it is internally caused. If I explain it as a function of the economic system, then my ideology centers on a belief that the market economy is implicated in poverty. Each of these positions is an ideology, based on a system of interdependent beliefs and values about things that cannot be proved but are deeply held. All of us have ideologies about the causes of social problems and the usefulness of current social policies. We also have ideologies about possible solutions—what could work to solve problems and what will not. Therefore the term *ideology* is not a negative one, implying thoughtless opinions, but refers to explanations of why things are the way they are. A more formal way of defining ideologies is as normative structures of values and meanings that provide pathways for our apprehension of the reality we encounter.

Much of the time, we don't think about our ideologies, but if asked to explain a problem in the world, we would make our ideological positions evident. Religious ideologies are powerful explanations that inspire people to great sacrifice and altruism as well as to violence and inhumanity. Political ideologies drive electoral and often legislative wrangling in this country. Disparate political beliefs have inspired wars; those held in common have led to nation building. Social ideologies can be powerful assumptions about groups. In American history, prevailing ideologies in the 19th century about gender relegated women to subordinate roles, just as prevailing ideologies about some ethnic groups led to their oppression and to unjust policies. Ideologies are often held in common by groups of people who have had similar historical experiences. Ideologies may have been created at a historical moment and passed down to succeeding generations without being questioned or verified. These systems of belief have been reified and legitimized over decades and are often very hard to modify. Individuals develop ideological positions largely based on what they learn from others, including family, peer groups, educational experience, government, popular culture, and media. In order to think critically about the prevailing ideologies in a society at any one time, individuals must see them as elaborate social constructions whose truth is not self-evident. Some ideologies are easier to pierce than others. Ideologies in the United States about the need for military intervention might be questioned more than those supporting capitalism and democracy, for instance. This is because military intervention involves a specific historical event and the period before the intervention is within the memory of observers, whereas few people have had experience with other forms of political or economic organization and therefore there is little perspective about their socially constructed nature. Most dominant ideologies are by definition conservative, as they are developed to explain and maintain the status quo.

Even though ideologies are socially constructed, they have important functions: (a) they offer a systematic explanation of reality internally congruent with other prevailing explanations; (b) they reduce anxiety about the different or the unknown; (c) they have the potential for social control; (d) they offer a sense of predictability; and (e) they justify our behavior in a situation. Thus the prevailing explanation or ideology that would be summoned if one came unexpectedly upon a person who appeared to be acting in an insane manner might be that this person is mentally ill. This explanation is congruent with the scientific worldview currently legitimized. Anxiety would be reduced once this explanation was accepted. Based on these beliefs, action might be taken to control the presumed mentally ill person through medical care or confinement. In this way the explanation of mental illness would allow the observer to control future anxiety-provoking behavior. Ideologies, then, are templates, or reassuring explanatory structures that can explain contingencies, both the unexpected and the taken-for-granted aspects of the social order. Elaborate belief systems or ideologies can be thought of as metanarratives, or overarching explanations shared by large numbers of people who have the power to define reality. The belief that White middle-class women are more delicate and less intellectually capable than men or that Whites are intellectually superior to other groups were metanarratives that dominated the social and political landscape for a great deal of our history. These ideologies had a self-realizing power; that is, they tended to create the conditions they described. White middle-class women were confined to situations where their delicacy was emphasized, and they were not encouraged to use their intellectual abilities. Non-White groups were systematically deprived of access to positions of power and influence, giving force to beliefs that they were less capable.

● U.S. EXCEPTIONALISM

Some historians have described the differences characterizing the U.S. historical development as American *exceptionalism*.[1] Clearly there is no way to "prove" that the United States is unique, and further there is no normative standard by which we can all agree that this difference, if it exists, makes us better or worse than other countries. Nevertheless there are certain historical signposts that suggest that the United States developed in ways that are qualitatively different from other industrialized countries.[2] This uniqueness lies in the values, beliefs, and ideologies that developed in this country in the 18th century and 19th century, partly brought as cultural baggage by early English settlers, partly brought by later immigrants, and partly brought as a consequence of the abundance of land and resources already here. We will now examine some of these cultural ideologies brought by early settlers and immigrants that continue to underlie social problems and social policies in the United States.

● INDIVIDUALISM

The generations that participated in the American Revolution and wrote the Constitution were deeply influenced by John Locke's ideas of individual liberty. Locke, a 17th-century English philosopher, believed that monarchy and established or state religion were not consistent with individual liberty, which he also identified with the individual freedom to acquire property and the rule of law. The revolutionary nature of Locke's ideas can only be understood in the context of 17th- and 18th-century Europe, in which absolute monarchies ruled. Locke's influence on the Revolutionary generation in this country is clear in the Declaration of Independence, which speaks of the individual's rights to "life, liberty and the pursuit of happiness," which government may not abridge.[3] Of course, these rights were thought to reside in White men, not in other residents of the new republic. The antigovernment emphasis of the Revolutionary generations discussed in Chapter 2 also carried with it a revulsion toward social class hierarchy and established church control over government or individual liberties,

Signers of the U.S. Constitution

SOURCE: From the Library of Congress, the Theodor Horydczak Collection.

as well as a deep respect for the liberties of thought, speech, and press. Locke was one of the philosophers (along with Hume and Rousseau) who developed the social contract theory of government, where the authority of the state rests on the consent of the governed.[4] The American experiment with self-governance (for it was seen as experimental at the time) included a strong emphasis on liberty and individual rights. Some see this early emphasis on liberty and individual rights as part of the exceptional nature of the American republic. According to this narrative, the United States forged its unique character based on its original commitment to individual rights in a republic where representative democracy depended on educated citizens.[5] The creation of a federal government and a constitutional guarantee of freedom of religion and the separation of church and state are other cases of American exceptionalism, according to this version of the origins of the United States.

The dominant narrative is only a part of a much broader story. The commitment to individual rights and liberty was and continues to be seriously limited. Many groups then and now have continued to be involved in an ongoing struggle to achieve even the minimum rights to life, liberty, and the pursuit of happiness. Nevertheless the rhetorical emphasis on political individualism was unique to this country and did influence the response to social problems as well as add to their creation.

Other early experiences in the colonies promoted individualism. The Puritans of 17th- and 18th-century New England believed that salvation depended on individual covenants or contracts with God and that grace would come to an individual directly from God, rather than through the intercession of a minister. Salvation was an individual matter from start to finish; God's grace might come to a husband but not a wife, and no amount of intercession would change God's will.[6]

This early emphasis on the rights of the individual or individualism among the authors of the founding documents (including the Bill of Rights) has been seen as a hallmark of the narrative Americans tell about themselves since the late 18th century.[7] This valorization of individualism includes a belief that the United States has been characterized by what one historian called a "reality of atomistic social freedom."[8] Since there are no hereditary class lines in the United States, it seems true theoretically that individuals are free to move through the social order. In actuality, economic resources and factors of discrimination often substantially limit their potential to take advantage of this formally class-less structure. This ideology about individual social freedom is held as an obvious truth to many, not subject to empirical verification. The myth of individual freedom has defined much of our political discourse and contributed to the creation of many social problems in the United States, including poverty and discrimination. The ideology of individualism limits our ability to create social policies that would promote social equality similar to those enjoyed by other industrialized democracies. Because of this belief that individual liberty is already ensured in the United States, social problems are instinctively viewed as the result of individual action or failure to act. This belief in individualism has served as a covering ideology, obscuring the failure of some individuals to attain their rights to life, liberty, and the pursuit of happiness.

The ideology of individualism that began in the American Revolution has not waned; if anything, this belief in the importance of individual rights and responsibilities has grown over the centuries. Paradoxically, this ideology supports both oppression and liberation of disenfranchised groups. The emphasis on individual rights has been important in the struggle to attain civil and legal rights for some oppressed groups, if not for the poor, including African Americans, gays and lesbians, and persons with disabilities. The ideology of individualism can serve as a platform for asserting the need for legal and political reform and advancement of rights of other oppressed groups as well. When it can be shown that individual rights are abridged unfairly, Americans may respond. Social workers and others concerned with social justice can use the commitment to individual liberty to advance their agendas.

INDEPENDENCE ●

Both individualism and its corollary, independence, are core American values.[9] Geographic mobility, which demands a high degree of independence from family of origin, has characterized American society since the beginning of the 19th century. The willingness to move away from family to begin the search for work is a hallmark of industrial societies in general, but it also has been seen as quintessentially American. Tocqueville noted the restlessness of Americans in the 1830s and their constant movement across state boundaries.[10] Dependence, on the other hand, is not functional in a geographically mobile society, where employment opportunities may necessitate movement away from family and friends. We will explore the relationship of independence to the functioning of the market economy in Chapter 4. For now it is important to note that the ideologies of individualism and independence have been powerful in the American imagination since the American Revolution.[11] These ideologies inform our political and economic lives and serve to punish those who cannot live up to their strict demands. Most Americans believe that independence is far superior to dependence as a way of living one's life.[12]

The belief in the value of independence and individualism functions as a narrative or story about the American character. Of course, no one can live a really independent life. Instead we depend on others in our every waking moment—from the products we use that are made by others to the rationality of others we assume when we interact with them. We need and depend on products picked, made, processed, or refashioned by others. Our dependence on electricity, for example, is starkly revealed during blackouts. During these and other crises of dependence such as weather disasters—hurricanes, blizzards, and so forth—people feel free to depend on each other in ways they would never consider under normal circumstances. While the belief in the value of independence is merely that, a belief, like other ideologies discussed in this chapter, its power in the culture lies in the legitimation of these ideologies; insofar as people believe this is how the world should work, those who do demonstrate these qualities may be punished. Other cultures may value interdependence rather than independence.[13] When Americans come into contact with persons with these values, they may see them as not only different but odd or inferior as well. The story of immigration in the 19th and 20th centuries was at least partly the story of the immigrants' struggle to assimilate and resist the key American values of individualism and independence.

● THE PROTESTANT WORK ETHIC

An important argument about U.S. exceptionalism was offered by Max Weber in his classic book *The Protestant Ethic and the Spirit of Capitalism*.[14] Weber argued that the Puritans who settled New England in the 17th and 18th centuries were followers of John Calvin, the Scottish Protestant reformer, who preached the doctrine of predestination. According to this doctrine, God chose some persons to be saved and others to be dammed to hell. Since there was no way to know whether one was saved or dammed, living with the uncertainty while maintaining one's piety and religious devotion was a challenging proposition. Calvinists believed that nothing could alter the ultimate fate God had chosen for one; no good works or prayer could influence the selection of those chosen by God for salvation. It was the duty of every person to believe that he or she was chosen, however, for to doubt it was a sure sign of lack of faith and ultimate damnation.[15]

The Puritans who settled in New England were a very pious group; they had left England in order to practice their religion freely. As Calvinists, they believed that each person had a *calling* from God to fulfill his duty in this world—to work to his fullest capacity. (They thought only men had such a calling.) The Puritans who came to New England believed that working hard at one's calling was a sign that one would be saved. Further assurance of salvation could be taken from the accumulation of worldly goods or wealth as a result of working hard at one's calling. This in essence is the Protestant work ethic: Hard work and success at this work in the form of wealth were signs that one had been chosen by God to be saved rather than dammed. Those who did not work hard at their calling and did not accumulate wealth were surely dammed. Because the anxiety associated with predestination was so overwhelming, Weber argued that achieving certainty about one's fate through the performance of one's calling in this world was crucial for these Protestant believers. Weber argued that this internal commitment to hard work and the accumulation of wealth in the first generations of Puritans was the reason that modern capitalism took hold so quickly and easily in 19th-century America. Puritans were committed to acting in *this world,* rather than focusing on the next, according to Weber. Calvinism supplied the inner drive that allowed for a disciplined commitment to work, as well as the drive for accumulation of wealth characteristic of the capitalist entrepreneur.[16] Puritans emphasized saving, not spending, wealth. They valued self-discipline, not consumption, making it easier to accumulate wealth. It was because of their belief that wealth was a sign of salvation that men were willing to work so hard to achieve it. These values led to the accumulation of wealth in the late 18th and 19th centuries among Puritans and later Protestants in general who shared the belief in frugality and in dedication to work as a holy enterprise. Both the value attached to wealth and the belief in the value of hard work are legacies of the Puritans, according to Weber.

Weber was struck by the rapid ascendance of the United States into the position of world economic leader around 1900. He connected this economic success to the Protestant religious traditions, which had characterized the United States for much of the 18th and 19th centuries.[17] Like Marx, Weber saw the successful development of capitalism depending on the development of "formally free labor and the rational, continuous pursuit of profit."[18]

Whether the link between the Puritan beliefs and the economic growth of the United States in the 19th century existed need not concern us here. The importance of Weber's contribution lies in the recognition that work and wealth have been highly valued in American history. Emptied of the religious content, there continues to be a moral imperative to hard work and a secular valorization of wealth in the United States. "The Puritan wanted to work in a calling; we are forced to do so," Weber noted.[19] The work ethic is now part of American culture.[20] Whether because of the influence of the Puritans or for other reasons, it is clear that Americans have a strong work ethic compared to workers in other countries. We work more weeks in a year and longer hours each week than do persons in industrialized countries in Europe.[21] Workers in this country have less leisure time than do workers in other countries, take fewer vacations, and are more likely to work overtime and work more than one job.[22] The number of hours worked per week in the United States has increased over the past 30 years, while it has decreased in Germany, France, and Spain.[23] Younger Americans continue to adhere to a strong work ethic, as do Americans from various ethnic and religious backgrounds.[24] Those who self-identify as Evangelical Christians are more likely to have values consonant with the Protestant work ethic than persons from other Protestant groups, including Lutherans and Methodists.[25] This makes sense, because the early Calvinists were more like the fundamentalist Christians of today than other Protestant denominations. Their beliefs in individual salvation, a direct relationship with God, and the necessity of an adult conversion experience are similar to the beliefs of fundamentalist Christians.[26] The link between the inner commitment to hard work and religion has been explored without conclusive results, but the belief in the importance of hard work, especially among Protestant Americans, has been found repeatedly.[27]

The belief that wealth is accessible for Americans who work hard has not been dislodged by the growing wealth inequality that has characterized the United States over the past 30 years.[28]

What are the implications of this belief that hard work and wealth are signs of personal and moral worth? The consequences of these values for persons who cannot work, are unemployed, or are working at marginal jobs are punishing. If hard work is a measure of one's drive, discipline, and worth, then not working is a sign of moral flaws or even failure. Even more punishing is the lingering idea that wealth is a measure of personal worth. While Americans do not believe that wealth is an insurance against damnation as the Puritans did, there is a strong value placed on material prosperity.[29] Those who have a great deal of wealth, especially those who became wealthy on their own without inheriting money, are widely admired. Many Americans hope to become wealthy themselves and expect their children to accumulate even more.[30] Yet many people work hard all their lives and accumulate little wealth. Persons working for minimum wage or below minimum wage have little hope of becoming wealthy. Perhaps that is why state lotteries are so popular with economically marginalized persons: They represent a chance for wealth.

In a society that believes material prosperity will follow hard work, the working poor may be seen as not having a proper or sufficient work ethic, in spite of the fact that they may work more than one job in punishing conditions (see Chapter 4). Thus poverty may be ignored or even disdained by those who have achieved wealth. The poor are not just poor; they are inferior, according to this way of thinking. These attitudes, even if shared by only some Americans, can have profound consequences for welfare policy and may have limited the possibilities for health care policy, housing policy, and other public provisions of policies and services.

● THE FRONTIER AND SELF-RELIANCE

Another factor frequently cited as a mark of American *exceptionalism* is the existence for much of the 19th century of a frontier that prompted westward expansion. Historians have been struck with the vast land that the English settlers had at their doorstep after the American Revolution when they were free to move into that land as well as the impact of the possibility of westward expansion on the American character.[31] Frederick Jackson Turner offered a seminal argument at the end of the 19th century when he announced prematurely in a speech to historians that the West was closed because all the land had been settled. While westward expansion continued through the early decades of the 20th century, Turner's words caught the attention of many intellectuals as he lamented the end of the frontier, which he felt had a salutary effect on the country and on the American character. He thought that the ever-moving Western frontier and the expansion of Americans into these lands had encouraged the growth of "free" institutions there, specifically capitalism, democracy, and individualism. He also saw the frontier as demanding a stern self-reliance from those who moved there, since they had to leave all previous ties and supporting institutions behind.[32] This self-reliance, a close cousin to individualism and independence, is part of the myth of the frontier that has been valorized in popular culture.[33] In fact, the survival of White settlers in frontier towns was marked by a high degree of mutual aid and solidarity, as few isolated farmers managed to survive the challenges of the environment. Yet the ideology of the frontier as a place where courageous, self-reliant, masculine energy forged a new society in the face of great odds contributed to the belief in the value of individual effort. Stories of frontier survival and rough justice reinforced the belief in self-reliance and individualism in the Eastern cities. The sense that westward expansion was always a possibility encouraged the notion of the West as a "safety valve" for urban discontents and deepened the ideological commitment that people functioned at their best without government intervention.[34]

Of course, this narrative about the frontier has been considerably revised, if not exploded, by the tardy recognition that other people already lived in this vast Western land and were killed, harassed, and moved against their will to make way for White settlement. It has now been acknowledged that women were an integral part of frontier life, as revealed by historical scholarship over the past 30 years. African American migrants moved West along with European settlers.[35] Mexican citizens lived in some of the Western lands, which White settlers coveted and eventually took from Mexico. All these historical facts have not altered the outlines of the original narrative about the West for many: The self-reliance demonstrated by men at the Western frontier was responsible for the spread of free institutions. It is just this self-reliance that some conservatives lament has now drained from American life, as we have become more dependent on the government to meet our needs.

The frontier also gave Americans a false sense of entitlement to expansion and conquest. After 1845, many political leaders believed in the concept of "manifest destiny" and argued that America's superior institutions and culture gave them a God-given right and obligation to spread their way of life across the continent. This was a way of thinking about the United States as an "exceptional" or unique country with a God-given mission, akin to that of the Puritans in the 17th and 18th centuries.[36] The commitment to Manifest Destiny fueled the annexation of Texas as well as the war with Mexico that resulted in the acquisition of California, Nevada, New Mexico, Arizona, Utah, and parts of Colorado in 1847. This treaty effectively set the stage for the dispossession of the Mexican landlord and the creation of the Mexican farm worker, with all the discrimination that status change implied in the territories acquired from Mexico.[37] Manifest Destiny was used to legitimize the federal government's claim of sovereignty over Oregon and Washington in 1846, at the expense of the British who claimed the territories as their own. Manifest Destiny justified these wars and expansionist policies. It rendered the killing of Native Americans morally defensible to many, since they were standing in the way of God's plan for the continent. Westward expansion had a direct influence on the expansion of slavery. The successful growth of cotton depended on the acquisition of arable land as cotton depleted the soil. This was the case, for instance, in Texas, where White farmers imported slaves from other states for cotton production. As Southern states looked West in the 1840s and 1850s, they sought to bring slaves with them. Westward expansion and the frontier encouraged the growth and expansion of slavery, the oppression of Native Americans, and the dispossession of Mexicans in the Southwest. These narratives were not told for many generations; instead another story was told—that of the self-reliant White male who "conquered" the land and its inhabitants. While White settlement of these lands brought benefits to other Whites who followed the first settlements, there was a deep cost for other groups. The narratives about hardiness and courage at the frontier are only a small part of the whole story of Western expansion.

● IMMIGRATION

The vast majority of persons now living in the United States descended from immigrants. Exceptions include Native Americans who lived here for centuries before English settlement and Latinos whose ancestors lived in the Southwest before the acquisition of their land from Mexico in 1847. For the rest of us, immigration is what brought our people here. The first wave of immigration was, of course, British in the 17th and 18th centuries. After the English culture and institutions took root in the 18th and early 19th centuries, the United States welcomed successive waves of European immigrants throughout the 19th century, beginning with the Irish immigration to the Northeast in the late 1840s and continuing with Germans, Scandinavians, and Northern Europeans in the mid-19th century. Between 1880 and 1920, large numbers of Southern and Eastern European immigrants came to the United States, over 13 million between 1866 and 1900 and 43 million total by 1910.[38] More than a million

Immigrants arriving from Europe

SOURCE: From the Library of Congress. Illustration by The Maltine Company.

Chinese and Japanese immigrants came to the West in the late 19th century. Some historians argue that the great migration of people to the United States is the factor that accounts for American *exceptionalism,* since this migration is unequaled in human history.[39] This is a convincing argument, given the economic benefits of large-scale immigration at the end of the 19th century. Could the industrial growth that characterized the United States in this period have occurred without the large supply of inexpensive labor supplied by these immigrants? The answer is clearly no: Economists and historians agree that an unregulated labor market allowed owners in the manufacturing and mining industries to pay low wages and still find all the workers they needed. The majority of immigrants in this period worked in the coal, iron, steel, meat packing, construction, and clothing industries.[40] This massive movement of people westward to the United States was an unmitigated economic boon for employers. It contributed significantly to the rise of large cities in the Midwest and led to an increase in population in the older cities on the eastern seaboard.[41]

Culturally, immigrants changed the landscape of the United States, beginning with the Irish, who brought Catholicism and a more fatalistic view than the Protestant natives, who dominated the Eastern urban areas in the mid-19th century. The Irish were a peasant migration; that is, they came from rural Ireland where they worked the land. Forced off their land by the English, the Irish came to the United States with little education, few job skills, and little or no money. They experienced the first anti-immigrant sentiments later to be suffered by other immigrant groups.[42] The cultural diversity the Irish offered the native English stock or "Yankee" was not appreciated at first; in fact, it was denigrated until the Irish worked their way into city government and local institutions at the end of the 19th century. The "new" immigrants came from Italy, Poland, Austria-Hungary, Russia, Greece, and Turkey to the United States from 1890 to 1920. American businesses promoted—and friends and family encouraged—this "new" immigration. Like the Irish immigrants earlier in the century, these new immigrants came largely from rural areas and possessed few skills suitable to industrial work. While male immigrants were welcome additions to the low-cost labor pool, families suffered greatly from terrible living conditions in urban areas and from anti-immigrant sentiment. In the West during the latter part of the 19th century, the Chinese and Japanese migrated to the United States where the Chinese suffered from extreme anti-immigrant feeling, also known as nativism.

Immigrants' migration patterns often featured families and neighbors following each other in migration chains. In the United States, immigrants had extensive social support networks during the first generation in particular. This pattern of social migration is also characteristic of contemporary migration from Mexico, Puerto Rico, and parts of Central and South America, as well as Korea, Japan, and China. These social support networks functioned as economic pathways to jobs in low-paying sectors of the economy, where immigrant groups tended to cluster by ethnicity, especially in the first generation.[43] Instead of complete assimilation to American values, new research on immigration has emphasized "resilient ethnicity" as the process by which 19th- and 20th-century immigrants and their descendents adapted to the United States.[44] Immigrants maintained their primary culture in various ways, especially in their enduring ethnic identities, social relations, and cultural institutions and practices, thereby enriching the tapestry of life in this country. Catholic immigrants and their leaders questioned the emphasis on individualism, which appeared to conflict with the ordered hierarchy of Catholicism. Both Catholic and some Protestant leaders worried that a moral relativism, corresponding to the emphasis on the importance of individualism, would overshadow the commitment to one faith among their followers.[45]

Some argue that immigrants tended to contribute to a conservative moral and political perspective. Comparing the conditions in the United States to the agricultural scarcity and famines they may have experienced in Eastern and Southern Europe, immigrants were somewhat more likely to look past unequal and unjust social and economic conditions that fueled the labor movements at the end of the 19th century, for example. Immigrants were reluctant to join labor protests and labor unions during the 19th and early 20th centuries because they came to this country to work, often with the intention of returning home. Some of them took jobs as scabs during strike actions, alienating nonimmigrants trying to win recognition for unions.[46]

Another factor that influenced the generally conservative perspective of immigrants was the fact that they had made a choice to come to the United States, regardless of how constrained that choice was by poverty and the lack of options in their home country. Seriously questioning the conditions in this country and especially taking public action to change them could call into question their own decisions to emigrate. In the first generation, immigrants spoke a variety of languages and so did not present a cohesive group that might be mobilized for political action. In the 19th and 20th centuries, many immigrants faced with anti-immigrant attitudes made attempts to assimilate or at least not bring public attention to themselves by participating in protests or in radical organizations. Finally, immigrants often brought with them traditional values from their countries of origin; these values did not encourage rebellion against authority.[47] This is especially true of the immigrants who practiced Catholicism, a conservative religion in the 19th and 20th centuries that did not promote radicalism among its working-class adherents.[48] Ironically, immigrant groups have been blamed for radical protests and strikes, even though most immigrants did not participate. The labor union movement, socialism, and communism all were thought to have immigrant roots at various times in the 20th century. Immigrants have been identified with ideologies that seem "anti-American," and sometimes their very presence has been seen as an assault on American values.

Some immigrants questioned the emphasis on material wealth they felt characterized American culture. Religious leaders from immigrant groups, especially Catholic priests, worried that the commitment to money overshadowed the commitment to morality.[49] Immigrants brought with them these and other values of their countries of origin (see Table 3.1), contributing to, rather than losing, their cultures as they became accustomed to life in this country. Immigrants were therefore critical in the development of the pluralistic, diverse, democratic society that sustained both the idea and the reality of the United States from the 19th century to the present.

TABLE 3.1   **Region of Birth of Immigrants to the United States: 1850–1990**

Percent Distribution for Region of Birth Reported	Region of Birth Reported						
	Total	Europe	Asia	Africa	Oceania	Latin America	Northern America
Year							
1990*	100.0	22.9	26.3	1.9	0.5	44.3	4.0
1980*	100.0	39.0	19.3	1.5	0.6	33.1	6.5
1970*	100.0	61.7	8.9	0.9	0.4	19.4	8.7
1960*	100.0	75.0	5.1	0.4	0.4	9.4	9.8
1930	100.0	83.0	1.9	0.1	0.1	5.6	9.2
1920	100.0	85.7	1.7	0.1	0.1	4.2	8.2
1910	100.0	87.4	1.4	–	0.1	2.1	9.0
1900	100.0	86.0	1.2	–	0.1	1.3	11.4
1890	100.0	86.9	1.2	–	0.1	1.2	10.6
1880	100.0	86.2	1.6	–	0.1	1.3	10.7
1870	100.0	88.8	1.2	–	0.1	1.0	8.9
1860	100.0	92.1	0.9	–	0.1	0.9	6.0
1850	100.0	92.2	0.1	–	–	0.9	6.7

SOURCE: U.S. Census Bureau, Population Division.

* Indicates sample data.

● **UPWARD MOBILITY**

Most Americans believe in the reality of upward mobility. They believe that anyone who works hard can move up the economic ladder. The concept of upward mobility was uniquely American in the 19th and for most of the 20th century. It was not present in agricultural societies or in European societies with an aristocratic heritage. The idea of social mobility emerged in the 19th century, partly as a reflection of the reality of increased economic opportunity in manufacture and industry and partly as a mythic narrative to explain what was different about the United States from Europe. With no aristocracy or inherited social status and no fixed class structure, it seemed that no law or rule could stop any American from achieving economic success and from moving from poverty to wealth. Comparing the United States with France, Tocqueville was struck in 1830 with the openness of American society, although he recognized that there was a great deal of inequality of wealth and income among its citizens.[50] The lack of codified rules for social behavior and the laissez-faire atmosphere of the unregulated market economy together made it seem that the possibilities for economic success were boundless. Examples of captains of industry like John Rockefeller and Andrew Carnegie solidified the ideology of pulling oneself up by the bootstraps, as it was known in the 19th century, since both men came from poor families. Their successes were widely advertised in the 19th century, in self-help manuals, sermons, magazine articles, and lectures. In reality, upward mobility was an important narrative that outlined a potential path out of poverty, slum living, terrible work conditions, poor health, and general oppression. It described a true trajectory for some White middle- or upper-class men in the 19th century (Rockefeller and Carnegie were exceptions) who rose to the ranks of heads of industry and made enormous fortunes. For the vast majority of new immigrants, for African Americans, and even for Irish urban dwellers, upward mobility was only a myth. Even with education, the latter two groups were virtually unable to rise to positions of wealth and power and stayed in low-paying, unskilled jobs all their lives—one reason why the success of the Kennedy family in Boston in the early 20th century was so unusual. African Americans were systematically shut out of skilled jobs in the 19th and early 20th centuries; they were restricted to unskilled work. Among other immigrants, second-generation workers did better than first-generation workers, sometimes moving from unskilled jobs to white-collar jobs by the end of the 19th century when such jobs were opening up in the new corporations.[51]

Whatever the case in the 19th and early 20th centuries, by the latter part of the 20th century the opportunities for upward mobility had diminished for all groups, largely due to the nature of the occupational structure. With fewer entrepreneurial opportunities in industry as well as fewer manufacturing jobs, the economic structure became less open than it was in the 19th century, and the ethnic disparities for African Americans, Latinos, and other marginalized groups were even more pronounced.[52]

If the ideology of upward mobility has had limited basis in fact and even then been applied only to White nonimmigrant men, why has it been accepted as part of the American experience and character? The answer to that question may lie in the origins of the ideology of social mobility. Beginning in New England in the 1850s, a new ideology of mobility was introduced that posited a completely open social and economic order and equated social status and economic success with individual merit. Community and church leaders, politicians, magazines, newspapers, and commencement addresses, all popular culture outlets, emphasized the situation of pure competition they argued characterized this new social and economic order. Why did this ideology emerge in the mid-19th century? The catalyst for this ideology was the appearance of an apparently permanently poor class of Irish immigrants who were not easily absorbed into the economic and social structure of the region's manufacturing life. Faced with crowds of poor immigrant men looking for work and unnerved by the threat they saw in their Catholicism, leaders reassured themselves, their neighbors, and even those who were looking for work that "life in America was an endless race open to all, one in which all began on an equal footing, regardless of social background and training."[53] Believing that those who wanted to become prosperous would do so was a way of telling Americans that they did not have a fixed class system similar to the one that existed in Europe at the time. Those who were talented would rise socially and economically; those without talent would not. This belief in upward mobility took away any responsibility from the prosperous to change anything or even to aid the poor. More important, it offered poor immigrants hope that one day they would climb the economic and social ladder to success. Their condition was only temporary. There was "no reason for discontent." With the right virtues—especially unflagging hard work[54]—anyone could succeed. Those who remained poor did so because of their "habits of extravagance"—in not using and saving their money wisely.[55]

In the 19th century, this ideology was used to promote social control and to allay feelings of unrest. Those who believed it were convinced that there was no social injustice causing poverty. The injunction for hard work was delivered to poor and working-class persons in various ways, including newspapers and broadsides. For some immigrants in the 19th century, the message was more muted: Upward mobility was for one's children, not oneself. With this belief, a lifetime of hard work with little reward could be justified as long as the hope for one's children remained strong.[56] In this way, the ideology would not be undermined by the failure of one generation to become upwardly mobile.

This message and the promise it offers continues to be powerful. In 2003, a Gallup poll found that one third of Americans polled believed that they would be rich one day.[57] Many economically marginalized persons may believe that through their hard work and discipline they can attain higher status, better-paying occupations, and ultimately wealth. The implication is that failure to attain this promise is laid at the door of the individual. Even people who are economically marginalized continue to believe in upward mobility, according to this poll. The belief in upward mobility may serve to keep less privileged groups from developing a critical consciousness about inequality and the lack of economic opportunity they face. Such ideologies have a conservative effect, maintaining the support for the prevailing economic and political structures.

EQUAL OPPORTUNITY ●

A corollary to the ideology of upward mobility is the belief in equal opportunity. According to this ideology, all persons start the race for prosperity and economic success at the same place—"on equal footing" as quoted above. Tocqueville, the French aristocrat who visited the United States in the 1830s, was struck by how the concept of individualism was expanded to include the idea of equality of opportunity. He marveled at the uniqueness of this belief in the United States and noted that a similar belief did not exist in European countries.[58] Immigrants believed in the reality of upward mobility and equal opportunity as much as native-born Americans did. In fact, the optimism of immigrants about their future was remarkable, considering the living conditions many of them endured.[59]

According to the ideology of equal opportunity, everyone begins the race at the same place, but it was clear even in the 19th century that not all could be victorious.[60] What marks the difference between those who succeed and those who do not? While the answer was initially hard work, by the end of the 19th century, the belief in merit had replaced the belief that hard work alone could win the race. The concept of a meritocracy where one's fate and fortune are determined by one's merit grew out of the growth of the common school movement in the 19th century.[61] By the end of the 19th century, most White children in the United States had the right to a free public education through sixth grade, although immigrant children often worked in factories rather than completing their primary education because their parents needed their income.[62] The functions of public education were complex. First and foremost, public schools were designed to encourage the assimilation of immigrant children into the American culture. Second, schools served as the means of socializing the workforce for the discipline of factory work. And finally, they were a way for Americans to assure themselves that everyone had *equal opportunity* for upward mobility.[63] If *equal opportunity* was an integral part of the American ideology, public education was the insurance that equal opportunity was a reality, not a myth. With the creation of public high schools in the early years of the 20th century, the role of public education became even more central to the narrative of equal opportunity. Designed to train inner-city poor youth to work in the demanding industrial sector, high school education soon became a necessity for success in the workplace and the guarantee of equal opportunity.[64] It is a heavy burden to place on public education, a burden that it has not been able to meet.

The belief in equal opportunity has not stood up to empirical studies of social mobility in the United States, which have consistently shown that economic achievement is related to social origins.[65] Moreover, both these narratives about equality and upward mobility were stories for White males—not for women, who were not thought to be in economic competition with men, and not for African Americans.[66] Americans who currently believe in equal opportunity view it ambiguously and disagree on what is meant by it—for many, differences in beginning circumstances, such as gender, economic background, and ethnicity, are not important as long as there are no explicit, legal barriers to deter any group from competing.[67] Legal barriers have been largely eliminated due to court rulings; the remaining barriers are much more difficult to detect and resolve. But as will be discussed in Chapters 4 and 5, economic inequality and discrimination erect barriers to equal opportunity, a concept whose power is more important as a dream than as a reality.

PROGRESS

Americans in the 19th century believed that God and history were on their side and that the country was on an inexorable trajectory of positive change that would lead to more knowledge, more control over disease, greater economic growth, and a stronger nation. The American Revolution was thought to be a chapter in the struggle to achieve human rights. Pride in the Constitution and the political experiment it codified made it a patriotic duty to believe that the United States represented the highest achievement of humankind and was a direct reflection of God's will. The belief in Manifest Destiny discussed above was a part of the idea of progress and God's will for the country's expansion.[68]

Educated persons believed deeply in the idea of progress in medical knowledge, scientific development, political institutions, and even morality. Most Americans were convinced that their country was at the leading edge of history and was the most advanced and progressive country in all of human history. The growth of urban areas, the spread of public education, and the expansion into Western lands all convinced Americans that change was rapid and moving in a positive direction.[69] Things, in other words, were bound to continue to improve in the United States, which had turned away from the centuries of stagnation and stasis represented by European societies. Reformers in the Progressive Era at the beginning of the 20th century were heady with the possibilities that a new era of urban and political reform might bring.[70] The idea of progress is a complex mix of religious, scientific, and political ideology. Some believed that Americans were God's chosen people, others believed that science eventually would solve most human problems, and others believed that democracy would provide Americans and others with the best political institutions and provide an engine for economic progress.

Clearly this narrative about America's progress toward the good left out many important stories of those who did not share in the social or economic progress but contributed to it at great personal loss of terms. While many Americans may acknowledge this fact, most Americans have continued to believe in scientific and medical progress and are not ready to dismiss the idea of economic progress as part of the American dream, even after the disillusionment of the late 20th century.[71]

SOCIAL DARWINISM ●

The idea of progress took a dark turn with the rise of Social Darwinism at the end of the 19th century. Social Darwinism was an attempt to bring Darwin's theory of evolution to human society. Darwin's *On the Origin of Species,* published in 1859, described the struggle for existence among various species in the animal world. Social Darwinists attempted to apply this theory to one species—human beings—in order to account for the differences in material wealth, power, and privilege evident in the United States, especially in the large industrial cities of the Northeast and Midwest. There immigrants lived in appalling conditions and were paid very little for extremely hard work in heavy industries such as coal, steel, and railroads. American promoters of Social Darwinism, such as William Graham Sumner, argued that the struggle for existence among humans led to the "survival of the fittest," who he concluded were the Anglo Saxons at the helm of government and industry in the United States. The least fit, on the other hand, were the "new" immigrants who lived in urban slums, had large families, and were on the verge of starvation.[72] According to this theory, the poor were the weakest of the human species and, like animals not adapted to their environment, should die out. Helping the poor in any way, especially through government action, would only prolong their misery and keep the entire human race at a low level of development.

[handwritten margin note: The Jungle by Upson Sinclare]

Social Darwinists feared that because of their large family size, the poor would take over the social order, leading to the demise of the American way of life. They were convinced that no efforts should be made to intervene with the natural workings of industrial capitalism in order to protect the poor, lest they multiply and pass down their defective genes to future generations, retarding the process of evolution.[73] Social Darwinism thus justified laissez-faire capitalism and gave a seemingly biological imperative to massive inequality and injustice. Society was exactly the way it was meant to be since evolution was always moving forward progressively; therefore, no steps should be taken to interfere with the course of human evolution.[74] While Social Darwinism was a theory known mostly to educated elite, it was widely accepted by them during the last 3 decades of the 19th century.[75] The influence of Social Darwinism among the educated gave a quasi-scientific imperative to racism, eugenics, and other perspectives that argued for biological differences among ethnic groups in the 20th century. The impact of Social Darwinism was much more muted outside the United States. It was primarily among the educated and privileged classes in the United States that inequality was viewed as a law of nature and the inevitable end game of the "survival of the fittest."

In the early 20th-century reform Darwinism replaced Social Darwinism as a covering explanation among the intellectual elite in the United States. The reform Darwinists argued that evolution was an ongoing process, that human beings had evolved to a higher level than the primitive necessities of survival of the fittest, and that cooperation and altruism were called for in the continued improvement of the human race.[76] Reform Darwinists also believed that environment, rather than biology or heredity, was the key variable determining outcomes in human circumstances. Creating a better environment would lead to a better world and influence the course of human evolution; change was within human reach, not a slow process spanning centuries, reform Darwinists felt.[77] The belief in reform Darwinism encouraged the spirit of reform in the 20th century, during what was known as the Progressive Era. Experts in criminal justice, law, psychology, and the new profession of social work all embraced the notion that changing the environment would profoundly alter the circumstances of immigrants living in urban poverty and children working in factories and languishing in adult prisons, along with others who were suffering from poverty and oppression. Reform Darwinists such as Jane Addams believed that conditions of inequality could be transformed through rigorous efforts to achieve social justice. (See Chapter 6.)

Currently few Americans would openly espouse the principles of Social Darwinism. Yet the periodic suggestion that biological differences are at the root of differing and unequal conditions in ethnic minority groups suggests that these ideas have not completely died out. While there is no scientific basis for belief in these so-called genetic differences among ethnic groups, discrimination and prejudice make some Americans susceptible to the myths of biological differences. (See Chapter 5.)

THE ABSENCE OF A RADICAL POLITICAL TRADITION   ●

An important argument frequently made for U.S. *exceptionalism* is the fact that the United States has no radical political party or standing left party offering a substantial critique of the economic system. Of course, there have been Socialist candidates for president and other offices at various periods in our history, but those offering a serious political critique of our economic institutions have never achieved the status of a major political party. This is unlike other industrialized countries in Europe, where left-of-center parties earn substantial minorities and sometimes majorities in national elections. This absence of a significant Socialist movement in U.S. history has been seen as the defining quality of American exceptionalism by some.[78]

Over the last 150 years, the political parties have demonstrated a remarkable consensus about the main issues facing our country. As mentioned in the previous chapter, for instance, there has been very little political debate about the nature of our economic system or about the longstanding institutional racism and other forms of deep oppression that have characterized our history. Some argue that the reason for this anomaly is the lack of a feudal tradition in American history: Since we have no class oppression in our past, we have little interest in an ideology that promotes class conflict.[79] The argument is that because there is no inherited system of social classes, there are no corresponding political parties to represent these classes. Most Americans instead believe in an open-opportunity structure and a lack of serious political divisions; they appear essentially content with what they choose to see as a democratic and egalitarian society.[80] Some even see "Americanism" itself as an ideology that embodies the essence of socialism's values: equality and fairness; therefore, they see no need for a Socialist political tradition or party.[81]

As we have seen in Chapter 2, for much of our history there has been remarkably little political debate about the role of the federal government in social and economic life: The consensus was that there should be as little government interference as possible. Until the New Deal in the 1930s, the prevailing ideology was economic individualism and laissez-faire government. Since the New Deal, there has been some debate between liberals, mostly Democrats, and conservatives, mostly Republicans, over the role of the federal government. Even this debate has taken place within narrow grounds: no questioning of the fundamentals of the economic system or political system and strict adherence to the Constitution, for example. Socialist candidates, who call for fundamental change in the economic system, are marginalized; few know who they are, and fewer still vote for them. The exception was the presidential election of 1912 when the Socialist Party candidate, Eugene Debs, polled 6% of the national vote, the most a Socialist candidate has ever achieved.[82] Woodrow Wilson, a Democratic Party candidate, won the election, but he was influenced by Debs's view of monopoly power of corporations. Thus Wilson continued the task of trust busting begun by one of his predecessors, Teddy Roosevelt. Otherwise, Debs left no lasting mark on American politics. Even the New Deal, as we shall see, was focused more on conserving the market capitalism and the key political structures than on redesigning them.

Similarly, no political party has seriously questioned the legitimacy of the Constitution as the supervening authority over the federal and state governments. Yet Thomas Jefferson, for one, believed that each generation should write a new Constitution, for one generation should not bind another to its laws. Recognizing the socially constructed nature of the Constitution and other laws, Jefferson did not see the Constitution as a sacred document but saw it as one that could and should be rewritten to suit changing times.[83] For example, slavery was recognized in the Constitution in the "three fifths" clause. Each Southern state could count slaves as three fifths of a person when determining the size of their population and the number of representatives they could elect to the House. The Constitution gave only White men the right to vote, forbade a direct tax on income (today known as income tax), and did not include the important civil and due process rights later enshrined in the first 10 amendments known as the Bill of Rights. Thus the Constitution has changed through the process of Constitutional amendment, while its core political structures, including the legislative, executive, and judicial branches, remain intact. The amendment process gives the Constitution some flexibility to evolve with changing circumstances. Yet some political leaders refer to the Constitution as a document reflecting natural law that cannot be altered, even though it is a human creation that could be altered or rewritten entirely if a majority wished to do so. The idea that the original intent of the framers of the Constitution must be the guide to what government can and cannot do is clearly false. All our institutions—political, economic, and social—are designed by humans, are kept in place by us, and can be changed.

PROFILES IN LEADERSHIP

Frederick Douglass, 1817–1895

Frederick Douglass dedicated his life to the abolition of slavery and the promotion of human rights for all people. Because of his achievements against great odds, he is recognized as the most significant African American leader of the 19th century. Born into a slave family, he went on to gain admiration and respect as a moral crusader, an intense advocate of human rights, and a leader in the abolitionist movement. His birth mother, Harriet Bailey, was a slave, and his father was a White man, possibly a slave owner. When he was a child, he was taken from his mother and forced to live on a plantation several miles away. He only saw his mother a few times after their separation at night when she visited him. At age 8, he was sent to Baltimore to work as a house servant. It

Frederick Douglass

SOURCE: From the Library of Congress.

was here that his education began when the wife of his "owner" began to teach him the alphabet, and he then taught himself to read by observing White children in his neighborhood reading. He soon realized that the lack of education for slaves was a deliberate attempt to keep them powerless.

At the age of 16, he was sent back to work in the fields. He attempted to escape several times, but each time he was caught. Finally, he succeeded in escaping and fled to New York.

(Continued)

(Continued)

There he eventually met and married Anna Murray, and soon after that they moved to Massachusetts where he obtained work in the shipyards. Although he had escaped from a plantation and was no longer working in the fields, the institution of slavery was still intact, so he had to use caution to make sure that he was not identified and recaptured as a runaway slave.

In 1841, several incidents charted a new direction for Douglass's life. He had developed impressive skills as an orator, and he honed these skills by speaking out against slavery at public gatherings. He was eventually offered a position as a lecturer for the Massachusetts Anti-Slavery Society. This position also gained him increasing recognition as a public speaker on important issues of the day, including the abolition of slavery. Douglass's best known work is his autobiography, *Narrative of the Life of Frederick Douglass, an American Slave,* published in 1845.

Soon he realized that his public recognition might expose his background as a runaway slave, so he left the United States for the British Isles, where he made speeches condemning slavery across the country from 1845 to 1847. Frederick Douglass returned to the United States a free man, British supporters having purchased his freedom. Upon returning to New York, he established a weekly journal entitled the *North Star.* In addition to abolition issues, the publication also included articles promoting vocational education for all African American youth. Douglass also became involved in other social reform movements, including the rights of women to vote. Douglass recognized that the Civil War was the beginning of the crusade to end the institution of slavery in the United States. His support for the Union cause led him to recruit African American men, including his two sons, to assist in the war effort. After the war, he continued to press for equality for newly freed slaves and argued for their right to vote. Douglass also spoke out against segregation, disenfranchisement, and lynching of African Americans.

In 1877, Douglass was appointed as a marshal for the District of Columbia, which marked the first time in the history of the United States that an African American had held public office. In 1889, he was appointed consul general to the Republic of Haiti. Douglass died in 1895 having led a remarkable life as a champion of human rights and an advocate for social justice. Frederick Douglass is an inspiration to generations because he would not let the forces of oppression silence him; he used the fundamental rights of expression granted in the Bill of Rights to free himself and other African Americans born into slavery.

● ALTRUISM AND BENEVOLENCE

The United States has always been one of the most religious countries in the world, in terms of those who say they believe in God and those who worship regularly.[84] In 2005, over 75% of persons surveyed said they believe in God.

Only 10% said they never pray, while the majority (59%) stated they pray at least once a day.[85] The power of the religious values and beliefs has had both positive and negative consequences for marginalized groups: Some religious groups have demonstrated hostile attitudes toward lesbians, bisexuals, gays, and transsexual persons and sought to enact policies that would discriminate against them. The Southern Baptist denominations supported slavery in the 19th century.[86] But religious values have also fostered the growth of altruism and benevolence in American life, encouraging the impulse to donate to causes and organizations that serve the poor and oppressed. The three major denominations in American history—Judaism, Protestantism, and Catholicism—all have strong traditions of altruism and benevolence.[87] Voluntary societies organized by church groups worked throughout the 19th century on various church-related causes. Women affiliated with Protestant churches formed benevolence societies in the North in the 19th century. The tradition of Christian women

Dr. Martin Luther King, Jr., leading a civil rights protest

SOURCE: Getty Images.

reformers was important in the founding of Charity Organization Societies that delivered systematic aid to poor immigrants.[88] Frances Willard, the founder and most influential member of the Woman's Christian Temperance Union, was a deeply committed Christian and feminist.[89] A general belief in the 19th century that women were more naturally benevolent than men spurred their voluntary participation in charitable causes. The so-called friendly visitors, who presaged the development of social work, were largely motivated by belief in the Christian imperatives of charity and good work.

In the early 20th century, many women and men involved in social reforms were allied with a particular form of Protestantism known as the Social Gospel movement, which was part of the progressive response to immigration, industrialization, and urbanization in the late 19th century. Its proponents were Protestant men and women who turned away from sectarianism and embraced the commitment to social reform implicit in their understanding of early Christianity. Some of these women were Christian Socialists; others were members of Protestant denominations that included Presbyterians, Congregationalists, Baptists, and Methodists. Social Gospelers were action-oriented Christians committed to broader social change, particularly in urban areas of the Northeast, where their influence was the strongest.[90]

Christian women, excluded from practicing in the Christian ministry, were particularly drawn to the Social Gospel movement as a means of religious and reform expression. These early social reformers were energized by the Social Gospel's commitment to social justice and the accompanying belief that salvation depended on social as well as personal reform. Transforming personal behavior was not sufficient, according to these Christians, because large-scale social and political reform was part of the Christian mission to the world. These reformers rejected individualistic versions of Christianity, which ignored the social causes of sin. Social Gospelers believed that both social science and democratic politics were legitimate tools to be harnessed in the struggle for social justice.[91] Many women recognized as founders of the social work profession, including Jane Addams, were inspired by religious ideals. (See Chapter 6.)

In the period before the Civil War, some religiously motivated women turned to the antislavery movement for their benevolent work.[92] The movement for the abolition of slavery before the Civil War was inspired by deeply religious men and women and encouraged by religious revivals throughout the North.[93] Religious groups and their leaders were again at the forefront in the social justice movements in the 1960s, including the civil rights movements. Religious fervor was a driving force of the civil rights movement of the 1960s. Martin Luther King, Jr., a Baptist minister, was inspired by the religious ideals of Christianity and the moral ideals of Gandhi. His nonviolent resistance was the hallmark of the movement, which drew its strength largely from the intense religious commitment of his followers.[94] While religion is not the only impetus to altruism and benevolence, it has been a strong force in the pursuit of social justice in American history.

FAIRNESS ●

The values of altruism and benevolence are encouraged by religious groups, but there is also a strong secular current of altruism based on an implicit sense of fairness first evident in the arguments made for the American Revolution and enshrined in the Declaration of Independence. Americans believe that their society should be fair; the main argument for the American Revolution was the unfairness the colonists perceived in England's policy of taxation without representation.[95] The commitment to fairness was a prime reason for the adoption of the Bill of Rights. The belief that the United States is a fair country is one of the main reasons for the continued belief in upward mobility and equal opportunity, in spite of clear evidence to the contrary in the lives of oppressed groups, especially ethnic minorities. Fairness is certainly a more limited concept than equality, yet it can be asserted as a principle to ensure equal access and even-handed rules that apply equally to all persons.[96] Insofar as outcomes and policies seem *unfair,* Americans can be persuaded that they should be changed. For example, when people attain wealth by hard work, they are admired, but when they become wealthy through what is perceived as unfair advantage or bending the rules, there is protest.[97] Adverse outcomes in sports, gambling, and other games that depend variously on some combination of skill and chance are accepted as long as the rules are fairly upheld. Those who cheat and unfairly gain resources that should belong to others are excoriated, as in the case of the corporate leaders of Enron. Thus the concept of fairness is a powerful tool for those seeking social justice; it was at the heart of the civil rights movement of the 1960s, as well as the women's movement and the gay liberation movement. All these social movements made essentially the same argument: We are unfairly denied our rights as Americans and shut out of social spaces that we have a right to inhabit. In spite of long-held feelings of discrimination, the concept of fairness was a powerful bridge to more socially just policies and institutions for these groups.

Americans may not be committed to equal outcomes, but they believe themselves to be committed to equal opportunity and equal access (see Table 3.2). If it can be shown that a group was unfairly denied that opportunity or access through no fault of its own, the momentum often shifts away from individual blame for outcomes such as poverty and homelessness to some consideration of the conditions that led to the outcomes. This is a strong motivation for social workers and others interested in social justice to thoughtfully research the causes of unequal conditions so that the fairness argument can be made.

TABLE 3.2 **Summary of Values, Beliefs, and Ideologies From American History**

Values, Beliefs, and Ideologies	Time Frame	Influences	Impact on Social Problems and Social Policies
Exceptionalism	18th and 19th centuries	• Cultural baggage of English settlers • Later immigration • Abundance of land and resources in United States	• Development of United States is qualitatively different from that of other industrialized countries in that it has a federal government and a constitutional guarantee of freedom of religion
Individualism	Began in 17th century and continues to grow over the centuries	• Social contract theory of government developed by Locke that focused on liberty and individual rights	• Individual freedom emphasized over the collective good, leading to social problems such as poverty and discrimination • Ideology supports oppression and liberation of disenfranchised groups
Independence	Since the American Revolution	• Geographic mobility and willingness to move away from family for work	• Informs our political and economic lives and punishes those who cannot live up to this ideology • Conflicts with those persons who may value interdependence rather than independence
Protestant work ethic	17th and 18th centuries	• Puritans who were followers of John Calvin • Other Protestant religious traditions	• Hard work and wealth are signs of personal and moral worth • Those who are poor are considered as not having a proper or sufficient work ethic and are often considered inferior
Self-reliance	19th and 20th centuries	• Westward expansion • Frontier survival and rough justice	• Concept of Manifest Destiny • Expansion of slavery • Oppression of Native Americans • Dispossession of Mexicans in the Southwest
Upward mobility	19th and 20th centuries	• Reflection of increased economic opportunity in manufacturing and industry • Lack of codified rules for social behavior • No aristocracy, inherited social status, or fixed class structure • Laissez-faire attitude toward market economy	• A myth for many new immigrant families and marginalized groups such as African Americans and Latinos
Equal opportunity	19th century	• Corollary to ideal of upward mobility	• Inequalities in education and labor market

Values, Beliefs, and Ideologies	Time Frame	Influences	Impact on Social Problems and Social Policies
		• Immigrants and native-born Americans believed in this myth	• Largely for White males and not women and other marginalized groups
Progress	19th and 20th centuries	• Complex mix of religious, scientific, and political ideology	• Left out many stories of those who did not share in social or economic progress

PROFILES IN LEADERSHIP

Ida B. Wells, 1862–1931

Ida B. Wells was born a slave in 1862 in Mississippi; she and her parents were freed at the end of the Civil War. She was the eldest of eight children and had to be self-sufficient at a very early age. She lost her parents and a sibling to a major disease sweeping the South (yellow fever) and at age 16 became responsible for raising her brothers and sisters. To keep the family together she took a job as a teacher in a country school. Wells attended Rust College and was considered an excellent student. After passing the teachers' examination, she found a teaching job at a rural community outside of Memphis, Tennessee.

A pivotal event occurred in her life when she was on a train in Tennessee, having purchased a first-class train ticket. She was seated in the ladies' first-class car when a conductor demanded that

IDA B. WELLS.

Ida B. Wells

SOURCE: From the Library of Congress.

(Continued)

(Continued)

she move to a segregated Blacks-only coach. She refused and was physically thrown off the train for her refusal to move.

She was outraged and successfully sued the railroad and was awarded $500 in damages. However, this decision was overturned by the Tennessee Supreme Court, which ruled that she had received "like accommodations" on the railroad. This rationale was similar to the "separate but equal" argument offered to justify racial segregation in Southern schools under the Supreme Court ruling of 1896, *Plessy v. Ferguson.*

Wells began to write articles and stories about the oppression experienced by Blacks and other poor people. Wells became a co-owner of a Black-owned weekly newspaper, and this gave her the opportunity to speak out against violence and discrimination against Blacks in fiery editorials. She gained a reputation as a fearless advocate for justice and freedom in Memphis. Tensions increased between Blacks and Whites in Memphis and reached a boiling point when a mob of White men destroyed the presses of the weekly newspaper and then threatened Wells with death if she continued to write about the plight of poor Blacks and the violence of Whites.

Wells traveled to New York, and while there, she began to write articles for the *New York Age,* a weekly newspaper. She spoke out against the lynching of Blacks and the double legal standards applied to Whites and Blacks, applying different laws to the two groups. She wrote a famous antilynching pamphlet in 1892, *Southern Horrors: Lynch Law in All Its Phases,* that presented her extensive research on lynching in the South.

She traveled extensively throughout the Northeastern states and then to England, where she spoke out against the oppression of Blacks in the United States. In 1895, she married Ferdinand Barnett, a lawyer who owned a weekly Black newspaper. They had four children. As violence against Blacks increased throughout the 1890s, Wells spoke out more vigorously, and her outspoken voice sometimes brought her criticism from Blacks who proposed a more moderate approach. She was involved in the founding of several important Black organizations including the National Association for the Advancement of Colored People, the National Association of Colored Women, the Negro Fellowship League, the Afro-American Press Association, and the National Afro-American Council and League.

Ida B. Wells was a champion of civil rights, a fierce defender of the rights of Blacks, and an outspoken critic of the laws and policies that oppressed Blacks. She was a strong activist at a time when women were not expected to speak out or to write about the oppression of Blacks, and she was particularly outraged about the practice of lynching, which she frequently spoke out against. At the end of her life, she was recognized by the Tennessee Historical Commission for her work on behalf of the Black community.

Ida B. Wells exemplifies a courageous person who used the power of free speech and the free press to challenge orthodoxy and to confront the oppressive power and policies that were barriers to social and economic justice for Black Americans.

FREEDOM OF SPEECH, PRESS, AND ASSEMBLY   ●

The freedoms of religion, speech, press, and assembly and to petition the government for grievances are guaranteed in the first 10 amendments to the U.S. Constitution, known as the Bill of Rights. All are critical to the pursuit of social justice. Without these guaranteed rights, there would be no ability to protest government actions or inaction, either individually or in social groups. All social movements in the United States have depended on these freedoms, although for many groups they have been honored in the breach as much as in actual practice. Workers trying to organize labor unions in the 19th and early 20th centuries, for example, often were met with armed resistance by state and federal troops.[98] Workers and their families in the mining, coal, steel, railroad, and automobile industries persisted in their protests and ultimately prevailed when their right to organize was firmly established by the federal government in 1935, in the Wagner Act. Freedom of the press was important in reforms in the Progressive Era in the early 20th century, both in city newspapers detailing the lives of factory workers and in the publication of books such as Upton Sinclair's *The Jungle* and Jacob Riis's *How the Other Half Lives,* which chronicled the suffering of immigrants and their families in the meat packing industry and the streets of New York.[99] Both books were instrumental in the fight against child labor, which resulted in the passage of child labor laws in most states in the early 20th century.

The civil rights movement depended on the right of assembly and free speech, although both were limited by local jurisdictions, sometimes with tragic results, during the civil rights protests in the 1960s. Movements for women's rights, for gay and lesbian rights, and for Chicano and Native Americans rights in the 1970s were all made possible by the rights to free speech, press, and assembly. All these social movements resulted in deep legal and cultural changes in relationships among groups, in political rights, and in rights to both public and social spaces.

A free press is fundamental to a democratic country; it is only through the institution of the free press that a sustained critique of government actions can be mounted and reach a sufficient number of persons to pressure politicians for a change in policy. During the Vietnam War, the publication of the Pentagon Papers by *The New York Times* in 1971 was a turning point in political support for the war, demonstrating a systematic conspiracy to lie to the American people about the nature of the war.[100]

In spite of the difficulties presented by economic inequality and discrimination that will be discussed in the next two chapters, these freedoms in the First Amendment to the Constitution have real meaning; they can come to life whenever individuals or groups choose to call upon them. With some egregious exceptions, such as the McCarthy era of the 1950s, which limited freedom of speech within the entertainment industry, these legal rights allow Americans to speak freely about the political leadership, the cultural practices, and the economic structures of their country.[101] These are not small things; instead, they are the foundations of our freedom to construct the kind of society in which we wish to live.

CONCLUSION

Many of the values discussed in this chapter originated in the first 100 years of American history, initially part of the cultural baggage of British immigrants and their immediate descendants. A good number were adopted by later immigrants to this country in the 19th and early 20th centuries.[102] Whether or not they have been embraced by new immigrant groups from Latin America and Southeast Asia or by those African Americans and Native Americans who continue to suffer from oppression is questionable. The socially constructed nature of these values and their obvious conflict with the reality of life in economically marginalized communities of immigrants and African Americans may have diminished their self-evident qualities. The ideologies discussed in this chapter are neither true nor untrue; instead, they are metanarratives that justify and legitimize the unequal circumstances of persons living in this country. Demonstrating the contradictions between these socially constructed values and current realities in the United States constitutes one of the most powerful tools social workers can mobilize in the struggle for social justice. If persons who believe in these ideologies can be shown that they do not necessarily reflect reality, the sense of inevitability and complacency about an economic meritocracy will be lost. Real examination of our economic and social structures that continue to oppress a significant number of Americans can then begin.

Let us revisit the idea of U.S. *exceptionalism:* To what extent has the historical development of this country been distinct from that of other industrialized countries? By the end of the 20th century, disillusionment with the concept of American exceptionalism had grown, as more democratic, industrialized nations began to resemble each other. Yet some of the key ideologies discussed in this chapter originated at specific periods in American history and therefore can be thought of as particularly American values and beliefs. The beliefs in upward mobility and in the moral value of hard work are uniquely American, as is the ideology, if not the practice, of individualism. We were the only industrialized country to have a vast expanse of land available for migration. More immigrants have come to the United States since the mid-19th century than to any other industrialized country. The impact of Social Darwinism and the overall

concern with so-called racial and ethnic differences have been more pronounced in this country than in other industrialized countries, although some
European nations are now engaging in the debates about ethnic differences, due
to increased migration of immigrants to their countries. Finally, the United
States has had no strong left tradition in its political history and no standing
political party that offers substantial challenge to the economic system or political institutions. These socially constructed traditions and beliefs are unique to
the United States, especially when taken as a whole.

These ideologies are important because they have contributed to the creation
of social problems and limited the social policy solutions developed in the United
States to solve those problems. Believing in the individual locus of control and in
the moral value of hard work and material goods puts at jeopardy those who are
unemployed or marginally employed in low-paying jobs. According to this ideology, hard work should lead to success and upward mobility, and those who do
not achieve either are judged as personally, if not morally, inadequate. The punishing nature of these beliefs for social work clients is obvious.

This judgment of personal blame for one's economic fate also turns attention
away from the economic structures that create and sustain poverty and underemployment. As we will see in the next chapter, poverty is a corollary of the
market economy. Yet assuming that poverty need not exist except for individual
failure is not only incorrect, it diminishes the ability to develop socially just policies for economically marginalized persons. It also eliminates almost completely
a more challenging task: the development of policies that would substantially
alter the way the economy operates in order to diminish poverty in the first
place. Since there is no major political party in the United States offering a critique of the market economy, it is unlikely that most people will think critically
about its role in ongoing poverty and oppression. Ongoing immigration contributes to the failure to question the basic economic structures of the United
States insofar as immigrants have been politically conservative in their struggle
to adjust to conditions here.

There are exceptional opportunities offered by these values as well. The
belief in fairness and equal opportunity can be a powerful force for positive,
even substantial change in our policies and even in our economic arrangements.
The legal guarantees of free speech, press, and assembly are the tools social
workers can utilize to move closer to their vision of just society. Those who hold
the ideologies discussed in this chapter are not likely to have developed a critical consciousness about the causes of social problems in this country. Without
piercing the fictive web of narratives about who we as Americans are, no substantial progress can be achieved in advancing social justice and social change
(see Table 3.3).

TABLE 3.3   Using the Web to Determine Your Values, Beliefs, and Ideologies

There are a number of Web resources to help you develop a basis for your beliefs and match personal views on social policies and problems with political parties that share those same views. While these resources are by no means a final authority on understanding your ideologies, they may be a helpful start in using your beliefs and values to create positive social change on issues important to you and social work practice.

- Go to http://typology.people-press.org/typology/ to take a typology questionnaire online and determine which typology group you fit into. The Pew Research Center also provides an analysis of where your typology group lines up on major social issues of today at http://typology.people-press.org/data/.
- Go to http://66.241.213.91/idealog.asp?ClassID = for an online quiz application to analyze your political values, created by Northwestern University political science professors Kenneth Janda and Jerry Goldman. The IDEAlog application features an introduction, a tutorial, and a self-test on political ideology.
- Go to http://www.theadvocates.org/ and take the World's Smallest Political Quiz, sponsored by Advocates for Self-Government, which describes itself as a "a non-profit, non-partisan libertarian educational organization." Rather than predicting a political party identification, the site predicts which political philosophy you inhabit.
- The PartyMatch Quiz of Party Platforms at http://www.ontheissues.org/Quiz.htm is sponsored by On the Issues, devoted to providing information to voters on issues. The online quizzes offer detailed explanations for the different stances (*strongly support, support, oppose,* and *strongly oppose*) on particular issues.

DISCUSSION QUESTIONS

1. Individualism, self-reliance, and independence are strong values in the United States. What are some values held by other cultures as important? Is there a way to ascertain which values are better or worse? Consistent with social justice?

2. What are the consequences of believing in the importance of individualism and self-reliance for social work clients? For ourselves? How are these values limiting?

3. Other countries do not value work as highly as the United States. Some might value leisure, others spirituality, and others family. What do you think would be some consequences in shifting our priorities away from work to valuing other things?

4. Why was the story of westward expansion focused on strong, self-reliant males to the exclusion of women and other groups at the frontier? Why did this dominant narrative, told until the 1970s, obscure the reality of conquest and genocide on the frontier?

5. Immigrants have presented enormous opportunities to the United States as well as eliciting a substantial amount of nativism and discrimination. Why have Americans been so hostile to immigrants, in spite of our rhetoric about being a nation of immigrants?

6. Is there any trace of the ideology of Social Darwinism in U.S. culture today? Give examples.

7. Have you participated in discussions questioning the economic or political structures of the United States? Have you witnessed others doing so? If so, what was the context of their remarks? If not, why do you think such discussions are relatively rare?

8. Social workers rarely discuss religion, yet religious groups have been prime factors in social reform in the course of American history. What social reforms are currently being undertaken by religious groups?

9. How has the concept of fairness been important in your life? Do you think people intuitively recognize when something is unfair, or do you think it must be pointed out to them?

10. Can you give other examples of the role of the Bill of Rights in securing social justice in the United States?

NOTES

1. Louis Hartz, *The Liberal Tradition in America* (New York: Harvest/Harcourt Brace Jovanovich, 1991); see also Seymour Martin Lipset, *American Exceptionalism: A Double-Edged Sword* (New York: Norton, 1996), 17–30.

2. Lipset, *American Exceptionalism*, 31–113.

3. Thomas Jefferson, *The Declaration of Independence* (Philadelphia, 1776).

4. John Locke, *Social Contract: Essays by Locke, Hume and Rousseau* (New York: Oxford University Press, 1960).

5. Ari Hoogenboom, "American Exceptionalism: Republicanism as Ideology," in Elisabeth Glaser and Hermann Wellenreuther, eds., *Bridging the Atlantic: The Question of American Exceptionalism in Perspective* (New York: Cambridge University Press, 2002), 43–69.

6. David Hackett Fischer, *Albion's Seed: Four British Folkways in America* (New York: Oxford University Press, 1989), 16–19; Don Fehrenbacher, ed., *History and American Society: Essays of David Potter* (New York: Oxford University Press, 1973), 232.

7. See Lipset, *American Exceptionalism*, 17–28, for a discussion of the importance of individualism.

8. Hartz, *The Liberal Tradition in America*, 62.

9. Lipset, *American Exceptionalism*, 128–130, 237–238.

10. Alexis de Tocqueville, *Democracy in America: Volumes I and II* (New York: Knopf, 1966).

11. Fischer, *Albion's Seed,* 3–13.

12. Lipset, *American Exceptionalism,* 267–292.

13. Lipset, *American Exceptionalism,* 211–253.

14. Max Weber, *The Protestant Ethic and the Spirit of Capitalism,* trans. Talcott Parsons (London: Routledge, 1992).

15. Weber, *The Protestant Ethic and the Spirit of Capitalism,* 66–68; Perry Miller, *Errand Into Wilderness,* (Cambridge, MA: Harvard University Press, 1956), 95–97.

16. Anthony Giddens, "Introduction," in Weber, *The Protestant Ethic and the Spirit of Capitalism,* xiii.

17. Lutz Kaelber, "Introduction," in William Swatos and Lutz Kaelber, eds., *The Protestant Ethic Turns 100* (London: Paradigm Publishers, 2005), xv–1.

18. Martin Riesebrodt, "Dimensions of the Protestant Ethic," in *The Protestant Ethic Turns 100* (London: Paradigm Publishers, 2005), 23–51, 32.

19. Weber, *The Protestant Ethic and the Spirit of Capitalism,* 123.

20. Joel Blau with Mimi Abramovitz, *The Dynamics of Social Welfare Policy,* 2nd ed. (New York: Oxford University Press, 2007), 155.

21. Jerry Jacob and Kathleen Gerson, "Who Are the Overworked Americans?" *Review of Social Economics* 56 (Winter 1998): 442–459.

22. Juliet Schor, *The Overworked American: The Unexpected Decline of Leisure* (New York: Basic Books, 1991), passim.

23. Joshua Berek, "Economists Want to Know: Do Europeans Work Less Because They Believe Less in God?" *Christian Science Monitor,* February 22, 2005, http://www.csmonitor.com/2005/0222/p12s01-woeu.html, accessed July 27, 2007.

24. Diane Wentworth and Robert Chell, "American College Students and the Protestant Work Ethic," *American Journal of Social Psychology* 137 (June 1997): 284–296; David Woehr, Luis Arciniega, and Doo Lim, "Examining the Work Ethic Across Populations," *Educational and Psychological Measurement* 67 (February, 2007): 154–168, http://epm.sagepub.com/cgi/content/abstract/67/1/154, accessed August 2, 2007.

25. Jai Ghorpade, Jim Lackritz, and Gangaram Singh, "Correlates of the Protestant Ethic of Hard Work: Results From a Diverse Ethno-Religious Sample," *Journal of Applied Social Psychology* 36 (October 2006): 2449–2473.

26. Miller, *Errand Into Wilderness.*

27. Harold B. Jones, "The Protestant Ethic: Weber's Model and the Empirical Literature," *Human Relations* 50 (July 1997): 757–778.

28. Economic Policy Institute, "Wealth Inequality Is Fast and Growing," August 23, 2006, http://www.epi.org/economic_snapshots/entry/webfeatures_snapshots_20060823/, accessed July 28, 2007.

29. Brent Gilchrist, *Cultus Americanus* (Lanham, MD: Lexington Books, 2006), 258–259.

30. James Kluegel and Eliot Smith, *Beliefs About Inequality: Americans' Views of What Is and What Ought to Be* (New York: Aldine, 1986); Kevin Smith and Lorene Stone, "Rags, Riches and Bootstraps: Beliefs About the Causes of Wealth and Poverty," *The Sociological Quarterly* 30 (March 1989): 93–107.

31. Fehrenbacher, *History and American Society*, 111–134; Henry Nash Smith, *Virgin Land* (Cambridge, MA: Harvard University Press, 1950), 258–263; Richard Slotkin, *The Fatal Environment: The Myth of the Frontier in an Age of Industrialization, 1800–1890* (New York: Atheneum, 1985), 31–36.

32. Frederick Jackson Turner, *The Frontier in American History* (New York: Henry Holt, 1920), 35–38; Ray Billington, *Frederick Jackson Turner* (New York: Oxford University Press, 1973); Fehrenbacher, *History and American Society*, 111–134.

33. Slotkin, *The Fatal Environment*, 15–32; Gilchrist, *Cultus Americanus*, 242–244.

34. Slotkin, *The Fatal Environment*, 36–40, 281.

35. Lucy Murphy and Wendy Venet, *Midwestern Women: Work, Community and Leadership at the Crossroads* (Bloomington: Indiana University Press, 1997); Dee Garceau-Hagen, *Portraits of Women in the American West* (New York: Routledge, 2005).

36. Gilchrist, *Cultus Americanus*, 241–245.

37. Carey McWilliams, *North From Mexico: The Spanish-Speaking People of the United States* (New York: Greenwood Press, 1990).

38. Roger Daniels, "The Immigrant Experience in the Gilded Age," in Charles Calhoun, ed., *The Gilded Age: Perspectives on the Origin of Modern America* (Lanham, MD: Rowman and Littlefield, 2007), 75–111; Gary Nash and Julie Jeffrey, *The American People: Creating a Nation and a Society*, 2nd ed. (New York: Pearson), 594.

39. Bernard Bailyn, *The Peopling of British North America* (New York: Vintage, 1986); Bernard Bailyn, *Voyagers to the West: A Passage in the Peopling of North America* (New York: Vintage, 1986).

40. Ewa Morawska, "The Sociology and Historiography of Immigration," in Virginia Yans-McLaughlin, ed., *Immigration Reconsidered: History, Sociology and Politics* (New York: Oxford University Press, 1990), 191–219.

41. David Ward, *Cities and Immigrants: A Geography of Change in Nineteenth Century America* (New York: Oxford University Press, 1971).

42. Oscar Handlin, *Boston's Immigrants: A Study in Acculturation* (Cambridge, MA: Harvard University Press, 1961); Charles Fanny, *New Perspectives on the Irish Diaspora* (Carbondale: University of Illinois Press, 2000).

43. Morawska, "The Sociology and Historiography of Immigration," 191–219, 194.

44. Morawska, "The Sociology and Historiography of Immigration," 211–212.

45. Jon Gjerde, "Immigrant Encounters With the Republic," in Donna Gabaccia and Vicki Ruiz, eds., *American Dreaming, Global Realities: Rethinking U.S. Immigration History* (Urbana: University of Illinois Press, 2006), 24–26.

46. Nash and Jeffrey, *The American People*, 618.

47. Morawska, "The Sociology and Historiography of Immigration," 216–218; Jon Gjerde, "The Burden of Their Song: Immigrant Encounters With the Republic," in Donna Gabaccia and Vicki Ruiz, eds., *American Dreaming, Global Realities: Rethinking U.S. Immigration History* (Urbana: University of Illinois Press, 2006), 9–35.

48. Marc Karson, *American Labor Unions and Politics, 1900–1918* (Carbondale: Southern Illinois University Press, 1958).

49. Gjerde, "Immigrant Encounters With the Republic," 9–35.

50. Tocqueville, *Democracy in America: Volume I*, 51–54.

51. Nash and Jeffrey, *The American People*, 602–603.

52. Adalberto Aguirre, Jr., and David Baker, *Structured Inequality in the United States* (New York: Pearson, 2008), 1–39, 187–243.

53. Stephan Thernstrom, *Poverty and Progress* (Cambridge, MA: Harvard University Press, 1964), 63.

54. *Boston Herald,* July 4, 1877, quoted in Thernstrom, *Poverty and Progress,* 64.

55. *Boston Herald,* March 1, 1856, quoted in Thernstrom, *Poverty and Progress,* 66.

56. Thernstrom, *Poverty and Progress,* 78–79.

57. Thomas DiPrete, "Is This a Great Country? Upward Mobility and the Chance for Riches in Contemporary America," *Research in Social Stratification and Mobility* 25 (1, 2006): 89–95, http://www.elsevier.com/wps/find/journaldescription.cws_home/706924/description#description, accessed August 1, 2007.

58. Tocqueville, *Democracy in America: Volumes I and II,* 148; Lipset, *American Exceptionalism,* 19, 113–116.

59. Gjerde, "Immigrant Encounters With the Republic," 14–16.

60. Thernstrom, *Poverty and Progress,* 63.

61. Lipset, *American Exceptionalism,* 53–54.

62. David Nasaw, *Schooled to Order: A Social History of Public Education in the United States* (New York: Oxford University Press, 1981), 7–80.

63. Thernstrom, *Poverty and Progress,* 77–78, 145–146.

64. Nasaw, *Schooled to Order,* 87–156.

65. Lipset, *American Exceptionalism,* 83.

66. Alice Kessler Harris, *Out to Work: A History of Wage-Earning Women in the United States* (New York: Oxford University Press, 1982); Thomas Dublin, *Women at Work* (New York: Columbia University Press, 1979).

67. Richard Ellis, *American Political Culture* (New York: Oxford University Press, 1993), 62–64.

68. Arthur Ekirch, *The Idea of Progress in America, 1815–1860* (New York: Columbia University Press, 1944); Richard Hofstadter, *Progressivism in America* (New York: New Viewpoint, 1974), 3–15; Ralph Gabriel, *American Values: Continuity and Change* (Westport, CT: Greenwood Press, 1974).

69. Slotkin, *The Fatal Environment,* 33–34.

70. David Marcell, *Progress and Pragmatism: James, Dewey, Beard and the American Idea of Progress* (Westport, CT: Greenwood Press, 1974), 15–27; Gabriel, *American Values,* 74–75.

71. Robert Nisbet, *History of the Idea of Progress* (Edison, NJ: Transaction Press, 1994).

72. William Graham Sumner, *Social Darwinism* (Englewood Cliffs, NJ: Prentice Hall, 1963).

73. Rick Tilman, "Introduction," in Rick Tilman, ed., *Social Darwinism and Its Critics* (Bristol, England: Thoemmes Press, 2001), ix–xxii.

74. Mike Hawkins, *Social Darwinism in European and American Thought, 1860–1945* (Cambridge, England: Cambridge University Press, 1997).

75. Eric Goldman, *Rendezvous With Destiny* (New York: Alfred Knopf, 1966), 91–93; Richard Hofstader, *Social Darwinism in American Thought* (Boston: Beacon Press, 1959).

76. Tilman, "Introduction," xv.

77. Goldman, *Rendezvous With Destiny,* 93–128.

78. Lipset, *American Exceptionalism,* 23–25; Hartz, *The Liberal Tradition in America,* 228–255.

79. Hartz, *The Liberal Tradition in America,* 3–32; Lipset, *American Exceptionalism,* 17–23.

80. Lipset, *American Exceptionalism,* 21, 81–84.

81. Michael Harrington, *Socialism: Past and Future* (London: Pluto, 1993), 118; Gary Gerstle, "The Ideas of the American Labor Movement, 1860–1950," in Peter Coclanis and Stuart Bruchey, eds., *Ideas, Ideologies and Social Movements: The American Experiment Since 1800* (Columbia: University of South Carolina Press, 1999), 72–90.

82. Nash and Jeffrey, *The American People,* 712.

83. Thomas Jefferson, *Notes on Virginia* (Richmond, VA: Randolph, 1853); David Mayer, "By the Chains of the Constitution: Separation of Powers Theory and Jefferson's Conception of the Presidency," *Perspectives on Political Science* 26 (3, 1997), 140–149.

84. Howard Karger and David Stoesz, *American Social Welfare Policy* (Boston: Pearson, 2006), 39.

85. The Association of Religion Data Archives, "QuickStats: U.S. Surveys," http://www.thearda.com/quickstats, accessed July 20, 2007.

86. Donald Matthews, *Religion in the Old South* (Chicago: University of Chicago Press, 1977).

87. Sydney Alstrom, *A Religious History of the American People* (New Haven, CT: Yale University Press, 1972).

88. Lori D. Ginzberg, *Women and the Work of Benevolence* (New Haven, CT: Yale University Press, 1992).

89. Carolyn Gifford, "The Women's Cause Is Man's: Frances Willard and the Social Gospel," in Wendy Edwards and Carolyn Gifford, eds., *Gender and the Social Gospel* (Urbana: University of Illinois Press, 1993), 21–35.

90. Robert Trawick, "Dorothy Day and the Social Gospel Movement: Different Theologies, Common Concerns," in Wendy Edwards and Carolyn Gifford, eds., *Gender and the Social Gospel* (Urbana: University of Illinois Press, 1993), 139–150.

91. Wendy Edwards and Carolyn Gifford, "Introduction: Restoring Women and Reclaiming Gender in Social Gospel Studies," in Wendy Edwards and Carolyn Gifford, eds., *Gender and the Social Gospel* (Urbana: University of Illinois Press, 1993), 1–21.

92. Ginzberg, *Women and the Work of Benevolence.*

93. James Monroe, *Hellfire Nation: The Politics of Sin in American History* (New York: Alfred Knopf, 2003), 123–222.

94. David Chappell, *A Stone of Hope: Prophetic Religion and the Death of Jim Crow* (Chapel Hill: University of North Carolina Press, 2004).

95. Gordon Wood, *The Radicalism of the American Revolution* (New York: Vintage Books, 1993).

96. Bruce Jansson, *The Reluctant Welfare State* (Stamford, CT: Brooks Cole, 2001), 23.

97. Michael Graetz and Ian Shapiro, *Death by a Thousand Cuts: The Fight Over Taxing Inherited Wealth* (Princeton, NJ: Princeton University Press, 2005), 177–178.

98. David Brody, *Workers in Industrial America: Essays on the Twentieth Century Struggle* (New York: Oxford University Press, 1980); Eric Arnesen, "American Workers and the Labor Movement in the Late Nineteenth Century," in Charles Calhoun, ed., *The Gilded Age: Perspectives on the Origins of Modern America* (Lanham, MD: Rowman and Littlefield, 2007), 53–75.

99. Upton Sinclair, *The Jungle* (Cambridge, MA: R. Bentley, 1946); Jacob Riis, *How the Other Half Lives* (New York: Scribner's Sons, 1891).

100. John Prados and Margaret P. Porter, *Inside the Pentagon Papers* (Lawrence: University Press of Kansas, 2004).

101. David Oshinsky, *A Conspiracy So Immense: The World of Joe McCarthy* (New York: Free Press, 1985).

102. Fischer, *Albion's Seed,* 3–13.

CHAPTER

4

The Economic System and Social Justice

CHAPTER QUESTIONS

1. What are the perceived benefits of the market economy in the United States?

2. What are the main problems or externalities caused by market capitalism? Is poverty necessary in a market economy?

3. Why is there ongoing poverty in the United States in spite of the fact that this is the most prosperous country in the world?

4. Why has there been increasing income and wealth inequality in the United States over the past 30 years?

5. What are the consequences of the concentration of wealth and corporate power in the United States?

6. What role does tax policy play in social and economic justice?

7. How has supply side economics limited the development of economic programs?

● ● ●

Most social workers do not think of economic policy when they think of social policy, yet economic policies are fundamental to the issues that social workers care most about, including inequality, poverty, and ethnic discrimination. Many of the ideologies and beliefs discussed in Chapter 3 depend on the fairness of the economic system for their realization. These include upward mobility, equal opportunity, and the power of self-reliance and individual effort. In this chapter we will be challenging these ideologies when we discuss the economic system of the United States, known as market capitalism.

85

● TASKS OF THE ECONOMIC SYSTEM

Every society must have an economic system to produce and allocate resources, including food and shelter, to its members. Since these resources are scarce, rather than infinitely abundant, not having such a system would lead to anarchy and disorder. Economic policies are socially constructed ways of developing and distributing these resources. Clearly there are various ways of organizing this system of production and distribution, some more humane than others. For example, a purely communist system, which exists primarily in religious orders, would feature equal sharing of all resources. In reality, countries that have called themselves communist were more centralized systems, where elite leaders controlled the means of production and the distribution of resources within the country, with little or no democratic input. Another possible economic system is socialism, where the government owns the means of production and oversees distribution by setting prices and wage levels. If this government is subject to regular elections, such a system would be known as democratic socialism. Conversely, dictatorships can claim to have socialist economic systems, with a centralized government owning the means of production and controlling the distribution of resources, as in Nazi Germany's National Socialist German Workers' Party. Mercantilism was an economic system that dominated Western Europe from 1400 to 1800. In this system colonies and colonizers interacted in a synergetic economic system in which both parts worked together to produce and allocate resources for the whole: The so-called mother country (as in the case of England) imported raw materials from the colonies, which were not allowed to manufacture goods. Instead, England manufactured goods from these raw materials and then sold these finished goods to the colonies for a profit. The colonies existed to benefit the colonizers.

At the end of the 18th century, the old mercantile economies of Western Europe were breaking down as former colonies waged successful wars of independence (including the British colonies, which became the United States). During this period of transition a new economic system emerged known as the market economy, where goods would be produced and allocated not according to government design or control but according the operations of the free market, or the market economy.

Before we look at the market economy in depth, let us step back to a more general look at the functions of an economic system, in order to determine what might be possible. Depending on one's goal, various economic policies will do the job of ensuring the production and allocation of goods, as we have seen. For instance, economic systems could promote individual freedom, as we say the market economy does. Or they could promote individual gain or wealth. Or they could promote fairness and distributive justice.

John Rawls examined how a social order handles the "problem of justice." Rawls noted that any social order must address conflict over the distribution of goods and services; who will receive what share of the goods produced, and how will rights and duties be allocated? According to Rawls, in most societies these decisions are determined by the social position into which persons are born, since "the institutions of society favor certain starting places over others." These initial differences in circumstances over which a person has no control lead to "deep inequalities" that follow a person throughout his or her life. Ultimately, the distribution of goods, rights, and duties is therefore determined by those born into high positions of status and power.[1] Rawls's argument is that if persons were to create a society where they did not know into which social circumstances they would be born, they would rationally choose an "initial position of equality," rather than a system of inequality where an accident of birth could deny them resources.[2] Rawls used Locke's concept of the social contract to hypothesize an analogous situation of persons who knew they would live in a society but did not know their social conditions upon birth. They functioned under what Rawls called "a veil of ignorance."[3] What kind of system would they choose? According to Rawls, they would choose equality, not only in resources but in rights, power, and opportunities, because they would not agree to a system that rests in inequality—that is, a system where one person is rewarded substantially less than others. Rawls gave the following example: If a man knew he were to be wealthy, he would find taxes to support welfare programs to be unjust, whereas if a man knew he were to be poor, he would find the opposite true. Rawls was making the point that many of our positions about what is just are informed by our own self-interests. Only by imagining no foreknowledge of our circumstances can we reason to a set of just principles. He thought, for example, that persons in the original position under the veil of ignorance might decide to reward physicians at a higher level than others, because all would desire to maximize their health and longevity. Since it would be to everyone's advantage to have physicians treating illness, this inequality would be agreed upon in advance as an incentive. Rawls summarized these principles as "justice as fairness":

1. Each person has an equal right to liberty that is compatible with the liberty of others.

2. Any social or economic inequalities must be to everyone's advantage.[4]

In contrast to Rawls's position is the utilitarian principle, which states that the greatest good for the greatest number should be the overarching principle of a social order. This principle was formulated by Jeremy Bentham, an 18th- and 19th-century British philosopher.[5] Bentham's *utilitarianism* was expounded in his *Introduction to the Principles of Morals and Legislation,* where he argued that the principle of utility approves of an action insofar as it has an overall tendency to promote the greatest amount of happiness. Bentham's principle has been described as the utilitarian calculus, or the greatest good for the greatest number, and was shared by other utilitarian thinkers, including his follower, John Stuart Mill.[6]

The utilitarian principle is in direct contrast to Rawls's principle of justice as fairness. Rawls posed the difference between the two philosophical positions in the following way: "The question is whether the imposition of disadvantages on a few can be outweighed by a greater sum of advantages enjoyed by others; or whether the weight of justice requires an equal liberty for all and permits only those economic and social inequalities which are to each person's interest."[7] This question goes to the heart of the values of social work: Can the good of many outweigh the disadvantage or suffering of a few? Most social workers would answer no, suggesting that the utilitarian calculus is based on majoritarian rather than ethical reasoning.

In this chapter we will see that the *utilitarian* principle is central to understanding the role of the market economy in the creation of social problems and the construction of social policies. Under this principle the welfare of the majority outweighs the disadvantages suffered by a minority. The principle of *justice as fairness* may be thought of as a principle leading to equal opportunity and social justice for everyone.

● MARKET CAPITALISM AND ADAM SMITH

Capitalism is seen by many in the United States as the best, if not the only, natural way an economy can function. Market capitalism is not "natural" any more than is any other socially constructed institution. Market capitalism demands government protection of private property, including the police power of the state, in order to function.[8] Persons who claim that capitalism is the most natural economic order see it as a perfect corollary to human nature because of its dependence on competition and self-interest. Those who feel this way clearly have a fixed view of human nature that does not emphasize cooperation or altruism.

Adam Smith, an 18th-century British philosopher and the founder of microeconomic theory, was the earliest proponent of the market economy.[9] He wrote the *Wealth of Nations* to describe how a market economy worked.[10] In this and other writings Smith argued that an economic system was separate from all other social systems and functioned perfectly according to its own law: that individual selfishness would lead to the common good. Smith believed that under the market economy an "invisible hand" would ensure that individuals pursuing their own selfish pursuits in the market economy would promote maximum benefit for all.[11] Seeking to give an intellectual rationale for the growth of a free market economy, Smith described his faith that self-interest in the pursuit of market exchanges would lead to the common good. This has been a hallmark of proponents of a free market economy ever since. Smith supported the utilitarian view that the greatest good for the greatest number should be the guiding principle of society and that the market economy would provide this greatest good. Ensuring a free market economy was the way governments could protect this principle. Smith was a strong proponent of a laissez-faire government. He believed that any government interference with the workings of the market economy, including tariffs and or any other government regulations, would undermine or even destroy it.

Adam Smith

SOURCE: From the Library of Congress, stipple engraving by MacKenzie.

Rather than regulating the market economy, Smith believed that governments should establish laws supporting free market functioning; these included laws regulating private property rights and enforcing contracts involving the right to property.[12] Smith's theory that the common good is promoted by individual acts of economic self-interest has never been proven; instead, it is taken on faith and has been called Smith's "logical fallacy."[13] With this unalloyed and unproven belief in the widespread benefits of the market economy, the social costs of capitalist economic development are ignored.[14]

Market capitalism, a system where most property is privately owned, has resulted in the accumulation of great wealth in the hands of some, technological progress for many, and poverty for others. Its benefits are far from equally shared. Under this system economic development is accompanied by "moral and social conflicts," which need to be addressed by policymakers as they emerge.[15]

Social policies must address this harm or social cost because the market itself will not absorb or defray it. The rest of this chapter will examine some of these social costs of market capitalism and discuss the social policies that have been developed to address them in the United States.

● SUPPLY, DEMAND, AND THE PRICE SYSTEM

Market Economy Ideal

Smith, along with many others since him, believed that the market economy is the most efficient way to produce and allocate goods and services. In a market economy decisions about production and allocation of resources are determined by supply and demand in the markets for goods and services. Individual decisions to produce or consume goods and services are determined by the price system. Private firms will *supply* goods that their consumers *demand* at a *price* they can afford. That stated simply is the essence of the model of the market economy taught in microeconomics courses. Let's see how this system is supposed to work. First we must ask what a market is. Rather than describing it as a physical place where people bring goods, economists describe markets as "mechanisms through which buyers and sellers interact to determine prices and exchange goods and services."[16] According to microeconomic theory, demand for goods results in production of those goods because producers are motivated by the profit motive to meet the demand (price includes profit). As the demand rises, the price rises until the supply of goods meets the demand point. At that point an equilibrium price will be reached. If the supply increases beyond the demand, the price will go down, as each producer will compete to sell its goods at the lowest possible price. However, prices cannot go down too far, since producers must maintain a profit margin. Higher prices, on the other hand, draw other producers into the market to make a profit, and thus more goods will be available (supply), ultimately reducing the price. If one producer tries to sell the goods for too high a price, other producers will compete to sell the goods at a lower price, thus capturing the market and shutting out the other producer.

This model of the market economy seems democratic: Goods and services will be produced or made available according to what most people want; their prices will not be more than what most people can afford, and producers will reap a fair profit.[17] This situation is described as a self-regulating market, constantly readjusting to reach equilibrium in supply and demand. This model of the market economy, which has been taught to many generations of college students, depends on perfect *competition*. The assumption is that the market consists of many producers competing to sell us goods at the lowest prices (while maintaining their profit margin). This kind of market is known as an open or competitive market. In an open market producers are likely to enter as long as the price of the good is higher than the cost of producing the good. Clearly this kind of market holds benefits for consumers, as firms compete to sell goods as the lowest price commensurate with profit.[18] Open, competitive markets are very sensitive to the demand of consumers: When demand rises, prices and production go up; when demand declines, prices and production go down.

Imperfect Competition

Most markets in the United States today exist in a condition of *imperfect competition* in which sellers have more control over the price than buyers. The most common forms of imperfect competition are markets dominated by oligopolies or monopolies. Other forms include sectors of the economy that are dominated, if not controlled, by larger businesses that have achieved economies of scale; that is, these larger businesses can make many units of their product at a lower cost, through large-scale production, than can smaller industries, whose cost per unit is greater. Another factor leading to imperfect competition consists of the barriers to entry that characterize some industries, such as automobiles. The cost of producing cars is a barrier to new producers entering the automobile market.[19] Other industries may have legal barriers to entry, such as drug patents.

Industry and businesses traditionally have avoided open competitive markets due the risk of business failure that accompanies these markets: Since the desire to maintain profit margins is paramount, reducing prices to capture demand threatens business and industry viability. Competitive, open markets limit the profit any supplier can make because of the need to keep prices low.[20] American industry and small businesses have sought to exert control over market forces by limiting the supply of goods they sell and reducing and eliminating the need to reduce prices.

One way to reduce competition and control price is to merge with other companies. One type of merger is known as vertical integration, which has characterized American business since the late 19th century. With vertical integration businesses seek to control the cost of raw materials needed for production of the final goods by buying companies that produce these materials.[21] Monopolies and oligopolies are two examples of horizontal integration, where one company merges with its competitors in order to control the supply of goods and limit the impact of demand on prices, with the goal of maximizing profits.[22] In a monopoly a producer controls virtually the entire supply of a good or service. An example of this is Microsoft Windows, the computer operating system that possessed monopoly power in the PC operating systems market and harmed consumers by stymieing competition, according to a federal court ruling in 1999. A drug company that receives a patent has a monopoly over that drug for the length of the patent, and its price will not be affected by competition from other suppliers. While monopolies were rampant in the economy in the late 19th and early 20th centuries, national monopolies are relatively rare today, due to Justice Department actions against them ("trust busting"). Local monopolies persist in cable companies and in public utilities, such as household water and electricity suppliers. While these utilities are quasi-regulated by local governments, they have real monopoly power since there is no alternative source of supply for the goods they deliver.

Oligopolies are more common than monopolies. In these markets a few suppliers dominate and often influence the prices of each other. Price setting, instead of open competition, is the norm: Industries agree to conform to each other's prices.[23] The automobile industry, the airline industry, and the household appliance industry are clear examples of oligopolies, as is the breakfast cereal industry (in spite of the many varieties of cereals available).[24] Consumers have far less ability to shape price in these markets than they would in more competitive markets, although firms are sensitive to price changes by other industries within the same sector (airlines lowering prices can set off a price war). All these industries characterized as oligopolies have certain things in common: They all function with significant economies of scale, meaning large firms can produce items more cheaply than small firms, and they all have barriers to entry, usually in terms of cost. Both the commercial airline industry and the automobile industry have high costs of entry that limit the number of new firms that emerge. In both industries a handful of firms dominate the market.

Large-scale industries and financial concerns that wield great power in the market economy in the United States are known as corporations.[25] A corporation can be defined as a business organization charter in a state that is owned by a large number of individual stockholders (as opposed to a family-owned business).[26] Many of these United States–based corporations operate in the global economy; that is, they have operations in countries outside the United States. The impact of the global economy will be discussed further in Chapter 11. Within the United States, while there are over 18 million businesses operating today, a few hundred corporations dominate the economy in terms of sales and assets, as well as in political and economic power.

Demand Manipulated

We have just considered the ways that suppliers avoid the situation of pure competition in the U.S. economy. Now let us turn to demand. Is demand a real reflection of the needs of consumers? On the one hand, yes, because this demand is expressed through a concrete act: spending money on goods and services. On the other hand, demand is manipulated through advertising. Advertising is the way that firms convince us that their products are more desirable than those of other firms. Advertising can build product loyalty, and the battle for consumer dollars can be fierce and expensive: Coca-Cola and Pepsi spend hundreds of millions of dollars per year convincing consumers that their products are the best, for example.[27] Advertising does more than inform consumers of potential products; many feel that it involves manipulating the desires of consumers.

The power of advertising is important to imperfect competition because the advertised products may be owned by one firm, and the sale of any of them will benefit that firm. This is the case, for example, with much of the advertising for breakfast cereals. The consumer vote on the matter of breakfast cereal will therefore not impact the supplier profit. The idea of this wide product differentiation is to discourage potential competitors.[28] If one manufacturer of many brands of cereal can appeal to various sectors of the market through brand differentiation, then consumers should not have to turn to another supplier to meet their preferences. Advertising thus contributes to oligopoly power and diminishes the power of the consumer over prices. These strategies that attempt to gain control of the market are counter to the interests of consumers.[29] At a deeper level of meeting human needs, money spent on advertising is wasted because it does not contribute to meeting human needs but contributes to increasing the profit of the firms advertising their goods.

Another problem with the demand side of the microeconomic model is the fact that those with low income have little impact on suppliers of goods and therefore little impact on price, even in the most competitive markets. Those with the ability to spend a great deal of money will have far more influence on types of products produced and their price than will persons with less money who vote with fewer dollars.[30] If the market economy model is akin to a democratic system, then money is tantamount to votes. Those with the most money will have the most to say about market operations, including the supply and price of goods.

As discussed early in this chapter, the market economy is neither natural nor inevitable, but it is a social construction that relies on law, regulation, and custom. Laws supporting the market economy include the U.S. Constitution, contract law, laws against thefts and bribery, and taxation law. A great deal of the power of the federal and state governments is dedicated to protecting private property rights and ensuring the smooth operation of the market economy. The notion that the United States has a private, free market economy is "fiction."[31] In the United States the federal government and the Supreme Court protected the market economy throughout the 19th and early 20th centuries. Property rights were routinely upheld by federal courts, to the exclusion of worker rights. Two versions of federal child labor laws were declared unconstitutional by the Supreme Court, one in 1918 and one in 1922. Federal and state governments sought to prevent workers from labor organizing, often through violent means, because unions represented interference with private enterprise, and federal courts upheld these actions.[32]

As we can see, there is a wide gap between the microeconomic model of the market economy and the reality. In fact, the only place where the microeconomic model of the market economy seems to prevail is in sectors of the economy dominated by small businesses owned by one person, known as "mom and pop" stores. Such firms have a very short life span; the average lifetime of a small store is approximately 1 year.[33] Yet it is these high-risk sectors of the economy that most closely reflect the model outlined early in the chapter. The "free" in free market economy refers not just to freedom from government intervention but also to freedom for pure competition, as in freedom from producers' control of the market through the mechanisms discussed above. Yet, as we have seen, producers do not want to operate in a free market and will do everything possible to avoid it. Many owners of small companies are hoping to be bought out by larger companies where they will avoid the exigencies of competition. Even though the free market economy is largely a myth, belief in its existence and the importance of protecting it has driven political ideology in the United States since the 19th century.

● THE LABOR MARKET

The market for human labor is different from all other markets, such as the market for corn or automobiles. It involves a necessary transaction: Individuals need to sell their labor for wages in order to survive. Since individuals need wages to survive but employers do not need a specific number of workers to survive, the balance of power in the labor market is with the employer: The labor market is not an even exchange.[34] Microeconomic theory predicts that wages should be determined by the same supply and demand factors that influenced the price of goods and services. The price of labor (wages) would be a function of the demand for a particular skill and the number of others supplying that skill. Professions with high demand and relatively low supply, such as physicians, should be remunerated at a higher wage than jobs with high demand and high supply (such as teachers) or jobs with low demand and high supply (such as day laborers). The supply of surgeons, for example, is severely limited by the cost of medical school training, the limited number of accredited medical schools, and the need for medical licensing. Approximately 50,000 surgeons are working in the United States, but the demand for surgery is growing, as is the demand for all health care services. As a result of the relatively high demand and low supply, the average salary of a surgeon was $331,970 per year in 2007.[35] Workers in fast food industries, on the other hand, have little entry requirements (training) and compete with an increasing supply of persons willing to work in this sector. The average fast food cook made an average of $16,860 in 2007.[36]

Under the labor market model wages reflect an individual's *investment in human capital,* or the kind and amount of training and education someone has received. A good investment in human capital means that the cost of the education or training is matched by an increase in productivity and wages.[37] Obviously little education or training represents a poor investment in human capital, but so does education in something not in high demand. A PhD in the humanities, for example, would not be as wise an investment in human capital as a PhD in economics. This is because while a person with a PhD in the humanities would be targeting higher educational institutions for employment, a PhD in economics can work in industry or in higher education; demand for this degree is higher. Thus the decision to work for graduate education in humanities may not pay off in the long run in terms of high wages. On the whole, though, education is a good investment; increased education usually leads to higher salaries. This is why most Americans believe that education is the most important means of achieving economic success.[38]

This model of the labor market assumes that skills in demand and in short supply will be rewarded with relatively high wages, while skills either not in demand or in high supply will be compensated with far lower wages. However, wages are not set only by supply and demand but are deeply influenced by the attitudes of those employing labor. The foremost attitude affecting wages is discrimination according to ethnicity, gender, or religious beliefs. Economists know that discrimination is a factor in wage differentials and therefore in income inequality; they call the impact of discrimination an "imperfection in the market." The fact that African Americans and Latinos generally receive lower wages, regardless of their investment in human capital, and therefore have lower levels of income and wealth is acknowledged by economists, as is the fact that many high-paying jobs are closed to women.[39] To explain these market anomalies, economists developed the idea of a "taste for discrimination"—that is, some firms do not like to hire minorities or women.[40] Here is an example from an economic textbook of how "broad-based discrimination" might work in the labor market. Imagine two job markets: The first requires higher-than-average skills and training and pays relatively higher wages; the second requires less skills and training than the first and pays lower wages. If a group of persons faces broad-based discrimination from other workers that limits their hiring in the first job market, they will leave that job market and move to the second job market, increasing the supply of labor there and reducing wages. Their exit from the first job market will leave those workers who do the discriminating in that market with lower supply of workers and consequently higher wages for themselves and their worker colleagues. Thus "broad-based" (as opposed to employer-based) discrimination would economically benefit or reward those workers who discriminate. The gains to those who discriminate are high, making "broad-based" discrimination difficult to eliminate. This form of discrimination contributes heavily to income inequality.[41] Of course, if management, not workers, are the ones with the "taste for discrimination," they would not benefit directly from these higher wages and would be acting solely out of prejudice. This kind of discrimination would be easier to root out through legislation.

It is clear that discrimination is an important intervening variable in the U.S. labor market. Both women and minorities on average earn less than White men. According to the Bureau of Labor Statistics, wages varied by ethnicity in 2006 and 2007, with Whites and Asian Americans earning the most weekly wages and African Americans and Latinos earning the least. The average weekly wage for a White worker in 2007 was $713, for an Asian worker it was $765, for an African American it was $562, and for a Latino it was $503. In each category men earned more than women.

In January 2009 median earnings for Black men working at full-time jobs were $618 per week, 74.2% of the median for White men ($833). See Figure 4.1 for variation in income by ethnicity.[42]

Part of the reason that Latino workers received the lowest wages is the fact that immigrants from Mexico represented 40% of the Latino workforce in the United States in 2000. Mexican immigrants are more likely to have not finished high school than native-born workers of Mexican ancestry, one reason that immigrants from Mexico received the lowest wages of all Latino subgroups. By contrast, fewer African American and White natives were high school dropouts in 2000 than in 1980, leaving fewer of each group in the unskilled workforce. In 2000, African Americans were 13.5% of low-wage workers, Asians 3.4%, and Latinos 24.6%. This represented a decrease in the percentage of African Americans in this group and an increase in the percentage of Latinos.[43]

Will the "new" Latino immigrants achieve the social mobility enjoyed by some earlier immigrants in the late 19th century? It seems unlikely, due

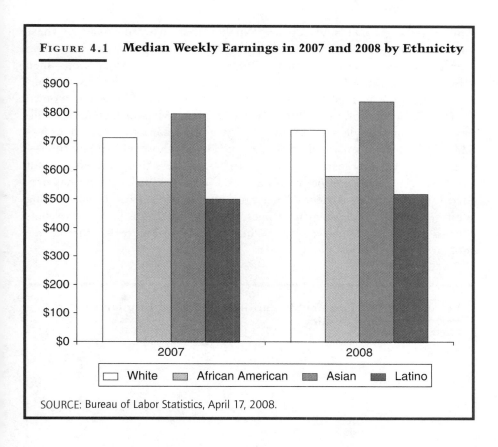

FIGURE 4.1   **Median Weekly Earnings in 2007 and 2008 by Ethnicity**

SOURCE: Bureau of Labor Statistics, April 17, 2008.

to the decline of the manufacturing sector that has characterized the U.S. economy since the 1980s and the high value currently placed on a skilled and educated labor force. The opportunities for social mobility, limited as they were, are very constricted today.[44]

Though poor women have always worked and middle-class women joined the workforce in record numbers in the 1970s, women's wages have continued to lag considerably behind men's wages. This gender gap can be partially explained by the existence of a gender-segregated labor market consisting of occupations traditionally filled by women that pay less than work traditionally done by men. These occupations include professional occupations such as nursing, teaching, and social work, as well as lower-paying jobs such as cosmetologists, child care workers, and home health aides. But even within nongendered occupations where men and women both work, men make more money than women.[45] From 1990 to 2007, in every category of jobs listed by the Bureau of

Labor Statistics, men's wages were higher than women's wages. These included management, professional, and related occupations (men earned on average $1,159 per week, women $829); sales and service occupations (men earned on average $492 per week, women $389); and office occupations (men earned on average $667 per week, women $534).[46] In 2007, women earned 77.5 cents for each dollar earned by men. Median income for full-time year-round male workers in 2007 was $44,255; for women it was $34,278.[47] For women an additional gap occurs for those who are mothers—women with children earn on average 10%–15% less than women without families.[48] The wage gap between male and female skilled workers has narrowed more among African Americans and Latinos than it has among Whites, primarily because men's wages in these two groups have not risen as consistently as have the wages of White men.[49] See Figure 4.2 for income comparisons by ethnicity and gender.

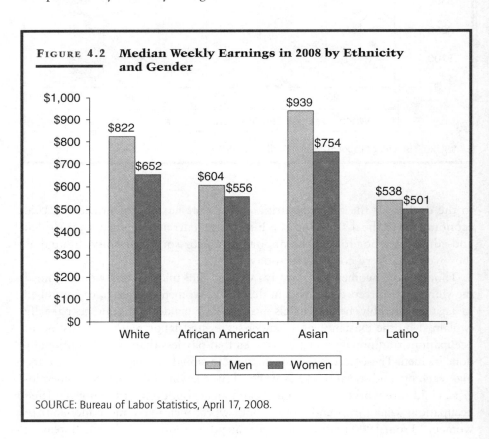

FIGURE 4.2   Median Weekly Earnings in 2008 by Ethnicity and Gender

SOURCE: Bureau of Labor Statistics, April 17, 2008.

DUAL LABOR MARKET ●

Why are some groups persistently poor? Why do women and certain ethnic minority groups make less than others? Why does upward mobility not work for those groups who are persistently poor? In the 19th and early 20th centuries, immigrants from Southern and Eastern Europe provided the cheap labor for heavy industry. They lived in poverty in urban slums and waited for their opportunity to move up the economic ladder. Without any federal or state policies to protect them and their families from the terrible working and living conditions they endured, most had to spend their lives in poverty. Some,

Agricultural workers

SOURCE: From the Library of Congress, photo by Ansel Adams.

like John Rockefeller and Andrew Carnegie, did become wealthy, but the vast majority died poor and counted on their children to reap the material rewards of their sacrifices. Currently certain ethnic groups and many women work at the bottom of the labor market, holding low-paying jobs with little job security, hoping for a better life for their children. Some economists explain the wage discrepancies by arguing that some groups have "lower attachment to the work force" and therefore have a "higher propensity to quit and therefore lower motivation." These characteristics are likely to be found, according to this theory, among "part time workers, youth, women and . . . workers from disadvantaged neighborhoods."[50]

In contrast, Michael Piore argued that those who held the lowest-paying jobs in the U.S. economy were really working in a separate labor market from middle-class skilled and professional workers.[51] He posited that there were dual labor markets—primary and secondary. In the primary labor market, jobs are characterized by relatively high wages, job security, good working conditions, and opportunities for advancements. Many of these jobs have benefits, such as health insurance. Secondary labor market jobs, on the other hand, feature low wages, no benefits, poor working conditions, no opportunity for advancement, and no stability; in fact, they are often temporary jobs. Piore argued that poor persons are confined more or less permanently to the secondary labor market, with little chance for advancement to the primary. One reason for this is that returns to education are less in the secondary labor market; therefore, training and education programs are not useful ways to reduce poverty in the secondary labor market.[52] Another reason for the lack of mobility between the secondary and primary labor markets is the fact that entry into the primary labor market requires a stable job history or recent college graduation, which most people in the secondary labor market cannot demonstrate. Piore recognized that discrimination also funneled some workers into the secondary labor market; he included "race, demeanor and accent" as factors that are discriminated against in the primary labor market. Since discrimination increases the supply of labor in the secondary market, it lowers wages that employers in this market must pay. Thus, Piore reasoned, secondary labor market employers have a stake in the continuation of discrimination in the primary labor market, as do primary labor market workers, who benefit from having a smaller supply of workers eligible for jobs in that market, as discussed above. Keeping secondary labor market workers poor is thus in the interests of many players in the economy.[53]

The segmented labor market theory is useful in understanding the poverty of some ethnic groups in U.S. history. During the late 19th and early 20th centuries, "new" immigrants, including Italians, Poles, and other immigrants from Eastern and Southern Europe, worked in the secondary labor market. Over the past 40 years women and African American and Latino men have been "confined" to the secondary labor market, while the primary labor market has been traditionally the market employing White men. Since the women's movement of the 1970s, many middle-class, college-educated women have moved into the primary labor market.

The dual labor market, like the idea of the "market" for labor, is a social construction—a theory to explain deep inequality in income. It can be a useful way of explaining income inequality and the persistent poverty of some groups. The dual labor market theory continues to be explored in economic research. Generally economists place professionals, secretaries, and other permanent white-collar workers, as well as industrial workers, such as automobile workers, in the primary sector because these jobs require training and skills. Laborers, temporary hotel and restaurant workers, and service workers are located in the secondary labor market.[54] White men and, to a lesser extent, White women continue to dominate the primary labor market, with ethnic minority men and women overrepresented in the secondary labor market.[55] Gender disparities in income are represented in all segments of the labor market; see Figure 4.3.

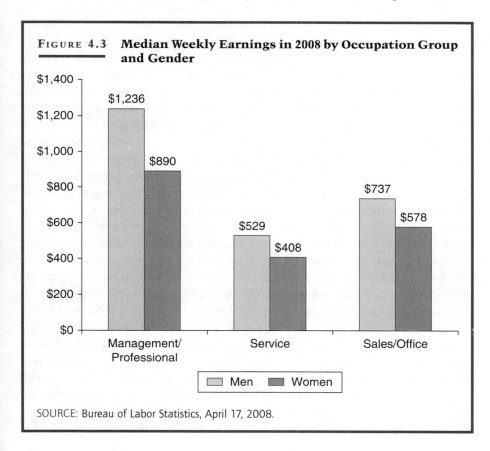

FIGURE 4.3   Median Weekly Earnings in 2008 by Occupation Group and Gender

SOURCE: Bureau of Labor Statistics, April 17, 2008.

The segmented labor market theory is different from the human capital model of the labor market, which asserts that education and training will significantly raise wages, thereby reducing inequality. As we have seen, education and training will not significantly raise earnings in the secondary labor market, since workers in these jobs cannot receive substantially higher wages in these low-wage jobs, even if they invest in education and training. Secondary labor market workers are often trapped in low-paying temporary jobs, earning, at best, the minimum wage. Mobility between the two labor markets during the course of an individual labor market career is severely limited, as employers in the primary labor market are looking for a work history that reflects specific skills and especially job stability, something secondary labor market workers do not have, as discussed above. A person's first job in the labor force is the best predictor of his or her future labor force trajectory. One exception might be the case of White males who hold secondary labor force jobs in high school and are able to move to the primary labor force in adulthood. Otherwise, ethnicity and sex are fairly accurate predictors of labor market at time of entry into the job market.[56]

There continues to be a wide gap between the median income of White workers and that of workers of color.[57] Workers in the secondary labor market are rarely offered the opportunity for overtime pay; instead, employers will hire part-time workers at low pay. Raisings wages for all jobs at the bottom of the income distribution scale is the only sure way to raise the standard of living of workers in this segment of the economy.[58] Until this is accomplished, there needs to be a potential labor force poor enough to be willing to work in these low-wage jobs. While jobs in the primary labor market are rationed, jobs in the secondary labor market are not but are subject to extra labor market influences, such as tourism and weather.[59] When there is a need to fill secondary labor market jobs, there must be persons willing to work in these low-paying jobs who are not otherwise employed in higher-paying jobs. In other words, there needs to be people in the economy who are worse off than the members of the secondary labor market. Since jobs in the secondary market expand and contract according to seasons (farm workers) or according to economic boom times or recession (hotel and restaurant workers tend to lose jobs in economic downtimes because spending on entertainment diminishes, as do construction workers when the housing market falls), people in these markets will be periodically without work. Leaving jobs to the vagaries of the market economy with no government floor on wages ensures that some will be underemployed, working part-time jobs or not working at all, waiting for their chances in the secondary labor market. Those who are looking for jobs in the secondary labor market can be thought of as a tertiary labor market. Some may be eligible temporarily for welfare; others may be homeless or marginally housed; others may be managing day-by-day on limited resources. As the secondary labor market contracts, the tertiary labor market expands. People in the secondary and especially the tertiary labor markets are the most economically marginalized of all workers; their *poverty is a necessity in an unregulated market economy*, as the above analysis demonstrates.

PROFILES IN LEADERSHIP

Dolores Huerta, 1930–

Dolores Fernández was born on April 10, 1930, in Dawson, New Mexico. Her father worked as a mine worker, as a union activist, and eventually as a farm worker. When Dolores was age 6, her parents divorced, and she and her mother moved to Stockton, California. Her mother began running a hotel that rented rooms to migrant farm workers who worked in the local fields. Even as a child, Dolores was a responsible child helping her mother with chores around the hotel and working during school vacations picking apricots.

In 1948 Dolores married her high school sweetheart. At the age of 20 after having two children, she was divorced from her first husband and began taking night classes to earn a teaching credential. As a schoolteacher she realized that her assistance to the poor children in her classes

Dolores Huerta, 1968

SOURCE: Getty Images.

(Continued)

(Continued)

was limited, and she concluded that she could be more effective in improving the lives of poor children and families if she devoted her time to organizing the farm workers. This desire led to a position with the Community Service Organization (CSO) of Stockton, California. This organization was committed to increasing the political power of farm workers who toiled in the fields receiving low wages and working in miserable conditions. Among other things, this organization led voter registration drives, advocated for more Latinos on the police force, and lobbied for more Spanish-speaking staff in hospitals and government offices.

After her leadership qualities with the organization were recognized, she was promoted to work as a full-time lobbyist representing her organization at the state capitol in Sacramento, California. As a lobbyist, she was instrumental in pushing through numerous items of legislation particularly focused on benefiting the Latino community. Despite these achievements, she realized that farm workers needed to be organized in order to effectively demand higher pay and improved working conditions. While in Sacramento, she met and married a man named Ventura Huerta, and they eventually had a large family. A critical moment happened in her life when she met another activist with similar ideas related to social justice, Cesar Chavez. When the two met in 1955, it was clear that they would form a powerful partnership to fight for the rights of farm workers. Chavez had resigned from the CSO after the organization balked at the idea of unionizing the farm workers. In response, he decided to form an organization and develop a union himself. Chavez and Huerta established the Farm Workers Association (FWA), an organization that would work to unionize farm workers and advocate on their behalf. Both Chavez and Huerta were aware of the challenges ahead and the resistance they would receive from growers and the business community. Their first task was to travel throughout California speaking to workers and asking them to support the new organization. Convincing the workers was a monumental task, as most had been poor for generations and could not conceive of how a farm worker's union could make demands of the powerful growers.

In 1962, the FWA held its first convention in Sacramento, California, attended by over 300 delegates from around the state. Chavez was elected president, and Huerta was elected vice president. For 3 years, they struggled to bring more members into the FWA in order to make it self-supporting. This was finally accomplished, and they decided to change the name of the FWA to the National Farm Workers Association (NFWA). This was done with the hope that one day this organization would represent all farm workers across the country.

The first official strike occurred when the membership agreed with the leadership of the NFWA to support the Filipino farm workers who were already on strike protesting poor wages. In response to the strike, growers were removing workers from their shacks and patrolling the fields with guns. Despite being beaten and threatened, the strikers did not back down or resort to violence. As a show of support, Huerta would often bring her children directly to the site of the strike to show solidarity with the workers. As the strike continued, other supporters including religious leaders, civil rights workers, and college students joined in the protest efforts. Chavez and Huerta decided they needed more effective tactics, so they organized an economic boycott of table grapes. Despite limited organizing success in California, they decided to expand their boycott nationally in order to have more impact on the resistant growers and to enlist additional support from other national groups. Soon their efforts in California began to pay off, and the union was able to bring a number of companies to the bargaining table. Huerta became the chief negotiator for the contracts signed by the growers.

In January 1968, Huerta and others traveled to New York to economic boycotts aimed at convincing consumers not to buy table grapes. There was a groundswell of support, and soon pickets were established at markets in small towns and big cities across the country.

Dolores Huerta continued to be in charge of negotiations with the growers as grape sales plummeted, and growers concluded that they were fighting a losing battle. Demands included an increase in base pay and a process to regulate the use of pesticides. In order to gain more leverage, many growers signed up with the Teamsters Union, which resisted the union growers' contracts, and this led to farm-labor strife resulting in mass arrests and two deaths of farm workers. Continued strife eventually led Governor of California Edmund Brown to establish the Agricultural Labor Relations Board to hear unfair labor practices and to conduct labor elections. This board helped farm workers win the right to join the union and to take control of their economic futures. The economic boycott had been extremely effective and had forced growers to the bargaining table.

In 1988, union supporters held a rally in San Francisco to protest Vice President George Bush's opposition to the ongoing grape boycott. The rally resulted in police brutality, and Huerta and others were severely beaten. Huerta and others sued the city, and she was awarded $825,000 as the result of police misconduct. Huerta continues to work as the union's vice president and has won numerous awards for her tireless work on behalf of the nation's farm workers. She was inducted into the Women's Hall of Fame and won the NAACP Martin Luther King Jr. award for her outstanding work and leadership. She devoted her life to achieve social justice for farm workers against great odds. She is a powerful role model for others who will continue to fight for social justice for workers across the nation.

POVERTY AND INEQUALITY   ●

Economists acknowledge the existence of poverty but may argue that the market usually solves the problem: Poverty is uncomfortable, and people seek to move out of it by acquiring training and education to improve their jobs, thereby escaping poverty.[60] Economists recognize that challenges to law and order resulting from persistent poverty, however, both on the part of economically marginalized persons and on the part of those concerned for moral reasons about poverty, are disruptive to market functioning and prosperity. Therefore many economists today advocate some sort of government safety net as an "insurance policy" to protect the market system.[61]

How is poverty officially defined in the United States? The first official calculation of what constitutes poverty in the United States took place in the 1960s. The poverty level was established by estimating that a family needed to spend about one third of its income on food to sustain an adequate diet. Therefore three times the cost of a "nutritionally adequate intake" was considered the poverty level—families who made less than that were considered officially poor.[62] Living above the poverty level means that the federal government has determined that a family's income is sufficient for basic food, shelter, clothing, and other essentials. As defined by the Office of Management and Budget and updated for inflation using the Consumer Price Index, the poverty line for a family of four in 2009 was $22,050; for a family of three, it was $18,310; for a family of two, it was $14,570; and for unrelated individuals, it was $10,830.[63]

There were 37.3 million people in poverty in 2007.[64] The poverty line, then, is the demarcation between those who are officially poor and those who are not; it is adjusted for inflation each year. The poverty line does not take into account regional differences in cost of living, thus disadvantaging some economically marginalized persons in high-cost urban areas, where rent may be much higher than in rural areas, for example. Another problem with the poverty line is that it overestimates how much families typically spend on food (now closer to 18% of their budget) and underestimates how much they spend on rent, health care, child care, and transportation, all necessities for wage earning.[65] The poverty line is important because the federal government uses it to establish eligibility for a host of programs, including Temporary Assistance for Needy Families (TANF) and Supplemental Security Income (SSI). The poverty threshold, a lower figure, is used to determine eligibility for other programs, including Head Start and the Supplemental Nutrition Assistance Program, or SNAP (food stamps). Thus it is more difficult to qualify for these programs than it is to qualify for TANF and SSI.

Single-headed families and families from certain ethnic groups are overrepresented among those living below the poverty line. Women-headed families on average bring in less money than families with male heads of households, because on average women make less money than men (see discussion above).

The term *feminization of poverty* refers to the disproportionate number of women living at or below the poverty line in the United States. Poverty rates are highest for families headed by single women, particularly if they are Black or Hispanic. In 2007, 28.3% of households headed by single women were poor, while 13.6% of households headed by single men and 4.9% of married-couple households lived in poverty.[66] (See Figure 4.4.)

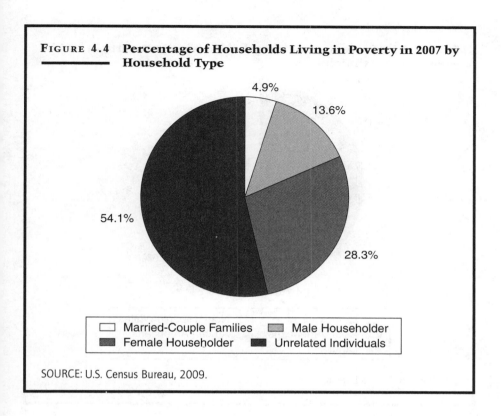

FIGURE 4.4   **Percentage of Households Living in Poverty in 2007 by Household Type**

SOURCE: U.S. Census Bureau, 2009.

Ethnic differences in household income are significant. Median household income in the United States for all households was $50,740 in 2007. The median income for non-Hispanic White households was $55,096, for Asian American households it was $66,935, and for Hispanic households it was $40,766. African American households had the lowest median income at $34,001.[67] Clearly a disproportionate number of African American and Hispanic families had household incomes below the national median. For Hispanics, 20.6% were living below the poverty line in 2007, whereas 10.2% of non-Hispanic Whites and 10.6% of Asian Americans lived in poverty. The highest rate of poverty was experienced by African Americans; 24.7% were living in poverty in 2007.[68] These differences are startling. Factors related to this inequality of income among ethnic groups will be discussed in Chapter 5. (See Figures 4.5 and 4.6.)

Families living at or below the poverty line are in the secondary or tertiary labor market. We see them every day but often do not notice their work, which frequently revolves around serving us or cleaning up after us. Some of these workers are not part of the formal economy as they are paid in cash and may not report

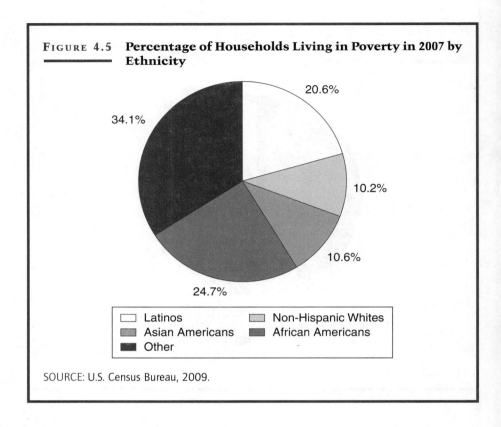

FIGURE 4.5   **Percentage of Households Living in Poverty in 2007 by Ethnicity**

34.1%

20.6%

10.2%

10.6%

24.7%

Legend:
- Latinos
- Asian Americans
- Other
- Non-Hispanic Whites
- African Americans

SOURCE: U.S. Census Bureau, 2009.

their income. Their invisibility has led some to call these workers part of the shadow labor market. The shadow economy includes legal and illegal transactions whose proceeds may not be reported as taxable income.[69] None of these workers are reflected in unemployment figures; their absence makes the unofficial unemployment figures an underestimate of those who are marginally unemployed. Persons actively seeking work who register for unemployment benefits are reflected in the unemployment figures published by the federal government. Persons working in the secondary labor market may not be eligible for unemployment benefits. Unemployment figures exclude so-called discouraged workers who are considered out of the labor force. On the other hand, part-time workers are considered employed, even though they would rather work full-time, as are those who are working at lower-paying jobs than their skills should command. Both of these groups are considered underemployed but are included in the employed group, underestimating the problem of unemployment.[70] Unemployment rates vary by ethnicity and gender: African Americans and women are more likely to be unemployed than other groups.[71]

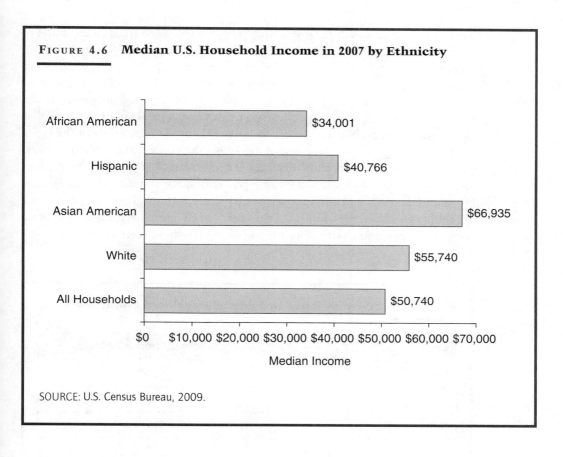

FIGURE 4.6   **Median U.S. Household Income in 2007 by Ethnicity**

SOURCE: U.S. Census Bureau, 2009.

Inequality of income has increased since 1980. Since 1970, pretax income inequality has increased significantly, with the share of income going to the top 1% of households more than doubling between 1970 and 2000. In 2005, households in the top 1% received about $500,000 more annually than they did in 1970. In 2005, the top 1% of households in the United States received 21.8% of all pretax income, which is the greatest concentration of income since 1928, the year before the Great Depression. The share of income going to the poorest fifth of the population has declined since 1980: from 5.4% in 1975 to 3.5% in 2001. This is in contrast with the share of income going to the richest fifth of the population, which increased from 15% to 22.4% between 1975 and 2001. Most of these income gains went to the top 0.1% of households.[72]

Economists explain the rising inequality in several ways: government programs to aid economically marginalized persons were cut in the 1980s and have not been restored; the wealthiest groups were aided by tax cuts made in the pursuit of *supply side economics* during this period; there has been increased compensation for CEOs of major corporations, as well as an increased number of births to single women, who have lower salaries than men and higher rates of poverty. Another factor in the growing inequality is the increased wage gap between college graduates and high school graduates that occurred between 1980 and 1997, with workers at the lower tiers of the labor market earning far less by the end of the 1990s than they had in previous years. A major factor in the decline of wages for high school graduates was the loss of manufacturing jobs and the waning power of labor unions to protect wages in manufacturing and services sectors of the economy. Real wages for the working class have been flat for 3 decades.[73] See Figure 4.7 for a comparative look at the percentage of persons living in poverty in selected countries.

FIGURE 4.7   Poverty Rates in Selected Developed Countries

Country	Percent Below Poverty
Poland	5%
Sweden	7%
Netherlands	7%
Austria	8%
Belgium	8%
Germany	8%
Canada	11%
United Kingdom	12%
Italy	13%
Ireland	17%
United States	17%

SOURCE: Adapted from T. Smeeding, "Poor People in Rich Nations: The United States in Comparative Perspective," *Journal of Economic Perspectives, 20*(1), 2006. Used with permission.

PROFILES IN LEADERSHIP

A. Philip Randolph, 1889–1979

A. Philip Randolph was born on April 15, 1889, in Crescent City, Florida. He was born into a poor family with strong religious values. Randolph spent most of his youth in Jacksonville, Florida, one of the most integrated towns in the South with Blacks represented in all areas of the city's structure and local businesses. Children in this town had an opportunity to attain higher education, unlike most children in other Southern cities. During Randolph's youth he was

A. Philip Randolph

SOURCE: From the Library of Congress.

not exposed to the rigid segregation and oppression experienced by other Blacks in much of the South. Fortunately, he was exposed to Blacks in positions of authority, and he had a very strong role model in his father. His father was a descendent of slaves but became educated by Northern White missionaries from the Methodist Church and eventually became a minister in the African Methodist Episcopal Church.

Young Randolph received a strong religious background from his father and often went to hear the sermons offered by his father at the Bethel Baptist Church in Jacksonville. From his father he learned very valuable lessons such as being independent, fighting racial discrimination, taking responsibility for the needy, and providing leadership to local causes. Social conditions began to change for the worse at the turn of the century (1900), when a major fire destroyed much of Jacksonville, resulting in a sharp rise in racial tension and conflicts. Jim Crow laws that existed in other parts of the South began to be implemented in Florida, barring Blacks from voting, holding government positions, and using the same public

(Continued)

(Continued)

facilities as Whites. During this period, Randolph attended public schools while being home schooled by his father in more academic subjects. At age 14, he was accepted at the Cookman Institute that offered college prep and trade-oriented courses. He excelled in his studies and other school-related activities. Upon graduation, he worked at many types of jobs, but he had determined that he was not interested in the ministry as a career like his father. At this time, he was very influenced by the beliefs of W. E. B. Du Bois in the system of racial injustice in the United States and the need for racial equality. In 1911 at age 22, he decided to leave Jacksonville and seek his future in New York City, ending up in Harlem. During the early decades of the 20th century, Randolph was one of a large number of Blacks moving from the South seeking economic opportunity and freedom from oppression. Harlem at this time was an exciting and challenging place for a young man from the South. He struggled to find work and even tried to become a professional actor until he became discouraged. He turned to politics and took classes in political science, history, and economics and became involved in a debating society. He soon discovered the writings of Karl Marx and came to believe that socialism was the best means for achieving racial equality in America. In 1914, Randolph met and married a 31-year-old beautician named Lucille Campbell Green; their marriage lasted almost 50 years.

In 1917, Randolph and a close friend, Chandler Owen, began a magazine that they named the *Hotel Messenger*. This magazine became the vehicle for speaking out against discrimination and instilling Black pride. The magazine was soon described as a radical magazine by Whites as advocating revolutionary change. In the mid-1920s, Randolph was asked to organize a porters' union for the sleeping car porters who worked for the Pullman Company. These workers were overworked and underpaid and were often away from home for extended periods. White railroad workers had been able to form a union, but Blacks found an unresponsive company and hostile responses at every attempt to form a union for Black porters. In 1925, Randolph and others decided to form a new organization, which they called the Brotherhood of Sleeping Car Porters. The response to the new organization from the workers was very favorable; soon large numbers of porters were joining the union from many states where the Pullman Company operated. Stunned by the success of the fledgling union, the Pullman Company mounted a hostile campaign against Randolph, calling Randolph a radical and threatening the workers with dismissal from their jobs. Randolph soon realized that the union could never succeed completely until there were changes in the federal labor laws. The new union hired lawyers and lobbyists to press for federal action and acceptance of the union. After a protracted struggle, Randolph and others felt that the only way to fight the Pullman Company for workers' rights was to threaten a strike. Because of the intense resistance to the new union, Randolph soon realized that the workers would lose their jobs, so he backed off from proposing a workers' strike. Randolph decided that the Brotherhood union could benefit from membership in the American Federation of Labor (AFL), America's largest labor federation. He believed that this would provide leverage in dealing with the Pullman Company and provide needed prestige for the new union. Despite these and other efforts, union membership began to decline, and soon the depression of the 1930s began to also have a negative effect on organizing efforts. The Brotherhood union experienced very difficult times until the election of Franklin D. Roosevelt who supported organizing efforts of workers.

After continuing struggles, collective bargaining negotiations began between the Brotherhood union and the Pullman Company in 1935. After 2 years of discussions, the Pullman representatives finally signed an agreement that gave the workers the wage and work-hour concessions that the union had demanded. The long bitter battle that had left Randolph exhausted and at times penniless was finally over.

The success of the Brotherhood union gave Randolph national recognition as a major leader and spokesperson for the Black workers of America. He then turned his attention to issues of discrimination and racism in other parts of the country. Recognizing that only intense pressure would result in positive social change, he threatened to organize a march on Washington of thousands of Black workers unless racial discrimination in the armed forces and the defense industries was prohibited by law. In 1941, President Roosevelt signed an executive order making discriminatory laws in the defense industry and the federal government illegal, as well as establishing the Fair Employment Practices Committee. Once again, Randolph prevailed in his quest for justice and equal rights for Black workers.

Randolph continued to be very active in civil rights struggles until he passed away at the age of 90. He had received the Medal of Honor from President Lyndon B. Johnson for his outstanding work on behalf of the workers of America. He has been recognized as the person who laid the foundation for the civil rights movement that swept the nation in the 1950s and 1960s. Randolph made major contributions to achieve social justice and social change in this country, and he influenced many other leaders who came after him who recognized his courage and vision for a better America.

Inequality of wealth has been growing over the past 10 years in the United States. The richest 1% of U.S. households own 34.3% of the nation's private wealth, more than the combined wealth of the bottom 90%. The top 1% also own 36.9% of all corporate stock.[74] When looking at median net worth by ethnicity, the figures are startlingly discrepant (see Figure 4.8). White non-Hispanics' median net worth was $140,700 in 2004, African Americans' median net worth was $20,600, and Hispanics' median net worth was $18,600.[75] Distribution of wealth is much harder than income distribution to determine, as wealth is not directly reported, whereas income is reported every year through taxes. High salaries are a source of wealth. In 2005, American CEOs earned 411 times as much as average workers, up from 107 times in 1990. Top executives in the United States now make about twice the pay of their counterparts in France, Germany, and the United Kingdom and about four times that of Japanese and Korean corporate chieftains.[76] The richest 1% of wealth holders had 190 times as much wealth of the median household in 2005, a 50% increase from 1965.[77] See Figure 4.8 for disparity in wealth in the United States by ethnicity.

FIGURE 4.8   **Median Net Worth by Ethnicity**

Ethnicity	Median Net Worth
White	$140,700
African American	$20,600
Hispanic	$18,600

SOURCES: White: From B. K. Bucks, A. B. Kennickell, and K. B. Moore, "Recent Changes in U.S. Family Finances: Evidence From the 2001 and 2004 Survey of Consumer Finances," *Federal Reserve Bulletin*, Vol. 92, February 2006, Table 3; African American and Hispanic: A. B. Kennickell, "Currents and Undercurrents: Changes in the Distribution of Wealth, 1989–2004," *Survey of Consumer Finances Working Paper*, January 30, 2006; Retrieved from http://www.demos.org/inequality/numbers.cfm on March 9, 2009.

● TAXES AND INEQUALITY

Governments at all levels provide public goods through taxation, including sales tax, federal excise taxes on alcohol and gasoline, income taxes, and corporate taxes. Sales taxes and federal excise taxes are taxes on consumption and are generally regressive; that is, they consume a larger proportion of the income of low-income families than of high-income families. The payroll tax collected for Social Security Insurance is also regressive. Sales tax and Social Security wage taxes are "flat" taxes because the rate of taxation does not increase as income increases. Income and corporate taxes, along with taxes on capital gains, are progressive taxes because the rate of taxation goes up with the amount of money taxed. Economists assess whether a tax is progressive by determining whether after-tax income is more equally distributed than pretax income.[78] Capital gains are taxes on wealth; they tax profits on sales of assets such as stock, land, or a business. Capital gains are taxed at a maximum rate of 15%, while ordinary income (including wages and interest) is taxed at a maximum rate of 35%. Thus the tax system favors wealth over income.

Tax Cuts: Who Benefits?

Congress has cut taxes every year since 2001. The 2001–2006 tax cuts reduced most individual tax rates, including those on capital gains and dividends; gradually phased out the limitations on itemized deductions and personal exemptions for high-income taxpayers; and phased out the estate tax. In 2005, the richest 10% of households got more than 90% of the capital gains tax benefits, diminishing the progressive nature of the capital gains tax.[79] Almost all of these tax cuts end by 2011 and must be renewed by Congress to continue. The revenue cost of the tax cuts will be approximately $2 trillion over the 2001–2010 period. Annual costs will rise if Congress extends the tax cuts beyond 2010. These tax cuts disproportionately benefit high-income taxpayers. In 2007, the tax cuts raised after-tax income by 0.3% for the lowest quintile, by 2.4% for the middle quintile, and by 3.2% for the top quintile. The top fifth of income earners received 67% of the tax cuts in this period.[80] Thus the tax cuts favored the wealthy: In 2006, households in the bottom 20% received only $23 due to the Bush tax cuts. Households in the middle 20% received $448. Families in the top 1% received $39,020. And households in the top 0.1% received $200,523.[81] Largely as a result of the these tax cuts, in 2005 income concentration at the top of households in the United States increased dramatically. Between 2004 and 2005 the average income of the top 1% of U.S. households, adjusting for inflation, increased by $102,000 while the average income of the bottom 90% of households increased by only $250. (See Figure 4.9.)

To compound the trend toward income inequality discussed above, since the 1960s the progressivity of the federal tax system has declined dramatically. High-income households have seen sharp drops in their federal tax rates since that date, even before the Bush tax cuts. After-tax income saw the same trends in inequality as before-tax income. In 1970, the top 1% paid 47% of their income to taxes; in 2004, they paid an average of 30% of their income. The difference is a gain of more than $200,000 in after-tax income to these households.[82] (See Figure 4.10.)

Tax cuts are not just a way to preserve income for the wealthy; they are part of a deep belief in the value of the market economy. The belief is that if profits (as in capital gains) and high income are taxed, the incentive for investment will be diminished. Taxes are levied because of a collective commitment to the social goods provided by governments, yet for some this collective commitment

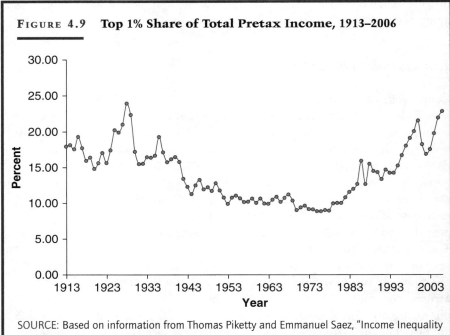

FIGURE 4.9   **Top 1% Share of Total Pretax Income, 1913–2006**

SOURCE: Based on information from Thomas Piketty and Emmanuel Saez, "Income Inequality in the United States, 1913–1998," *Quarterly Journal of Economics,* 118(1), 2003. Updated to 2006 at http://emlab.berkeley.edu/users/saez. Adapted from Inequality.org.

undermines individual incentives for risk taking in the market economy. Those who took market risks and are rewarded with high income or wealth should not be taxed deeply, goes the argument; instead, they should be rewarded in order to encourage others to invest in the economy. Not only taxes but government regulation of the marketplace in any form, including environmental regulations and oversight of worker conditions, is considered interference with the free market.

Earned Income Tax Credit

The Earned Income Tax Credit (EITC) is a federal program that uses the tax system in a wholly different way by providing tax refunds to the working poor. Established in 1975, the EITC uses public funds to subsidize the wages of some low-income workers, thereby reducing the labor costs of employers. Low *wages,* not poverty itself, are the established criteria for this program. The value of the EITC is based on earnings and the number of children, if any, raised by

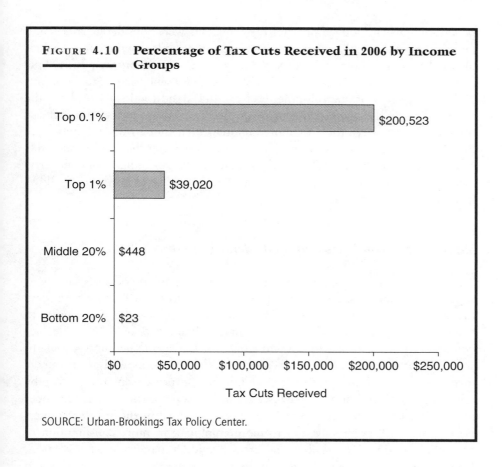

FIGURE 4.10 **Percentage of Tax Cuts Received in 2006 by Income Groups**

Top 0.1% — $200,523

Top 1% — $39,020

Middle 20% — $448

Bottom 20% — $23

Tax Cuts Received

SOURCE: Urban-Brookings Tax Policy Center.

a worker. In 2006, a family earning between $11,340 and $14,810 received the maximum credit of $4,536. The maximum EITC for families with one child was $2,747 and for childless workers was $412. EITC benefits are adjusted for inflation, and thus they go up every year.[83] The threshold for eligibility for the EITC in 2006 was $37,783 for a household with two children; for a household with no children, the threshold was $12,590.[84]

According to the Center on Budget and Policy Priorities, the EITC lifts more children out of poverty than any other single program or category of programs. Just as important as the direct effect of the EITC is the indirect effect: Studies have consistently found that the EITC increases labor force participation substantially for single mothers because it effectively increases wages by several thousand dollars, thus encouraging work.[85] Since the minimum wage has not kept up with inflation, the value of the EITC has diminished. In 1998, a typical family of four with a full-time, minimum-wage worker had income above the poverty line when food stamps and EITC benefits were considered. In 2006, a family of four with only one minimum-wage earner had a total income (including food stamps and the EITC) of $18,950, some $1,550 *below* the poverty line. Raising the minimum wage to $7.25 an hour in 2009 will bring a family of four with one parent working full-time receiving EITC and food stamps above the poverty line.[86] One of the problems with the EITC is that it does not increase for families that have three or more children, even though those families are more likely to be living in poverty than families with fewer than three children.[87] Many states also have EITC benefits; these states can reduce child poverty, increase the total income coming into the household, and cut taxes for low-income working families.

Supply Side Economics and the Federal Deficit

The political ideology supporting tax cuts for wealthier Americans is known as supply side economics. The term *supply side* comes from the emphasis on using the tax system to encourage productivity and the *supply* of goods, in order to stimulate buying and eventually employment. Proponents of supply side economics argue that cutting the capital gains tax will encourage more people to sell their capital assets, thereby increasing tax revenues, as well as encourage investment of the remainder of the capital gains in private enterprise, thereby strengthening the economy. Likewise, cutting personal income taxes for upper income brackets is believed to be an incentive for investment in private enterprise, which will eventually lead to more employment, more consumption of new goods produced, more economic growth, and ultimately more taxes paid.[88] Ronald Reagan was the first president to advocate tax cuts on both wages and corporations for these reasons in the 1980s. Supply side economists influencing Reagan argued that high taxes reduced the incentive to work and the supply of capital. The result of this first experiment with supply side economics was not what proponents expected: The expected growth in private investment in the United States was not seen, nor was the expansion of jobs; instead, the reduction in tax revenues meant that the federal government spent more than it brought in, leading to a large budget deficit.[89] President Bill Clinton turned away from supply side economics and raised taxes on the wealthy in 1993 to offset the growing budget deficit. This measure, along with the booming economy of the 1990s, resulted in a federal budget surplus by 1998. This federal surplus was subsequently eroded by fears of terrorism, wars, and a stock market decline. But the main growth in the federal deficit occurred in 2001, after George W. Bush persuaded Congress to enact large across-the-boards tax cuts.

Bush used supply side reasoning to argue that the tax cuts would stimulate the economy by raising the long-run rate of economic growth.[90] Another set of tax cuts followed in 2003, and combined with an increase in military spending to fund the war in Iraq and Afghanistan, served to further deepen the federal deficit.[91] Internal Revenue Service data demonstrate that the Bush tax cuts did not result in increased revenue to the federal government, contrary to what the administration predicted about economic growth. In 2003, the year tax breaks for capital gains and dividends, as well as reductions in marginal tax rates and other tax cuts, were enacted by Congress, the lower tax rates resulted in a 6.1% decrease in total income tax revenues.[92]

Social Work and the Federal Deficit

What are the implications of the large federal deficit for social workers? One of the most severe consequences of the deficit is the pressure to cut social programs.[93] Borrowing money to fund the federal government has become routine since 2001, and paying the yearly interest on the federal deficit is extremely costly, increasing the deficit more. The strategy of driving up the federal deficit in order to deny funds for social programs and reduce the size of government is known as "starving the beast." The idea is to cut taxes before cutting spending and then use the resulting deficit as a political argument to reduce spending. This strategy has been used by both Reagan and George W. Bush.[94] The reasons for the popularity of the policy of "starving the beast" include a distaste for federal spending that has consistently characterized conservatives since the founding of the country, along with a belief that increasing the deficit is a more politically palatable way of reducing spending than a direct attempt to cut spending on potentially popular programs. This belief drives supporters of regressive tax cuts on upper-income households, even though military spending continues to increase. Making the tax cuts of 2001 and 2003 permanent would represent a loss of $3.0 trillion over the next 10 years (fiscal year 2008 through 2017), according to Joint Committee on Taxation and Congressional Budget Office estimates.[95] Furthermore, the Congressional Budget Office estimates that if the tax cuts are made permanent and future costs for the wars in Iraq and Afghanistan follow the Congressional Budget Office's most optimistic scenario, the deficit will climb to $1.7 trillion by the end of 2009.[96]

Meanwhile federal revenue from corporate taxes is decreasing. Like the tax rate on upper-income households, the corporate tax burden has fallen substantially since 1990.[97] Corporate revenues have fallen consistently since 2000 and represent a smaller percentage of overall tax revenue every year.[98] Although the

United States has a corporate tax rate commensurate with that of other industrialized countries, because of special corporate tax breaks, our *effective* corporate tax rate is among the lowest in the developed world. Corporate tax revenue data demonstrate this point. In 2005, the most recent year for which data are available, U.S. corporate tax revenue as a share of gross domestic product (GDP) was only 2.6%, lower than in all but two developed countries.[99]

The United States remains one of the least taxed industrial countries. We rank 28th in taxes paid among the 30 Organisation for Economic Co-operation and Development (OECD) countries. Only Korea and Mexico had lower taxes.[100] Partly as a result of the tax policies outlined above, the United States spends a smaller percentage of its GDP on social policies than any other industrialized nation.[101]

● TAX EXPENDITURES

The federal government offers fiscal benefits to individuals and corporations through the tax system. These benefits are called tax expenditures because they represent money that would come into the federal budget without specific provisions that allow businesses and individuals to keep revenue and avoid taxation. Tax expenditures therefore result in loss of federal revenue in the same ways that direct spending does. These tax policies represent billions of dollars of lost revenue to the federal government every year. The sum of tax expenditure revenue loss was $730 billion in 2004. Tax expenditures have exceeded discretionary spending for most years in the last decade.[102] According to the Joint Committee on Taxation of the U.S. Congress, tax expenditures for fiscal years 2005–2009 are estimated to exceed $2.1 trillion. Among the largest tax benefits were employer-provided health insurance, the mortgage interest rate deduction, and reduced tax rates on dividends and capital gains taxes (taxes on wealth).[103]

The most widely used tax incentive for individuals is the mortgage interest tax deduction. Homeowners can deduct a percentage of the interest on their mortgages, depending on their income—a benefit renters do not receive. The amount of the deduction parallels the amount of yearly taxable income—the more income, the greater the deduction.[104] Introduced along with the income tax in 1913, the mortgage interest deduction was little used until the post–World War II suburban boom of the 1950s. In 2006, it cost the U.S. Treasury approximately $76 billion. Since the benefit increases with household income, a little more than half of this tax benefit is utilized by the top 12% of taxpayers with incomes of $100,000 per year and more.[105] See Chapter 10 for an in-depth discussion of federal housing policy, including the mortgage interest deductions.

The tax deduction for employee health insurance benefits businesses that offer health insurance to their workers. This tax break for businesses serves as an incentive to private enterprise to offer health insurance through the private market economy, thereby benefiting private insurance companies and reducing the demand for national health insurance that would likely grow if there were no employee participation in worker health care.[106]

Other federal outlays that directly, rather than indirectly, subsidize corporate interests are called "corporate welfare" by their critics. These involve direct subsidies to corporations and private sectors such as agriculture. The Export-Import Bank uses taxpayer dollars to provide subsidized financing to foreign purchasers of U.S. goods. Its activities include making direct loans to those buyers at below-market interest rates, guaranteeing the loans of private institutions to those buyers, and providing export credit insurance to exporters and private lenders. Another example is the Commerce Department's Advanced Technology Program, which gave research grants to consortiums of some of the nation's largest high-tech companies. Those grants allowed private companies to use taxpayer dollars to help them develop and bring to market profitable new products.[107]

A major corporate welfare program is designed to help large corporate farmers. Farmers are disadvantaged in a free market economy because if each farmer grows all he or she can in order to maximize his or her income, the prices of farm goods will fall because of oversupply. Farm subsidies were begun in 1935 to protect the income of working farmers whose production of farm commodities led to excess supply and lower prices. It is now a complex infrastructure of entitlements that has cost $172 billion over the past decade. Between 1995 and 2005 approximately $165 billion in subsidies were paid by the federal government to farmers; some are paid not to grow crops; others have their income supplemented by the federal government if prices fall below a certain level. Two thirds of farmers do not qualify for federal subsidies because their acreage is too small. Of those who do receive subsidies, about 10% collected 73% of all subsidies paid, amounting to $120 billion over 11 years.[108] This subsidy program puts small farmers at a serious disadvantage compared to large corporate farmers, who often use their payments to buy up smaller farms. Nationwide, the federal government paid at least $1.3 billion in subsidies from 2000 to 2006 to individuals who did no farming at all. The payments now account for nearly half of the nation's expanding and complex agricultural subsidy system. In 2005 alone, when pretax farm profits were at a near-record $72 billion, the federal government handed out more than $25 billion in aid, almost 50% more than the amount it pays to families receiving welfare.[109] This massive welfare payment to farmers is rarely questioned and even more rarely compared to welfare payments to mothers raising children.

● **PUBLIC BENEFIT, PRIVATE PROFIT**

The public sector benefits the private sector in many ways aside from the direct tax expenditures described above. The government provides public goods that can be enjoyed by everyone. Since the benefits of highways, clean water, and other public health measures are widely available, it is not feasible for one firm to produce them for a profit.[110] Libraries and public transportation systems may have a user's charge, but these charges are not high enough to create or sustain these public services. Thus government becomes responsible for delivering public goods, including police, sanitation, and fire departments. One of the biggest government benefits to the corporate sector was enjoyed by the automobile and oil industries in 1956, when the Eisenhower administration funded the largest public works project in American history and authorized $26 billion to build a federal highway system, rather than encourage the development of a mass transit system. One of the unintended consequences of this policy was to encourage the national dependence on oil, a problem driving our foreign policy in the Middle East. This policy also encouraged suburban development and the White middle-class housing boom after World War II, at the expense of persons living in the inner cities, many of whom were ethnic minorities who would have benefited from a mass transit system.[111]

In addition to the provision of public good that benefits private enterprise, the public sector has absorbed much of the cost of educating the workforce through publicly subsidized education from primary grades through public universities and subsidizes much of the transportation costs in the journey to work that labor market participation demands through highway systems and mass transit. Social insurance programs stimulate consumer demand by transferring income to groups with less purchasing power. Employment and training programs sponsored by the federal government have subsidized the wages of disadvantaged workers from low-income areas for limited periods. In-kind benefits such as food stamps allow some employers to pay such low wages that their workers may qualify for these benefits.[112]

Public benefits that shore up the income of economically marginalized persons, such as welfare, food stamps, and the EITC, reduce the worst effects of the inequality caused by the market economy. In so doing they reduce potential tension and dissatisfaction with the inequality that is a necessary corollary of a market economy. It can be argued that corporate and business interests have the most to gain from these social welfare programs, since they preserve the structures of wealth and income inequality from angry and disgruntled persons who might seek deep change in the system otherwise. Finally, social welfare benefits such as SNAP and entitlement programs such as Social Security help the corporate sector by increasing consumer demand; with increased resources, both cash and in-kind benefits, consumers will purchase more goods and services, thereby contributing to corporate profits. In sum, the public goods provided by all levels of government—local, state, and federal—are indispensable to the survival of the market economy.

SOCIAL COSTS AND EXTERNALITIES ●

Economists refer to unemployment and other problems that accompany the market economy as externalities or social costs. Both terms refer to a cost that is not reflected in the market transaction and impacts persons not part of market exchange. Like monopolies and oligopolies that restrict perfect competition, all externalities and social costs are described as "market failures" by economists.[113] Social costs include environmental pollution and worker health and safety hazards. Since the New Deal, many of these social costs have been met by the government through publicly supported social policies, such as Unemployment Insurance Benefits and the Occupational Safety and Health Act. Assigning social costs to the public sector and profits to the private sector is a trade-off that benefits corporations, regardless of complaints about government interference or government spending.

Much of the debate between the major political parties in the United States has focused on how much of these social costs should be a collective responsibility met by the public sector. Conservatives are likely to argue that these costs are private, should be absorbed by the individuals who sustain them, and should not be taxpayers' responsibility, while progressives argue that many of these costs should be considered a collective burden met by government. For example, the costs of child care can be considered social costs of maintaining an active labor force sufficient to meet the needs of business. Should the government assume a collective responsibility for child care, or should individuals bear the burden of child care alone? A third alternative would be to make businesses bear the cost of child care for their employees, but since this would reduce profits, few businesses are willing to accept these costs. The cost of child care is not part of the national political debate because the two alternatives, business absorption of cost and taxpayer commitment to working families, do not enjoy broad support. The fact that child care costs are social costs of families' participation in the labor market is rarely if ever mentioned in policy discussions or political discourse.

Conservatives who want to control government spending on social programs have their own excessive spending to explain. According to the Congressional Budget Office, spending increased under George W. Bush at twice the rate of his

Democratic predecessor, Bill Clinton. Domestic discretionary spending, entitlement spending, and military spending all increased under Bush.[114] Bush expanded federal non-entitlement programs in his first term almost twice as fast each year as Lyndon Johnson did during his entire presidency.[115] Combining military and nonmilitary spending, under Bush federal spending increased at the fastest rate in the last 30 years. Conservatives may be ideologically opposed to federal spending for social welfare policies, but they are not necessarily opposed to federal spending for other policies they support.

While in developing countries, few if any social costs are addressed in public policy (see Chapter 11); in developed countries like the United States there are laws to control certain externalities such as air and water pollution, hazardous wastes, unsafe food and drugs, and other dangerous substances like radioactive materials.[116] Economists agree that government intervention should address some public costs of market transaction, either through regulation or taxation on negative externalities.[117] Below we will discuss the social policies designed to protect human beings from some of the social costs of the market economy.

● SOCIAL POLICIES DESIGNED TO AMELIORATE SOCIAL COSTS OF THE MARKET ECONOMY

Many social policies already in place are designed to deal with some of the social costs or externalities that accompany the operation of the market economy. In this section we will briefly review the ones that exist in the United States. Several of them will be explored fully in subsequent chapters.

Under market capitalism, business cycles of inflation, recession, and depression occur inevitably in the absence of government intervention. Inflation can occur when high employment and increased investment lead to high consumer demand that outstrips limited supply, driving up prices. This results in increases in employment levels, as businesses attempt to meet the increase in demand by producing more goods and hiring more workers. The demand for more workers drives up wages, which in turn drives up prices further due to an increase in consumer demand.[118] When prices rise, the value of the dollar is less since it takes more money to buy the same goods. The opposite of inflation is recession and depression. Recessions typically last less than a year and are characterized by a decline in economic growth, income, and employment; depressions are prolonged periods of high unemployment, low output and investment, falling prices, and business failures.[119] Depressions, in other words, are severe recessions in which demand shrinks dramatically; as a result, businesses stockpile goods and lay off workers to cut costs. This increase in unemployment reduces demand further and can lead to dramatic increases in poverty, as in the Great Depression of 1929, when market capitalism seemed to be collapsing.[120] These business cycles can continue unabated and are accompanied by much human suffering, especially for those who have lost their jobs. The Great Depression was characterized by as much as a 25% unemployment rate in large urban areas. What measures are taken to regulate the business cycle?

The Federal Reserve Board is the major federal regulatory body attempting to influence the cycles of inflation, recession, and depression. Established in 1913, the board sets the interest rates at which banks can borrow money and therefore indirectly determines the interest rates charged by banks to consumers. In a situation of inflation with high demand and high prices, the board slows down the economy by raising interest rates, thus discouraging borrowing and ultimately reducing demand. Lowering demand will ultimately lead to more unemployment, as businesses cut payrolls in the face of lower prices. These measures are not worker friendly but promote the interest of lenders (inflation reduces the value of money paid back in the future) and businesses.[121] In recessions or near recessions when demand is low, the board may reduce interest rates to encourage borrowing and, ultimately, demand. Increased demand should eventually lead to hiring by businesses and decreased unemployment.[122] As employment and demand increase, the inflationary side of the business cycle may begin again. The Federal Reserve can also affect the business cycle by selling government bonds and by changing the reserve requirements for banks, both of which tighten the money supply and reduce demand.[123] Of course, none of these measures are foolproof, and all are subject to extramarket influences, such as war, which have an independent effect on the business cycle. Banks and businesses generally prefer high unemployment to inflation because (a) more people are affected by inflation than unemployment (illustrating the importance of the utilitarian calculus), and (b) inflation favors borrowers rather than lenders, since the value of the money borrowed decreases over time.[124]

Under the Social Security Act of 1935 (see Chapter 7), Unemployment Insurance Benefits (UIB) are provided by a federal-state partnership. Employers who participate (largely in the primary labor market) contribute to a trust fund through a federal payroll tax administered by the federal government. States provide coverage for 26 weeks; benefits can be extended for an additional 13 weeks if unemployment rates in states rise. Not every worker is eligible for unemployment; part-time workers or persons looking for part-time work are ineligible for benefits in some states, as are temporary workers, low-wage workers who may fail to meet minimum earning requirements. Another problem with UIB is the low level of benefits. Benefits have been declining, after adjusting for inflation, over the past 20 years. UIB excludes approximately one half of jobless workers from benefits, especially those who are considered "discouraged" workers (see above). UIB was designed to aid workers temporarily unemployed, not those whose loss is permanent, as in downsizing or plant closing due to the rise of overseas manufacturing. Women are less likely to be eligible for UIB than men, partly because their lower wages and periodic employment make it harder for them to qualify.[125] Another problem is the relatively low rate of benefits; unemployment insurance in the United States replaces 54% of an average worker's pay, while unemployment insurance programs in Western Europe replace an average of 79%. Over the past 10 years, less than 40% of the unemployed in the United States received benefits.[126]

Policies already in place to provide income transfers to groups disadvantaged by the economic system include Social Security Insurance for older persons, TANF for poor women and children, SSI for older persons and disabled persons of limited means, and the EITC for low-income households. Policies that deliver in-kind benefits, which persons with low income may not be able to purchase in the market economy, include food stamps, Medicare, and Section 8 housing vouchers.

Some economists argue that policies promoting economic equality, like the above policies, undermine efficiency. The argument is that the market economy operates to produce an abundance of goods; if measures were taken (such as income transfers through the tax system or measures to ensure hiring and wage equity) to promote equality, then the incentive to invest in private enterprise would be diminished because profits would be limited by increased taxation and measures to guarantee worker income and fairness. However, more income equality would mean more purchasing power among less affluent groups, who spend a greater percentage of their income on consumption than do more affluent consumers. The increase in consumer demand for goods and services that would result from greater equality would be likely to stimulate investment in the economy.[127]

Social policies designed to promote equity in employment practices include the Fair Employment Practices Commission founded in 1935, which prohibits discrimination in hiring on the basis of race; the Age Discrimination in Employment Act of 1967, which prohibits discrimination in employment on the basis of age; and Title IX of the Education Amendments of 1972, which prohibits educational institutions from discriminating on the basis of gender. These policies do little to affect the problem of workers in the secondary labor market who are consigned to low-income jobs with little upward mobility.

Social policies that are regulatory protect workers' rights in the market economy. These include the minimum wage, first enacted during the Great Depression, which mandates how much employers must pay to workers in certain sectors of the economy. While important in principle, the minimum wage has not kept pace with inflation. Since 1997, the cost of living has risen 26%, while the minimum wage has fallen in real value due to inflation. The minimum wage will be gradually raised to $7.25 an hour effective July 24, 2009, after being set at $5.15 an hour from 1997 to 2007. States can set their own minimum wage laws; most, but not all, have minimum wage levels higher than the federal government. Minimum wage is not enough to keep a household with children above the poverty line. It is estimated that 13 million workers will benefit from a raise in the minimum wage. Adults (not teenagers as some economists contend) make up the largest share of workers who would benefit from a minimum wage increase: 79% of workers whose wages would be raised are adults. Single mothers will also benefit from the raise in the minimum wage: 59% of workers who would benefit are women. As might be expected, a disproportionate amount of benefits will help households at the bottom of the income scale. While households in the bottom 20% received only 5% of national income in 2006, 38% of the benefits of a minimum wage would go to them. The raise in the minimum wage is critical in the effort to reduce inequality and poverty.[128]

Another important social policy designed to protect workers is the Occupational Safety and Health (OSH) Act, which seeks to protect workers from serious recognized hazards and other dangers in the workplace. The Occupational Safety and Health Administration (OSHA) was created by Congress in 1971 to enforce the OSH Act. The agency has regulatory power over businesses and corporations through inspections, consultations, and technical assistance. OSHA claims to have cut workplace fatalities by more than 60% and occupational injury and illness rates by 40%. It is responsible for more than 135 million employees at 8.9 million work sites. States oversee Workers' Compensation programs, which mandate that employers cover the cost of death benefits, disability benefits, medical assistance, and survivor benefits to families affected by job injury or death.[129]

Other government measures that will be discussed in later chapters include child labor laws, meat inspection laws, and laws guaranteeing unions the right to organize. These policies were put in place during the Progressive Era and the New Deal in the early 20th century. Social workers were instrumental in the passage of many of these policy "reforms," which limited the power of owners of businesses and corporations and ended the laissez-faire political climate that had allowed private enterprise to operate in an unregulated market economy. While these reforms protected workers, they also conserved market capitalism by protecting it from potential unrest and rebellion from those suffering from its worst excesses. Historians argue as to whether the New Deal was a radical change in the operations of the economy or a fundamentally conservative adjustment designed to preserve market capitalism, with most supporting the latter position.[130] See Chapter 7 for further discussion of New Deal policies.

While many of the social policies discussed above are designed to protect the market economy from its own excesses, others are designed to "redeem the failures of the economy" to promote the common good.[131] In this chapter the argument has been made that unregulated market capitalism carries with it negative consequences for many people; these consequences include inequality, poverty and economic insecurity, and what one economist calls other "pain and difficulties."[132] The economic system as it functions in the United States is not based on Rawls's principle of "justice as fairness" but rather is based on the utilitarian calculus, where the interests of the majority dominate the needs of the minority. The successful functioning of market capitalism demands government intervention and stable social structures. Those who complain about the so-called welfare state fail to recognize that the existence of the social policies discussed above and explored in later chapters of this text are the main reasons that market capitalism has survived in the United States. However, much more needs to be done to redirect and regulate the market economy to ensure the well-being of oppressed groups and to reduce inequality and poverty. Developing bold policy initiatives involving a new social contract laying out the expectations and obligations among workers, employers, government, and society as a whole is the next step in the struggle to achieve an economic system that is guided by the "justice as fairness" principle.

CONCLUSION

The United States is only one of many industrialized countries in which the market economy is the means of producing and allocating resources. In all of these societies the socially constructed system of market capitalism creates a host of social problems, many of which are discussed in this chapter. Most of these other countries, however, have a greater variety of social policies in place designed to mitigate these consequences.[133] Some of these social policies, as well as other policies consonant with our historical values and ideologies, could significantly reduce the burden of inequality, poverty, and economic insecurity that accompanies market capitalism in this country, while preserving the essential productive capacity and flexibility that has led to economic growth over the last century. The remaining chapters of this text will suggest policies that would be effective in accomplishing these goals.

The United States is *exceptional* in its values and ideologies as well as in the paucity of social policies that protect workers and families who suffer as a result of market capitalism.[134] The most important reasons that the United States has so few social policies are the ideologies discussed in Chapter 3. The power of these ideologies limits Americans' recognition that economic structures are the major cause of poverty and many other social problems. The social meanings attached to hard work, self-reliance, and individualism are transformed once the realization emerges that commitment to these values has little relationship to one's economic situation. Many economically marginalized persons work very hard, and many affluent persons benefit from demographic fortune or social connections (social capital), which are the antithesis of individualism and self-reliance. The facts on the ground suggest that economic structures are more important than personal behavior or personal ideology in predicting one's economic fortune. This is a reality many Americans may find difficult to accept, but it is an understanding that social workers can offer to those who have not thought critically about the conflict between our ideologies and the economic realities.

Social workers can be at the forefront of the development of social policies that protect individuals and families from unregulated market capitalism. The economic system is embedded in a wider social structure; it should not be the dominant system determining one's life situation. Other values operate outside the market economy and should control its impact; these include human dignity, justice, equity, diversity, equality of opportunity, and the right to have one's essential human needs met.[135] These are values that the social work profession embraces and can seek to realize in social policy transformation.

DISCUSSION QUESTIONS

1. Why are some ethnic groups overrepresented among economically marginalized groups?

2. Why do most Americans not recognize the amount of poverty in the United States?

3. Why is there no discussion of the market economy's limitations in mainstream policy or political debate in the United States today?

4. Why is the tax rate in the United States lower than that in other industrialized countries?

5. What are some examples of how corporate and wealth interests influence social policy?

6. Why are subsidies for farmers supported but subsidies for women and children through welfare not supported?

7. Why does the United States have fewer social policies to mitigate the effects of market capitalism?

NOTES

1. John Rawls, *A Theory of Justice* (Cambridge, MA: Harvard University Press, 1971), 7.
2. Rawls, *A Theory of Justice*, 11.
3. Rawls, *A Theory of Justice*, 137.
4. Rawls, *A Theory of Justice*, 60.
5. Rawls, *A Theory of Justice*, 33.
6. John Stuart Mill, *Utilitarianism* (London: Longman's, Green & Co., 1897), especially Chapter 4.
7. Rawls, *A Theory of Justice*, 33.
8. William Roth, *The Assault on Social Policy* (New York: Columbia University Press, 2002), 15.
9. Paul Samuelson and William Nordhaus, *Economics* (New York: McGraw-Hill, 2005), 5.
10. Adam Smith, *An Inquiry Into the Nature and Causes of the Wealth of Nations*, Vols. 1 and 2 (London: Dent and Sons, 1904).
11. Smith, *An Inquiry Into the Nature and Causes of the Wealth of Nations*; Duncan Foley, *Adam's Fallacy* (Cambridge, MA: Harvard University Press, 2006), 2–44.
12. Foley, *Adam's Fallacy,* 38–39.
13. Foley, *Adam's Fallacy,* 3.
14. Ibid.
15. Foley, *Adam's Fallacy,* 226.
16. Samuelson and Nordhaus, *Economics,* 26.
17. Samuelson and Nordhaus, *Economics,* 25–31; Arline Prigoff, *Economics for Social Workers* (Stamford, CT: Brooks Cole, 2000), 16–25.
18. Arline Prigoff, *Economics for Social Workers*, 19.
19. Samuelson and Nordhaus, *Economics,* 17–176.
20. Prigoff, *Economics for Social Workers,* 21.
21. Alfred Chandler, *The Visible Hand: The Managerial Revolution in American Business* (Cambridge, MA: Harvard University Press, 1977).
22. Thomas Karier, *Beyond Competition: The Economics of Mergers and Monopoly Power* (Armonk, NY: M. E. Sharpe, 1993), 130–137.
23. Prigoff, *Economics for Social Workers,* 22–29.
24. Samuelson and Nordhaus, *Economics,* 166–173.
25. Samuelson and Nordhaus, *Economics,* 119.
26. Ibid.
27. Samuelson and Nordhaus, *Economics,* 173.
28. Ibid.

29. Prigoff, *Economics for Social Workers*, 23.

30. Prigoff, *Economics for Social Workers*, 38.

31. Roth, *The Assault on Social Policy*, 14–15.

32. Gary Nash and Julie Jeffrey, *The American People: Creating and Nation and a Society*, 7th ed. (New York: Pearson Longman, 2006), 612–619.

33. Samuelson and Nordhaus, *Economics*, 119.

34. Joel Blau with Mimi Abramovitz, *The Dynamics of Social Welfare Policy*, 2nd ed. (New York: Oxford University Press, 2007), 64.

35. Federal Register, Vol. 72, No. 21, Thursday, February 1, 2007, http://bulk .resource.org/gpo.gov/register/2007/2007_04824.pdf, accessed March 31, 2009.

36. Bureau of Labor Statistics, "May 2007 National Occupational Employment and Wage Estimates, United States," http://www.bls.gov/oes/2007/may/oes_nat.htm#b35-0000, accessed March 31, 2007.

37. Lester Salamon, "Why Human Capital? Why Now?" in David Hornbeck and Lester Salamon, eds., *Human Capital and America's Future* (Baltimore: Johns Hopkins University Press, 1991), 1–43.

38. Allan Ornstein, *Class Counts Education, Inequality and the Shrinking Middle Class* (Lanham, MD: Rowman and Littlefield, 2007), 174–176.

39. Samuelson and Nordhaus, *Economics*, 257–263.

40. Samuelson and Nordhaus, *Economics*, 258; Jan Hogendorn, *Modern Economics* (Englewood Cliffs, NJ: Prentice Hall, 1995), 326.

41. Jan Hogendorn, *Modern Economics*, 326–327; Samuelson and Nordhaus, *Economics*, 239, 257–263.

42. Bureau of Labor Statistics, "Labor Force Characteristics by Race and Ethnicity, 2007," http://www.bls.gov/cps/cpsrace2007.pdf, accessed August 20, 2007; "Earnings of Men and Women by Race and Ethnicity, 2007," http://www.bls.gov/opub/ted/2008/oct/wk4/art04.htm, accessed March 28, 2009; "Usual Weekly Earnings of Wage and Salary Workers News Release," January 2009, http://www.bls.gov/news .release/wkyeng.htm, accessed March 28, 2009.

43. George Borjas, "Wage Trends Among Disadvantaged Minorities," in Rebecca Blank, Sheldon Danziger, and Robert Schoeni, eds., *Working and Poor: How Economic and Policy Changes Are Affecting Low-Wage Workers* (New York: Russell Sage, 2006), 59–86.

44. Borjas, "Wage Trends Among Disadvantaged Minorities," 80–81.

45. Ruth Sidel, *Keeping Women and Children Last* (New York: Penguin, 1998).

46. U.S. Census Bureau, "Poverty: 2007 Highlights," http://www.census.gov/hhes/www/poverty/poverty07/pov07hi.html, accessed March 30, 2009.

47. U.S. Census Bureau, Table 7, "Income, Earnings, and Poverty Data From the 2007 American Community Survey," http://www.census.gov/prod/2008pubs/acs-09.pdf, accessed March 30, 2009.

48. Samuelson and Norhaus, *Economics*, 260.

49. Rebecca Blank and Heidi Shierholz, "Exploring Gender Differences in Employment and Wage Trends Among Less-Skilled Workers," in Rebecca Blank, Sheldon Danziger, and Robert Schoeni, eds., *Working and Poor: How Economic and Policy Changes Are Affecting Low-Wage Workers* (New York: Russell Sage, 2006), 23–59, 25–28.

50. Gilles Saint-Paul, *Dual Labor Markets: A Macroeconomic Perspective* (Cambridge, MA: MIT Press, 1996), 67.

51. Michael Piore, "The Dual Labor Market," in David Gordon, ed., *Problems in Political Economy* (Lexington, MA: DC Heath, 1977), 90–94.

52. Saint-Paul, *Dual Labor Markets,* 67.

53. Piore, "The Dual Labor Market," 93.

54. T. D. Boston, "Segmented Labor Markets: New Evidence From a Study of Four Race-Gender Groups," *Industrial and Labor Relations Review* 44 (1, 1990): 90–115.

55. Rudy Fichtenbaum, Kwabena Gyimah-Brempong, and Paulette Olson, "New Evidence: The Labor Market Segmentation Hypothesis," *Review of Social Economy* 52 (Spring 1994): 20–39.

56. David Gordon, *Theories of Poverty and Unemployment* (Lexington, MA: DC Heath, 1972), 45–53.

57. Deborah Figart, "Labor Market Policy: One Institutionalist's Agenda," *Journal of Economic Issues* 37 (June 2003): 315–323.

58. Figart, "Labor Market Policy," 315–323.

59. Saint-Paul, *Dual Labor Markets,* 3, 62.

60. Hogendorn, *Modern Economics*, 330.

61. Hogendorn, *Modern Economics*, 331; Samuelson and Nordhaus, *Economics,* 389–392, 395–397.

62. Hogendorn, *Modern Economics*, 330.

63. 2009 Federal Poverty Guidelines, http://www.atdn.org/access/poverty.html, accessed March 29, 2009.

64. U.S. Census Bureau, "Income, Earnings, and Poverty Data From the 2007 American Community Survey," http://www.census.gov/prod/2008pubs/acs-09.pdf, accessed March 30, 2009.

65. Blau with Abramovitz, *The Dynamics of Social Welfare Policy,* 73.

66. Ibid.

67. U.S. Census Bureau., "Income, Earnings, and Poverty Data From the 2007 American Community Survey," http://www.census.gov/prod/2008pubs/acs-09.pdf, accessed March 30, 2009.

68. Ibid.

69. Frederick Schneider, "Hiding in the Shadows: The Growth of the Underground Economy," The International Monetary Fund's *Economic Issues* 30 (March 2002), http://www.imf.org/external/pubs/ft/issues/issues30/index.htm, accessed September 9, 2007.

70. Michael Lewis and Karl Widerquist, *Economics for Social Workers* (New York: Columbia University Press, 2001), 114–116.

71. Lewis and Widerquist, *Economics for Social Workers,* 116.

72. Samuelson and Nordhaus, *Economics,* 390–391.

73. Samuelson and Nordhaus, *Economics,* 391–392.

74. Inequality.org, "By the Numbers," http://www.demos.org/inequality/numbers.cfm, accessed September 9, 2007.

75. Ibid.

76. Ibid.

77. Economic Policy Institute, "Wealth Inequality Is Vast and Growing," August 23, 2006, http://www.epi.org/economic_snapshots/entry/webfeatures_snapshots_20060823/, accessed September 27, 2007.

78. Aviva Aron-Dine, "New Study Finds 'Dramatic' Reduction Since 1960 in the Progressivity of the Federal Tax System," Center on Budget and Policy Priorities, http://www.cbpp.org/cms/index.cfm?fa=view&id=2657, accessed September 14, 2007.

79. Tax Policy Center, Urban Institute, and Brookings Institute, "End the Break on Capital Gains," July 30, 2007, http://www.taxpolicycenter.org/publications/url.cfm?ID=901101, accessed September 14, 2007.

80. Tax Policy Center, "The Bush Tax Cuts: If We Account for How the Cuts Are Paid for, Who Benefits From Them?" http://www.taxpolicycenter.org/briefing-book/background/bush-tax-cuts/account.cfm, accessed March 28, 2009.

81. Ibid.

82. Aron-Dine, "New Study Finds 'Dramatic' Reduction Since 1960 in the Progressivity of the Federal Tax System," http://www.cbpp.org/cms/index.cfm?fa=view&id=2657; Aviva Aron-Dine, "New Data Show Income Concentration Jumped Again in 2005," Center on Budget and Policy Priorities, March 29, 2007, revised October 24, 2007, http://www.cbpp.org/cms/index.cfm?fa=view&id=2656, accessed March 28, 2009.

83. Jason Furman, "Tax Reform and Poverty," Center on Budget and Policy Priorities, April 10, 2006, www.cbpp.org/4-10-06tax.pdf, accessed September 20, 2007.

84. Internal Revenue Service, "EITC Thresholds and Tax Law Updates," http://www.irs.gov/individuals/article/0,,id=150513,00.html, accessed September 20, 2007.

85. Furman, "Tax Reform and Poverty," www.cbpp.org/4-10-06tax.pdf, retrieved September 20, 2007.

86. Jason Furman and Sharon Parrot, "A $7.25 Minimum Wage Would Be a Useful Stop in Helping Working Families Escape Poverty," Center on Budget and Policy Priorities, January 5, 2007, http://www.cbpp.org/cms/index.cfm?fa=view&id=1027, accessed September 20, 2007.

87. Ifie Okwuje and Nicholas Johnson, "A Rising Number of State Earned Income Tax Credits Are Helping Working Families Escape Poverty," Center on Budget and Policy Priorities, October 20, 2006, http://www.cbpp.org/cms/?fa=view&id=733, accessed September 20, 2007.

88. Samuelson and Nordhaus, *Economics,* 703.

89. Hogendorn, *Modern Economics*, 553–554.

90. Samuelson and Nordhaus, *Economics,* 703.

91. William Gale and Peter Orszag, "Bush Administration Tax Policy: Starving the Beast?" *Tax Notes*, Tax Policy Center, Urban Institute and Brookings Institution, November 15, 2004, http://www.taxpolicycenter.org/publications/url.cfm?ID=1000705, accessed September 16, 2007.

92. Richard Kogan, Isaac Shapiro, and Aviva Aron-Dine, "Spurring Economic and Revenue Growth: New IRS Data Confirm Tax Cuts Lose Revenue," Center on Budget and Policy Priorities, October 6, 2005, http://www.cbpp.org/10-6-05bud3.pdf, accessed September 21, 2007.

93. Frances Fox Piven, *The War at Home* (New York: Free Press, 2004), 43–46.

94. Jonathan Barn and Edward McCaffey, "Starving the Beast: The Psychology of Budget Deficits," September 2004, http://law.bepress.com/usclwps/lewps/art22/, retrieved September 16, 2007.

95. The Urban Institute, "Bush Tax Cuts," January 16, 2008, http://www.urban.org/decisionpoints08/archive/01bushtaxcuts.cfm, accessed March 28, 2009.

96. Congressional Budget Office, "A Preliminary Analysis of the President's Budget and an Update of CBO's Budget and Economic Outlook," Table 1.3, March 2009, http://www.cbo.gov/ftpdocs/100xx/doc10014/03-20-PresidentBudget.pdf, accessed March 27, 2009.

97. Roth, *The Assault on Social Policy*, 34.

98. Tax Policy Center, Urban Institute, and Brookings Institute, "Corporate Income Tax as a Share of GDP, 1946–2004," http://www.taxpolicycenter.org/taxfacts/displayafact.cfm?Docid=263, accessed September 20, 2007.

99. Citizens for Tax Justice, "Bush Administration Gets It Half Right on Corporate Tax Reform," August 9, 2007, http://www.ctj.org/pdf/bushcorporatetax proposal.pdf, accessed September 21, 2007.

100. Citizens for Tax Justice, "United States Remains One of the Least Taxed Industrial Countries," April 2007, http://www.ctj.org/pdf/oecd07.pdf, accessed September 21, 2007.

101. Roth, *The Assault on Social Policy*, 34.

102. Government Accountability Office, "Tax Expenditures Represent a Substantial Federal Commitment and Need to Be Reexamined," September 2005, http://www.gao.gov/cgi-bin/getrpt?GAO-05-690, accessed September 21, 2007.

103. Joint Committee on Taxation, "Estimates of Federal Tax Expenditures for FY 2005–2009," January 13, 2005, http://www.house.gov/jct/s-1-05.pdf, accessed September 21, 2007.

104. Mimi Abramovitz, "Everyone Is Still on Welfare: The Role of Redistribution in Social Welfare Policy," *Social Work* 46 (October 2001): 297–308.

105. Roger Lowenstein, "Who Needs the Mortgage-Interest Deduction?" *New York Times*, March 5, 2006, http://www.nytimes.com/2006/03/05/magazine/305deduction.1 .html?ex=1299214800en=e, accessed September 21, 2007.

106. Blau with Abramovitz, *The Dynamics of Social Welfare Policy*, 24.

107. Cato Institute, *Cato Handbook for Congress*, http://www.cato.org/pubs/handbook/handbook107.html, accessed September 21, 2007.

108. Environmental Working Group, "Farm Subsidy Database," http://www.ewg .org/farm/region.php?0000fibs, accessed September 27, 2006.

109. Dan Morgan, Gilbert Gaul, and Sarah Cohen, "Farm Program Pays 1.3 Billion to People Who Don't Farm," *Washington Post*, July 2, 2006, http://www.washington post.com/wpdyn/content/article/2006/07/01/AR2006070100962.html, accessed September 27, 2007.

110. Samuelson and Nordhaus, *Economics,* 37.

111. Nash and Jeffrey, *The American People*, 866.

112. Blau with Abramovitz, *The Dynamics of Social Welfare Policy*, 35.

113. Samuelson and Nordhaus, *Economics,* 30.

114. Daniel Mitchell, "Bring Back Clinton," Cato Institute, March 20, 2007, http://www.cato.org/pub_display.php?pub_id=8137, accessed September 22, 2007.

115. Ibid.

116. Samuelson and Nordhaus, *Economics,* 36–37.

117. Roth, *The Assault on Social Policy*, 53; Hogendorn, *Modern Economics*, 255–256; Samuelson and Nordhaus, *Economics,* 35–38.

118. Lewis and Widerquist, *Economics for Social Workers,* 117–118; Samuelson and Nordhaus, *Economics,* 676.

119. Samuelson and Nordhaus, *Economics,* 736, 749.

120. David Potter, "American Individualism in the Twentieth Century," in Don Fehrenbacher, ed., *History and American Society: Essays of David M. Potter* (New York: Oxford University Press, 1973), 267.

121. Blau with Abramovitz, *The Dynamics of Social Welfare Policy,* 79.

122. Lewis and Widerquist, *Economics for Social Workers,* 118.

123. Blau with Abramovitz, *The Dynamics of Social Welfare Policy,* 78–79.

124. Samuelson and Nordhaus, *Economics,* 672–673.

125. Karger and Stoesz, *American Social Welfare Policy,* 256–258.

126. Richard Freeman, *America Works: The Exceptional U.S. Labor Market* (New York: Russell Sage, 2007), 15.

127. Samuel Bowles, David Gordon, and Thomas Weisskopf, *After the Wasteland* (Armonk, NY: M. E. Sharpe, 1990), 220–221.

128. Economic Policy Institute, "Minimum Wage," http://www.epi.org/publications/entry/issue_guide_on_minimum_wage/, accessed September 22, 2007.

129. U.S. Department of Labor, "OSHA's Role," http://www.osha.gov/oshinfo/mission.html, accessed September 23, 2007

130. Paul Conkin, *The New Deal* (Arlington Heights, IL: Harlan Davidson, 1992); Richard Kirkendall, The *New Deal: The Historical Debate* (New York: Wiley, 1973).

131. Roth, *The Assault on Social Policy,* 10.

132. Richard Swedberg, "The Economic Sociology of Capitalism: An Introduction and Agenda," in Victor Nee and Richard Swedberg, eds., *The Economic Sociology of Capitalism* (Princeton, NJ: Princeton University Press, 2005), 2–28, 15.

133. Neil Fligstein, "States, Markets and Economic Growth," in Victor Nee and Richard Swedberg., eds., *The Economic Sociology of Capitalism* (Princeton, NJ: Princeton University Press, 2005), 120–143.

134. Freeman, *America Works,* 7–17.

135. Freeman, *America Works,* 16–18.

5

Discrimination and Social Justice in the United States

CHAPTER QUESTIONS

1. What are the most grievous examples of social policies based on discrimination in U.S. history?

2. What factors contribute to ongoing discrimination in the United States?

3. What is the meaning of the term *race*? Does racism exist, and if so, in what forms?

4. What is meant by the term *ethnicity*? How are the members of one ethnic group alike, and how are they different?

5. What is the difference between personal racism and institutional racism?

6. What is White privilege, and what does it mean to be White in the United States?

7. How have federal policies manifested racism toward Native Americans, African Americans, Latinos, and Asian Americans?

8. How do economic inequality and discrimination interact to produce poverty and restricted opportunities for members of some ethnic groups?

9. Why does discrimination against women persist in spite of political and social advances promoting equality?

10. How are women disadvantaged economically?

11. Why are LGBT persons denied rights that other Americans take for granted?

12. How have social movements created by oppressed ethnic groups and women inspired social policy change in the United States?

● ● ●

Discrimination has taken many forms in American history. This chapter will focus on historical and current discrimination against ethnic groups and women in the United States. While many groups have been actively discriminated against in the past, currently African Americans, Latinos, American Indians, and Asian Americans are the ethnic groups that experience the brunt of discriminatory attitudes and practices, both informal and institutional. Before we explore the origins of discrimination against these groups, we will explore the nature and causes of discrimination in the United States.

It is important to distinguish between prejudice and discrimination. Prejudice can be thought of as negative attitudes based on false beliefs about ethnic or gender differences (e.g., women are not as intellectually capable as men). These false beliefs can become the basis for discriminatory actions, such as excluding women from certain professions or refusing to hire Latinos. When these discriminatory practices deprive individuals of access to public goods, such as education, they can be contested through legal means; hence we have laws against discrimination in education and in the workplace. However, the complex system of unfounded beliefs about certain ethnic groups, combined with the inequalities based in market capitalism discussed in Chapter 4, has led to a far more insidious and subtle pattern of discrimination that cannot be rooted out by legal means alone. Passing laws against discrimination in hiring is one example. It is not easy to prove that a person was not hired based on his or her ethnicity; thus, violations are difficult to prove and prosecute. When the field of applicants is limited by the lack of access to education on the part of some groups, how can legal measures compensate for this inequality of opportunity? The answer is they cannot. Ethnic and gender discrimination are far reaching; they begin with the accident of birth that locates each person in a certain gender and ethnic group. The life opportunities of every individual are greatly influenced by his or her initial ethnic and gender status. Thus discrimination includes economic and social variables, not just legal ones. It is these economic and social barriers enmeshed in the texture of society that are extremely difficult to root out and are not easily ameliorated by legal remedies. Clearly other more substantial measures are needed to unravel the constriction of life opportunities that flow from discrimination and economic inequality. Affirmative action measures are efforts to ameliorate the limited life opportunities facing some persons, but currently they have fallen out of favor with many Americans who see them as reverse discrimination.

Discrimination exists within the complex web of institutions, culture, economic structures, and habit that make up social life in the United States. To describe only one example of the complex nature of discrimination, consider the case of public education. While there have been no laws mandating separate schools or unequal conditions in public schools since the 1954 Supreme Court decision,

Brown v. Board of Education, local funding through property taxes inevitably leads to unequal resources in public education: Wealthy areas will support schools richer in resources than those in economically marginalized areas. Thus students from affluent families will receive on average a better education than students from poorer areas. These funding structures perpetuate inequality, and since ethnic minorities are overrepresented in poorer areas, discrimination in public education exists whether or not any school officials are prejudiced. Laws regulating individual behavior cannot end this pattern of discrimination. Similarly, the fact that certain ethnic groups are overrepresented in the secondary labor market is the result of a complex pattern of historical discrimination and residential and educational segregation, along with a host of factors that lead to restricted opportunities for some groups. The reasons for the disproportionate number of African Americans, Latinos, and women in the secondary labor market will be explored later in this chapter.

Many White persons believe that racial animus must exist for discrimination to be experienced by ethnic minorities. The above examples demonstrate that the texture of discrimination is historically rooted and does not depend on individual racism. Individual racism becomes institutionalized racism, which needs no individual intentionality to continue racist practices. In other words, it takes on a life of its own.

RACE AND RACISM ●

What is the meaning of the idea of race? The concept of race emerged in the United States in the latter half of the 19th century as a way of asserting biological differences between White ethnic groups. These socially constructed biological differences were used to explain differences in social and economic conditions among these groups. During this period immigrants from Southern and Eastern Europe experienced deep poverty and poor living conditions compared with native-born White groups, many of whom lived prosperous lives and enjoyed political, economic, and social power. The idea of race was a social construction that asserted that biological differences underlay this inequality. Specifically, the proponents of the race theory believed that some ethnic groups had evolved further than others and were biologically capable of greater achievements. The concept of race thus can be seen as an ideological tool developed to promote the interests of groups in power at the end of the 19th century. Contemporary social scientists agree that there is no scientific validity to the concept of race, because there is no biological or genetic substrata corresponding to our idea of race. Scientists note that ethnic groups differ genetically among themselves more than they differ from other ethnic groups. As the American Anthropological Association noted: "There is greater variation within 'racial' groups than between them."[1] In other words, where race is concerned, there is no independent biological existence, only social constructions created to maintain power and privilege in dominant groups. The Human Genome Project has established conclusively that all humans share the same basic genetic components, ordered in exactly the same way.[2]

Where did the concept of race get its power? To answer that we must look back to the discussion of Social Darwinism in Chapter 3. Social Darwinism, closely aligned with the concept of race, was used in the late 19th and early 20th centuries to justify the power and privilege of the dominant Anglo Saxon group at the expense of the newer immigrants. Looking at the history of the concept of race in this country illuminates its socially constructed nature. In the late 19th century when the concept of race emerged, the Irish, English, Italians, Austrians, and Greeks and all immigrants from countries other than the United States were thought to be separate races.[3] By the end of the 20th century, these White ethnic groups were assimilated into one ethnic group and were considered one "Caucasian race."[4]

Currently the idea of biological differences is applied to groups who continue to be discriminated against by the White majority: African Americans, Latinos, Asian Americans, and American Indians. These groups are not biologically distinct; they exist as categories only with respect to their treatment by others. Because of the power of the social constructions of race, many people treat persons from these groups as though they are biologically distinct. This erroneous belief typically leads to discrimination against group members and a resulting experience of oppression. The idea of racial difference therefore has a self-realizing power; being treated negatively leads to the formation of group identity, which in turn reinforces the notion of group difference within and outside the group. Paradoxically, then, while race itself does not exist, the fact of racism— or prejudiced attitudes and behavior toward persons perceived to be of another race—is real, powerful, and destructive. As Miller and Garran noted: "Racism is much more than the sum of individual prejudices and attitudes; it is systemic, institutional, and sustained by a collective discourse of privilege and denigration."[5] Race, like all social constructions, is fluid, contingent, and contested.[6] It is a political and moral concept, not a biological one.

● THE RACIAL CONTRACT

According to critical race theory, race is "sociopolitical, rather than biological."[7] It is a real category through which hierarchies and domination are created and sustained. Mills argued that a "racial contract" has existed between Whites and persons who were colonized by European powers since the 18th century. Under this "contract," humans are divided into two groups: Whites and non-Whites; the latter are given "inferior moral status" and "subordinate civil standing" and are subjected to various forms of discrimination, including employment and housing discrimination.[8] In the case of African Americans this subordinate status was originally maintained through slavery; currently other measures are necessary to enforce this "contract." The need to ensure the subordination of non-White persons calls on the "coercive arms of the state," including the police and the penal system, according to this theory. The racial contract is one way to explain the ongoing police brutality to African Americans as well as the uneven application of the death penalty to Whites and African Americans.[9] Whites may maintain their innocence with respect to charges of racism because the racial contract offers a "racialized moral psychology," which prevents them from seeing the racist effects of their actions, according to Mills. White privilege prevents White realization of the impact of discrimination on the oppressed group. Some Whites may consciously refuse to take part in this contract and actively fight against it. Even they will have limited identification with oppressed groups, however, because they remain privileged by the color of their skin.[10]

Another way of understanding why Whites may not see their role in racial domination is standpoint theory, first introduced by feminists in the 1980s.[11] Standpoint theory is derived from the argument elaborated by the German philosopher Karl Mannheim in the early 20th century: One's perception and knowledge of reality are influenced by one's place in the social structure.[12] Our standpoint influences how we socially construct the world. Since inequalities of different social groups create differences in perceptions, a subordinated group will experience and understand the world differently than will an oppressed group; in other words, those who are oppressed perceive and understand racism more clearly than those who are not oppressed. Non-Whites see discrimination in their lives every day; Whites need to have it pointed out. Similarly to oppressed ethnic groups, women experience and construct the world differently than men. Based on their social location as a subordinated group, their knowledge will be different than the standard male-based conventional wisdom.

For these reasons, most White persons, even the most liberal and well-meaning, have only a vague idea of what persons from oppressed groups experience in their daily lives and cannot fathom the impact of racism on the self and on social relationships. Not to understand is part of White privilege, which means that it is a privilege not to experience racism. Looking at White privilege in all its manifestations is an important task for the deconstruction of racism in American culture. White ignorance of privilege and of the impact of racism on persons from oppressed groups means that dialogues between Whites and members of oppressed groups are essential if racism is to be first deconstructed and then eliminated from American life.

● AVERSIVE RACISM

Many social workers will dispute or vehemently reject the idea that they are racist. Most people who decide to become professional social workers do not actively seek to discriminate against ethnic groups or women. Nonetheless, most, if not all, members of certain ethnic groups living in the United States today have direct and sustained experiences of racism. Some liberal, educated persons who do not consider themselves racist might benefit from considering the concept of aversive racism. Social scientists define aversive racism as a subtle form of bias existing below conscious deliberation, which allows an individual to discriminate as long as the situation allows him or her to "maintain a positive view of the self."[13] One form of aversive racism found by researchers is the tendency to give members of one's own group, who are marginally qualified, the benefit of the doubt in hiring or admission decisions, while judging marginal members of other groups more harshly. This bias often manifests itself as preferences for one's own group and avoidance of other groups, often to their detriment. The decision not to hire African Americans can be an example of aversive racism, although those making the decision will deny that racism operated in their preference for White employees. Aversive racism is difficult to combat, since those practicing it are unlikely to acknowledge personal prejudice. Instead of feelings they identify as racist, they may feel discomfort or anxiety around persons from certain ethnic groups, feelings that may be evident to persons of color.[14]

An interesting question to consider is what will happen when Whites are no longer the clear majority of the population of the United States. By 2050, ethnic minority groups will account for nearly 50% of the population.[15] Will the racialization of the population continue, and will socially constructed racial categories have the same power they do now to control non-White access to power and resources?

● WHITENESS

What does it mean to be "White"? It is clearly more than the color of a person's skin, as color differentiation is only a vague marker for ethnic identification in the United States. Persons designated as African American, Latino, or White come in various hues, and there is a great deal of overlap among the ethnic groups, something apparent to anyone who has been to an urban center in the United States. Whiteness is not a color and certainly not a race, but it is a status or privilege. According to some, Whiteness denotes a positive status defined simply as "not Black." The degree to which other ethnic groups are viewed as White will determine whether they share in the privileges of Whiteness, while those who are viewed as more Black than White will face the restrictions and oppression that African Americans do. For some, "Whiteness" may be thought of as the defining quality of who is and who is not an American.[16] Whiteness has been a legal identity in America's past; during the Jim Crow period in the South, legal privileges were given to Whites, and legal restrictions were imposed on Blacks. It continues to be a social identity that opens many doors in education, in employment, and in housing, to name a few. Whiteness, in other words, has social and economic value that persons identified as White may be reluctant to share with others. Resentment over affirmative action or any policies that attempt to increase ethnic equality may be the result of this "possessive investment in Whiteness" on the part of the privileged group.[17]

Whiteness is a standpoint, not a biological characteristic. In this way, "Whiteness is not a color at all, but a set of power relations."[18] In the United States, Europeans and their descendants are seen as "White" and assume the dominant position in the racial contract, but there is nothing intrinsic about their being White that gives them this position; rather, their dominance is a function of a contingent set of historical circumstances. Whatever the personal attitudes of individual White persons with respect to their superiority to other groups, their Whiteness has been assigned the status of "normal" whereas other groups have been given the status of other, minority, or culturally different.[19] Thus Whiteness is a complex social, political, and economic identity that many Whites misread as a simple color descriptor. Persons from oppressed ethnic groups are unlikely to see Whiteness that simply.

The concept of White privilege is familiar to social workers. White privilege can be thought of as all the unearned benefits Whites receive from their membership in the dominant group. These benefits are not just economic and social benefits but adhere to virtually every aspect of public life; they affect the education systems, the criminal justice system, and the political system. Some White privilege is less tangible, such as the ability to represent only oneself and not an entire ethnic group in public interactions, the freedom to ignore one's ethnicity as a factor in one's interactions, and the presumption of acceptance in social settings, residential areas, and other public interactions, including shopping in retail outlets.[20] Privilege adhering to Whiteness in these situations is likely to be invisible to White persons, whereas it will be very visible to those who do not share in it. White privilege does not depend on racial animus, prejudice, or any other negative feelings on the part of White persons; it accompanies them wherever they go; they are as likely to be oblivious to it as to the air they breathe.

As a corollary, racism is so pervasive in the United States that it does not depend on individual intent for its effect to be felt. Discrimination against ethnic groups may be "passive and unobtrusive," but its effects are significant in shaping opportunities and life outcomes.[21] While there is legal recourse for egregious conscious acts of personal discrimination in employment and in educational systems, the subtlety of this broader *institutional racism* is more difficult to unravel because it depends on many complex factors, many of which appear "race neutral." Examples include the public education system (K–12) discussed above. Likewise, residential segregation is strongly encouraged by biased policies of lending institutions and real estate agents. In the cases of public education and housing, discrimination in the form of institutional racism operates from a complex system of historical custom and habit whose origin is difficult to unravel because these systems interact to produce and reproduce inequalities.[22] We will look at how discrimination contributes to the social construction of problems in the United States and informs the creation of specific social policies to solve these problems in the rest of this text. For a summary of federal and state policies impacting ethnic groups in the United States see Table 5.1.

●   **ESSENTIALISM**

The recognition of gender, ethnic, and sexual orientation diversity over the past 30 years has been an important paradigm shift in social work and in the broader culture. While understanding and embracing diversity was absolutely critical to the advancement of social justice and equality, the new paradigm is in danger of becoming as rigid a template as the earlier monolithic view, which substituted White as a hidden descriptor for most persons discussed in the social work literature. One problem with the way we think about ethnic diversity lies in the danger of essentialism, which is the implied belief that diverse groups, such as African Americans or Latinos, *have an underlying and unchanging essence.* This Platonic view of diversity assumes that there is a referent in the real world for the concept of African American or Latino (or woman or gay man), as though being assigned to this group offers a compelling and definitive explanation of a person. The term *Latino* is a demographic descriptor and is imperfect in its differentiation; that is, there are many kinds of Latinos in

TABLE 5.1 Summary of Federal and State Policies Impacting Ethnic Groups in the United States

Native Americans		African Americans		Latinos		Asian Americans	
Year and Policy	Description	Year and Policy	Description	Year and Policy	Description	Year and Policy	Description
1887 Dawes Act	Ended recognition of tribes as sovereign nations	1880s through 1950s "Jim Crow" laws 1896—*Plessy v. Ferguson*	Legal segregation	1846 Treaty of Guadalupe Hidalgo	Legal annexation of almost half of Mexico to United States	1852 California Foreign Miner's Tax	Drove Chinese out of mining and into agriculture
1924 Indian Citizenship Act	Native Americans made citizens	1954 *Brown v. Board of Education*	School segregation unconstitutional	1855 California Anti Vagrancy Act	Banned vagrancy among Mexicans causing them to be farm and day laborers rather than landowners	1882 Chinese Exclusion Act	Banned immigration of the Chinese to the United States
1934 Indian Reorganization Act	Authorized funding for tribal land and self-government of Indian reservations	1964 Civil Rights Act	Outlawed racial discrimination in all public accommodations	1994 Wet Foot, Dry Foot Policy	Allows Cuban immigrants who reach American soil the opportunity to stay; those found in the water are returned to Cuba	1908 Gentlemen's Agreement between Roosevelt and prime minister of Japan	Limited immigration of Japanese laborers
		1965 Voting Rights Act	Authorized federal examiners to register African American voters who had been denied registration in the South			1941 Executive Order 9066	Ordered the removal of all Issei and Nisei on the West Coast to detention camps run by the federal government

terms of ethnicity—persons whose ethnic origin is Mexico, Puerto Rico, Cuba, Honduras, and so forth. All may be called Latino in the United States, but persons in these groups may see themselves as very different from each other and do not think of themselves as Latino when they are living in their country of origin. It is when they migrate to the United States that they are designated as Latino, in the same way that persons from Korea, Japan, or China are given the name Asian American when they come here. The designation African American does not hold up to logical scrutiny either; other groups are not called by the name of their country of origin anymore (Italian Americans), and most African Americans come from families that have been in this country for generations and are not from Africa. Thus all the designations are merely convenient ways of labeling people who seem different from the dominant White groups. The reason for this distinction is not biological but in reality is based on the need of the dominant group to distinguish the "other" in its midst. Common ground within these groups arises from their experience of oppression, not because of an underlying quality Latinos or African Americans necessarily have in common. The notion that there exists an essential quality of being Latino, African American, or Asian American shared by all persons in each group is false. Ethnicity is a social construction created by dominant groups for many reasons, one of which is to reduce the threat of diversity.

Generalizing about diverse ethnic groups can elevate cultural patterns to reified truths. Such generalizations ignore the multiplicities of experiences that characterize persons within ethnic groups. These reifications may be strengthened by social science research when research results are generalized to all members of an ethnic group. While categorical thinking may be necessary in the pursuit of knowledge, postmodernism rejects essentialist categories as falsely universal and therefore problematic. Instead we need to substitute a more fluid and plural understanding of diversity.[23] Some Latinos may have certain characteristics in common, but Latinos cannot be summed up according to overarching generalizations. The same is true for African Americans. All groups and all persons are "hybrids of multiple social practices, cultural traditions and ethnic customs."[24] Individual identities are multiple, based on our gender, ethnicity, age, and family roles. No one can be defined solely or even primarily by his or her ethnicity.

Social workers need to recognize the multiplicities of experiences within ethnic groups and be careful of metanarratives that seek to explain any group by a series of attributes, values, or beliefs. All these categorical efforts belie the heterogeneity, fragmentation, and nonreplicability of the lived experience. Even benign generalizations distort individual reality and give us a false sense of ease that comes with untested assumptions about others. Categorizing "the others" according to a fixed set of themes is one way to marginalize them and contain the threat they pose as the unknown. Thus Whites will seek generalizations about ethnic groups in order to reduce the anxiety of working with someone perceived to be different. These constructed meanings serve to reduce the unpredictability associated with ethnic or gender or sexual orientation difference. Sometimes these social constructions are embraced and turned on their head by members of ethnic groups who seek to recast stereotypes as cultural strengths, in this way owning the essentialist dialogue about themselves and turning a perceived deficit into a strength.[25]

In sum, narratives about ethnic groups are often linear and reductive. While it may be important to learn about a group's historical experiences, presenting them as culturally monolithic is counterproductive because it increases stereotypes, which is the real danger of essentialism. One theme members of certain ethnic groups in the United States have in common is their experience of oppression, both historical and contemporary. Rather than offering metanarratives or overarching descriptions that attempt to totalize and universalize the experiences of Latinos, African Americans, American Indians, and Asian Americans, we will now turn to historical flashpoints that illustrate each group's experiences of oppression.

NATIVE AMERICANS ●

What should the original inhabitants of North America be called? Naming a group, as we have seen, is a political act freighted with connotations of power and domination. The name *Indian* was given to the inhabitants of the Americas by Christopher Columbus, who thought he was going to India. Later Amerigo Vespucci, another Italian navigator, gave the name *America* to the continents in the Western Hemisphere. Thus *American Indian* was the name given to the original tribes inhabiting this continent. Beginning in the 1970s, *Native American* emerged as the preferred name among academics and activists to emphasize tribal members' original, nonimmigrant status. Neither name was what tribal members called themselves; both names were given by Whites to designate people from various tribes, such as Cherokee, Chickasaw, Choctaw, Mohawk, Navajo, Seminole, Hopi, and Wampanoag. *American Indian* is the term used in the 2000 U.S. census, but most social work publications use the term *Native American,* ostensibly because it is less offensive than *American Indian.* Clearly, there is no good resolution to the question of what to call the first peoples of what is now the United States.

Native American mother and child

SOURCE: From the Library of Congress, copyright 1901 by Howard D. Beach.

When examining the history of the contact between Europeans and Native Americans, the power of the racial contract is evident. At every point of contact between Whites and Native Americans, conquest has been the driving theme. To compound the offense, the narrative about this interaction was told from the point of view of Whites: Brave White men fought marauding Indians. Only since the 1970s has the outline of a more accurate narrative been made clear, recounting the White massacres of Native American men, women, and children from the 17th to the end of the 19th century. This revision of the history of the relationship of Whites to Native Americans was made possible not by the discovery of new scholarship about Native Americans, since many of these facts were already known by historians of the Old West, but by the emergence of a movement for Indian rights in the late 1960s. The American Indian Movement (AIM) was founded in 1968 to resist police brutality toward Native Americans in the Midwest. The movement achieved national status when activists occupied the former federal penitentiary at Alcatraz Island in San Francisco in 1969, claiming the island belonged to Native Americans under a federal law that gave them first refusal on surplus federal lands. This action led to a floodtide of protests over the federal government's broken treaties since the founding of the United States, as well as a broader outrage among Native Americans over their racist treatment over the centuries of White expansion and genocide. The climax of the AIM actions was the occupation in 1973 by Native American activists of Wounded Knee, South Dakota, the scene of a massacre of 200 Sioux by federal troops in 1890. The occupation lasted for 71 days and drew worldwide attention to the Native American cause. Non-Indians were awakened to the historical injustices perpetrated on the native population, seeing the tragedy of Wounded Knee as a symbol of countless other atrocities the Native Americans suffered at government hands. The history of the oppression and violence Native Americans suffered at the hands of Whites was finally made known.

Since the 1970s, other aspects of Native American history have undergone substantial revision. The first revision involves the origins of the indigenous population in North America, which has been established at 10,000 BC or even earlier, according to archaeologists.[26] Early White settlers had assumed that the Native Americans they encountered had arrived in the "New World" just a few hundred years earlier than they had. The assumption of recent arrival would be used to justify the rapacious approach to Native Americans and their land. The fact that Native Americans had lived on this continent for thousands of years before White settlement demonstrates their status as the original settlers of North America, persons who created a culture and a way of life that had continued undisturbed until Whites came to their land. Similarly, early estimates of the number of people living in the area now known as the United States were very small, around 100,000. Newer scholarship conclusively demonstrates that at least 4 million people lived in the area north of Mexico before White settlement, 700,000 of whom lived on the eastern seaboard before the first English settlements were established.[27] The English colonists were moving not to the wilderness they described in letters to England but to a country already inhabited by people with an established culture and way of life.

Colonial Settlements and Native Americans

Native Americans were quickly branded as uncivilized by early English settlers; it has taken 400 years for White Americans to begin to understand the true complexity of Native American culture, since many of their beliefs ran directly counter to the individualistic values of the White settlers. The English believed that property was individually owned and that land was a private resource to be exploited for personal gain. Native Americans, on the other hand, believed that land possessed sacred value and should be held in common by tribes. Most tribes believed in sharing resources, not in accumulating individual resources at the expense of others. Most tribal societies were matrilineal, where family membership was determined through the female line; English society was patrilineal and patriarchal. Women had more power in the Native American tribes than women did in English settlements; Indian women often choose the village leaders.[28] Religious life was distinctly different in the two societies: English were Christians who used Bibles and church structures to inform their religious beliefs; Native Americans were pantheists who saw divinity in nature. Indians had a more mystical, diffuse sense of the supernatural than did Christians, who personified the deity into God the father and God the son.

In spite of these cultural differences, the main issue dividing English settlers and Native Americans was the settlers' desire to own the land the Native Americans occupied. War, death, broken treaties, and relocations are the themes driving the history of Native Americans after English settlement. In the first century after the establishment of the American republic, all 370 treaties with Native Americans were broken by Whites.[29] Desire for unfettered territorial expansion, along with ethnocentrism and racism about Native American culture and religion, was used to legitimize violence and brutality against tribes along the eastern seaboard in the 17th century. Missionary work to "Christianize" Native Americans led to about 1,000 Native Americans living in "praying villages" in New England, in an effort to show them how to live like the English.

The Spanish and English both brought deadly diseases, such as smallpox, measles, influenza, and diphtheria, to the Native Americans in the areas they conquered. A visit by English fishermen to New England in 1616 resulted in the death of 125,000 Native Americans due to smallpox and respiratory viruses; smallpox returned to the area in 1633, killing thousands more. English settlers interpreted this disaster as God's plan to free the land for their settlement.[30]

Cherokees and Creeks

Andrew Jackson gained renown as an "Indian fighter" before he was elected president of the United States in 1828. In 1814 he led the U.S. Army in an attack on the Creek nation near the Florida border at Horseshoe Bend in retribution for an earlier Creek attack in the area. It was the bloodiest attack of White men on Native Americans in the 19th century. Afterward Jackson stripped the remaining Creek of more than half the land under their control in Alabama and Georgia. President Jackson developed the policy of removal, where Native Americans in the Southeast were forcibly removed to undeveloped lands west of the Mississippi, the majority to Oklahoma. Members of the so-called Five Civilized Tribes—Cherokee, Choctaw, Chickasaw, Creek, and Seminole—who had developed agricultural settlements in fertile valleys in the Southeast, were removed to make way for White settlements. Making new treaties while breaking old ones, the federal government decided to effect the forced removal of the Cherokees, notwithstanding the ruling by the Supreme Court Chief Justice John Marshall in 1832 that Native American tribes retained their "original natural rights" and that treaties made with them by the federal government were binding. Marshall viewed tribes not as independent nations but as "domestic dependent nations"; he ruled that their rights were not absolute but coexisted with states' rights.[31] Federal officials ignored this decision and forced the Cherokees to leave their land in Georgia and march westward to Oklahoma in 1838. This forced march, known as the Trail of Tears, killed more than 8,000 Cherokees. Altogether more than 100,000 Native Americans were forced to leave their lands in the Southeast and marched west across the Mississippi as a result of the removal policy. In Oklahoma, the federal government promised the displaced Indians they could stay forever. In the 1880s, oil was discovered in Oklahoma, and the next generation was forced off their land again.

Plains Indians

During the 1840s, White Americans came into contact with the Plains tribes for the first time as they continued their westward migration. Approximately one quarter of a million Native Americans occupied the area from Colorado to Ohio. Many of them had never seen a White person, while some males had seen them only as occasional trading partners. The tribes were different from each other: Some, such as Pawnee, Omaha, and Oto, lived in agricultural settlements; others, like the Oglala Sioux, Cheyenne, Shoshone, and Arapaho, roamed the plains following the buffalo; while the Southwestern tribes, including the Comanche, Ute, and Hopi, had borrowed aspects of Spanish culture and had domesticated animals, including sheep and cattle. All the Plains tribes had horses, which were introduced by the Spanish in the 16th century, giving them access to buffalo, which became central to their survival. Problems developed when White settlers brought cattle to graze on the grasslands the buffalo needed for food and began to hunt the buffalo for sport. The gold rush to California after 1849 drew so many Whites across the plains that the buffalo were in danger of being wiped out, at the same time as thousands of Native Americans were wiped out by cholera brought by emigrating Whites. Tribes warred among themselves for the remaining limited hunting grounds. In 1851, the federal government called a tribal council at Fort Laramie, Wyoming, where officials announced to the tribal chiefs who attended that the days of unlimited movement in the plains were over; instead the federal government drew up tribal boundaries and developed the reservation system where tribes would be limited to one geographic area to be determined by the federal government. The Sioux, Apache, and Comanche refused to sign the treaty. Violence continued between the White settlers and tribes during what is known as the Great Plains Wars. In 1864, a massacre of 600 unarmed members of the Cheyenne tribe at Sand Creek, Colorado, by the state militia was followed by greater brutality on the part of Whites, who punished members of the Cheyenne tribe for responding to the massacre with force. In 1867 and again in 1868, the government met again with tribal leaders, urging them to relocate to western South Dakota or Oklahoma to reservations and adapt to White culture.[32]

The tribes who did settle on the reservations after 1868 found the wildlife there too sparse to support them and moved back to their hunting lands. In response the federal government ordered the U.S. Army to go to war against the Plains tribes. Fighting continued as the transcontinental railroad was built in 1869. Railroad officials wanted White settlement to surround the railroad lines to make their investment profitable; they also demanded the right of way through tribal land. The destruction of the buffalo herds (by 1883, 13 million animals had been killed by White miners and hunters) led to a weakening of the Plains tribes, whose livelihood was increasingly tied to compliance with White demands.

In 1887, Congress passed the Dawes Act, ending the recognition of tribes as sovereign nations. The purpose of the act was twofold: to free land for White use and to end the tribal system. Under it, reservation land would be distributed to individuals, not tribes. Holding land in common was thought to encourage tribes to be un-American. Common land was sold to White settlers, leaving the tribes with even less land than they had before. In 1880, before the Dawes Act, approximately 150 million acres were under tribal title. By the end of the century, two thirds of that land was in White hands.[33] The Dawes Act, also known as the Allotment Act, attempted to transform Native American families from extended forms to nuclear ones. Close family members were given plots of land distant from each other, and long-established kinship ties were destroyed. Previous treaties that had given the Plains tribes large amounts of land in permanent reservations were abrogated, as small parcels were distributed at the will of the federal Indian affairs agent.[34]

Not only the land but the culture of Native American tribes was the target of federal policy. The concept of "wardship" was an ideology adopted earlier in the 1830s by the federal government to justify the seizure of tribal lands and the creation of a system of total social control of Native Americans. Under this concept the federal government argued that Native Americans were wards of the federal government. The Bureau of Indian Affairs was established to hold Native American lands and resources in "trust."[35] The system of social control was overseen by General Richard Pratt, who wanted to ensure that Native Americans assimilated to White culture. Beginning in 1900, boarding schools for Native American children were established that were run with army-style discipline, where student life was regimented and all tribal identity and manifestations of tribal culture were forbidden. Children wore uniforms, had their hair cut, and were taught Christianity. Virtual prisoners, the Native Americans lived similar lives to the early California natives who were forced to build missions for the Spanish Franciscans in the late 18th and early 19th centuries. Later in the early 20th century, vocational training predominated as Native American children and adolescents were trained to work in industrial society at these "Indian schools."[36]

Native Americans were not made citizens of the United States until the Indian Citizenship Act of 1924. Congress passed the Indian Reorganization Act in 1934, abolishing the allotment program and authorizing funding for tribal land acquisition. Under this act the federal government encouraged self-government of Indian reservations. Currently there are 561 federally recognized tribal governments in the United States, all with the right to govern themselves, to tax, and to enact their own laws. Courts have ruled that tribes are equal to states in making their own laws and are subordinate only to the federal government.

Once called the vanishing Americans, Native Americans are now the fastest-growing ethnic group in the United States. This is at least partly due to the policy of the Census Bureau in 2000 allowing respondents to identify more than one ethnic background. This astonishing reversal of the decline of the Native American population is at least partly due to the power of the social movement of Native Americans to rewrite their history and demand long-suppressed rights from federal and state governments.

AFRICAN AMERICANS ●

While everyone in the United States no doubt knows that Africans were brought to the United States as enslaved persons, few understand the impact of that experience on African Americans, and fewer still know about the immediate

Housing for enslaved persons

SOURCE: From the Library of Congress, photo by T. H. O'Sullivan.

consequences of slavery in the postslavery South. The importance of slavery in U.S. history is indicated by the fact that most U.S. presidents before the Civil War were slaveholders, as were the majority of men signing the Declaration of Independence and the Constitution. Thomas Jefferson, author of the Declaration of Independence and slaveholder, worried about the future of a country that allowed slavery to flourish. "We have the wolf by the ears," he wrote, "and we can neither hold him nor safely let him go. Justice is in one scale, and self preservation in the other." Jefferson hoped that the United States would abolish slavery; he feared the consequences of slavery, especially the anger of those enslaved, would destroy the new country. He worried about "deep-rooted prejudices entertained by the whites and ten thousand recollections, by the blacks of the injuries they have sustained . . . ," which he thought would eventually end with the destruction of either the Blacks or the Whites.[37] Jefferson's prescience was not shared by most of his Southern colleagues, who saw slavery as the most economical means of growing rice, tobacco, and cotton, thereby ensuring their economic fortunes.[38] That slavery and its aftermath did not destroy African Americans and permanently poison all White/Black relationships was due, for the most part, to the resilience and courage of African Americans, in slavery and in freedom.

The Jim Crow South

The immediate aftermath of slavery in the South was intended to be almost as soul-crushing as what it replaced. Southern life was in chaos after the Civil War, thanks in part to the economic destruction brought on the region by the war but also because of the newly fluid relationship of Whites and Blacks. No longer enslaved persons, African Americans could and did move freely throughout the Southern states, searching for family members who had been sold during slavery and looking for work in the increasingly marginalized rural communities. Since the South had been a largely rural economy before the war, there were few jobs in manufacturing or in urban areas, unlike in the North. To compound the economic devastation of the Civil War, formerly enslaved persons were given no financial help by the federal government. Whites in the South reacted with alarm and a shocking violence to the presence of free Blacks in their midst. Lynching, beatings, and general intimidation of African Americans across the South became the White means of attempting to reassert control over Blacks. Obviously the end of slavery did not mean the end of racist attitudes among most White Southerners, for though these attitudes had developed as a way to justify enslaving human beings, they did not disappear with the end of the institution of slavery. Instead violence, fueled by the same racist ideology, replaced legal ownership of African Americans. The situation was so dangerous, for Whites and Blacks alike, that Southern state legislatures, in an effort to keep Blacks and Whites apart and so contain the violence, began to pass so-called Jim Crow laws in the 1880s and 1890s. These laws did several things: (a) ensure that no Black man could vote in spite of the Fifteenth Amendment to the Constitution giving all men the right to vote; (b) assure Whites that African Americans would be confined to separate spheres in all public places by segregating public restrooms, restaurants, drinking fountains, post offices, waiting rooms, parks, cemeteries, toilets, hospitals, hotels, and any place where people

Segregated public facilities

SOURCE: Associated Press.

could mingle in public; and (c) subordinate and control African Americans to replicate as closely as possible the system of slavery.[39]

Even the economic situation of African Americans mimicked slavery: Most African Americans in the South were sharecroppers who lived and grew crops on White-owned farmland. Their cash proceeds of their crops were "shared" with the owner of the land, who received one third, and the supplier of seed and fertilizer at the local store who typically received another third, thereby leaving the sharecropper with one third of the proceeds of his or her labor. A much smaller number of African Americans worked in the newly established factories in Southern coastal cities, particularly in coal mining and steel mills. But their main sustenance was in the rural economy, where they were kept in penury through the iron grip of sharecropping.[40] Violence and economic marginalization dominated the lives of African Americans in the South.

"Jim Crow" dominated Southern race relationships until the mid-20th century when legal segregation, upheld in 1896 by the Supreme Court decision *Plessy v. Ferguson,* began to unravel thanks to the 1954 Supreme Court decision, *Brown v. Board of Education.* Overturning *Plessy v. Ferguson,* the Supreme Court found that school segregation was unconstitutional. Legal segregation; the sharecropping system, which became the main source of support for African Americans in the South; lynching; and violent assaults on African American men and women—all occurred as the result of federal and state social policies; all were encouraged, if not mandated, by government-sponsored force.

The Move North

Against these overwhelming odds, African Americans in the late 19th and early 20th centuries struggled to support their families and to survive in a hostile White world. In the early 20th century, African Americans began migrating to the Northeast and Midwest, searching for work in the thriving factories and for the economic opportunity that accompanied steady employment as well as escape from the uncertainties of sharecropping and the violence still endemic in the Southern towns and cities. In the North they were met with discrimination and industrial workplaces that generally shut them out.

African American women in Northern states held a variety of jobs, from domestic work to laundry work. Racism generally kept them out of the higher-paying clerical jobs that opened up for Whites in the 1920s and 1930s. African American women shared their wages with family members who stayed in the South. Extended family systems provided financial and caretaking support of children.[41] During the Great Depression in the 1930s, African American women lost their jobs to White women who entered the labor force to help support their families.[42] Although kinship networks in urban areas were strained by the financial crisis families faced, it was through these same networks of kin and close friends or fictive kin that African Americans survived the Great Depression.[43]

African American men initially were shut out of industrial jobs in the North and forced to work in unskilled jobs. A few employers hired African Americans to subvert efforts of White workers to form unions, hoping to use racism to divide the workforce. As they predicted, violence against African Americans by White workers was common. Until the 1930s, when the United Mine Workers union began to recruit African American workers, no union allowed Black workers to be members.[44] African Americans formed their own union, the Brotherhood of Sleeping Car Porters, led by A. Philip Randolph, in 1937. With the advent of World War II, African Americans joined the armed forces, where they were forced into segregated units, overseen by White officers. The discrimination they experienced as civilians followed them into the service. A. Philip Randolph decried the discrimination against African Americans in the armed forces and threatened President Roosevelt with a massive march on Washington if he did not desegregate the troops. Roosevelt refused but signed an executive order banning discrimination in defense industries and government jobs and creating the Fair Employment Practices Commission to enforce the order. The armed forces were not desegregated until President Truman issued an executive order to that effect in 1948.

African American Resistance

African Americans did not endure their treatment at the hands of White society passively. During the 19th and early 20th centuries, leaders emerged to inspire resistance in African Americans and mobilize them to work for social justice. Frederick Douglass, the famous orator and former enslaved person, urged African Americans to seek justice through the political process but on his death bed in 1895 spoke his last words: "Agitate! Agitate! Agitate!" Ida B. Wells launched an antilynching campaign in the early 20th century and founded the Negro Fellowship League in Chicago to help Black migrants there. W. E. B. Du Bois urged Blacks to demand their rights and founded the Niagara Movement in 1905 to enlist African American leaders and White liberals to promote equality for African Americans. He predicted that the problem of the 20th century would be the "problem of the color line."[45] The Niagara Movement became the National Association for the Advancement of Colored People (NAACP) in 1910. Marcus Garvey and the organization he founded, the Universal Negro Improvement Association (UNIA), were an important part of the struggle for freedom and justice in the African American community. Garvey was the leader of the largest organized mass movement in Black history; he was a progenitor of Malcolm X, the influential leader of a militant Black movement of the 1960s. Garvey is remembered for his advocacy of a Back to Africa movement, which he firmly believed was the only way for Blacks to achieve social justice. Garvey urged African Americans to resist the pressure to submit to White domination, which he viewed as the covert goal of efforts to assimilate; instead he wanted African Americans to build separate institutions and reclaim their own culture.[46]

The civil rights movement was the climax of these early movements for African American freedom. Several factors converged in the late 1950s and early 1960s and led to the creation of a powerful social movement of African Americans in Southern states to throw off the shackles of "Jim Crow." Southern resistance to enforcement of school desegregation made federal law in *Brown v. Board of Education* led President Eisenhower to send federal troops to Little Rock, Arkansas, to escort African American children to public school. This scene was repeated several times in other school districts and nationally televised, galvanizing national sympathy for African American victims of Southern racism. The civil rights movement will be discussed later in this chapter as an example of a social movement by oppressed persons.

African American Identity

African Americans, like other oppressed ethnic groups, Asian Americans and Mexican Americans, have two names: one identifying their country of origin and one designating their country of residence. The designation *African American* was made popular by the Reverend Jesse Jackson in the late 1980s as a way of linking persons in this country to their African ancestry. It has largely replaced the term *Black* in popular culture and public documents. *Black* replaced the earlier term *Negro* in the 1960s and 1970s, as a more positive designation associated with the movement for Black pride and Black power. Malcolm X was an important leader of the Black Power movement; a charismatic leader and Nation of Islam minister, Malcolm X emphasized Black pride and Black separatism. Disillusionment with the leadership of the Nation of Islam in 1964 led him to broaden his message to include a critique of capitalism and an identification with other oppressed groups. Malcolm X was assassinated in 1965.[47]

Why have African Americans suffered so much from racism in the United States? Winthrop Jordan argued that this animus stems from the British fear of Africans during the colonization of Africa in the 16th century. Jordan argued that the British fear of Africans and their guilt over their brutal treatment of Blacks on the continent led them to construct negative stereotypes about Blacks. These racist beliefs about Africans that the British brought with them to North America became the basis for their willingness to buy enslaved persons and institute slavery there.[48] Jordan explained racism against African Americans in terms of ideology; another perhaps more powerful explanation is economic. In the first half of the 17th century, African Americans worked alongside White indentured servants in the tobacco and cotton fields of the South. By the end of the 17th century, Southern states had passed laws making slavery lifelong and hereditary for Blacks, largely because of the economic benefits to the planters of a self-perpetuating workforce of free labor. The predisposition of English to view Africans as fundamentally different from themselves may also have played a role in their eagerness to make Black, but not White, indentured servants into enslaved persons.[49]

Whatever the reason, African Americans have a unique history in the United States. No other group was brought to this country involuntarily and forced to live as enslaved persons; nor has another group been systematically segregated from Whites even while living in their midst. Like the British fear, guilt over colonization, the guilt and fear that developed as a result of the institution of slavery and the brutality of segregation in the South, may have fueled much of the ongoing racism against African Americans in the United States.

In spite of all the overt and more subtle forms of racism directed against them, African Americans continue to demonstrate the strength, resistance, and resilience they have throughout American history. In the 1990s, many African American professionals moved up the economic ladder, and the number of African American firms increased, as did the percentage of home ownership.[50] Yet by 2005, some of these gains were eroding. The overall unemployment rate for African Americans is consistently about twice that for White Americans; African American men have the lowest employment and labor force participation rates of all racial and ethnic groups.[51] The earnings of African American men were 25%–30% lower than those of White men with the same educational attainment, while earnings for Black and White women with similar educational attainment were more comparable. Persistent discrimination and geographic mismatch between jobs and workers are two of the factors responsible for the disparate wages of African American and White men.[52] This difference between the educational achievements and earnings of African American men and women may reflect the intensity of the problems of discrimination faced by African Americans of all ages in American society. Thus, while some African Americans have overcome great odds, many continue to suffer from unequal social and economic conditions that are legacies of oppression. Considerable research demonstrates that young, less educated African American men experienced a decline in employment and labor market participation rates in the 1980s and 1990s, as compared with young White and Latino men and women, whose economic conditions improved.[53] Economic predictors for the coming decade for unemployment rates of less skilled young adults, including African American men, are dismal, unless public policy focuses on investment in skills for these potential workers, raising the value of work through raises in the minimum wage and Earned Income Tax Credit, making access to transportation a greater priority to increase access to jobs in the suburbs, and easing the negative impact of incarceration for young men reentering the labor market.[54]

In Chapter 4 we saw how income and wealth inequality has impacted African Americans in the United States. Without specific social policies designed to positively impact the labor market prospects of young African Americans, this economic inequality is likely to magnify and lead to detrimental outcomes for African American children and their families in the coming decades.

The impact of welfare policies, housing policies, and child welfare policies on African American families will be discussed in succeeding chapters.

LATINOS ●

The word *Latino* is used to refer to a wide variety of people originally from areas colonized by the Spanish in the 18th and 19th centuries. It includes persons from Puerto Rico, Cuba, Mexico, Central America, and South America and their descendants. The majority of Latinos in the United States are of Mexican descent; over 18 million people identified their ethnic origins as "Mexican" in 2006. Out of a total Latino population of 43.2 million, 65.5% were of Mexican origin, approximately 14.2% were of Central American or South American origin, 8.6% identified as Puerto Rican, and 3.7% identified as Cuban Americans. The majority of Mexicans live in the West and South, the majority of Puerto Ricans live in the Northeast, and the majority of Cubans live in the South. More Latinos live in the West (26.6%) than in any other region of the country.[55] Latinos are a relatively young population, with 34% under the age of 18. In 2006, approximately 40% of the Latino population was born outside the United States.[56]

Mexican Americans

The history of Mexican Americans begins with a war waged by the United States against Mexico in the 1840s. Most Americans know that much of the Southwest was once part of Mexico and came to be part of the United States after an invasion of Mexico. It was the Treaty of Guadalupe Hidalgo, signed in 1846, that resulted in what are now California, New Mexico, and Arizona and parts of Colorado, Nevada, and Utah being ceded to the United States.[57] The war and the annexation of almost half of Mexico was driven by the belief in "Manifest Destiny," a belief held by many Americans, that the superiority of the Anglo Saxon "race" must prevail over all other peoples living in the lands desired by the United States. In spite of this hubris, some Americans expressed anxiety about the annexation of Mexican lands, fearing that that the Mexicans living there might overwhelm and pollute the Anglo Saxon majority.[58]

The relationship between the United States and Mexico in the 19th century was complex. Texas, originally a part of Mexico, became an independent republic and later a state after an armed insurrection of American settlers in Texas in 1836. The settlers wanted to maintain slavery in Texas, which the Mexican government had outlawed, and the government of Mexico had prohibited further immigration from the United States into the Texas territory. The story of the battle of the Alamo is the story of White Americans staking their claim to Texas and fighting against the Mexican government at least partly to preserve the institution of slavery. Stephen Austin, a leader of the rebellion, characterized war as between the "mongrel Spanish-Indian and negro race" and "civilization and the Anglo American race."[59]

The aftermath of the Treaty of Guadalupe Hidalgo was not beneficial for the Mexicans living in the areas affected. After establishing territorial governments, White settlers began systematically stripping Mexican landowners of their land. Violence against Mexicans was common all over the Southwest.[60] Within 1 year of the discovery of gold in California in 1849, American settlers streamed into the state, outnumbering the Mexican inhabitants by 100,000 to 13,000. Mexicans mined for gold alongside Anglos, so successfully that by 1850 when California was admitted to the Union as a state, one of the first acts of the legislature was to impose a miner's tax on "foreigners." In 1856, the legislature passed the "Greaser Law," which banned vagrancy among Mexicans. Divested of their land through laws and taxation, Mexicans in California went from landowners to farm and day laborers in less than a generation in the 19th century.[61] Their language and culture were marginalized and sometimes brutally suppressed. Living in poverty, the Mexicans had become the Mexican Americans and were "foreigners in their native land."[62] The image of the Mexican American as a docile worker had taken root in the Anglo mind and the struggle against that image would galvanize Latino activists for the next 100 years.[63]

Mexicans were recruited to work in agriculture and on the railroads in the Southwest and Midwest between 1880 and 1930. During the lean years of the Great Depression, over 1 million Mexicans were deported under force to Mexico. After World War II the demand of farmers for cheaper labor led to the institution of the Bracero Program, which brought Mexicans back to work in the farms and on the railroads again. Mexican immigrants to the Southwest have been at the mercy of the economic tides ever since.[64]

Puerto Ricans

The story of Puerto Rico is another story of conquest and occupation. The Spanish American War in 1898 freed Cuba and Puerto Rico from Spanish rule but ultimately subjected Puerto Rico to U.S. colonization. As a U.S. territory, Puerto Rico has suffered many indignities, including lack of self-rule and economic exploitation by U.S. corporations that destroyed much of Puerto Rico's agricultural economy. Migration to the United States, most significantly to New York City, exploded in the early 1950s. There Puerto Ricans encountered discrimination and economic marginalization, similar to what they endured in Puerto Rico. The migration continues; the number of persons identifying themselves as Puerto Rican living in the United States increased by 40% between 1990 and 2000, when over 2.5 million persons self-identified as Puerto Rican on the U.S. census.[65] Puerto Ricans are the most economically marginalized of all Latino groups, with 26% living below the poverty line, compared with 21% of Mexican Americans and 16% of Cuban Americans.[66]

Cuban Americans

The majority of Cubans living in the United States are those who left Cuba after Fidel Castro came to power in 1959 and their descendants. Cuba itself has had a long relationship with the United States, first as a protectorate in 1902 and thereafter as a virtual economic colony. The first immigrants from Cuba in the 1960s and 1970s were mostly from the upper and middle echelons of Cuba society who came to the United States with professional and technical skills. As a result, they soon became the most prosperous Latino group in the United States. Beginning in 1980 with the Mariel boatlift operation, which brought 125,000 Cuban refugees to the United States in a period of 6 months, Cuban immigrants were more economically marginalized and generally had darker complexions than the lighter-skin earlier wave of immigrants. These immigrants evoked nativist and racist sentiments from White Americans; their differences from the earlier immigrants, as well as their swelling numbers, led to a change in U.S. immigration policy toward Cuban immigrants.[67] Even Cubans who migrated earlier resented the new migrants; prejudice against darker skin is not solely a White phenomenon. Even among members of oppressed ethnic groups, discrimination on the basis of skin color is common, with lighter skin being privileged over darker skin, leading to discrimination and racism within ethnic groups.[68]

In 1994, the United States announced a "wet foot, dry foot" policy, wherein Cuban immigrants who reach American soil are allowed to stay, while those who are apprehended by immigration officials while still in the water are returned to Cuba.[69] Meanwhile, the United States has continued its economic blockade against Cuba as a way of protesting the government of Fidel Castro, increasing poverty for those Cubans left behind.

Central Americans

More than 2 million immigrants from Central America were living in the United States in 2000; of these, 817,336 were from El Salvador, and 480,665 were from Guatemala. Significant immigration to the United States from Central America began in the 1980s, when civil wars in Nicaragua, El Salvador, and Guatemala led many to leave the region. Other periods of increased immigration have followed natural disasters, such as Hurricane Mitch in 1998, two earthquakes in El Salvador in 2001, and Hurricane Stan in 2005. U.S. immigration policy toward Central America has been dictated by foreign policy concerns. While approximately one fourth of the political asylum applications from Nicaragua were approved between 1984 and 1990, under 3% of the 45,000 political asylum claims from El Salvador and less than 2% of those from Guatemala were approved in the same period. The difference in the asylum rate is due to the U.S. policy of supporting immigration from countries considered to be communist (Cuba and Nicaragua), while opposing immigration from regimes its supports, such as El Salvador, regardless of the level of violence. During this period the U.S. government was supporting the Salvadoran government against a Marxist insurgency and did not wish to grant political asylum as this would be a commentary on Salvadoran established government.[70]

Latino Identity

In the 1960s cultural nationalism emerged among Latino activists, who created ethnic movements rejecting the assimilationist goals of more traditional group members, who had identified as Mexican Americans. Leaders of this movement advocated a separate identity as Chicanos, which reflected their commitment to a transformative political struggle for liberation.[71] Today the term *Latino* has largely replaced the term *Hispanic,* which was adopted by the U.S. Department of Health, Education, and Welfare in 1973 to designate people whose origins are tied to Spain or Spanish-speaking Latin American countries, including the Caribbean. The term *Latino* was a reaction to the imposed term *Hispanic,* as many felt that it defined a group solely in terms of its relationship to Spain and marginalized indigenous cultures.[72] Currently the U.S. Census Bureau uses the terms *Hispanic* and *Latino* interchangeably.[73]

Immigration

Since the 1990s, immigration from Latin America, both legal and illegal, has increased nativism and discrimination against Latinos in the United States. The backlash against immigration stems from several factors. One is the critical mass factor described by Allport in the classic study *Nature of Prejudice*. Allport noted that a region can absorb some people of different backgrounds comfortably, but when the numbers reach a critical mass, the native population reacts strongly to the threat of loss of dominance with discrimination.[74] Allport also noted that the formation of ethnic enclaves, while helpful for new immigrants to an area, may elicit nativist attitudes. Insofar as ethnic enclaves serve to meet most needs—including financial, religious, and social needs—of immigrants, they may limit the efforts to assimilate that majority groups expect from immigrants. Majority groups resent the lack of assimilation, which they view as the price immigrants must pay to come to this country. Many Latino groups today, like earlier immigrants in the 19th century, live in close proximity to those who have similarly immigrated from their countries of origin, where Spanish-language institutions, newspapers, and churches predominate. It is these so-called ethnic enclaves that may stir resentment in the wider population and contribute to discrimination felt against immigrants. Continuing immigration from Latin America refreshes these ethnic enclaves, even as some members leave and move to other neighborhoods. Allport also noted that those who are downwardly mobile, suffering loss of economic status, are more likely to discriminate against others. These groups may need to find a scapegoat to blame for job loss and financial hardships. As an example of the power of downward mobility to fuel anti-immigrant sentiment, observers noted that the wave of resentment against Latino immigrants in California coincided with an economic downturn in the region, as natives may falsely perceive that immigrants are taking their jobs.[75] The reaction to Latino immigration by some Americans can be seen as an example of the racial contract: Immigrants from Latin America elicit racist reactions from some, who view them as inferior and not equal to Americans.

The entry of undocumented immigrants into the United States is not new. As discussed above, the Southwest was originally part of Mexico, and the artificial nature of the borders is perhaps more apparent to those South of this border than to persons living in the United States. Historically the Southern border of the United States has been permeable, with migration back and forth from

Mexico and Central America. The perception that more undocumented persons are entering the country than in previous decades accounts for much of the negative sentiment against all immigrants and, in some cases, against Latinos. The number of immigrants nationwide reached an all-time high of 37.5 million in 2006. This number represents 12.4% of the population. Yet annual rates of immigration declined between 2001 and 2004, partly as a result of an economic downturn in the United States.[76] The number of undocumented persons entering the country annually is impossible to determine. Based on analysis of U.S. census data and other data sources that offer indications of the growth in the foreign-born population, the Pew Hispanic Center estimated that there were 11.5 million to 12 million "unauthorized migrants" in the United States in 2006.[77]

The rate of naturalization of immigrants has increased since 2000. The proportion of all foreign-born residents who have become naturalized U.S. citizens rose to 52% or 12.8 million in 2005, a historic high, according to an analysis by the Pew Hispanic Center. Naturalized citizens accounted for slightly more than 1 in 2 (52%) legal foreign-born residents. Among all 36 million foreign-born residents in 2005, naturalized citizens made up a slim plurality (35%) over legal noncitizens (33%) and unauthorized migrants (31%).[78]

Attitudes toward undocumented immigrants have not shifted over the past 40 years, in spite of the recent public interest in the issue. Polls conducted in 2006 indicate that a majority of Americans think immigrants are taking jobs Americans don't want.[79] Research has consistently found no link between growth in immigration and a decline in employment for Americans.[80] Perhaps recognizing the economic advantages of undocumented immigration, a majority of Americans appear to favor measures that would allow undocumented persons currently in the United States to remain in the country. Only a minority favors deporting all illegal migrants or otherwise forcing them to go home.[81]

Immigrants may be better off economically in the United States than in their country of origin, but they do not benefit as much from immigration as does the native U.S. population. The poverty rate for immigrants and their U.S.-born children (under 18) is two thirds higher than that of natives and their children. Immigrants and their minor children now account for almost 1 in 4 persons living in poverty. Children of immigrants continue to face greater hardship than children of native parents. Immigrants are workers, many filling jobs in the secondary labor market. Of the 18.9 million employed foreign-born workers, 7.1 million (37%) were from Mexico and Central America, 4.9 million (26%) were from Asia, 2.4 million (12%) were from Europe, 1.7 million (9%) were from the Caribbean, and 1.3 million (7%) were from South America. (See Figure 5.1.)

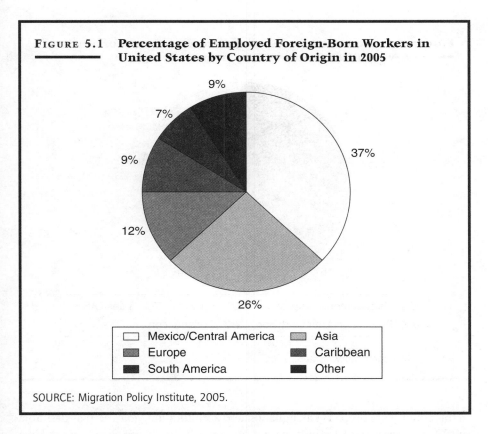

FIGURE 5.1   **Percentage of Employed Foreign-Born Workers in
United States by Country of Origin in 2005**

SOURCE: Migration Policy Institute, 2005.

Immigrants work primarily in the managerial/professional fields, in service occupations, and in technical or sales occupations.[82] (See Figure 5.2.) In spite of their dispersal across occupational levels, Latinos are generally poorer than Whites. While Hispanics represented 13.3% of the total population, they constituted 24.3% of the population living in poverty. In addition, Hispanic children younger than 18 years of age were much more likely than non-Hispanic White children to be living in poverty (28.0% compared with 9.5%).[83]

Latino immigrants contribute to American society in a variety of ways, not just in the stereotype of low-wage workers but as professionals, as carriers of culture, and as an important and political force. Continued migration from and to Mexico and Central America nourishes the culture and language of the Southwest and gives this region a different history, demography, and political and economic reality than the rest of the country. Latinos have been part of the American cultural landscape since the early 19th century, contributing to economic, political, and social institutions alongside other immigrants; their roots

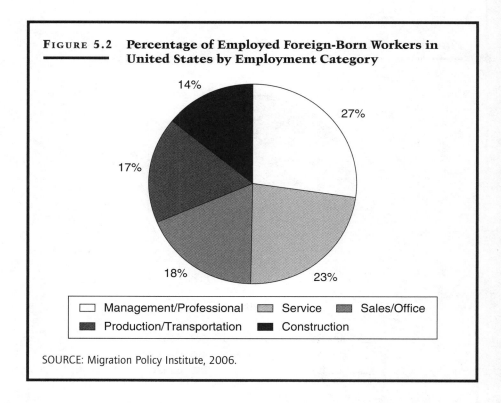

FIGURE 5.2   **Percentage of Employed Foreign-Born Workers in United States by Employment Category**

Management/Professional   Service   Sales/Office

Production/Transportation   Construction

SOURCE: Migration Policy Institute, 2006.

in this country are deep. Yet assimilation and acculturation, goals seen as desirable by White observers of Latinos, cannot extinguish the reality that Latinos have a culture; when they come to the United States, they bring cultural baggage as did the Puritans 300 years earlier. The major difference between the two cultural transplantations is the discrimination faced by the Latinos who sought to make their home in the United States.

As the United States faces a growing shortage of young workers and an aging White population, immigrants from Latin America will be needed to fill the need for labor in the health care and social service sectors as well as pay into the Social Security system. As U.S. corporations move into Latin America over the next 20 years, more workers there will be displaced and migrate north (see Chapter 11). This region will continue to serve as a "labor reserve" for the United States, ready to serve the needs of "capitalist expansion and contraction" regardless of political rhetoric about immigrants.[84] The move for immigrant rights will only become more powerful as their necessity becomes more evident.

Immigration is not just important to the United States economically; immigrants uphold the narrative of the United States as a refuge for seeking a better life and as the cradle of democratic aspirations for the entire world. Immigrants evoke the central American narrative; the United States is special, God's chosen place where people across the globe wish to live. Immigration to the United States, both legal and illegal immigration, affirms our singular place in the world.[85]

ASIAN AMERICANS   ●

Asian American is a convenient term used to describe persons whose origin can be traced to one of several countries: Japan, China, Korea, or the Philippines; *Southeast Asian* is used to refer to persons whose origin can be traced to India, Vietnam, Cambodia, Laos, Malaysia, Thailand, or Indonesia, according to the U.S. census.[86] In reality, the term *Asia* was constructed by non-Asians to describe a part of the world that seemed to be similar, both in geographic location and in culture. Therefore the concept of Asia is a good example of standpoint theory—from the standpoint of persons in the United States or Europe, these countries can be considered as one geographic region, but persons living in these countries do not consider themselves Asians. Thus *Asian* is a Western term that has replaced the earlier designation, *Oriental*. According to Edward Said, the concept of the Orient was created by the West and offers a reverse image of what is inferior to the West and alien to Westerners (the Other).[87] Since the end of the 19th century, the term *Oriental* has been a pejorative one, associated with coded racism. *Asian* is clearly a less demeaning term than *Oriental*, but it is still a social construction developed for the convenience of Westerners.

The classification *Asian or Pacific Islander* first appeared in the U.S. census in 1980; before this date Asian Americans were classified as other. In 1990, the census asked respondents to identify one country associated with their ancestry; these included Chinese, Japanese, Filipino, Korean, Vietnamese, and Thai, along with others. All these are grouped under the classification of either Asian American or Pacific Islander by the U.S. census.

Chinese Americans

In U.S. history, two groups currently categorized as Asian Americans suffered deeply as the result of discriminatory policies by the U.S. government. The first were the Chinese. Chinese immigrants came to this country beginning in 1849 to work on the transcontinental railroad and later the silver mines of the Western states. Like many other immigrant groups, the lure of jobs was a powerful one for the Chinese, whose country was experiencing wars, turmoil, and harsh economic conditions. The Chinese were primarily a bachelor migration, with men planning to work temporarily in the United States and return to their families with economic resources once their labor contracts, promoted by Chinese labor brokers, were fulfilled. Most Chinese immigrants borrowed the money for their passage to the United States from these labor brokers and were forced to pay this back with high interest charges; most never returned to China. Initially welcomed to California and other Western states where they settled, their presence soon led to brutal outbreaks of racism and violence. Once the railroad was finished, these immigrants worked in the gold fields and silver mines of California and Nevada, where they were viewed as competition by the Anglo settlers trying to establish dominance in the region. The California legislature enacted a second foreign miners' tax in 1852 (the first had been aimed at the Mexicans) and drove many Chinese out of mining and into agriculture as well as into the urban areas of San Francisco and Sacramento. Even there the Chinese were viewed with suspicion and resentment. Chinese were imagined to have similar qualities that White Americans had assigned to African Americans during slavery: They were thought to be childlike, morally inferior, and savage. Fear of their religion and their cultural differences, as well as more primitive fears of the Chinese as a threat to White racial purity, led to an anti-Chinese crusade by some newspapers and White elites.[88] Discrimination pushed the Chinese into defined areas of cities, known as Chinatowns. Many Chinese were forced to seek self-employment in stores, restaurants, and laundries, due to the discriminatory practices of employers in the West. Hostility and violence toward the Chinese immigrants culminated in the passage of the Chinese Exclusion Act in 1882, which banned immigration of Chinese to the United States.[89] This legislation was the first and last time that an entire ethnic group was banned from the United States; it demonstrates the economic and cultural threat that the Chinese had become to Whites in this country. As a result of the earlier 1790 Naturalization Law, which stated that no non-White persons could be naturalized as citizens, Chinese were not allowed to become citizens, no matter how long they had lived in this country. Chinese continued to live in a male-dominated society in the United States; even in 1905, only 5% of Chinese immigrants were women.[90] The male character of the migration may have contributed to the nativist response since "bachelors" are seen as more threatening than families. The Chinese Exclusion Act threatened to freeze the bachelor society in place.[91] The act was not repealed until 1943,[92] when leaders in the United States perceived another "Asian" group as a more serious threat.

Japanese Americans

The main Japanese migration to the United States took place in the last decades of the 19th century. Theirs was a migration of women as well as men, for the Japanese government promoted female emigration. Japanese immigrants worked in agriculture, railroads, and mining. Japanese immigrants grew the majority of fruit and vegetables in California, shipping their products to the East. Their agricultural success became a source of prosperity. By the early 20th century, White farmers began to envy the success of Japanese immigrants in the rich farmlands of California and sought ways to displace them. As a result of the growing anti-Japanese sentiment in California, in 1907 President Theodore Roosevelt negotiated a so-called Gentlemen's Agreement with the Prime Minister of Japan to limit immigration of Japanese laborers. California and other states passed laws excluding Japanese from owning lands, based on their ineligibility for citizenship in the same 1790 law that refused citizenship to the Chinese. In 1924, Congress passed a general immigration law, which severely restricted Japanese immigration to this country.[93] Like the Chinese

Japanese families en route to Manzanar Internment Camp, California

SOURCE: From the Library of Congress, photo by Ansel Adams.

immigrants, Japanese Americans lived in ethnic enclaves where they sought support from the discrimination of White society. As in the case of other ethnic groups, this solidarity led Whites to criticize the Japanese for not assimilating.[94]

First-generation Japanese Americans, known as Issei, hoped that their children born in the United States, known as Nisei, would be accepted in the United States and prosper. Yet the Nisei too suffered discrimination at the hands of Whites and were perceived as foreigners, even though they were born in the United States. Most Nisei worked for other Japanese Americans, as White employers would not hire them. Looking different from White Americans, second-generation Japanese learned that education and assimilation were not enough: Physical characteristics continued to mark them as the "other." Nisei formed the largest group within the Japanese American community: On the eve of World War II, they constituted 63% of the Japanese Americans.[95]

After Japan's attack on Pearl Harbor, the Navy base in Hawaii, on December 7, 1941, the Japanese Americans were perceived by some as direct threats to American security, especially in California. The leaders of the movement to punish or detain Issei and Nisei came from farming interests in California, who wanted the lands that Japanese Americans had farmed with great success. Anti-Japanese hysteria, especially on the West Coast, was fueled by the racist sentiments that had followed the Japanese since the end of the 19th century. This racist anxiety culminated in the infamous Executive Order 9066 of President Franklin Roosevelt that ordered the removal of all Issei and Nisei on the West Coast to detention camps run by the federal government. Approximately 110,000 Japanese, including 60,000 American citizens, were forced to leave their homes, farms, and businesses.[96] Japanese Americans lost their possessions and their economic resources. The transfer of agricultural wealth sought by White farmers for 50 years was complete. Why were the Japanese Americans removed and the much larger groups of German Americans or Italian Americans left in place? Clearly the reason was the fact that the Japanese looked different from most Americans and therefore were an easy target for scapegoating. It was not until 1988 that Congress voted for limited compensation in the amount of $20,000 each for persons relocated during World War II and offered an apology for the actions of the U.S. government.

Asian Americans as a "Model Minority"

Asian Americans have been constructed as a "model" minority when compared to other racial minorities in the United States. Proponents of the "model" minority point to higher levels of education and income in certain Asian American groups, especially Chinese and Japanese, while ignoring the hardships and economic marginalization faced by Asian Americans who migrated to this country more recently, including Vietnamese, Cambodians, and Filipinos. These latter groups have experienced economic hardships and discrimination in the United States, often in spite of relatively high educational achievements.[97] For example, Filipino Americans make up 2.4 million of the 11.9 million Asian Americans in the United States. They are the second largest Asian subgroup in this country, closely trailing the 2.7 million Chinese Americans. Filipinos provided the largest number of immigrants from any Asian group between 1981 and 1998. While their level of education is above the national average, their income is below the mean income of all groups in the United States.[98]

The narrative of the "model minority" carries an implicit reproach to other ethnic groups who have not fared so well in the American economy; why can't all ethnic groups be like Asian Americans? With this concept Asian Americans are collapsed into one group and serve as an object lesson to other oppressed groups.[99] (See Table 5.2.)

POVERTY AND DISCRIMINATION ●

Why are African Americans and Latinos disproportionately poor, many working in the secondary labor market? One reason is the residency patterns that have dominated many urban areas since the 1960s. As African Americans and Latinos migrated to the large urban centers of the Northeast, Midwest, and West, they formed ethnic enclaves, partly by choice and partly because of constricted job opportunities and residential segregation. As manufacturers pulled their plants out of the inner city in the 1960s and later out of the country altogether (see Chapter 11), African Americans and Latinos became economically and socially isolated in inner city areas, far from job opportunities in the suburbs that were encouraged by the federal government support of highway construction. Another factor contributing to suburban growth after World War II was the GI Bill, which gave low-cost housing loans to former members of the armed forces, encouraging housing construction in suburban rings. This move to the suburbs meant that between 1970 and 1990 the White population in the major cities declined and the African American and Latino population increased.[100] Of course, some African Americans and Latinos did leave the inner cities, move to the suburbs, and join professionals and others in the primary labor market, leaving the poorest to remain in the inner city. Another policy increasing inequality is the public education system in the urban core.

**TABLE 5.2   Historical Flashpoints of Ethnic Groups' Experiences of Oppression
in the United States**

Year and/or Period	Event and Description
Native Americans	
Colonial Period	Indian removal from land by early English settlers through war, death, broken treaties, and relocations
1814	Andrew Jackson led U.S. Army in attack on Creek nation and developed policy of removal where Native Americans in Southeast were forcibly removed
1830s	Concept of "wardship" adopted by the federal government
1838	Trail of Tears—a forced march that killed more than 8,000 Cherokees and forced removal of more than 100,000 Native Americans
1840s	Removal of Plains Indians during westward migration by Whites
1851	Tribal Council at Fort Laramie, Wyoming, where federal government developed the reservation system to limit tribes to one geographic area
1864	Great Plains War—massacre of 600 members of the Cheyenne tribe
1867 and 1868	Forced removal of Cheyenne tribes to reservations
1887	Dawes Act—ended recognition of tribes as sovereign nations
1900	Boarding schools for Native American children were established to maintain social control
1924	Indian Citizenship Act—Indians allowed to become citizens of United States
1934	Indian Reorganization Act abolished allotment program and authorized funding for tribal land acquisition
African Americans	
Civil War	Ended slavery in the South, but freed slaves were given no financial help by the federal government
1880s–1890s	"Jim Crow" laws—legal segregation of Blacks and Whites
1896	*Plessy v. Ferguson* upheld "Jim Crow" laws, which allowed legal segregation, the sharecropping system, lynching, and violent assaults against African Americans
1954	*Brown v. Board of Education*—school segregation was unconstitutional
19th and early 20th centuries	Leaders such as Frederick Douglass, Ida B. Wells, W. E. B. Du Bois, and Marcus Garvey inspired resistance in African Americans
1950s–1960s	Civil rights movement, Black Power movement

Year and/or Period	Event and Description
Latinos	
1836	Battle of the Alamo in which White Americans staked their claim to Texas and fought against Mexico's government in order to preserve institution of slavery in Texas
1840s	U.S. war against Mexico resulting in Treaty of Guadalupe Hidalgo
1850	California imposes a miner's tax on foreigners
1855	California Anti-Vagrancy Act against Mexicans passed
1898	Spanish American War that brought Puerto Rico under U.S. control
1880–1930	Mexicans recruited to work in agriculture and on the railroads
Great Depression	Over 1 million Mexicans deported under force to Mexico
After World War II	*Bracero* Program brought Mexicans back to work in farms and on railroads
1960s	Cultural nationalism among Latino activists
1980s	Mariel boatlift operation, which brought 125,000 Cuban refugees to the United States
	Significant immigration to the United States from Central America, but policy toward Central America has been dictated by foreign policy concerns
1990–2000	Puerto Rican migration increased by 40% due to lack of self-rule and economic exploitation by U.S. corporations
1994	"Wet foot, dry foot" policy adopted by United States
Asian Americans	
1849	Chinese immigrants (primarily men) came to United States to work on railroad and silver mines
1852	California legislature enacts a foreign miner's tax, which drove many Chinese out of mining and into agriculture
1882	Chinese Exclusion Act—banned Chinese immigration
1924	Japanese immigration was severely restricted
1942	Executive Order 9066 by President Franklin Roosevelt that ordered the removal of all Issei and Nisei on the West Coast to detention camps run by the federal government
1988	Congress gave limited compensation in the amount of $20,000 each for persons relocated during World War II and offered an apology for the actions

The property tax base in low-income urban areas does not support a public school system rich in resources, further disadvantaging those who attend these schools. Factors limiting the ability of those living in the urban core to secure primary labor market jobs in the suburban ring include transportation costs, child care costs, and other job-related expenses, which may be prohibitive for those living at the poverty level.

Vast differences in wealth accumulation, the result of generations of discrimination, mean that ethnic minorities have fewer economic resources to fall back on to fund their movement into the middle class. Periods of unemployment and economic recession will be more devastating for those who have not accumulated capital. The large gap in median net worth between Whites and Latinos and African Americans known as the wealth gap is remarkable. As of 2004, the latest year for which data are available, the median Hispanic household had a net worth of $18,600, and the median African American family had a net worth of $20,600, meaning that half of the households in those groups had less and half had more. The median White household, by contrast, had more than 7 times either amount—$140,700. Nearly a third of Blacks and over a quarter of Hispanic households had zero or negative net worth in 2002, compared with 13% of Whites. The net worth of Hispanic and Black households fell 27% from 1999 through 2001, while White household wealth rose 2% during the same period.[101]

Another economic limitation on the family income of certain ethnic groups is the fact that there are more children born to single-parent families among African Americans and, to a lesser extent, Latino families than there are to White and Asian American families.[102] Since women, on average, earn less income than men, families headed by women are more economically disadvantaged than those headed by two wage earners. But family structure is not the most powerful explanation of economic inequality, since the poverty rates of nonworking African American and Latina mothers in two-parent households where the spouse is working are nearly identical to those of employed single African American and Latina mothers. Latina mothers are more likely to be married than African American women, and their families are more likely to be headed by two persons, but Latino children are just as likely to be poor as African American children. Family structure is not the determining variable that predicts poverty among African Americans and Latinos.[103] Withdrawal of jobs from urban areas, marginalized public education, limited economic resources, and outright discrimination have combined to push African Americans and Latinos into the secondary labor market and consequently into poverty.[104] Affirmative action will not improve the economic condition of persons in the secondary labor market, regardless of their ethnicity. Racism is an ideological component of the complex nexus of inequality; that is, it creates, justifies, and increases the unequal conditions of oppressed persons.[105]

GENDER DISCRIMINATION   ●

Gender is an overlapping category, since women are represented in all the groups discussed in this chapter. Can gender be a category of analysis in the discussion of discrimination? There are many different kinds of women; ethnic, age, and sexual orientation differences are just a few ways that gender can be subdivided in the United States. The experiences of women in each subcategory are different from each other. Like ethnic categories, the category of women carries with it the dangers of essentialism and the idea that all women are fundamentally the same, a presumption that ignores the power of ethnicity, class, and sexual orientation to shape experience. On the other hand, gender discrimination affects all women, and there are certain forms of discrimination that affect only women. While recognizing the multiplicity of women's identities, talking about women as a group is central to understanding the impact of gender discrimination.

After acknowledging problems with the category of women, we can affirm that being born a woman rather than a man has led to a different set of life experiences for most women in American history. Women did not participate in public political life for much of our history; instead, they were consigned to the home, where their labor as homemakers and mothers was uncompensated. Women who did work were forced to work in low-paying, low-status jobs and endured worse working conditions than men; subject to sexual harassment, women were given the less desirable jobs than their male counterparts and were paid less.

In Chapter 4, we saw how women suffer from economic discrimination and consistently earn less money than men. Why is this so? One reason is the weight of historical expectations. Until the women's movement of the 1970s, middle-class White women were thought to be working to supplement the family income, not to support a family. Employers therefore felt justified in giving them a lower wage. Women were also believed to be less reliable workers; they took time off for childbirth and child care and generally were not considered to be as steady workers as men, and hence they were paid lower wages. These assumptions have been proven wrong since the 1970s, as many women support families without a second income, and notions of women as unreliable workers have largely dissipated. Yet these beliefs continue to inform labor market practices. Why?

If we look more deeply at the wage discrepancy, we also see a disregard for women implicit in the economic inequality they suffer. For much of European and American history, women were thought to be less intellectually capable than men—more emotional and less rational, less reliable and less dependable. These beliefs are the not-so-subtle subtexts of the unequal pay given to women. Feminists believed that it was important to advance the argument that gender roles are socially constructed and that the gendered division of labor that characterized U.S. history until relatively recently was fundamentally unfair.

Women Working

There were 152 million women in the United States at the end of 2006; 82.5 million of them were mothers.[106] In 2008, women made up about 48% of the labor force and men 52%.[107] In 2004, almost 60% of women over 16 were in the labor force; African American women had the highest participation rate at 61.5%, and Latinas had the lowest at 56.1%. Higher educational attainment meant higher labor force participation. Women with a B.A. or higher had a 73% participation rate in 2004.[108] That same year 70% of mothers with children under 18 were in the labor force, and 77% of mothers with children 6–17 worked.[109] All these women faced greater odds of low wages than did men in their ethnic groups. Women working

Woman waitress, circa 1920

SOURCE: © 2009 Jupiterimages Corporation.

in low-paying jobs often received no benefits. Over 17 million women had no health insurance in 2007. Since more women than men are insured as dependents on their spouse's insurance policy, they are more likely to be without insurance in the case of divorce or death of spouse. Low-income women and women of color, especially Latinas, are more likely to be uninsured than other groups.[110]

Child Care

Lack of affordable child care is one of the most significant obstacles to women's economic well-being, especially considering the high number of mothers in the workforce. While the availability of child care has increased over the past 20 years, there is still not sufficient quality child care available for many working mothers. The United States has no overall child care policy and does not subsidize child care for working mothers, unlike Great Britain, which has a policy of ensuring adequate child care for working mothers.[111] Thus every parent must purchase child care or arrange for free child care with relatives.

In 2007, 3 out of 4 mothers with children under 18 worked full-time, compared with one half in 1975. All these mothers need child care. For single mothers, minimum wage will return $10,712 per year, and child care costs may be nearly impossible to meet.[112] Single parents with two children will spend on average between 47% and 113% of their state's median income on child care. The average cost across the country for child care for preschoolers ranges from approximately $4,000 to $11,000 per year; for infants the cost is from $5,000 to $14,500 per year. Families on average spend more on child care than they do on rent or food. The burden of child care arrangements and costs falls primarily to women.[113]

Political Power and Gender

Gender discrimination is subtle and far reaching. While there are no laws prohibiting women from holding political office, the proportion of political power accorded to women has been slight compared to that for men, far less than in European democratic countries. Why is this? Conceptions of femininity have limited the possibilities and contributed significantly to gendered arrangements that discriminate against women. Beliefs that women are more delicate, emotional, and fragile than men arose in the 19th century partly to explain why women were left at home to manage the household and children while men went off to the new jobs created by the rise of manufacturing and, later in the 19th century, industrialization. A "cult of true womanhood" dominated middle-class White culture, in which social and religious leaders praised the womanly virtues of piety, domesticity, purity, and submissiveness. Many thought these qualities were natural to good women and sadly missing in sinful women.[114] Of course, immigrant women, poor women, and women from oppressed groups such as African American women did not have the luxury of staying at home and practicing these womanly virtues. For many White middle-class women, these stereotypes became constraining; men who were opposed to women's suffrage argued that these qualities of piety, domesticity, purity, and submissiveness made women unfit for the rough and tumble of politics. This argument was so persuasive that women did not win the right to vote until 1919, when the Nineteenth Amendment to the Constitution was ratified. Yet women also enjoyed special treatment because of the social construction of gender roles; they were supported economically and protected from hard work outside the home.

PROFILES IN LEADERSHIP

Elizabeth Cady Stanton, 1815–1902

Elizabeth Cady Stanton

SOURCE: From Library of Congress, photo by Veeder.

Elizabeth Cady Stanton was born on November 12, 1815, and died in 1902 in New York.

She was one of 10 children and was fortunate to be born into a wealthy family with both parents involved in politics. Her father, judge of the state Supreme Court, passed on his skills in legal argument and oral debate to his daughter, who eventually became recognized for her logic, clear speaking, and strong arguments on social issues of the day.

Stanton was raised in a home with strict discipline and a strong religious atmosphere.

She lived an enviable life, with all the comforts of a well-to-do family, but at an early age she began to understand that only the privileged few could live a life such as hers. At her father's law office, she learned about gender inequity in property and inheritance law. She began to see that there was great injustice and discrimination against women and began to think of herself as a social reformer. Her father was embarrassed by her reform efforts and tried to discourage her from speaking out for women's rights in public.

In the 19th century, women were thought to be biologically and psychologically more suited for domestic tasks such as raising children and tending to the household than for public roles. To speak out for women's rights, such as voting and divorce, was considered outrageous, and Stanton experienced considerable hostility mostly from men. It was clear that Elizabeth Cady Stanton was a woman far ahead of her time who had strong opinions about social justice and would not be silenced by her critics.

Elizabeth married her husband, Henry Stanton, over her father's objections, but she refused to say the word *obey* in the marriage ceremony. Her husband influenced her to become involved in the abolitionist movement. She and her husband traveled to England where he was to attend the World Anti-Slavery Convention. After returning to the United States, she began a speaking tour traveling to various cities speaking about women's rights and the abolition of slavery. She believed that women's dependence on men would not change until women became educated enough to become self-sufficient.

In 1848, the first women's rights convention took place in Seneca Falls, New York.

The timing was good because only a few months earlier the New York State Legislature had passed legislation allowing women limited rights to the ownership of property. At this convention, Stanton introduced a resolution that women be given the right to vote. The reaction of the press and the pulpit was predictable: They responded with hostility and venom and ridiculed the ideas presented by Stanton.

In 1866, Elizabeth Cady Stanton was the first woman to run for Congress. She lost, but the message was clear that she would not be stopped by convention or by opponents. She soon obtained a position as a writer for a newspaper called *The Revolution* where she had the opportunity to freely argue her views about the oppression of women. Her point of view was that women should be equal to men in all areas of society and that all occupations should be open to women. It was not until 1920, 18 years after Stanton's death, that the Nineteenth Amendment was approved in Congress and ratified by the states, giving women the right to vote after many years of struggle.

In her 80s, Stanton began to study socialism to expand her ideas about equality. She also became recognized as the individual who began the women's movement, who contributed to the public debate about the oppression of women, and who articulated the rights and needs of women when others were too timid or afraid of speaking out. She was a fighter for social justice and a champion for women.

Many of these attitudes about what women should be have lingered in the culture and inform policies directed specifically to women, such as welfare (see Chapter 7). These socially constructed beliefs about women's nature limited women's economic, political, and social roles and fueled the feminist movement of the 1970s. In this movement, middle-class women, primarily White, sought to overturn what they considered sexist notions about gender roles and gender arrangements that dominated middle-class culture (with a brief exception during World War II when middle-class women entered the workforce) for much of the 20th century. As a result of their focus on socially constructed gender roles, many of the issues raised by these feminists were personal, related to gender roles within families and relationships between men and women. Arguing that the personal is political, feminists made the argument that the gender division of labor that assigned women to the household and men to the public sphere was unjust and served to exclude women from centers of economic, political, and social power.[115]

The feminist movement of the 1970s did not embrace the agenda of poor and working-class women, especially women from ethnically oppressed groups, who had neither benefited nor been limited by the social constructions of the cult of true womanhood or from being limited to the private sphere. Poor women, including immigrant women and women of color, had been forced to work in low-paying jobs throughout the 19th and 20th centuries to ensure their families' survival. For these women, issues related to gender relationships were not as important as economic marginalization and discrimination that interfered with their ability to meet their families' needs. Women from oppressed ethnic groups turned the agenda of middle-class White women on its head; instead of wishing for more time to work away from domestic life, women of color wanted more time for family life and less pressure to work in low-paying jobs. The experience of oppression was located outside the family, in the discrimination and exploitive conditions found in the workplace. For economically marginalized women, the home was a place of support more than it was a place of confinement. While White feminists struggled with gender roles with the nuclear family form, families were more diverse among some ethnic groups, particularly African Americans, whose struggle with economic hardship and discrimination resulted in the creation of extended families, consonant with their cultural legacy. These extended African American families demonstrated great resilience in the face of adversity.[116]

In spite of these differences, all women have common concerns related to the abuses of power inherent in a patriarchal society, especially violence against women and children and the need for reproductive rights. All women who assume the major responsibility for childrearing and household maintenance are performing uncompensated labor benefitting the capitalist economic structure.

Household labor and socialization of children constitute necessary work in any society, work that would have to be compensated in lieu of volunteer labor provided by women for their families. This vast pool of unpaid labor is willingly given by most women to their families, but the benefits to the market economy are significant; without this donated domestic labor, wages would have to be higher to compensate workers for purchasing these services. Thus women's unpaid domestic work increases the profits of private enterprise and benefits the market economy.[117] Women have been primarily responsible for social reproduction, which includes bearing and socializing children to perform expected adult roles; caring for family members, old and young; and meeting basic needs of family members. In the United States, there are very few government policies designed to assist with social reproduction; thus, the burden falls on women to care for their families, in spite of gains made by the feminist movement of the 1970s. Since all these tasks are necessary for social stability and the maintenance of the economic system, women who perform them for their families without compensation are contributing to the social and economic good. Women who work for low wages must perform these tasks in absence of public policies, such as subsidized child care, that would make the burden of social reproduction less onerous.[118]

LGBT: LESBIAN, GAY, BISEXUAL, AND TRANSGENDERED PERSONS ●

The history of groups whose sexual orientation is different from the socially constructed version of normality known as heterosexuality has been marked by oppression, stigma, and outright violence in the United States. Members of LGBT groups continue to live under circumstances of oppression in the workplace, in schools, in their rights to legalize their domestic unions, in the military, and in the unregulated spaces of the social order where casual harassment takes place every day. The history of LGBT persons in the United States cannot be told separately from the history of homophobia, a deep-seated attitude of hostility or fear of gay people and homosexuality. Homophobia has many manifestations, ranging from dislike and avoidance of LGBT persons to active harassment and, finally, to violence.

Discrimination Against LGBT Persons in U.S. History

In early American history, the colonies enacted stiff criminal penalties for any sexual acts that were considered nonprocreative or that took place between persons unmarried, including heterosexuals. In the 19th century, a psychological view of sexuality slowly overtook the legal and moral perspective, at least among educated groups. Homosexuality was thought to be a sign of psychological pathology by some, although Freud believed that all human beings were innately bisexual and that their early experiences with their parents determined their ultimate sexual orientation. Freud did not view homosexuality as a pathology but as a variation of sexuality.[119]

In spite of Freud's views about the universality of bisexuality, a deep-seated fear of homosexuality led to many restrictive laws in the United States. Until the U.S. Supreme Court's ruling in *Lawrence v. Texas* in 2003, sodomy laws in 13 states criminalized sexual relationships between gay men and lesbians. Although these laws were rarely enforced, they stigmatized LGBT persons as criminals, thereby deterring the passage of antidiscrimination laws, serving to drastically limit parenting rights of gay men and lesbians, and delaying the recognition of the right to marry. By contrast, decriminalization of sexual conduct by LGBT persons was achieved in Canada in 1969, leading to earlier recognition of the right to marry and the passage of antidiscriminatory laws in that country.[120]

In the United States, it was not until 1986 that the American Psychiatric Association (APA) removed "homosexuality" from its list of mental disorders, published as the *Diagnostic and Statistical Manual of Mental Disorders,* and that was only after pressure from gay activists. In the 1980 edition, *DSM-III,* the APA had attempted to satisfy its critics by substituting the concept of "ego-dystonic homosexuality" for the term *homosexuality,* making a diagnosis of mental disorder only for LGBT persons unhappy as a result of their sexual orientation. Given the oppression and resulting repression of sexual orientation that resulted from centuries-long hostility toward LGBT persons in the United States, unhappiness with homophobic reaction to one's sexual orientation was a normal reaction and not a sign of mental disorder. However, the psychiatric profession did not assign an external cause to unhappiness experienced by LGBT persons but preferred to focus on internal causes. In this way, LGBT persons could be encouraged to seek psychiatric treatment.

Gay Liberation Movement

The gay liberation movement emerged first in New York City after the famous Stonewall uprising in 1969, when New York City police raided a popular gay bar in Greenwich Village. While these raids were not unusual, a massive street protest followed the police action, as hundreds of gay men protested the unjust treatment by law enforcement. This spontaneous uprising was a catalyst for a wider gay and lesbian liberation movement in the 1970s that accompanied the women's movement and the movements for ethnic equality discussed earlier in this chapter. A general celebration of sexual freedom swept through many college campuses and helped to carry the gay liberation movement forward. One of the achievements of the gay liberation movement was the election of Harvey Milk as the first openly gay man to hold office in the United States to the San Francisco City Council in 1977. Although Milk was assassinated a year later, his life and work had deep influence on LGBT culture, especially among young people in the late 1970s and early 1980s.

The gay liberation movement was derailed in the late 1980s and early 1990s by the HIV/AIDS crisis in the United States, for which gay men were blamed by many Americans. The apparent initial concentration of the epidemic in the gay community fueled existing homophobia and resulted in an extreme backlash against gay men, temporarily undermining the achievements of the gay liberation movement. Ultimately, however, members of the LGBT community transcended the stigma and pain of the HIV/AIDS epidemic and reemerged stronger and with a new emphasis on diversity within their communities.[121]

Employment Discrimination

Although the LGBT movements have made a strong positive impact on popular culture, the strong role homophobia and discrimination continue to play in the United States is evident in the failure of all but 11 states to pass laws prohibiting discrimination against LGBT persons in the workplace. Employers continue to be free to refuse to hire lesbians, gay men, or transgendered persons in 39 states and can deny them promotions, fire them, or otherwise discriminate against them in the workplace.[122]

By the close of 2008, there was no federal law to protect individuals from job discrimination on the basis of sexual orientation or gender identity. Federal law prohibits discrimination against women or members of ethnic groups in the workplace, but LGBT persons are not protected by federal law. Title VII of the Civil Rights Act of 1964 prohibits discrimination based on sex, race, color, religion, and national origin but not on the basis of sexual orientation or gender identity. The Equal Employment Opportunity Commission (EEOC), established to enforce the Civil Rights Act, will not hear cases of discrimination based on sexual orientation or gender identity. While numerous efforts to add sexual orientation to the act have been mounted in Congress since the 1970s, none have been successful.[123] As a consequence of the refusal of the federal government to ensure the protection of employment rights for lesbians and gay men, as well as for bisexual and transgendered persons, it is up to states to ensure economic rights for these groups. As we have seen, the vast majority of these states have not done so. Some localities have banned discrimination against gays and lesbians in public jobs, but this piecemeal approach to ensuring the rights of these groups is inadequate and often not enforced. Not only have most states failed to include protection for LGBT persons in employment practices; some localities have passed antigay ordinances to forestall inclusion of these groups in discrimination laws, including those related to employment and housing.[124] It will be astonishing for social workers who are not members of LGBT groups to realize that discrimination against these Americans is legal in so much of the country.

Same-Sex Unions

Another more well-known area of discrimination against LGBT persons is the fact that gay men and lesbians are denied the right to marry in all but six states: Massachusetts, Connecticut, Vermont, Maine, New Hampshire, and Iowa. Same-sex marriage was declared a fundamental constitutional right by the California Supreme Court in 2008, only to be "overturned" in a ballot proposition by voters later that same year. During the period before the ballot proposition passed, more than 18,000 same-sex couples married in the state.[125] The California Supreme Court has agreed to rule on the legality of the proposition seeking to amend the state constitution in 2009. By 2007, 30 states had passed constitutional amendments restricting marriage to opposite-sex couples, while another 15 states have forbidden same-sex marriages directly. All these state laws prohibiting same-sex marriages were given legitimacy by the 1997 passage of the federal Defense of Marriage Act (DOMA), which defined marriage as restricted to heterosexuals and barred federal recognition of same-sex couples for purposes of federal benefits, even if states have made such marriages legal. This law made it impossible for same-sex partners to receive Social Security benefits and other federal benefits given to married couples (see Chapter 7). Under DOMA, if one state recognizes same-sex unions, no other state has to honor those unions.

Seven states offer domestic partnerships or civil unions, which give many of the state benefits to same-sex couples, but cannot give them federal benefits and do not call these unions "marriage."[126] Civil unions and domestic partnerships allow same-sex couples to name each other as dependents in health care and other employee-related benefits. The goal of lawmakers who have sponsored these same-sex unions is to grant same-sex couples the same rights as married couples without incurring the opposition of religious groups who oppose same-sex marriage. In Europe most countries have legalized same-sex unions without calling them marriages. By contrast, in 2005, the Canadian Parliament made marriage between same-sex couples legal throughout the country.[127]

Why is the concept of same-sex marriage so contested? Much of opposition is based on religious beliefs about the nature of marriage. Yet if marriage is conceived as a social construction (see Chapter 1), then the idea of persons from the same sex marrying in order to legalize their relationship, insure their mutual property interests, and raise children is not controversial but rather another way of thinking about marriage. Cultural beliefs and institutions are in constant flux, as we have seen from how the ideas about African Americans and American Indians have evolved over the past 200 years. Similarly, LGBT persons are more likely to be "out" and claim their identities than at any other time in our history. The pressure to keep one's sexual orientation or gender identity hidden from others still exists, most strongly in the U.S. military as we will see, but it is less than in the 19th century or the bulk of the 20th century.[128] However, the infusion of the idea of marriage with religious meaning, along with the belief of some fundamentalist Christians that the LGBT lifestyle is immoral, has delayed the natural evolution of thinking about the rights of LGBT persons to formalize their unions in recognized marriages. The consequences of this opposition to the rights of LGBT persons are profound. Marriage carries economic and legal rights as well as social recognition. The right to be declared "next of kin" in health and other emergent situations is situated in marriage, which trumps all other relationships in every legal and social circumstance. The rights to inherit and to be awarded community property in divorce settlements are only two of the economic rights accrued to marriage. Additionally, the rights to raise children and to share in their custody in case of divorce or dissolution are attached to the married state. All these rights can be granted by same-sex unions, but the social recognition inherent in marriage cannot be.

Sectarian or religious arguments about same-sex marriage should not be established as law, since such laws violate the principle of the separation of church and state and advance "constitutionally forbidden intolerance."[129] Marriage is ultimately a civil union, sanctioned by the state, and carries no necessary religious meaning. Whatever the cause of the opposition to same-sex unions, Christian religious belief or outright homophobia, it is still discrimination and an assault on social justice as well as being counter to the National Association of Social Workers' *Code of Ethics,* which states that social workers should act to prevent discrimination against any person, group, or class on the basis of race, ethnicity, national origin, color, sex, sexual orientation, age, marital status, political belief, religion, or mental or physical disability.[130]

Adoption and Foster Care

In November 2008, Arkansas voters passed a ballot proposition that banned gays and lesbians as well as unmarried heterosexuals from becoming foster parents or adopting children. Arkansas thus joined Utah in effectively banning same-sex couples from fostering or adoption. Unmarried heterosexuals were added by antigay groups after the Arkansas Supreme Court struck down an earlier law banning only gays and lesbians from adopting as unconstitutional.[131] Mississippi also bans same-sex couples from adopting. Only one state, Florida, explicitly bans gay men and lesbians from adopting children, both as single persons and as couples, while allowing them to be foster parents.[132] The recent passage of the Arkansas proposition (by 57% of voters) is a chilling reminder that discrimination and homophobia still have enough resonance to achieve policies that both deprive LGBT persons of social justice and thwart the child welfare system from pursuing the best interests of the child in making decisions.

Difficulties faced by LGBT youth in the foster care system are widely acknowledged in the social work literature. These youth are less likely to be reunited with their birth families and may lack permanent connections with their families of origin that make it very difficult for them to transition out of foster care. Especially in group care facilities, LGBT youth may be subject to harassment and even violence from their peers, as well as group care staff.[133]

Military Service

Another example of discrimination against LGBT persons is the fact that more than 12,500 service members have been discharged as a result of the "Don't Ask, Don't Tell" policy passed by Congress in 1993. "Don't Ask, Don't Tell" is the law banning openly lesbian, gay, and bisexual Americans from serving in the military. According to a 2005 Government Accountability Office report, nearly 800 of those discharged were "mission-critical" specialists—including pilots, intelligence analysts, medics, and linguists. A Blue Ribbon Commission report found that the cost to replace and train service members discharged from fiscal years 1994 through 2003 exceeded $363.8 million.[134]

Prior to the passage of "Don't Ask, Don't Tell" in 1993, homosexuality in the military was banned by regulation. Although President Bill Clinton pledged to lift the ban during the presidential campaign of 1992, the attempt failed after much congressional and military opposition. Congress then passed the "Don't Ask, Don't Tell" law as a compromise allowing gay men and lesbians to serve if they kept their sexual orientation secret. The policy was based on the justification developed by the military known as "social cohesion"; the argument was that combat groups would lose social cohesion if an openly gay person was serving with them, thus endangering the unit's safety and fighting ability. These notions are socially constructed legitimations of homophobia, implicitly acknowledging its existence in the military and allowing homophobia to continue to deprive LGBT persons of their rights. Opposition to the "Don't Ask, Don't Tell" policy has coalesced around the Military Readiness Enhancement Act, introduced in 2007, which would repeal "Don't Ask, Don't Tell" and establish a policy of nondiscrimination for members of the armed services. Barack Obama has pledged to support this bill and to overturn the "Don't Ask, Don't Tell" policy during his presidential administration.[135]

Struggling against tremendous odds, including every form of discrimination and outright violence, LGBT persons have continued to assert their rights and made much progress in overturning longstanding attitudes and actions based on ignorance and homophobia. As we can see from the above, much more needs to be accomplished before LGBT persons achieve social justice and full parity with all Americans.

PERSONS CONSIDERED DISABLED ●

The definition of "disability" is socially constructed and relative. Differing views of what constitutes disability affect the number of persons identified as disabled. According to a U.S. Census Bureau report released in December 2008, based on 2005 data, there were 54 million persons who had some form of disability, representing 19% of the population. More than 10 million Americans needed some assistance with at least one activity associated with daily living, such as bathing. Approximately 3 million Americans use a wheelchair, and more than 9 million use some form of ambulatory aid, such as a walker. More than 16 million Americans have some kind of cognitive or mental disorder that interferes with daily activities. Other impairments include those related to sight and hearing. Disabled persons had a lower median income than nondisabled persons, $22,000 compared to $25,000. Persons with a severe disability had a median income of $12,800.[136] Nearly half of U.S. citizens with disabilities have been employed over the past few years.[137] The number of disabled persons is likely to increase over the next 10 years as the population of baby boomers ages, since age itself is a major risk factor for disability.[138] The return of veterans from Iraq and Afghanistan will also increase the number of disabled persons.

Concepts of Disability

Currently there are two competing or contested views of disability in the United States. The first and arguably the dominant one is the medical view. Under this view, a disabled person is defined by what he or she is unable to do, and disability is seen as a deficit or based on a medical condition, such as visual impairment or paralysis. This model of disability is the basis for the federal Social Security Disability Insurance program (see Chapter 2), which gives grants to low-income persons with disabilities whose ability to work is compromised.

A newer and more empowering view of disability focuses on the reaction of others to disabled persons. Under this perspective, disabilities are socially constructed categories that stigmatize and discriminate against those categorized. This view of disability has led to a disability rights movement, which was instrumental in the passage of the Americans with Disabilities Act in 1990. The central tenet of the disability rights movement, similar to that of the civil rights movement, is that differences should not be grounds for discrimination. Disability is primarily an oppressive social construct, according to this view, not an individual, medical phenomenon. It is the individualistic model of disability that gave rise to the stigmatization and shunning characterizing the reaction to disabled persons historically. Instead, activists see disability as an environmental problem based on external constraints that keep persons with impairments from living a full life.[139]

According to this social model of disability, physical impairments or differences are distinct from the social situation or "disability" of persons, which is socially constructed. Physically impaired persons or persons who are different from others are placed in a disabled category, isolated and excluded from full participation in all aspects of society. Exclusion is the result of ignoring persons with impairments or differences when making social and physical arrangements.[140]

It is clear that the concept of disability is a contested one, with the medical and federal welfare establishment resting on one assumption and the disability rights community resting on another. While not ignoring the need for medical treatment in some cases of impairment and not discounting the importance of federal programs like Supplemental Security Income as well as state programs to meet the needs of low-income persons, disability rights activists do not want to be defined by their impairment or difference but rather want to broaden the view of normalcy. In their view, impairment is an ordinary part of life that can affect any person during his or her life, as a result of accident, injury, or chronic illness. Being nondisabled or "able bodied" is at best a temporary state.[141] Instead of focusing on the impairment, disability rights activists want to focus on removing social and environmental barriers.[142]

The origin of both the new definition and the struggle for the rights of persons called disabled first emerged in the 1970s. The movement to reframe disability as related to social exclusion was a profound paradigm shift that began the process of examining environmental and social constraints limiting the full opportunities of disabled persons. This paradigm shift meant that the disadvantage of disability lies in the social reaction to a condition and the unequal status given to the disabled person, not in the condition itself. If all buildings were accessible to wheelchairs, for example, then being in a wheelchair would not be a disadvantage.[143]

Disability Rights Movement

With the disability rights movement, persons who were considered disabled became agents in their own lives, rather than passive recipients of help. Many persons involved with this movement, which culminated in the Americans with Disabilities Act discussed below, had experienced impairment later in life, after living under the guise of "normality" for many years. They thus understood the fluidity of the status of disability and brought a sense of relativity to the experience of oppression and discrimination shared by persons considered disabled.[144]

The initial gains in the disability rights movement came via court rulings. In 1971, the U.S. District Court for the Middle District of Alabama ruled in *Wyatt v. Stickney* that people in residential state schools and institutions have a constitutional right "to receive such individual treatment as (would) give them a realistic opportunity to be cured or to improve his or her mental condition." Disabled people could no longer simply be locked away in "custodial institutions" without treatment or education.[145] This decision was a crucial victory in the struggle for deinstitutionalization as well as the beginning of the modern disability rights movement. In 1972, the U.S. District Court for the District of Columbia, in *Mills v. Board of Education,* ruled that the District of Columbia cannot exclude disabled children from the public schools.[146] Similarly, the U.S. District Court for the Eastern District of Pennsylvania, in *PARC v. Pennsylvania,* struck down various state laws used to exclude disabled children from the public schools.[147] These decisions were crucial to the passage of the Education for All Handicapped Children Act of 1975, now known as IDEA (Individuals with Disabilities Education Act). According to this act, states must develop and implement policies that ensure a free appropriate public education to all children with disabilities in order to receive federal funds.[148]

Access to public transportation was another milestone achieved through court struggles. The Paralyzed Veterans of America, the National Paraplegia Foundation, and Richard Heddinger filed suit to force the Washington Metropolitan Area Transit Authority to incorporate access into their design for a new, multibillion-dollar subway system in Washington, D.C., in 1973. The suit eventually became a landmark in the struggle for accessible public mass transit when courts ruled in the plaintiffs' favor in 1990.[149]

In 1973, another significant milestone in the struggle to end discrimination against persons considered disabled was achieved when Congress passed the Rehabilitation Act, mandating that programs receiving federal funds not discriminate against otherwise qualified individuals who were disabled.[150] Court struggles that followed the passage of the act featured concepts important to the disability rights movement, including "reasonable accommodation," which was central to the Americans with Disabilities Act of 1990. Other milestones of the 1970s included the founding of several disability rights interest groups. As a result of the Rehabilitation Act of 1973, the U.S. Supreme Court ruled in 1987 that persons with infectious diseases who are otherwise qualified for their jobs cannot be fired solely as a result of their contagious condition. This ruling was advanced for persons with HIV/AIDS and tuberculosis, as well as for other groups.[151]

The Americans with Disabilities Act of 1990

The Americans with Disabilities Act (ADA) was an important civil rights measure aimed at eliminating discrimination against individuals who have physical or mental impairments. The act was the result of years of struggles in courts and in legislatures by advocacy groups. Its signing in 1990 was witnessed by thousands of disability rights activists. It mandates that local, state, and federal programs be accessible to all persons, that businesses with more than 15 employees make "reasonable accommodations" for disabled workers, and that public accommodations such as restaurants, hotels, and stores make "reasonable modifications" to ensure access for disabled members of the public. The act also mandates access in public transportation, communication, and other areas of public life, including all levels of education. The act sought to eliminate all discrimination against disabled persons in employment, transportation, public accommodations, communications, and governmental activities. Under the provisions of the ADA, there are three ways one can be deemed disabled: (a) a person has a physical or mental impairment that substantially limits one or more major life activities; (b) a person has a record of such impairment; or (c) a person is regarded as having such impairment. If a person is judged to be disabled, "reasonable accommodations" must be made for that person, unless that creates an "undue hardship."[152] Major life activities were not originally defined in the 1990 act, leaving that task to the agencies responsible for enforcing the ADA and the courts. The initial legal battles about enforcement of the act focused on who was disabled in terms of the law. Courts mandated that an impairment must restrict the person from doing activities of central importance to most people's lives—not just a certain activity. These decisions were criticized by many who claimed that truly disabled individuals were being denied coverage.

The ADA Amendments Act of 2008 was designed to enlarge coverage of the ADA by overturning a series of U.S. Supreme Court cases, which limited the number of persons who could demonstrate they were disabled. These new amendments call for "the definition of disability to be construed in favor of broad coverage of individuals," shifting the burden of proof to those who would deny disabled persons the protection of the law. The amendments favor broad coverage of conditions that interfere with activities of daily living, as well as thinking and learning, working, lifting, and speaking. Unfortunately, the amendments did not clarify the important question in the ADA of what are "reasonable accommodations" that employers must make for disabled persons. Under the amendments, Congress recognized that disabled persons are often denied the right to participate fully in society because of social prejudice, as well as due to the existence of societal and institutional barriers.

With these amendments, Congress embraced the social model of disability.[153] The problem is now assumed to rest on the discriminatory behavior and attitudes of the larger society, not on the impairment or difference presented by persons considered disabled. This represents a sea change in federal policy about disability, mandating that persons with impairments be treated equally to all other persons. Even though there are still areas of difficulty and local failures to comply with the law, the ADA is one of the most important advances in the rights of oppressed groups in American history.

SOCIAL MOVEMENTS AMONG ETHNIC GROUPS AND WOMEN   ●

According to Marx, ethnic and gender conflict is deliberately introduced into capitalist societies as a way of dividing the working class so that its members will not perceive their common economic interests and instead focus on the gender and ethnic tensions that divide them.[154] While it is impossible to determine whether these divisions have been purposely manipulated or have merely grown out of the historical experiences of ethnic groups and women, it is clear that tensions among oppressed groups have been exacerbated by economic inequality. The picture is not bleak, however, as a look at the history of social movements among oppressed groups demonstrates. Every social movement is an implicit challenge to the legitimacy of the prevailing social order, as its goals are sought through unconventional, extrapolitical means.[155] Social movements begun by oppressed groups over the past 50 years have dramatically challenged the status quo in political, cultural, and social arrangements. Their impact has been substantial. Legally segregated public schools are outlawed, as are separate public facilities. Some persons from oppressed ethnic groups and some women have advanced economically into positions of power and wealth. How was Jim Crow overturned? How did Latinos overcome a century of oppression to become a major political and economic force in the Southwest? How did Native Americans achieve a ban on use of American Indian mascots during postseason college games? How did women achieve so much mobility in professions from which they had been virtually excluded? How did a woman and an African American man become major candidates for the presidency in 2008? All these gains began with social movements led by oppressed persons who made demands on government, educational institutions, private enterprise, media, and institutions of power, transforming conditions of oppression and discrimination.

PROFILES IN LEADERSHIP

Martin Luther King, Jr., 1929–1968

Dr. Martin Luther King, Jr.

SOURCE: From the Library of Congress, Prints & Photographs Division, LC-USZ62–100009.

Martin Luther King, Jr., was born on January 15, 1929, in Atlanta, Georgia. His father was a Baptist minister and head of the middle-class family in which Martin was raised. His father hoped that one day he too would become a minister. But deciding to become a minister took years, as the young King considered other careers such as medicine and the law. As a child, many noticed that at an early age he had developed an extensive vocabulary and an impressive way of speaking. As a youngster he was very athletic and participated in many sports, excelling in most of them. His parents often took him to smaller parishes where the young King sang religious songs. King's father made Ebenezer Baptist Church into one of the largest and most prestigious Baptist churches in Atlanta. King's father was also a very accomplished person as he was one of the charter members of the Atlanta Negro Voters League, an active Republican, and a graduate of Morehouse College.

His family's wealth helped to insulate the young King from the worst abuses suffered by poor Blacks in Atlanta at that time. Taking advantage of a special program for gifted students, King was admitted to Morehouse College at the age of 15. He remained living at home during his college years. King was determined to study medicine, which he considered a respectable and socially beneficent profession. However, he eventually came to realize during his college years that he was not suited temperamentally or intellectually for the profession. He changed his mind and decided to major in sociology with the idea that he might eventually pursue a career in the legal profession. Toward the end of his college years, King became very impressed with the comments of the president of the college Dr. Mays during the chapel meetings. Eventually Dr. Mays began to visit the King home and engage the young King in discussions about religion and social issues. Soon after these visits began, King announced to his family that he had decided to enter the ministry.

King attended the prestigious Morehouse College, in Atlanta, a traditionally Black college where his father and grandfather had graduated. Later on King went on to study at Crozer Theological Seminary and Boston University, where he received his PhD. This advanced study gave him the opportunity to study social movements and intellectual leaders, which enabled him to develop his own views about nonviolence, social justice, inequality, and racial issues. King was subsequently introduced to Coretta Scott, who was a graduate of Antioch College. Their courtship culminated in their marriage in 1953 in Alabama. The couple then returned to Boston where King continued his doctoral studies. After his doctoral studies were completed, King returned to the South to become the pastor of Dexter Avenue Baptist Church in Montgomery, Alabama. He had held this post for about a year when Rosa Parks refused to give up her seat on a Montgomery city bus to a White person. News spread fast regarding the arrest of Mrs. Parks, and a major mobilization of Black people was quickly underway.

King was soon recruited to sit on a committee to organize and plan a boycott of the public bus system in Montgomery. King and others contacted community leaders to become involved in the boycott. In addition to this activity, King gave sermons at his church from the pulpit talking about the current crisis, the abuse suffered by Blacks, and the need for the community to protest. What began as a bus boycott in Montgomery was soon to be repeated in urban areas throughout the South mainly for the same reasons. The reaction of the White community was one of shock and in some cases led to violence and bombings. After weeks of tension and protest, the U.S. District Court in 1956 ruled that Alabama's laws requiring segregation on Montgomery public buses were unconstitutional. Reprisals continued for a time, but social justice had finally been achieved, and King had played a key role and was now recognized as a major civil rights leader.

(Continued)

(Continued)

The South resisted integration fiercely, particularly in public institutions like schools and businesses and restaurants and hotels. This triggered massive protests by Black young people who became involved in the famous "sit-ins" at Woolworth's and other restaurants throughout the South. King exhorted federal officials to intervene, with limited success. King soon realized the need for an organization to spearhead the efforts and the need for a nationwide campaign to reward progressive businesses and punish those businesses that remained segregated. He continued to emphasize that nonviolence as a strategy was the best means to achieve the goals of integration, a philosophy he had learned from Gandhi. During the next few years, King spoke out at numerous events and participated in various protests, and he was jailed many times with trumped-up charges.

Having created the Southern Christian Leadership Conference, he struggled to keep up with the demands of this organization and the needs of his congregation. In addition, he was needed in other areas of the country to speak out and to participate in protests and rallies to end segregation. Despite its message of nonviolence, the frustration of the Black community, particularly student members of the Student Nonviolent Coordinating Committee, sometimes led to violent protests and mass arrests. Some criticized King for being too conservative with his nonviolence philosophy.

By the time President Kennedy was assassinated in 1963, King had become nationally recognized as a major civil rights leader. Three months before Kennedy's death, King had led a March on Washington to protest segregation and demand equality for Blacks. It was here, in front of the Lincoln Memorial, that King gave his famous "I have a dream" speech. He had met personally with President Johnson and many of the federal law enforcement officials to discuss the situation in the South. Johnson, at King's urging, had lobbied Congress to pass the Civil Rights Act of 1964 and the Voting Rights Act of 1965, landmark changes that continued to be resisted by Southerners.

As King traveled to Northern cities, he began to see that the exclusive focus on problems in the South had shifted attention away from the severe ghetto conditions in many Northern cities. He also began to speak out against the war in Vietnam and to focus on the issues impacting the poor across the country. King organized a Poor People's march on Washington to focus attention on the needs of the poor and the need for a federal mandate to provide funds to help local communities. King worked with many civil rights leaders from various parts of the country, and they were not always in agreement on tactics and strategies. But King's influence as the moral leader never diminished, and his leadership was inspirational to millions of poor and Black people.

In 1968, an assassin with a high-powered rifle shot and killed Martin Luther King. He may have ended Dr. King's life, but he did not extinguish the dream and the promise that King spoke of, which was to have one America with freedom and justice for all. Dr. King continues to be seen as this country's greatest civil rights leader. In 1964, Dr. Martin Luther King received the Nobel Peace Prize for his struggles for racial equality and social justice.

A social movement, as opposed to a short-lived explosion of protest, grows out of a group consciousness of shared injustice; is triggered by a spontaneous insurgency, such as a work stoppage, a strike, or a bus boycott; features charismatic leadership to articulate the group grievances; establishes a structure or organization external to this leadership to carry on the work of the movement; and is animated by an ideology that lays out a vision of a "just future."[156] All the ethnic groups discussed in this chapter had a consciousness of shared injustice. Each movement for equality and social justice was sparked by individual protests. Consider the refusal of Rosa Parks to move to the back of the bus in Montgomery, Alabama, in 1955. This act of defiance led to the Montgomery bus boycott and brought Martin Luther King, Jr., a Southern Baptist minister from Atlanta, Georgia, into national prominence as an organizer and spokesman for the boycott, in which 50,000 African Americans refused to ride the city buses. King sparked national attention as the leader of the civil rights movement in the South. His oratorical abilities were unmatched, and his leadership was largely responsible for the swelling protests that tore through the South and ultimately touched Northern cities in the 1960s. King's passionate oratory, demonstrating the injustice of segregation, moved Whites across the country, resulting in the end of legal segregation in the South.[157]

In 1957, King, along with other Protestant leaders, founded the Southern Christian Leadership Conference, which was committed to nonviolent resistance. In 1956, the Supreme Court declared laws requiring segregation on buses unconstitutional. The sit-in phase of the civil rights movement began in 1960, when four college students decided on their own to sit at a "Whites-only" lunch counter in Greensboro, North Carolina. In 3 months, sit-ins took place at over 60 public establishments; soon they spread all over the South. Out of this spontaneous movement of students, another new organization was formed, the Student Nonviolent Coordinating Committee, or SNCC. The civil rights movement exposed White Americans in the Northern cities to the injustice of the segregated South; racism seemed to have a face in a police chief setting dogs on young African Americans; other officials used cattle prods and high-powered hoses to break up marches as King called for "freedom and justice."

The legacy of the civil rights movement became permanent when many of its demands were institutionalized in court rulings and federal laws. In 1964, Congress passed—and President Lyndon Johnson signed—a Civil Rights Act outlawing racial discrimination in all public accommodations and forbade discrimination in hiring on grounds of race, gender, religion, or national origin. In 1964, a movement of college students from across the country known as Freedom Summer sponsored a voter registration drive in the South. Three students working in the effort, two Whites and one African American, were murdered, and almost 100 others were beaten by Southerners who objected to their efforts to register African Americans to vote. Congress responded by passing the Voting Rights Act of 1965, which put federal registrars in districts where local officials were obstructing registration of African American voters. As a result of the effort to enfranchise African Americans in the South, the number of Black elected officials there tripled (from 1,000 to 3,000 from 1969 to 1975), and more than 930,000 new African American voters were added to registration rolls in the South.[158]

When civil rights leaders, including King, turned their attention to the Northern cities, the situation was more complex; instead of laws mandating segregation, reformers found patterns of residential and economic segregation that had existed for 100 years and were resistant to simple legal change. Northern Whites, who were sympathetic to African American efforts to overturn Jim Crow in the South, were hostile to activists marching in Northern cities demanding that their way of life change. More militancy among some African American leaders resulted in Northern Whites turning away from demands for equality and social justice, and the movement all but died out, with much left undone.

Why did the movement for civil rights begin in the 1950s and swell in the 1960s? The economic growth, educational expansion, and geographic mobility that occurred in the United States after World War II encouraged a new vision

Civil rights protesters

SOURCE: From the Library of Congress, U.S. News & World Report Magazine Photograph Collection.

of a moral order based on equality and social justice. The immediate impetus of the civil rights movement was the 1954 Supreme Court decision *Brown v. Board of Education*, which declared segregated schools unconstitutional. But the civil rights movement caught fire as a result of the spontaneous uprising of African Americans in the South. Assertion of ethnic pride and protest against unequal treatment were features of other movements for social justice during this period, which were inspired by the original civil rights movement.[159]

PROFILES IN LEADERSHIP

Fannie Lou Hamer, 1917–1977

Fannie Lou Hamer was born in 1917 in Montgomery County, Mississippi. She was 1 of a large family of 20 children. Her parents were sharecroppers, and her grandmother had been enslaved. When she was 2 years old, the family moved to the Delta, a rich agricultural area near the Mississippi River. The family made a living chopping cotton, growing vegetables, and doing odd jobs. Her father was a well-known and respected man in the community, and Hamer benefited from living in a family with a positive reputation in the local area. At that time, Mississippi was a very poor state, and income disparity was the greatest of any state in the union. The Ku Klux Klan was very active, and there were frequent murders and assaults of Blacks.

In 1929, the family's fortune seemed to change for the better. Hamer's father was able to lease land and move the family to a new farm. He bought an automobile and purchased farm equipment and animals to work his own land.

Fannie Lou Hamer

SOURCE: From Library of Congress, U.S. News & World Report Magazine Photograph Collection.

(Continued)

(Continued)

It appeared that the family could finally leave the life of sharecropping, where families would work the land owned by Whites in exchange for access to free housing, seed, and farm equipment. Unfortunately, at the end of the year, there would be no profit for the family as the White owner would deduct the cost of the seed and equipment, leaving the family with nothing.

As things were looking up, tragedy struck when one of the White neighbors poisoned the family's farm animals, making it impossible to farm the land. The family had to return to sharecropping and was even worse off than before. Hamer had to quit school and work full-time in the fields. She deeply regretted leaving school as she had been an excellent student. Having left school, her only option to learn was to read the Bible in Sunday school. She had left school in the sixth grade, which was as much school as the majority of Blacks completed in the public education system at the time. At that time, the educational system in Mississippi was controlled by the plantation owners, and expenditures on Black education were outrageously low, even though Blacks made up 50% of the state's population. Under the Jim Crow laws of the South, Blacks were not allowed to attend the University of Mississippi and could not eat in restaurants, and all accommodations were listed as White or Colored.

In 1940, Hamer met and married Perry Hamer, a tractor driver on a nearby farm. They moved from the family home and settled in the community of Ruleville, Mississippi. Hamer and her husband never had any children of their own, but they did take in two girls whom they raised as their own. The owner of the plantation where her husband worked realized that Fannie Hamer was smart, literate, and good with figures. He hired her as a timekeeper, and this helped keep her from farm work. Mississippi had remained relatively unchanged since the end of Reconstruction in 1875. Segregation in all areas of life was maintained under Jim Crow. This system began to change after World War II, as thousands of young Black men who had served in the armed forces began to return to Mississippi. These young men had been exposed to other parts of the country and the world where segregation was not the norm. They were outraged when they realized that in Mississippi they could not vote, attend college, or find a decent job. Many refused to accept the status quo and began to push for social and economic justice.

In 1954, the Supreme Court ruled in *Brown v. Board of Education* that racially segregated public schools were illegal and unconstitutional. This major court decision had far-reaching impact in the South. In response to the Supreme Court's ruling, a group of White men in Mississippi created the White Citizens' Council, essentially making it impossible for anyone who advocated desegregation to find and hold a job, obtain credit, or renew a mortgage. Soon after, there were several brutal murders of young Black people who were trying to register Black people to vote. Despite the continued activities of the Ku Klux Klan, such as burning crosses on people's front yards to terrify them, resistance to the segregated system was beginning to grow. In Alabama, federal troops had to be brought in to integrate

Little Rock Central High School in 1957, and in some communities "sit-ins" were being mounted to desegregate lunch counters. In addition, "Freedom Riders" were taking interstate bus trips to challenge Jim Crow customs and local laws.

Hamer became interested in the voting rights issue after attending a meeting of the Southern Christian Leadership Conference. She realized that social and economic change would only come to Mississippi when Black people could vote and achieve political power. In 1962, Hamer traveled by bus to the county courthouse in Indianola to try to register. At that time, there were many barriers such as literacy tests, poll taxes, hostile city police, and local public officials who strongly discouraged Blacks from voting with the threat of force.

At the age of 45, Hamer was invited to attend a leadership training conference in Nashville, Tennessee, participating in workshops about voter registration and nonviolence and communication skills. She was a natural leader, was fearless, and continued to try and register herself and others to vote. In 1963, she passed the literacy test administered by the White registrar and was finally able to vote. Hamer continued to try to educate other Blacks about how to register, how to pass the literacy tests, and other details of the Mississippi voting laws. In 1963, she attended a voter registration workshop in South Carolina, and while returning with others by bus, they were stopped and arrested by local police. All were taken to the local jail, charged with challenging the segregation laws. Most of those incarcerated were beaten, but Hamer received the worst injuries and was hospitalized. Hamer's injuries were so severe that even her family was not allowed to visit her for weeks while she recovered from the severe beating.

In 1964, Hamer shocked the television audience at the National Democratic Convention by challenging the legitimacy of the all-White Mississippi delegation. This act outraged the credentials committee of the Democratic Party and others including President Lyndon Johnson who was himself a Southerner. She exposed the racist practices of Mississippi and revealed to the nation the brutal oppression that had kept Black and poor people powerless. President Johnson was so furious that he quickly called a national press conference to make a few announcements in order to shift media attention away from Hamer's remarks. It was too late, as the media printed articles about conditions in Mississippi and Hamer's comments. With national recognition, she was now invited to speak across the country at major political events, and she continued to raise money for local projects in Mississippi. The 1964 Civil Rights Act and the 1965 Voting Rights Act finally provided federal marshals at polling places, eliminated White-only primaries, and provided basic constitutional voting rights for Black people.

In the early 1970s, Hamer's health began to deteriorate, and she was hospitalized several times. She died of heart failure in March 1977, at the age of 59. She was instrumental in bringing social, economic, and political change to one of the most segregated and oppressive states in the country. She had a vision for social justice that she never lost, and she was fearless in pursuing her dream. She was never afraid to speak out for poor and oppressed people, and she helped to bring major change not only to her state but to the nation as well.

As a result of the Black Power movement, which followed the initial movement for civil rights led by King, the meaning of Black identity was politicized and reframed from an emphasis on individual struggle to collective action.[160] The same transformation was to occur subsequently in the Chicano and American Indian movements.[161] In this way the civil rights movement was a direct model for the other ethnic movements of the 1960s and 1970s and an indirect model for the feminist movement, the gay and lesbian movement, and the student movement against the Vietnam War.[162]

The civil rights movement was one impetus for the feminist movement in this period. Women's liberation, as the feminist movement of the 1970s was known, grew out of women's participation in the civil rights movement in the South. As women worked alongside men, they told of being marginalized and assigned gender-related tasks. Many of these women became leaders of the feminist movement when they returned home.[163] Meanwhile, Betty Friedan's *The Feminine Mystique,* published in 1963, galvanized middle-class White women living the lives of domesticity and submissiveness urged on them a century earlier. As the cultural leader of the feminist movement, Friedan was responsible for the overturning of the Cult of True Womanhood among educated, middle-class, White women, who were its original targets in the 19th century. College attendance and labor force participation among middle-class White women increased dramatically in the 1960s and 1970s, setting the stage for a rejection of the notion that the domestic sphere was the only appropriate one for women. Friedan was one of the founders of the National Organization for Women (NOW) in 1966, an organization with half a million members. Soon after its founding, NOW sponsored the Equal Rights Amendment (ERA) to the U.S. Constitution, which would have guaranteed equal rights for women. However, the ERA was not ratified by a sufficient number of states and was never revived. While the cultural aspects of the feminist movement continued among middle-class women, the movement never regained its original political momentum. After the 1980s, the feminist movement moved away from a sole focus on concerns of White middle-class women and embraced the perspectives of women of color, including race and class identities. Activists were committed to demonstrating how these multiple identities interact simultaneously in women. In this way, feminism has moved away from the limited standpoint of White middle-class women to encompass the diverse standpoints of all women.[164]

PROFILES IN LEADERSHIP

Cesar Chavez, 1927–1993

Cesar Chavez, community activist, moral leader, and union organizer, was born in 1927 in Yuma, Arizona, to a small-scale farmer and his wife. Although the family was poor, his early life was fairly stable, and he was surrounded by a loving extended family. All this was to change in 1937 when the family was forced to leave the farm because it was unable to pay the increased property taxes. The uprooted family members fled to California where they became migrant farm workers. A few years later, to add to the family's misfortune, Chavez's father was injured in an automobile accident and was unable to work. This forced young Cesar to quit school and work in the fields full-time along with his brother and sister.

Cesar Chavez

SOURCE: Corbis.

As farm workers, Chavez and others were confronted by miserable and dangerous working conditions, exploitation by wealthy farm owners, and the experience of feeling powerless to make any changes or improvements in their lives. They lived in numerous migrant camps and were often forced to sleep in their car. Chavez himself attended more than 30 elementary schools. The family traveled constantly across the state, seeking one harvesting job after another. After several years of toiling in the fields, Chavez decided to join the Navy in 1944, where he served in World War II. Exhausted by years of working in the fields, he hoped to acquire a skill or trade

(Continued)

(Continued)

that would provide an avenue for advancement. Chavez experienced substantial racial discrimination in the military as a Latino. Upon discharge from the military, he sought work away from the fields, but he was unsuccessful, so he returned to farm work where this type of work was plentiful.

After he returned from service in World War II, Chavez began to read about labor history, along with biographies of Gandhi, whose philosophy of nonviolence impressed him greatly. In 1952, Chavez met Fred Ross, who was part of a group called the Community Service Organization (CSO) founded by Saul Alinsky. As a result, he began organizing Mexican American farm workers throughout California, urging them to register and vote. One of his responsibilities in the CSO was to examine the California Bracero Program, which brought workers from Mexico to work in the fields during harvest season. Chavez believed that this program was exploitive of farm workers, and he worked to propose changes to improve the program. In 1962, Chavez left the CSO to form the National Farm Workers Association (NFWA), later changed to United Farm Workers (UFW). At this time, he moved to Delano, California, in the central valley of the state where many farm workers lived and worked. He took a deep interest in the potential of unions to fight for the rights of farm workers and to advocate for better working conditions. He realized that the power of the farm owners could not be challenged unless the farm workers had a vehicle to speak for them. Unions had been successful in other industries in other parts of the country, and they had won a number of successful victories. Unions, however, had not been organized in the agricultural sector of the California economy, due to strong objections from business and agricultural farm owners.

Chavez struggled to recruit union members as he traveled to various parts of the state. In addition to growers' opposition to unionize their workers, he also had to convince the workers that it was possible to improve their working conditions. Worker skepticism was based on the belief that the powerful growers could not be persuaded or influenced by large numbers of low-income farm workers. Chavez worked tirelessly to recruit new members, and by 1970, he had effectively organized over 50,000 dues-paying members.

From 1965 through the early 1990s, the NFWA organized and carried out a series of protest marches and boycotts designed to expose the dangerous and poor working conditions of farm workers. These activities of the NFWA resulted in intense opposition and confrontation by antiunion forces. During this period, thousands of workers were arrested, hundreds of strikers were beaten, dozens were shot, and two were murdered. Chavez himself, as the leader of the protest movements, was jailed. Chavez increased his efforts to pressure legislators and was able to obtain public attention by organizing a Delano grape strike, mounting a 340-mile march by hundreds of workers from Delano to Sacramento and, like Gandhi, engaging in public fasts that brought national attention to the issues facing farm workers. He was also able to enlist the support of organized labor, religious groups, ethnic communities, political figures, major entertainment people, and students across the country. Through all of this, Chavez continued his commitment to nonviolent protest, believing that hard work, faith, and a willingness to sacrifice would eventually prevail despite the overwhelming opposition.

In 1975, with the support of Governor Brown and intense support and pressure from other prominent Americans after much conflict, the California legislature finally passed the California Labor Relations Act that provided for elections, the right to boycott, voting rights for union members, and provisions related to the timing of elections. This landmark legislation finally recognized the legal rights that had been demanded by the NFWA and opened the way for workplace improvements for farm workers. In 1988, at the age of 61, Chavez began his last public fast to call attention to the farm worker families affected by dangerous pesticides used in the fields on various crops. In 1993, Cesar Chavez died in his sleep. In 1994, President Clinton awarded Chavez the Medal of Freedom, America's highest civilian honor, after his death. The president commended Chavez for overcoming formidable, often violent opposition while pursuing his mission with dignity and a commitment to nonviolence.

Coming from a humble background, Cesar Chavez rose to a position of leadership because of his determination in the face of major opposition, his courage to keep fighting for the rights of workers, and his unwavering belief that social justice should be extended to everyone. His legacy of courage and leadership improved the lives of generations of farm workers, and he will be particularly remembered for his efforts on behalf of the millions of people who quietly toil in the agricultural fields of California.

The Chicano movement began in the agricultural fields of the Southwest. Migrant farm workers, most of them Mexican American, had been left out of the New Deal reforms that promoted the rights of workers, including the right to unionize, the right to be covered by the federal minimum wage, and the right to receive Unemployment Insurance Benefits. Farm workers were not covered by Social Security and thus had no federal protection for retirement. Their working conditions were poor; they received low wages, were forced to live in substandard housing provided by growers, and had no benefits or protections from job-related injuries. In 1965, the Filipino grape workers walked out of the vineyards in Delano, California, to protest the low wages and poor working conditions maintained by the growers. Cesar Chavez and the farm workers he represented joined the strike action in Delano, and the United Farm Workers organization was founded. Growers refused to negotiate with the union, evicted farm workers from their living quarters, and hired strikebreakers. The Delano grape strike lasted 5 years and became the grape boycott, attracting widespread national support and bringing Chavez international recognition as the leader of oppressed farm workers in the Southwestern states. While the grape strike ended in 1970 with a contract between the growers and the workers, another strike began that same year when vegetable workers walked off the fields in Central California. The largest farm labor strike in U.S. history followed. The strike was marked by violence and intimidation on the part of the growers, who resisted Chavez's union efforts. Labor protest continued until 1975, when the state of California signed a law giving farm workers the right to organize and bargain collectively. However, labor unrest continued in California, and as growers continued to resist unionization, Chavez undertook a series of fasts to protest the actions of growers, especially their continued use of harmful pesticides in the fields. By galvanizing public support for the farm workers and by institutionalizing farm workers' right to unionize for the first time, Chavez, along with Dolores Huerta, the vice president of the United Farm Workers, achieved a monumental legal and moral victory.[165] Later, political considerations muted the progressive effect of the Agricultural Labor Relations Board created by the state to oversee relations between the union and growers, when conservatives appointed representatives from agribusiness to the board. As a consequence, the conditions under which farm workers live and work continue to be oppressive.

Inspired by his Catholic faith and his own suffering as a migrant worker from the age of 10, Chavez fought discrimination and economic deprivation. His sole goal was to organize farm workers so that the unjust conditions of their lives would be eliminated. In 1984, he wrote, "I have been driven by one dream, one goal, one vision: To overthrow a system that treats farm workers as if they are not important human beings."[166]

While most Latinos in the United States were not farm workers, the union movement brought visibility to the unequal conditions suffered by urban Latinos. A Chicano movement emerged in the late 1960s and 1970s, emphasizing ethnic nationalism and pride in Mexican heritage. Eventually cultural nationalism and ethnic pride spread to all Latino ethnic groups, especially Puerto Ricans. Latino groups fought for political empowerment and an end to discrimination and engaged in struggles for community control in urban areas dominated by Latinos. The movement was important on college campuses, where a sense of Chicanos as colonized people and a rejection of assimilationist strategies emerged.[167] The Chicano movement was an example of "resilient ethnicity," which has emerged as a new model of ethnic reality in the United States. Under this model of ethnicity, asserting one's ethnic difference with pride replaced the drift toward assimilation. The Black Power movement in the

1960s—and its charismatic leader Malcolm X—was the first such movement, now the norm among oppressed ethnic groups seeking social justice.[168] Closely aligned with nationalism, the reassertion of a distinct and coherent ethnicity sometimes called on an idealized past and a rootedness outside the United States, in Africa or Mexico.[169] Even as European immigrant groups continued to merge into the "White" group, after 1965, African Americans, Latinos, Native Americans, and Asian Americans developed separate and distinct identities and began to compete for cultural and political recognition.[170]

We have already seen how Native Americans rewrote the history of their interaction with Whites and reclaimed their culture in the American Indian movement of the 1970s. As we look at the effects of social movements, we can see some concrete legal changes along with policies recognizing the rights of oppressed groups (such as the Indian Child Welfare Act of 1978; see Chapter 8). Social and cultural changes have also flowed from these social movements; perhaps the best example is the cultural reframing of gender for middle-class women and men and a revision of working conditions for women (sexual harassment laws). In terms of lasting political and especially economic changes, the effects are less clear. Political marginalization has not been substantially reduced. The vast majority of the members of Congress are White men, as are most of the governors of the 50 states. See Table 5.3 for a summary of social movements by oppressed groups.

TABLE 5.3   Social Movements Among Oppressed Groups in the United States

Year and/or Period	Movement and Description
1950s and 1960s	Civil Rights Movement—ended legal segregation in the South
1960s	Black Power Movement—meaning of Black identity and focus on collective action rather than individual struggle
1970s	American Indian Movement—rewrote history and reclaimed their culture
1970s	Feminist Movement—women's liberation and equal rights for women
1960s and 1970s	Chicano Movement—improved labor conditions for farm workers, Chicano nationalism and pride
1960s and 1970s	Gay and Lesbian Movement—equal rights
1960s and 1970s	Student Movement—against Vietnam War
1970s and 1980s	Disability Rights Movement

As we have seen in Chapter 4, economic inequality is still pronounced along ethnic and gender lines. Some argue that the so-called politics of identity, which involves a recognition and appreciation of cultural diversity, has become a distraction from the deeper problem of economic inequality, discussed in Chapter 4.[171] Of course, these issues are intertwined, not mutually exclusive; a recognition of cultural and ethnic diversity does not preclude an examination of economic inequality, but neither does such a recognition solve the problems of poverty and inequality.

All these movements for social change featured the core elements of a social movement, including charismatic leadership and the establishment of an ongoing organization. All promoted an ideology of a socially just future and, with the exception of the feminist movement, were inspired by a spontaneous insurgency, including the occupation of Alcatraz by Native Americans discussed earlier in this chapter. Each movement was fueled by group consciousness of unjust treatment. Inspired by the civil rights movement, most of these movements were nonviolent and democratic, protesting unjust conditions with the only strategy likely to move the consciences of a majority of Americans, nonviolence.[172]

Social movements have traditionally emerged outside of the political process, because oppressed persons have little access to political structures to effect change. Only with actions outside the political mainstream have social actors been able to move the political process, by galvanizing political opinion in their favor. Piven and Cloward argue that the politics of disruption is the only method poor people and others with little or no power have to influence the political process in their favor.[173] The social movements discussed above embraced the idea of rights, along with freedom and equal opportunity. All the social movements of the last 50 years were built on the ideologies discussed in Chapter 3, including equality of opportunity, liberty, and fairness, as well as freedoms of speech, press, and assembly. Thus these movements drew on American values and utilized the opportunities for free speech and assembly to promote their positions. One of their legacies is the realization that despite centuries of oppression, collective action on the part of groups can be successful in promoting social justice in the United States. What are the possible configurations of a social movement that would unravel the remaining patterns of discrimination discussed in this chapter? The civil rights movement succeeded in overturning Jim Crow because it focused on a clear target in a drama peopled by real heroes and villains. Currently, the racial hegemony of Whites is more systemic, and the targets, embedded in a complex structure of social and economic power, are more obscure.[174] Yet there is no question that all is possible, that discrimination can be unbundled and institutional racism dismantled through collective will, since the entire structure of discrimination is human in origin and held in place by our assent, as with all other social arrangements.

In this chapter we have seen how historical and contemporary forces of *discrimination* have operated to create and continue oppression of certain ethnic groups and women in the United States. Interacting with both the historical values developed in the United States and the economic inequalities sustained by market capitalism, the ideologies that promote discrimination are part of a worldview of many Americans. The consequence of their unblinking acceptance has been the social construction of devastating social problems, as well as of social policies inadequate to their solution. The following chapters of the text will illustrate how these forces inform major social welfare policies in the United States.

DISCUSSION QUESTIONS

1. What are the sources of racism in American society? Do you think the "racial contract" is a useful way of thinking about discrimination in the United States?

2. What is the difference between race and ethnicity?

3. What are the dangers of essentialism in discussing gender and ethnicity?

4. Do you think racism still affects African Americans and members of other ethnic groups? Give examples to support your opinion.

5. Why are Americans so ambivalent about immigrants from Latin America? What is the source of the nativism against Latino immigrants?

6. Why were Asians considered the "model minority"? Why do we lump all Asians together as one group?

7. What policy changes would substantially reduce the effects of discrimination on oppressed ethnic groups?

8. Why were many Americans unwilling to ratify the Equal Rights Amendment to the Constitution protecting women from various forms of discrimination?

9. What policy changes would promote social justice for women? For LGBT persons?

10. Are there social movements you can identify in the United States today? Where do you see the next important social movement emerging?

NOTES

1. American Anthropological Association, "Statement on Race," May 17, 1998, http://www.aaanet.org/issues/policy-advocacy/AAA-Statement-on-Race.cfm, ¶ 1; Scott MacEachern, "The Concept of Race in Anthropology," in *Race and Ethnicity* (New York: Prentice Hall, 2003), 24–26.

2. Human Genome Project, "Insights Learned from the Human DNA Sequence," http://www.ornl.gov/sci/techresources/Human_Genome/project/journals/insights.shtml, accessed October 7, 2007.

3. Jennifer Guglielmo and Salvatore Salerno, eds., *Are Italians White? How Race Is Made in America* (New York: Routledge, 2003).

4. Timothy Meagher, "Racial and Ethnic Relations in America, 1965–2000," in Ronald Bayor, ed., *Race and Ethnicity in America* (New York: Columbia University Press, 2003), 193–241.

5. Josh Miller and Ann Marie Garran, *Racism in the United States* (Belmont, CA: Brooks Cole, 2008), 22.

6. Miller and Garran, *Racism in the United States,* 26.

7. Charles Mills, *The Racial Contract* (Ithaca, NY: Cornell University Press, 1997), 125–126.

8. Mills, *The Racial Contract,* 11.

9. Mills, *The Racial Contract,* 85.

10. Mills, *The Racial Contract,* 60, 93.

11. Donna Haraway, "Situated Knowledges: The Science Question in Feminism and the Privilege of Partial Perspective," *Feminist Studies* 14 (Fall 1988), 575–599.

12. Karl Mannheim, *Ideology and Utopia* (San Diego, CA: Harcourt Brace Jovanovich, 1936/1985), 3–16.

13. Gordon Hodson, John Dovidio, and Samuel Gaertner, "The Aversive Form of Racism," in Jean Lau Chin, ed., *The Psychology of Prejudice,* Vol. 1 (Westport, CT: Praeger, 2004), 119–137, 120.

14. Miller and Garran, *Racism in the United States,* 96.

15. Howard Karger and David Stoesz, *American Social Welfare Policy: A Pluralist Approach* (Boston: Pearson, 2006), 61.

16. Michael Brown, Marin Carnoy, Elliott Currie, Troy Duster, David Openheier, Marjorie Shultz, and David Wellman, *White-Washing Race* (Berkeley: University of California Press, 1993), x–xi.

17. George Lipsitz, *The Possessive Investment in Whiteness: How White People Profit From Identity Politics* (Philadelphia: Temple University Press, 1998).

18. Mills, *The Racial Contract,* 127.

19. Miller and Garran, *Racism in the United States,* 27.

20. Mary E. Swigonski, "Challenging Privilege Through Africentric Social Work Practice," *Social Work* 41 (March 1996): 153–161; Peggy McIntosh, "White Privilege and Male Privilege: A Personal Account of Coming to See Correspondences Through Work in Women's Studies," in Margaret Anderson and Patricia Hill Collins, eds, *Race, Class and Gender: An Anthology* (Belmont, CA: Wadsworth, l992), 70–81.

21. Brown et al., *White-Washing Race,* 18.

22. Miller and Garran, *Racism in the United States,* 63–66.

23. Catrina Brown, "Feminist Postmodernism and the Challenge of Diversity," in Adrienne S. Chambon and Allan Irving, eds., *Essays on Postmodernism and Social Work* (Toronto, Ontario, Canada: Canadian Scholar's Press, 1994), 33–45.

24. Alan Dawley, "Is Race the Problem for the 21st Century?" in *African American Urban Experience* (New York: Palgrave Macmillan, 2004), 31–334, 320.

25. George Frederickson, *Racism* (Princeton, NJ: Princeton University Press, 2002), 155.

26. Bruce Johansen, *The Native Peoples of North America* (New Brunswick, NJ: Rutgers University Press, 2005), 12–14.

27. Gary Nash and Julie Jeffrey, *The American People: Creating and Nation and a Society,* 7th ed. (New York: Pearson Longman, 2006), 17.

28. Nash and Jeffrey, *The American People,* 20–21.

29. Miller and Garran, *Racism in the United States,* 38.

30. Nash and Jeffrey, *The American People,* 88.

31. Johansen, *The Native Peoples of North America,* 211–213.

32. Ronald Takaki, *A Different Mirror: A History of Multicultural America* (Boston: Little, Brown, and Co., 1993), 228–233.

33. Johansen, *The Native Peoples of North America,* 300–301.

34. Takaki, *A Different Mirror,* 238.

35. Johansen, *The Native Peoples of North America,* 307.

36. Johansen, *The Native Peoples of North America,* 308–315.

37. Thomas Jefferson, *Notes on the State of Virginia* (Philadelphia: Pritchard and Hall, 1800), 157; Thomas Jefferson to John Holmes, April 22, 1820, in Paul Ford, ed., *The Works of Thomas Jefferson,* Vol. 13 of 20 (New York: T. MacCoun, 1892–1899), 159.

38. Edmund Morgan, *American Slavery, American Freedom: The Ordeal of Colonial Virginia* (New York: Norton, 1975); Barbara Fields, "Slavery, Race and Ideology in the United States of America," *New Left Review* 181 (May 1990): 95–118.

39. C. Vann Woodward, *Origins of the New South* (Baton Rouge: Louisiana State University Press, 1951); Rayford Logan, *The Negro in American Life and Thought: The Nadir, 1877–1901* (New York: Van Nostrand Reinhold, 1970).

40. Nash and Jeffrey, *The American People,* 536–537.

41. Jillian Jimenez, "The History of Grandmothers in the African American Community," *Social Service Review* 76 (December 2002): 523–551.

42. Lois Rita Hembold, "Beyond the Family Economy: Black and White Working-Class Women During the Great Depression," in Melvin Dubofsky and Stephen Burwood, eds., *Women and Minorities During the Great Depression* (New York: Garland, 1990), 630–645.

43. Jimenez, "The History of Grandmothers in the African American Community," 535–541.

44. Takaki, *A Different Mirror,* 368.

45. Quoted in Nash and Jeffrey, *The American People,* 578.

46. Timothy Meagher, "Racial and Ethnic Relations in America, 1965–2000," 193–241.

47. Meagher, "Racial and Ethnic Relations in America, 1965–2000," 195.

48. Winthrop Jordan, *The White Man's Burden* (New York: Oxford University Press, 1974).

49. Edmund Morgan, *American Slavery, American Freedom,* 65–71.

50. Karger and Stoesz, *American Social Welfare Policy,* 62–63.

51. Economic Policy Institute, "African Americans in the Current Recovery," April 6, 2005, http://www.epi.org/economic_snapshots/entry/webfeatures_snapshots_20050406/, accessed October 23, 2007; Ronald Mincy, "Preface," in Ronald Mincy, ed., *Black Males Left Behind* (Washington, DC: The Urban Institute Press, 2006), ix–1, xiv.

52. Harry Holzer, "Expanding the African American Middle Class: Improving Labor Market Outcomes," Testimony before the U.S. Commission on Civil Rights, July 15, 2005, http://www.urban.org/UploadedPDF/900828_holzer_072905.pdf, accessed October 23, 2007.

53. Harry Holzer and Paul Offner, "Trends in the Employment Outcomes of Young Black Men, 1979–2000," in Ronald Mincy, ed., *Black Males Left Behind* (Washington, DC: The Urban Institute Press, 2006), 11–39.

54. William M. Rogers, "Forecasting the Labor Market Prospects of Less-Educated Americans," in Ronald Mincy, ed., *Black Males Left Behind* (Washington, DC: The Urban Institute Press, 2006), 39–67.

55. U.S. Census Bureau, "Hispanic Population 2006," http://www.census.gov/population/socdemo/hispanic/cps2006/CPS_Powerpoint_2006.pdf, accessed March 31, 2009.

56. Ibid.

57. Tom Gray, "Teaching With Documents: The Treaty of Guadalupe Hidalgo," The National Archives Web site, http://www.archives.gov/education/lessons/guadalupe-hidalgo/, accessed March 31, 2009.

58. Juan Gonzalez, *Harvest of Empire: A History of Latinos in America* (New York: Penguin Books, 2000), 44.

59. Takaki, *A Different Mirror,* 172–177.

60. Juan Gonzalez, *Harvest of Empire,* 100–102.

61. Earl Shorris, *Latinos: A Biography of the People* (New York: Norton, 1992), 32.

62. David Weber, *Foreigners in Their Native Land: Historical Roots of the Mexican Americans (*Albuquerque: University of New Mexico Press, 1973), vi.

63. Shorris, *Latinos,* 40–41.

64. Gonzalez, *Harvest of Empire,* 202–203.

65. U.S. Census Bureau, http://factfinder.census.gov/home/saff/main.html?, accessed November 3, 2007.

66. Roberto R. Ramirez and G. Patricia de la Cruz, "The Hispanic Population in the United States," March 2002, Current Population Reports P20–545, U.S. Census Bureau, June 2003, http://www.census.gov/prod/2003pubs/p20–545.pdf, accessed November 19, 2007.

67. Gonzalez, *Harvest of Empire,* 108–114.

68. Margaret L. Hunter, "If You're Light, You're Alright: Light Skin Color as Social Capital for Women of Color," *Gender and Society* 16 (April 2002): 175–193; Ronald E. Hall, "A Descriptive Methodology of Color Bias in Puerto Rico: Manifestations of Discrimination in the New Millennium," *Journal of Applied Social Psychology* 32 (July 2002): 1527–1537.

69. U.S. Immigration Support, "History of Cuban Immigration to the United States," http://www.usimmigrationsupport.org/cubanimmigration.html, accessed November 4, 2007.

70. Megan Day, The Central American Foreign Born in the United States, Migration Information source, April 2006, http://www.migrationinformation.org/US focus/display.cfm?ID=38535, retrieved November 9, 2007.

71. Michael Omi and Howard Winant, *Racial Formation in the United States From the 1960s to the 1990s* (New York: Routledge, 1994), 108–109.

72. Jeffrey Schultz, *Encyclopedia of Minorities in American Politics* (New York: Greenwood Press, 2000), 402.

73. Roberto R. Ramirez and G. Patricia de la Cruz, "The Hispanic Population in the United States," March 2002, Current Population Reports P20–545, U.S. Census Bureau, June 2003, http://www.census.gov/prod/2003pubs/p20–545.pdf, accessed November 19, 2007.

74. Gordon Allport, *The Nature of Prejudice* (Reading, MA: Addison, Wesley, 1979), 227–229.

75. Gonzalez, *Harvest of Empire,* 232–273.

76. Jeffrey Passel and Roberto Suro, "Rise, Peak and Decline: Trends in U.S. Immigration 1992–2004," Pew Hispanic Center, September 25, 2005, http://pewhispanic.org/reports/report.php?ReportID=53, accessed November 8, 2007.

77. Jeffrey Passel, "The Size and Characteristics of the Unauthorized Migrant Population in the U.S.," March 7, 2006, http://pewhispanic.org/files/reports/61.pdf, accessed November 9, 2007.

78. Jeffrey Passel, "Growing Number of Immigrants Choosing Naturalization," Pew Hispanic Center, March 28, 2007, http://pewhispanic.org/reports/report.php?ReportID=74, accessed November 9, 2007.

79. Pew Hispanic Center, "The State of American Public Opinion on Immigration in Spring 2006," May 17, 2006, http://pewhispanic.org/factsheets/factsheet.php?FactsheetID=18, accessed November 9, 2007.

80. Passel, "The Size and Characteristics of the Unauthorized Migrant Population in the U.S."

81. Pew Hispanic Center, "The State of American Public Opinion on Immigration in Spring 2006."

82. The Migration Policy Institute, "What Kind of Work Do Immigrants Do?" January 2005, http://www.migrationpolicy.org/pubs/five_industry_occupation_foreign_born.pdf, accessed November 9, 2007.

83. Roberto R. Ramirez and G. Patricia de la Cruz, "The Hispanic Population in the United States," March 2002, Current Population Reports P20–545, U.S. Census Bureau, June 2003, http://www.census.gov/prod/2003pubs/p20–545.pdf, accessed November 19, 2007.

84. Gonzalez, *Harvest of Empire,* 204, 205.

85. Ali Behdad, *A Forgetful Nation: On Immigration and Cultural Identity in the United States* (Durham, NC: Duke University Press, 2005), 16–17.

86. Jessica S. Barnes and Claudette E. Bennett, "The Asian Population: 2000," U.S. Census Bureau, February 2002, http://www.census.gov/prod/2002pubs/c2kbr01–16.pdf, accessed November 13, 2007.

87. Edward Said, *Orientalism* (New York: Vintage Books, 1979).

88. Takaki, *A Different Mirror,* 405–406; Elmer Sandmeyer, *The Anti-Chinese Movement in California* (Urbana: University of Illinois Press, 1991), 25–40.

89. Takaki, *A Different Mirror,* 191–215, 205; Nash and Jeffrey, *The American People,* 673.

90. Sucheng Chan, "The Exclusion of Chinese Women, 1870–1943," in Wang Gungwu, ed., *Chinese America: History and Perspectives* (Brisbane, CA: Chinese Historical Society, 1994), 75–127.

91. Takaki, *A Different Mirror,* 209.

92. Him Mark Lai, *Becoming Chinese American* (Walnut Creek: CA, Alta Mira Press, 2004), 20–21; Benson Tong, *The Chinese Americans* (Boulder: University of Colorado Press, 2003), 30–66.

93. Takaki, *A Different Mirror,* 272–274.

94. Miller and Garran, *Racism in the United States,* 45.

95. Takaki, *A Different Mirror,* 273.

96. Nash and Jeffrey, *The American People,* 838–839.

97. Kathy Rim, "Model, Victim, or Problem Minority?" Paper presented at the annual meeting of the American Political Science Association, Marriott, Loews Philadelphia, and the Pennsylvania Convention Center, Philadelphia, August 31, 2006, http://www.allacademic.com/meta/p153419_index.html, accessed November 13, 2007.

98. Veltisezar Bautista, *The Filipino Americans (1763–Present): Their History, Culture, and Traditions,* 2nd ed. (Naperville, IL: Bookhaus, 2002).

99. Takaki, *A Different Mirror,* 416–417.

100. Bruce Jansson, *The Reluctant Welfare State* (Belmont, CA: Brooks Cole, 2001), 266–267.

101. Pew Hispanic Center, "Wealth Gap Widens Between Whites and Hispanics," October 18, 2004, http://pewhispanic.org/newsroom/releases/release.php?ReleaseID=15, accessed November 24, 2007.

102. The Annie Casey Foundation, "Children in Single-Parent Families by Race (Percent): 2005," http://www.kidscount.org/sld/compare_results.jsp?i=722, accessed April 21, 2009.

103. Brown et al., *White-Washing Race,* 88–89.

104. Susan Williams McElroy, "Black+Woman=Work: Gender Dimensions of the African American Experience," in Joe Trotter, ed., *African American Urban Experience: Perspectives From the Colonial Period to the Present* (New York: Palgrave Macmillan, 2004), 141–156.

105. Dawley, "Is Race the Problem for the 21st Century?," 327.

106. U.S. Census Bureau, "Women by the Numbers," http://www.infoplease.com/spot/womencensus1.html, accessed November 25, 2007.

107. U.S. Department of Labor, Bureau of Labor Statistics, "Women's Share of Labor Force to Edge Higher by 2008," February 14, 2000, http://www.bls.gov/opub/ted/2000/feb/wk3/art01.htm, accessed November 25, 2007.

108. U.S. Department of Labor, Women's Bureau, "Women in the Labor Force in 2004," http://www.dol.gov/wb/factsheets/Qf-laborforce-04.htm, accessed November 25, 2007.

109. U.S. Department of Labor, Bureau of Labor Statistics, "Mothers in the Labor Force, 1955–2004," http://www.infoplease.com/ipa/A0104670.html, accessed November 25, 2007.

110. Kaiser Family Foundation, "Women's Health Insurance Coverage," February 2007, http://www.kff.org/womenshealth/upload/6000_05.pdf, accessed November 28, 2007.

111. Every Child Matters, "Early Years and Childcare," http://www.everychildmatters.gov.uk/earlyyears/, accessed November 28, 2007.

112. Almanac of Policy Issues, "Minimum Wage," http://www.policyalmanac.org/economic/minimum_wage.shtml, accessed November 29, 2007.

113. NACCRA, "Parents and the High Price of Child Care, 2007," http://www.naccrra.org/docs/press/price_report.pdf, accessed April 1, 2009.

114. Barbara Welter, "The Cult of True Womanhood," in Mary Gordon, ed., *The American Family in Social- Historical Perspective* (New York: St. Martin's Press, 1978), 313–334.

115. Mimi Abramovitz, *Regulating the Lives of Women* (Boston: South End Press, 1988).

116. Jillian Jimenez, "The History of Grandmothers in the African American Community," 523–551.

117. Mimi Abramovitz, "Ideological Perspectives and Conflicts," in Joel Blau and Mimi Abramovitz, eds., *The Dynamics of Social Welfare Policy*, 2nd ed. (New York: Oxford University Press, 2006), 169–170.

118. Mimi Abramovitz, "Poor Women in a Bind: Social Reproduction Without Social Supports," *Affilia: A Journal of Women and Social Work* 7 (Summer 1992): 23–44.

119. Allen Omoto and Howard Kurtzman, eds., *Sexual Orientation and Mental Health: Examining Identity and Development in Lesbian, Gay, and Bisexual People* (Washington, DC: American Psychological Association, 2006); Gregory M. Herek, "Facts About Homosexuality and Mental Health," http://psychology.ucdavis.edu/rainbow/html/facts_mental_health.html, accessed January 12, 2009.

120. Miriam Smith, *Political Institutions and Lesbian and Gay Rights in the United States and Canada* (New York: Routledge, 2008), 6.

121. Gregory Herek, "The HIV Epidemic and Public Attitudes Toward Lesbians and Gay Men," in Martin Levine, Peter Nardi, and John Gagnon, eds., in *In Changing Times: Gay Men and Lesbians Encounter HIV/AIDS* (Chicago: University of Chicago Press, 1997), 191–221; Jane Ward, *Respectably Queer: Diversity Culture in LGBT Organizations* (Nashville, TN: Vanderbilt University Press, 2008), 27–50.

122. Human Rights Campaign, "2008 Presidential Questionnaire: Senator Barack Obama," http://a4.g.akamai.net/f/4/19675/0/newmill.download.akamai.com/19677/anon.newmediamill/pdfs/obama.pdf, accessed January 9, 2009; Smith, *Political Institutions and Lesbian and Gay Rights in the United States and Canada*, 5.

123. Smith, *Political Institutions and Lesbian and Gay Rights in the United States and Canada*, 41.

124. Human Rights Campaign, 2007, http://www.hrc.org/search.asp?site=www_hrc_org&client=hrc_search_results&output=xml_no_dtd&proxystylesheet=hrc_search_results&turl=10.88.88.227&q=anti-gay+ordinances, accessed January 11, 2009.

125. Jesse McKinley, "Across U.S., Big Rallies for Same-Sex Marriage," *New York Times,* November 15, 2008, A25.

126. Smith, *Political Institutions and Lesbian and Gay Rights in the United States and Canada*, 4–5.

127. Ramon Johnson, "Where Is Gay Marriage Legal?" http://gaylife.about.com/od/samesexmarriage/a/legalgaymarriag.htm, accessed January 9, 2009.

128. John D'Emilio and Estelle Freedman, *Intimate Matters: A History of Sexuality in America* (Chicago: University of Chicago Press, 1998), 171–239.

129. David Richards, *Identity and the Case for Gay Rights* (Chicago: University of Chicago Press, 1991), 112.

130. National Association of Social Workers, *Code of Ethics of the National Association of Social Workers* (Washington, DC: Author, 2006), 27.

131. *New York Times,* "Arkansas Ban of Gay and Lesbian Adoption Unconstitutional," January 6, 2009, A20.

132. Amanda Ruggeri, "Emerging Gay Adoption Fight Shares Battle Lines of Same-Sex Marriage Debate," *U.S. News,* October 31, 2008, http://www.usnews .com/articles/news/national/2008/10/31/emerging-gay-adoption-fight-shares-battle-lines-of-same-sex-marriage-debate.html, accessed January 11, 2009.

133. Jill Jacobs and Madelyn Freundlich, "Achieving Permanency for LGBTQ Youth," *Child Welfare* 85 (March/April 2006): 299–316.

134. Servicemembers Legal Defense Network, http://www.sldn.org/, accessed January 12, 2009.

135. Peter Baker, "Economy May Delay Work on Campaign Pledges," *New York Times,* January 11, 2009, A17.

136. U.S. Census Bureau, "Americans with Disabilities, 2005," released December 2008, http://www.census.gov/prod/2008pubs/p70–117.pdf, accessed January 14, 2009; University of Maryland Health Sciences & Human Services Library, "More Than 54 Million Disabled in U.S., Census Says," in *Health News,* December 18, 2008, http://www.hshsl.umaryland.edu/general/news/health/2008/12/more-than-54-million-disabled.html, accessed January 15, 2009.

137. Employers' Forum on Disability, "Nearly 50 Per Cent of US Disabled People in Employment," December 30, 2008, http://efd.org.uk/media-centre/news/nearly-50-cent-us-disabled-people-employment, accessed January 17, 2009.

138. Susan Landers, "Number of Disabled Expected to Rise," *American Medical News,* May 21, 2007, http://www.ama-assn.org/amednews/2007/05/21/hlsb0521.htm, accessed January 16, 2009.

139. Barbara Fawcett, *Feminist Perspectives on Disability* (Essex, England: Pearson Education, 2000), 16–20.

140. Michael Oliver, *Understanding Disability: From Theory to Practice* (Basingstoke, England: Palgrave Macmillan, 1996), 19–30.

141. Carol Thomas, *Sociologies of Disability and Illness: Contested Ideas in Disability Studies and Sociology* (Basingstoke, England: Palgrave Macmillan, 2007), 76.

142. Rachel Hurst and Bill Albert, "The Social Model of Disability, Human Rights and Development Cooperation," in Bill Albert, ed., *In or Out of the Mainstream* (Leeds, England: The Disability Press, 2006), 24–40.

143. Peter Burke, "Disadvantage and Stigma: A Theoretical Framework for Associated Conditions," in Peter Burke and Jonathan Parker, eds., *Social Work and Disadvantage: Addressing the Roots of Stigma Through Association* (London and Philadelphia: Jessica Kingsley Publishers, 2007), 11–27, 20.

144. Doris Zames Fleischer and Freida Zames, *The Disability Rights Movement: From Charity to Confrontation* (Philadelphia: Temple University Press, 2001), 200–215.

145. U.S. Court of Appeals, 11th District, *Wyatt v. Stickney,* Nos. 95–6637, 95–6875, http://caselaw.lp.findlaw.com/cgi-bin/getcase.pl?court=11th&navby=case& no=956637man, accessed January 18, 2009.

146. U.S. District Court, District of Columbia, *Mills v. Board of Education of District of Columbia,* 348 F. Supp. 866 (D. DC 1972), http://outreach.umf .maine.edu/docs/EDU%20550/millsvboardofed.pdf, accessed January 17, 2009.

147. U.S. District Court, *PARC v. Pennsylvania,* 334 TF. Supp. 1257 (E.D. PA 1972), http://www.faculty.piercelaw.edu/redfield/library/case-parc.pennsylvania.htm, accessed January 18, 2009.

148. Public Law 94–142, http://www.scn.org/~bk269/94–142.html, accessed January 19, 2009.

149. U.S. Court of Appeals, District of Columbia Circuit, *Paralyzed Veterans of America et al. v. Washington Metropolitan Area Transit Authority*, 894 F. 2d 458, January 30, 1990, http://cases.justia.com/us-court-of-appeals/F2/894/458/306686/, accessed January 18, 2009.

150. "The Rehabilitation Act Amendments of 1973, as Amended," http://www.access-board.gov/enforcement/Rehab-Act-text/intro.htm, accessed January 19, 2009.

151. U.S. Supreme Court Center, *School Board of Nassau County v. Arline*, 480 U.S. 273 (1987), http://supreme.justia.com/us/480/273/, accessed January 18, 2009.

152. U.S. Equal Opportunity Employment Commission, Disability Discrimination, "The Americans with Disabilities Act of 1990, Titles I and IV," January 15, 1997, http://www.eeoc.gov/policy/ada.html, accessed January 18, 2009.

153. Louise Fenner, "Protections for America's Disabled Workers Expanded Under New Law," October 9, 2008, http://www.america.gov/st/diversity-english/2008/October/20081009111835xlrenneF0.9165918.html, accessed January 17, 2009; U.S. Equal Employment Opportunity Commission, Disability Discrimination, "The Americans with Disabilities Act Amendments of 2008," December 9, 2008, http://www.eeoc.gov/policy/adaaa.html, accessed January 18, 2009.

154. Steven Buechler, *Social Movements in Advanced Capitalism* (New York: Oxford University Press, 2000).

155. Steven Buechler, *Social Movements in Advanced Capitalism*, 92.

156. Hugh Davis Graham, "The Role of Ideas in the African American Civil Rights Movement," in Peter Coclanis and Stuart Bruchey, eds., *Ideas, Ideologies and Social Movements: The United States Experience Since 1800* (Columbia: University of South Carolina Press, 1999), 119–146, 123.

157. Taylor Branch, *Parting the Waters: America in the King Years, 1954–1963* (New York: Simon and Schuster, 1988).

158. Meagher, "Racial and Ethnic Relations in America, 1965–2000," 193–241; Hugh Davis Graham, "The Role of Ideas in the African American Civil Rights Movement," 139.

159. Meagher, "Racial and Ethnic Relations in America, 1965–2000," 193–241; Buechler, *Social Movements in Advanced Capitalism*, 131.

160. Omi and Winant, 95–96.

161. Buechler, *Social Movements in Advanced Capitalism*, 132–133.

162. Buechler, *Social Movements in Advanced Capitalism*, 134.

163. Sara Evans, *Personal Politics: The Roots of Women's Liberation in the Civil Rights Movement and the New Left* (New York: Vintage Books, 1979).

164. Buechler, *Social Movements in Advanced Capitalism*, 140–141.

165. Frederick John Dalton, *The Moral Vision of Cesar Chavez* (Maryknoll, NY: Orbis Books, 2003), 15–19.

166. Quoted in Dalton, *The Moral Vision of Cesar Chavez*, 9.

167. Omi and Winant, 108–110.

168. Ewa Morawska, "The Sociology and Historiography of Immigration," in *Immigration Reconsidered: History, Sociology and Politics* (New York: Oxford University Press, 1990), 192–215.

169. Omi and Winant, Racial Formation in the United States, 108–109, 132–205; George Sanchez, *Becoming Mexican American: Ethnicity, Culture and Identity in Chicano Los Angeles, 1900–1945* (New York: Oxford University Press, 1993).

170. Meagher, "Racial and Ethnic Relations in America, 1965–2000," 194.

171. Walter Benn Michaels, *The Trouble With Diversity: How We Learned to Love Identity and Ignore Inequality* (New York: Metropolitan Books, 2006), 1–20.

172. James Juhnke and Carol Hunter, *The Missing Peace: The Search for Nonviolent Alternatives in United States History* (Kitchener, Ontario, Canada: Pandora Press, 2001), 215–216.

173. Frances Fox Piven and Richard Cloward, *Poor People's Movements: Why They Succeed, How They Fail* (New York: Vintage Books, 1977).

174. Buechler, *Social Movements in Advanced Capitalism,* 133–134.

CHAPTER

6

The Social Work Profession and Social Justice

CHAPTER QUESTIONS

1. What does the history of the social work profession reveal about the social work profession's commitment to social justice?

2. To what extent has the social work profession been engaged in efforts at social control?

3. Why have most social workers been women?

4. What has been the role of Christianity in the development of the social work profession?

5. What was the impact of the professionalization of social work on its commitment to social justice?

6. How did social work come to be identified with children's issues and child welfare?

7. How did the emergence of psychiatric social work impact the social work profession?

8. What are some challenges facing the social work profession today?

● ● ●

In this chapter we will consider the social work profession as a force for social justice, working to ensure the well-being of marginalized populations and, alternately, as a force for social control of oppressed populations. The social work profession has engaged in both kinds of activities, beginning with the first stirrings of altruism evident in the friendly visitors in the late 19th century, as well as in the settlement houses established to bring social programs and social justice to poor immigrants in the same period. Social work is a paradoxical profession, with a complex relationship to the larger economic, social, and political structures of American society. Social workers have worked extensively to secure social justice for their clients, in the form of local, state, and federal policies, as well as in neighborhood empowerment. On the other hand, social workers have worked in institutions that are at least partly dedicated to social control of marginalized populations, including juvenile justice, mental hospitals, welfare bureaucracies, and public schools. Social workers have been the lead professionals in the most important system affecting the relationship between parents and children, child welfare. All these systems contain elements of both social control and social justice.

● THE ORIGINS OF THE SOCIAL WORK PROFESSION

The social work profession first emerged at the end of the 19th century, during the period of reform known as the Progressive Era, when rapid industrial growth overtook the eastern urban areas of the United States. Industrialization was accompanied by a concentration of economic power and wealth in the hands of a few who benefited from the new opportunities for industrial growth and investment. Monopolies controlled the largest industries, and self-made men, like Andrew Carnegie and John Rockefeller, made quick fortunes in railroads, steel, and oil, living out the dream of upward mobility. The state governments—and especially the federal government—were beholden to wealthy industrialists; officeholders at the federal level were wealthy White men. Wealth was highly concentrated: 1% of the population owned 50% of the wealth.[1]

During this period, middle-class reformers began noticing the severely marginalized living conditions of Eastern and Southern European immigrants crowded together in urban tenements, struggling in poverty with minimal food, shelter, and clothing, while they worked or waited to work in the factories of the industrial revolution. Living conditions for the 20 million immigrants who came to the United States between 1880 and 1914 were harsh. Tenements were poorly built; many of them were fire traps made more dangerous by overcrowding. In some cities, 40% of the population was immigrants, mostly from Italy, Eastern Europe, and Russia. Most immigrants from Italy and Eastern Europe had been rural peasants in their home countries; Russian Jews were fleeing religious persecution and came from urban areas. Living in ethnic enclaves, these immigrants created mutual aid societies, newspapers, and banks to meet the needs of the group. Bringing their cultural traditions with them, immigrants brought religious diversity to the United States. Catholic churches and synagogues aided immigrants in their neighborhoods and provided continuity with their cultural origins. Local politicians in Eastern cities provided an informal welfare system for immigrants. The political machine, as it was known, traded fire, police protection, and jobs for immigrant votes. In the industrial workplace, immigrants were forced to work 12-hr days, 6 days a week, and unions were generally outlawed by court rulings. Working conditions were dangerous, especially in the coal mines, railroads, and steel mills. Over 25,000 workers were killed in industrial accidents every year. Courts ruled that workers were responsible for industrial accidents, not industry.[2] To survive, most family members, including children, worked. Industrial jobs were gendered; men worked with heavy machines, and women did laundry, domestic work, or cleaning in the factories. Children worked in cigar factories, meat processing, and light manufacturing.[3]

The majority of African Americans lived in the South in this period, where they provided cheap labor for Southern agriculture. White immigrants provided the cheap labor for industrial plants in the North and Midwest. After World War I began, immigration to Northern cities from Southern and Eastern Europe slowed down. At the same time, Southern agriculture became mechanized, and African Americans began the northward migration that would continue throughout the 1920s.

The marginalized conditions of immigrants, with many families living in one- and two-room apartments with no indoor plumbing or running water, did not move politicians to extend aid or develop social policies to benefit the tenement dwellers. During this period of American history, even sanitation services were private, not public, so poorer families had no access to indoor plumbing. The immigrants' plight did, however, move some college-educated, middle-class women and men to try to help the immigrants at the end of the 19th century. These women and men were the prototypes for social workers in the 20th century, who participated in the first major reform movement in the 20th century known as the Progressive Era.

INTELLECTUAL ANTECEDENTS OF SOCIAL WORK: THE PROGRESSIVE ERA ●

Before the Progressive Era could emerge in the United States, the belief that biological imperatives caused social problems, such as inequality and poverty, had to be relinquished by intellectuals, college-educated persons, and potential reformers. This ideology, known as Social Darwinism (see Chapter 3), was replaced by reform Darwinism, a theory that human evolution would move in a positive direction if environmental conditions were changed to promote human well-being. In their belief in the importance of the environment in shaping future evolution, reform Darwinists like the social activist Jane Addams were hopeful that improving the living conditions of immigrants through changes in local, state, and federal policy would result in positive outcomes for those living in unjust conditions. Addams and other reformers believed that all persons, including the immigrants, possessed the same potential as the educated middle class. In order to provide an environment that would promote human potential, progressive reformers believed that certain policy changes were necessary, such as child labor laws, safer working conditions, and public sanitation, which they believed would ensure that immigrants would have access to the equal opportunity currently denied them. Progressive reform was not radical by today's standards; few progressive reformers talked of whole-scale revisions to industrial capitalism (although a few others did; see section below on Eugene Debs) or argued for income transfers to economically marginalized populations; instead, they wanted to pass legislation that would protect those vulnerable to the new social order, especially children and women.[4]

Progressive reformers were not monolithic; some were passionate about business reforms (the antitrust movement, railroad regulation), others wanted improvement in workers' rights and conditions (union movements), others were concerned for women and children's rights, and still others were interested in personal moral reforms embodied in the temperance movement and feminist struggles (the suffrage movement). Some progressives were concerned with ensuring more efficient and democratic local governments, working to reduce the influence of machine politics on local governments and promoting democracy through the use of the initiative and referendum. In all these streams of Progressivism, the early social workers played a part, making their greatest contribution in the promotion of women and children's rights. Women were central to progressive reform, including the struggle for unionization of women workers. Their arguments for reform seem quaintly old-fashioned today; they often called upon the general belief in women's special qualities as nurturers and homemakers to justify their efforts to clean up the city and to protect other women and children in the workplace. However, they were merely capitalizing on prevailing ideologies about women's nature; to directly countervail them would have led them down a different, less effective road.[5]

PROFILES IN LEADERSHIP

Mother Jones (Mary Harris Jones), 1838–1930

Mother Jones was born in Cork, Ireland, in 1838; her family immigrated to America soon after her birth. Her father was a laborer on the railway construction crews, a job that took him to Canada. The family moved to Toronto where Jones attended public schools and eventually graduated from a teachers' college. Mother Jones was a well-educated woman for the times. Although she could have married into the middle class, she decided to marry George Jones, an itinerant blacksmith who was an organizer for the Iron Moulders' Union in Memphis, Tennessee. Jones and her husband had four children: three boys and a girl. They lived in a poor section of Memphis. In 1867, there was an epidemic of yellow fever in Memphis that devastated the town and particularly the poor, who had limited medical care and could not leave the area to escape the epidemic. All of Jones's children and her husband succumbed to the yellow fever and died.

Mother Jones

SOURCE: From the Library of Congress, by Bertha Howell.

After this terrible experience, she packed up her meager belongings and moved to Chicago where she eventually opened a dress shop. She began to speak out against the injustices experienced by the mineworkers and organized meetings to blast the mine owners and

(Continued)

(Continued)

elected officials who ignored pleas from miners' families and others to improve working conditions and wages. In 1871, another tragedy struck Mother Jones when the Great Fire of Chicago devastated the city, killing hundreds and leaving thousands homeless. Jones lost her business and all of her personal possessions. Once again, she had lost everything precious to her.

After the fire, Jones became more and more involved in the labor struggles of the day and the living and working conditions of the poor and working people of Chicago. She began attending meetings of a labor organization called the Knights of Labor, and this opened up a new world to her. She was exposed to the ideas of socialism and learned about labor history in Europe. She was sent out to the community by the Knights of Labor to speak to potential union workers and to recruit them to join the union. She began to attract large audiences and developed her public speaking skills with a commanding presence. Her fiery presentations aroused audiences to adopt action and move away from apathy. She developed a strong friendship with the leader of the Knights of Labor, Terrence Powderly, and this relationship would last most of her life. Powderly had very progressive ideas embodied in his union although unions were often depicted as evil socialist organizations. Although Mother Jones had a strong sense of religion, she had very little faith in the Catholic Church to help working people because it would not support unions due to what it believed were their socialist tendencies.

In 1897, she began working with the coal miners of West Virginia and Pennsylvania as a field organizer. Mother Jones was not identified as an early social worker although she began to work for social justice for miners at about the same time as Jane Addams was working to improve the lives of immigrants in Chicago. Although involved in many types of labor strikes including textile strikes, streetcar strikes, silk mill strikes, ironworker strikes, and railroad strikes, nothing impacted her more than the working conditions and struggles of the mine workers. The plight of mine workers toiling far beneath the earth in dirty dangerous conditions with their families barely able to survive in company-owned shacks made Jones more determined than ever to fight the oppression of the mine owners. One example of this was the strike at the Drip Mouth Mine in Pennsylvania that had been going on for 5 months. Fighting the mine owner who brought in substitute workers, she organized the miners' wives into an opposing force that finally brought the strike to an end. She also became involved in the Kensington, Pennsylvania, strike involving textile workers, many of whom were children. Child labor was common in many industries and had received little attention despite the dangerous and dirty work performed by thousands of poor children. Mother Jones eventually brought public attention to this tragedy by organizing a march of mill children across several states, eventually meeting with President Roosevelt. At that time, workers, including children, were under the complete control of factory owners, who rejected child labor legislation as interfering with their rights.

In 1905, Jones traveled to Chicago to attend the first meeting of a new radical organization called the Industrial Workers of the World. It was inclusive in that it included workers of all types and all racial groups. It was dedicated to revolutionary labor relations and to changing American society in major ways. To try to defeat the unions, business leaders and corrupt public officials made up false charges to frame labor leaders for crimes they did not commit. Eventually the three defendants were acquitted, helping to increase the legitimacy of union organizations.

One of the most ferocious battles in the history of American labor was in 1913 and 1914 in the coalfields of Colorado. The strikers were demanding improved pay, improved working conditions, and other benefits, but the company refused to negotiate. The mines were owned by absentee-owner John D. Rockefeller, and he clung to the principle that business owners had the right to hire and fire at will. Again outside workers were brought in to work as substitutes for the strikers. The situation worsened, and eventually the Colorado National Guard fired machine guns into a striker encampment, killing many women and children. President Roosevelt then sent in the U.S. Cavalry to restore order, and this eventually led to the settlement of the strike. Public sentiment turned against the Rockefellers and the union owners. Media coverage finally informed the public about the abuses and terrible working conditions of the miners. Mother Jones met later with President Roosevelt; during the meeting he attempted to convince her of the legitimacy of the mine owner's response. Jones was not convinced and would not be swayed from her convictions by the royal treatment offered to her at the White House.

Mother Jones is considered a major figure in the American labor movement. Her courage in fighting oppression, her unfailing commitment to social justice, her speaking out to end unfair and unjust working conditions for working people, and her fight to end child labor made her an inspiration to millions of working Americans.

College Education and Women

In the latter decades of the 19th century, middle-class White women began entering colleges in the United States. Before this time, the constricted gender roles available to women precluded all but the most daring from entering colleges, few of which accepted women even in the second half of the 19th century. The expansion of private women's colleges in the Northeast and the growing acceptance of coeducation by Midwestern public universities meant that a new class of educated women were looking to use their education outside the home.[6] College education itself was undergoing a transformation at the end of the 19th century, as social sciences began to be introduced into the academy. Sociology, economics, political science, and especially psychology offered new perspectives that sought to apply theory to contemporary social problems, including poverty.[7] The social sciences represented a move away from the classical education offered to college students earlier in the century, which included Greek, Latin, philosophy, and other more traditional disciplines. The new social sciences offered theories of "systematic social reform" to students who would later answer the call for reform in their own lives.[8]

It was primarily from this group of college-educated women that the first social workers emerged. These women provided an important impetus to the voluntary movement to ameliorate the problems of immigrants in urban areas of the Northeast. Many of these college-educated women remained unmarried; those who did marry did so later in life and had fewer children.[9] While college education, particularly at the new women's colleges, gave women a sense of options and possibilities, women were barred from all but a few occupations, such as nursing and teaching. Rejecting domesticity in their own homes, women reformers moved to clean up urban slums and the family life of others. The Woman's Christian Temperance Union, which urged abstinence from alcohol, benefited from the work of these women reformers, as did other women's voluntary associations to promote religious causes and reform causes, including women's suffrage. One of the most important volunteer efforts of these college-educated women in the late 19th century was the settlement house movement.

Settlement House Movement and Jane Addams

The settlement house movement began in 1889, when two college friends, Jane Addams and Ellen Gates Starr, moved into Hull House in a poor immigrant neighborhood in Chicago. Addams was a wealthy young woman who had experienced a period of personal turmoil after college graduation and wanted to do something meaningful with her life and her fortune. She decided to dedicate her life to helping immigrants and worked to offer services and promote policies that would serve the needs of the neighborhood. The settlement house movement spread to the major cities of the Northeast, and by 1900 there were almost 100 of them. Women who lived in the settlement houses attracted other likeminded reformers who contributed to the reform goals of the settlement workers. At Jane Addams's Hull House, a variety of services were offered to immigrants in the local area, including

Hull House

SOURCE: Associated Press.

vocational training, crafts, cultural events, and English classes.[10] While some of the features of settlement houses, such as citizenship and housekeeping classes, may be viewed as patronizing today, the decision of settlement house volunteers to live in poor neighborhoods suggested a strong and selfless commitment to social justice.

In 1893–1894, shortly after the first settlement houses were established, a devastating depression threw thousands of workers out of their jobs in the Northeast, leaving many homeless and starving. Settlement houses became important sources of activism and refuge for immigrants, who learned about politics and social action by working with settlement leaders like Jane Addams and Florence Kelley to form alliances of working-class women, such as the Illinois Woman's Alliance. These women worked for sanitation reforms and protective labor legislation for women and children. Settlement house workers joined with the growing women's club movement in efforts to help young women and children from immigrant groups. Child labor laws and mothers' pensions, which offered state support to

Child labor

SOURCE: From the Library of Congress, from the records of the National Child Labor Committee.

widowed mothers and their children, were two of the most important reform activities of these college-educated women, reform-minded women in women's clubs and settlement houses, who offered their time and fortunes to the cause of social reform.[11]

The Social Gospel Movement

Jane Addams and her colleagues were motivated by more than reform Darwinism in their dedication to those struggling under impoverished and unjust conditions. They, like other reformers in this era, were inspired by a Protestant movement known as the Social Gospel movement. This form of

Protestantism was different from the more inner-directed forms of other Protestant religions. Social Gospelers emphasized the importance of doing God's work *in* the world, rather than retreating from it, as the way to ensure salvation. Social Gospelers were action-oriented Christians, men and women committed to broader social change in urban areas of the Northeast, where their influence was the strongest.[12] Women, who were excluded from Christian ministry at this time, were particularly drawn to the Social Gospel movement as a means of religious and reform expression. These social reformers were energized by the Social Gospel's commitment to social justice. Transforming personal behavior was not sufficient, according to Social Gospelers, because large-scale social and political reform was part of the Christian mission to the world. These women and men believed that both social science and democratic politics were legitimate tools to be harnessed in the struggle for social justice. These beliefs provided a powerful backdrop for many women reformers, who sought to embody their faith in broader legislative reforms. Comporting with the prevailing gender ideology of the time, women concentrated their efforts on measures that would improve the well-being of families, especially women and children.[13] While gender discrimination within the Protestant establishment motivated some women to join the Social Gospel movement, even there women were not given leadership roles. The settlement house movement itself can be seen as a reaction to the male domination of the Social Gospel movement. Settlement women considered their work to constitute the practical side of the Social Gospel movement.[14]

The leader of the settlement house movement, Jane Addams, based her commitment to reform both on her participation in the Social Gospel movement and on her intellectual embrace of reform Darwinism. While Jane Addams and her colleagues were deeply committed to their vision of Christian reform, they were not interested in converting anyone to their religious beliefs; instead, these leaders wished to be involved in reform efforts that would be supported by all progressives.[15] In her essay "The Subjective Necessity for Social Settlements," Addams wrote that the social settlement movement reflected the "renaissance of early Christian humanitarianism."[16] Addams, Ellen Gates Starr, and Florence Kelly, another Hull House colleague, believed that their commitment to Christian principles demanded social action on behalf of immigrants and children. While their reform efforts have been portrayed in social work literature as largely secular, they were all active Christians, energized by the Social Gospel movement, who saw no contradictions between their religious beliefs and their public work as women reformers.[17]

PROFILES IN LEADERSHIP

Jane Addams, 1860–1935

Jane Addams

SOURCE: From Library of Congress.

Jane Addams was born on September 6, 1860, in Cedarville, Illinois, and was the youngest of eight children. From an early age she exhibited a strong interest in civic duty, and she was a hard worker by choice. She became a nationally recognized social reformer committed to social change and social justice. A debilitating illness forced her to drop out of the Women's Medical College in Philadelphia, where she had hoped to become a doctor. She then shifted her attention to mission work and the establishment of settlement houses in the United States. She had become familiar with settlement houses after traveling to England and observing the operations of the Toynbee Hall project. This project trained members of the clergy in working with the urban poor of London. Addams was so impressed with this program that she vowed to replicate such a program in the United States.

In 1889, Addams and others acquired the Charles J. Hull mansion that later became known as Hull House. This project differed from the Toynbee Hall project in that the people who came to Hull House to learn about providing social services to poor immigrants were young, middle-class women, not clergy. Hull House grew to eventually comprise 13 buildings staffed by 65 college-educated women. In addition to providing much needed services, Hull House became an important training center for several well-respected social workers. Under the direction of Jane Addams, Hull House became recognized as a leader in the social reform movement.

By 1895, Addams had shifted her attention to improving the working conditions of the city's workers. She became a labor rights activist and participated in a number of strikes against various industries. By 1898, Addams had expanded her focus on national issues to the promotion of world peace and the achievement of social justice. As a pacifist she began presenting public lectures and writing about reforming the political systems and ending war. She became recognized as a leader in the peace and social reform movement.

However, the coming of World War I would shift public attitudes toward her due to her pacifist views and lead to criticism that she was either a communist or a German sympathizer. Despite the attacks on her, she continued to press for social justice and improvements in working conditions for the poor.

Addams continued to work at Hull House after World War I, seeking reforms and social justice for those most vulnerable in our society. She was awarded the Nobel Peace Prize in 1931 for her dedication and work on behalf of the poor. Her accomplishments serve to inspire others, and she has continued to be seen as a pioneer advocating for social justice and a strong role model for generations of social workers. Jane Addams died in 1935.

Social Workers as Social Feminists

If social work's founding women were self-professed Christians, they were also feminists, insofar as they were women who operated independently from male authority and who led public lives of service and political action.[18] Jane Addams, Florence Kelly, and others stepped out of comfortable and expected personal and social contexts of women of their day to forge new pathways. As advocates, they lived lives of feminists, whether they articulated explicit feminist ideology or actively worked for feminist causes, like suffrage. Settlement house workers have been called "social feminists," who believed their "womanly benevolence" was critical to successful urban reform.[19] Social feminists believed that women had a more highly developed moral sense than men and could be particularly skilled in areas of urban reform. Central to the development of modern feminism, women reformers in the Progressive Era included maternal and child welfare, as well as poverty relief, as part of their distinct mission in social change.[20]

Charity Organization Societies

Another stream of primarily women reformers in the late 19th century who contributed to the emergence of the social work profession were those who volunteered in the Charity Organization Societies. COS, as they are commonly known, were voluntary organizations depending on contributions from wealthy persons who were often influenced by their religious beliefs. Local Charity Organization Societies were established in major urban areas in the Northeast and Midwest in order to deliver systematic aid to poor immigrants. Most of

Friendly visitor with immigrant family

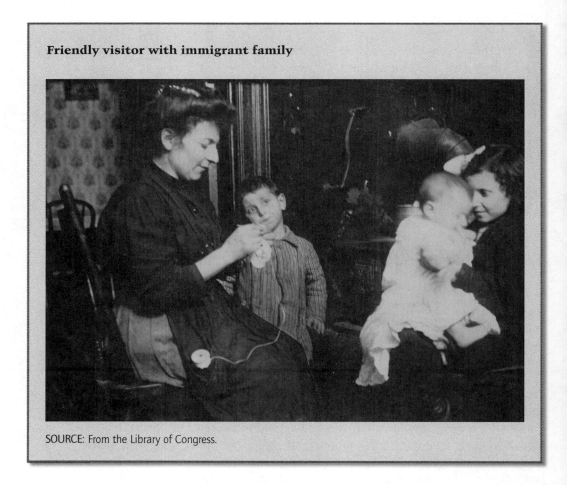

SOURCE: From the Library of Congress.

these voluntary philanthropic efforts took place in areas that experienced large-scale European immigration at the end of the 19th century. In the South, these voluntary efforts were more scattered, were less influential, and followed the established patterns of segregation. One example of this reform effort was spearheaded by Charles Loring Brace, who worked with children of immigrants and developed the "orphan train" system of aid discussed in Chapter 8.

A general belief in the 19th century that women were more naturally benevolent than men spurred women's voluntary participation in charitable causes, including the COS.[21] Volunteers were known as "friendly visitors"; they were motivated by their belief in the Christian imperatives of charity and good work.[22] Their job was to screen out poor persons who were not suitable for aid, since COS sought to distinguish between the worthy and unworthy poor. These women volunteers were also asked to monitor the recipients while they received charity donations to ensure that they were complying with the expectations of the donors. The "friendly visitors" were expected to conduct research on the families receiving aid, with the goal of describing their living conditions and moral progress. The "friendly visitors" were also urged to offer moral instruction to recipients to encourage proper living habits. Serving as an example of a successful, moral life, the middle-class volunteering woman was believed to be a positive influence on poor families, one that could help them escape poverty and the moral problems such as alcoholism that were believed to keep them in poverty.[23] The vast majority of clients of the COS were poor women and children.

A national organization of COS was formed in 1884, naming itself the National Conference of Charities and Corrections. COS were by nature more conservative than the settlement houses; they were bureaucratic organizations controlled by the voluntary patrons who funded them. Those working for the Charity Organization Societies, whether as volunteers or paid employees, had limited autonomy and had little incentive to identify with a profession outside the bounds of the organization. Paid staff began to replace the volunteer "friendly visitors" at the end of the 19th century; they became the country's first caseworkers.[24] COS addressed social problems on an individual, family-by-family basis; they neither developed nor advocated for policy initiatives that carried the reform impulse of the Progressive Era.[25]

Mary Richmond

One of the early icons of the social work profession, Mary Richmond, served for 20 years as director of the Charity Organization Department of the Russell Sage Foundation. In this capacity, she laid the groundwork for the development of the social work profession's belief in systematic casework as essential to work with and empowerment of clients. Richmond's famous book *Social Diagnosis,* published in 1917, laid out the casework principles she believed should be at the center of any work with individuals; some of her concepts are still taught in social work education today. Richmond said she had little interest in women's rights. Yet she was a strong advocate of social reform in the individually oriented practice of charity; she wished to systematize good works and believed in the organized delivery of charity, attempting to integrate religious and social science values to humanitarian ends. At the same time she emphasized the importance of experiential and personal knowledge, urging caseworkers working with the poor to conduct research and arrive at a social diagnosis to determine the cause of the individual problems. Richmond's casework solutions were not on the grand scale of the settlement house movement; she did not advocate changing laws to positively affect the environment, but she did understand that individuals needed resources in the community to improve client functioning and well-being.[26]

Like the work of the settlement house reformers, Richmond's work in urban charity grew out of her Christian beliefs in the necessity of alleviating poverty.[27] The casework methods she advocated involved interacting with neighborhood environments to seek out resources that could meet the needs of clients.[28] While casework emphasized working with individuals, Richmond and her followers did not see individual well-being as separate from the environment. In this respect, her work fell squarely in the tradition of progressive reform.

Richmond's belief in the importance of social diagnosis convinced her that skills and training were necessary in social casework. She wanted to take casework out of the hands of the volunteer. She worked to establish the first program of social work education, known as the New York School of Philanthropy, which was established in 1910. This 2-year curriculum in professional social work was later to become the Columbia University School of Social Work. Other schools of social work were established within a few years across the urban centers of the Northeast and Midwest. These new graduate programs were dominated by casework, which focused on individual work with clients and their families. In 1907, leaders of the settlement house movement established a different kind of social work program at the University of Chicago, with an emphasis on policy and administration, which became the School of Social Service Administration.[29] The Chicago program emphasized social science and interdisciplinary studies of social problems, creating a program that was distinct from the casework approaches of the other social work programs.[30]

Settlement House Movement and COS Influence on Social Work

Both the settlement house movement and the Charity Organization Societies were progenitors to the social work profession. Only one, however, contributed significantly to the institutionalization of the profession through social work education: the Charity Organization Societies.[31] While it would be too simplistic to align the settlement house movement with efforts for social justice and the Charity Organization Societies movement as an example of social control, there is some truth in that distinction. The early social workers visiting families under the COS model emphasized investigation of clients and assessment of their status as worthy recipients. These actions were not linked to broader actions seeking to change the conditions under which the clients lived. As a consequence, it was under the auspices of COS that detailed information about the lives of poor families was first gathered, often with few results. Settlement house volunteers did research too, but the intended consumers of the data were political actors who could make policy changes. Research on economically marginalized persons with no meaningful policy changes linked to the results was a trend that continued throughout the 1920s and up to the present day. By 1927, almost 3,000 surveys of poor families had been conducted by early social workers, none of which resulted in broad policy changes.[32]

The settlement house movement emphasized changing living and working conditions of poor and immigrant persons in their neighborhoods. Settlement workers were less interested in visiting poor immigrants in their households; instead, they provided a refuge for them at settlement houses, where they could receive well-baby care, receive child care, and learn new skills. Settlement house workers sought to interact with political actors who had the power to change the conditions of the immigrants. Those who lived with immigrants in their neighborhoods were likely to understand the environmental conditions that led to poverty and were less likely to assign personal blame for poverty.[33] Charity Organization Societies staff and volunteers, on the other hand, believed that individual, personal change was the way to reform. This ideology contrasted strongly with the settlement house movement. While the casework method outlined by Richmond was far more sophisticated, less moralistic, and more empowering of clients than the earlier methods of the COS, the focus on individual treatment ignored the importance of broad social reforms to ensure client well-being.

This tension between broad policy change and focus on individual well-being through casework has been evident since the beginning of the social work profession. Social work emerged in a society committed to a laissez-faire attitude toward government, where virtually no federal social policies to limit the worst effects of market capitalism existed. In the rare case when a federal social policy was enacted that would regulate the labor market—the law outlawing child labor passed by Congress in 1916—it was declared unconstitutional by a conservative Supreme Court in 1918. Social work could have embraced a more radical path, but most social workers became caseworkers, working within the existing establishment. When looking at the history of the settlement house workers, it is clear that the profession might have gone another way.[34]

Socialism in the Progressive Era

The inequality and suffering of workers and the poor in the American economic structure during this period led to the rise of political opposition in the form of

Socialism as well as to ongoing efforts of labor unions to achieve legitimacy and, ultimately, collective bargaining rights. Both these groups offered a critique of market capitalism not shared by most social workers. Workers fought for the right to unionize throughout the Progressive Era. The success of this struggle was undermined by the fact that labor was in high supply due to continuing immigration and that the immigrant workforce was more conservative than the native workers (see Chapter 3).[35]

Two settlement house social workers, Ellen Gates Starr and Florence Kelley, who lived and worked at Hull House in the 1890s, did become Socialists as a result of their work there.[36] While at Hull House, Kelley conducted research on the sweatshop system in Chicago's garment industry; she and other Hull House residents lobbied fiercely to end child labor in the garment industry and to improve working conditions for women. Her efforts were successful; in 1893, the Illinois state legislature passed a law prohibiting child labor, limiting working hours for women, and regulating sweatshops. Kelley was made the first chief factory inspector in the state, charged with enforcing the new legislation.[37]

The Socialist Party elected more than 1,000 to state and local offices in the 1912 election, when Eugene Debs was the national candidate of the Socialist Party for President of the United States.[38] Debs captured over 1 million votes out of 15 million cast—a not-insubstantial percentage.[39] Several early social workers, like Florence Kelley and Ellen Gates Starr, were both members of the settlement house movement and Socialists. Kelley and Starr embraced Socialism as the way to redress the poverty and inequality they believed were caused by unregulated industrialization.[40] Most social workers, however, continued to work within the prevailing economic structure, some attempting to mitigate its worst excesses.

● ACCOMPLISHMENTS OF EARLY SOCIAL WORKERS

Although the reforms actually passed during this period do not seem as radical as those 25 years later in the New Deal, social workers and others did accomplish a few key policy initiatives that protected vulnerable groups. Social workers were part of the effort at state levels to pass the first child labor laws. During the 19th century, children had worked in mines, glass factories, textiles, agriculture, canneries, home industries, and slaughterhouses. Although the U.S. Supreme Court overturned the federal child labor law in 1918, by then several states had passed laws restricting child labor, something that was often seen as unwelcome by immigrants who depended on the wages of their children. Jane Addams was instrumental in the passage of a child labor law in

Illinois, as well as a law to restrict women's working hours to 8 hours a day. Addams was also instrumental in establishing the first juvenile court in the nation in Illinois, offering an opportunity for the rehabilitation of youthful offenders who had previously been housed in jails with adults.

Women working with Jane Addams at Hull House were also active in broader social reforms during this period. These women included Florence Kelley discussed above, Alice Hamilton, Julia Lathrop, Ellen Gates Starr, Sophonisba Breckinridge, and Grace and Edith Abbott, all of whom became well-known activists as a result of their experiences at Hull House. The Abbotts lobbied the Illinois state legislature to pass progressive policies protecting women in the workplace as well as compulsory education laws.[41] After her successful effort to pass child labor laws in Illinois, Florence Kelley founded the National Consumers League, which advocated family subsidies to soften the impact of withdrawal of children from the labor market. The league was considered a radical group in its time. A limitation of Kelley's and other progressive women's reform efforts lay in their focus on White women and children in the workplace; all these reformers ignored the fact that African American women were forced to work in even more degrading and low-paying positions as domestic servants, laundry workers, and unskilled laborers.[42]

Florence Kelley was also a leader in the effort to create the federal Children's Bureau, and with other settlement house reformers, she was an architect in 1909 of the first White House Conference on the Care of Dependent Children. It was here that support for a federal Children's Bureau coalesced; Congress passed a law establishing the bureau in 1912, at the height of the progressive reform movement. Jane Addams, Florence Kelley, and other Hull House women testified before Congress about the importance of the bureau, whose mandate was to "investigate and report upon all matters pertaining to the welfare of children," including infant mortality, orphanages, and juvenile courts.[43] The mission of the bureau did not extend to political advocacy for children, but rather the bureau was to focus on research about children's needs. Julia Lathrop, a Hull House alumnae, was appointed the head of the new Children's Bureau, becoming the first woman to head a public agency in the federal government. The Children's Bureau quickly assumed the national leadership role in child welfare. Lathrop's appointment of other women reformers to important positions within the bureau established women as the leaders in child welfare (see Chapter 8).[44]

Jane Addams is often considered the founder of the social work profession, although she certainly did not identify as a social worker during her lifetime. For her time, Addams was a radical: She lived near her clients; advocated social policy reforms, which had never been passed before; and spoke her conscience about World War I, which she opposed on the grounds of pacifism. She was condemned for her outspoken opposition and vilified by politicians and the press.[45] Addams was animated not by Socialism but by her father's Quaker religion, by the Social Gospel movement, and by her own experiences in witnessing the struggles of the poor.[46] She and others in the settlement house movement believed in the right to unionize and in women's suffrage and reproductive rights and advocated for improvements in public health and sanitation.[47] From our contemporary point of view, Addams and most of her colleagues fell short of a systematic critique of industrial capitalism; with the exception of mothers' pensions, they advocated no permanent reforms addressing the growing inequality caused by the robust industrial growth. Addams supported efforts to unionize women workers but was not directly involved in union struggles. She did not call for redistribution of income through the income tax system, though the Sixteenth Amendment to the Constitution authorizing an income tax was ratified in 1916. Yet these early social workers were forward thinking in their grasp of the fact that government policies were needed to reign in the worst excesses of industrialization and protect the most vulnerable Americans. Other Americans, aside from union organizers and Socialists, appear to history to have been unconcerned with the rights of vulnerable populations. Social workers, along with other progressive reformers, set the stage for the New Deal, which did institutionalize several policies that seriously limited the effects of industrial capitalism on these populations.

Mothers' Pensions

Mothers' pensions were state efforts to meet the needs of poor women and children in the early decades of the 20th century. Women, mostly widows, who were seen as "poor and worthy," could receive a small stipend for the support of their children. While these policies constituted a change from the prevailing government policies of laissez faire, they were based on the distinctions between worthy and unworthy poor raised first in the Elizabethan Poor Laws.[48] Illinois was the first state to pass legislation for mothers' pensions, which were administered by Children's Court. Many states adopted similar policies between 1911 and 1919, but because of strict eligibility requirements few mothers were actually aided; residency laws also excluded many immigrants.[49] Mothers' pension laws were a good example of reform Darwinism realized in social policy. Those who supported them believed that, with aid, mothers would improve and become good mothers.[50] While many early social workers supported mothers' pensions, some did not, fearing that such state efforts would take the place of private charity given by nonprivate groups staffed by friendly visitors.[51]

Mothers' pensions, which will be discussed in detail in Chapter 7, are a good example of the limits of progressive reform: efforts to mitigate human suffering with no deep understanding of the causes of this suffering.

SOCIAL WORK AND THE END OF REFORM ●

The Progressive Era ended by the 1920s, with the reform impulse extinguished by World War I and the apparent return to normalcy that typically follows major wars in the United States. It was in this period of conservative consolidation that social work moved seemingly inexorably from a voluntary, altruistic pursuit of those able to dedicate their lives to the work of social change and helping others to a profession of those looking for a paid career in organizations employing social workers. Several historical trends diminished the interest in the problems of poverty and immigration, issues that early social workers had taken on as their own. The drive for reform was replaced by the desire for legitimacy.

The reasons for the decline of reform had little to do with social work. A revival of nativism swept across the country, as the so-called Red Scare and the reemergence of the Ku Klux Klan effectively shut down most dissent. Much of this repression was the result of renewed immigration after the war, as well as the large-scale migration of Southern tenant farmers, including African Americans, to Northern cities, looking for work. Riots against African Americans broke out in urban areas in the North, at the same time as the fear of socialism and communism among immigrant populations led to draconian measures, including loyalty oaths for teachers and other public employees. In the infamous Palmer raids of 1920, U.S. Attorney General A. Mitchell Palmer supervised the rounding up of 4,000 persons suspected of being radical aliens in one night. In this atmosphere, social reforms seemed un-American at best and communist at worst. Union leaders were jailed and their organizing efforts co-opted, as industry organized company unions in which workers played the role of union members under the authority of company executives. After winning suffrage in 1920, feminists retreated into the background. A new consumer society born of the mass production of automobiles, radios, refrigerators, and the like seemed to promise the middle class unlimited prosperity. Those left out of the boom in consumer goods, including farmers, industrial workers, and immigrants, did not have a voice that could penetrate the self-satisfaction of the postwar generation of middle-class consumers.[52]

In this atmosphere, the profession of social work emerged, not as a catalyst for social change but as a woman-identified service organization concerned with issues of socialization and, to some extent, social control. During the 1920s, social workers struggled to become identified as a "profession," not a volunteer activity of altruistic reformers. It was this struggle to professionalize that shaded the next decades of social work's development.

Social workers in the 1920s, even those who continued the work in settlement houses, were embarrassed by the religious idealism of the initial settlement house workers.[53] What led to this turning away from religious and spiritual values among social workers? The secularization of American culture after the 1920s and the disillusionment with reform after World War I were critical to marginalizing the Social Gospel movement and undermining the idealism of religious-based reform. For the social work profession, a key moment occurred in 1915, when Abraham Flexner, a physician, delivered the keynote address to the National Conference of Social Work and argued that social work was not an established profession because it had little intellectual authority, no clear educational discipline, and indefinite ends. Social work could not stand on its own as a profession; instead, it was a "mediating profession" according to Flexner, upheld by the "unselfish devotion" of its practitioners.[54] Flexner thought of social work as a feminine profession that emphasized womanly, nurturing values, rather than more masculine, scientific, and rational ones.[55]

Many social workers took Flexner's words seriously and concluded that religious values had no place in the rigorous intellectual underpinnings that Flexner insisted were necessary for autonomous professions. The social feminism that had inspired the settlement house and other reform movements receded, along with the religious inspiration of an earlier generation, as social workers in the 1920s and later adjusted to the formal bureaucracies in which they began to work.[56] Echoing the earlier spirit of reform that had animated social work, Mary Richmond, at a national conference for social workers in 1922, used the language of the Social Gospel movement to call on her audience to "bear faithful witness to the need for social reforms whenever their daily work reveals the need."[57] Yet just as the progressive reform spirit did not survive the postwar ennui, neither did the settlement house movement, with its religiously fueled optimism and appetite for broader reform. By the end of the 1920s, social work was a thoroughly secular profession, neither feminist nor fond of social reform.

Social Work: A Scientific Profession?

As the social work profession embraced scientific casework in the 1920s, the quest for professional status demanded an even more rational and systematic approach to work with individuals than had been suggested by Richmond. The first professional association of social workers, the American Association of Social Workers (AASW), was founded in 1921. It adopted as its goal raising professional standards in the social work field to the level of doctors, lawyers, and other professional groups who had professional organizations, membership requirements, and education requirements. Schools of social work joined with the association to promote their belief that their programs were essential for the professionalization of social work. Flexner's words had a strong impact on social workers all through the 1920s. The AASW insisted that social workers should be recognized as autonomous professionals, not as semiprofessionals (as they were described in the federal census in 1929) who could function only as adjuncts to physicians, lawyers, and other recognized professionals.[58] The medical profession became the standard by which the AASW measured social work; it emphasized social workers' scientific knowledge, especially its objectivity, reliability, and neutrality.

Recognizing that scientific knowledge, not social reform, was highly valued in American culture, professional social workers focused on making casework more scientific. The practice of casework was designed to follow the scientific method, including observation of the facts of the "case," generation of hypotheses about these "facts," and then controlling these "facts for new ends."[59] The emphasis on "facts" was meant to reassure the profession about the scientific nature of casework. According to this idea, social workers practicing casework, which was defined as the diagnosis and treatment of individual problems, were no different from other professionals, including physicians.

Others outside the profession, however, continued to view social workers as charity workers and could not make the transition to viewing the profession on par with medicine or law. Thus one of the central dilemmas of the social work profession in the 20th century became the question of how social workers could gain respect for the special and skillful work they do, as opposed to being identified with the well-meaning friendly visitor or charity worker dispensing alms to the poor. In response to the public identification of social work with issues related to poverty and injustice, professionals began to turn away from the goal of social justice and instead embraced a personal, psychological perspective of human problems suitable to their casework methodology. Of course, change does not come that swiftly, and some social workers did continue to emphasize the problems of the social environment, but they became increasingly isolated from the mainstream of the profession.[60]

Social Work: A Women's Profession?

The apparent feminine nature of the profession was also viewed as a drawback by social workers in the 1920s and 1930s. As we have seen, social work was initially animated by social feminism; most of its early icons were women, and in the new casework positions social workers increasingly occupied, most of their clients were women. Yet some social work leaders felt that acknowledging the gender basis of their profession would have further eroded respect for social work, since women's work was not held in high esteem. The general belief in this period was that women's work depended on emotion and sympathy, not scientific reasoning. Yet since the census reported in 1930 that over 70% of social workers were women, it was difficult to banish feminine qualities from the profession. One solution offered in 1923 was to divide the profession into the casework aspect, which women could dominate, and the public agency and administration aspect, which would be controlled by men.[61]

The irony of a profession founded by women turning so quickly to men to enhance its prestige was not lost on women social workers in the 1920s and 1930s, but they recognized the paradoxical nature of the concept of a woman professional in a culture where middle-class women were barely entering public life.[62] Even in social work, women worked in lower-paying positions and with less autonomy than men.[63] In order to advance the position of women in the profession, some social workers resorted to arguing that, as mothers, women knew more about the personal work of social work than men; others emphasized the neutrality of the female social worker who, they argued, strips away all feminine sensitivity in order to become an effective practitioner.[64] Social work continued to attract women, in spite of efforts to degender the profession, because employers were willing to hire women who they believed possessed the nurturing qualities central to the work.

Social Work's New Clients

Class issues that reduced the status of the social work profession were as important as gender issues. Social workers were linked with poor people in the public mind during the 1920s. This was a dilemma for the profession, since the ascendance of business interests in the federal government and the rise of consumerism did not give much support for concern about poverty. Social work attempted to make its way out of this thicket of constricted possibilities by emphasizing its role as providers of individual casework to middle-class persons. This effort was important if social work was to be a self-sustaining profession; counting on the wealthy to sponsor philanthropic activities would not be sufficient. Where was social work to find middle-class clients who could pay for their services? The solution that emerged in the 1920s was to align the profession with psychiatry and, in so doing, adopt psychoanalytic theory to strengthen its professional credibility. This would give social work both a client base and an enhanced professional status. Psychoanalytic theory could stand on its own or could be blended with social casework to offer individual treatment to clients. Social workers worked in industry, in mental hygiene clinics, in child guidance clinics, in state hospitals for the mentally disordered, and in newly established veterans' hospitals. Child guidance clinics, especially, supported the emergence of the psychiatric social worker, who worked in a team with psychiatrists and psychologists to treat disturbed children and their families. While some of these families were referred by courts, others were sent by family physicians and schools, and some came willingly on their own.[65]

Psychoanalytic theory was welcomed by some social workers because it was more complex and carried the prestige of the psychiatric profession, whereas casework had only the social work profession to give it legitimacy. Many social workers drew on a hybrid of both methods; social casework continued to be practiced by most social workers in agencies.[66] While neither method was completely successful in the treatment of mental disorders, psychoanalytic methods were useful as a legitimizing professional tool. As a result, by the end of the 1920s, psychoanalytic theory was accepted by many social work professionals as the gold standard in individual treatment and the surest way for social workers to achieve full professional status. Psychoanalytic theory had little room for an environmental analysis of impact on individual well-being; instead it focused on the personal histories of the clients. Concerns about the broader social structure or the community problems that had moved settlement house workers were not relevant to psychoanalytic theory, which argued that poverty was an expression of childhood dependency needs. These views were not detrimental to disadvantaged clients, since only the middle class and wealthy persons could afford the intensive and expensive treatment. Not all social workers embraced the intricacies of psychoanalytic theory, or psychotherapy as it came to be called. Many continued to adhere to social diagnosis and casework. Whatever the differences between the two groups, it was the individual treatment model that dominated the social work profession after the 1920s.[67]

Like the rest of American society in the 1920s, most social workers were tired of social reform and hopeful about economic progress and the continued growth of the consumer society. The drive to professionalize included a new emphasis on the scientific values of objectivity and neutrality, moving social workers further from the social reform efforts of the Progressive Era. The choice to professionalize, rather than to unionize, was a significant one for social workers in this period. Professionalization was consonant with the middle-class background of most social workers; unionization would have aligned social work with the interests of oppressed groups and the immigrants and working-class persons for whom the settlement house workers had sought political reform.[68]

Social Work and the New Deal

As the worst economic depression in U.S. history threw millions of workers into unemployment and threatened families across the country with economic catastrophe, mayors and governors in the early 1930s called on President Herbert Hoover, an advocate of laissez-faire government, to design federal programs to supplement the depleted state and local relief efforts. By 1930, there were 40 social work schools across the nation, most of which were deeply committed to the casework approach, rather than social reform or social policy. One of the main concerns of the profession was the low supply of trained workers, which in the face of increasing demand led many agencies employing social workers to train them on the job, keeping social work salaries low.[69] The question of whether these trained staff were professional social workers was answered definitively: Only professional education in a graduate social work program could make one a social worker. As a result of this assumption, social work leaders were concerned with ways to increase the professional education of social workers, which they assumed would increase their status and pay. Most educators in graduate programs in social work were more concerned with these issues of professionalization than they were with federal policies to mitigate the effects of the depression, yet it was through the development of welfare capitalism in the New Deal that social work found its biggest and most powerful sponsor: the federal government.

The impact of the Great Depression on families and the New Deal policies that emerged to help them will be discussed in Chapter 7. For now the key point is that these New Deal policies provided a new, permanent niche for social workers in the political economy of the United States. The federal government, under the leadership of Harry Hopkins, a social worker with much experience in child welfare, recruited prominent social workers, both those who were professionally trained and those who had experience working as social workers, to fill key positions in the Roosevelt administration. Frances Perkins, Secretary of Labor, had worked as a social worker and, along with Hopkins, was instrumental in designing the Federal Emergency Relief Administration in 1933 and later the Social Security Act (see Chapter 7). Hopkins wanted social workers to become involved in determining eligibility and in managing the welfare relief bureaucracy.[70] Under his influence, social workers were appointed to the Federal Bureau of Public Assistance, which oversaw the new state-operated welfare system known as Aid to Dependent Children. Hopkins also supported professional social work education with direct grants. In spite of the support for social work within the Roosevelt administration, professional schools of social work were, on the whole, uninterested in designing content on social legislation or public welfare, preferring to adhere to the individual casework approach, which had defined the profession. Thus the profession as a whole did not seize the opportunity to become involved with the development of the new public policies of the New Deal, including the Social Security Act; instead, social work leaders and the AASW focused their efforts on the staffing requirements of public welfare, hoping to increase the demand for professional social workers. Social work efforts to professionalize welfare staff failed, as they refused to compromise on the less intensive training programs the newly created public agencies wanted for their employees. Professional social workers returned to their casework interests and private agency work, leaving public welfare to staff not formally trained in social work. Ironically, after the New Deal the entire social work profession became identified in the public mind as the deliverers of the welfare state.[71]

The expansion of public sector social work was accompanied, if not matched, by the growth of the voluntary sector, with organizations such as the Red Cross, the Community Chests, and United Way growing rapidly to deliver charity dollars to local groups in need.[72] Social work now had to fit into a whole new set of bureaucratized, regulated, and standardized roles that increased the demand for its services but reduced professional autonomy.

Even in the face of widespread economic suffering, most social workers were loath to abandon the individual casework approach and recommend broader economic and political solutions to the problems of those suffering from economic dislocation and unemployment. Advocating for public programs seemed a move into partisan politics, a betrayal of the profession's recent commitment to impartiality.[73] This position was not in keeping with the earlier involvement of early social workers in advocating for public policies during the Progressive Era, and it is at odds with the current efforts of social work organizations like the National Association of Social Workers to advocate for policies at state and federal levels. The failure to become involved in the designing of New Deal policies is one sign of how insecure many social workers were about their new professional status.

The Rank and File Movement

A counterweight to the emphasis on professionalization that guided the social work profession in the 1920s and 1930s emerged in a movement of rank and file social workers staffing public relief agencies. This so-called rank and file movement emphasized the solidarity of social workers with other workers who were struggling with their marginalized status during the depression. Embracing working-class consciousness, these social workers began to look to unionization, not professionalization, as the means to increase their autonomy and ability to exert control in the workplace. Reaching a peak in 1936, the rank and file movement was fueled by a large number of social service workers who did not have professional social work education and were suffering under stressful working conditions. Their work investigating eligibility status of potential relief recipients was met with hostility and little gratification. Some social work leaders supported the rank and file movement for unionization, which reached a peak membership of 15,000 in the mid-1930s. The rank and file movement sought to steer social work on a more progressive course than the more established AASW, which did not accept members without professional social work education. The rank and file social workers formed local unions across the country, such as the Social Service Workers Union in Chicago. Its members advocated radical reforms of the economy, ideas that grew out of a Marxist analysis of the depression; they criticized professionally oriented social workers as instruments of social control, working for state-run bureaucracies. After 1937, the reforms of the New Deal, especially the Social Security Act, opened up more jobs for rank and file social workers. The rank and file movement ended at the end of the 1930s, as a new civil service bureaucracy was created to protect public sector jobs, co-opting union efforts to stabilize employment in the public sector.[74] Social work efforts to unionize were not over, however; they have continued up to the present day in public sector social work. The question of whether social workers should unionize divides the field: Some think that social work's professional status would be undermined by union identification; others think that the progressive nature of social work would be strengthened by unionization and that the status of social work would be elevated through collective bargaining.[75]

● SOCIAL WORK IN THE POST–WORLD WAR II ERA

Social workers, while increasing their position in the administration of federal and state welfare bureaucracies, generally did not engage in social action in the postwar period, concentrating instead on organizing separate professional groups within the growing social work profession, which included psychiatric social workers, medical social workers, and school social workers.[76] In an effort to consolidate the profession and distinguish themselves from public welfare workers, the separate professional organizations merged in 1954 to create the National Association of Social Workers (NASW). A 2-year graduate degree in social work was required to be a member of NASW, excluding large numbers of social workers who were not professionally trained, most of whom worked in public agencies. By 1960, when approximately 105,000 social workers were working in the United States, only 20% had completed a 2-year graduate program. NASW committed itself to enhancing the professional status of social workers and adopted a cautious posture toward social action and political involvement.[77]

Social Work and the War on Poverty

In the late 1960s and early 1970s, social work benefited greatly from the policies adopted by the Lyndon Johnson administration to eradicate poverty in the United States through the so-called War on Poverty and the passage of the Economic Opportunity Act in 1964. While most antipoverty programs were based on the culture of poverty model, which rested on the assumption that cultural factors were causes of poverty, some programs did encourage empowerment of economically marginalized and politically disenfranchised persons. Under the Office of Economic Opportunity created by the Johnson administration, community representatives were given power to make decisions about how federal resources would be used in their communities and neighborhoods. These programs, known as Community Action Programs, were created in impoverished urban areas to encourage local indigenous leaders to set up community organizations to both work with existing resources and seek new resources in order to alleviate poverty in their communities. The phrase *maximum feasible participation* signaled the desire of the Office of Economic Opportunity to include poor persons in these Community Action Programs.[78] Under these programs, community members were included in every step of program development. The emphasis on maximum feasible participation was short-lived; in 1967, Congress amended the Economic Opportunity Act, which funded the War on Poverty, putting local mayors in charge of federal money, not community action boards. Community members were relegated to honorary positions that involved advice giving to local political leaders.[79]

Other programs that emerged during the activism of this period included the Mobilization for Youth program developed out of the Henry Street Settlement House on the Lower East Side of Manhattan. This community program was instrumental in the establishment of the welfare rights movement in the Northeast. Academic activists Richard Cloward and Frances Fox Piven were important in the establishment of the National Welfare Rights Organization (NWRO) in the 1960s; by 1969, there were more than 20,000 dues-paying members of the NWRO across the country. Members of the NWRO were preponderantly women receiving Aid to Families With Dependent Children; they complained about the social workers in the welfare bureaucracy dehumanizing them. Even though most of these social workers were not professionally trained, the critique of social workers as agents of social control was deeply felt. The NWRO succeeded in increasing the welfare rolls and publicizing the rights of welfare recipients, who had been ignored by the welfare bureaucracies. Ironically the growth in the welfare rolls and the increasing advocacy of welfare recipients about their rights contributed to the hostile public climate toward welfare in the late 1970s and 1980s.[80] Advocating for a federally guaranteed annual income policy, the leaders of the NWRO wanted to do away with the welfare system entirely.

As a result of these policies, a new movement of paraprofessionals emerged from the ranks of local leaders. Working at public and private agencies as intermediaries between clients and social workers, paraprofessionals could claim knowledge of culture and community that had eluded social workers, many of whom were White middle-class professionals with academic credentials. The social work field was in a quandary about the growing number of paraprofessionals; on the one hand social workers committed to social action in the 1960s and 1970s welcomed the empowerment of community workers, but on the other hand there were concerns about the challenge to professionalism they seemed to represent.

The possibility of an undergraduate social work degree was also viewed as a challenge to the professionalization of social workers. Federal funding of undergraduate education that began in the 1960s was seen as a threat to the standards necessary to maintain professionalism. The need for undergraduate education was finally recognized by NASW in 1969, when the organization decided to open membership to those who had undergraduate social work degrees, thereby recognizing the bachelor of social work (BSW) as an entry-level degree. Some argued that the BSW would serve to depress the demand for masters of social work, thereby contributing to deprofessionalization and a lowering of standards and salaries; others argued that it was necessary to increase the supply of trained workers in the human services systems.[81]

The failure of the War on Poverty to end poverty and inequality led many in the United States to become cynical about the ability of social workers and social welfare programs to alleviate poverty and inequality.[82] Similarly, many gave up on the idea that liberal, government-sponsored programs could ameliorate social conditions among economically marginalized inner-city populations. A backlash against antipoverty programs began in the 1970s and has never subsided. Responding to these public attitudes, social workers were even more reluctant to ally with public welfare programs or to engage in social action efforts to improve welfare policies after the demise of the War on Poverty. As it turns out, the progressive impulse that overtook the profession in the 1960s and 1970s was a function of federal funding; little had changed in the profession's view of itself.

See Table 6.1 for a history of significant events related to the profession of social work.

TABLE 6.1   Timeline of Significant Events Related to the History of the Social Work Profession

Year	Significant Events
Late 19th Century	• Charity Organization Societies established to deliver systematic aid to poor immigrants • Contributed to the emergence of the social work profession with volunteers known as "friendly visitors" (college-educated, middle-class women) who screened persons on whether they were suitable for aid • Paid staff began to replace volunteer "friendly visitors" and were considered first caseworkers; they addressed social problems on an individual and family basis but did not advocate for policy initiatives of the Progressive Era • National Conference of Charities and Corrections (national organization of COS) was formed in 1884 • Contributed significantly to institutionalization of the profession by establishing social programs for poor immigrants • Reform Darwinism ideology emerged that focused on environmental conditions being changed to promote human well-being • Progressive reformers developed the antitrust movement, railroad regulation, union movements, women's and children's rights, the suffrage movement, and the rise of political opposition in the form of Socialism • First social workers emerged from this group of college-educated women
1889	• Settlement house movement began with Jane Addams, Florence Kelley, and Ellen Gates Starr at Hull House in a poor neighborhood of Chicago • Provided a variety of services to immigrants • Settlement houses became important sources of activism and refuge for immigrants • Sanitation reforms and labor legislation for women and children were some of the reforms from this activism • Social Gospel movement and social feminists influenced this work also
1899	• Jane Addams was instrumental in establishing the first U.S. juvenile court as part of the Circuit Court of Chicago
1907	• Leaders of the settlement house movement established a social work program at the University of Chicago focused on policy and administration
1909	• The National Child Labor Committee, organized by a combination of New York and Chicago settlement groups, became primarily responsible for the 1909 White House Conference on the Care of Dependent Children
1911	• The first mothers' aid law was enacted in Illinois for mothers' pensions
1912	• The Children's Bureau Act was passed on April 9. It established the U.S. Children's Bureau as a separate government agency, based on an idea initiated by Florence Kelley and Lillian Wald; Julia C. Lathrop was appointed the first chief

(Continued)

TABLE 6.1 (Continued)

Year	Significant Events
1915	• Abraham Flexner in his address to the National Conference of Social Work delivered a keynote address on "Is Social Work a Profession?" He stated social work does not qualify as a bona fide profession, consequently stimulating continual definition efforts by social workers
1917	• Mary Richmond published *Social Diagnosis* that laid out casework principles from her work as director of the Charity Organization Department of the Russell Sage Foundation • Book laid the groundwork for the social work profession's belief in systematic casework with clients • Richmond established the first program of social work education in 1910 at the New York School of Philanthropy (later became the Columbia University School of Social Work) • COS contributed significantly to institutionalization of the profession through social work education
1920s	• Palmer raids that rounded up 4,000 persons suspected of being radical aliens were examples of events leading to a decrease in social reform after the Progressive Era • Social workers struggled to be identified as a profession rather than volunteers motivated by religious idealism
1921	• Quest for professional status of social work was focused on scientific casework rather than social reform
1923	• Profession begins to divide into casework (primarily women) and public agency and administration (primarily men)
1926	• The American Association of Psychiatric Social Workers, originally a section of the American Association of Hospital Social Workers, was organized. This began the profession's attempt to align with psychiatry and adopt psychoanalytic theory to strengthen professional credibility
1932	• President Herbert Hoover signed the Emergency Relief and Construction Act (Ch. 520, 47 Stat. 709) into law on July 21; a provision of the act enabled the Reconstruction Finance Corporation to lend money to states for relief purposes, moving federal government into the field of public relief • New Deal policies provided a new niche for social workers in the political economy of the United States
1933	• The Civilian Conservation Corps Act was passed by Congress on March 31. The act was established to meet part of the need caused by the Great Depression by providing work and education programs for unemployed and unmarried young men ages 17 to 23 years

Year	Significant Events
	• The Federal Emergency Relief Act was passed on May 12. It created the Federal Emergency Relief Administration (FERA), which provided 25% matching and direct grants to states for public distribution for relief. Social worker Harry Hopkins became the director on May 22
1941	• The United Service Organization was incorporated in February to coordinate services provided to armed forces and defense workers by six voluntary agencies: (1) National Jewish Welfare Board, (2) National Catholic Community Service, (3) National Traveler's Aid Association, (4) Salvation Army, (5) YMCA, and (6) YWCA
1954	• NASW commenced operation on October 1 through a merger of five professional membership associations—(1) American Association of Group Workers, (2) American Association of Medical Social Workers, (3) American Association of Psychiatric Social Workers, (4) American Association of Social Workers, and (5) National Association of School Social Workers—and two study groups—(1) Association for the Study of Community Organization and (2) Social Work Research Group
1960s	• National Welfare Rights Organization established by Richard Cloward and Frances Fox Piven
1964	• The Economic Opportunity Act (PL 88452) passed by Congress on August 20, establishing the Office of Economic Opportunity and calling for the creation of Volunteers in Service to America, Job Corps, Upward Bound, Neighborhood Youth Corps, Operation Head Start, and Community Action Programs • This gave community representatives power to decide how federal resources would be used in their communities and neighborhoods • Social work benefited greatly from policies adopted by the Lyndon Johnson administration
1969	• The bachelor of social work degree was recognized for NASW membership as a result of a national membership referendum and is implemented in 1970

CONCLUSION

The profession of social work has continued to be motivated by the desire for legitimacy and professional recognition; NASW has recently sponsored legislation in several states to outlaw the use of the designation *social worker* by those who have not graduated from a social work program.[83] Social workers continue their efforts to control the market for their services by establishing licensing requirements and working to maintain reimbursement from federal programs like Medicare.[84]

Yet the progressive aspects of social work have not been extinguished; they reappear periodically. While the necessity for most professional social workers to find paid employment has limited the possibilities for social workers to engage in free-standing social reform and political action, social work education continues to be a center of progressive thought.[85] Progressive social workers emphasize egalitarian relationships between clients and workers and continue the struggles to combat racism, sexism, agism, and other facets of discrimination.

Social reform efforts by social workers appeared to detract from professionalism of social work in the 1920s, and this tension continued in the profession to the present day. The question of whether social work should put aside social activism in order to maintain its professionalism was raised repeatedly at professional conferences and in journals throughout the 20th century.[86] For various reasons, the prime one being the belief that professionalization demanded political and policy neutrality, social work did not seize the opening represented by the Great Depression or to collaborate on policies to regulate the market economy, even though it did benefit from the opportunities created by the public programs of the New Deal. The mixed blessing of being identified as the workforce in public welfare—and especially child welfare—emerged as the most recognizable role for social work in the United States after the New Deal. However, social work education in the main has avoided taking the opportunity to shape the policies of the welfare state. This failure to act for the benefit of social work clients and oppressed groups in general reminds us that social work practice is political, either supporting the status quo or seeking to change it.[87] Seeking the false objectivity of political neutrality in policies affecting clients' well-being is turning away from our singular professional commitment to social justice, shared by no other profession.

Paradoxically, social work is identified as a liberal or even radical profession by many persons in the United States. The reason for this perception is not so much that social workers or their professional organizations have pushed for radical reforms but rather that the profession is seen as promoting government-sponsored social programs. From the point of view of our history, the question social workers themselves might ask is whether the drive for professionalism contributes to our becoming agents of social control, rather than social justice.[88] The potential for social workers to be agents of social change is high, since with more professional autonomy, social workers have more room to work for social reform and potentially do more good for clients.[89]

As can be seen from this chapter, the history of social work illuminates the tensions and paradoxes of the profession today. Many of the first conflicts present in the Progressive Era continue to characterize social work. In spite of the similarities, there are important differences. It is far more difficult for social workers to mobilize for social action and social change today than it was in the Progressive Era, when settlement workers pledged their own fortunes to sustain themselves and their colleagues through acts of social protest and social reform. The wealthy donors who supported the work of Jane Addams and her friends now give money to umbrella nonprofit agencies like United Way. Funneling philanthropic money through umbrella agencies means that the work of social work will be done by agency personnel, with accountability to managers and donors, not just to clients and their own consciences. While the federal government sponsored programs to question its own policies during the War on Poverty, today the government does not encourage radical action against itself. Other impediments to social work being a force for social justice and social change include the profession's continuing emphasis on casework, in its educational programs, in the workplace, and as it is tied to funding sources that want accountability in terms of individual clients served. This focus on individual clients tends to emphasize individual responsibility for problems and takes the focus away from structural factors impinging on individuals, like the inequities of the market economy.

On balance, social work has been a strong force for social justice, as the *only* profession committed to securing social change for marginalized and oppressed populations. Social work began as a religious profession; it has now embraced a secular faith in diversity and multiculturalism, values critical to all clients, especially those from oppressed groups (see Chapter 5). However, a commitment to diversity alone does not illuminate issues related to social class and inequality, which are equally important to clients' well-being. Multiculturalism is only one path to social justice; by itself it will not result in a redistribution of resources to clients suffering from the inequities of the economic system. In spite of the obstacles currently in its path, social work must reown its unique and primary commitment to work for social policy change in the pursuit of social justice.

See Table 6.2 for a list of Web resources to help you learn more about the history of social work and the influences on the social work profession.

TABLE 6.2   **Using the Web to Understand the History of the Social Work Profession**

There are a number of Web resources to help you learn more about the history of social work and the influences on the social work profession.

- Go to http://www.idbsu.edu/socwork/dhuff/XX.htm to take a cyber history tour of social work's formative years. This Web site was developed by Dan Huff at Boise State University. It includes narrative on the early history, a pictorial history, and links to Web sites (excursions) that will help you further develop your knowledge of the history of social work.
- Go to http://www.uic.edu/jaddams/hull/hull_house.html for further information about Jane Addams and the Hull House Museum.
- Go to http://newdeal.feri.org/ and learn more about the New Deal. It contains information, links, and pictures of what the Franklin and Eleanor Roosevelt Institute (FERI) created. The New Deal Network is a research and teaching resource on the World Wide Web devoted to the public works and arts projects of the New Deal.
- Go to http://www.hartford-hwp.com/archives/45/index-be.html for reprints of articles related to the history of social legislation and welfare in the United States.
- Go to http://womhist.alexanderstreet.com/ for more information on women and social movements in the United States, 1830–1930. This site is organized around 79 documents with 2,400 primary documents on women and social movements.
- Go to http://www.policymagic.org/resources.htm for an exhaustive list of Internet links to resources related to social work policy and the profession of social work. This site is maintained by John McNutt and the social welfare policy and practice group created to encourage the study and teaching of social welfare policy and policy practice within social work education. The group is further concerned about the creation of optimal social policy and social welfare policy. This group sponsors the social welfare policy symposium at the Council on Social Work Education's Annual Program Meeting and the *Journal of Social Policy.*

DISCUSSION QUESTIONS

1. Has the social work profession been more of a force for social justice or social control? Give examples of efforts for social control and struggles for social justice.

2. Which factor in social work history has had more influence on the development of the profession: the settlement house movement or the Charity Organization Societies?

3. Has the drive to professionalize social work contributed to or detracted from social work's original commitment to social change on behalf of oppressed groups?

4. How has the fact that social work continues to be a gendered profession impacted its public image? Its ability to serve clients? To work for effective policy change?

5. How has social work's commitment to multiculturalism and diversity empowered the profession and its clients? What are the limitations of this approach?

6. How important was religious belief to the origins of the social work profession? Is there any element of moral suasion in social work education today? How much room is there for dissent from the central precepts of the social work profession?

7. Is the main emphasis in social work education on work with individuals (casework)? How much emphasis is given to community action and social policy change in the social work curriculum?

8. Do you feel prepared to work for social policy change once you complete your social work degree? What else would help you become effectively engaged in the social policy arena?

9. What are the challenges facing social work in the policy arena today? How can social work engage in the political struggle necessary to advance social justice?

10. What were your reasons for deciding to pursue social work education? How do your aspirations fit with social work's unique commitment to social justice?

NOTES

1. John Ehrenreich, *The Altruistic Imagination: A History of Social Work and Social Policy in the United States* (Ithaca, NY: Cornell University Press, 1985), 22–23.

2. Bruce Jansson, *The Reluctant Welfare State: American Social Welfare Policies—Past, Present and Future* (Belmont, CA: Brooks Cole, 2001), 124–127; Gary B. Nash and Julie Jeffrey, *The American People* (New York: Pearson Longman, 2006), 695–696; David Brody, *Workers in Industrial America: Essays on the Twentieth Century Struggle* (New York: Oxford University Press, 1980).

3. Otto Bettmann, *The Good Old Days—They Were Terrible* (New York: Random House, 1974).

4. Daniel Levine, *Poverty and Society: The Growth of the American Welfare State in International Comparison* (New Brunswick, NJ: Rutgers University Press, 1988), 151–152.

5. Robyn Muncy, *Creating a Female Dominion in American Reform, 1890–1935* (New York: Oxford University Press, 1991), 35–37.

6. David M. Austin, "Greeting the Second Century: A Forward Look From a Historical Perspective," in June Gary Hopps and Robert Morris, eds., *Social Work at the Millennium* (New York: Free Press, 2000), 18–41; Muncy, *Creating a Female Dominion in American Reform, 1890–1935*, 4–5.

7. Austin, "Greeting the Second Century," 21.

8. Austin, "Greeting the Second Century," 22.

9. Sara Evans, *Born for Liberty: A History of Women in America* (New York: Free Press, 1997), 147.

10. Jansson, *The Reluctant Welfare State*, 139.

11. Evans, *Born for Liberty*, 149–150.

12. Robert Trawick, "Dorothy Day and the Social Gospel Movement: Different Theologies, Common Concerns," in Wendy Edwards and Carolyn Gifford, eds., *Gender and the Social Gospel* (Urbana: University of Illinois Press, 2003), 139–150.

13. Wendy Edwards and Carolyn Gifford, eds., *Gender and the Social Gospel* (Urbana: University of Illinois Press, 2003), 1–17.

14. Eleanor Stebner, *The Women of Hull House: A Study in Spirituality, Vocation and Friendship* (Albany: State University of New York Press, 1997), 1–5.

15. Stebner, *The Women of Hull House*, 12–15.

16. Jane Addams, *Twenty Years at Hull House* (New York: Signet Classic, 1910), 20.

17. Kathleen Sklar, "Beyond Materialism: Protestant Women and Social Justice Activism: 1889–1920," in Margaret Bendroth and Virginia Brereton, eds., *Women and Twentieth Century Protestantism* (Champaign: University of Illinois, 2002), 3, 2–7.

18. Kathleen Tangenberg, "Linking Feminist Social Work and Feminist Theology in Light of Faith-Based Service Initiatives," *Affilia 18* (November 2003): 379–394.

19. Barbara Simon, "Building on the Romance of Women's Innate Strengths: Social Feminism and Its Influence at the Henry Street Settlement, 1893–1993," in K. J. Peterson and A. A. Liberman, eds., *Building on Women's Strengths* (New York: Haworth Press, 2001), 23–39.

20. Nancy Cott, *The Grounding of Modern Feminism* (New Haven, CT: Yale University Press, 1987); Lori Ginsberg, *Women and the Work of Benevolence: Morality, Politics and Class in the Nineteenth Century United States* (New Haven, CT: Yale University Press, 1990), 2–20.

21. Ginsberg, *Women and the Work of Benevolence*, 4–10.

22. Jansson, *The Reluctant Welfare State*, 157.

23. Roy Lubove, *The Professional Altruist: The Emergence of Social Work as a Career* (Cambridge, MA: Harvard University Press, 1971), 12–13; Jansson, *The Reluctant Welfare State*, 157–158; Ehrenreich, *The Altruistic Imagination*, 61–62.

24. John Ehrenreich, *The Altruistic Imagination*, 60–61.

25. Austin, "Greeting the Second Century," 23; Levine, *Poverty and Society*, 164.

26. Ehrenreich, *The Altruistic Imagination*, 63–65.

27. Elizabeth Agnew, "Shaping a Civic Profession: Mary Richmond, the Social Gospel and Social Work," in Wendy Edwards and Carolyn Gifford, eds., *Gender and the Social Gospel* (Urbana: University of Illinois Press, 2003), 116–139.

28. Lubove, *The Professional Altruist*, 81–82.

29. Jansson, *The Reluctant Welfare State*, 158.

30. Muncy, *Creating a Female Dominion in American Reform, 1890–1935*, 81.

31. Austin, "Greeting the Second Century," 21–25; Jansson, *The Reluctant Welfare State*, 136–137.

32. Linda Gordon, *Pitied but Not Entitled: Single Mothers and the History of Welfare, 1890–1935* (Cambridge, MA: Harvard University Press, 1994), 170.

33. Ehrenreich, *The Altruistic Imagination*, 63.

34. Michael Reisch and Janice Andrews, *The Road Not Taken: A History of Radical Social Work in the United States* (New York: Brunner-Routledge, 2001), 23–37.

35. David Brody, *Labor Embattled: History, Power and Rights* (Urbana: University of Illinois Press, 2005).

36. Reisch and Andrews, *The Road Not Taken*, 16–17.

37. Muncy, *Creating a Female Dominion in American Reform, 1890–1935*, 25–26.

38. Reisch and Andrews, *The Road Not Taken*, 19.

39. Jansson, *The Reluctant Welfare State*, 144.

40. Reisch and Andrews, *The Road Not Taken*, 14–17.

41. Harvard University, Open Collections Program, "Women Working, 1800–1930: Jane Addams," http://ocp.hul.harvard.edu/ww/people_addams.html, accessed January 15, 2008.

42. Mimi Abramovitz, *Regulating the Lives of Women: Social Welfare Policy From Colonial Times to the Present* (Boston: South End Press, 1988), 184–185.

43. Muncy, *Creating a Female Dominion in American Reform, 1890–1935*, 47.

44. Muncy, *Creating a Female Dominion in American Reform, 1890–1935*, 62.

45. Reisch and Andrews, *The Road Not Taken*, 13–18.

46. Stebner, *The Women of Hull House*, 2–6.

47. Reisch and Andrews, *The Road Not Taken*, 27.

48. Abramovitz, *Regulating the Lives of Women*, 200–206.

49. Jansson, *The Reluctant Welfare State*, 137–138.

50. Levine, *Poverty and Society*, 164.

51. Jansson, *The Reluctant Welfare State*, 139.

52. Ehrenreich, *The Altruistic Imagination*, 43–52.

53. Clark Chambers, *Seedtime of Reform: American Social Service and Social Action, 1918–1933* (Minneapolis: University of Minnesota Press, 1963), 148.

54. Abraham Flexner, "Is Social Work a Profession?" in *The Proceedings of the National Conference of Charities and Correction* (Chicago: Hildmann Printing, 1916), 577–578.

55. Agnew, "Shaping a Civic Profession," 128.

56. Leslie Leighninger, *Social Work: Search for Identity* (Westport, CT: Greenwood Press, 1987).

57. Mary Richmond, *What Is Social Casework?* (New York: Russell Sage Foundation, 1922), 225.

58. Regina Kunzel, *Fallen Women, Problem Girls: Unmarried Mothers and the Professionalization of Social Work, 1890–1945* (New Haven, CT: Yale University Press, 1993), 37–41.

59. Virginia Robinson, "Analysis of Processes in the Records of Family Case Working Agencies," NCSW Proceedings (1921), 253, cited in Kunzel, *Fallen Women, Problem Girls*, 41.

60. Ehrenreich, *The Altruistic Imagination*, 59, 83; Reisch and Andrews, *The Road Not Taken*, 59–60.

61. James Tufts, *Education and Training for Social Work* (New York: Russell Sage Foundation, 1923), 73.

62. Regina Morantz-Sanchez, *Sympathy and Science: Women Physicians in American Medicine* (New York: Oxford University Press, 1985).

63. Kunzel, *Fallen Women, Problem Girls*, 46.

64. Kunzel, *Fallen Women, Problem Girls*, 48.

65. Ehrenreich, *The Altruistic Imagination*, 69–70.

66. Wenocur and Reisch, *From Charity to Enterprise: The Development of American Social Work in a Market Economy* (Urbana: University of Illinois Press, 2001), 101.

67. Ehrenreich, *The Altruistic Imagination*, 67–68, 71–74.

68. Wenocur and Reisch, *From Charity to Enterprise*, 86–89.

69. Wenocur and Reisch, *From Charity to Enterprise*, 117, 134.

70. Wenocur and Reisch, *From Charity to Enterprise*, 170–173.

71. Leighninger, *Social Work*, 87–88, 93–95.

72. Wenocur and Reisch, *From Charity to Enterprise*, 152–153.

73. Leighninger, *Social Work*, 55–57.

74. Wenocur and Reisch, *From Charity to Enterprise*, 182–207.

75. Mimi Abramovitz, "Social Work and Social Reform: An Arena of Struggle," *Social Work 43* (November 1998): 512–527.

76. Wenocur and Reisch, *From Charity to Enterprise*, 233–240.

77. Leighninger, *Social Work*, 200–203.

78. Ehrenreich, *The Altruistic Imagination*, 170.

79. Ehrenreich, *The Altruistic Imagination*, 179.

80. Reisch and Andrews, *The Road Not Taken*, 143–152.

81. Wenocur and Reisch, *From Charity to Enterprise*, 266–269.

82. Leighninger, *Social Work*, 216.

83. NASW Missouri Chapter, "'Social Worker' Word Protection Information," http://www.nasw-mo.org/title_protection.htm, accessed February 13, 2008.

84. Wenocur and Reisch, *From Charity to Enterprise*, 91.

85. Reisch and Andrews, *The Road Not Taken*, 165.

86. Ehrenreich, *The Altruistic Imagination*, 59–60.

87. Joel Blau with Mimi Abramovitz, *The Dynamics of Social Welfare Policy*, 2nd ed. (New York: Oxford University Press, 2007), 182.

88. Reisch and Andrews, *The Road Not Taken*, 234.

89. Mimi Abramovitz, "Social Work and Social Reform: An Arena of Struggle," *Social Work 43* (November 1998): 512–527.

CHAPTER

7

Policies to Support Income

Welfare and Social Security

CHAPTER QUESTIONS

1. How were dependent women and children and elderly perceived and cared for in early American history?

2. What market failures led to the creation of the New Deal and the Social Security Act in 1935?

3. What were the assumptions behind the creation of the first welfare policy in the Social Security Act in 1935?

4. What were the assumptions underlying the creation of the first Social Security policy in 1935?

5. How did the welfare system change in 1996?

6. What is the relationship between TANF and the labor market?

7. What is the impact of TANF on poor women and children?

8. What are the successes and limitations of the current Social Security system?

9. How does Social Security discriminate against some groups?

10. How can we keep Social Security solvent for coming generations?

The need to care for those who cannot care for themselves exists in every society, and each society meets these needs in different ways. In the United States several factors combine to influence how we will meet the needs of the poorest and most vulnerable among us. The most important of these are our *historical values and ideologies,* the *demands of the market economy,* and the *legacy of discrimination* that informs all social welfare policies. In this chapter we will see how those three forces have come together to construct the social problems that underlie both welfare policies and income maintenance policies for elderly Americans as well as shape the solutions to these social problems. We begin our narrative in the colonial period.

● ENGLISH LEGACY: THE ELIZABETHAN POOR LAWS

England was the first country in the Western world to institute laws to protect and care for dependent children with no source of support. In 1601 the Elizabethan Poor Laws were passed by Parliament to ensure that children without parents or other caretakers would be cared for by local authorities, paid for by local taxes. These poor laws were part of the cultural baggage of the colonists who came to this country from England. The colonists instituted similar policies that mandated that all relief be local relief and that those who needed relief must return to their town of residence (normally where they were born) in order to be eligible for aid. In the colonies the aid usually consisted of goods in kind, meaning that poor women and children received shelter, food, perhaps some wood for fuel, and some clothing. No cash was given out in this cash-poor economy; the colonies were not allowed to print their own money and had to use scarce English money to pay their taxes to the mother country. This first welfare system established several important principles: Benefits would be given in kind; residence was required for eligibility; and perhaps most important, the law distinguished between two kinds of poor folk: worthy and unworthy. The former category consisted of widows and their children, elderly, and disabled, especially those who were blind. All others were thought to be able bodied and therefore unworthy of aid. This distinction between worthy and unworthy poor is with us today.

Another British principle of poor relief that took hold in the United States is the principle of less eligibility, which the British, the colonists, and welfare policymakers in the United States since saw as a way to keep the numbers of persons receiving aid low. Under this principle payments (whether benefits or cash) to poor persons must be lower than the wages of the poorest worker.

We saw in Chapter 3 the importance of work in early American history and to contemporary American culture. In the colonial poor laws this meant that those who were able to work were not eligible for help, whether or not work was available. This is an important distinction that has been maintained to this day in the U.S. welfare system: Only dependent children and their caretakers are eligible for welfare, as are some disabled persons with low income. Able-bodied persons with no children are not eligible for federal or state welfare, regardless of economic conditions. Of course, workers can receive Unemployment Insurance Benefits (UIB) temporarily, but part-time workers and secondary labor market employees usually do not qualify for UIB, as we have seen in Chapter 4. Thus welfare programs have been and continue to be restricted to a small group of dependent persons, who apparently have no responsibility for their plight because they are unable to work.

AID TO WOMEN AND DEPENDENT CHILDREN ●

In the early period of American history there were two ways poor women and children could be helped. The first form was known as outdoor relief, where someone eligible for town aid could receive a small amount of food, wood, or clothing. Under this arrangement poor persons might be boarded out to other householders in the local area, who would be paid to keep poor persons under their roof if there was no other shelter available to them. Some towns auctioned the poor off to the lowest bidder who would care for them (usually women and children or elderly) in return for a small fee paid by the town. In return the poor families were expected to work.[1] Some towns, like Boston, sent male paupers to jail, having no other places to confine them in the 18th century.[2]

The second form of aid was known as indoor relief, where poor persons would be confined to local almshouses, separated by gender and given work to do to repay their board and care. Almshouses were built in England in the 18th century, but in the United States the great wave of almshouse establishment did not occur until the early 19th century.[3] During the almshouse period, poor persons, mostly women and children, who needed assistance were given no choice but to go into almshouses and work for their keep. Children, as well as adults, were kept in local almshouses, whose construction was underwritten by local taxes but whose ongoing operation was expected to be self-sustaining, based on the work of the poor confined there. Women and children worked at spinning cotton, weaving, and shoemaking. In keeping with the distinctions mandated by the colonial poor laws, men were generally not allowed in almshouses unless they were attached to a family, but even then some almshouses refused to admit them. When men were admitted to almshouses, they were expected to perform manual labor.

Antipathy toward aiding the poor, especially through outdoor relief, grew in the second half of the 19th century, as rapid industrialization, urbanization, and immigration seemed to exacerbate the problem of poverty. Social Darwinism provided a convenient explanation for the causes of poverty and an even more convenient justification for refusing to aid poor persons outside the almshouse. Almshouses, also known as workhouses or poorhouses, became increasingly places of reform rather than places of refuge. Residents lived under strict rules and rigorous schedules, which included religious worship and moral education.[4] These measures rested on the belief that poverty was related to personal moral character, an ideology related to the Protestant work ethic. If poverty was caused by moral failings, it might be reversed by moral transformation.

By the last decades of the 19th century when immigration from Southern and Eastern Europe was on the rise, it was clear that poorhouses could not solve the problem of poverty. Crowded and unsanitary, these places of confinement could not escape the spread of disease. The lack of classification of the residents meant that children and adults of both genders wandered freely throughout the poorhouses. Mentally ill persons, women, children, persons with disabilities, and the elderly suffered greatly in these almshouses as they received no treatment or special care. In 1872 at least 1,300 children lived in poorhouses in New York state. Some cities attempted to separate the worthy poor into almshouses and the unworthy idle poor into workhouses, but this arrangement was too expensive for most localities.[5]

In spite of serious objections to aiding the poor outside of a confined and controlled environment, more costly indoor relief was replaced by outdoor relief in the early years of the 20th century, as the cycle of relief came full circle. Poorhouses were transformed into old-age homes, and the other dependent populations in poorhouses—women, children, and mentally ill—were the subject of other arrangements; women and children would receive mothers' pensions and later Aid to Families With Dependent Children (AFDC), orphans and children without functioning caretakers would go to existing state-run orphanages and later the child welfare system, visually impaired persons would go to institutions for the blind, developmentally disabled persons would go to custodial hospitals, and the mentally ill would be placed in state-run mental hospitals. Able-bodied men in poorhouses would be sent to flophouses in urban areas.[6]

● MOTHERS' PENSIONS AND ADC

The limitations of indoor relief for poor women and children in the early 20th century necessitated the development of another means of aiding children living with their mothers. As discussed in Chapter 6, mothers' pension laws were passed by the majority of states between 1911 and 1920. The programs were designed for poor single (mostly) mothers with children. By 1930, 46 states had passed mothers' pension or mothers' aid laws; these laws were the model for the first federal welfare program, Aid to Dependent Children (ADC), passed under the Social Security Act in 1935. The struggles over the form that mothers' pensions should take presaged concerns about welfare for single mothers that dominated discussions throughout the 20th century. Advocates for the programs and state legislators were concerned that programs for single mothers did not encourage single motherhood. Advocates believed that mothers' aid programs could supplement the low income of working single mothers and signal the public value of mothering. Critics saw these programs as too radical and as undermining the dependence of women on men; even though most states earmarked the money for widows, women whose husbands had deserted them as well as unmarried mothers inevitably received some of the funds. As if to allay these fears, most states included a program to supervise the mothers who received mothers' pensions. Some states assigned the administration of these programs to juvenile courts that could monitor whether mothers receiving aid were providing "suitable" homes for their children.[7] These kinds of programs were noncontroversial and raised few objections from local officials.

The decision to offer state grants to low-income mothers was a fateful one. Instead of an alternate strategy of working to increase women's wages, most reformers in this period preferred a small stipend for needy mothers. Likewise, efforts to initiate child care programs for working mothers, although considered by some reformers, were not pursued. Women's wages were lower than men's not only because of the gendered nature of the workforce but because the prevailing concept of a family wage meant that men were expected to support the unpaid labor of their wives at home, while women were not expected to need wages to support others.[8] Mothers' pensions can thus be seen as a gendered policy whose goal was to keep women in the home, fulfilling the duties of motherhood, rather than assuming an equal place in the workforce. By upholding the public, social significance of the maternal role, women reformers promoted the maternalist or family ethic that ratified women's gender role assignment and their responsibility for reproduction and domestic life.[9] While the financial stipends given to mothers and children were inadequate and the number of women aided was much smaller than that of those eligible (93,000 families out of an eligible 1.5 million received aid in 1930),[10] mothers' pensions did establish the precedent that government should help this population of so-called worthy poor. The return to outdoor relief was a monumental shift in attitudes toward poor mothers and children, as was the effort to keep families together, rather than attempting to place the children in orphanages or in the privately run foster care system. In spite of their limitations, mothers' pensions represented a clear turn away from laissez-faire government and Social Darwinism.

● SOCIAL SECURITY AND ADC: THE FIRST WELFARE SYSTEM

What led the United States to pass the first federal welfare bill for women and children in 1935 in the New Deal, as well as old-age insurance in the form of Social Security pensions? To understand the origins of both Social Security and welfare we must understand the economic conditions that presaged the New Deal. What caused the U.S. economy to collapse in the early 1930s?

In the late 1920s the U.S. economy was highly stratified, with the majority of resources in the hands of the top third of the population. The poorest third were struggling to survive and unable to buy the new consumer goods, such as automobiles and refrigerators. Stocks were overpriced due to high demand by the wealthiest Americans, but the price of most stocks did not reflect the value of the corporations. In 1929 the price of stocks fell dramatically as the great sell-off began, implicating banks and the entire credit structure. Many wealthy Americans had purchased stocks on the margin, putting as little as 10% down and borrowing the rest, expecting to pay off their loans when their stocks were

Soup kitchen

SOURCE: From the Library of Congress, National Photo Company Collection.

Unemployed persons seeking government assistance during the Great Depression

SOURCE: Associated Press.

sold at a profit. When these loans were not paid off, banks were unable to meet their deposits, having lent these monies to those buying stocks on the margin. Manufactured goods began stockpiling because of a dramatic decline in consumer confidence, resulting from the stock market collapse and the corresponding collapse of banks. As a result corporations laid off workers in order to cut costs, further diminishing demand for goods. The Great Depression was in essence a collapse of demand, which caused corporations to seek to protect their profits by laying off more workers, which in turn caused more decline in consumer demand as families had no income to buy goods. Farmers were especially hard hit, as the agricultural sector had suffered from overproduction and low prices. Many farmers had difficulty paying their mortgages and lost their farms as prices of farm commodities continued to tumble.[11]

How did all this affect families? A flurry of movement took place across the United States, as impoverished farmers and other residents of rural areas migrated to cities looking for work. Young men and women rode the rails, traveling from state to state in empty railroad cars; approximately 700,000 men and women were ejected from trains in 1932 alone. African Americans left for the North, as the Southern agriculture economy was near collapse. Families camped out after losing their homes, and breadlines in urban areas and cities swelled around city blocks. Men who had lost their jobs left families behind while they became transients, looking for work, a handout, and a fresh start. The movement out of the cities was almost as large as the migration in, as young men and women wandered from state to state, looking for work. In 1933 the federal Women's Bureau estimated that 10,000 women, most under 30, were migrants, without homes. Unwelcome in small towns, migrants kept moving from one urban area to another. Every large city, including New York City, had an area that was essentially a village of shacks and huts made of cardboard, newspapers, and corrugated iron. Here transients were welcome. Diseases spread in these grueling living conditions; most had little food or clothing and suffered greatly in the winter and during inclement weather. Children in particular suffered; some died of malnutrition in urban areas like New York City, where tuberculosis and other infectious diseases spread among the young. Child labor in sweatshops returned as families desperate for income sent their children to work in makeshift arrangements for low wages.[12] Married women entered the labor force, many for the first time, working at whatever low-paying, unskilled jobs they could find.[13]

The federal government did not respond to the crisis during the first 3 years of the depression. The ideology of laissez faire discussed in Chapter 3 had dominated the federal government throughout the 1920s. While state and local relief agencies, based on the principles of the English Poor Laws, still existed in the 1920s and early 1930s, these local sources of relief were quickly exhausted as the depression threw families into poverty and economic dependence. The massive unemployment in Northern and Midwestern cities, as high as 25% in the early '30s, led to uprisings against local relief offices and growth in membership in the Socialist and Communist parties. Herbert Hoover was president during the initial years of the Great Depression. He was firmly committed to the laissez-faire ideology that had driven the federal government under Republican and Democratic administrations throughout the 19th century and during the 1920s. He felt federal involvement in the economic disaster would only make it worse.

The number of unemployed men and women was catastrophic and unprecedented; salaried and professional workers who had escaped unemployment in previous downturns were laid off alongside manufacturing workers. The marriage and birth rates declined dramatically. With local governments continuing to bear the burden of relief as they had since the colonial period, they could not meet the demand for aid and quickly ran out of funds. Some families did manage to qualify for limited aid. In 1934 the average person on relief was a 38-year-old White male household head with an elementary school education and 10 years' work experience in manufacturing who had lost his job in the past 2 years. These men headed families struggling to survive on the very limited resources offered by the local relief offices. The vast majority (82% in one study) had never applied for relief before the Great Depression. In large cities relief offices were able to give out small amounts of food to some families. In 1932, New York City was offering the families who had reached the relief offices first an average of $2.75 a week. State governments did not have the resources to help local governments, even if they had wanted to, which many did not. Private agencies that traditionally had dispensed charity to the poor staggered under the burden, and many collapsed.[14]

Into the breach stepped the federal government with the programs known as the New Deal. Franklin Roosevelt was elected president in 1932 and turned the federal government from a laissez-faire one to an activist one by encouraging the development of many policies designed to aid those affected by the Great Depression. Most of the New Deal programs targeted the recently unemployed primary labor force, consisting predominantly of White men. Farmers, who had demanded price supports periodically since the 1880s, were helped with the Agricultural Adjustment Act, which offered price supports to large farmers but hurt African American sharecroppers when farmers were paid not to grow. The Civilian Conservation Corps offered work and room and board to 2.5 million young men from urban areas. The Public Works Administration and the Works Progress Administration offered federally supported jobs to unemployed men to engage in public works, such as road, bridge, and dam construction. Few of the New Deal programs were targeted for women or members of oppressed ethnic groups. An early New Deal program, the Federal Emergency Relief Administration, designed to give aid to individuals and families in need due to the breadwinner's unemployment or underemployment, was an effort to shore up local relief efforts. Designed as a temporary program (it ended in 1935), the Roosevelt administration—in particular the social worker Harry Hopkins—wanted to put money in the hands of families who needed it. Without categorical restrictions, the only eligibility criterion was economic need. Some working poor received funds under the federal program, which was administered by state officials.[15]

In terms of social welfare policies, the most important achievement of the Roosevelt administration, which forever changed the social welfare landscape in the United States, was the Social Security Act, which was passed in 1935. Its provisions included ADC, UIB, Social Security pensions for older Americans, Aid to the Blind (AB), and Old Age Assistance (OAA). Two of the programs, Social Security and UIB, were designed to be self-funding insurance programs; three (AB, ADC, and OAA) were aid programs funded through general revenue

**President Franklin D. Roosevelt signing the
Social Security Act**

SOURCE: From the Library of Congress, Farm Security Administration and Office of War
Information Collection.

and the tax system. Additionally a small amount of money was given to state
agencies to administer child welfare programs and public health programs. This
marks the first time that the federal government gave direct grants to states and
individuals for social welfare needs.

Was the New Deal a set of radical programs, attempting to move the United
States closer to socialism, or was it a conservative program, establishing social and
economic programs that would protect market capitalism from the collapse of
demand and popular unrest? Most historians argue that the New Deal was

fundamentally conservative in its efforts to stabilize market capitalism but also forward thinking by committing the federal government to intervene in the lives of individuals and the operation of corporations (the minimum wage law of 1937 is cited as an example of this).[16] The New Deal established a new role for the federal government, one that demanded intervention when economic and social crises befell Americans. This is one reason why the federal response to Hurricane Katrina on the Gulf Coast was so disappointing to many: Since the New Deal, federal response to disaster has been seen as a necessary intervention, not as charity.

PROFILES IN LEADERSHIP

Harry Lloyd Hopkins, 1890–1946

Harry Hopkins

SOURCE: Getty Images.

Harry Hopkins was born on August 17, 1890, in Sioux City, Iowa, and was one of five children. His father was a harness maker and did so well that eventually the family opened a store where they sold a variety of products including harnesses. Harry's mother was president of the Methodist Home Missionary Society of Iowa. Hopkins graduated from Grinnell College with honors in 1912. Hopkins's career in social work began during the Progressive Era when he worked in the settlement house movement. He held a variety of positions working with poor immigrants. He worked for a time with the Red Cross in New Orleans and Atlanta during World War I. In 1922, he returned to New York and was later appointed the director of the New York Tuberculosis Association. Later in 1931, Hopkins was appointed

(Continued)

(Continued)

executive director of the New York Temporary Relief Administration to provide relief for unemployed Americans, a very innovative program at the time, since previous to this program only women and children could receive state relief. In the early 1930s, Hopkins and Frances Perkins (another settlement house alumni) served on President Roosevelt's Committee on Economic Security. Out of this experience they developed the framework for the Social Security Act and the Works Progress Administration Act of 1935. Earlier, in May 1933, Hopkins had been appointed the chief administrator of the Federal Emergency Relief Administration by Roosevelt, which gave states and localities over $3 billion to operate local work projects. Later he would supervise the Works Progress Administration. These programs were hailed as critical components of the recovery effort during the Great Depression.

In 1938 President Roosevelt appointed Harry Hopkins Secretary of Commerce as World War II approached and the need for preparedness and wartime policies surfaced.

In this position he developed plans to meet England's need for supplies and headed the Lend-Lease program. He also served as envoy to the British and Soviet governments and attended the Yalta Conference. Clearly he was a valuable resource to President Roosevelt and bravely continued his duties even though he was struck with cancer. In 1945 President Truman awarded him the Distinguished Service Medal. Harry Hopkins died in New York City in 1945.

Hopkins has been referred to as the "bishop of relief" because of his role in providing millions of Americans with relief during one of the worst economic periods of American history. His contributions as an administrator and planner helped a nation get back on its feet, and his creativity in designing and delivering government-sponsored programs and services chartered a new role for government that had not existed before. Social workers today can point with pride to Harry Hopkins for his vision and dedication to social justice in one of the darkest periods of this nation's history.

● AFDC

The one program designed to meet the needs of children and their caretakers would prove to be the most controversial of all the New Deal programs: Aid to Dependent Children. ADC was originally conceived as a short-term program to help widows and children survive the depression. The grants were only for children with one caretaker (hence no mention of families in its name).

With this program the federal government assumed the responsibility for children whose caretakers could not support them. What was the significance of ADC? On one level the federal policy was simply an extension of the mothers' pension programs already passed by most states. From another perspective, the federal government had for the first time taken responsibility for social reproduction, which included raising and socializing children, a sphere previously left to families. ADC was a radical shift away from the laissez-faire philosophy that the market economy could meet the needs of families. Only with the massive unemployment of White men in the primary labor market could such a change have taken place. Under this policy the federal government did not aid all poor children, only those who were "deprived of parental support by death, continued absence from the home, or physical or mental incapacity . . ."[17] In this way ADC substituted the federal government for one parent, most often the father.

The growth in the number of single mothers during the Great Depression alarmed policymakers; in addition to the approximately 100,000 single mothers receiving mothers' pensions in 1934, it was estimated that another 300,000 single-headed families would need financial assistance as the depression deepened. The provision for single-headed families in the Social Security Act was made grudgingly and with the intention of freeing single mothers from the obligation to work at low-paying jobs so that they might care for their children. Unlike mothers' pension programs in states, which gave localities great leeway in determining how and whether to grant relief, ADC programs were required in every state, though some states delayed until the 1940s to start up their programs. The federal part of the grants was very low, with a maximum of $18 per month for the first child (compared to $30 per month for recipients of OAA), and no money was allotted for a caretaker (usually the mother) until 1950. In every state since the program's inception, grant levels have been set below the prevailing wage level in keeping with the Poor Law tradition of less eligibility. Consequently, grants have varied considerably from state to state to avoid competing with low-wage labor. Aid to Families With Dependent Children (AFDC) grants (the name was changed in 1962) have always been lower than the Supplemental Security Income (SSI) grants (the program, established in 1974, that combined Aid to the Blind, Aid to the Permanently and Totally Disabled, and Old Age Assistance).[18]

ADC was designed for single mothers, just as mothers' pensions had been. The implementation of ADC/AFDC carried a moral imperative similar to the earlier policy: Mothers must provide a "suitable home" to remain eligible for welfare. This criterion was sanctioned by the Federal Bureau of Public Assistance in the 1939 amendments to the Social Security Act and joined by another criterion used by some states that "employable mothers" should not be given ADC, since it would undermine their availability for low-wage work. The "employable mother" rule was used to disqualify African American women from receiving welfare in Southern states, along with the "man in the house" rule (see below). Until the end of World War II, the majority of women on ADC continued to be White widows.[19]

ADC was the only New Deal program that directly benefited women. Unemployment insurance was limited to full-time, mostly unionized occupations that principally employed White men. Most women who worked during the Great Depression worked in domestic service or as part-time workers, occupations not covered by UIB.[20] During the period of the Great Depression there was a consistent effort to persuade or force married women to leave the labor force so that unemployed men could have their jobs.[21] The provisions of the Social Security Act reinforced the traditional gender role assignment of women by ensuring that women without husbands to support them would not enter the labor force but could receive ADC to stay home and care for their children.

● ATTITUDES TOWARD WOMEN ON WELFARE

The number of women on welfare grew by 107% from 1960 to 1969.[22] Although never a popular program, ADC/AFDC became even more unpopular when the numbers of women, particularly African America women, receiving aid increased dramatically. The "problem" of unmarried motherhood had begun to be constructed differently for White and African American women: For White women out of wedlock, pregnancy was seen as an individual psychological problem; for African American women, the same was seen as a sign of "cultural pathology."[23] As the costs of welfare increased along with the number of women and children receiving grants, the focus of welfare changed from a program designed to help White widows to one aiding unmarried, separated, and divorced women.[24] As a result of this shift, during the 1950s and 1960s, states with large African American populations began enacting "suitable home" and "man in the house" rules, allowing welfare officials to deny aid to mothers whose moral standards they disapproved of.[25] The "man in the house" rule was based on the original 1935 law stipulating that only children deprived of both caretakers were eligible for aid; while mothers had been added to the ADC in 1950, a man in the house was presumed to be acting as a second caretaker of the child, rendering the child ineligible for aid. Welfare offices hired investigators to check up on women applying for or already on welfare, sometimes in infamous "midnight raids" when investigators hoped to surprise a "man in the house." Some states also questioned the suitability or moral fitness of a mother applying for welfare if one of her children was illegitimate.[26]

The economic functions of AFDC were well established by 1960. Instead of being a system of charity for women without men to support them, AFDC became a stabilizer of the secondary labor market, with the number of women on welfare expanding at the same time as low-paying jobs were contracting and diminishing as more low-wage workers were needed. This expansion and contraction of the welfare population was accomplished by states tightening eligibility rules with requirements such as the suitable home rule, which was used to disqualify women applying for welfare and to remove other women from the welfare rolls. These rules were relaxed as low-wage jobs became scarce, allowing more women to receive welfare for their children. Thus welfare shadowed the market economy, providing workers willing to work for low wages and, according to Piven and Cloward, functioning as a safety valve for discontent among marginalized populations, reducing the chances of unrest and challenges to market capitalism.[27]

The number of women entering the welfare system after 1950 included larger proportions of African Americans than before, as women left the depleted agricultural employment of the South and went north looking for work, where they were restricted to low-paying and temporary jobs.[28] When these jobs ended, African American women sought public assistance. States sometimes removed children from homes of African American women who applied for welfare on grounds of neglect, utilizing the "suitable home" rule; in other cases they simply denied aid to these families.[29] In 1960, in the Fleming rule, the federal government ordered states to provide for children removed from homes of welfare recipients on the grounds of neglect; the next year Congress passed a law authorizing AFDC funds for children who were placed in foster care as the result of the suitable home regulations. Thus the transfer of children from the welfare system to the child welfare system began, and the movement of African American children from informal community care to public foster care was launched[30] (see Chapter 8).

In the 1960s while Whites still outnumbered African Americans on welfare, the public perception of welfare, fueled by racism and ignorance of economic realities, had hardened. In the South, the Supreme Court decision desegregating public schools in 1954, combined with the emergence of the civil rights movement in the 1960s, evoked widespread fear that the established ways of racial segregation were ending. The presence of African American women on the welfare rolls fed stereotypes about promiscuity that had haunted them since slavery days, even though the birth rate to single mothers in all ethnic groups grew during the 1960s. Racial animus, fueled in some places by the civil rights movement and the push for integration, increased the condemnation of African American welfare mothers.[31] In 1968 the Supreme Court declared the "man in the house" laws to be unconstitutional, an easing of restrictions that brought more mothers onto welfare. Then as now, welfare grants were insufficient to stave off poverty; many families on welfare lived in inadequate shelters and suffered from food insufficiency.[32]

● **ENDING WELFARE AS WE KNEW IT:
THE PERSONAL RESPONSIBILITY AND
WORK OPPORTUNITY RECONCILIATION ACT**

The biggest change in welfare for needy mothers and children since the passage
of the Social Security Act occurred in 1996, when Congress approved the end

**President Bill Clinton signing the Personal
Responsibility and Work Opportunity
Reconciliation Act**

SOURCE: AP Photo/Rod Edmonds.

of AFDC and replaced that program with Temporary Assistance for Needy Families (TANF). The key word in the new policy was *temporary;* the entitlement to federal support was replaced with a short-term program whose aim was to end welfare by moving adult caretakers of eligible children into the workforce. The federal grants that had funded AFDC were folded into block grants and allocated to states based on the number of persons who had received grants under the AFDC program; the initial grants were to be reduced by 10% each year. States, in essence, were allowed to run their own welfare programs with federal monies; the restrictions were time limits: TANF recipients could receive welfare for 2 years consecutively and 5 years lifetime. Work requirements of 30 hours a week for adult caretakers of eligible children meant that welfare no longer supported domesticity and maternalism; instead, mothers had to join the labor force, look for work, or be trained to join the labor force. With this law, those living in poverty were no longer entitled to federal support. Other provisions of the law included restricting aid for unmarried minor parents who did not live with an adult caretaker, usually their parents. States had options to enact a "family cap," which limited the amount of aid states could pay to the number of children of a recipient upon entering TANF; subsequent children were not given additional monies. States also had the option to deny TANF for life to a woman convicted of a drug felony. Recipients receive Medicaid while they are participating in TANF; after they leave the welfare rolls, parents can apply for Medicaid for their eligible children.[33]

While previous efforts at welfare reform sought to mandate work, this is the first policy that terminates welfare regardless of the caretaker's employment status.[34] Why was the entitlement to welfare ended in 1996? According to its critics, AFDC enrollment had soared to an all-time peak in 1994, covering 5 million families and more than one eighth of U.S. children. More than half of AFDC children were born outside marriage, and three fourths had an able-bodied parent who lived away from home.[35] But deeper reasons lay behind the antipathy toward welfare; even at its peak, AFDC accounted only for approximately 1% of the federal budget; cost alone was not a major reason for the effort to end women and children's entitlement to welfare. In fact the congressional hearings on the Personal Responsibility and Work Opportunity Reconciliation Act (PRWORA) reveal an antipathy toward welfare mothers based on deep-seated values about women's place in American society. The welfare reform bill targeted long-term welfare families, who were in the minority of those receiving aid in the 1990s. The legislation was specifically targeted toward unwed mothers, particularly African American women.

Public hostility toward unwed mothers gained new strength from the conservative counterrevolution that emerged in the wake of the feminist and other social movements of the 1960s and 1970s. The feminist movement challenged traditional beliefs about what a woman should be. Previous to modern feminism the qualities of domesticity, piety, submissiveness, and purity were thought to be central to the character of a good woman, to her femininity, and to the fulfillment of her cardinal roles: wife, mother, and daughter. Feminists reshaped the beliefs about the inevitability of women's gender roles, arguing for the plasticity of gender. While feminism made a difference for middle-class White women, it did not affect the lives or opportunities of poor women or women from oppressed groups, who had never lived under the privileges or strictures of these so-called feminine characteristics.

The conservative backlash to feminism, inspired by a wave of Protestant fundamentalism in the 1990s, led some to believe that feminism had encouraged a widespread sexual promiscuity among women.[36] Some conservatives wished to impose sexual discipline on women who they believed were benefiting from the looser sexual morals and having children out of wedlock in order to gain welfare benefits.[37] While this belief was refuted by the fact that most (73%) women on welfare had only one or two children, the ideological position against supporting women having children out of wedlock remained firm. Even liberals argued that women on welfare had failed to make responsible reproductive decisions. With these ideologies dominant in the 1990s, the passage of a bill to "end welfare as we know it" seemed all but inevitable.

During the congressional hearings on welfare reform it became clear that traditional beliefs about gender dominated the thinking of most lawmakers. Welfare itself was cited for promoting nonwork and illegitimacy. The "problem of illegitimacy" was mentioned repeatedly, with one witness testifying that it was "the most serious problem facing our country today."[38] "Marriage and reducing out of wedlock births" were central goals of welfare reform: The belief was that if welfare became temporary and work oriented, women would choose marriage over dependence on the federal government. The hearings were laced with coded references to sexual promiscuity; racism was thinly disguised. Birth rates of single African American mothers were presented separately from those of other groups. Some testifying before Congress argued that even applying for welfare ought to disqualify women from retaining custody of their children; in these cases the father should be granted custody.[39] Reminiscent of the ideology that underlay the "man in the house" rules of the 1950s, the congressional hearings reflected assumptions that most welfare mothers were immoral, raising children who joined gangs and used drugs. The message was clear: Women on welfare needed to be disciplined; since most women were now working outside the home, women on welfare needed to be sent to work. The reality of the feminization of poverty and the exigencies of the secondary labor market never emerged during the hearings. The conservative counterrevolution focused on welfare mothers, but much of its anger was directed at feminists who refashioned the modern understanding of gender roles. The failure of feminists to recognize a common ground with women on welfare and other economically marginalized women left these women helpless in the face of the punitive policy of welfare reform.

TANF was reauthorized in 2006 (in the Deficit Reduction Act of 2005) after much congressional debate. This act substantially increases the proportion of recipients who had to participate in work activities for a specified number of hours each week. The new policy emphasizes "work first," over education or training, increasing the work requirements to 35 hours a week. As a result states have implemented work-first programs that stress job search and rapid entry into employment. State programs also have focused on supporting work by permitting recipients to keep a part of their welfare check when they become employed. The reauthorization of TANF allows education leading to a baccalaureate or advanced degree to count as vocational educational training, for a maximum of 12 months.[40]

The reauthorization put new emphasis on marriage promotion, offering states federal grants to promote marriage among welfare recipients. The Bush administration was committed to the assumption that marriage will solve the problem of poverty for many women seeking public assistance, even though in economically marginalized groups the pool of marriageable men is smaller than in the middle class and men often work at low-paying, temporary jobs in the secondary labor market. While two-headed families have an economic advantage over single-headed families, especially those headed by women, the use of federal policy to encourage marriage for welfare mothers is heterosexist and paradoxical, considering the Defense of Marriage Act (DOMA). Passed in the same year (1996) as PRWORA, DOMA outlaws federal recognition of gay and lesbian marriage. Encouraging marriage for poor women but outlawing it for gays and lesbians is a clear introjection of religious values in social policy.

Child care funds for TANF recipients are paid for out of block grants given to states for this purpose, as well as from a separate federal fund known as the Child Care and Development Fund. States have a great deal of flexibility as to how to meet child care needs for TANF recipients. The funds are provided in the form of vouchers designed to meet 75% of child care costs in local communities, but the demand for child care has far outstripped the supply, both in terms of federal funding and in the availability of child care facilities. Many low-income families, including those on TANF, receive no help with child care, and the costs of licensed child care are often prohibitive. These families must settle for substandard child care arrangements, even though research suggests that good child care can have positive long-term consequences for children's cognitive, emotional, and social well-being.[41] Child care support generally ends as soon as the TANF grants end or shortly thereafter.

Efforts to secure child support from the fathers of children on welfare were increased under TANF. Applicants who do not verify paternity can be denied welfare or receive reduced benefits. Payments secured while families receive TANF must be paid to the federal government and the states to repay welfare payments, resulting in no net benefit for families. Enforcing child support payments is far more difficult than it would appear. Many men, especially in the African American and Latino community, may not have the resources to pay child support due to discrimination, poor education, lack of jobs in inner cities, and other factors that limit their economic mobility[42] (see Chapter 4).

The impact of TANF on federal support of poor women and children was profound. In the first 6 years after its passage, the federal contribution to welfare decreased by $55 billion.[43] The amount of welfare payments declined from 2000 to 2005, reducing the program's ability to lift families out of poverty (see Table 7.1).

TABLE 7.1   Income, Earnings, and Benefits of Welfare Recipients (2000 and 2005)

	2000	2005	Change
Annual Mean TANF Family Income	$25,528	$22,733	−$2,795
Annual Median TANF Family Income	$16,904	$15,405	−$1,499
TANF Family Income Relative to Poverty (%)			
< 50% Poverty	25.3	31.6	6.3*
50%–100% Poverty	31.2	27.6	−3.6
100%–150% Poverty	16.6	16.8	0.1
150%+ Poverty	26.9	24.1	−2.8

SOURCE: From "TANF Caseload Composition and Leavers Synthesis Report," by Gregory Acs and Pamela Loprest, 2007, Washington, DC: The Urban Institute.

*indicates change is significant at the 90% confidence level

Has TANF reduced welfare dependency? The short answer is yes. TANF has been successful in reducing welfare rolls, especially during the initial years after passage of the policy. More than 50% of welfare recipients left the welfare rolls between 1996 and 2005. Of these approximately one half were working. However, most parents who left TANF for work had low earnings and were unable to increase their wages or earnings significantly over time. Many families unable to secure stable employment face serious barriers. These range from mental and physical health problems to domestic violence, substance abuse, and unstable housing.[44] While progress in reducing welfare dependency has been substantial, reduction in poverty of families who would have previously qualified for welfare has not been as great. In most states, families lose eligibility for TANF cash assistance at income levels that are well below the poverty line. Most employed TANF leavers earn low wages over time and continue to face hardships in making ends meet. Those who leave TANF voluntarily or who are forced off welfare due to time limits lose their Medicaid coverage and their automatic entitlement to food stamps. In some cases only eligible children are receiving a reduced grant because their caretaker has been sanctioned by the state or because of immigration status.[45] In 2002 one study found that two thirds of former welfare recipients had incomes below the poverty line.[46] While slightly more than half of those who left the welfare rolls before 2000 were working, from 2000 to 2005 that percentage dropped to 39%, and the yearly income of leavers declined after 2000. In 2007 about 20% of leavers were not working, were not living with a working spouse, and received no public assistance.[47] For these leavers TANF was not a success. See Figure 7.1 for the decline in the number of welfare recipients since 1996.

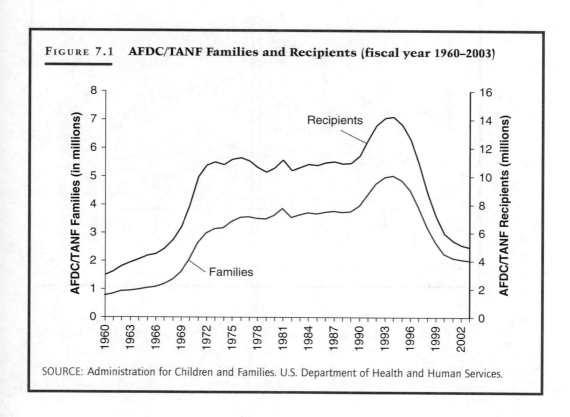

FIGURE 7.1   AFDC/TANF Families and Recipients (fiscal year 1960–2003)

SOURCE: Administration for Children and Families. U.S. Department of Health and Human Services.

In other developed countries the rate of poverty among single-parent families is much lower than it is in the United States, largely due to labor market policies that promote wage equity and social policies that offer children's allowances to each child in a family. The availability of subsidized child care and national health insurance likewise reduces poverty in single-parent families in these countries.[48]

The relationship between welfare and the labor market is reciprocal—as one expands, the other contracts. Piven and Cloward argued that welfare policies are cyclical and move from liberal to restrictive depending on the conditions in the labor market.[49] Unemployment rates in the United States were relatively low throughout the 1990s, compared to the late 1970s and 1980s, making the restrictive policies of TANF more feasible; as fewer people are unemployed, welfare is harder to access.[50] See Figure 7.2 for unemployment rates in the United States since 1960. Note the decline in unemployment at the time TANF was passed in 1996.

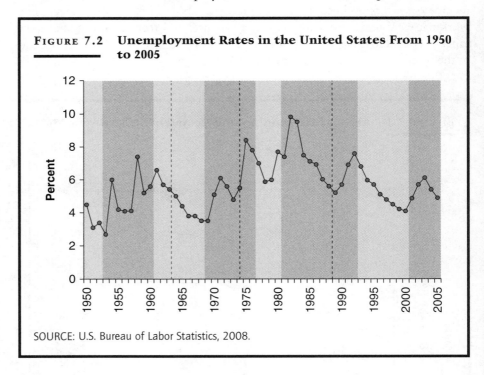

FIGURE 7.2   **Unemployment Rates in the United States From 1950 to 2005**

SOURCE: U.S. Bureau of Labor Statistics, 2008.

A promising development is the fact that a few states have begun programs to pay income supplements to working families who have left TANF for periods ranging from a few months to 2 years; other states are considering such laws. These policies can improve employment outcomes for families by offering incentives for former recipients to secure and keep jobs. Such policies can reduce poverty by providing income assistance on top of the earnings families receive when they leave the welfare rolls and go to work.[51]

The PRWORA also made legal immigrants ineligible for food stamps and SSI. These measures have been largely overturned since the passage of the act. Legal immigrants who have been in the United States for 5 years, as well as immigrant children and immigrants with disabilities, are now eligible for food stamps. SSI and Medicaid were restored to most legal immigrants living in the United States in 1997.[52]

MISSED OPPORTUNITIES OF TANF ●

TANF represents the acknowledgment of a new reality for American women: Most work, and working has been normalized, even in a two-parent, middle-class family. The cultural changes that led to the shift to work over welfare are perhaps inescapable. However, the policy was also fueled by a dislike of poor women and a racial animus against African American women, who now, along with Latinas, represent the majority of women receiving TANF.[53] Regardless of the ideology behind its passage, TANF would have been far more successful in lifting women out of poverty if a public jobs program had been part of the policy, similar to the one designed for men in the primary labor market during the New Deal. Public jobs for welfare mothers were not considered at any point in deliberations about TANF. Depending on secondary labor market jobs to lift women out of poverty was bound to be a failed effort, especially with the lack of national health insurance or subsidized child care.

It is clear that ending poverty was not a goal of welfare reform; rather, it was ending welfare. Women and children are no longer entitled to public support if they cannot make it in the labor market. All women must now make their way in the market economy, bringing their children with them, for better or worse. Poor children are the official target group of any welfare policy, but over the years this has been forgotten as their mothers increasingly have become the target of the moral reform efforts that drive welfare policy.

SOCIAL SECURITY ●

Social Security, the second major income maintenance program in the United States, has been far less controversial than welfare policy, either AFDC or TANF. While both Social Security and welfare can be linked historically to the English Poor Laws, and while both trace their origin to the Social Security Act of 1935, the differences between them are more striking than the similarities.

Older Americans in adult services center

SOURCE: © PhotoDisc.

A major reason for the differing public attitudes toward the two policies is the fact that Social Security (OASDI, or Old-Age, Survivors, and Disability Insurance) is an insurance-based program, paid for by a wage tax on workers in the United States, whereas TANF is a direct transfer of funds from the tax-supported general revenue funds of the federal and state governments. The Social Security retirement program is much larger than TANF; in fact, it is the largest social program in the United States.

More than 49 million people receive monthly OASDI benefits (see Figure 7.3). About 91% of the population age 65 and older received benefits in the form of old-age pensions at the end of 2006. The majority of these, about 33 million, were retired workers and their dependents; about 7 million were survivors of deceased workers; and about 8 million were disabled workers and their dependents. The total amount of monthly benefits paid during 2006 was about $553 billion, for an average monthly check of $1,031. Benefits are paid out without respect to income; unlike TANF, Social Security is not means tested (see Table 7.2).

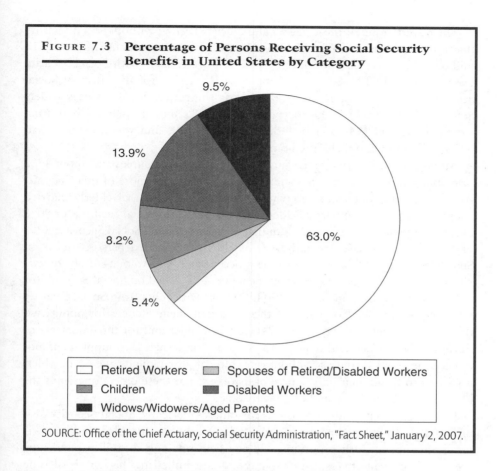

FIGURE 7.3   **Percentage of Persons Receiving Social Security Benefits in United States by Category**

9.5%

13.9%

8.2%

5.4%

63.0%

☐ Retired Workers   ☐ Spouses of Retired/Disabled Workers

☐ Children   ■ Disabled Workers

■ Widows/Widowers/Aged Parents

SOURCE: Office of the Chief Actuary, Social Security Administration, "Fact Sheet," January 2, 2007.

TABLE 7.2   **How Much Did Beneficiaries Receive in 2006?**

Average Monthly Retirement Benefits	
Retired Worker	$1,031
Retired Worker and Spouse, Ages 62 and Older	$1,712
Average Monthly Survivor Benefits	
Aged Widow(er) Alone	$1,008
Widowed Parent and Two Children	$2,147
Average Monthly Disability Benefits	
Disabled Worker, Spouse Under 65, and One Child	$1,642

SOURCE: Office of the Chief Actuary, Social Security Administration, Fact Sheet, January 2, 2007, Table C.

The poverty rate for those age 65 and older is 10.1%; without Social Security that rate would rise to 46%. Nationwide, Social Security benefits lift nearly 13 million seniors age 65 and older above the poverty line. With Social Security benefits just 1 in 12—8.7%—is poor.[54] See Table 7.3 for the effect of Social Security on poverty rates of seniors across the states. Wealth varies widely among the elderly. In 2000, the poorest fifth of senior households had a net worth of $3,500 ($44,346 including home equity), and the wealthiest had $328,432 ($449,800 including home equity).[55]

Among Social Security beneficiaries, 21% of married couples and about 43% of unmarried persons rely on Social Security for 90% or more of their income. Among *African Americans* receiving Social Security, 32% of elderly married couples and 54% of unmarried elderly persons relied on Social Security for 90% or more of their income in 2004. Among *Latinos* receiving Social Security, 39% of elderly married couples and 58% of elderly unmarried persons relied on Social Security for 90% or more of their income in 2004. Among *elderly unmarried women* receiving Social Security benefits, 46% relied on Social Security for 90% or more of their income in 2004.[56] Monthly benefits from Social Security represent at least half or more of the total retirement income for about two thirds of all Social Security recipients age 65 or older and for three quarters of those age 75 or older. Although Social Security was designed to supplement, not replace, personal savings, for about one third of all recipients age 65 or older, it is close to being their only source of income.[57] For these older Americans the loss of Social Security would be catastrophic.

In addition to providing pensions for older Americans, Social Security also provides disability payments to those who qualify as disabled and to their family members. Both programs, old-age pensions and disability payments, are based on wage taxes, and the payouts are linked to the length of time worked; a minimum of 10 working years is required. The Social Security Act also provided federal grants-in-aid to the states for the means-tested programs of Old Age Assistance, Aid to the Blind, and Aid to the Totally and Permanently Disabled, which were replaced by the Supplemental Security Income program in 1972. These programs supplemented the incomes of persons who were ineligible for Social Security (OASDI) or whose benefits could not provide a basic living.[58]

● SOCIAL SECURITY AND THE NEW DEAL

The United States was the last country in the industrialized world to enact a system for pensions for the elderly. Based on the model of veterans' pensions

TABLE 7.3   Effect of Social Security on Poverty Among Seniors

Persons Age 65 and Older	Percent Below the Federal Poverty Line		Number Lifted Above Poverty Line by Social Security
	Excluding Social Security	Including Social Security	
U.S. Total	**46.8%**	**8.7%**	**12,896,000**
Alabama	53.1	13.2	222,000
Alaska	31.7	5.9	11,000
Arizona	43.2	6.8	235,000
Arkansas	58.1	11.8	180,000
California	39.8	7.9	1,065,000
Colorado	42.9	7.3	151,000
Connecticut	37.0	5.0	157,000
Delaware	40.9	6.0	34,000
District of Columbia	41.8	16.3	17,000
Florida	50.2	8.7	1,116,000
Georgia	47.8	11.8	273,000
Hawaii	27.8	5.6	35,000
Idaho	48.0	5.1	63,000
Illinois	47.6	7.2	569,000
Indiana	51.5	8.1	341,000
Iowa	52.9	7.4	179,000
Kansas	46.1	6.3	150,000
Kentucky	54.6	10.7	216,000
Louisiana	49.5	12.6	192,000
Maine	56.0	7.2	97,000
Maryland	40.1	9.0	196,000
Massachusetts	46.9	8.4	316,000

(Continued)

TABLE 7.3 (Continued)

Persons Age 65 and Older	Percent Below the Federal Poverty Line		Number Lifted Above Poverty Line by Social Security
	Excluding Social Security	Including Social Security	
Michigan	48.6	8.0	461,000
Minnesota	43.2	7.7	171,000
Mississippi	53.3	15.8	120,000
Missouri	43.8	5.8	249,000
Montana	50.6	7.8	55,000
Nebraska	47.0	8.4	79,000
Nevada	40.6	6.0	82,000
New Hampshire	43.6	4.9	63,000
New Jersey	45.6	6.2	456,000
New Mexico	47.2	13.4	78,000
New York	44.4	8.4	872,000
North Carolina	50.1	12.1	370,000
North Dakota	55.9	10.3	39,000
Ohio	46.2	6.6	563,000
Oklahoma	48.8	10.7	171,000
Oregon	47.8	4.7	168,000
Pennsylvania	50.2	6.9	737,000
Rhode Island	49.8	5.6	70,000
South Carolina	49.2	11.6	194,000
South Dakota	51.7	8.9	44,000
Tennessee	54.7	12.6	265,000

Persons Age 65 and Older	Percent Below the Federal Poverty Line		Number Lifted Above Poverty Line by Social Security
	Excluding Social Security	Including Social Security	
Texas	48.5	12.5	757,000
Utah	37.6	8.6	51,000
Vermont	54.7	7.4	35,000
Virginia	41.8	9.1	264,000
Washington	44.7	7.2	251,000
West Virginia	58.1	9.3	137,000
Wisconsin	44.8	7.1	253,000
Wyoming	50.4	6.4	26,000

SOURCE: CBPP tabulations of the Current Population Survey for March 2001, 2002, and 2003.

NOTE: Income is family cash income after taxes plus EITC and certain noncash benefits (food, housing, and energy assistance). Figures are 3-year averages for 2000 through 2002.

enacted after the Civil War, Social Security drew on a long tradition in Western capitalistic countries that elderly people needed government protection and should not be forced to depend on their own savings or on their families when they could no longer work. However, before the Great Depression the expectation in the United States was that the elderly would save enough money for their nonworking years or, failing that, be able to depend on their family. In other words, the ideology of the work ethic, combined with the commitment to laissez-faire government, precluded a government policy to support older Americans.

Veterans' Pensions

Veterans' pensions were established by Congress in 1862 and covered Civil War veterans and their dependents. In 1890 the pensions were expanded to cover any veteran who had served in the Civil War for at least 90 days along with his dependents. The sole criterion was an inability to perform manual labor, satisfied fully by old age. Disabled veterans were given pensions in 1906. Pensions were a drain on the federal government; in fact, the United States spent more on its veterans' pensions than Great Britain did on its old-age pensions. When the Civil War generation died out around 1910, pressure for a new system of old-age assistance grew. Unions demanded a system of pensions paid for by the federal government out of general tax revenue, but businesses opposed a federally supported pension and wanted workers to pay. While some businesses did institute pension plans in the beginning of the 20th century, most did not, and the vast majority of American workers had no pensions as they moved into old age.

The concept of providing for workers in retirement was based on a relatively new concept of old age that emerged in this country at the end of the 19th century at the same time as the growth of heavy industry, which made it difficult for older persons to continue to work in the labor-intensive jobs. Before this period the United States had been a rural and manufacturing economy, where the concept of retirement was unknown. Most people worked until their death or until sickness or disability forced them to withdraw from the labor market. Those who were unable to support themselves through work depended on and lived with their children. Older Americans without children or other family members willing to care for them went to the local poorhouse. As the number of elderly increased due to increasing longevity and industrialization and urbanization pressured immigrant families, fewer elderly were able to live with their families, and poorhouses were transformed into old-age homes.[59]

The United States came into the Great Depression naked as far as policies for older Americans were concerned. There were no guaranteed pensions; nor was there any sort of income support for retired persons or persons too old to work, with the exception of a federal pension program for federal employees funded entirely by employee contributions. A movement for old-age pensions had emerged in the 1920s among many groups of Americans, all of whom shared the common fate of growing old. This movement encouraged some businesses to offer pension plans, usually funded entirely by workers, but during the Great Depression this limited number of private pension plans went bankrupt.

President Roosevelt decided to create an old-age pension system, along with another important protection for workers, Unemployment Insurance Benefits, as well as aid to mothers and children. These were incorporated into the Social Security Act of 1935. In deciding to include old-age pensions in the act, Roosevelt was influenced by political pressure from older Americans that emerged on two fronts. The Townsend movement was begun by a California dentist, Francis Townsend, who was said to have a following of almost 5 million people. He and his supporters promoted the Townsend Old Age Revolving Pension Plan, asking the federal government to give $200 a month to all persons over 60 who would leave the workforce and spend the money in the same month they received it. While the plan never moved beyond the petition stage, Townsend's discontent with federal policy was matched by Louisiana Governor Huey Long's plan to "Share the Wealth" by guaranteeing $2,000 a month to all American families (which would have been twice as much as the $1,000 a month almost 20 million American families were earning in the early 1930s). Long wanted to tax oil refineries in Louisiana to pay for his plan and raise taxes on the wealthy. Both these plans frightened Roosevelt, who saw that the Great Depression was giving birth to policies that threatened the capitalist economic structure. These were important reasons why Roosevelt supported both old-age insurance and unemployment insurance (UIB).[60]

During the debate about the form old-age pensions were to take, there was a division in the country between those, including unions and progressives, who wanted old-age pensions to be funded entirely out of tax revenue with no worker contributions, and those, represented by conservatives and business interests, who wished it funded out of employee contributions alone, with no contributions from employers or taxpayers. A compromise was reached after prolonged debate and resulted in old-age pensions being funded from two sources: employee contributions and employer contributions, making neither side of the debate happy. In its first iteration in 1935, the Social Security pension system excluded farm workers and domestic workers, effectively shutting out the majority of African Americans and Latinos, who predominated in these secondary labor market occupations.[61] The payouts originally were not scheduled to begin until 1942 in order to allow the wage taxes to accumulate, but due to continuing economic distress suffered by older Americans, Social Security payouts began in 1940.

While Roosevelt had included a plan for national health insurance in the Social Security Act, Congress dropped it because of the opposition of the American Medical Association. Even though the United States is and was the only industrialized country to mandate that workers pay a regressive wage tax to fund a social insurance program, for some the program was too radical because it was not voluntary. Business interests, represented by the National Association of Manufacturers, decried the Social Security Act and its old-age pension provisions as undermining self-reliance and independence.[62]

While Social Security is essentially an insurance program, it also has the characteristics of a welfare program, due to the redistributive aspects of the benefits structure (see below). Social Security is unlike traditional insurance where the payout only comes with a disastrous event (death, sickness, accident). With Social Security the payout is expected and, depending on individual life span, universal. See Figure 7.4 for how important Social Security is to the well-being of many older Americans.

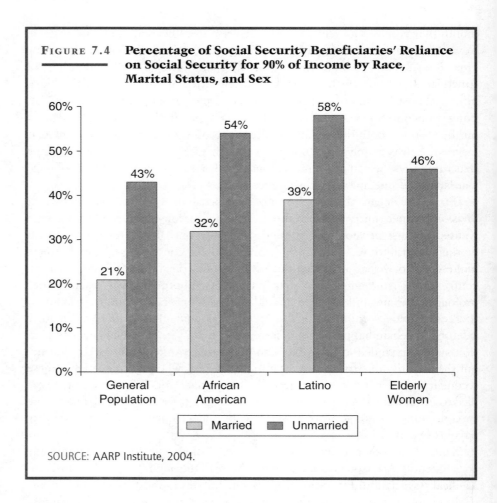

FIGURE 7.4   **Percentage of Social Security Beneficiaries' Reliance on Social Security for 90% of Income by Race, Marital Status, and Sex**

SOURCE: AARP Institute, 2004.

● HOW DOES SOCIAL SECURITY WORK?

Social Security is funded through a wage tax known as FICA (Federal Insurance Contributions Act), which is composed of 6.2% of a worker's salary up to the income cap, plus 1.45% of all earnings for Medicare funding. The income cap governs how much of one worker's income can be taxed for Social Security; it is raised every year to keep up with inflation. In 2008 the income ceiling for Social Security taxes was $102,000; workers earning more than that pay no wage tax on their additional wages. Employers pay the same Social Security tax (6.2%) as workers but do not pay into Medicare. Persons who are self-employed must pay both employer and employee contributions. Every year payments into Social Security that exceed payments going to current retirees are put into the Social Security Trust Fund. The federal government uses the extra funds (or surplus) from the Social Security Trust Fund to buy U.S. Treasury bonds, thereby loaning itself money from the Social Security Trust Fund. In 2006, the trust fund (in the form of Treasury bonds) had a balance of over $2 trillion, largely due to the number of baby boomers working and paying into the fund. Baby boomers are paying for current retirees, which is why the Social Security Trust Fund is currently awash with a surplus of money. Until the baby boomers retire beginning in 2010, there will be more workers paying into Social Security than there are retirees withdrawing funds. However, as baby boomers retire and begin to collect Social Security, the fund will be depleted because the replacement ratio (ratio of workers to retirees) will diminish and the payouts will exceed the wage taxes of the workforce, which will be smaller than the number of baby boomers currently working.

In order to prolong the life of the Social Security system, in 1983 the age of retirement and eligibility for full benefits from Social Security was raised from 65 to 66 for those born between 1943 and 1960 and to 67 for those born after 1960. Social Security benefits can be accessed at age 62, but benefits will be permanently reduced for those who do. The maximum Social Security benefit for individuals in 2008 was approximately $2,185, and each member of a married couple can collect that amount if he or she qualifies for the highest payments; the so-called marriage penalty was ended under the Bush administration. If one spouse dies, the remaining spouse can continue to receive his or her own benefit or 100% of his or her spouse's benefit, whichever is higher.

Equity Issues in Social Security

Social Security payments replicate the inequality in the labor market: Those who earn more in their lifetime (primary labor market workers) will receive higher Social Security benefits. However, Social Security payments have a redistributive aspect, since lower-paid workers receive a larger proportion of their wages in the form of benefits than do higher-paid workers, even though higher-paid workers will receive higher benefits. Most Americans who live long enough to collect benefits will take more money out of Social Security than they put in.

The Social Security wage tax is a regressive tax because all income earners pay the same amount; therefore, the tax is a greater proportion of the income of low-wage workers. This is slightly offset by the redistributive aspects of Social Security payments discussed above. While low-income, ethnic minority workers are likely to receive a good return on their Social Security wage tax, there is one important caveat that may eliminate the redistributive impact of Social Security pensions for some members of this group: African American men have a shorter mean lifespan than other groups (African American men's average age of death in 2003 was 63), precluding many from collecting a Social Security pension.[63] Persons retiring at 62 collect only 70% of their Social Security benefit, limiting those African Americans who decide to retire early to a reduced benefit. For those engaged in physical labor, working past 62 may be a physical hardship or impossibility, due to poorer health and higher rates of self-perceived disability. Older African American men are already less likely to work than their White counterparts, largely due to these factors. Fewer African American men and women report retirement as the reason for not working; instead they report poor health or disability. Unemployment rates increase among African American and Latino men as they age. Raising the age of eligibility for collecting Social Security benefits hurts workers in the secondary labor market, especially African American men, who are likely to have no other source of income in the years before they can collect Social Security.[64]

Women face a different set of issues with Social Security. When the program was founded in 1935, the expectation was that most women were traditional homemakers who would not be employed outside the home once they married and had children. Of course this assumption ignored immigrant and ethnic minority women, who continued to work in low-paying jobs when they married as well as women who did not marry. These traditional, class-bound assumptions about women's roles led to the homemaker policy: Married women can collect 50% of their husband's Social Security or, if they worked, their own. Among women collecting Social Security to date, most have elected to take their husband's Social Security rather than their own, due to low wages and low benefits. This provision privileges married, heterosexual women and discriminates against lesbians and single women. Since a woman has to be married to a man for at least 10 years to be eligible for his Social Security, it also discriminates against divorced and widowed women not married for 10 years. Women must be at least 62 to collect benefits based on a former spouse's Social Security; generally women who remarry are not eligible for any benefits of a former spouse. Married women who take one half of their husbands' Social Security lose all their own contributions to Social Security over their working life. Some have suggested income sharing between spouses as a way to calculate benefits more equitably. Under this arrangement the income of spouses would be combined and then split, with benefits based on each equal half.

Women are far more likely to be poor after age 65 than men, for various reasons, including low wages and time taken out for childbirth and childrearing. They are more likely than men to count on Social Security as their only income and not have pensions from their years of employment. Since women on average live longer than men, they are more likely to spend their final years in poverty. More than 40% of elderly women depend on Social Security for more than 90% of their income, compared with 28% of elderly men. More than 20% of unmarried women over 65 are poor, but only 5% of married couples over 65 are poor.[65] Without Social Security, half of all women over 65 would live in poverty.[66] Social Security combats poverty in the elderly with little of the stigma attached to welfare for mothers and children. It provides purchasing power, thereby increasing demand among an increasingly large population of older Americans. By these measures, it is a successful program.

SURVIVORS' BENEFITS AND DISABILITY INSURANCE ●

In 1939, Congress made the old-age insurance system a family program, by adding benefits for dependents of retired workers and surviving dependents of deceased workers. No major changes were made again in the program until the 1950s, when it was broadened to cover many jobs that previously had been excluded, including regularly employed farm workers (not secondary labor market migrant workers) and domestic workers. The scope of Social Security was also widened in 1956 through the addition of disability insurance. Benefits were provided for severely disabled workers aged 50 or older up to 65 and for adult disabled children of deceased or retired workers. In 1958, the Social Security Act was further amended to provide benefits for dependents of disabled workers similar to those already provided for dependents of retired workers. After 2 years of receiving Social Security Disability Insurance payments, workers and their surviving spouses and children are eligible for Medicare. An important change took place in 1972, when amendments provided for automatic cost-of-living increases for Social Security recipients.[67]

THE FUTURE OF SOCIAL SECURITY ●

As the United States as a whole grows more diverse, so does the population age 65 and older. In 2003, older Americans were 83% non-Hispanic White, 8% Black, 6% Hispanic, and 3% Asian. By 2030, an estimated 72% of older Americans will be non-Hispanic White, 11% will be Hispanic, 10% will be Black, and 5% will be Asian American. African Americans and Latinos over age 65 rely on Social Security payments much more than do other Americans (see Figure 7.5).[68] Most astonishing, the U.S. population age 65 and over is expected to double in size within the next 25 years. By 2030, almost 1 in

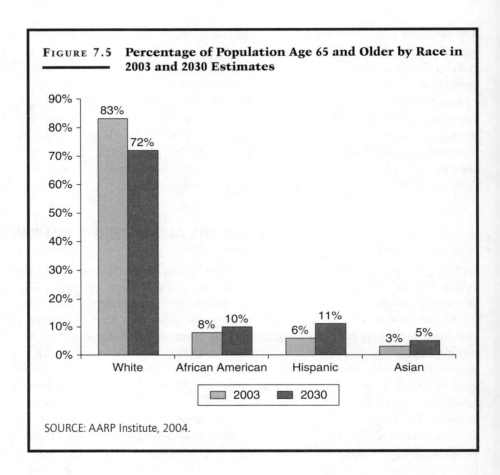

FIGURE 7.5   **Percentage of Population Age 65 and Older by Race in 2003 and 2030 Estimates**

SOURCE: AARP Institute, 2004.

5 Americans—some 72 million people—will be 65 years or older. The age group 85 and older is now the fastest-growing segment of the U.S. population.[69]

Fixing Social Security

Due to the demographic imperative discussed above, the Social Security Trust Fund is projected to run out of funds sometime in the middle of the 21st century. In reality, there is no Social Security Trust Fund, but instead the federal government has used the trust fund monies to buy U.S. Treasury bonds as discussed above, effectively lending itself the Social Security trust funds. These funds will have to be paid back. The date when benefits exceed Social Security tax revenues is projected to be 2017, at which time the gap will be covered by redemption of the Treasury bonds bought by the Social Security Trust Fund. Policymakers fear that the Social Security Trust Fund will run out of money completely by 2041 (this date changes frequently). By this time the dependency ratio, or the number of workers it takes to support a retired person, will be 2.1 to 1, a dramatic change from 1960 when there were 5 working persons for each retired person.[70]

Reform of Social Security was given a sense of urgency as company failures resulted in the loss of private pension funds set aside for employees, as happened in the case of Enron's collapse in late 2001. Many private companies have been cutting back on guaranteed pensions for workers, and some public pension funds are in jeopardy as well. Traditional defined benefit plans that guarantee a monthly income after retirement are giving way to defined contribution funds, where employees put aside tax-deferred income each month and companies contribute a partial match to the retirement fund. In 2005 only 20% of American workers were covered by traditional defined benefit retirement plans.[71] Well-publicized corporate failures, like the collapse of the large investment firm Bear Stearns in 2008, are often accompanied by the loss of employee pension funds. These economic collapses have brought the problems in the Social Security system to the fore but also served to make many less anxious to subject Social Security to the vagaries of American enterprise. Private pension plans cover only workers in the primary labor market and are not a hedge against loss of income in later years for workers in the secondary labor market, in any case. These funds have contributed to the inequality of income among older Americans. Yet now even primary labor market workers cannot rely on pension plans.

What are the options to keep Social Security viable for the next generations of retirees? The first question to consider is whether there will be a political will to continue to support Social Security through wage taxes. Future generations may decide to change or eliminate the system of old-age pensions created in the New Deal, although it is unlikely that no system of protection will succeed Social Security. The political power of older Americans will preclude that outcome.

Raising the Income Cap

Options to increase the Social Security reserves for future generations include raising the income cap so that all income will be taxed. The reason not to do this is the political reality that wealthier Americans may oppose Social Security if they are taxed on more of their income, especially since they are unlikely to retrieve their contributions the way Social Security benefits are structured. The income over the income cap could be taxed at a lower rate than 6.2%, at 2% or 3%, serving the goal of increasing Social Security reserves without incurring a strong political backlash. Another option is to make the wage tax progressive: That is, it could be lower at lower incomes and higher at higher incomes. However, this measure may reduce the amount of money available in the trust fund.

Making Social Security Benefits Means Tested

Another less popular and politically more dangerous remedy would be to make the benefits means tested according to the incomes of older Americans. In this plan older Americans with a higher level of income would receive smaller amounts of Social Security benefits than those with less income. This policy may jeopardize the Social Security program by making it appear similar to TANF; one of its strengths politically has been the argument that it is viewed as an insurance system, not a welfare system. As we have seen, welfare is subject to political vagaries that Social Security has thus far escaped. Making Social Security like welfare would not be to its advantage, especially given the fact that all workers have to pay into it (but some may receive very little in benefits if they are means tested). One way around this dilemma would be to give all retirees a basic minimum benefit and supplement this grant with another monthly benefit based on need. This would preserve the social insurance aspects of the plan for everyone, while going further to meet the financial needs of the poorest elderly. The problem with this plan is similar to the purely means-tested plan discussed above; the wealthiest Americans would receive less return on their Social Security investment than they do now (but at least they would receive something).

Borrowing From the Social Security Trust Fund

Since the late 1980s, the federal government has borrowed some of the Social Security Trust Fund (in Treasury bonds) to pay for other government programs when the federal budget has been in deficit. After the Clinton administration ended in 2000, there was hope that the federal budget surplus would be used to repay the Social Security Trust Fund.[72] However, with the second Bush administration, the federal surplus quickly disappeared, largely due to the war in Iraq and Afghanistan; the deficit soared, and repayment of the Social

Security Trust Fund never happened. Repaying the money owed to the Social Security Trust Fund and maintaining its integrity would go a long way to preserving the fund for future generations.

Reducing Cost-of-Living Adjustments

The federal government offers Cost-of-Living Adjustments (COLAs) to Social Security and SSI recipients based on the increase in the Consumer Price Index, which is designed to measure the inflation rate. In 2007 the COLA was 2.3%, only marginally helpful to those depending primarily on Social Security. Reducing the COLA further or eliminating it would amount to a tremendous hardship for these persons.[73] Over the past few years the COLA has lagged behind rising health care costs, particularly the Medicare premiums that most people in Social Security pay. While Social Security checks have increased by about 3% each year, Medicare Part B premiums (Part B pays for a part of physician costs and other services) have risen on average by almost 10% annually.[74]

Rescinding Tax Cuts for the Wealthy

A more indirect but important solution to the future of Social Security lies in rescinding the tax cuts for the wealthy passed by the Bush administration (see Chapter 4). Rescinding the tax cuts and staunching spending on the war in Iraq would easily cover the deficit in the Social Security Trust Fund over the next 75 years.[75] In fact, wiping out the Social Security shortfall over the next 75 years would be only one third the cost of extending the Bush tax cuts through that period.[76]

Privatization

With the beginning of the Bush administration, the idea of privatizing Social Security came to life and became a central lynchpin of the domestic policy agenda. President Bush appointed a Social Security commission in 2001 to study the feasibility of privatizing Social Security. The commission offered three plans, all of which involved cutting benefits to retirees.[77] Many suggestions about how privatization might work have been offered since 2001. Some plans were based on so-called add-ons, where individuals would be taxed at a slightly higher rate than 6.2%, at 7.7% to 8.2%, in order to fund the individual investment accounts. Money made in the individual accounts would be paid out upon retirement and would be in addition to the basic pensions guaranteed by Social Security. Most proposals for privatization called for reducing Social Security benefits in order to maintain the future viability of the Social Security Trust Fund.[78] President Bush, for example, proposed to fund the private accounts through reduction in Social Security benefits.[79] Other privatization plans featured so-called "carve-out" plans, which would take part of the money now paid as a wage tax and invest it in individual accounts. This plan would substantially reduce Social Security benefits, as there would be less money in the Social Security Trust Fund. It would negatively impact the retirement resources for low-income retirees, especially women, who generally receive lower payments than men. Women especially lose the redistributive effect of Social Security payments (see above) under the smaller guaranteed pensions of a privatized system. Low-income workers in general have less education, have less access to investment advice, and are less able to weather the fluctuations and downturns of the financial markets.[80] Another negative feature of private investment accounts would be their high administrative costs, with commissions to brokerage firms constituting a large share of these costs.

Proponents of privatization argue that the return to investment on private accounts is likely to be higher over the long run than the interest paid on U.S. Treasury bonds (5.2% in 2007), where the Social Security funds now sit.[81] The problem with this approach is that individual investment decisions can vary widely, and the risk for persons unschooled in investment strategy, including the working poor, could be high. The Bush plan exempted individuals who were 55 years and older, reasoning that older Americans should not take a risk with funds they will need in the short run. Democratic members of Congress and the public did not respond with enthusiasm to the privatization initiative, and the decline of the stock market after 2005 did not encourage Americans to cast their retirement hopes toward Wall Street. See Table 7.4 for a summary of options for preserving Social Security.

● SUMMARY: COMPARISON OF SOCIAL SECURITY AND TANF

Social Security is a contract among future workers, current workers, and older Americans. Each one of these groups has a vested interest in another group if Social Security is to survive. Older Americans collecting benefits and those about to retire need the salaries of workers contributing to Social Security to be as high as possible to support their level of benefits and future COLAs. Current workers who are contributing to the system have an interest in the education and well-being of children who are the future contributors to their

TABLE 7.4   Summary of Options for Reforming Social Security

Option	Pros	Cons
Raising the income cap so that all income will be taxed	Increases Social Security reserves	Wealthier Americans may oppose Social Security if they are taxed on more of their income
Making Social Security benefits means tested	Matter of fairness that higher level of incomes should receive fewer benefits than those with lower incomes	May weaken support of social security program as it may seem more like a welfare program than an insurance system
Stop borrowing from Social Security Trust Fund	Repaying money owed to Social Security would preserve the fund for future generations	No money for other government programs when federal budget is in deficit
Reduce Cost-of-Living Adjustments	Would close about 17% of Social Security's financing gap	Add hardship to those depending primarily on Social Security
Rescind tax cuts for the wealthy	Would cover the deficit in the Social Security Trust Fund over the next 75 years	Wealthier Americans may oppose Social Security if they are taxed on more of their income
Privatization	Returns on private accounts are likely to be higher than interest paid to fund benefits now	Investment decisions can vary widely, and risks for working poor could be high

Social Security benefits. All three generations are linked if the long-run viability of Social Security, which is projected to offer lifetime benefits of $470,000 to a low-income elderly married couple by 2030, is to be maintained.[82]

Since today's children will be the workers of tomorrow, supporting old-age pensions for adults currently working, policies that deprive children of what they need to grow into healthy and productive adults, are shortsighted. Likewise, discrimination against certain members of the labor force, restricted educational opportunities, and low-paying jobs in the secondary labor market may result in future generations being unable or unwilling to support a system of old-age pensions. Because all generations are linked in these ways, childrearing should be viewed as a collective responsibility, and childrearing activities of parents should be rewarded when calculating Social Security payouts. Time taken out for childrearing should be credited by the Social Security system in the same way paid labor is. This policy change would give single mothers and mothers not married for 10 years access to the same benefits as women married for 10 years.

In summary, welfare and Social Security/Disability are linked as two halves of the policy that provide a floor under the income of our most vulnerable groups. Both are descended from the English Poor Laws brought to this country by colonists who recognized that the Protestant work ethnic must make exceptions for members of society who are unable to work: children, disabled persons, and elderly persons. While the policies are interrelated, the attitudes they inspire and the benefits they offer are very different. Far more federal resources go to older adults than to poor mothers and children. Though children, like elderly persons, cannot be expected to work, the punitive aspects of the welfare system belie this commonsense understanding. Mothers and children on welfare are pitied or scorned; elderly receiving Social Security benefits are collecting what is due them and what they have a right to receive. Social Security is earned, and welfare is seen as charity, something arbitrary, subject to cuts when economic times are bad and altruism is constricted. This attitude toward welfare did not predominate at the time welfare was initiated; in 1935 the policy was viewed as a necessary support to women who were raising children without adequate means. The adoption of TANF in 1996 demonstrated a new attitude toward welfare; it was now seen as a temporary gift for which the adult recipients (not the children) needed to demonstrate correct behavior in the form of work. Similar to the poorhouses of the late 19th century, welfare now demands reciprocity beyond the tasks of parenting. Work of some sort is required, both during and after participation in TANF.

Four reasons stand out for the differences in the public support of Social Security and TANF. First, Social Security is based on work previously done; TANF is based on the inability (or, some would say, refusal) to work since most believe that if women were working, they would not need welfare. Second, Social Security is viewed as old-age insurance that people pay for themselves (even though there are redistributive aspects to Social Security), while TANF is viewed as an outright handout from taxpayers. Third, older Americans constitute a strong political lobby with great influence over policymakers, especially through the power of their organization, the AARP. The initiative to privatize Social Security, for example, was met with strong resistance from AARP, which launched a $5 million campaign against the Bush plan in 2004.[83] Fourth and finally, each of these income support programs has a different relationship to the *market economy*. Social Security allows individuals to opt out of the labor market if they wish (although they may work and collect benefits), while under TANF mothers must work while they receive funds.

Welfare is central to market capitalism, serving a necessary function of providing a tertiary labor market that can expand into the secondary labor market. While Social Security benefits reflect the inequities of the labor market during the working lifetime of older Americans, there is nothing demanded of its recipients. Neither lack of reciprocity nor their behavior can disqualify them from their entitlements (see Table 7.5).

TABLE 7.5   Summary of Differences in Public Support of Social Security and TANF

Social Security	TANF
Based on work previously done	Unable to secure employment
Old-age insurance program that people pay for themselves	Viewed as outright handout from taxpayers
Has a strong lobby particularly through AARP	Does not have a strong lobby given views on welfare and political powerlessness of poor persons
Can opt out of labor market	Recipients must work while they receive funds

CONCLUSION

Due to the inequality inherent in the unregulated *market economy,* some groups cannot meet their minimum economic needs. Two of these groups were central to the worthy poor of the colonial poor laws: women/children and elderly. Two policies have been created to offer these "worthy" groups economic resources: welfare and Social Security. However, as a result of the *historical ideologies* toward poor women and children, welfare involves temporary assistance and is a far more punitive policy than Social Security. The comparative generosity of Social Security is related to the fact that older Americans have worked in order to qualify for benefits. Even in this more generous policy, the values of self-reliance and independence are evident: In the United States Social Security is an insurance-based system that requires workers and employers to contribute to retirement income so that elderly will not be reliant on taxes. This retirement system is unlike that of other industrialized countries where public resources in the form of taxes have been used to support the income of elderly persons. In both cases members of certain ethnic groups who have suffered from our *legacy of discrimination* have benefited less from both policies than have White persons.

The success of Social Security suggests how welfare can be reformulated as a more socially just policy. An income maintenance system, similar to Social Security, should be given to all families in the form of an income transfer out of general tax revenues and returned through the tax system by families whose earned income is at predefined level. This family allowance would eliminate the stigma and the calls for character reformation that accompany TANF, which has not lifted women and children out of poverty but tied them inextricably to low-paying jobs in the secondary labor market. We already have an Earned Income Tax Credit system in place to deliver the resources to families. Under this policy universal entitlement for older Americans would be paired with universal entitlement to a minimum level of income for families and children, lifting them out of poverty just as Social Security has done for older Americans.

While the answer to the problem of welfare seems simple, the political will to make it happen needs to be developed. The social work profession is uniquely positioned to begin the political dialogue that can result in the transformation of welfare into a universal system of entitlements.

For further understanding of Social Security, consider the Web resources listed in Table 7.6.

TABLE 7.6   Internet Resources for Understanding Social Security

Organization	URL	Description
AARP	http://www.aarp.org/research/socialsecurity/overview.html	Excellent Web site that provides lots of data on Social Security benefits
Campaign for America's Future	http://www.ourfuture.org/socialsecurity	Lots of information on effects of privatization of Social Security
National Senior Citizens Law Center (NSCLC)	http://www.nsclc.org	Promotes the independence and well-being of low-income elderly and disabled Americans and offers information on Social Security
Center for Policy Research	http://www-cpr.maxwell.syr.edu/gero_ed	Policy-oriented curriculum components in aging and social sciences—has an excellent module on the economic issues of aging
Social Security Online	http://www.ssa.gov	Official Web site of the U.S. Social Security Administration
Center on Budget and Policy Priorities	http://www.cbpp.org/pubs/socsec.htm	Information on putting Social Security debate in context

1. Why is welfare for farmers not seen as negatively as welfare for women and children?

2. Why was a public jobs program not part of the welfare reform effort?

3. Why are women on welfare blamed for their situations?

4. What are the advantages and disadvantages of TANF as it is now constructed?

5. What are the advantages and disadvantages of the privatization of Social Security?

6. How could the Social Security system be transformed to be more equitable to poor women and ethnic minorities?

7. What are the advantages and disadvantages of raising the income cap on Social Security? Making the wage tax progressive?

8. What are the advantages and disadvantages of tying Social Security benefits to need?

9. Why is Social Security a more generous policy than TANF?

10. What changes would be necessary to refashion TANF into a more socially just income maintenance program for women and children?

The following is an example of a policy analysis of TANF. Each policy analyst will have his or her own point of view of what the problem is and what the causal hypotheses are that account for the problem. In an actual policy analysis, references would be used to support the argument. In this analysis, a brief example of the first section is offered.

Part One: The Social Problem Addressed by the Policy

1. What is/are the problem/s to be solved in the most fundamental terms?

The question addressed by TANF is whether children whose caretakers cannot support them adequately should receive public resources. The default assumption in the United States is that children will be provided for by their parents' income received as a result of their labor or through accrued wealth. When parents or other caretakers are unable to provide the basic necessities for their minor children, should society in the form of taxpayers be expected to support children and, by extension, their caretakers, or should

(Continued)

(Continued)

children be left to the exigencies of the market economy? The historical ideologies that have dominated this country since the colonial period suggest that self-reliance and individualism and hard work should be guiding principles in determining the economic fate of all individuals. Since children are not responsible and are considered vulnerable if not innocent, the question of their material well-being and survival may be different from that of responsible adults.

2. What is the history of the problem in the United States?

Beginning with the colonial poor laws in the 17th century, women and children have been considered worthy poor and eligible for local aid. The first system of welfare for mothers and children was local, funded by towns and administered by town officials. It consisted primarily of boarding out women and children with local families who were reimbursed for their care. This system lasted until the mid-19th century when some states build almshouses for poor women and children. The system of indoor relief replaced the older outdoor relief. Within the almshouses women were expected to work at domestic labor and attend religious services, as well as care for their children. This system was replaced by outdoor relief at the beginning of the 20th century as almshouses fell out of favor.

Under the efforts of progressive reformers, some states passed mothers' pensions legislation, which gave grants to a limited number of poor women and children. This system was replaced by the first federal system of aid to mothers and children passed under the Social Security Act of 1935. Aid to Families With Dependent Children (AFDC), as it came to be known, was an entitlement program wherein

every mother and child who qualified on the basis of income was eligible for federal/state aid. This changed in 1996 when the Personal Responsibility and Work Opportunity Reconciliation Act was passed, creating Temporary Assistance for Needy Families, which replaced AFDC.

3. What are the various theories about the cause/s of the problem? Based on this, what do you think is/are the most important cause/s of the problem?

What causes poverty? Before the passage of the Social Security Act in 1935, most Americans thought that poverty among children was due to the absence of a father and husband. Pauperism, as it was known, was largely taken for granted as an aberration in the American story of upward mobility. Even with the passage of the Social Security Act in 1935 when economically marginalized "widows and orphans" were the targets of Aid to Dependent Children, most Americans assumed the lack of a husband was the cause of poverty. It was not until the numbers of women and children grew in the 1960s that the question of why they turned to welfare was raised as worthy of investigation. Since then, many theories have been advanced to explain why women turn to welfare to support their children and themselves. These theories include morally based ones, such as poor character, sexual promiscuity, lack of discipline, and laziness. Others have posited a culture of poverty where intergenerational transmission of values such as inability to delay gratification and lack of appreciation for education were responsible for promoting welfare reliance. Some of the above theories were thinly veiled racial arguments. Currently the notion of work readiness is used as an explanatory variable: Women on welfare do not have the work habits or experience that other women have, and this deficit explains their dependence on government assistance. All these theories are based on the assumption that the economic system provides adequate employment to all who seek it.

A perspective that locates the cause of the problem primarily outside the agency of women on welfare looks to the economic structure to explain the difficulties some women experience in providing for their children. Low-paying jobs in the secondary labor market, inadequate education, and discrimination are thought to be factors related to poverty among women with children. The feminization of poverty might be cited by those who support this theory.

The reasons for women seeking government assistance to provide for their children are multifocal. Economic factors combine with educational limitations and discrimination to present obstacles to self-sufficiency for many women with children. Lack of publicly supported health care in secondary labor market employment, lack of subsidized child care, and economic fluctuations, such as recessions and layoffs, push some women and their children into poverty.

NOTES

1. Mimi Abramovitz, *Regulating the Lives of Women: Social Welfare Policy From Colonial Times to the Present* (Boston: South End Press, 1988), 86–87; David Rothman, *The Discovery of the Asylum: Social Order and Disorder in the New Republic* (New York: Walter de Gruyter, 2003), 20–26.

2. Mary Ann Jimenez, *Changing Faces of Madness: Early American Attitudes and Treatment of the Insane* (London: University of New England Press, 1988).

3. Rothman, *The Discovery of the Asylum*.

4. Michael Katz, *In the Shadow of the Poorhouse: A Social History of Welfare in America* (New York: Basic Books, 1986), 3–36.

5. Katz, *In the Shadow of the Poorhouse*, 30.

6. Katz, *In the Shadow of the Poorhouse*, 86.

7. Linda Gordon, *Pitied but Not Entitled: Single Mothers and the History of Welfare* (Cambridge: Harvard University Press, 1994), 45.

8. Gordon, *Pitied but Not Entitled*, 62.

9. Gwendolyn Mink, *The Wages of Motherhood: Inequality in the Welfare State, 1917–1942* (Ithaca, NY: Cornell University Press, 1995), 27–53; Abramovitz, *Regulating the Lives of Women*, 8–11, 181–206.

10. Gordon, *Pitied but Not Entitled*, 49.

11. John Galbraith, *The Great Crash, 1929* (Boston: Houghton Mifflin, 1957); Irving Bernstein, *The Lean Years: A History of the American Worker, 1920–1933* (Boston: Houghton Mifflin, 1960), 312–334; Robert McElvaine, *The Great Depression: America: 1929–1941* (New York: New York Times Book Co., 1984), 25–50; Gary Nash and Julie Jeffrey, *The American People: Creating a Nation and a Society*, 7th ed. (New York: Pearson Longman, 2006), 792–794.

12. Bernstein, *The Lean Years*, 325–332.

13. Abramovitz, *Regulating the Lives of Women*, 223.

14. Katz, *In the Shadow of the Poorhouse*, 208–217.

15. Bruce Jansson, *The Reluctant Welfare State* (Belmont, CA: Brooks/Cole/Thompson, 2001), 177–184.

16. Katz, *In the Shadow of the Poorhouse,* 207–208.

17. Jansson, *The Reluctant Welfare State,* 206.

18. Abramovitz, *Regulating the Lives of Women,* 315–317.

19. Abramovitz, *Regulating the Lives of Women,* 319.

20. Mink, *The Wages of Motherhood,* 127.

21. Gordon, *Pitied but Not Entitled,* 183–199.

22. Catherine Pelissier Kingfisher, *Women in the American Welfare Trap* (Philadelphia: University of Pennsylvania Press, 1996), 31.

23. Regina Kunzel, *Fallen Women, Problem Girls: Unmarried Mothers and the Professionalization of Social Work* (New Haven, CT: Yale University Press, 1993), 163.

24. Abramovitz, *Regulating the Lives of Women,* 324–332.

25. Kenneth Neubeck and Noel Cazenave, *Welfare Racism: Playing the Race Card Against America's Poor* (New York: Routledge, 2001), 60–61.

26. Neubeck and Cazenave, *Welfare Racism,* 69–75.

27. Frances Fox Piven and Richard A. Cloward, *Regulating the Poor: The Functions of Public Welfare,* 2nd ed. (New York: Vintage, 1993).

28. Abramovitz, *Regulating the Lives of Women,* 320–321; Neubeck and Cazenave, *Welfare Racism,* 62–65.

29. Abramovitz, *Regulating the Lives of Women,* 325–329.

30. Abramovitz, *Regulating the Lives of Women,* 327; Jillian Jimenez, "The History of Child Protection in the African American Community: Implications for Current Child Welfare Policies," *Children and Youth Services Review* 28 (2006): 888–905.

31. Neubeck and Cazenave, *Welfare Racism,* 35–38.

32. Abramovitz, *Regulating the Lives of Women,* 336.

33. Personal Responsibility and Work Opportunity Reconciliation Act, Public Law 104–193, 104th Congress, August 22, 1996, www.fns.usda.gov/FSP/rules/Legislation/pdfs/PL_104–193.pdf, accessed March 7, 2008.

34. Jill Duerr Berrick, "Income Maintenance and Support: The Changing Face of Welfare," in James Midgley and Michelle Livermore, eds., *The Handbook of Social Policy* (Thousand Oaks, CA: Sage, 2009), 336–347.

35. Committee on Ways and Means, *Green Book 2004* (Washington, DC: U.S. Government Printing Office), http://www.gpoaccess.gov/wmprints/index.html, accessed March 8, 2008.

36. Margaret Bendroth, *Fundamentalism and Gender, 1875 to the Present* (New Haven, CT: Yale University Press, 1993), 3–10.

37. Mary Ann Jimenez, "A Feminist Analysis of Welfare Reform: The Personal Responsibility Act of 1996," *Affilia: Journal of Women in Social Work* 14 (Fall 1999): 278–291.

38. U.S. Congress, Senate, *Hearing Before the Committee on Finance, 104th Congress, 1st Session, March 9–29* (Washington, DC: U.S. Government Printing Office, 1995), 612, 795.

39. Jimenez, "A Feminist Analysis of Welfare Reform," 283.

40. Liz Schott, "Summary of Final TANF Rules: Some Improvements Around the Margins," Center on Budget and Policy Priorities, February 20, 2008, http://www.cbpp.org/cms/?fa=view&id=1084, accessed April 21, 2009.

41. Josefina Figueira-McDonough, *The Welfare State and Social Work: Pursuing Social Justice* (Thousand Oaks, CA: Sage, 2007), 251–254.

42. William M. Rodgers, "Forecasting the Labor Market Prospects of Less-Educated Americans," in Ronald Mincy, ed., *Black Males Left Behind* (Washington DC: The Urban Institute Press, 2006), 39–67.

43. Figueira-McDonough, *The Welfare State and Social Work*, 183.

44. Center on Budget and Policy Priorities, "Implementing the TANF Changes in the Deficit Reduction Act: 'Win-Win' Solutions for Families and States," February 9, 2007, http://www.cbpp.org/cms/?fa=view&id=1176, accessed March 5, 2008.

45. Figueira-McDonough, *The Welfare State and Social Work*, 185.

46. Pamela Loprest, "Making the Transition From Welfare to Work: Successes but Continuing Concerns," in A. Weil and K. Finegold, eds., *Welfare Reform: The Next Act* (Washington, DC: The Urban Institute Press, 2002), 17–32.

47. Gregory Acs and Pamela Loprest, "TANF Caseload Composition and Leavers Synthesis Report," March 28, 2007, The Urban Institute, http://www.urban.org/publications/411553.html, accessed March 9, 2008.

48. Figueira-McDonough, *The Welfare State and Social Work*, 256.

49. Frances Fox Piven and Richard Cloward, *Regulating the Poor: The Functions of Public Welfare* (New York: Random House, 1971), 2–8.

50. Mehmet Ugur, *An Open Macroeconomics Reader* (New York: Routledge, 2002), 475.

51. Liz Schott, "Using TANF or MOE Funds to Provide Employment Assistance to Low Income Working Families," September 8, 2008, Center on Budget and Policy Priorities, http://www.cbpp.org/cms/?fa=view&id=312, accessed March 7, 2008.

52. Figueira-McDonough, *The Welfare State and Social Work*, 273.

53. Congressional Research Service Reports for Congress, "Welfare Reform: TANF Trends and Data," March 12, 2003, http://digital.library.unt.edu/govdocs/crs/permalink/meta-crs-5708:1, accessed March 12, 2008.

54. Arloc Sherman and Isaac Shapiro, "Social Security Lifts 13 Million Seniors Above the Poverty Line," Center on Budget and Policy Priorities, February 24, 2005, http://www.cbpp.org/cms/?fa=view&id=1111, accessed March 18, 2008.

55. AARP, "Social Security Benefits," January 2007, http://www.aarp.org/research/socialsecurity/benefits/, accessed March 18, 2008.

56. Alison Shelton, "Social Security: Basic Data," AARP Public Policy Institute, June 2007, http://www.aarp.org/research/socialsecurity/general/dd159_ss.html, accessed March 18, 2008.

57. American Academy of Actuaries, "Social Security Issues," July 2007, http://www.actuary.org/socsec/index.asp#2007, accessed March 14, 2008; Social Security Administration, "2006 OASDI Trustees Report," http://www.ssa.gov/OACT/TR/TR06/II_highlights.html#wp76460, accessed March 14, 2008.

58. Committee on Ways and Means, *Green Book 2004*.

59. Katz, *In the Shadow of the Poorhouse*, 200–202; David Hackett Fischer, *Growing Old in America* (New York: Oxford University Press, 1978), 3–11.

60. Katz, *In the Shadow of the Poorhouse*, 234–236.

61. Katz, *In the Shadow of the Poorhouse*, 244–245.

62. Nash and Jeffrey, *The American People*, 802–804.

63. Thomas La Veist, "Racial Segregation and Longevity Among African Americans: An Individual-Level Analysis," *Health Service Research* 38 (December 2003): 1719–1734.

64. Namkee Choi, "Potential Consequences of Raising the Social Security Eligibility Age on Low-Income Older Workers," *Journal of Aging and Social Policy* 11 (4, 2000): 15–38.

65. American Academy of Actuaries, "Social Security Issues."

66. AARP, "Social Security Benefits."

67. Committee on Ways and Means, *Green Book 2004.*

68. AARP, "Social Security Benefits."

69. U.S. Census Bureau, "Dramatic Changes in U.S. Aging Highlighted in New Census," March 9, 2006, http://www.census.gov/Press-Release/www/releases/archives/aging_population/006544.html, accessed March 18, 2008.

70. Social Security Administration, "History of SSA, 1993–2000," http://www.ssa.gov/history/ssa/ssa2000chapter3.html, accessed March 15, 2008.

71. U.S. Administration on Aging. *Profile of Older Americans, 2005.* www.aoa.gov/stats/profile. accessed March 20, 2008.

72. The Social Security Network, "What Do the Social Security Trust Funds Consist Of?" http://www.socsec.org/publications.asp?pubid=540, accessed March 16, 2008.

73. Social Security Administration, "Cost-of-Living Adjustments," October 2007, http://www.ssa.gov/OACT/COLA/colaseries.html, accessed March 20, 2008.

74. William D. Novelli and Edward Langston, "Social Security COLA Fails to Keep Up With Rising Costs," October 25, 2007, http://thehill.com/letters/social-security-cola-fails-to-keep-up-with-rising-costs-2007–10–25.html, accessed March 20, 2008.

75. Robert Greenstein and Chad Stone, "What the 2008 Trustees' Report Shows About Social Security," March, 27, 2008, Center for Budget and Policy Priorities, http://www.cbpp.org/cms/index.cfm?fa=view&id=64, accessed April 3, 2009.

76. Ibid.

77. Joel Blau with Mimi Abramovitz, *The Dynamics of Social Welfare Policy,* 2nd ed. (New York: Oxford University Press), 302.

78. Ibid.

79. Jason Furman, "The Impact of the President's Proposal on Social Security Solvency and the Budget," Center for Budget and Policy Priorities, July 22, 2005, http://whitepapers.silicon.com/0,39024759,60135894p,00.htm, accessed March 20, 2008.

80. John Williamson and Sarah Rix, "Social Security Reform: Implications for Women," *Journal of Aging and Social Policy 11* (4, 2000): 41–68.

81. Social Security Administration, "Trust Fund FAQs," http://www.ssa.gov/OACT/ProgData/fundFAQ.html#n3, accessed March 20, 2008.

82. C. Eugene Steuerle and Adam Carasso, "Lifetime Social Security and Medicare Benefits," The Urban Institute, March 31, 2003, http://www.urban.org/publications/310667.html, accessed March 22, 2008.

83. *New York Times,* "AARP Fights Social Security Plan," December 30, 2004, http://money.cnn.com/2004/12/30/news/economy/aarp_socialsecurity/index.htm, accessed March 22, 2008.

8

Responses to Child Maltreatment

Child Welfare Policy

CHAPTER QUESTIONS

1. When and why did the concept of child abuse emerge in the United States?

2. What factors contributed to the emergence of the public child welfare system?

3. What are the value conflicts at the heart of the public child welfare system?

4. What have been the major federal policies underlying the development of child welfare?

5. What are problems of discrimination in the current public child welfare system?

6. How have African American children been served by the public child welfare system?

7. What are the limitations of current policies to ensure the protection of children from maltreatment?

8. How can child welfare policies be refashioned to ensure social justice for children and their families?

● ● ●

Portions of this chapter have been reprinted from *Child Welfare Issues and Perspectives*, 2009, edited by Steven J. Quintero, with permission from Nova Science Publishers, Inc.

The protection of children from harm by their families and the provision of safe havens for children who are maltreated in their home environment are the twin goals of child welfare policy. In this chapter we will look at the emergence of the concept of child abuse, the evolution of the system of public child welfare, and the problems in developing policies to ensure children's safety, family functioning, and the development of alternative places of care for children. While public child welfare is now the dominant provider of protection and care for maltreated children, we will explore another system of child protection that developed in the African American community during the long period in which these children were excluded from public child welfare. After exploring the limitations of current child welfare policies, we will suggest other policies that would protect children and enhance family functioning without the limitations of our current policies.

In this chapter the *inequalities accompanying the market economy* in the United States will be seen as contributing to the problem of child maltreatment. Discrimination against these families has limited the resources and services the federal government is willing to commit to empower them to adequately meet the needs of their children, as *historically based negative ideologies about poverty and poor families intersect with discrimination against oppressed ethnic groups* serving to turn away from families of origin in the effort to ensure safety for children.

● THE CONCEPT OF CHILD ABUSE

While there are many issues in current child welfare policy in the United States, the fact that any society has a child welfare policy is a relatively new phenomenon. For much of human history parents have had sole control over the lives of their children, including how to discipline or punish them, what to feed them, and how much they should learn. Childhood itself has evolved over the course of human history, from being viewed as a period where children provide economic benefit to parents in rural economies to a more current conception in which children have become an economic liability for parents, costing far more than the economic utility they provide. Similarly, the emotional elements of parenting have been transformed in modern industrial societies. In the United States concern about children's survival has been largely replaced by concern about children's emotional, social, and intellectual well-being.

Since children were not seen as existing fully independently from their parents until relatively recently, the possibilities for protection of children from parental harm were virtually nonexistent. In fact, the role of children was subservient to the needs of parents in the largely agricultural societies that characterized most human settlements before the 18th century. Most residents of these earlier societies did not see childhood as a distinct developmental interlude but rather saw it as a period of miniature adulthood, where children were thought to be very similar to adults. Children in European families and in the British colonial families were viewed as economic assets, whose labor in and later out of the home was essential to families' economic survival. In colonial America outside the South, White children were considered future workers and sent to live with neighbors after age 7 to work as indentured servants (girls to assist the mothers and boys to learn a trade) in order to learn the value of work and responsibility. Parents, especially fathers, had complete control over children's lives; in the case of indentured servants, the male authority figure in the home had the final say. Parents were generally free to punish their children any way they wished, short of killing them. In general indentured servants were protected from abuse of masters far more than children were protected in their own homes.[1] Children had so few rights with respect to parental control that the state augmented parental power by bringing wayward children into the criminal justice system. For example, in 1641 the colony of Massachusetts passed a law known as the Stubborn Child Act, which allowed parents to bring disobedient children to court to appear in front of a judge. If a child was found guilty, the punishment could include capital punishment in the form of death by hanging.[2]

Local governments were not involved in protecting children through much of American history, with rare exceptions, until the end of the 19th century.[3] It is fair to say that during this period the concept of child abuse did not exist. Parents were normally considered immune from prosecution in cases of parental abuse, and there was no child protective service system; nor was there provision for out-of-home care. Children bound out as indentured servants were occasionally removed and placed in almshouses during the 19th century in cases of cruelty and gross neglect.[4] Parents, however, were free to punish their children through whipping, locking in small spaces without food and water, and hitting with objects such as tree limbs. While some states had laws on the books forbidding cruelty or neglect of children, there were no local jurisdictions that assumed responsibility for enforcing laws.[5] It is clear that even harsh corporal punishment was not thought to be cruel; teachers in the new public schools that opened in the mid-19th century had authority to punish children. Many had whips or paddles in the classroom, which they used freely.[6]

Life for most children was hard. While public schooling up to sixth grade began in the Northeast in the 19th century, many families, especially immigrant families, needed the income from child labor and could not afford to send their children to school. Elementary education was not compulsory in every state until 1918.

High schools were created in the early 20th century, after child labor laws forced most children to leave the full-time labor force. High schools were first established in urban areas, where they were viewed as necessary for training an industrialized workforce and socializing an immigrant population to American values.[7]

In spite of the growing opportunities for public education, the majority of children in the United States worked well into the 20th century. While the U.S. Census Bureau acknowledged that 1 of every 6 children worked in 1900, the numbers are thought to be far higher, as the census did not count children under 10; nor did it include children who worked informally for their parents in sweatshops or on farms.[8] By 1930 the number of children who worked had declined dramatically, largely due to child labor laws passed by the states in the Progressive Era, which led to the gradual acceptance by state authorities that children should be in school until they are 16.

Other factors important in the substitution of school for work included the increase in European immigration at the end of the 19th century discussed in Chapter 3. Adult immigrants began competing with children for work during this period, and employers began to see children as less desirable. Technological innovations in the industrial workplace and the need for a skilled, educated workforce encouraged employers to demand adult labor.

The removal of children from the labor market was also the result of a cultural change in how children were understood. The value of children moved from economic to emotional, as parents began to be seen as instrumental to their children's well-being.[9] This sentimental attitude toward childhood depended both on the removal of children from the workplace and on the emergence of the discipline of psychology in the universities. Cognitive and developmental psychology were the first aspects of academic psychology to gain credibility; each showed that children were not miniature adults but had specific developmental stages that must be negotiated for fully functioning adulthood. Another factor raising the importance of children in the American culture was the contraction of the birth rate among wealthier families in the early 20th century, which meant that children in White middle-class families were fewer in number and each came to be regarded as a precious resource. Urbanization rendered the necessity of large families to work the farmlands moot. In the new relations of parents and children, not only did parents forego the money children had brought into the family in the form of wages; they also were expected to give children an allowance out of their wages. Thus had the role of parent and child reversed, with parents now being responsible for meeting all the needs of a smaller number of children.[10]

White, middle-class attitudes toward childhood made it difficult for parents to send their children to work; instead they must spend their time at school, at home, and in play. This was truly a revolution that overturned centuries-long beliefs that children were economically important to parents, sent to work to help support the family. Immigrant and more economically disadvantaged families fought this new social construction of childhood because it served to limit family income. Yet it was this new paradigm about the meaning of childhood that both supported and made inevitable the emergence of child welfare.

The Emergence of Child Welfare

Central to the recognition that children were different from adults—that they were vulnerable and passed through distinct developmental stages—was the emergence of the social work profession. Perhaps the first organized effort to help abandoned children, outside of orphanages, took place in New York City in the mid-19th century under the auspices of Charles Loring Brace. Earlier in the 19th century the movement to house the poor in almshouses had been accompanied by an effort in some states to remove children from almshouses and place them in orphanages, where it was believed they would receive more appropriate treatment to meet their needs.[11] Charles Loring Brace, the founder of the voluntary society the Children's Aid Society, developed a "placing out" system that he believed was superior to orphanages in providing for homeless and destitute children. Children were shipped to the Midwest on so-called orphan trains and placed with farm families looking for help with farm labor as well as additions to their families. Brace's idea was that both parties to the transaction would receive ample rewards. Children would have a family, learn a trade and responsibility, and have a chance at upward mobility. Farm families would have the extra help needed in a rural economy and add to their family's prosperity and well-being. Society would benefit because the process would lead to the socialization of immigrant children, who had little to look forward to in overcrowded urban areas, into the classic American values of hard work and thrift. Brace believed in these rural parts of the United States the influence of school and religion would serve to uplift children from their poverty background.[12] Foster care programs in other urban areas developed under the auspices of voluntary organizations, which focused on removing children from single mothers who were living in urban poverty. Most of these child removals were voluntary, since the states had no authority to remove children from homes in the early part of the 20th century. While these first foster care programs were based on an altruistic impulse to save children who were neglected, abandoned, or living in economically marginalized homes, there was little or no supervision of children once they were removed. Today it seems very shortsighted to ship children out of urban areas away from their families and in the process effect a cultural transfer from immigrant culture to Yankee culture. Yet the outlines of this early foster care system and the current one are similar, with child removal rather than economic and social changes that would enable families to provide safer and better homes for their children the default child welfare strategy.

As discussed in Chapter 6, precursors to social workers, known as friendly visitors, visited immigrant families in other to both help and reform them. It was one of these friendly visitors volunteering with a charity organization society in New York who found Mary Ellen, a young indentured servant about 9 years of age who was being whipped, kept locked in a home, and frequently left alone in New York City. When the friendly visitor approached the New York Society for the Prevention of Cruelty to Animals for help, the director visited the child and was instrumental in her removal and placement with the friendly visitor, Etta Wheeler. The case was made famous by *The New York Times* and has been emblematic of the recognition of child abuse ever since. As a result of the publicity engendered by the case, the New York Society for the Prevention of Cruelty to Children (NYSPCC) was founded by wealthy volunteers. Mary Ellen married at 24 and lived until her 80s, thus giving a happy ending to her story and a beginning to official efforts to rescue children from unsuitable homes, later known as child protective services. After this several states in the Northeast founded voluntary societies similar to the NYSPCC (see Chapter 6).

The White House Conference on Children and Youth in 1909 brought together some of the new experts on foster care and the emerging field of child welfare. Surprisingly, given the movement toward foster care that had burgeoned since the latter decades of the 19th century, participants reached agreement that children should not be removed from their homes simply because their parents were poor. These early social workers at the conference objected to the practice of removing children from the homes of poor single mothers that was becoming common at the end of the 19th century. The first stirrings of the family preservation movement were apparent at the conference when family care was strongly endorsed as an alternative to foster care. The emphasis on family preservation gave an important boost to the efforts of progressive reformers to provide state support for single mothers and their children in the form of mothers' pensions.[13]

In 1912 the federal government moved permanently into the field of child welfare with the establishment of the Children's Bureau, which was headed by Julia Lathrop, formerly of Hull House in Chicago. The bureau was concerned with both maternal and child welfare, but its mission was to collect data on children, not to sponsor policy initiatives. Its first strategy was to focus on infant mortality and infant health. Infant mortality rates were high in 1900; almost

1 in 5 infants died in their first year of life.[14] In 1913 the Children's Bureau sponsored research on the issue of infant mortality in Johnston, Pennsylvania, a steel town with a large immigrant population. Results indicated a strong correlation between infant mortality and poverty, as measured by father's income. Its findings constituted a marked departure from assumptions that permeated the child-saving movement that maternal deficits caused infant death.[15] Yet the finding made little impact on child savers and others concerned with child welfare in urban areas, who continued to blame family deficits and heredity for problems experienced by children. These assumptions contributed to the foster care initiatives, not to family preservation efforts. Perhaps inevitably, given the prevailing attitudes of the Progressive Era, large-scale economic changes that would improve the wages of families were rarely seen as a strategy to improve child welfare. While income of single mothers was a concern to reformers who promoted mothers' pensions, by and large policies designed to promote the economic advancement of families were not promoted by child welfare advocates. Modifying the economic structure seemed like the long way around compared to removing children from poor families and placing them with families with greater means.

One policy designed to reduce infant mortality rates was the Sheppard-Towner Act, also known as the Maternity and Infancy Protection Act, passed in 1921. The bill had broad support from women, middle-class reformers, working-class women, and women from rural areas. Designed by Children's Bureau head Julia Lathrop, the bill provided federal matching funds to states to fund prenatal and child health clinics sponsoring educational efforts to encourage healthy practices in infant and child care. Improvements in sanitary conditions were urged by the clinics, as was breast feeding and education about well-baby care and child development. These educational efforts contributed to a decline in infant mortality rates after 1920.[16] Even though the act embodied a public health approach to infant mortality rather than a medical one, it was vigorously opposed by many in the medical profession and by conservative activists. These opponents stripped the medical care and nursing care for infants and children that were featured in the original legislation from the final bill. Opponents saw even health education as the first step to state-run medicine and viewed the act as undermining mothers' individual responsibility for children's well-being.[17] The program was terminated in 1929 as a result of conservative fears that the program would be a precursor to other large-scale social welfare programs. The same belief in individual responsibility for health and well-being is also at the heart of the arguments of those who oppose national health insurance today (see Chapter 9).

While not directly concerned with child maltreatment, the Maternity and Infancy Protection Act was the first federal effort to reach into families and offer support for parents and children; in this way the policy promoted child welfare. Under the Social Security Act of 1935, maternal and child welfare services were restored when the Children's Bureau was expanded with a mandate to oversee newly created state-run child welfare services to protect dependent and neglected children. These child welfare services were located in public welfare departments and therefore were offered only to poor families, implicitly acknowledging the link between poverty and certain forms of maltreatment on the one hand but serving to stigmatize welfare recipients as likely to maltreat their children on the other hand. The creation of public child welfare had commenced.

● PUBLIC CHILD WELFARE

There were three principles underlying the public child welfare system as it emerged in the 20th century: the colonial poor laws, the principle of *parens patriae,* and the concept of the legal contract. In the 19th century the poor laws were the basis of state action to care for dependent children from poor families. Children might be removed by state agencies like the Massachusetts State Board of Charities and placed with other families where their labor would be useful or placed in almshouses. Later in the century the child savers, like the one who rescued Mary Ellen, had more altruistic motives to help children in dire circumstances, which usually meant extreme poverty, by removing them to institutions or other homes.[18]

A second legal principle undergirding the public child welfare system is the English common law principle known as *parens patriae,* which establishes the state as the ultimate parent for children without parental oversight. This principle was to establish legal guardianship when a child inherited property. Today this principle is frequently cited as authorizing state protective service workers to remove children from their homes, although its original meaning did not include this.[19]

The third principle underlying public child welfare is that of the legal contract, an assumption that formal, individual responsibility for a child must be established by courts or agency jurisdiction. Similar to the state's efforts to determine property rights through the enforcement of property law, the child welfare system seeks to establish unitary responsibility for the child's welfare, which includes either the parent, the state (under the aegis of foster parents), or new adoptive parents. The idea that one party is solely responsible for the child is central to the public child welfare system, which seeks to establish clear lines of responsibility for children. This linear, unitary responsibility for children does not allow for shared legal responsibility among several parties.[20] Together these three principles establish the right of state child welfare systems to oversee the well-being of children in their jurisdictions, without the consent of parents.

History of African Americans in the Child Welfare System

In the 19th and for much of the 20th century, African American children were raised under an entirely distinct set of circumstances from that of White children, with families who had a different view of childrearing. These differences were based on both African cultural roots and the oppression African American families endured under slavery and afterward. The social construction of parenting was very different in the African American community than it was in the White majority community. The unitary view of individual legal responsibility for children that characterized child welfare law is opposed to the tradition of kin and community responsibility for childrearing in the African American community. Kinship care in these communities was partly a response to discrimination and economic hardship, but it was also part of the African cultural heritage that continued to inform life in the slave quarters and during late 19th- and 20th-century America. West African society featured an intensive kinship network where family relations were widespread and the responsibility for childrearing was collective. In Africa and later during slavery, extended families shared responsibility for parenting tasks, including community surveillance and discipline, daily care and nurturance of children living with parents, and substitute care for children whose biological parents could not care for them.

Substitute care was arranged informally by kinship networks, especially grandmothers. Sometimes, especially in Northern urban areas, fictive kin would assume responsibility for children when families were unable to or had moved away to find work. When parents returned, kin caretakers returned the children to them or joined with them in raising the child. This is one reason why African American families were reluctant to adopt children: The idea that parental rights had to be terminated (necessary for legal adoption) was an unwelcome idea, since boundaries of responsibility for children were fluid. The White model of closed adoption that dominated in the courts and child welfare system for decades was based on a fiction: Adoptive parents acted as if they were the biological parents, even substituting another birth certificate for the original one. This denial of the biological parents' connection to the child was unheard of in African American families, where the connection between parent and child was not denied, even in cases of informal adoption. Informal adoption of African American children by kin or fictive kin meant that children did not go to orphanages, which did not accept African American children in any case; nor were they adopted under the aegis of the formal legal public system. Because of the practice of informal adoption, few African American children became wards of the state before the 1960s. This informal system of child welfare was a necessary substitute for the formal White system of child welfare. It drew on the strengths of communities tested by discrimination and economic deprivation.[21] It was not until the 1960s that African American children were welcomed to private orphanages, which then were transformed into residential treatment centers when the federal government began to reimburse states for placement of foster children in these group homes.

The history of collective informal efforts in African American communities to ensure the protection and well-being of their children suggests that the public child welfare system, with its emphasis on unitary, singular responsibility for children, was not a good fit with African American families. The principle of *parens patriae,* where the state assumes responsibility for children whose parents cannot raise them, was meaningless for African American children until the 1960s, when African American children were brought into the public child welfare system. As local welfare jurisdictions began removing African American children from economically marginalized families at a much higher rate than other children, the early colonial poor laws were the most applicable legal precedent underlying child welfare practice.[22]

● FEDERAL CHILD WELFARE POLICIES

From the 1920s through the 1950s the social problem of child abuse receded from public awareness.[23] Those professionals who were concerned with child abuse worked in public welfare departments and were focused on removal of children from welfare families.

In a 1959 study of children in foster care, most of whom were removed from their homes due to neglect or economic hardship, Maas and Engler found that a negative correlation existed between the size of the Aid to Families With Dependent Children grant received by the family and the removal of children from their homes. Families who received larger grants were less likely to have children placed out of the home, suggesting that economic deprivation was directly linked to removal. Mass and Engler also found that many children in foster care lingered or *drifted* through the system for many years, although their placement was initially thought to be temporary.[24] Foster care had become substitute care, a modern replacement for the orphanage.

The social movements of the late 1960s and 1970s led to a new interest in children's rights, tying the denial of these rights to the oppression of women.

Disillusionment with public authority linked to the Vietnam War increased the sense that all sources of authority, including parental authority, were potentially oppressive. In this climate the radiologist C. Henry Kempe in 1962 published the article "The Battered Child Syndrome" in the *Journal of the American Medical Association,* in which he demonstrated that radiological examinations proved that childhood injuries were sometimes caused by parental abuse.[25] The publicity generated by this article led every state to enact legislation between 1963 and 1967 encouraging the reporting of child abuse.

The Child Abuse Prevention and Treatment Act (CAPTA) passed by Congress in 1974 was the federal response to the growing perception that child abuse by parents was a problem in some psychologically disturbed families, calling for government-sponsored professional intervention in family life. CAPTA established standard definitions of child abuse and neglect, authorized limited government research in child abuse prevention and treatment, and established funding incentives to tighten the state reporting laws that had been passed in the 1960s. In order to qualify for federal funds for foster care available under the 1961 Social Security Amendments, states were required to have staff and facilities available for treatment of children who were found to have been abused as a result of the mandatory reporting laws. Soon after the federal law was passed, states added protective custody provisions to their mandatory reporting laws.[26] While the original idea behind CAPTA was an assumption that only a small number of psychologically disturbed parents abused their children, by the time of congressional hearings to renew the legislation in 1977, the perception was that the problem had grown to near "epidemic proportions."[27] Several states reported a dramatic increase in the reports of child abuse since the passage of CAPTA. State child welfare representatives asked Congress for more professional training of social workers and more funding for services to help abusing families. However, Congress did not allow any significant increase in funding for families; instead subsequent extensions of the bill in 1977 and 1981 rested on the assumption that mandatory reporting alone could solve the problem of child abuse. The inference was that public exposure and the ensuing shame would be enough to deter families from abuse, even though state officials testified that they were inundated with so many reports of child abuse that they could not investigate them.[28] Yet Congress did not authorize more funds to help families at risk; instead, federal funding for foster care of children was increased.[29]

One important consequence of CAPTA was increased state intervention, represented by the presence of professionals, especially social workers, in the lives of families. The psychological paradigm underlying CAPTA encouraged the dispersal of caseworkers into homes to offer psychological interventions that might prevent abuse. Like other, earlier approaches to child maltreatment, the structural factors linked to abuse, such as the lack of child care services, economic inequality, and joblessness, were overlooked. Without funding to deliver critical resources to families and without the time to engage families in intensive counseling, social workers in public child welfare had one recourse when suspecting abuse: placement in foster care, the only service funded by the federal government. Many children, especially African American children, were moved from foster home to foster home without a clear plan and with little hope of reunification with their families.[30]

Adoptions Assistance and Child Welfare Act of 1980

In 1986 the National Center on Child Abuse and Neglect reported that the number of reports of abuse had doubled between 1976 and 1986.[31] This was to be expected with the adoption of mandatory reporting laws in every state; whether or not most of these cases reflected actual abuse was unknown. The accompanying trend toward increased foster care placement that followed CAPTA and the lack of money for services for families led some child welfare professionals to argue that family preservation could serve a child at risk for maltreatment while eliminating the trauma of removal and foster care placement for the child. The concept of family preservation was predicated on a service-intensive approach to family maintenance, where caseworkers would be available 24 hours a day to support troubled families and offer a range of services.[32] The side benefit to an emphasis on family preservation was its cost-effectiveness; these services would be far less expensive than foster care.

　　Another factor leading to the passage of the 1980 Adoptions Assistance Act was the perceived antagonism between child welfare workers and the needs of families who came under the aegis of the child welfare system. To some it seemed that child welfare workers were functioning more as detectives and prosecutors than as empathetic caseworkers. Added to this was the research on foster care "drift" discussed above, which seemed to make child protective service workers enemies, rather than protectors, of children's best interests. The capriciousness of social workers' decisions to remove children was roundly criticized in congressional hearings for the new act, as was their failure to promote family visits to children in foster care. Child welfare departments were seen as lacking accountability and as having an antifamily bias. The problems of foster care, along with the cost savings anticipated from family preservation, were frequent arguments presented by political leaders and child development experts, as well as by a powerful group of parents who claimed to be victims of overzealous investigations by child protective service workers known as

VOCAL (Victims of Child Abuse Legislation). These latter testified at the hearings, citing the arbitrary actions of child welfare workers.[33]

The assumptions behind the 1980 Adoptions Assistance and Child Welfare Act were that families could best serve the needs of their children; the job of child welfare was to help them to do so. The beliefs on which the act was passed were that every child deserved a permanent home and, when families were unable to care adequately for children, adoption was a far better option than foster care. Family preservation was another version of family privacy, reasserted after the interference resulting from CAPTA. The act mandated that reasonable services were to be delivered to families in the child welfare system, to aid in maintaining the family unit (family maintenance) and reunifying families who had been separated by child protective services (family reunification). Legislators may have had many services in mind when the bill was passed, but little in the way of new services emerged from the legislation. While federal funding was part of the 1980 legislation, appropriation of these funds was not carried through by the Reagan administration, leaving family preservation as a rhetorical ideal, rather than a substantial policy.[34]

Effects of CAPTA and the Adoptions Assistance Act

The assumption that foster care was harmful to children was not supported by research; in fact, the opposite was true: Foster care was generally safer than leaving a child in a home where previous abuse had occurred, especially without extensive services.[35] The combined effects of the two federal policies was to bring more families into the child protective service system through mandatory reporting, while leaving them on their own with few services except for occasional visits by social workers. This was an incendiary mix as families suffered the interference of the child welfare system without a gain in services to meet their needs. Partly as a result of the ideological shift toward family preservation that occurred without a corresponding increase in funding for child welfare services, the number of child deaths increased dramatically from 1986 to 1991, the overwhelming majority at the hands of biological parents.[36]

While the number of children in foster care declined immediately after the passage of the act, beginning in 1982, the number of children in foster care began to increase and continued to increase every year until 2000.[37] It is important to note that the number of children dying from maltreatment increased during the years in which children were returned to their families with no substantial increase in services.

Since funding for family preservation had been virtually nonexistent from 1980 to 1992, in 1993 the Clinton administration sought to reverse this trend and allocated $930 million for family preservation services in the Omnibus Budget Reconciliation Act. Conservative groups intent on protecting the family from government intervention had applauded the turn toward family preservation in 1980 and offered little objection to the funding offered by the Clinton administration, reasoning that preserving families would eventually eliminate the need for foster care and even child welfare workers. While the research on family preservation did not support the unalloyed hope that it would become a panacea for troubled families, the values of child welfare experts and other interested observers mandated a shift toward leaving children with their families, rather than removing them to foster care. In spite of these values, as noted above, the number of children in foster care continued to increase even after 1993 and the infusion of federal funding. At the same time news stories about children killed by their parents after being returned home by child welfare departments operating under family preservation policies proliferated.[38] Clearly the limited federal funding of family preservation offered by the Clinton administration in 1993 was not enough.

Adoptions and Safe Families Act of 1997

As a result of the apparent failures of family preservation and the policies represented by the Adoptions Assistance Act of 1980, the Clinton administration shifted gears and supported the Adoptions and Safe Families Act of 1997 (ASFA). This policy represented a 180-degree turn away from family preservation and toward parental termination and adoption. The theory behind the policy was that children should have a limited amount of time in foster care before their permanent futures were decided and those who could not be safely returned should be legally severed from their families and adopted by other families. As a result of this sea change in federal policy, the weight of the federal government came down fully against biological families, although the act contained lip service about reasonable efforts to serve families. As opposed to helping families provide adequate care for children, ASFA put child welfare agencies in the position of planning for termination of their parental rights. Many states passed concurrent planning laws, mandating that child protective service workers develop two plans simultaneously when a child was removed: one to reunify children with families, one to terminate parental rights and find permanent adoptive homes. Part of the rationale for ASFA was research that indicated that children reunited with their parents were at higher risk for reabuse than those who were not reunited. Under ASFA parents were given 12 months, rather than the 18 allowed under the 1980 act, to reunify with their children. ASFA allowed child welfare agencies to deny reunification services to families who committed certain kinds of abuse, including murder or manslaughter of another

Mother and child needing assistance

SOURCE: © 2009 Jupiterimages Corporation.

child or other aggravated circumstances as determined by the state, including abandonment, torture, chronic abuse, and sexual abuse.[39]

Clearly, ASFA was not targeted toward parents who were at risk for abusing children; there were no extra funds for services for families, and instead the funds went to counties as incentives for finding permanent adoptive homes for children in foster care. For many states the federal law gave an excuse to states to deny reasonable efforts to most clients in the child welfare system. California, for example, has added 15 conditions under which reunification services can be denied.[40] ASFA puts the weight of federal law on the side of children's rights and child safety and away from efforts to help biological families develop the resources to care for their children adequately. While both goals could conceivably be met in a child welfare policy, to date they have not been. See Table 8.1 for a summary of federal child welfare policies.

TABLE 8.1 **Summary of Federal Child Welfare Policies From 1921 to 1997 With Provisions and Impact on Problem**

Federal Policies	Time Frame	Provisions	Impact on Problem and How It Redeemed Failures of Previous Policies
Maternity and Infancy Protection Act (*also known as Sheppard-Towner Act*)	1921	• Provided federal matching funds for states to set up prenatal and child health clinics to encourage healthy practices in infant and child care	• First federal effort to offer support to parents and children, thus promoting child welfare • Contributed to decline in infant mortality rates after 1920 • Program was terminated in 1929 due to concerns of it being a state-run medical system and a precursor to other large-scale social welfare programs
Social Security Act	1935	• Maternal and child welfare services were restored with a mandate to encourage state-run child welfare services to protect dependent and neglected children	• Programs were located in public welfare departments, and services were only available to poor families • Linked poverty and some forms of child maltreatment but stigmatized welfare recipients to likely maltreat their children
Child Abuse Prevention and Treatment Act (CAPTA)	1974 Extensions of bill in 1977 and 1981	• Federal response to child abuse and neglect calling for government-sponsored professional intervention in family life • Established standard definitions of child abuse and neglect and protective custody provisions • Authorized limited government research in child abuse prevention and treatment • Established funding incentives to tighten state reporting laws	• Several states reported a dramatic increase in the reports of child abuse after CAPTA • Assumption that mandatory reporting would solve problem of child abuse • No significant increase in funding for families despite increases in reports • Federal funding was focused on children in foster care, thus the increase in foster care rather than in helping families • Increased state intervention, represented by the presence of professional social workers, in the lives of families

Federal Policies	Time Frame	Provisions	Impact on Problem and How It Redeemed Failures of Previous Policies
Indian Child Welfare Act (ICWA)	1978	• Federal response to concern about large number of placements of American Indian children outside tribal areas with White families • Child protective service agencies were mandated to make active efforts to keep American Indian children with their families and involve tribal courts in decisions regarding the welfare of these children	• Multiethnic Placement Act of 1994 exempted Indian children from its provisions • Became more difficult for child protective agencies to place Indian children outside their homes; however, lack of state compliance has been a problem due to lack of allocated funds • Indian children still continue to be at risk for removal due to high poverty rates and later policy changes focused on child removal
Adoptions Assistance and Child Welfare Act	1980 1993 Omnibus Budget Reconciliation Act allocated more funds	• Federal response to higher number of child abuse reports and increased foster care placement and foster care "drift" • Focus on family preservation and families serving the needs of their children rather than child welfare agencies	• Focus on family preservation was another version of family privacy, reasserted after the interference of CAPTA, giving families more rights but not more services • Little funding by Reagan administration so primarily a rhetorical idea rather than a substantial policy • Child deaths increased dramatically from 1986 to 1991 due to lack of funding for services • Number of children in foster care declined in 1982 after passage of act but began to increase steadily until 2000 • Limited federal funding increase in 1993 did not lower number of children in foster care
Multiethnic Placement Act (MEPA-IEP)	1994	• Prohibited the use of race, color, or national origin to deny or delay child placement in ethnically diverse foster or adoptive homes • Required that states diligently recruit foster and adoptive parents who reflect the racial and ethnic diversity of the foster care population	• Promoted adoptions of ethnic minority children by White families

(Continued)

Table 8.1 (Continued)

Federal Policies	Time Frame	Provisions	Impact on Problem and How It Redeemed Failures of Previous Policies
Adoption and Safe Families Act (ASFA)	1997	• Federal response to failures of family preservation and policies of the Adoption Assistance Act of 1980 • Focus was on limiting time in foster care and getting permanent placements for children through adoption • Parents were given 12 months rather than 18 months to reunify with their children • Allowed child welfare agencies to plan for termination of parental rights and promote legal adoption and kinship care through adoption tax credits and TANF reimbursement • Provided financial rewards to states that increased their numbers of finalized adoptions • Required that states file a petition to terminate parental rights for children who have been in foster care for 15 of the 22 most recent months	• Shift toward parental termination and adoption rather than family preservation • States were easier able to deny reasonable efforts for reunification services • Law supported children's rights and child safety rather than efforts to help families develop resources to care for their children • Law gives clear preference for nonbiological families over birth families • Foster care adoptions increased by 78% as a result of ASFA

Legal Adoption

One of the most controversial aspects of ASFA was its intention to promote legal adoption of children in the child welfare system and termination of parental rights.

Adoptions of children with special needs are subsidized by states and the federal government, and adoption tax credits are given by the federal government to all adopting families. These policies have increased the pool of adoptive parents, many of whom were originally foster parents to the adopted child.[41] More policies offering permanent adoption subsidies to families who adopt children from foster care would increase the number of adopted children. According to the most recent data available, 114,000 children in the U.S. foster care system were waiting to be adopted in 2005. During that same year, however, only 51,000 children were actually adopted. Older children and sibling groups are the least likely to be adopted. Children who are adopted are younger by an average of 2 years than those who are not adopted.[42]

Foster care adoptions increased by 78% from 1996 to 2000, as a result of ASFA and earlier state initiatives. It is estimated that ASFA requirements and incentives have resulted in an additional 34,000 adoptions from 1998 to 2000 that would not have otherwise occurred.[43] Sixty percent of children waiting to be adopted were either African American or Latino; 70% of children had been waiting for 2 or more years.

The history of collective informal efforts in African American communities to ensure the protection and well-being of their children suggests that legal adoption, with its emphasis on unitary, singular responsibility for children, may not be a good fit with African American families. Contrasting formal, legal adoptions with informal adoption reveals the contractual relationship at the heart of legal adoption, which creates parenthood by law and replaces biological families with legally constructed ones.[44] In African American communities the idea of termination of parental rights and exclusion of biological parents from the child's life is not culturally congruent, as discussed above. Parties to informal adoptions made room for the return or involvement of the biological parents, no matter how intermittent. Informal adoptions were part of a natural kinship strategy, not a legal contract creating a fictive parent-child relationship. This tradition should be incorporated into child welfare policy to encourage African American families to adopt children who are kin or nonkin.

Kinship Care

ASFA encouraged kinship or relative care of children removed from their homes and allowed relatives to be reimbursed in the same way as nonrelative foster parents, providing they received a foster care license from the state. Several types of kinship care exist; the most formal type is kinship foster care, where children are in state custody and then placed with relatives; other types include informal or voluntary kinship care, where families are not supervised by child welfare officials and not compensated at the foster care rate. Instead these families, who are not licensed, receive the lower Temporary Assistance for Needy Families (TANF) reimbursement. Largely because of the lower rate of reimbursement for many kinship care families and the lack of services, children in this form of home care are thought to face more barriers and to fare less well than children in their own homes or in supervised foster placements.[45] The economic deprivation experienced by many kinship families is one important reason for the difficulties faced by children placed there. On the other hand, advantages to kinship care include the family continuity and support it offers and the relative stability it offers children; children in kinship care are less likely to be moved than children in nonrelative foster care.

Kinship care may seem like a natural fit for African American children in the child welfare system, since it draws on the historical and cultural strengths of African American families. Indeed over the past 20 years more African American children than any other children have been in some form of kinship care. In 2004 more than half of the approximately 400,000 children in the more formal, supervised, kinship foster care were African American, and almost half of the 2.2 million children in kinship care were African American.[46] While kinship care is not a panacea for African American children, it stands on solid historical ground as the natural system that developed in African American communities to ensure the welfare of children. However, depending on nonreimbursed kinship care as a major policy meeting the needs of African American or any children is a flawed strategy, as it compounds the economic disadvantage experienced by minority families. Only when families have the economic and emotional resources to take on what is clearly an extra burden should kinship placements be made.[47]

Federal and state funds should be provided for all families who take in children related or nonrelated, as should child welfare services. Why have kin been utilized as a low-cost way to meet the needs of many African American children? Ambivalence over reimbursement of family members for care may be at the heart of the reluctance. However, socially just policies would mandate that both legal guardians and kin caregivers be reimbursed for their efforts to care for children, who would be placed in federally funded, nonrelated foster homes should relatives refuse to take on this responsibility. Redressing the financial inequities inherent in current kinship care policies is crucial to protecting and promoting the well-being of African American children. Reimbursing all kin at the same rate as nonrelatives and offering child welfare services to all children in kinship families are crucial first steps in promoting the welfare of African American children in kinship care.

Legal Guardianship

Legal guardianship, which is an arrangement wherein kin or others assume legal custody of children whose birth parents may retain certain rights, such as the right to visitation, the right to consent to adoption, and the responsibility for child support, may be more culturally congruent with African American communities. As discussed above, African American families may not wish to become involved with permanent adoptions of their family members because of longstanding cultural traditions that work against parental termination. Yet legal guardianship may pose a financial hardship for many families, since in most cases the federal government does not subsidize the care of children in guardianship arrangements. Guardians of children eligible for TANF may receive compensation that is approximately one third to one half of the rate the federal government pays to foster parents, who also care for dependent children. The answer may lie in subsidized guardianship, where guardians (usually kin) are reimbursed at the higher foster care rate. These subsidized guardianships have been approved under a federal waiver in eight states, including Illinois. Research indicates that subsidized guardianships do result in permanency for African American children. In one study in Illinois, relatives in subsidized guardianship arrangements converted their informal arrangements into formal, open adoptions in greater numbers than in nonsubsidized guardianships; these adoptions accounted for 58% of all adoptions in the state of Illinois in 1999.[48] Making subsidized guardianship available in all states would increase the options for permanency with kin for African American children in the child welfare system.

Indian Child Welfare Act

In 1978 Congress recognized the cultural assault on American Indian identity represented by the large number of placements of American Indian children outside tribal areas with White families. Citing a longstanding government campaign to place these children in White institutions that began in the early 20th century, the Senate held hearings in which witnesses testified that from one quarter to one third of American Indian children had been separated from their families by child protective services. Infants were particularly at risk for adoption by Whites. Witnesses blamed culturally biased standards of child raising for the high number of removals, mostly on grounds of neglect or "social deprivation."[49] Congress declared that both the continued existence of tribes and tribal sovereignty were threatened by the actions of state child protective service workers. Under the new law child protective service agencies were mandated to make active efforts to guarantee that American Indian children remain with their families and to turn cases of child endangerment over to tribal courts, who would make decisions regarding the welfare of American Indian children. The law applies to foster placements, termination of parental rights, and adoptions. The Indian Child Welfare Act (ICWA) defines "Indian child" as a child who is a member of a federally recognized Indian tribe or is eligible for membership in such a tribe and the biological child of a member. The Multiethnic Placement Act of 1994 exempts Indian children from its provisions, in keeping with the goals of ICWA. States are allowed to oppose transfer to a tribal court in cases where good cause exists, including the non-existence of such tribal courts. However, state agencies must make every effort to locate the tribe to which the child may belong, even if this is not immediately apparent. The act establishes a minimum federal standard if a state wishes to remove American Indian children from their home. It is more difficult for child protective service agencies to place Indian children outside their homes, and these placements are with Indian homes wherever possible.

In spite of clearly stated federal intention, lack of state compliance with this act is a problem; some states decline to enforce it. While some states have passed their own laws to support the federal law, in other states Indian children have been removed from their homes and placed in non-Indian foster or adoptive homes.[50] Since the federal government did not allocate funds to tribes to implement ICWA, there is little recourse in cases of state indifference to the act, and even cooperative state child welfare agencies may find limitations in how tribes can supervise their child welfare responsibilities. The federal government still has not allocated funds for tribal child welfare services.[51] As a result of these factors, ICWA has not been fully implemented.

Indian children continue to be at risk for removal on grounds of child neglect, due to the high poverty rates experienced by the American Indian families. In 2000, 22% of American Indian children lived below the poverty level in the United States. Recent policy changes may put these families at greater risk for child removal. Families on economically marginalized reservations and in rural areas have long depended on welfare, since there are few employment opportunities in these areas. Poverty in reservation families may be exacerbated by the 5-year time limit for receiving TANF (see Chapter 7), and pressure for permanency through adoption and parental termination may undermine the goals of ICWA in families who are not returned to tribal jurisdictions and are subject to the oversight of state child protective service agencies.[52]

Multiethnic Placement Act

In 1994 Congress passed the Multiethnic Placement Act prohibiting the use of race, color, or national origin to deny or delay children placement in ethnically diverse foster or adoptive homes. Combined with the Adoptions and Safe Families Act of 1997 requiring that children who are not reunited with their parents be placed in adoptive homes, these two policies together serve to promote adoptions of ethnic minority children by White families. Critics argue that removing African American children from their families and giving them to White families to adopt is often a mistake because it strips children of their historical and cultural legacies. In 1972, the National Association of Black Social Workers (NABSW) had announced that it was opposed to adoptions that placed Black children into White families (known then as transracial adoptions), a stance that had strong repercussions for child welfare policy until the Multiethnic Placement Act. The NABSW now focuses its efforts on encouraging adoptions within the African American community.[53] Ironically, most of the children who are considered examples of transracial adoptions over the past 10 years are not from the United States but are from outside the country. Adoption of foreign-born children has increased dramatically to over 20,000 a year.[54] The concept of transracial adoptions has lost its meaning since the Multiethnic Placement Act was passed, and the need to widen the pool of adoptive applicants has emerged as a pressing policy issue.

As we have seen, there is a cyclical nature to child welfare policy. Each federal policy seeks to redeem the failure of the previous one. Beginning with CAPTA, federal policies moved between opposing goals: The first goal was to grant child welfare agencies the power to intervene with families; reaction to child protective service intervention and the rising number of foster care placements came in 1980, when the Adoptions Assistance Act gave families more rights but not more services. When this apparently resulted in more child endangerment, the reaction was to redirect child welfare agencies away from services to families and to grant them unprecedented power to initiate the process of legally terminating the parent-child relationship.

CHILD ABUSE AND CHILD WELFARE IN THE 21ST CENTURY ●

In 2006, the last year for which data are available, 510,000 children lived in foster care, which represented a decline of over 40,000 since 2000. The average placement time in foster care was 32.6 months.[55] Of children in foster care, 41% were classified as White, non-Hispanic; 32% were Black, non-Hispanic; 18% were Hispanic; and 8% were from other ethnic groups. Approximately one fourth of children in foster care were in relative homes. Of children who left foster care, 54% were reunited with their families. The number of children waiting to be adopted (whose rights had been terminated) increased from 114,000 on September 30, 2005, to 129,000 on the same day in 2006. There was a significant increase in children in foster care with parental rights terminated for all living parents—from 66,000 in 2005 to 79,000 in 2006.[56] See Figure 8.1 for the proportion of children in foster care by ethnicity.

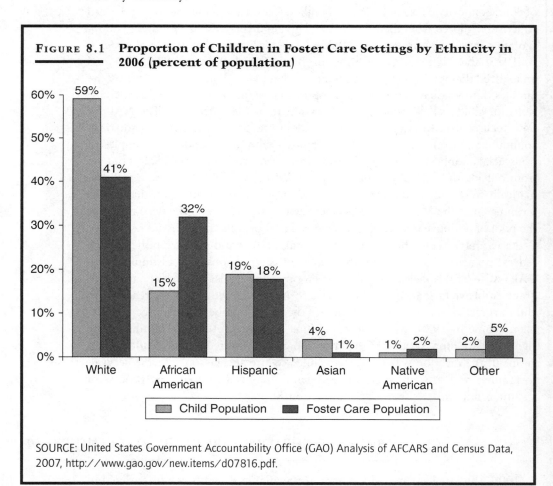

FIGURE 8.1   **Proportion of Children in Foster Care Settings by Ethnicity in 2006 (percent of population)**

SOURCE: United States Government Accountability Office (GAO) Analysis of AFCARS and Census Data, 2007, http://www.gao.gov/new.items/d07816.pdf.

PROFILES IN LEADERSHIP

Marian Wright Edelman, 1939–

Marian Wright Edelman was born on June 6, 1939, in South Carolina. She was the youngest of five children; her father was a pastor in Shiloh Baptist Church. She was influenced by her father to pursue higher education and to serve the local community. In 1956, Wright completed high school and entered Spelman College in Atlanta. She was soon involved in civil rights activities and was arrested for participating in a sit-in at Atlanta's City Hall. Following that experience she decided to pursue a career in law and was admitted to Yale Law School.

Marian Wright Edelman

SOURCE: Centers for Disease Control and Prevention.

While in law school, Wright became involved in voter registration drives and eventually became an intern for the NAACP Legal Defense and Educational Fund. After passing the bar, she opened a law office in Mississippi, primarily to work on behalf of civil rights activists who had been jailed. In 1968, she received a foundation grant and moved to Washington, DC, where she met her husband, Peter Edelman. In 1971, the couple moved to Boston, where Peter became vice president of the University of Massachusetts and she obtained a position as the director of the Harvard Center for Law and Education.

In response to her growing concern regarding the well-being of children, in 1973 Wright Edelman founded the Children's Defense Fund, a nonprofit child advocacy organization. She and her husband returned to Washington in 1979, and her husband took a teaching position at Georgetown University. Wright Edelman increased her work on behalf of

(Continued)

(Continued)

disadvantaged, poor, and minority children and was recognized for her work with the award of a MacArthur Foundation Fellowship. She also began lecturing at Harvard University and began to collect data and statistics to document the plight of poor children in America. She also organized major demonstrations on behalf of poor children and raised awareness about the needs of the nation's youth. She also authored a book, *Guide My Feet: Prayers and Meditation on Loving and Working for Children,* which reflects on the lessons she learned in childhood and emphasizes the importance of the values of faith in God, integrity, and service to the community.

Her courage and determination were evident in her commitment to fighting obstacles in the way of achieving social justice for children. She built networks and coalitions with other social institutions, including churches, to support the causes of poor children. She established a variety of institutes for child advocacy to educate and raise awareness of the needs of poor children. Wright Edelman expanded the vision of the social gospel to include the civil rights movement, a woman's right to choose, and child advocacy. Her vision of the future envisioned a time when we could develop a more just, sustainable, and holistic community that would include people of all races and ethnic backgrounds living in harmony. Wright Edelman, like Martin Luther King, Jr., had a vision of a future full of promise and opportunities for all and the elimination of discrimination, exploitation, and poverty.

Marian Wright Edelman lobbied Congress to pass new legislation strengthening foster care, supporting adoption, and meeting the needs of abused and neglected children. She has been one of the strongest child welfare advocates in the United States, fighting to bring social justice to the nation's forgotten children.

According to the National Child Abuse and Neglect Data System (NCANDS), there were an estimated 1,460 child fatalities, or 1.96 per 100,000 children, in 2006. This translates to a rate of 2.03 children per 100,000 children in the general population. NCANDS defines "child fatality" as the death of a child caused by an injury resulting from abuse or neglect or where abuse or neglect was a contributing factor. Children under 3 years of age account for almost 50% of child fatalities; the most common cause of all deaths was parental neglect. Three quarters of the perpetrators were the child's parents. Experts agree that the number of child fatalities is underreported, as investigators are often unable to pinpoint causes of child death. Some studies have found that as many as 50% of child fatalities are unreported. While most data on child fatalities come from state child welfare agencies, states are also able to draw on other data sources, including health departments and fatality review boards to make their estimates of child fatalities.[57]

WHAT CAUSES CHILD MALTREATMENT? ●

There is strong evidence that child maltreatment is related to economic stress and poverty, both social costs of the market economy. Economic stress includes unemployment, migration, marginalized housing and food insecurity, and lack of adequate support systems in periods of economic crisis.[58] High concentrations of female-headed households, high crime rates, and high rates of families living in public housing have been found to be correlated with high risk of child maltreatment.[59] These factors accompany poverty and economic marginalization in urban communities; together they interact to increase stress on families and reduce their ability to meet the needs of their children. Members of certain ethnic groups, including African Americans, Latinos, and American Indians, are more likely to live in economically marginalized communities and may be at risk for either child maltreatment or inclusion in the child welfare system[60] (see Chapter 4). Other factors linked to child abuse including domestic violence, parental stress and mental illness, parental incarceration, and death are associated with areas of concentrated poverty.[61]

TANF and Child Welfare

The majority of children in foster care are from families who either receive public assistance or qualify for it.[62] States receive federal reimbursement for welfare-eligible children in foster care; since children of color are overrepresented on TANF, this reimbursement policy promotes their overrepresentation on child welfare rolls. In fiscal year 2004, the date from which the latest funding figures are available, the federal government spent 10 times as much on children eligible for TANF (Title IV E) in child welfare funding as it did on children not eligible for TANF (Title IV B). The federal government accounts for almost one half of all child welfare spending, with states and localities making up the other half.[63] The federal government spent $285 million in 2007 on child welfare-related services to families under Title IV B but over $2 billion on foster care for children whose families were welfare eligible in the same period.[64]

Welfare reform, passed in 1996 (see Chapter 7), may impact the number of children in child welfare caseloads. The number of children in foster care increased in the first 2 years after the passage of TANF, although the mechanisms for this increase are unknown; speculation about factors associated with increases in the number of children in out-of-home care includes TANF's family caps, lifetime limits, and tough sanctions for noncompliance with work requirements. The relationship between welfare reform and foster care was most significant among African American children living in urban areas.[65] It might be expected that tightening welfare policies would drive more families into poverty, putting them at higher risk for child maltreatment or for charges of neglect related to poverty. Some research suggests that lower welfare benefits are associated with more reports for neglect and more children entering foster care.[66]

● ETHNICITY AND CHILD WELFARE

According to NCANDS, African American, American Indian or Alaska Native, and Pacific Islander children have higher rates of reported child maltreatment than do other children. In 2005, African American children had a reported maltreatment rate of 19.5 per 1,000 children, Pacific Islander children had a reported maltreatment rate of 16.1 per 1,000 children, and American Indian or Alaska Native children had a reported maltreatment rate of 16.5 per 1,000 children, compared with 10.8 per 1,000 non-Hispanic White children, 10.7 per 1,000 Hispanic children, and 2.5 per 1,000 Asian children.[67] It is important to note that these statistics are based on cases that are reported to child welfare agencies and found to be credible; earlier larger studies known as the National Incidence Studies of Child Abuse and Neglect, undertaken by the federal government in 1980, 1986, and 1993, found no ethnic effect on child maltreatment. These large-scale federal studies found an economic effect: Poorer families were more likely to maltreat their children, regardless of ethnicity.[68] The results of the Fourth National Incidence Study will be available in 2010. The 1993 National Incidence Study found that compared to children whose families earned $30,000 per year or more, children in families with annual incomes below $15,000 per year were more than 22 times more likely to experience some form of maltreatment. The statistics gathered in these National Incidence Studies are more accurate than the NCANDS reports, which depend solely on cases of child maltreatment that have been reported to child protective service agencies. The National Incidence Studies draw from a wider range of reporters who may or may not have interacted with the local child protective service agencies. The National Incidence Study (NIS) design assumes that the maltreated children who are investigated by child protective services (CPS) represent only the "tip of the iceberg," so while NIS estimates include children investigated at CPS, they also include maltreated children who are identified by a wide range of professionals in representative communities. These professionals, called "sentinels," are asked to remain on the lookout for children they believe are maltreated during the study period.[69] Thus while there are ethnic differences in the children who are reported to CPS, there apparently is no ethnic difference established in actual maltreatment, according to these broader studies.

Why is this? Many observers note that there is a class and ethnic bias in the reporting and investigation systems found in CPS systems across the country; poorer families, including families from some ethnic groups, are overrepresented, while middle- and upper-class families are underrepresented. If there is no significant ethnic difference in child maltreatment, as the National Incidence Studies have found, then the fact that some ethnic groups are overrepresented in the child protective service caseloads is due to systemic problems in child welfare oversight. African American children and American Indian children are the most overrepresented groups; they are in foster care at twice the rate their numbers in the population would predict. On the other hand, Latino and Asian American children tend to be underrepresented in child protective service caseloads, as are White non-Hispanic children. What factors account for these differences? Some research suggests that differences in reporting exist; poorer communities have more surveillance in terms of who tends to report abuse: educational staff, law enforcement, and social service personnel.[70] Both public and private hospitals have been found to overreport abuse among Blacks and underreport it among Whites. Controlling for actual injury due to abuse, another study found that children of color were more likely to be reported for physical abuse than White children, even when White children were injured by their caretakers. African American women are more likely to be reported for abuse when their newborns test positive for drug use than White women. While some research did not find these ethnic discrepancies, the bulk of the research has found these discrepancies.[71]

Not all allegations of child maltreatment lead to investigation by CPS agencies; approximately one third of reports are screened out by hotline workers and not investigated. Ethnicity has been found to be a strong predictor of investigation in cases of alleged physical abuse and neglect. While Whites are more likely to be investigated in cases of sexual abuse, African Americans are twice as likely to be investigated for physical abuse and neglect as Whites.[72] Are reports of abuse more likely to be substantiated—that is, found to be correct—for African American children? Research suggests that this is indeed the case.[73] Once maltreatment is found to be substantiated by the child welfare system, are there ethnic differences in whether children remain in their homes or are placed in foster homes? According to national data, African American children are much more likely than White victims of abuse and neglect to be placed in foster care.[74] Regional studies have also found that after controlling for gender, age, and reason for referral, African American children were slower to exit foster care and less likely to be reunited with their biological parents than White children.[75] Finally, children of color receive fewer services than White children while in the

Foster children at play

SOURCE: © 2009 Jupiterimages Corporation.

child welfare system.[76] For the differences in the percentage of African American children and White children in the child welfare system see Figure 8.2.

The overrepresentation of African American children in the child welfare system parallels their overrepresentation in the juvenile justice system, the subject of concern for over 40 years.[77] As we have seen, there are many decision points in the child welfare system, from the first reports to child protective services through the decisions to place children in foster care or reunify them with their biological parents. Many different outcomes are possible for children in the child welfare system, including monitoring in the home, foster care, group homes, and adoption. Are African American children overrepresented because child welfare practices at these decision points are influenced by racism and/or discrimination? Or are African American children more likely to be abused and thus more in need of child welfare services? The National Incidence Studies seem to indicate that their overrepresentation can be explained by overreporting of child maltreatment in African American families, underreporting of White children, and differences in investigation of cases and in substantiation rates. In fact, the National Incidence Studies discussed above acknowledged the high risk factors experienced by African American families in terms of low income, single-parent status, and welfare status but still found lower incidence of child

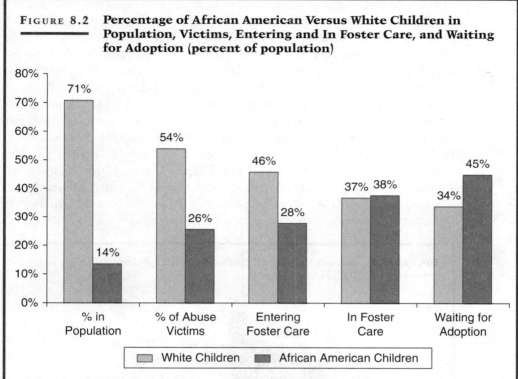

FIGURE 8.2   **Percentage of African American Versus White Children in Population, Victims, Entering and In Foster Care, and Waiting for Adoption (percent of population)**

SOURCE: U.S. Department of Health and Human Services, Administration for Children and Families: *Child Maltreatment 2002* (http://www.acf.hhs.gov/programs/cb/pubs/cm02/chapterthree.htm#race) and "The AFCARS Report: Final Estimates for FY 1998 through FY 2002" (http://www.acf.hhs.gov/programs/cb/stats_research/afcars/tar/report12.htm).

maltreatment in African American families compared to other groups with these same factors. Perhaps these risk factors are not as salient for African American families. Mediating factors that reduce the risk may include the cultural strengths of African American families discussed above. If so, differences in treatment during the child welfare decision-making process explain the disproportionality.[78]

Latino Children in the Child Welfare System

Latinos have received fewer social services than non-Hispanic Whites for much of the 20th century in a wide range of areas, including health and mental health services.[79] While African American children historically have suffered the worst outcomes in the child welfare system, Latino children tend to be processed into the child welfare system more quickly and have a higher percentage of cases substantiated than White non-Hispanic children; one study attributed this to the higher number of Latino clients receiving public assistance. Latino children are in out-of-home placement longer than White children and are less likely to be reunified than White children.[80] Latino children have been found to enter the system at a younger age than White non-Hispanic children, suggesting a bias on the part of the child welfare system as to the risk factors affecting younger children. In California, where more than 13 million Latinos make up 36% of the state's population, the number of Latino children in the child welfare system is much higher than in the rest of the nation, although not disproportionate with their numbers in the state population.[81] Less research has focused on Latino children in the child welfare system than on African American children,[82] although they constitute the second largest group in the child welfare system and are the majority in states with a larger Latino population, including California, Texas, and New Mexico. For the differences in ethnicity of children waiting for adoption, see Figure 8.3.

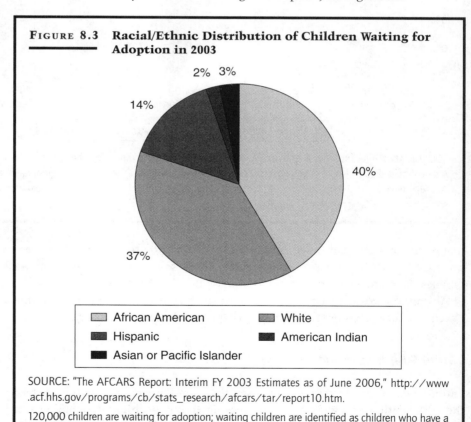

FIGURE 8.3   Racial/Ethnic Distribution of Children Waiting for Adoption in 2003

SOURCE: "The AFCARS Report: Interim FY 2003 Estimates as of June 2006," http://www .acf.hhs.gov/programs/cb/stats_research/afcars/tar/report10.htm.

120,000 children are waiting for adoption; waiting children are identified as children who have a goal of adoption and/or whose parents' rights have been terminated. Children 16 years old and older whose parents' rights have been terminated and who have a goal of emancipation have been excluded from the estimate.

NEW CHILD WELFARE POLICIES ●

*Fostering Connections to Success
and Increasing Adoptions Act, 2008*

In 2008 Congress passed the Fostering Connections to Success and Increasing Adoptions Act. Under this federal law states are given the option of using federal funds to reimburse themselves for part of the cost of providing kinship guardianship assistance to grandparents and other relatives. Family members must have cared for children for at least 6 months without reimbursement to be eligible for these funds and must meet the state foster family home licensing standards. Relatives must enter into a formal guardianship agreement with the guardian and be willing to commit to care for the children on a permanent basis. For relatives who cannot meet usual licensing standards, exceptions can be obtained from the Department of Health and Human Services on a case-by-case basis. Legal guardianship arrangements can be reimbursed only when the options of returning the child home and adoption have been ruled out. Additionally, the act expands the Adoption Assistance Program by mandating that all those who are adopting children from foster care be advised that they may be eligible for adoption tax credit. The act expands eligibility for federal adoption assistance by phasing out over time income criteria deemed too stringent that were based on cash welfare program rules.[83]

This act moves toward subsidized guardianship as a viable third option (after adoption and long-term foster care) in child welfare policies for children removed from home and demonstrates the federal government's willingness to view kinship placements as comparable to foster care placements in terms of reimbursement. However, the fact that exceptions to the licensing mandate for reimbursed relatives must be made by HHS on a case-by-case basis at the request of the state leaves questions about whether this is a significant change to child welfare policy. How many such exceptions is HHS likely to grant? The fact that relatives must care for children for 6 months with no reimbursement suggests that Congress wanted relatives to show their commitment first and meet all state standards for licensing and background checks before being eligible for reimbursement. Whether these provisions draw more relatives into permanent legal guardianship arrangements remains to be seen.

Child welfare policies that encourage the participation of families and community-based agencies in planning for the well-being of children have been utilized in some states on a pilot basis, and such experiments can lead the way to empowering families in the system to take some responsibility for their children even if they are placed in out-of-home care.[84] In this vein, the shared custody arrangement may be more useful than our current models for many families and children in the child welfare system. Under this model, which is similar to custody arrangements in divorce, biological parents would share responsibility with a permanent guardian (ideally a relative) acting under state supervision. The biological parents would continue to receive necessary services as long as they continued to be involved with their children. This model would go beyond the current contractual one mandating a single legal parent surrogate responsible for a child's well-being; instead it would offer parallel lines of responsibility for children in need of state supervision. The guardian would have permanent legal custody and the right to make all major decisions about the child. Biological parents would have specific responsibilities, outlined by the courts, as well as shared custody, where appropriate.[85]

All families in the child welfare system should receive services. Encouraging the delivery of services to parents who remain connected with their children in kinship care or in legal guardianship arrangements draws on the strengths of families. This would be a radical departure from the dichotomy currently driving child welfare policies; either deliver services to children in their families or deliver services to children outside their families. Kinship care would thus be conceptualized as a way to serve families and children, not as a way to replace them. Offering biological families resources while their children are in out-of-home placement would involve a paradigm shift for child welfare policy. Neither the 1980 Adoptions Assistance Act nor the 1997 Adoptions and Safe Families Act made specific provisions to help biological families meet the needs of children at risk for child maltreatment. Under ASFA, money goes to counties as incentives for adoption of children from foster care. Foster care reimbursement for eligible children continues to be funded by the federal government and states.

Why have biological families been ignored in policies designed to keep children safe? To understand this, it is necessary to examine the values and ideologies about families in the child welfare system. Many of these families are economically marginalized, some are on public assistance, and a majority come from oppressed ethnic groups. Historical ideologies about poverty and ethnic differences dominate public attitudes toward parents at risk for child maltreatment. Adding to these ideological biases, the assumption that all parents whose children are in the child welfare system are guilty of child maltreatment limits the political will to fund programs that would enable these families to overcome the economic and other deficits that are factors in their parenting limitations. The latest federal policy, ASFA, is a prime example of a clear preference for nonbiological families, in the form of foster parents and adoptive parents, over the birth families, who offer something irreplaceable to children: the feeling of belonging and continuity disrupted by foster care and adoption.

CONCLUSION

The footprints of the *market economy* are clearly visible in the patterns of child maltreatment. Parents maltreating their children are disproportionately low-income families. *Historical values about poverty and the poor* hinder efforts to make policy changes that would reduce inequality. *Discrimination against oppressed ethnic groups has meant that child welfare policies negatively impact these groups, especially African Americans.* Due to these factors child welfare policies have focused economic resources on substitute parents instead of families of origin, damaging many children who are left without a permanent home.

None of the child welfare policies discussed in this chapter have targeted the pervasive economic inequality and poverty that fuels at least some child maltreatment. Reducing inequality would go some way, though admittedly not all the way, toward reducing the problem of child abuse. Policymakers, for reasons discussed earlier, are not willing to take this step to try and ensure child safety and well-being. Instead, they prefer to switch children from economically marginalized, troubled families to more advantaged families whom government will pay to care for their children. While some out-of-home care may be necessary, creating federal policies that make no real effort to strengthen biological families is extremely shortsighted at best and discriminatory at worst. The fact that ethnic and cultural transfers occur as a result of placement in foster care or adoptive homes cannot be ignored: White families predominate among adoptive parents; ethnic minority children predominate among children in foster care.[86] The social work profession, as we have seen, has played the central role in the development of the child welfare system in the United States. Social workers can play a major role in reversing the policy priorities that have led to the child welfare arrangements reminiscent of the early orphan trains: Remove the children; ignore their families.

Example of Policy Analysis of the Adoptions and Safe Families Act:

Part Two: The Policy Objectives, Value Premises, Expectations, and Target Populations

1. Policy objectives: overt and covert objectives. What are the stated objectives of the policy? In your judgment what are the covert objectives of the policy?

The stated objectives of ASFA are to improve the safety of children, to promote adoption and other permanent homes for children who need them, and to support families. ASFA was passed after a series of publicized deaths of children in child protective service caseloads across the country led lawmakers to tighten requirements for parents accused of child maltreatment. To this end, ASFA has several key provisions, including imposing

(Continued)

(Continued)

a time limit on parents whose children have been placed in foster care to comply with court requirements and reunify with their children. Reunification services can be denied families who committed severe forms of abuse as determined by states. In order to reduce time spent by children in foster care, the law encouraged adoption of children from foster care, giving counties financial incentives for each child adopted.

What are the covert objectives of ASFA? Looking at the movement of children from their biological families to foster care to adoptive parents, the transfer of children from their families of origin to adoptive families seems to be a covert objective. This transfer involves an ethnic and cultural substitution of White middle-class families, more likely to adopt children, for the low-income, disproportionately ethnic families represented in the child welfare system. Public child welfare agencies are encouraged to pursue legal termination of parental rights when time limits have been exceeded and to concurrently plan for reunification and termination of parental rights when a child is placed in foster care. The covert values are suggested by the fact that few resources are targeted directly to families at risk for maltreatment in the legislation; instead federal resources are given to county child welfare departments to encourage adoption.

2. What are values underlying the policy objectives? What values are revealed by the overt and covert objectives?

The overt objectives rest on the value that children should be raised in safe homes and that government has a responsibility to ensure the safety of children. Additionally, the legislation is based on the value that permanency in living situations is necessary for optimal development of children. The needs of children for safety and permanency are more important than the rights of parents to raise their children. Likewise, the needs of parents for services and resources are secondary to the rights of children. The legislation sanctions kinship care, reimbursing it at the same rate as foster care as long as kin families obtain state foster care licenses. In this way kin are recognized as legitimate substitutes for parents in the protection of children.

The covert objectives rest on prevailing beliefs about parents in the child welfare system. The first of these is that maltreating parents are unfit to care for their children and therefore their children need to be protected from them. These beliefs are intensified by the fact that most parents in the child welfare system are from economically marginalized, ethnically oppressed groups. Ideologies about the causes of poverty, including the belief that poverty is due to individual limitations rather than structural imperatives, contribute to the negative evaluation of parents in the child welfare system. Discriminatory and racist beliefs about oppressed ethnic groups intensify the social distance that policymakers feel from these parents and encourage the acceptance of more punitive policies toward them.

Foster parents are viewed as inadequate substitutes for permanent families because, unlike families of origin, they are reimbursed for the care they offer children, reducing the perceived altruism of their motives. Foster care is seen as temporary, whereas children are viewed as needing permanent homes based solely on love, not on financial gain. For these reasons adoptive homes are viewed as more suitable for children. A class bias is evident in the preference for adoptive families, who tend to be White and middle class. Kin caregivers are eligible for long-term foster care placements and payments, as long as they are state licensed, as well as for eventual adoption.

Policies promoting kinship care serve to mitigate the class bias in the adoption policy of ASFA, although economic circumstances may make adoption difficult for kin caregivers.

3. What did the policymakers expect would be the result of the policy?

Lawmakers hoped that restricting the families to a shorter time frame for reunification would eliminate families from the reunification process who have low motivation for reunification or demonstrate serious problems that cannot be ameliorated in the time frames allowed. This would result in the freeing of children whose families cannot or will not care for them for permanency in adoptive homes or, in certain cases, in kinship care.

4. Target segments of the population at whom policy is aimed. Discuss the direct target of the policy in terms of size and other demographic characteristics. Who are the indirect targets of the policy?

Over 500,000 children are currently living in foster care in the United States. The largest percentage of children in foster care are White, non-Hispanic (41%); 32% are Black, non-Hispanic; 18% are Hispanic; and 8% are from other ethnic groups. Approximately one fourth of children in foster care are in relative homes. The number of children whose parents' rights have been terminated and who are waiting to be adopted is approximately 135,000.

African American children are overrepresented in the child welfare system, although their rates of maltreatment, controlling for economic status, are no higher than other groups. African American children are more likely to be placed in foster care than other children, more likely to be moved once in foster care, and less likely to return home.

Indirect target groups include families of origin, foster parents, and child welfare workers. Each county in the United States employs social workers or other human services in child protective service systems; these workers are all indirect targets of any federal child welfare legislation. The over half a million children in foster care in the United States have families of origin who are profoundly affected by the legislation, as are the foster parents and potential adoptive parents. Approximately 50,000 children are adopted yearly from foster care placements. The number of foster parents varies from state to state, but in general there are not enough foster parents for the number of children coming into the child welfare system.

DISCUSSION QUESTIONS

1. Why have child welfare policies ignored biological families in favor of substitute families?

2. Why has social work been the lead profession in shaping child welfare policies?

3. Why have African American children suffered the greatest inequities in the child welfare system?

4. What are the major causes of child abuse that public policy can address?

5. Why has the Indian Child Welfare Act been unsuccessful in meeting the needs of American Indian children?

6. Should other ethnic groups marginalized by the public child welfare system, such as African Americans, be able to establish and oversee a separate child welfare system?

7. What new child welfare policies do you think would meet the needs of children and families and promote social justice?

8. Which policies would you eliminate or change in the current child welfare system?

NOTES

1. Sallie Watkins, "The Mary Ellen Myth: Correcting Child Welfare History," *Social Work* 35 (6, 1990): 500–503.

2. Linda Gordon, *Heroes of Their Own Lives: The Politics and History of Family Violence* (Urbana: University of Illinois Press, 1988), 190–191; Phillip Greven, *The Protestant Temperament: Patterns of Child-Rearing, Religious Experience and the Self in Early America,* (New York: Meridian, 1979), 32–33; Martin Thomas, "Child Abuse and Neglect: Part 1: Historical Overview, Legal Matrix and Social Perspectives," *North Carolina Law Review* 50 (1997): 291–297.

3. Watkins, "The Mary Ellen Myth," 500–503.

4. Thomas, "Child Abuse and Neglect," 293–294.

5. Homer Folks, *Care of Destitute, Neglected and Delinquent Children* (New York: Macmillan, 1902), 34; Greven, *The Protestant Temperament,* 32–55.

6. Greven, *The Protestant Temperament,* 32–55; Philip Greven, *Spare the Child: The Religious Roots of Punishment and the Psychological Impact of Child Abuse* (New York: Knopf, 1998); Stephen Owens and Kenneth Wagner, "Explaining School Corporal Punishment: Evangelical Protestantism and Social Capital," *Social Justice Research* 19 (December 2006): 471–499.

7. David Tyack, *The One Best System: A History of American Urban Education* (Cambridge, MA: Harvard University Press, 2007), 39–59, 182–229.

8. Viviana Zelizer, "From Child Labor to Child Work: Changing Cultural Conceptions of Children's Economic Roles, 1870s–1930s," in Stuart Bruchey and Peter Coclanis, eds., *Ideas, Ideologies, and Social Movements: The U.S. Experience Since 1800* (Columbia: University of South Carolina Press, 2000), 90–101.

9. Michael Katz, *In the Shadow of the Poor House* (New York: Basic Books, 1986), 113–121.

10. Zelizer, "From Child Labor to Child Work," 110.

11. Duncan Lindsey, *The Welfare of Children* (New York: Oxford University Press, 2003), 15.

12. Lindsey, *The Welfare of Children,* 16.

13. Mary Ann Jimenez, "Permanency Planning and the Child Abuse Prevention and Treatment Act: The Paradox of Child Welfare Policy," *Journal of Sociology and Social Welfare* 17 (3, 1990): 55–73; Lindsey, *The Welfare of Children*, 24–25.

14. Lindsey, *The Welfare of Children*, 22.

15. Molly Ladd-Taylor, *Mother-Work: Women, Child Welfare, and the State, 1890–1930* (Urbana: University of Illinois Press, 1995), 86–87.

16. Lindsey, *The Welfare of Children*, 23.

17. Ladd-Taylor, *Mother-Work*, 169.

18. Leila Costin. "Cruelty to Children: A Dormant Issue and Its Rediscovery, 1920–1960." *Social Service Review* 66 (1992): 177–197.

19 Paul Pecora, James K. Whittaker, Anthony N. Maluccio, and Richard P. Barth. *The Child Welfare Challenge: Policy, Practice and Research*, 2nd ed. (New York, Aldine de Gruyer, 2000), 34–36; Jillian Jimenez. "The History of Child Protection in the African American Community: Implications for Current Child Welfare Policies." *Children and Youth Services Review* 28 (2006): 888–905.

20. Jimenez, "The History of Child Protection in the African American Community," 891.

21. Jimenez, "The History of Child Protection in the African American Community," 888–905.

22. Carrie Jefferson Smith and Wynetta Devore, "African American Children in the Child Welfare and Kinship System: From Exclusion to Overinclusion," *Children and Youth Services Review* 26 (May 2004): 427–466.

23. Leila Costin, Howard Jacob Karger, and David Stoesz, *Politics of Child Abuse in America* (New York: Oxford University Press, 1996), 8.

24. Henry Maas and Richard Engler, *Children in Need of Parents* (New York: Columbia University Press, 1959), cited in Lindsey, *The Welfare of Children*, 35–36.

25. C. Henry Kempe, "The Battered Child Syndrome," *The Journal of the American Medical Association 181* (January 1962): 17–24.

26. Jimenez, "Permanency Planning and the Child Abuse Prevention and Treatment Act," 60–61.

27. U.S. House Hearings, *Hearings on the Proposed Extension of the Child Abuse Prevention and Treatment Act. Committee on Education and Labor, 95th Congress, 1st Session, March 11, 1977* (Washington, DC: U.S. Government Printing Office), 28.

28. Jimenez, "Permanency Planning and the Child Abuse Prevention and Treatment Act."

29. Maternal and Child Health Library, "Five Decades of Action for Children," 1962, http://www.mchlibrary.info/history/chbu/2628.PDF, accessed April 29, 2008; Costin, Karger, and Stoesz, *Politics of Child Abuse in America*, 110.

30. Costin, "Cruelty to Children," 111.

31. Costin, Karger, and Stoesz, *Politics of Child Abuse in America*, 116.

32. Costin, Karger, and Stoesz, *Politics of Child Abuse in America*, 120–121.

33. Jimenez, "Permanency Planning and the Child Abuse Prevention and Treatment Act," 64–65.

34. Lindsey, *The Welfare of Children*, 85–86.

35. Jimenez, "Permanency Planning and the Child Abuse Prevention and Treatment Act," 68–70; Costin, "Cruelty to Children," 123.

36. Costin, "Cruelty to Children," 116.

37. Lindsey, *The Welfare of Children*, 86–87.

38. Ibid.

39. Amy D'Andrade and Jill Duerr Berrick, "When Policy Meets Practice: The Untested Effects of Permanency Reforms in Child Welfare," *Journal of Sociology and Social Welfare* 33 (March 2006): 31–52.

40. D'Andrade, "When Policy Meets Practice," 37.

41. Child Welfare Information Gateway, "Foster Parent Adoption," 2006, http://www.childwelfare.gov/pubs/f_fospro/f_fospro.cfm, accessed May 24, 2008.

42. Erica Zielewski, Karin Malm, Rob Geen, and Steve Christian, "Trends in U.S. Foster Care Adoption Legislation," The Urban Institute, November 16, 2006, http://www.urban.org/publications/411380.html, accessed May 23, 2008.

43. Evan B. Donaldson Adoption Institute, "Foster Care Facts, 2002," http://www .adoptioninstitute.org/FactOverview/foster.html, accessed April 21, 2009.

44. Judith Model, *Kinship With Strangers: Adoptions and Interpretations of Kinship in American Culture* (Berkeley: University of California Press, 1994).

45. Rob Geen, "The Evolution of Kinship Care: Policy and Practice," *The Future of Children,* Vol. 14 (Washington, DC: The Urban Institute, 2004), 115–129.

46. Ibid.

47. Julie Miller-Cribbs and Naomi Farber, "Kin Networks and Poverty Among African Americans: Past and Present," *Social Work* 53 (January 2008): 43–51; Jimenez, "The History of Child Protection in the African American Community," 900–902; Smith and Devore, "African American Children in the Child Welfare and Kinship System," 427–446.

48. Mark Testa, "The Changing Significance of Race and Kinship for Achieving Permanence for Foster Children," in Dennete Derezotes, John Poertner, and Mark Testa, eds., *Race Matters in Child Welfare: The Overrepresentation of African American Children in the System* (Washington, DC: Child Welfare League of America, 2005), 231–241.

49. Dorothy Roberts, *Shattered Bonds: The Color of Child Welfare* (New York: Basic Books, 2002), 248–250; Madeleine Kurtz, "The Purchase of Families Into Foster Care: Two Case Studies and the Lessons They Teach," *Connecticut Law Review,* 26 (1994), 1453–1475.

50. Andrea Wilkins, "The Indian Child Welfare Act and the States," The National Conference of State Legislatures, April 2004, http://www.ncsl.org/programs/statetribe/icwa.htmaccessed May 21, 2008.

51. Ann MacEachron and Nora Gustavsson, "Contemporary Policy Challenges for Indian Child Welfare," *Journal of Poverty* 9 (2, 2005): 43–61.

52. U.S. Census Bureau, and Alaska Natives by Tribe and Language: 2000: Part 1," 2003, 89, http://www.census.gov/population/www/socdemo/race/indian.html, accessed May 21, 2008.

53. Roberts, *Shattered Bonds,* 246–249.

54. "Transracial Adoption," http://racerelations.about.com/od/parentingrace/i/transracialadop_2.htm, accessed May 19, 2008.

55. Center for Law and Social Policy, "Child Welfare in the United States," http://clasp.org./publications/childwelfareinus06.pdf, accessed May 11, 2008.

56. U.S. Children's Bureau, "New Report on Adoption and Foster Care Numbers," May 2008, http://cbexpress.acf.hhs.gov/index.cfm?event=website.viewArticles&issueid=94&articleID=1550&keywords=report%20on%20adoption%20and%20foster%20care%20numbers, accessed May 9, 2008.

57. Child Welfare Information Gateway, "Child Abuse and Neglect Fatalities," 2008, http://www.childwelfare.gov/pubs/factsheets/fatality.cfm, accessed May 9, 2008.

58. Ruth McRoy, "The Color of Child Welfare," in King Davis and Tricia B. Bengt-Goodley, eds., *The Color of Social Policy* (Alexandria, VA: Council on Social Work Education, 2004), 44–45.

59. Alice Hines, Kathy Lemon, Paige Wyatt, and Joan Merdinger, "Factors Related to the Disproportionate Involvement of Children of Color in the Child Welfare System," *Children and Youth Services Review* 26 (June 2004): 507–527.

60. Dennete Derezotes and John Poertner, "Factors Contributing to the Overrepresentation of African American Children in the Child Welfare System," in Derezotes et al., *Race Matters in Child Welfare,* 1–25.

61. Hines, Lemon, Wyatt, and Merdinger, "Factors Related to the Disproportionate Involvement of Children of Color in the Child Welfare System," 507–527.

62. Robert Goerge and Bong Joo Lee, "The Entry of Children From the Welfare System Into Foster Care: Differences by Race," in Derezotes et al., *Race Matters in Child Welfare,* 173–186.

63. Center for Law and Social Policy, "Child Welfare in the United States," http://clasp.org./publications/childwelfarein us06.pdf, accessed May 11, 2008.

64. Technical Assistance Partnership, "Child Welfare Frequently Asked Questions," 2007, http://www.tapartnership.org/advisors/ChildWelfare/faq/sept07.asp, accessed May 11, 2008.

65. Jane Waldfogel, "Welfare Reform and the Child Welfare System," *Children and Youth Services Review* 26 (October 2004): 919–939.

66. Christina Paxon and Jane Waldfogel, "Welfare Reforms, Family Resources and Child Maltreatment," *Journal of Policy Analysis and Management* 22 (1, 2003): 85–113.

67. U.S. Department of Health and Human Services, Administration for Children and Families, *Child Maltreatment 2005* (Washington, DC: U.S. Government Printing Office, 2007), http://www.acf.hhs.gov/programs/cb/pubs/cm05/index.htm.

68. Robert Hill, "Synthesis of Research on Disproportionality in the Child Welfare System: An Update," Casey-CSSP Alliance for Racial Equity in the Child Welfare System, October 2006, http://www.racemattersconsortium.org/docs/BobHillPaper_FINAL.pdf, accessed May 11, 2008; Andrea J. Sedlak and Diane D. Broadhurst, "Executive Summary of the Third National Incidence Study of Child Abuse and Neglect," U.S. Department of Health and Human Services, 1996, http://www.childwelfare .gov/pubs/statsinfo/nis3.cfm, accessed May 10, 2008.

69. U.S. Department of Health and Human Services, "Fourth National Incidence Study of Child Abuse and Neglect," https://www.nis4.0rg/nishome.asp, accessed May 10, 2008.

70. U.S. Department of Health and Human Services, *Child Maltreatment 2003* (Washington, DC: U.S. Government Printing Office, 2005), www.acf.hhs.gov/programs/ cb/pubs/cm03/index.htm, accessed May 10, 2008.

71. Hill, "Synthesis of Research on Disproportionality in the Child Welfare System," 9; Hines et al., "Factors Related to the Disproportionate Involvement of Children of Color in the Child Welfare System," 10–11.

72. John Fluke, Ying-Ying Yuan, John Hedderson, and Patrick Curtis, "Disproportionate Representation of Race and Ethnicity in Child Maltreatment: Investigation and Victimization," *Children and Youth Services Review* 25 (5/6, 2003): 359–373; Andrea Sedlack and Dana Schultz, "Racial Differences in Child Protective Service Investigation of Abused and Neglected Children: Risk of Maltreatment in the General Child Population," in Derezotes et al., *Race Matters in Child Welfare,* 97–119; Brian Gryzlak, Susan Wells, and Michelle Johnson, "The Role of Race in Child

Protective Services Screening Decisions," in Derezotes et al., *Race Matters in Child Welfare*, 63–96.

73. Fluke et al., "Disproportionate Representation of Race and Ethnicity in Child Maltreatment," 359–373; Hill, "Synthesis of Research on Disproportionality in the Child Welfare System," 20–21.

74. U.S. Department of Health and Human Services, Administration for Children and Families, *Child Maltreatment 2005* (Washington, DC: U.S. Government Printing Office, 2007), http://www.acf.hhs.gov/programs/cb/pubs/cm05/index.htm.

75. Sheila Ards, Samuel Myers, and Allan Malkis, "Racial Disproportionality in Reported and Substantiated Child Abuse and Neglect: An Examination of Systematic Bias," *Children and Youth Services Review* 25 (5/6, 2003): 375–392; Yuhwa Lu, John Landsverk, Elissa Ellis-Mcleod, Rae Newton, William Ganger, and Ivory Johnson, "Race, Ethnicity and Case Outcomes in Child Protective Services," *Children and Youth Services Review* 26 (5, 2004): 447–461; Hill, "Synthesis of Research on Disproportionality in the Child Welfare System," 24.

76. Hill, "Synthesis of Research on Disproportionality in the Child Welfare System," 28; A. Garland, J. Landsverk, and A. Lau, "Racial/Ethnic Disparities in Mental Health Service Use Among Children in Foster Care," *Children and Youth Services Review* 25 (5/6, 2003): 491–507; McRoy, "The Color of Child Welfare," 36–65.

77. Derezotes and Poertner, "Factors Contributing to the Overrepresentation of African American Children in the Child Welfare System," 1–25.

78. Richard Barth, "Child Welfare and Race: Models of Disproportionality," in Derezotes et al., 25–47.

79. Kathleen Kilty and Vidal de Haymes, "Racism, Nativism and Exclusion: Public Policy, Immigration and the Latino Experience in the United States," in Vidal de Haymes, Kathleen Kilty, and Elizabeth Segal, eds., *Latino Poverty in the New Century: Inequalities, Challenges and Barriers* (New York: Haworth Press, 2000), 50–203.

80. Wesley Church, "From Start to Finish: The Duration of Hispanic Children in Out-of-Home Placements," *Children and Youth Services Review* 28 (9, 2006), 1007–1023; Roberts, *Shattered Bonds*, 48–49.

81. Wesley Church, Emma Gross, and James Baldwin, "Maybe Ignorance Is Not Always Bliss: The Disparate Treatment of Hispanics Within the Child Welfare System," *Children and Youth Services Review* 27 (12, 2005): 1278–1292.

82. Alice Hinex, Peter Lee, Kathy Osterling, and Laurie Drabble, "Factors Predicting Family Reunification for African, Latino, Asian and White Families in the Child Welfare System," *Journal of Child and Family Studies*, 16 (April 2007): 275–289.

83. Emilie Stolzgus, "Child Welfare: Fostering Connections to Success and Increasing Adoptions Act of 2008," Congressional Research Service, October 9, 2008, http://wikileaks.org/wiki/CRS:_Child_Welfare:_The_Fostering_Connections_to_Success_and_Increasing_Adoptions_Act_of_2008,_October_9,_2008, accessed April 7, 2009.

84. Jane Waldfogel, *The Future of Child Protection* (Cambridge, MA: Harvard University Press, 1998), 213–216.

85. Marcia Garrison, "Why Terminate Parental Rights?" *Stanford Law Review* 35 (1987): 423–450; Jimenez, "The History of Child Protection in the African American Community," 902.

86. Pauline Irit Erera, *Family Diversity: Continuity and Change in the Contemporary Family* (Thousand Oaks, CA: Sage, 2002), 63–65.

CHAPTER

9

Health Care Policy

CHAPTER QUESTIONS

1. Why is the United States the only country in the developed world without a national health care policy?

2. What have been the biggest impediments to the development of national health care?

3. Which Americans are most likely to be uninsured? How is their health impacted?

4. Why does health care cost so much in the United States, even though so many are uninsured?

5. What are the drawbacks and successes of the publicly funded health programs, Medicare, Medicaid, and SCHIP?

6. Why did previous efforts to reform the health care system fail?

7. What are some options for health care reform in the United States now?

● ● ●

THE DEMAND FOR HEALTH CARE ●

The fact that everyone dies means that everyone knows someone who has died, that everyone we know will die, and that we will also die. The end of life is generally something we wish to put off as long as possible. Similarly, most people do not wish to be sick or see their loved ones ill. The desire to avoid death and illness comprises two of the strongest human needs. Health care, along with prayer and other spiritual remedies, is seen as the main remedy for sickness and death. The demand for health care is infinite; most people would choose a medical intervention over sickness or death. Thus health care is fundamental to human well-being, and when a society has the resources to support a comprehensive health care system, presumably it will. All developed, industrialized societies have created a national health care system to allow all residents access to life-saving and life-prolonging treatment except one: the United States.

As noted above, the demand for health care is potentially infinite given the finality of death and the suffering associated with illness and disease. For this reason, all societies ration health care, most according to emergent need (how life threatening a particular condition is), but the United States and other nonindustrialized countries without adequate medical technology to serve everyone ration health care according to price. Those who can afford health care can purchase it; those who cannot do without. With some exceptions discussed below, the United States therefore has the same health policy as countries in nonindustrialized, developing areas of the world, in spite of the fact that the highest level of medical technology and trained workforce exists in this country. Why does this paradox exist? The rest of this chapter will address this question, detailing the consequences for persons living in this country, looking toward American history to explain the anomalous status of health care in this country, and suggesting models of health care that would promote more equitable access to health care.

This chapter will demonstrate how in the United States most health care is delivered through the *market economy,* which means that those with low incomes have great difficulty purchasing it if their employers do not offer it as a job-related benefit. The delivery of health care through a for-profit insurance system leads the United States to have the most expensive health care system in the world, even though 46 million persons have no insurance. The *historical ideologies emphasizing self-reliance and individualism* work against a collective view of health, which underlies national health care systems in other industrialized countries. *The legacy of discrimination against certain ethnic groups* results in persons in these groups having lower health status and greater difficulty accessing health care.

Access to Health Care in the United States

Health care, like other private commodities, is delivered through the price system. Individuals pay health care providers for their services, using either private insurance obtained through employers or public insurance (Medicare and Medicaid). Those with neither receive state-supported care in hospital emergency rooms across the country, the most expensive health care in the United States. Most people buy health care using insurance previously paid for and supplementing the insurance with funds of their own. In the United States health care is purchased through the mechanisms of the *market economy* just like other commodities, including food and shelter. In the United States those who can afford health care receive high-quality care; those who depend on government programs or who cannot afford any insurance may receive lower-quality care.

The United States is the only country in the industrial world to depend on employer-based, voluntary health insurance. Yet only a little more than half of insured persons received health insurance from their employers in 2007.[1] The vast majority (80%) of those covered by employers contribute to their own health insurance premium; for individuals the worker contribution averaged $694, and for family coverage the mean worker contribution was $3,281.[2] Having employer-based health insurance is a clear economic benefit to working families since the average cost of private insurance for a family of four in urban areas in the United States for those buying their insurance privately is $20,000–$40,000. Businesses incur costs for providing health insurance for their workers; the average cost to a business of insuring one worker is $12,000 per year, much of which is tax deductible for businesses as will be discussed later in this chapter.[3] The working landscape has shifted dramatically in terms of the availability of health insurance: Not all businesses offer insurance, largely because of rising health care premiums. The percentage of people covered by employment-based health insurance was 59.3 percent in 2007.[4] Even among businesses offering insurance, many of their workers cannot afford the premiums they themselves must pay. Health care premiums paid by workers have risen 143% since 2000. Workers are now paying $1,400 more in premiums annually for family coverage than they did in 2000.[5]

Who Is Uninsured?

The number of people uninsured in 2007 was approximately 46 million persons, or 15% of the population.[6] This number represents a 9 million-person increase since 2000 and a 40% increase since 1987. The vast majority of uninsured are either native or naturalized citizens, not undocumented immigrants as some suggest.[7] African Americans and Latinos have the highest percentage of uninsured persons; the uninsured rate for African Americans in 2007 was 19.5%, for Latinos the uninsured rate was 32.1%, for Asians it was 16.8%, and the percentage of uninsured White persons was 10.4 (see Figure 9.1).[8]

Even so-called middle-class families earning $50,000 a year or more are often unable to afford health insurance. Not surprisingly, national surveys show that

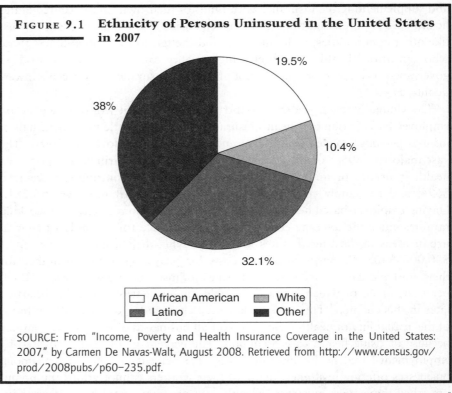

FIGURE 9.1   **Ethnicity of Persons Uninsured in the United States in 2007**

19.5%

38%

10.4%

32.1%

☐ African American   ▨ White
▧ Latino   ■ Other

SOURCE: From "Income, Poverty and Health Insurance Coverage in the United States: 2007," by Carmen De Navas-Walt, August 2008. Retrieved from http://www.census.gov/prod/2008pubs/p60−235.pdf.

the primary reason people are uninsured is the high cost of health insurance.[9] Those who change or lose jobs will lose their health insurance. COBRA, a program that allows individuals to buy continued group health insurance after they leave a job, is prohibitively expensive for many; only 7% of Americans who have lost employer-based coverage can afford to purchase COBRA, which averages $700 monthly for a family of four.[10]

Many Americans think that all children in the United States have health care. On the contrary, the number of uninsured children in 2007 was 8.1 million, which is more than 11% of children in the United States. These children are not covered by Medicaid, the government-sponsored insurance that covers some very poor children, or the State Children's Health Insurance Program, the government-sponsored program that allows families to buy low-cost insurance (see Figure 9.2). In 2007 the number of people insured by Medicaid was 39.6 million, or 13.2% of the population; by Medicare it was 41.4 million, or 13.8% of the population.[11] Largely because of the high number of uninsured, the health indicators traditionally used to measure a country's health are not particularly good for the United States, in spite of the fact that we spend more money on health care than any country in the world.

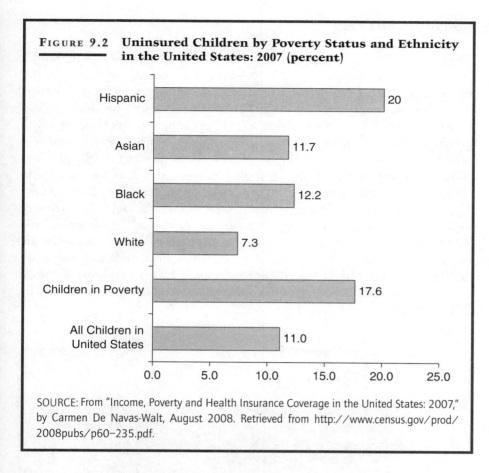

FIGURE 9.2   **Uninsured Children by Poverty Status and Ethnicity in the United States: 2007 (percent)**

SOURCE: From "Income, Poverty and Health Insurance Coverage in the United States: 2007," by Carmen De Navas-Walt, August 2008. Retrieved from http://www.census.gov/prod/2008pubs/p60–235.pdf.

Impact of Not Having Health Insurance

Those without health insurance are less likely to receive preventive care and are more likely to be diagnosed at advanced stages of diseases than those who have regular medical care through insurance. As a result, the uninsured have higher mortality rates than the insured. Those who have neither private nor public insurance are likely to receive their health care in the emergency room; approximately 20% of the uninsured report that their usual source of health care is the emergency room. While emergency rooms cannot turn very sick people away, many hospitals now require that uninsured persons pay for their care with their personal credit cards, driving many families to bankruptcy. Another cost incurred by having some persons uninsured is unnecessary hospitalizations; the uninsured are more likely to be hospitalized for a condition that could have been avoided. These hospital stays cost an average of $3,300 per stay.[12]

Cost of Health Care

The U.S. level of per capita health care expenditure is the highest in the world, more than twice as high as that of most other developed countries and 4.3 times the amount we spend on national defense. Higher costs for prescription drugs, hospital stays, and doctor visits are the main reasons for the high cost. In 2006 the United States spent over $7,000 per capita (per person) on health care, 53% more than the next highest-spending countries, Switzerland and Norway. We spend over 16% of our gross domestic product (GDP, all things produced in the United States) on health care, compared to 8% to 10% in other industrialized nations. Health care spending accounted for 10.9% of the GDP in Switzerland, 10.7% in Germany, 9.7% in Canada, and 9.5% in France in 2006, according to the Organisation for Economic Co-operation and Development.[13] In spite of this expenditure, the United States has a similar life expectancy as Cuba, which spends about 1/25th as much on health care as we do.[14] In 2006 the United States spent more than 16% of its gross domestic product on health care. It is projected that the percentage will reach 20% by 2016.[15] (See Figure 9.3.)

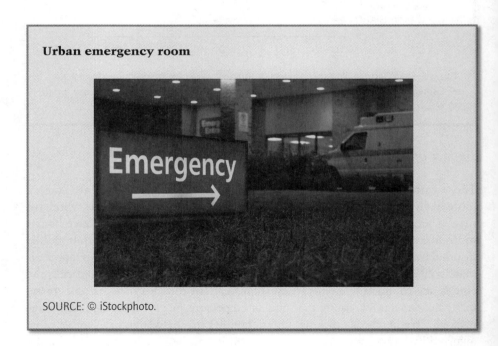

Urban emergency room

SOURCE: © iStockphoto.

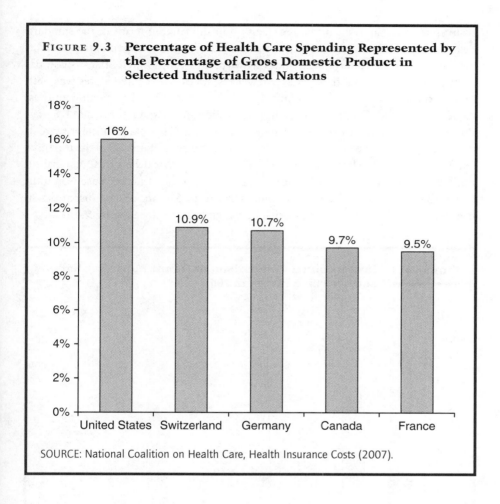

FIGURE 9.3   **Percentage of Health Care Spending Represented by the Percentage of Gross Domestic Product in Selected Industrialized Nations**

SOURCE: National Coalition on Health Care, Health Insurance Costs (2007).

One reason for the high cost of health care is the high number of uninsured persons. The United States spends $100 billion annually providing health care to uninsured persons; much of this cost comes from the considerably more expensive emergency room treatment and avoidable hospitalizations. Uncompensated health care provided to uninsured persons by hospitals totals $34 billion annually.[16] All these costs could be avoided with the adoption of national health insurance: postponed medical treatment, expensive and unnecessary treatment in emergency rooms, increased mortality, and anxiety about obtaining and paying for medical care.

In spite of the amount of money spent on health care, in terms of the standard health indicators commonly used to measure the health of a population—infant mortality rates, morbidity rates, and longevity rates—the United States is comparable to developing countries with far fewer resources. The United States was 48th in life expectancy and 42nd in infant mortality rates in 2006 among all countries. Chile, Cuba, and Greece have higher life expectancies than the United States; Puerto Rico has a higher life expectancy for women.[17] The infant mortality rate in the United States is 7 deaths per 1,000 live births, compared with 2.7 in the top three countries in terms of infant mortality.[18] In 2000, the World Health Organization ranked the United States 15th out of 25 countries in health care, based on indicators that include life expectancy, child survival to 5 years of age, disparities in health care, and out-of-pocket health care expenditures.[19] (See Figure 9.4.)

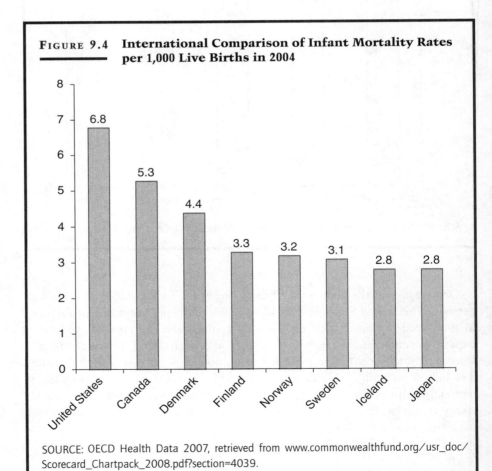

FIGURE 9.4 International Comparison of Infant Mortality Rates per 1,000 Live Births in 2004

SOURCE: OECD Health Data 2007, retrieved from www.commonwealthfund.org/usr_doc/ Scorecard_Chartpack_2008.pdf?section=4039.

Part of the reason for the low performance of the United States may be the high proportion of health resources that go to administrative costs: 31% in this country, compared to 17% in Canada, whose national health care system covers everyone. The United Kingdom spends 50% less per capita than the United States on health care, yet its population is much healthier than that of the United States. This health superiority is evident across all social classes. Great Britain has dramatically lower prevalence rates of heart disease, diabetes, hypertension, and cancer. Most analysts attribute the difference to the fact that preventive care is available to everyone in Britain through the national health care system.[20]

HISTORY OF BELIEFS AND VALUES ABOUT HEALTH   ●

Why doesn't the United States have national health insurance? An important reason for the failure of the United States to create a national health care policy lies in the history of our ideas about health. While institutional forces, including the American Medical Association and the private insurance and pharmaceutical sectors of the economy, have at various times played important roles in preventing the adoption of health care proposals by Congress, a deeper reason lies in the beliefs about the origins of sickness and health that emerged in the United States in the 19th century and had a unique power in this country. The conviction that health is a private good, achieved through personal struggle and discipline, is an important theme in American attitudes toward health. This theme first emerged in the religious revival movement of the 19th century, when a health reform movement surfaced to counter the fatalism about sickness and death characterizing the colonial period. The health reform movement had its origins in a religious movement emphasizing human perfectibility and optimism, known as the Second Great Awakening. These early health reformers believed that God intended every human to have perfect health; they saw ill health as the result of poor human choices. Diet, control of alcohol intake, exercise, and sleep habits were thought to be the lynchpins of good health since these behaviors were subject to individual control and health was a matter of individual responsibility. These first health reformers in American history discounted broader social forces that are commonly implicated in poor health today, including pollution, overcrowding in urban centers, and sanitation problems. The return to a simpler way of life emphasizing self-regulation and the avoidance of vices associated with urban areas were urged as crucial steps to the attainment of good health. One of the most famous health reformers in the 19th century was Sylvester Graham, inventor of the graham cracker, whose writing was widely circulated. Graham believed that there was a deep connection between health and moral character. Health was the result of self-discipline.[21]

This conviction that proper living can prevent disease continues to characterize our health beliefs. It underlies health promotion efforts of professionals who urge us to cease some habits and take up others.[22] At first glance it appears to be a benign philosophy, one likely to have positive effects on well-being. The dark side of this belief that health is an individual responsibility is the failure to recognize the collective aspects of health. Early public health reformers understood that public hygiene was central to good health; unhealthy air, water, and food were causes of disease that were subject to collective policy solutions, not individual self-regulation. As major epidemics of cholera, malaria, and typhoid swept urban areas in the Northeast and Midwest in the 19th century, public health experts worked to reform sanitary conditions there by pressuring city and state officials to purify water and milk supplies and to improve sanitation in poor communities.[23]

In spite of their success in public sanitation, by the early 20th century public health experts had been marginalized by medical professionals, who objected to the free clinics in immigrant neighborhoods that were established by public health officials. Physicians wanted to restrict public health officials to the diagnosis of contagious diseases such as tuberculosis.[24] The medical profession as a whole showed little interest in community prevention of disease; instead it focused on finding cures for known diseases. Public health became marginalized in local bureaucracies and charged with diagnosis and tracking of communicable diseases, not prevention or treatment. With the discovery of bacteriology, the notion that all disease had a single if invisible cause that could be treated only by a medical professional shifted attention away from the original mandate of public health to link diseases with larger urban problems. Public health officials joined physicians in urging personal hygiene (hand washing) as the best defense against disease. With the new emphasis on personal hygiene, as opposed to urban problems, the original emphasis on collective responsibility that had characterized the public health movement was lost.[25]

As Paul Starr describes it in his history of American medicine, the medical profession holds a rarefied place in American society.[26] As representatives of science, physicians are conversant with the most privileged and arcane form of knowledge, giving them status as keepers of the secrets of health and life itself. As witnesses/participants in the most intimate aspects of human life, they inspire sometimes desperate hope and trust. All these factors give physicians enormous power in our culture; combined with the fact that health care, which they

PROFILES IN LEADERSHIP

Margaret Sanger, 1879–1966

Margaret Sanger was born in 1879 in Ohio, and she was raised in poverty with loving parents who included a working-class father and a very ill mother. Margaret's father, although not formally educated, was well read and turned to social activism when he became outraged about the conditions of the working poor and eventually became a socialist. Margaret was the sixth of 11 children, and her frail mother became exhausted with the tasks of cooking and cleaning and caring for her very large family.

Margaret's two older sisters eventually scraped together sufficient funds to send young Margaret to Claverack College, which was a Methodist preparatory school not far from Hudson, New York. Margaret loved being at Claverack College; she was an excellent student and even dreamed of attending medical school at Cornell University. She developed a strong sense of self and was not shy about defending herself when necessary. Eventually she left

Margaret Sanger

SOURCE: From the Library of Congress.

Claverack and took a teaching job temporarily but had to return home soon to take care of her very ill mother. Later she decided to go to White Plains, New York, where she accepted a position as a nurse practitioner at White Plains Hospital. It was at White Plains Hospital that she began to understand women's health issues and focused on obstetrics as her main interest. It was also

(Continued)

(Continued)

here that she met and eventually married William Sanger, an architect. She and her husband had three children. During this time she developed tuberculosis and was quite ill for several years.

At the turn of the 20th century radical groups were openly challenging the brutal labor conditions that were being imposed by rich and powerful employers. Margaret became intensely involved in these issues, and eventually she and her husband became active socialists. As she became more involved in radical issues, she began delivering lectures on birth control and women's health issues. She was very much influenced by the massive and grinding poverty that she had experienced as a nurse in the Lower East Side of New York. She saw poor mothers who had repeated pregnancies and deteriorating health while trying to survive in deplorable living conditions. She was determined to help those women and became committed to overturning the federal Comstock law that had been passed by Congress in 1873. This law made it a crime to manufacture, sell, or send through the mail any articles or printed matter that prevented conception. The punishment was a fine of $5,000 and a jail sentence of up to 10 years.

Of course the wealthy continued to be able to obtain contraception, but poor families had to depend on illegal abortions, sometimes resulting in major health problems and even death. Margaret Sanger began to write a column in a local publication on the Lower East Side that provided valuable but forbidden information about birth control. These articles found their way into government publications for military personnel, making her more vulnerable to federal prosecution. These articles were titled "What Every Boy and Girl Should Know" and were distributed widely to many other publications.

In 1914 due to her radical activities and challenging of the Comstock law, Margaret was indicted by a grand jury on nine counts for publishing obscenities and was now facing the possibility of prison. Soon after being indicted, she and her husband fled to Europe.

While in Europe, Sanger visited a number of nearby countries to better understand how they had successfully established birth control clinics and overcome hostile prejudice and superstition regarding the termination of pregnancies. She felt that this knowledge would help her when she returned to the United States to continue her work.

When she returned to America in 1915 after a year abroad, she discovered a major change in public attitudes about birth control, and she soon received support and assistance from women's radical groups. Although there were pending charges against her, the government decided to dismiss all of them, and Sanger was able to return to the issue that had consumed her. She toured major American cities lecturing about the importance of birth control. Emboldened by her success in having the charges dropped, Sanger went on to establish the first birth control clinic in the country in Brooklyn, New York. Local authorities reacted by promptly arresting Sanger and a number of women who had been receiving birth control information and devices. Sanger was sentenced to 30 days in jail. Massive protest in the local community influenced her release. For the next few years Sanger busied herself with lecture tours, publishing articles and books, traveling to foreign countries, organizing national and international conferences on birth control, and developing strategies and plans for convincing Congress to pass major birth control legislation. All of this was during a time when large sections of the country still opposed birth control and maintained very conservative attitudes regarding sexuality and birth control.

Over time birth control became more acceptable in the United States, and finally in 1965, the U.S. Supreme Court ruled in *Griswold v. Connecticut* that use of birth control was a guaranteed constitutional right. Margaret Sanger's dream of making birth control legal and available had finally become a reality; she died a year after this decision. Sanger is recognized as a courageous leader who devoted most of her life to helping women to control their own bodies. Her fight was against tremendous obstacles including religious, cultural, and social objections, but she never wavered in her determination and courage as a pioneer for women's rights in the area of reproductive freedom.

provide, is a scarce and often expensive commodity, their authority may be unequalled. For these reasons physicians have had enormous power over the shape and content of health care policies and health care delivery. The power of physicians increased in 1915, when the accrediting body for medical schools in the United States standardized and consolidated schools offering medical education, decreasing their number from 131 to 95. Since that time the number of accredited medical schools has been strictly limited by the accrediting body of the American Medical Association; schools have been warned to keep the number of students low, with the clear result, if not the intention, of making the supply of physicians artificially scarce. In fact there are fewer physicians per population in the United States than in any other developed country.[27]

The Emergence of Private Insurance

Private health insurance did not exist until the 1930s, when hospitals began to sponsor prepayment plans, realizing that many patients could not afford their hospital bills. Blue Cross was the first private insurance plan for hospitalization, followed by Blue Shield for physicians' visits. Both these private for-profit insurance startups were sponsored by state medical societies. In 1943 the National War Labor Board ruled that employer contributions to employee benefit plans, including health insurance benefits, would not be counted as wages and therefore would not be taxable, in effect giving a tax benefit to workers. In 1951 the Internal Revenue Service gave even more encouragement to the development of private insurance by ruling that employers' costs for health care premiums were tax deductible. The rise of for-profit insurance led to increased utilization of physicians' services in the 1950s; some would call it overconsumption, which led to increased physician income and hospital profit. Between 1946 and 1957 the number of workers covered by health insurance plans rose from 1 million to 12 million, plus an additional 20 million dependents. The political motivation for national health insurance had been dimmed by the employer-derived tax-free health care benefits. Workers not covered by union contracts were far less likely to receive these health care benefits, just as workers in the secondary labor markets today are unlikely to receive them.[28] For example, fewer than half the workers in the retail sector of the economy are covered by health insurance from their employer.[29]

The above decisions about the tax implications of employer-sponsored health care, though little recognized by the general public, amount to a federal tax subsidy to workers covered by employer-based health insurance. Combined with the tax deductions claimed by businesses that pay health care premiums for their workers, these tax expenditures cost taxpayers $200 billion a year, money that ordinarily would come into the federal, state, and local treasuries as tax payments.[30]

● HEALTH DISPARITIES AMONG ETHNIC GROUPS: THE IMPACT OF DISCRIMINATION

In the United States access to health care is mediated by income, ethnicity, nativity, and gender. Access to health care is critical, not only because of the standard of fairness one would expect in a democratic society but because barriers to health care access have been demonstrated to be directly linked to poorer health.

One example of a health disparity is the fact that African Americans and Native Americans have higher death rates between the ages of 45 and 54, compared to Whites and Latinos. Differences in death rates in this age group are a good indicator of disparities in levels of disease, access to health care, and quality of health care.[31] African Americans are less healthy than all other ethnic groups throughout their lifespan; they experience both higher infant mortality and higher adult mortality. The life span of African American men is on average 8.3 years shorter than that of White men. African American men have an increased level of cardiovascular disease and higher rates of diabetes and infectious diseases—all of which lead to the shorter average life span they experience.[32] Additionally and perhaps more significantly, African Americans have higher rates *of mortality* from heart disease, cancer, diabetes, cerebrovascular disease, HIV/AIDS, unintentional injuries, pregnancy, and sudden infant death syndrome than do Whites.[33] African American infants are less likely to be healthy than White infants; in 2008, an African American baby born in the United States was 2.5 times more likely to die before his or her first birthday than a White baby.[34]

What accounts for these disparities? African Americans are less likely to possess private or employment-based health insurance than White Americans and are more likely to be covered via Medicaid or other publicly funded insurance.[35] See below for a discussion of the limitations of Medicaid. Add to this fact the lifetime of discrimination and accompanying stress experienced by many African Americans and the potential for greater health challenges in this group seems clear.

American Indians have the highest rate of mortality from diabetes; Latinos are twice as likely as Whites to die from this disease. These differences are related to socioeconomic status, not genetics, according to health researchers.[36] In terms of preventative health care, African Americans and Latinos are less likely to receive cancer screenings and influenza immunization, as well as (along with American Indian women) prenatal care and dental care.[37] African Americans, Latinos, American Indians, and Asian Americans are less likely to have health insurance, have greater difficulty accessing health care, and have fewer choices in health care services than Whites.[38] Discrimination contributes to inequality in education and income, which in turn perpetuates health discrepancies among ethnic groups by limiting access to adequate health care.

Poverty is the most powerful variable affecting health. Economic factors are strongly linked to health outcomes throughout the life span. Disparities in health status begin in utero, as the health of the fetus is dependent on the health of the mother. Multiple risk factors for adverse pregnancy and birth outcomes are associated with a mother's poverty. The most important problems associated with low income and lack of health care are premature birth and low birth rate, both of which are correlated with developmental problems in infants. Older children in lower-income areas are at greater risk of death from infectious diseases, accidents, and child abuse. They are more likely to suffer from lead poisoning and secondhand smoke and to develop asthma, as well as developmental delays. These children are more likely to be exposed to family and community violence. Adolescents in lower-income groups have higher rates of pregnancy and sexually transmitted diseases, depression, obesity, and suicide. Adolescents from economically marginalized families are more likely to drop out of high school or be killed. The health disparities continue into adulthood; adults who do not have a high school education have life expectancies that are 6 years shorter than those who complete college. Adults who are economically marginalized have higher rates of death across a wide range of diseases. They are at risk for earlier onset of hypertension, diabetes, cardiovascular disease, obesity, and depression. Health disparities among elderly persons are not as pronounced as in younger years, but older persons who live in poverty relative to others in their age cohort experience more disability, more limitations in activities of daily living, and more frequent and rapid cognitive decline. Why are these relationships between health status and economic status so powerful? One possibility is, of course, that for some, poor health precedes and causes economic marginalization. But the fact is that economic status in childhood predicts health in adulthood. There are many reasons this link occurs; research has established that chronic stress, such as that associated with poverty, has long-term and cumulative physiological effects. In the United States those with fewer economic resources have less access to health care, especially quality health care, and less access to preventive health care. Absence of health insurance itself has been consistently related to higher mortality in the United States. The effects of poverty are multiplied by the confluence of risk factors experienced by marginalized groups living in low-income neighborhoods under conditions of restricted access and discrimination. Researchers have found that residing in high-poverty areas is itself a risk for healthy people, putting all residents at risk of developing cardiovascular disease.[39]

● HEALTH CARE IN THE UNITED STATES: PUBLIC-PRIVATE MIX

The health care system in the United States is neither all private nor all public. Two major programs, Medicare and Medicaid, are publicly administered and financed, and even in the case of the private system, the federal, state, and local governments bail out hospitals that cannot recover their emergency room costs. Clearly the fact that employer-based health insurance is tax deductible for both the employer and the employee (who do not pay income tax on health benefits) is an important form of public support. Looked at this way, the government is responsible for 60% of national health care expenditures.[40]

As employers cease offering health care benefits due to high cost, many more persons become uninsured. This increase has already been reflected in higher Medicaid enrollment, which grew by almost 20% between 2000 and 2003.[41] Private insurance still outpaces public insurance; estimates are that 37% of health care expenditures are covered by private insurance, while 34% are covered by Medicare and Medicaid combined.[42] Various forms of medical delivery—fee for service, health maintenance organizations, and preferred provider organizations—are utilized by both the private and the public health care systems. (See Figure 9.5.)

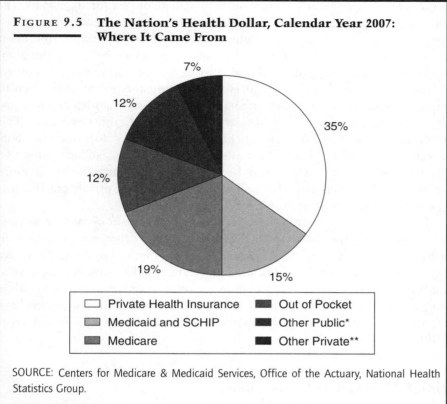

FIGURE 9.5   **The Nation's Health Dollar, Calendar Year 2007: Where It Came From**

Legend:
- ☐ Private Health Insurance
- ☐ Medicaid and SCHIP
- ☐ Medicare
- ■ Out of Pocket
- ■ Other Public*
- ■ Other Private**

SOURCE: Centers for Medicare & Medicaid Services, Office of the Actuary, National Health Statistics Group.

NOTE: Numbers shown may not add up to 100.0 because of rounding.

*Other Public includes programs such as workers' compensation, public health activity, Department of Defense, Department of Veterans Affairs, Indian Health Services, state and local hospital subsidies, and school health.

**Other Private includes industrial in-plant, privately funded construction, and nonpatient revenues, including philanthropy.

Fee for Service

Fee for service has been the traditional means of paying for medical care in the United States; when a health care provider offers a service or performs a procedure, the patient or the patient's insurance pays for the cost of the service, which normally includes a profit margin for the provider or the institution providing the service. In order to ensure that a variety of patients with varying economic means could afford their service, many physicians traditionally employed a sliding scale, offering lower fees to poorer patients. With the advent of health insurance, physicians' charges became more standardized, with one fee for all patients. The cost of fee for service is based on the number of procedures and physician visits. When private insurance companies reimburse physicians and other providers, they attempt to keep the costs of services down by setting standardized fees for which they will reimburse (a set fee for one visit to a doctor's office, for example). This is one way that insurance companies maintain their profit margins; other means include charging high premiums, requiring copayments, and restricting insurance for those with preexisting health conditions. This profit margin maintained by private insurance companies does not contribute directly to patient well-being. Most insurance benefits are paid according to a "usual, customary and reasonable fee," usually determined by the insurance company.[43] Physicians and other providers in free-standing private practice generally charge according to the fee for service model.

The drawbacks to fee for service include overutilization of medical services by patients and the use of excessive tests and procedures by physicians to increase their profit margins. Malpractice suits and the accompanying expensive malpractice insurance for physicians in private practice drive up the cost of medical care, resulting in higher insurance rates. Fee for service medicine drives up the cost of health care and is by its nature inflationary, since providers have incentives to multiply the medical events for which they are reimbursed, especially diagnostic tests.[44]

Health Maintenance Organizations

Health maintenance organizations, or HMOs, utilize a completely different form of financing for health care services. In HMOs the unit of remuneration is the person, not the medical service. Under a prepayment or capitation system, patients are covered for all medical expenses, exclusive of deductibles, for a specific period of time, normally a month. The cost of medical care comes out of the monthly prepayment; if there are no medical costs, the payment stays in the medical system. The incentive for HMOs is to control medical costs, not to offer more services. Prevention of disease is incentivized in health maintenance organizations; that is, it is in the physician's interest to offer access to early care to prevent later, more serious costs in terms of hospitalization and other more expensive medical tests and procedures.[45]

The drawback for HMOs is underutilization of necessary medical services; if the incentives for not offering care are too high, physicians and administrators may withhold services to patients in order to protect the revenue received from prepayments. This is especially true in for-profit HMOs, which have suffered from consumer complaints about difficulties accessing quality care. Nonprofit HMOs have been found to offer a higher standard of care.[46]

HMOs have existed in the United States since the 1930s, although their growth increased after the Nixon administration passed the HMO Act of 1973, requiring employers with more than 25 employees to offer an HMO option if one was available and to contribute to such plans an amount equal to what they contributed to fee for service plans. In general all forms of managed care attempt to contain health care costs by offering more efficient services and care driven by patient need, rather than by compensation rates. HMOs also seek to modify consumer behavior by controlling unlimited access to health care in various ways, including utilizing primary physicians to serve as gatekeepers to specialists.

Under HMOs patients agree to receive all their care from one group of physicians, which is paid a set fee per patient. The HMO then assumes responsibility for all health care for its patients. In the 1990s, HMOs suffered somewhat in competition with competing preferred provider organizations (PPOs) and point of service (POS) plans, loosely knit organizations of free-standing physicians, both of which offer employers low-cost insurance options. Under both of these latter plans, employees have more choice of providers than they do with HMOs. The PPO is basically a fee for service health care plan where a network of providers has agreed to give purchasers (employers) a discount.[47]

Efforts to Control Health Care Costs

The inflationary aspects of relatively unlimited access to health care on the part of those who could afford private insurance were not initially recognized. After the passage of the federal health care programs in 1965, Medicare and Medicaid (see below), the costs of health care began to be a concern to federal policymakers, as they perceived excessive testing and treatment to be an unintended consequence of the generous financing of fee for service health care, in both the private and the public sectors. Containing rising health care costs became the preoccupation of health policy experts, replacing earlier concerns with access and quality that had spurred the passage of Medicare and Medicaid.

Efforts to rein in health care costs began with the effort to limit health care consumption on the part of consumers. Higher deductibles, the use of primary physicians as gatekeepers, the proliferation of HMOs, and other more cost-effective health care delivery systems were encouraged by the federal government, as Medicaid patients were forced into HMOs and Medicare beneficiaries encouraged to join (often to little effect). Federal government reimbursement to hospitals under Medicare was regulated by a prospective pay plan beginning in the 1980s, in which a system of preestablished rates determined payment.[48] While these measures decreased the per-patient costs under Medicare, the enrollment in this federal entitlement has increased, limiting the overall savings.

One of the major inequities in the private insurance market is the right of insurance companies to deny individual applications for insurance for a preexisting condition that the company feels makes the individual at higher risk for claims against its policy. Group policies offered by employers minimize the risk of individual claims, but individual policy applicants are subject to the preexisting condition rule. An effort by Senators Kennedy and Kassebaum in 1996 to guarantee that workers changing jobs would be able to keep their original insurance coverage, bypassing the preexisting conditions policy of insurance companies, was strenuously opposed by insurance companies and resulted in a watered-down final bill that did not eliminate preexisting conditions.[49]

Medicare

Medicare is the federal health insurance program for the elderly in the United States, covering approximately 43 million Americans. Medicare benefits were $374 billion; net federal spending minus premiums paid by beneficiaries was $331 billion in 2006, or 14% of the federal budget. Medicare provides a variety of hospital services, as well as physician services and other services, including a prescription drug benefit. Medicare is financed through three sources: a wage tax paid by workers (1.45% of the FICA wage tax), premiums paid by recipients, and general tax revenues. Persons eligible for Medicare include persons 65 and over, disabled persons entitled to Social Security disability benefits, and end-stage renal disease patients. Medicare consists of four parts: Part A covers hospitalization, some posthospital care in skilled nursing facilities, and hospice care. Part B covers physician and physician-ordered services, including outpatient diagnostic tests. Part B does not cover dental care, eye exams or eyeglasses, hearing exams or hearing aids, or long-term custodial care, either in-home or nursing home care. While Part A is free to the recipient, Part B requires a monthly premium be paid to the government. Medicare generally pays only 80% of costs for Part B and requires a deductible for Part A. As a result of this, most Medicare beneficiaries have private Medigap health insurance policies to cover deductibles and the remaining 20% of the cost not covered by Medicare. Part C is known as the Medicare Advantage Plan. Added in 1987, Part C is the managed care part of Medicare, which allows HMOs and PPOs to enroll

Medicare beneficiaries and provide them with Medicare Part A, Part B, and in most cases Part D (see below).

In 2003 the federal government added Part D to Medicare, consisting of a prescription drug benefit, although Medicare Part D did not begin enrolling participants until 2006. Beneficiaries must pay an additional premium to receive this benefit, as well as pay a high percentage (75%) of drug costs up to the first $2,250 spent in one year. After that there is a gap (known as the "doughnut hole") where no drug coverage exists and beneficiaries must absorb the full cost of the drugs up to $3,100. After that amount has been reached ($5,100 total), Medicare Part D pays for 95% of the remaining drug costs for that year. On top of the premium paid to the government to participate in Medicare Part D, beneficiaries must buy a prescription drug plan from the private insurance market to secure their drug benefits. If they wish to be covered for the drug "doughnut hole," they must buy yet an additional private policy. The wide array of choices for prescription drug plans has proved confusing to some beneficiaries, as each plan covers different drugs at different rates. The doughnut hole was put into the bill at the insistence of the lobbying group for managed care firms, the American Association of Health Plans, which feared that Medicare beneficiaries would not join managed care plans (which offered extensive drug coverage) if they could receive similar drug coverage under Medicare Part D.[50]

Medicare Part D is projected to be one of the most expensive government programs ever passed, largely due to the provision in the law that forbids both government and health insurers from negotiating volume discounts with drug companies. In other words, even though the purchasing power of the federal government should result in a reduction in the price of drugs (the government will control a large part of the demand sector), the law does not allow the natural forces of the *market economy* to operate in the purchase of drugs for Medicare beneficiaries. This is unlike the Veterans Health Administration, which is allowed to negotiate the price of drugs with drug manufacturers. This provision was added to the law at the insistence of lobbyists for the pharmaceutical industry, who demanded that their revenue not be adversely affected through negotiation for lower prices. Instead, the pharmaceutical companies are in line to experience a tremendous increase in profit, as government subsidy allows more elderly to buy drugs that they previously could not afford. In spite of the cost, estimated at $675 billion in the next decade, the Congressional Budget Office estimates that the new drug benefit will cover only 22% of the drug costs of Medicare beneficiaries from 2004 to 2013, while premiums for prescription drug plans will increase by 78% over this same period. Medicare Part D is therefore a tremendous boon to pharmaceutical and private insurance companies, which sell the drug insurance policies to beneficiaries.[51]

Almost half of Medicare recipients (45%) have incomes below 200% of the poverty line; 15% are under 65 and permanently disabled. Medicare's high cost-sharing requirements mean that recipients pay a high share of their medical costs. Deductibles for Medicare Parts A, B, and C are $950, $124, and $250, respectively; on top of these costs, beneficiaries must pay monthly premiums for Part B ($90+/month) and Part D (average $25/month). For economically disadvantaged elderly, Medicare costs are burdensome. Medicare has contributed to cost inflation in health care largely because most elderly use their benefits to purchase fee for service medical care, not managed care. As discussed above, fee for service care is the most expensive care in the United States, as payments are based on medical events. The more care, including diagnostic tests, Medicare enrollees receive, the greater the expense. Since the demand for health care increases with advancing age and declining health, the costs of Medicare are very high and are likely to increase dramatically when the baby boomers retire.[52] The federal government has tried to reduce hospitalization costs through the Prospective Pay System (PPS) discussed earlier. Psychiatric facilities and children's hospitals have received a waiver from the Medicare administration and do not have to use the PPS. Under the PPS, payment is based on a predetermined rate system. If the hospital can provide care under this rate, it can keep the difference, but if the care provided exceeds the rate, the hospital must incur the loss. Clearly the incentives under PPS are to provide less, not more, care, which on the one hand may reduce the inflationary aspects of Medicare but on the other hand may result in excessively low levels of care and even patient jeopardy.

In the 1990s the federal government attempted to move the elderly away from fee for service to managed care plans, known as Medicare Advantage Plans, in the hope that Medicare costs could be contained. At the same time many HMOs left the Medicare market, claiming reimbursement was too low, sometimes leaving Medicare beneficiaries stranded with no coverage. In an effort to remedy this situation, in 2003 the Medicare Prescription Drug Improvement and Modernization Act raised the amount paid to Medicare Advantage Plans to an average of 111% of the amount paid for similar benefits in traditional fee for service plans, as a way of encouraging these plans to enroll Medicare beneficiaries.[53] In spite of these efforts, Medicare Advantage Plans currently enroll only 16% of Medicare beneficiaries.

Annual federal spending for Medicare is projected to grow to $524 billion by 2011. Annual growth in Medicare spending is influenced by increasing numbers of beneficiaries and increased cost of health care in the United States. Yet growth in Medicare's per-capita cost (8.9%) is lower than that of private insurance (9.9%), suggesting that Medicare has been relatively successful in controlling costs.[54] However, many experts are concerned about the long-term viability of Medicare because the demands on the fund will become increasingly higher as the baby boomers retire from the workforce and begin to enroll.

Medigap

Because Medicare does not pay all the costs for enrollees, most have supplemental coverage for the 20% that Medicare does not pay as well as the various deductibles. About a third of these beneficiaries receive this supplemental coverage through current or former employers, about one quarter have a private insurance policy known as Medigap, and the rest of the enrollees are either in Medicare-sponsored HMOs or are eligible for state-funded Medicaid, which pays their supplemental costs, including Part B premiums and deductibles.[55] Medigap insurance is expensive, since beneficiaries pay the full cost of the insurance.

The majority (70%) of persons eligible for both Medicare and Medicaid have incomes under $10,000 a year. Beneficiaries of both programs are more likely to be in poorer health and in institutional care than are Medicare beneficiaries who are not eligible for Medicaid.[56]

Long-Term Care Insurance

The federal government estimated that in 2007 approximately 9 million persons over 65 utilized some form of long-term care, either in home or out of home. By 2020, the government estimates that 12 million older Americans will need long-term care. Persons reaching age 65 have about a 40% chance of entering a nursing home. Most long-term care is custodial, helping persons with what are called activities of daily living, such as dressing, eating, and mobility. Medicare only pays for time-limited, medically necessary care linked to hospitalization. Therefore many families will find their financial resources stretched to pay for long-term care of elderly persons; 70% of long-term care is provided by family and friends.[57] The majority of elderly receive assistance at home, not in nursing homes. The proliferation of long-term care private insurance policies may change the face of long-term care for middle-income and wealthier families, but for now it is a largely unanticipated cost that can wipe out a family's savings until eligibility for Medicaid is established (see below). The bulk of spending on long-term care in nursing homes is through Medicaid and private out-of-pocket funding. In-home long-term care is far more economical than nursing home care, but it is only provided for Medicaid-eligible elderly. Long-term care will be an increasing policy need in the 21st century; clearly an expanded social insurance program that provides long-term in-home care is the best solution, although it is increasingly less likely with huge federal budget deficits and concerns about the viability of Social Security and Medicare.[58]

Reforming Medicare

There are many issues with Medicare, but the overriding policy issue lies in the increasing costs of the program. The worker-to-beneficiary ratio will decrease dramatically when the baby boomers become eligible for Medicare beginning in 2011. Exacerbating the cost of new enrollees is the fact that most Medicare beneficiaries receive care under the traditional fee for service plans, which are more expensive than HMOs. The cost multiplier inherent in fee for service medicine is an even greater problem in delivering health care to persons over 85, who are more likely to have chronic health problems, including cancer, asthma, arthritis, cardiovascular problems, and cognitive impairment, and who need help with daily activities. Because Medicare operates largely on a fee for service basis, with few real efforts to ration care, it is a costly system. Reimbursing providers based on the existing fee for service system ratifies a system that allows physicians to charge what they wish and patients to seek medical care they desire, with no oversight as to medical necessity. Under fee for service, patients can seek out repeated visits to providers and diagnostic tests whether or not they are medically indicated.[59] Having a fee for service medical system to provide medical care to persons whose health is increasingly frail is tantamount to providing unlimited vouchers to shoppers in a department store; depending on self-limitation in such circumstances is foolish. Of course, even though Medicare beneficiaries can see as many physicians as many times as they wish, they do not have long-term care or comprehensive drug coverage. So the picture is mixed, yet the costs are still very high. Only under managed care would medical decisions, not personal choice, govern medical utilization under Medicare. Congress has been reluctant to force Medicare beneficiaries into managed care, largely due to the powerful lobbying group, AARP, which opposes managed care.

Medicare is far from ideal, but it does offer the closest policy to comprehensive health care that exists in the United States, and there are many positive aspects to the program. Unlike Medicaid (see below), Medicare is a universal, stigma-free health insurance system that includes everyone over 65, regardless of work history, income, or other demographic characteristics. By 2030 most baby boomers will be eligible for Medicare, and 1 in 5 Americans will be 65 or older.[60] Yet even with this increase in their proportion of the population, the elderly will still be in the minority. While the health care needs of the elderly have not been completely met, there currently are 47 million non-elderly persons who are uninsured, many of whom are working to pay the Medicare wage tax that supports health care for the elderly. Since workers' wages have not kept up with inflation and since many workers either are not offered or cannot afford health insurance, some might wonder whether equity is served by supporting an expensive Medicare program that utilizes fee for service financing for much of its subsidized care and returns profits to private insurance and pharmaceutical companies. The cost of Medicare may outstrip our ability to fund it over the next 10 years. The best way to fix Medicare and ensure health care for the elderly is to enact a national health care system that would end the separate Medicare program and fold coverage for the elderly into a policy that ensures coverage for everyone.

Medicaid

Medicaid is the program delivering health insurance to the poor, funded by a federal state partnership, where the federal government pays from 50% to 76% of the costs, depending on a state's per-capita income. Medicaid is funded solely through federal and state tax revenues, unlike Medicare, which depends partly on a payroll tax and partly on beneficiary payments. While Medicare is a generous program that offers elderly persons virtually unlimited health care access, Medicaid is far more parsimonious and limited. The generosity of Medicare is based on the ideology that hard work during one's life should ensure adequate health care in old age. The major beneficiaries of Medicaid are children from low-income families. Economically marginalized persons are often presumed to be poor because of some individual flaw or failure. The differences in perceptions of the two groups are a major reason for the discrepancies in Medicare and Medicaid.

Overall, the federal government finances 57% of all Medicaid spending. In 2006, total Medicaid spending was over $300 billion, with most of the funds going to hospitalization and long-term care.

Medicaid has far less political support than Medicare; as a means-tested program, with strict requirements for eligibility, it is associated with low-income groups, ethnic groups, and welfare recipients. The program covers inpatient and outpatient services, diagnostic imaging, laboratory services, nursing home care, and home health care and physician services. Some states cover drugs under Medicaid. Medicaid constitutes the largest source of income for elderly in nursing homes.[61]

Unlike Medicare, the federal government has made a concerted effort to move Medicaid participants into managed care by forcing them to enroll in these programs in order to reduce costs.[62] In 2006, 64% of Medicaid participants were in managed care, helping to control the growth of Medicaid benefit levels. In spite of these efforts, total Medicaid expenditures have grown dramatically since 2001, due to the increase in the number of uninsured persons.[63] Every one-percentage-point rise in the unemployment rate leads to a 1.1 million-person increase in the uninsured population and a 1 million-person increase in those enrolled in Medicaid and the State Children's Health Insurance Program (SCHIP). Medicaid grew by 10.7% in the first 6 months of 2007, the biggest increase since 2001. Unlike Medicare, which is administered by the federal government, states are in charge of the administration of Medicaid and pay part of the costs. Many states are cutting funding for Medicaid in an effort to cope with budget deficits and control their costs.[64] In some states Medicaid spending is greater than state spending for K–12 education. Medicaid spending has outpaced state tax revenue growth since 2004. Cost-cutting measures already undertaken by states include controlling drug costs by limiting drugs covered by Medicaid, reducing or freezing provider payments, reducing eligibility and benefits, and imposing higher costs to Medicaid beneficiaries.[65]

More than 55 million persons were enrolled in Medicaid in 2006; they included children and their parents, persons with disabilities, and elderly persons who need Medicaid to pay for their uncovered Medicare costs. Approximately 40% of Medicaid funds go to persons also covered by Medicare, known as "dual eligibles."[66] Persons covered by Medicaid cannot afford private health insurance; without Medicaid they would join the ranks of the uninsured. Interestingly, in recent years Medicaid per-capita spending has grown more slowly than private health insurance. Until the passage of the 2005 Deficit Reduction Act, states were required to give all their Medicaid participants the same health services; after that date, states could limit health care services to some groups and require cost sharing and premiums from some Medicaid participants.[67]

In order to qualify for Medicaid, individuals must have income below a certain level and fall into a covered category of children, parents of dependent children, pregnant women, people with disabilities, and the elderly. Parents are eligible for Medicaid in only 42 states and only if their income is less than 70% of the poverty level; children are eligible for Medicaid or SCHIP if family income is below 200% of the poverty line if they are over 5 and below 133% of the poverty line if they are under 5. As a result, in many low-income families the children are insured, but the parents are not, or younger children are insured while older children are not. Federal funds cannot be used to cover childless adults, no matter how limited their income.[68]

While elderly persons and persons with disabilities make up just one quarter of all Medicaid participants, they account for 70% of Medicaid spending.

Nursing home care alone accounts for 44% of Medicaid spending; Medicaid covered 1 million nursing home residents in 2007.[69] As discussed above, Medicare does not pay for long-term care independent of acute hospitalization; in order to qualify for long-term care under Medicaid, participants have to spend their savings down to approximately $2,000 to qualify. Some have complained that middle-class families are using Medicaid as a "middle-class entitlement" to pay for nursing home care of elderly relatives by transferring assets to adult children so that elderly family will be eligible for nursing home care paid by Medicaid. Attempts to rein in what is seen by some as an abuse of Medicaid have been largely unsuccessful.[70]

Medicaid pays physicians much less than Medicare or private insurers pay them. While states differ in their payment rates, the average payment for an office visit to a physician is estimated to be only 65% of the average payment for Medicare patients, which is by law only 80% of the cost of the visit. This low rate of reimbursement drives many providers away from Medicaid. The only way for physicians to make close to a comparable income from Medicaid patients is through high volume.[71] For these reasons the medical care funded by Medicaid may not be as good as that funded by Medicare or private insurance. A recent study found that those covered by Medicaid, along with the uninsured, are more likely than those with private insurance to receive a diagnosis of cancer in late states, reducing their chances of survival.[72]

Medicaid is critical to the health of children in the United States. One in four children depends on Medicaid to pay for his or her health care.[73] Since states vary in whom they will cover and what the eligibility requirements are, only federal law can eliminate state variations in coverage across income levels and family composition. However, the federal government is moving away from standardization in Medicaid eligibility and funding; instead, consideration has been given to substituting block grants for direct federal funding, based on enrollment and costs. The shift toward block grants to states and away from federal entitlement would be a major assault on Medicaid's long-term viability, as states would not receive extra federal funding if Medicaid enrollment increased due to economic downturns.[74]

SCHIP

In 1997 Congress enacted the State Children's Health Insurance Program at the urging of the Clinton administration. SCHIP offers families living under 200% of the poverty line the opportunity to buy low-cost insurance that will cover their children's health care needs. While some states have received a federal waiver to cover parents, childless adults are not covered by SCHIP. This program provides federal matching funds for state-subsidized health insurance for parents whose income makes them ineligible for Medicaid but is considered too low to allow them to purchase insurance privately.

Overall, SCHIP has reduced the number of children from low-income families who are uninsured.[75] The percentage of low-income children in the United States without health coverage has fallen by one third since SCHIP was created in 1997, even though employer-based insurance has declined during this period. More than 4 million low-income children were enrolled in SCHIP in 2007. The number of uninsured children was estimated to be 8.7 million in 2007, but only 700,000 of these children were thought to be eligible for SCHIP.[76] In 2007, Congress passed a bill raising the income limit for eligibility for SCHIP, but President Bush vetoed the bill, saying it would interfere with the private insurance market. Unlike Medicaid, currently an entitlement program whose federal funding increases automatically to compensate for increases in health care costs, SCHIP is a block grant, which means it has a predetermined, fixed annual funding level. The federal SCHIP funding that states receive has not kept pace with the rising cost of health care or population growth. Since Congress refused to substantially increase funding for SCHIP in 2007, there will be eligible children who will not be covered in the coming years (see Chapter 11).[77]

Immigrants and Public Health Insurance

The passage of the Personal Responsibility and Work Opportunity Reconciliation Act in 1996 made it more difficult for immigrants, including legal immigrants, to qualify for Medicaid and SCHIP, increasing the disparity in health care between immigrants and nonimmigrants. Legal permanent residents are ineligible for Medicaid or SCHIP during their first 5 years in the United States. After 5 years, they are eligible for Medicaid and SCHIP if they meet the programs' other eligibility requirements. Undocumented immigrants are ineligible for either program. In seven states pregnant women, regardless of their immigration status, are eligible for Medicaid. Both legal and undocumented immigrants are eligible for emergency Medicaid for emergency health services in all states. One effect of the 1996 act was to shift much of the costs of covering immigrant health needs to states and localities. States with large immigrant populations have been particularly hard hit by the federal restrictions and the cost shifting. As economic times worsen, more states are expected to restrict their health care coverage of immigrants.[78] See Table 9.1 for a summary of types of health care delivery in the United States.

TABLE 9.1   **Summary of Health Care Delivery in the United States: Public-Private Mix**

Form of Medical Delivery	Provisions	Drawbacks of Delivery
Fee for Service	• Traditional means of paying for medical care in United States • Patient's insurance pays for service and includes profit margin for provider and insurance companies • Charges are standardized with one fee for all patients	• Overutilization of medical services by patients • Use of excessive tests and procedures by physicians to increase profit margins • Malpractice suits and insurance drive up costs of medical care and increase insurance rates • Insurance companies can deny coverage based on preexisting conditions
Health Maintenance Organizations (HMOs)	• Focus is on individual and not the medical service • Uses a prepayment or capitation system in which cost of medical care comes out of a monthly prepayment • Incentive is to control medical costs and not to offer more services • Focus is on prevention to reduce higher costs associated with treating a medical condition • Care is received by a group of physicians, which is paid a set fee per patient	• Underutilization of necessary medical services as physicians and plan administrators may withhold services to keep costs down • Consumer complaints about ability to access quality care
Preferred Provider Organizations (PPOs) and Point of Service (POS) Plans	• Like HMOs but employees have more choice of providers • Fee for service plan where a network of providers gives employers a discount	• Provided competition to HMOs in the 1990s
Medicare	• Federal health insurance for the elderly (over 65), disabled persons, and end-stage renal patients in the United States • Provides hospital services, physician services, and a prescription drug benefit • Funded by a worker tax, FICA tax by employer, premiums, and general tax revenues • Consists of four parts: Medicare Parts A, B, C, and D	• Most expensive government program ever passed (Part D) due to issues with prescription drug benefit • Recipients pay a high share of their medical costs • Costs of Medicare are high to the government, but the program appears successful in controlling costs

(Continued)

TABLE 9.1 (Continued)

Form of Medical Delivery	Provisions	Drawbacks of Delivery
Medigap	• Supplemental coverage for the 20% Medicare does not pay	• Insurance is expensive since beneficiaries pay the full cost of the insurance • Most people (70%) eligible for this insurance have incomes under $10,000 a year
Medicaid	• Program that delivers health insurance to the poor but majority of beneficiaries are children from low-income families • Federal government pays 50%–76% of costs, and states cover the rest • Funded through federal and state tax revenues • Far less political support than Medicare since it is associated with low-income families	• Efforts to move Medicaid patients into managed care programs to control growth of Medicaid benefit levels • Medicaid beneficiaries and costs continue to increase due to increased numbers of uninsured and unemployed
State Children's Health Insurance Program (SCHIP)	• Offers families living under 200% of the poverty line an opportunity to buy low-cost health insurance to cover children's health care costs • Has reduced the number of children from low-income families who are uninsured	• This is a block grant, so there is a fixed annual funding level • Has not been able to keep pace with rising costs of health care or population growth

● MENTAL HEALTH POLICY

Questions about the nature of mental disorder have confounded efforts to establish meaningful mental health policies in the United States. During the early part of American history mental disorder was thought to be an affliction from God or a test from the devil, and those so afflicted were left without treatment and rarely confined unless they seemed dangerous. Mental disorder was considered temporary or periodic, not permanent. With the emergence of the medical view of mental disorder in the 19th century, the idea that physicians should take charge of the mentally disordered and that society should confine them in mental hospitals led to the rise of public mental hospitals in every state. Although the motives of reformers who lobbied for public mental hospitals were clearly altruistic, by the end of the 19th century persons confined in these hospitals received little or no treatment and were subject to sometimes terrible mistreatment in the form of isolation, physical restraint, and heavy use of opium for sedation. Many were impoverished immigrants and elderly who were put in what were called insane asylums as a way of disposing of a problem that states had little interest in solving. The prospects of "cure" for those confined in these hospitals receded as did the prospects of release. State mental hospitals functioned as places of confinement for Americans others wished to ignore. Women had particularly difficult times in these mental hospitals; they were often subject to pelvic exams upon admittance on the theory that their mental disorders were caused by diseases of their reproductive organs. Confinement was relatively easy to arrange; husbands could ask for their wives to be confined, parents their children, and adult children their parents. Hospital physicians rarely refused admission to family members brought by other family members. In the early 20th century confined persons, falsely called "patients," languished in public mental hospitals overseen by a meager staff of hospital staff and hospital physicians, while the new medical specialty of neurology began the outpatient treatment of depressed women for "nervous prostration" or "neurasthenia."[79]

With the rise of outpatient child guidance clinics, the influence of Freud and other European analysts, and the emergence of the profession of social work in the 1920s, mental health treatment became outpatient treatment for middle- and upper-class persons who could afford it (see Chapter 6). Persons confined in public mental hospitals were largely forgotten. During this period in American history the conceptions of what constituted mental disorder changed: In the colonial period persons who were severely impaired were thought to be "distracted," and other behavior was not categorized. In the 19th century the medical profession added the category of melancholy. By the early 20th century the kinds of mental disorder had expanded to include neurasthenia and hypochondria, as well as depressed (for melancholy), mania, and dementia praecox. With the influence of Freud and other European psychiatrists in the 1920s and 1930s, the number of mental disorders expanded to include schizophrenia, manic depression, and postpartum depression. Currently the catalog of what is considered mentally disordered is kept by the American Psychiatric Association in the form of the *Diagnostic and Statistical Manual of Mental Disorders*. Somatic disorders such as dementia are included as are a growing variety of problems in living, such as the anxiety disorders and sleep disorders,

State mental hospital in Connecticut

SOURCE: AP Photo/Jack Sauer.

personality disorders such as borderline personality disorder, and serious and persistent mental disorders such as schizophrenia. The relationship between any of these categorized mental disorders and underlying physical or somatic processes is unknown, although research is ongoing, but the self-realizing power of the *DSM-IV,* along with its earlier versions, is considerable. Insurance companies and government health care programs such as Medicare will not reimburse practitioners for treatment of anything outside of the spectrum of the *DSM.* This may account for the ever-expanding inclusion of problems of living in the *DSM,* as clinicians wish to help persons in distress, so distress must be conceptualized as a mental disorder recognized by a professional organization.[80] While states played the central if not only role in public mental health policy until the 1960s, the increased number of persons, especially women, seeking outpatient treatment in the form of casework and therapy was the major source of growth for the mental health professions, particularly psychiatry, along with a few private asylums where distressed persons could receive intense medical and psychological attention.

By World War II a two-class system of mental health care had taken shape, one public, one private. The public one was virtually unnoticed as increasing numbers of disturbed and unwanted persons were warehoused in large state-run asylums, where ineffective and punitive treatments such as ice baths, insulin shock treatment, and even sterilization were common. The back wards of mental hospitals and institutions that confined the developmentally disabled persons were restrained and forgotten, constituting one of the great shames of our history.[81]

Deinstitutionalization

Several forces converged to lead to the movement to deinstitutionalization in the 1960s. States began to experiment with community-based care at the same time as cost-saving efforts turned policymakers away from large institutional care of persons in state mental hospitals and institutions for the developmentally disabled. The most important impetus to the concept of community care and its corollary, deinstitutionalization, was the passage of the federal Mental Retardation Facilities and Community Mental Health Centers Construction Act in 1963. Inspired by his family's experience with developmental disability, President John Kennedy introduced a federal plan for the construction of comprehensive community mental health centers. This served to hasten the movement toward deinstitutionalization, which had begun in the states. The plan was an ambitious one, with one mental health center envisioned for every 200,000 persons, but by 1980 only 750 centers had been established, and very few of them provided free or low-cost mental health services. Instead they were established on a fee basis. The act mandated that each center offer comprehensive mental health services, including inpatient, outpatient, emergency, and consultation and education to the broader community, as in public health. The comprehensive nature of these centers could not be sustained with federal funding, and states and localities did not contribute the savings accrued from the closure of state mental institutions as was initially hoped. As a result the centers that did exist began charging standard fees for outpatient mental health services, and the concept of serving the community was lost. While federal enthusiasm for mental health funding waned under the eras of Nixon and Ford in the 1970s, some community mental health centers continued to receive limited federal funding until the 1980s, when all funding ceased. Far from serving the clients deinstitutionalized from the state mental hospitals as its founders dreamed, the community mental health movement met the needs of very few ex–mental hospital residents. Instead in a process of transinstitutionalization, in the 1980s, these ex-patients found themselves in nursing homes, often in confined conditions, which were reimbursed by the newly funded Medicaid program; in local jails; or on the streets.[82]

Deinstitutionalization at the state level was accelerated by court decisions such as *Wyatt v. Stickney* in 1971 (see Chapter 5), mandating that persons confined in institutions receive treatment. In 1975 the U.S. Supreme Court ruled in *O'Connor v. Donaldson* that states could not confine persons in mental hospitals unless they were a danger to themselves or others and who were not being treated and who were able to survive outside the mental hospital. The impact of these rulings, as interpreted by the American Civil Liberties Union, was that states were deterred from involuntary commitments of persons who were not considered dangerous to themselves or others.[83]

After these rulings it became much more difficult to commit persons involuntarily to state mental hospitals, and most states had little interest in confining persons to mental hospitals voluntarily at public expense, especially if they had to provide treatment, as mandated in *Wyatt v. Stickney*. Court decisions hastened the release of former mental patients to the streets, nursing homes, and local jails, where many found themselves. Persons who were admitted to public mental institutions under these stricter criteria were often released after a short period of treatment and medication, but with no treatment readily available at the increasingly scarce public community mental health centers, some returned to hospitals in what has been called a revolving door syndrome.[84]

When states and localities attempted to establish residences for mentally disordered persons and former patients in the community, many residents reacted with outrage and refused to allow mentally disordered persons to live in their communities. This is now known as the NIMBY (Not in My Backyard) reaction and has emerged when ex-prisoners or any other group that is stigmatized and feared (homeless persons, persons with HIV/AIDS) tries to locate in group residences in local communities.[85]

Public Mental Health Policies in the 21st Century

Community mental health centers did not receive direct federal funding after the 1980s; instead the federal government combined mental health funds with funds for substance abuse programs in block grants to the states overseen by the Substance Abuse and Mental Health Services Administration (SAMHSA) of the Department of Health and Human Services. While the goals of the block grant program were to "provide financial assistance to states to enable them to carry out the State's Plan for providing comprehensive community mental health services to adults with a serious mental illness and to children with a serious emotional disturbance," the amount of federal money allocated has been, relative to the needs of the state public mental infrastructure, minimal.[86]

In theory children from economically marginalized families, who are in foster care, or who have a severe disability and receive Supplemental Security Income are eligible for mental health services through Medicaid.

However, use of mental health services under Medicaid varies widely from state to state, with some states offering little or no mental health care for eligible children. As discussed earlier, Medicaid is based on a federal-state partnership; states must spend money to use Medicaid funds. In states that enroll Medicaid recipients in managed care programs, mental health services are likely to be excluded.[87] For adults, few of whom are eligible for Medicaid, public mental health services are unreliable and largely unavailable. States have not taken advantage of the potential for mental health funding under Medicaid, largely because of the high cost of mental health services and the necessity of state participation in the delivery of Medicaid mental health care.[88] In spite of these limitations, Medicaid is the single largest payer for mental health services in the United States, a sign of how limited public mental health funding is. Each state that wishes to use Medicaid for mental health funding must formulate a state plan (subject to federal regulations and guidelines) outlining the nature and scope of the services to be provided in that state under Medicaid. Most states have enrolled Medicaid participants in managed care programs, which, as noted above, provide less-than-comprehensive mental health services to Medicaid recipients. Rates of psychiatric medication in some states, especially among young children, have increased under Medicaid, even as contact with therapists has diminished.[89] Other states have severely restricted the use of psychiatric medication for Medicaid participants in an effort to control costs.[90] Regardless of choices that states make in their Medicaid funding, it is clear that federal funding for mental health programs is inadequate and that the mental health policy has not emerged as a federal priority since the end of community mental health funding in the 1960s and 1970s.

Mental Health Parity Act

In 1996 Congress passed the Mental Health Parity Act, designed to go into effect in 1998. It required employers with 50 or more employees who offer mental health coverage to include mental health benefits comparable to health benefits.[91] However, the act did not require employers to offer mental health coverage and may have contributed marginally to the loss of mental health benefits in the workplace. In October 2008 a new Mental Health Parity Act was passed by Congress as part of the economic bailout plan, which attempted to close loopholes in the original act by requiring parity coverage for annual and lifetime dollar limits. Neither act requires employers to offer mental health coverage or covers uninsured persons, representing the greatest need for federal mental health programs.[92]

The Privatization of Mental Health

Social workers cannot help notice the paradox of mental health treatment: Those without private health insurance receive very little mental health treatment, while those with private insurance are increasingly turning toward the mental health professions—psychiatrists, clinical psychologists, and social workers—for medication and therapy. Many people receive outpatient services each year through private insurance. While persons with schizophrenia may receive mental health treatment in managed care, the worried well, as they are called, may not.

In 2005–2006, 15% of U.S. children aged 4–17 years had parents who talked to a health care provider or school staff about their child's emotional or behavioral difficulties. This included 18% of boys and 11% of girls.[93] Approximately 5% of children received "treatment other than medication" for emotional or behavioral difficulties. Most of these children—60%—received this treatment from a mental health private practice, clinic, or center.

● IMPLICATIONS FOR SOCIAL WORK

Most social workers are involved in some sort of case management or counseling in addition to their work with groups and with communities. The absence of an adequate public mental health infrastructure is vitally important to the social work profession, as many social work clients need mental health services but cannot afford to buy them on the private health care market. Many states have little or no public mental health services. In California the situation was so dire in terms of public mental health services that Proposition 63, introduced in 2004 and sponsored by social workers and other mental health advocates, was successful in imposing a 1% income tax on personal income in excess of $1 million. The resulting Mental Health Services Act increased funding, personnel, and other resources to support county mental health programs. More than $4 billion in additional revenues for mental health services were generated through the end of fiscal year 2008. However, the fiscal situation of the state has declined dramatically over the past year, and these funds may be captured for other uses in 2009.[94] Even so, the success of Proposition 63 demonstrates that there is a desire to provide low-cost public mental health services that can be tapped by mental health advocates.

PREVIOUS EFFORTS FOR HEALTH CARE REFORM   ●

The health care system as it exists in the United States today has developed largely without the direction of any government body; that is, it is largely the result of the actions of the *market economy*. The major exceptions to this are, of course, Medicare and Medicaid and the health care offered to veterans. Yet there have been serious efforts to reform the private health care system, beginning in the early 20th century. One of the major obstacles to reform has been the American Medical Association (AMA). By the early 20th century the AMA had succeeded in establishing professional dominion over medical practice, including midwifery, homeopathic medicine, and nursing. States enacted uniform standards of licensing that either forbade alternative practices or made the practitioners subject to the rule of physicians. Along with this dominance, professional medicine reaped the financial rewards of becoming the lead if not the only profession to minister to the sick and prevent debilitating disease. Throughout the 20th century the AMA responded forcefully to what it perceived as a direct threat to physician autonomy and income. The ideology of the AMA was that government-sponsored health insurance would interfere with the sacred physician-patient relationship upon which good health depended and would move the United States toward socialism or at least "socialized medicine," where the government determines treatment and squeezes out physician discretion. While Germany had adopted a national health insurance system (making health insurance compulsory with varying degrees of government subsidy) in 1883 and other European countries followed during the early 20th century, the United States did not formally consider enacting any form of national health insurance. The ideologies of laissez faire, self-reliance, and individualism, along with the faith in the operation of the market economy to distribute social goods, worked against the possibility of a serious consideration of national health insurance. While the AMA encouraged private insurance as a means of ensuring that patients had a way to pay for their care, the idea that the federal or state governments would become involved in subsidizing insurance or health care was unacceptable to the AMA.[95]

Abortive attempts to introduce national health care emerged periodically during the 20th century. The Sheppard-Towner Act of 1921 offered limited services to mothers and infants in the form of health education, but the treatment aspects of the legislation were opposed by the AMA and removed by Congress. It was largely due to the successful efforts of the AMA and other conservatives that this act was repealed in 1929. The new domain of "well-baby care" at the heart of the Sheppard-Towner Act was henceforth under the exclusive control of the medical profession. With the New Deal, another threat to the autonomy of physicians emerged as the Roosevelt administration planned to introduce national health care along with the other provisions of the Social Security Act of 1935. The AMA threatened to oppose the entire Social Security Act if health care were included; the Roosevelt administration backed away from national health care, and the moment of opening for substantial reform offered by the Great Depression passed. National health insurance came up again under the Truman administration after World War II but was opposed again by the AMA. In 1946 Congress passed the Hill-Burton Act, offering federal funds to states for hospital construction; this policy was acceptable to the AMA, as it offered more venues for medical practice. After World War II, unions began to include health benefits through private insurance in their collective bargaining efforts. Veterans received their own health care system in the form of the Veterans Health Administration hospitals. Thus the most vocal constituencies for health insurance reform were satisfied. The poor and others who could not afford to buy private insurance were left out.[96]

Not until 1965 was Congress able to overcome the opposition of the AMA and pass landmark legislation that involved the federal government in a health insurance program for the elderly, Medicare, and the poor, Medicaid. The AMA agreed to compromise on Medicare, providing that Medicaid would be means tested and its funding and administration left to the states. The most recent effort to enact national health insurance occurred under the Clinton administration in the 1990s. By this time the lobbying arm of America's Health Insurance Plans had gained considerable political clout and led the fight, alongside the somewhat diminished AMA and lobbyists for the pharmaceutical industry. Both sectors of the economy, insurance and pharmaceuticals, saw national health insurance as a threat to their profit margins. The AMA was more ambivalent, recognizing the groundswell for national health insurance, and the organization took a backseat to the efforts of the insurance and pharmaceutical sectors, whose survival in the profitable health care industry seemed to be at stake. Grassroots campaigning and media ad campaigns funded by the lobbyists for insurance companies and coalitions of manufacturing and business groups were instrumental in defeating the Clinton proposal, which was never brought to the floor of the Senate or House for debate.[97] The major theme in the campaign against national health care was "choice." Those opposed to the Clinton plan argued that Americans would have no choice in providers if it were enacted. Choice is one of the most salient issues in American attitudes toward health and must be confronted in any political effort for health care reform.[98]

● HEALTH CARE AND THE MARKET ECONOMY

As discussed earlier, the main objection to national health insurance has been the limitations in choice that opponents argue would result from any effort to offer universal health care. Yet within the for-profit health care field, there has been a movement to consolidate health care choice, in the form of nationally managed chains of nursing homes, national HMOs, medical groups, and so forth.[99] This movement is similar to all market movements for integration of firms that compete with one another. In other words, just as in other sectors of private enterprise, the effort to capture a larger share of the health care market is natural to the operation of the *market economy*. Thus "choice" in health care is at least partly an illusion, fostered by those opposed to government delivery of health.

Americans are opposed to rationing health care, but as we discussed in the beginning of this chapter, all societies must ration health care, since theoretically there exists a virtually infinite demand for it, given the possibility of sickness and the inevitability of death. Americans often assume that the *market economy* delivers goods and services efficiently, while maximizing individual choice, in health care, as in other sectors of the economy. Yet in our current public-private system we have seen how rationing occurs: Even persons with health insurance can obtain health care only after external bodies, such as insurance companies or health maintenance organizations, approve it. Those without insurance are largely shut out from non-emergent health care. Some implicit rationing occurs whenever health care is obtained through public or private insurance, rather than bought outright with private resources. The irony of the managed care movement in the 1990s was that managed care rationed health care more than the Clinton health care reform care plan would have. Since the 1990s managed care plans have seen their costs rise significantly, because when Americans expressed dissatisfaction with managed care, these plans relaxed many of the restrictions that made them cost-effective. While nonprofit managed care plans have proved to be effective in offering good disease management and quality control, the proliferation of for-profit managed care plans has not been as successful in offering quality medical care.[100]

Private health care delivery illustrates the illusion of Adam Smith's vision of the invisible hand guiding the *market economy* toward the greater good, for when individual actors pursue their own self-interest in obtaining health care, the public good is left far behind. From the point of view of the provider in fee for service medicine, giving as much care as can be medically justified can be considered as pursuing one's economic self-interest. Yet due to the high costs of fee for service medicine discussed above, the individual pursuit of economic self-interest does not advance the common good; instead, it detracts from it by driving up the cost of health care.

When those with no or inadequate insurance wait to obtain medical care until they are seriously ill, the costs of their care will fall to taxpayers and employers, when primary preventive care may have forestalled the need for costly hospitalization and loss of work time. This is an irrational use of health care resources. Far from being competitive, market mechanisms yield advantages for some providers, suppliers, and insurers, who benefit from the private financing of health care and wish to keep it that way. The profits to be made by pharmaceutical companies, insurers, and others in private health care offer strong motivation to fight against a national health care system.[101] This arrangement leaves the poor, those who are sick, and those who are unable to purchase affordable insurance due to the preexisting conditions rule left out of the insurance market.[102] Ironically, there are enough resources now being spent in the $1.4 trillion health care system (about $5,000 for each person in the United States) to finance universal coverage for all "if the for profit insurance industry were replaced by a single publicly administered insurance program."[103]

● HEALTH CARE REFORM: WHAT ARE THE POSSIBILITIES?

The United States spends six times more per capita on the administration of the health care system than its peer Western European nations.[104] As this chapter has indicated, there are serious flaws with the health care system, even with all the money we spend. One of the most pressing problems is the future expenditures mandated by Medicare. Since Medicare is a defined benefits program where beneficiaries are guaranteed benefits regardless of ability to pay or health status, the program represents an open-ended financial commitment by the federal government to pay for health care of all persons over 65. By 2011, when baby boomers begin to be eligible for Medicare, this obligation will increase dramatically and will continue to increase as successive waves of baby boomers reach retirement age. Since the effort to move Medicare beneficiaries to managed care has thus far not been successful, the demographic bubble represented by the baby boomer generation will present a serious challenge to the viability of Medicare.[105] Thus *Medicare presents the strongest argument for health care reform: As a country we may not be able to live up to our obligation to pay for the health care of elder Americans under our present system.*

Several suggestions have been offered by health policy experts to "save" Medicare and deliver less costly and more equitable universal health care. Many plans center on a *voucher* system, where the federal government would give all Americans, including Medicare beneficiaries, a fixed dollar amount for their health care in the form of a health care voucher, which would be used to purchase insurance in the private health care market. The difference between the voucher amount and the cost of private insurance plans would be borne by the beneficiaries as a substitute for Medicare Part B premiums for the elderly and as insurance premiums for all other Americans.[106] The appeal of the voucher plan is that the federal government would control the health care costs borne by taxpayers through the vouchers.

A related plan also promotes the use of health care vouchers for all Americans but adds another feature: *The amount of the voucher would be adjusted each year according to the health status of the beneficiaries, with sicker participants getting larger vouchers.* The federal government would determine what is affordable in terms of health care and issue these vouchers of varying value every year; the vouchers would be designed to pay for basic health care coverage, including drugs, home health care, and nursing home care. Insurance companies would compete for participants, willingly taking on those at higher risk of illness because their vouchers would be larger. Any difference in actual costs between the federally sponsored vouchers and the cost of the actual health care would be kept as profit by insurance companies (as is the case now with insurance premiums paid by employers and individuals). Medicare and Medicaid would be eliminated, along with employer health insurance tax breaks. Funding would come from general revenue (taxes). The plan would be affordable because the federal government would no longer be responsible for Medicare and Medicaid costs; both programs would be subsumed under the voucher plan.[107] This plan rations health care according to need and what the federal government determines it can afford. The problem with insurance companies avoiding persons with preexisting conditions would be eliminated, since such persons would receive larger federal vouchers. The serious drawback of both voucher plans is that they leave the private insurance market intact, maintaining the profit in the health care system and contributing to the high cost of health care.

Others argue that *Medicaid should be expanded to cover more working poor and that eligibility for the program should be based on income, not family status, thus making childless adults eligible.* The problem with this idea is that currently states are under strong economic pressure and are likely to be unwilling to extend Medicaid benefits beyond what they are currently paying. The sympathetic groups or "worthy poor" already have been given public health care subsidies: elderly, children, and disabled. The working poor adults are the last economically marginalized group without any subsidized health care; since they are not a particularly sympathetic group to the American public, no special programs are likely to be designed for them. Universal health coverage is the only option that would cover their needs.[108]

Making *tax credits available for the individual purchase of health insurance* is another idea that has been suggested; the drawback here is that such benefits may push some employers to drop their own coverage and even encourage some states to limit their Medicaid benefits, in the hopes that individuals would purchase their own insurance. Of course, tax credits would benefit middle- and upper-class families, not poor families who already have a comparatively low tax burden.[109]

Another reform idea is to *mandate and subsidize employer coverage;* smaller firms that cannot currently afford to cover their employees' health insurance would receive a federal subsidy to help them with their share of the costs. This plan would cover only full-time workers, leaving workers in the secondary labor market uninsured. Even if secondary labor market workers were somehow to be included, jobless persons and persons between jobs would not be. The cost of health insurance for uninsured persons who do not have employer-sponsored coverage is prohibitive; buying health insurance as an individual outside of a group would cost more than 20% of the income of most uninsured persons. Group health plans negotiate discounted rates for health care, something individuals cannot do. Because of this, in order for the uninsured not covered by an employer's group plan to receive adequate health care, some form of tax redistribution will be necessary.[110] Eliminating employer-sponsored insurance altogether and starting over with a wholly new health care system would replace an inefficient, unjust, expensive system with a more cost-efficient, fairer health care system that would function outside the market economy.

Some states, not willing to wait for federal action, have already passed their own health insurance reforms. The *Oregon Health Plan* admits new members, who are qualified by virtue of limited income, through a yearly lottery. Those who win the lottery are eligible to receive the standard benefit package offered at no or low cost by the state. The plan covers physician services, prescription drugs, mental health and chemical dependency services, emergency medical services, and some dental, hospital, and vision services. The lottery is necessary because state budget difficulties have squeezed the plan and limited the number of persons enrolled since its passage in 1996. Currently 18,000 Oregonians are enrolled in the health plan, but over 90,000 persons applied to be included via the lottery in 2008. The state health plan has room for only a few thousand more people, leaving the vast majority of those who apply uninsured.[111]

Massachusetts has a mandatory health insurance plan that requires everyone to take out health insurance or suffer tax penalties. Those who cannot afford to buy health insurance are subsidized by the state. Employers who do not offer health insurance must pay into a health insurance fund. In 2008, only half of the 650,000 uninsured had signed up for the state plan; those who do not will face stiff penalties in the coming year. In a step toward making private insurance affordable, the state held insurers to no more than 5% increases in premiums per year, a rate far lower than the national one. State officials have worked with private insurers to offer several moderately priced state-sponsored plans. Costs of the program have risen since its inception, largely because more uninsured persons have signed up than anticipated.[112] The Massachusetts plan follows the principle of enlarging the risk pool, where the costs of health care for the few who are sick are borne by a large number of people, in this case the whole state, thus minimizing the costs to any single person or entity.

Single Payer Plan

The best idea for health care reform is the *single payer plan* where the federal government through its tax revenues would become the single payer for all health care and all persons would be covered. Under a single payer plan that provides universal health care, all Americans would be covered in one risk pool, spreading the cost of health care to as wide a group as possible (all taxpayers in the United States), as opposed to the current system where the healthier and more affluent are in the private system and the poorer and sicker are in the public health care system. All Americans would contribute to health insurance through taxes and/or premiums, and all would be covered, regardless of health status. Under our current system federal, state, and local governments already pay 60% of the total national health expenditures, including the $200 billion yearly tax expenditures (payroll and income tax breaks) discussed earlier in this chapter. The costs will continue to shift to taxpayers, as the drug benefit enacted under Medicare Part D is utilized by the baby boomers and as employers continue to stop providing health care coverage for their workers, forcing more families onto Medicaid and SCHIP.

Under a single payer plan health care would be funded from general tax revenues, after eliminating Medicare and Medicaid. More affluent taxpayers could be required to pay a premium for their health care or for extra health care benefits (which they could purchase through private insurance plans), but a basic package that would include inpatient care, outpatient care, pharmaceuticals, diagnostic testing, basic dental health, long-term care, eye care, and necessary medical equipment would be available to everyone and would be free to those with lower incomes or who have very high medical bills. The government would pay providers directly, utilizing a fee schedule similar to the one currently used by the Medicare system. Medical providers, including physicians, would continue to practice medicine as they currently do; their payments would come from tax revenues, not insurance companies. Of course, there would be limits on medical care, just as there are now. Instead of for-profit insurance companies determining what will be covered, a government agency would make those decisions. Most health policy experts predict that physicians will have greater freedom than most currently do to practice discretionary medicine.[113]

A single payer plan would be far more *cost-effective* than our current mixed public-private system. One health policy expert suggests that the plan be called the "more choice, less cost" plan as consumers and health care providers would have more choice than they currently do.[114] The administration of health care would be public, saving money that under our current system goes to the private insurance sector and to middlemen operating under the aegis of insurance companies, health plans, and pharmaceutical companies. Estimates are that at least 20% of our current health care expenditures are spent on administration and bureaucracy and that we can save over $200 billion a year by reorganizing Americans into one risk pool and instituting a single payer plan.[115]

A great deal of the high cost of our current health care system is driven up by the profits made in the private sector, especially insurance companies and drug companies; the latter have the highest profit margin of all U.S. corporations.[116] Under universal health coverage, the federal government would determine the reimbursement rate for drugs covered under the basic plan. In spite of the high costs of the Medicare drug plan, it is estimated that under our current health care system less than 4% of the expense of each drug will go toward the actual cost of the drug, whereas 96% of the expense will be taken as profits by pharmaceutical companies and middlemen responsible for promoting the drugs to physicians.[117]

None of the previous efforts to contain health care costs have worked, largely because of the inexorable and unregulated rise in health care costs in the absence of a national health care policy. Under a single payer plan costs would be controlled because overhead would be far lower than in our current system with duplication of administration costs in every state and in every private insurance company. Removing profit from the health care system, just as with public education, would have a powerful impact on both cost and access. Much of the growth of medical costs is due to the profits sought and found in the system, not to increased efficiency and advances in clinical care of the sickest Americans.[118] While the *market economy* drives the delivery of health care for many Americans, the principles of market capitalism do not work in health care. Many consumers are priced out of the market and cannot access this literally life-sustaining good. The increased supply of health care that should be triggered with high demand has not occurred; competition is stalled as consolidation of health care providers increases prices and promotes wasted resources.[119] What would happen to insurance companies and their workers? Insurance companies could be contracted to administer the health plan on a nonprofit basis (as in Canada), limiting the impact on employment in the insurance sector of a single payer plan.

Under a single payer plan a collective, community-oriented approach to health care would replace the emphasis on self-reliance and individualism that has undergirded our health care system to date. The false issue of choice would be exposed: Most of the choices currently available only to some would be available to everyone; everyone could choose the health care provider that suits him or her; providers would continue to work for themselves, not for government-run hospitals and clinics. While the provision of health care would remain the same, the method of financing health care would be protected from the vagaries of the market economy. No one should have his or her health care be a function of income, any more than police or fire protection is. Both public goods were once private goods; the fire department would not help you unless you had paid an indemnity to it before your fire started! Politicians soon realized that putting out fires was a public function, not a private commodity to be withheld from those who could not afford it or who had not prepaid. The same should be true for health care: It is not a commodity like other goods and services traded in the marketplace. It connects with life and death, the most fundamental of human needs.

Can the United States afford universal health care? The answer is unequivocally yes. Remember that every other industrial country provides health care for everyone at considerably less cost than we provide coverage for only some. Many analysts have already demonstrated that universal health coverage with a simplified administrative structure (single payer plan) would cost less than what we are currently spending.[120] Universal health care would provide necessary care to everyone; just as in our current system, waiting times for appointments for non-emergent conditions would likely be a feature of the new plan.

The single payer plan is not the same as socialized medicine, where the government delivers the health care services. The single player plan refers only to the financing of health care. England's National Health Service is a system where health care providers are government employees, working in government hospitals and clinics. This is not a system that would be feasible in the United States; the British system also features a second, private tier of health care, giving more affluent persons the ability to opt out of public health care entirely. By contrast the single payer plan utilized in Canada depends largely on private delivery of health care; physicians are not allowed to practice outside the system, with the exception of plastic surgeons. See Table 9.2 for a summary of ideas for health care reform in the United States.

The reluctance of Americans to move to national health insurance is due to several factors. First, there has been a concerted effort to forestall any changes in our private-public health care system by the powerful industry lobbying groups: drug companies, private insurance companies, and physicians' groups such as the AMA. Other health care providers in the for-profit sector, such as nursing home alliances, have also fought any change in their profitable health

TABLE 9.2 **Summary of Health Care Reform Ideas in the United States**

Reform	Possible Ideas	Advantages/Drawbacks of Ideas
Reform of Medicare	• Voucher system in which all Americans get a fixed dollar amount for their health care in the form of a voucher • Voucher could be used to purchase insurance in the private health care market • Related plan is the amount of voucher would be adjusted based on the health status of the beneficiary	• Advantage is that the federal government could control the health care costs borne by taxpayers • Medicare and Medicaid would be eliminated along with employer health insurance tax breaks • Plan rations health care according to need and what the federal government determines it can afford
Expand Medicaid	• Base eligibility of program on income and not family status	• States would be unwilling to expand benefits beyond what they are paying for due to high costs
Tax credits	• Tax credits available for the purchase of health insurance	• Drawback is employers would drop their own coverage for employees and encourage states to limit their Medicaid benefits
Mandate and subsidize employer coverage	• Smaller firms would receive a federal subsidy to cover their employer's health insurance costs	• Plan only covers full-time workers and not secondary labor market workers, jobless persons, or persons between jobs
Single payer plan	• Federal government through tax revenues becomes the single payer for all health care, and all persons would be covered • Universal health care but not socialized medicine since the government is financing health care and not the market economy	• All Americans would contribute to health insurance through taxes or premiums, and all would be covered, regardless of health status • Would eliminate Medicare and Medicaid • Payments for services would be paid by government directly, using a fee schedule like the one used by the Medicare system • Government agency rather than a for-profit insurance company would determine what would be covered and what would not • More cost-effective as the reimbursement rate for services will be determined by the government and not the for-profit sector in our current health care system • Concerns from lobby groups that benefit from market economy of health care have stopped efforts • Fear that it is socialized medicine and our tradition of being responsible for our own health care and not seeing health as a collective good

care management. Second, Americans do not understand universal health care, especially the single payer plan, and falsely equate it with socialized medicine, which most fear. Third, we have a long *historical* tradition, as discussed earlier in this chapter, of believing that we are responsible for our own health. This has been translated into a conviction that we are also responsible for our own health care. The belief that health is a collective good has not yet taken hold in this country, although it dominates in every other developed country, which is why these countries all have national health insurance.

CONCLUSION

In this chapter we have seen how the *market economy* promotes inequity in access to health care and in health outcomes. Based on our *historical values* of self-reliance, individualism, faith in equal opportunity, and upward mobility, along with our longstanding distrust of government power, Americans have been reluctant to develop a national health care system. This has resulted in continuing *discrimination against oppressed ethnic groups*, in terms of both health outcomes and health care access. In spite of these obstacles, the time for health care reform may be approaching, as the deepening economic crisis reveals the extent of the inequities of our health care system and the resolve of the Obama administration to offer national solutions to the health care crisis (see Chapter 11).

Examples of a Policy Analysis of Medicare: Effects of the Policy

1. What are the intended effects of the policy?

Lawmakers intended to cover the vast majority of persons over 65 with Medicare health insurance. The coverage was intended to be comprehensive; seniors would be able to obtain the most comprehensive and up-to-date health care available with no restrictions. While Medicare covered up to 80% of the costs of health care, private insurance companies quickly moved to fill the gap and offered policies that paid the other 20%. Over 40 million persons are covered by Medicare; this number includes elderly Americans, persons covered by Social Security Disability Insurance, and end-stage renal dialysis patients. Medicare covers a majority of the hospitalization costs for these groups, as well as 80% of outpatient costs and most diagnostic tests. Medicare also covers some prescription drug costs for its recipients. To receive these benefits beneficiaries must pay monthly fees along with copayments. In sum, Medicare has provided a safety net for elderly Americans to ensure that they receive health care, though the program does not cover all the costs.

(Continued)

(Continued)

2. Unintended effects: What are the effects that the lawmakers did not foresee?

When Medicare was first passed, the elderly were a smaller portion of the population than they are today and than they will be in the coming decades. The costs of Medicare have grown exponentially over the past 10 years, even though policymakers have attempted to restrict access to the unlimited demand for health care represented by seniors. Cost-saving measures such as encouraging elderly persons to enroll in managed care have been only partially successful. The real problem with Medicare funding has been the higher cost of health care in general in the United States. Medicare Part D is projected to be especially expensive due to a law that keeps the federal government from negotiating volume discounts from pharmaceutical companies. In spite of its great costs, the drug provision will cover only a percentage of the drug costs for the elderly.

For elderly with low income levels, Medicare is increasingly expensive as the cost of the program and copayments continue to rise. The cost to the recipient of Part B is now almost $100 per month. For economically disadvantaged elderly, Medicare costs can be overwhelming. Medicare has contributed to cost inflation in health care largely because most elderly use their benefits to purchase fee for service medical care, not managed care. As discussed above, fee for service care is the most expensive care in the United States, as payments are based on medical events.

Estimates are that Medicare will run out of money by 2018, at which point the government may have to scale back the benefits and/or raise taxes to sustain the program. The high cost of Medicare, reflecting the high cost of health care in the United States, is an unintended effect of the policy, which was designed to be self-sustaining as it was meant to be paid primarily by a payroll tax.

3. Distinguish between short-range (under 5 years) and long-range (5+ years) effects of the policy.

The short-range effects of Medicare were almost all positive, as persons over 65 who had left the workforce without health insurance were now guaranteed coverage under a federal program. Similarly, patients with end-stage renal disease or certain disabilities were able to have most of their health care needs met by the taxpayers. Private insurance companies also benefited from Medicare in the short run, as to a lesser extent did pharmaceutical companies, since drugs were not covered until 2006. Physicians as well as allied health practitioners covered by Medicare expanded their practices as elder Americans were able to afford medical care previously out of their reach.

The long-range effects of Medicare have been less positive from a fiscal point of view. Costs have expanded beyond the ability of the program to be self-sustaining and are projected to continue to expand as the baby boom generation retires. The private insurance market has increased the cost of Medigap insurance, and beneficiaries must choose from plans with wide variations in cost. Some physicians have refused to accept Medicare because they believe the reimbursement rate is too low. Fewer beneficiaries than expected have enrolled in less costly managed care plans. The question of the future viability of Medicare has led many health policy analysts to suggest that it be replaced by universal health care in what is surely the most unintended of long-range consequences.

DISCUSSION QUESTIONS

1. What are the major reasons that the United States has not adopted universal health care?

2. What are the most serious consequences of not having a national health care policy?

3. Which groups are most severely impacted by the lack of a national health care policy?

4. What are the biggest problems with Medicare now and in the near future?

5. What are the limitations of Medicaid? Of SCHIP?

6. Why haven't the earlier efforts to enact national health care been successful?

7. What conditions would be necessary for the United States to adopt a national health care policy?

8. What kind of health care policy do you think the United States will adopt over the next 10 years?

9. In your judgment, what kind of national health care policy would meet the goals of social justice for groups currently without access to health care?

10. What political arguments might be useful to convince Americans to adopt national health insurance?

NOTES

1. Carmen de Navas-Walt, "Income, Poverty and Health Insurance Coverage in the United States: 2007," U.S. Census Bureau, August 2008, http://www.census.gov/prod/2008pubs/p60–235.pdf, accessed April 10, 2009.

2. Kaiser Family Foundation, "Employer Health Benefits," 2007, http://www.kff.org/insurance/7672/upload/Summary-of-Findings-EHBS-2007.pdf, accessed June 24, 2008.

3. Laurence Kotlikoff, *The Healthcare Fix: Universal Insurance for All Americans* (Cambridge, MA: MIT Press, 2007), 49, 7.

4. Carmen de Navas-Walt, "Income, Poverty and Health Insurance Coverage in the United States: 2007," August 2008, U.S. Census Bureau, http://www.census.gov/prod/2008pubs/p60–235.pdf, accessed April 10, 2009.

5. National Coalition on Health Care, "Facts on Health Insurance Coverage," http://www.nchc.org/facts/coverage.shtml, accessed June 24, 2008.

6. Carmen De Navas-Walt, "Income, Poverty and Health Insurance Coverage in the United States: 2007," U.S. Census Bureau, August 2008, http://www.census.gov/prod/2008pubs/p60–235.pdf, accessed April 10, 2009.

7. Kotlikoff, *The Healthcare Fix,* 6.

8. 9. National Coalition on Health Care, "Facts on Health Insurance Coverage," http://www.nchc.org/facts/coverage.shtml, accessed April 10, 2009.

10. National Coalition on Health Care, "Facts on Health Insurance Coverage," http://www.nchc.org/facts/coverage.shtml, accessed April 10, 2009; Carmen de Navas-Walt, "Income, Poverty and Health Insurance Coverage in the United States: 2007," U.S. Census Bureau, August 2008, http://www.census.gov/prod/2008pubs/p60–235.pdf, accessed April 10, 2009.

11. Carmen de Navas-Walt, "Income, Poverty and Health Insurance Coverage in the United States: 2007," August 2008, U.S. Census Bureau, http://www.census.gov/prod/2008pubs/p60–235.pdf, accessed April 10, 2009.

12. Kotlikoff, *The Healthcare Fix,* 7.

13. National Coalition on Health Care, "Facts on Health Insurance Coverage," http://www.nchc.org/facts/coverage.shtml, accessed June 24, 2008.

14. Robert Le Bow, *Health Care Meltdown: Confronting the Myths and Fixing Our Failing System,* rev ed. (Chambersburg, PA: Alan C. Hood, 2007), 27–28; Alma Koch, "Financing Health Systems," in Stephen Williams and Paul Torrens, eds., *Introduction to Health Services,* 7th ed. (Clifton Park, NY: Thomson, 2008), 77; Karen Davis, Cathy Schoen, and Stuart Guterman, "Slowing the Growth of U.S. Health Care Expenditures," The Commonwealth Fund, January 29, 2007, http://www.common wealthfund.org/publications/publications_show.htm?doc_id=449510, accessed July 3, 2008.

15. Kant Patel and Mark Rushefsky, *Health Care Politics and Policy in America* (Armonk, NY: M. E. Sharpe, 2006), 36–37.

16. National Coalition on Health Care, "Facts on Health Insurance Coverage," http://www.nchc.org/facts/coverage.shtml, accessed June 24, 2008.

17. Stephen Williams, "Population and Disease Patterns and Trends," in Stephen Williams and Paul Torrens, eds., *Introduction to Health Services* (Clifton Park, NY: Thomson, 2008), 52.

18. The Commonwealth Fund Commission on a High Performance Health System, *Why Not the Best: Results From a National Scorecard on U.S. Health System Performance* (New York: The Commonwealth Fund, 2006).

19. Geyman, "Myths as Barriers to Health Care Reform in the United States," 409.

20. Gunnar Almgren, *Health Care Politics, Policy and Services: A Social Justice Analysis* (New York: Springer, 2007), 188.

21. Mary Ann Jimenez, "Concepts of Health and National Health Care," *Social Service Review* 71 (1, 1997): 34–50.

22. Michael Goldstein, *The Health Movement: Fitness in America* (New York: Twayne, 1992), 3–6.

23. Jimenez, "Concepts of Health and National Health Care," 40–41.

24. Paul Starr, *The Social Transformation of American Medicine* (New York: Basic Books, 1982), 193–194.

25. Starr, *The Social Transformation of American Medicine,* 189–197.

26. Starr, *The Social Transformation of American Medicine,* 3–9.

27. Starr, *The Social Transformation of American Medicine,* 272; Patel and Rushefsky, *Health Care Politics and Policy in America,* 36–37.

28. Patel and Rushefsky, *Health Care Politics and Policy in America,* 37–38; Jill Quadagno, *One Nation Uninsured: Why the U.S. Has No National Health Insurance* (New York: Oxford University Press, 2005), 51–52.

29. Almgren, *Health Care Politics, Policy and Services*, 110.

30. Kotlikoff, *The Healthcare Fix*, 82.

31. Almgren, *Health Care Politics, Policy and Services*, 224–225.

32. Susan Brink, "The Toll of Racism," *Los Angeles Times*, September 24, 2007, F1.

33. Kevin Fiscella and David Williams, "Health Disparities Based on Socioeconomic Inequities: Implications for Urban Health Care," *Academic Medicine* 79 (12, 2004): 1139–1147; Antronette Yancey, Rosan Bastani, and Beth Glenn, "Ethnic Disparities in Health Status," in Ronald Andersen, Thomas Rice, and Gerald Kominski, eds., *Changing the U.S. Health Care System* (New York: Wiley, 2007), 33–57.

34. David Satcher and Eve Higginbotham, "The Public Health Approach to Eliminating Disparities in Health," *American Journal of Public Health* 98 (March 2008): 400–403.

35. Brian Smedley, Adrienne Smith, and Alan Nelson, *Unequal Treatment: Confronting Racial and Ethnic Disparities in Health Care* (Washington, DC: The National Academies Press, 2003), 84.

36. Fiscella and Williams, "Health Disparities Based on Socioeconomic Inequities," 1145.

37. Ed Kelly, Ernest Moy, Daniel Stryer, Helen Burstin, and Carolyn Clancy, "The National Healthcare Quality and Disparities Reports: An Overview," *Medical Care* 43 (3, 2005): 13–18.

38. Smedley, Smith, and Nelson, *Unequal Treatment*, 85.

39. Fiscella and Williams, "Health Disparities Based on Socioeconomic Inequities," 1144; Yancey, Bastani, and Glenn, "Ethnic Disparities in Health Status," 33–57.

40. Kotlikoff, *The Healthcare Fix*, 48–50.

41. Kotlikoff, *The Healthcare Fix*, 82–83.

42. Almgren, *Health Care Politics, Policy and Services*, 97.

43. Koch, "Financing Health Systems," 94–96.

44. Almgren, *Health Care Politics, Policy and Services*, 105.

45. Koch, "Financing Health Systems," 95.

46. Koch, "Financing Health Systems," 96; Eric Schneider, Alan Zaslavsky, and Arnold Epstein, "Quality of Care in For Profit and Not for Profit Health Plans Enrolling Medicare Beneficiaries," in Charlene Harrington and Carroll Estes, eds., *Health Policy: Crisis and Reform in the U.S. Health Care Delivery System* (Sudbury, MA: Jones and Bartlett, 2008), 221–226.

47. Koch, "Financing Health Systems," 124.

48. *Health Care Politics and Policy*, 225–252.

49. Jill Quadagno, *One Nation Uninsured*, 196.

50. Quadagno, *One Nation Uninsured*, 199.

51. Geyman, "Privatization of Medicare: Toward Disentitlement and Betrayal of a Social Contract," in Charlene Harrington and Carroll Estes, eds., *Health Policy: Crisis and Reform in the U.S. Health Care Delivery System* (Sudbury, MA: Jones and Bartlett, 2008), 323–324; Quadagno, *One Nation Uninsured*, 198–200.

52. Koch, "Financing Health Systems," 89.

53. Kaiser Family Foundation, "Medicare at a Glance," February 2007, http://www.kff.org/medicare/1066.cfm, accessed July 6, 2008.

54. Ibid.

55. Patel and Rushefsky, *Health Care Politics and Policy in America*, 141.

56. Kaiser Family Foundation, "Dual Eligibles: Medicaid's Role in Filling Medicare's Gaps," March 2004, http://www.kff.org/medicaid/upload/Dual-Eligibles-Medicaid-s-Role-in-Filling-Medicare-s-Gaps.pdf, accessed July 7, 2008.

57. U.S. Department of Health and Human Services, "Long Term Care," April 10, 2007, http://www.medicare.gov/longtermcare/static/home.asp, accessed July 7, 2008.

58. Patel and Rushefsky, *Health Care Politics and Policy in America*, 156–162.

59. Kotlikoff, *The Healthcare Fix*, 17–19.

60. Steven Wallace, Emily Abel, Nadereh Pourat, and Linda Delpt, "Long Term Care and the Elderly Population," in Ronald Andersen, Thomas Rice, and Gerald Kominski, eds., *Changing the U.S. Health Care System*, 3rd ed. (New York: Wiley, 2007), 341–363.

61. Almgren, *Health Care Politics, Policy and Services*, 131.

62. Kotlikoff, *The Healthcare Fix*, 43.

63. Ibid.

64. Kaiser Family Foundation, "Medicaid, SCHIP, and Economic Downturn: Policy Challenges and Policy Responses," April 2008, http://www.kff.org/medicaid/upload/7770ES.pdf, accessed July 8, 2008.

65. Quadagno, *One Nation Uninsured*, 195, 208.

66. Kaiser Family Foundation, "Medicaid, SCHIP, and Economic Downturn."

67. Almgren, *Health Care Politics, Policy and Services*, 133.

68. Patel and Rushefsky, *Health Care Politics and Policy in America*, 77–79; Almgren, *Health Care Politics, Policy and Services*, 134.

69. Quadagno, *One Nation Uninsured*, 207–210; Kaiser Family Foundation, Kaiser Commission on Medicaid Facts, "Medicaid and the Uninsured," March 2007, http://www.kff.org/medicaid/upload/7235–02.pdf, accessed July 8, 2008.

70. Patel and Rushefsky, *Health Care Politics and Policy in America*, 120–121.

71. Patel and Rushefsky, *Health Care Politics and Policy in America*, 102.

72. Kevin Sack, "Study Links Diagnosis of Cancer to Insurance," *New York Times*, February 18, 2008, A10.

73. Kaiser Family Foundation, "Medicaid and the Uninsured."

74. Patel and Rushefsky, *Health Care Politics and Policy in America*, 120–121.

75. Matthew Broaddus, Leighton Ku, and Mark Lin, "Chartbook: Improving Children's Health—The Roles of Medicaid and SCHIP," Center on Budget and Policy Priorities, January 1, 2007, http://www.cbpp.org/schip-chartbook.htm, accessed July 10, 2008.

76. Department of Heath and Human Services, "HHS Releases New Analysis of SCHIP Eligibility," June 2007, http://www.hhs.gov/news/facts/schip.html, accessed July 10, 2008.

77. Matthew Broaddus and Edwin Park, "Freezing SCHIP Funding in Coming Years Would Reverse Recent Gains in Children's Health Coverage," Center on Budget and Policy Priorities, February 22, 2007, http://www.cbpp.org/cms/index.cfm?fa=view& id=453, accessed April 10, 2009.

78. Kaiser Family Foundation, "Medicaid and SCHIP Eligibility for Immigrants," April 2006, http://www.kff.org/medicaid/upload/7492.pdf, accessed July 10, 2008.

79. Mary Ann Jimenez, *Changing Faces of Madness: Early American Attitudes and Treatment of the Insane* (Hanover, NH: University Press of New England); Gerald Grob, *Mental Institutions in America: Social Policy to 1875* (New York: Free Press, 1973); Gerald Grob, *The Mad Among Us: A History of the Care of America's Mentally Ill* (New York: Free Press, 1994); Nancy Theriot, "Women's Voices in Nineteenth-Century

Medical Discourse: A Step Toward Deconstructing Science," *Signs* 19 (1, 1993): 1–31; Andrew Scull, *Social Order/Mental Disorder: Anglo-American Society in Historical Perspective* (Berkeley: University of California Press, 1989); Michael Katz, *In the Shadow of the Poorhouse* (New York: Basic Books, 1996).

80. American Psychiatric Association, *Diagnostic and Statistical Manual of Mental Disorders*, 4th ed., text rev. (Washington, DC: Author).

81. James Trent, Jr., *Inventing the Feeble Mind: Mental Retardation in American History* (Berkeley: University of California Press, 1995).

82. Grob, *The Mad Among Us*, 249–279; Cynthia Moniz and Stephan Goran, *Health and Mental Health Care Policy*, 2nd ed. (Boston: Pearson, 2007), 43–44; Bonnie Lefkowitz, *Community Mental Health Centers: A Movement and the People Who Made It Happen* (New Brunswick, NJ: Rutgers University Press, 2007), 135–151.

83. Howard Karger and David Stoesz, *American Social Welfare Policy: A Pluralist Approach* (Boston: Pearson, 2006), 343; O'Connor v. Donaldson, 422 U.S. 563 (1975), http://www.psychlaws.org/LegalResources/Caselaws/Case1.htm, accessed January 22, 2009.

84. E. Fuller Torrey, *Out of the Shadows: Confronting America's Mental Illness Crisis* (New York: Wiley, 1998), 13–43.

85. Bernard Goldstein, "NIMBY," *Encyclopedia of Public Health*, http://www.enotes.com/public-health-encyclopedia/my-backyard-nimby, accessed January 22, 2009; Lois Takahashi, *Homelessness, AIDS and Stigmatization: The NIMBY Syndrome in the United States at the End of the Twentieth Century* (Oxford, England: Clarendon Press, 1998), 45–64.

86. Federal Grants Wire, "Block Grants for Community Mental Health Services," 93–958, http://www.federalgrantswire.com/block-grants-for-community-mental-health-services.html, accessed January 23, 2009.

87. Embry Howell, "Access to Children's Mental Health Services Under Medicaid and SCHIP," The Urban Institute, 2004, http://www.urban.org/Uploaded PDF/311053_B-60.pdf, accessed January 23, 2009.

88. Mental Health America, "Maximizing Medicaid Options for Mental Health Services," http://www1.nmha.org/shcr/community_based/medicaid_options.cfm, accessed January 22, 2009.

89. Centers for Medicare and Medicaid Services, "Mental Health Services," August 27, 2008, http://www.cms.hhs.gov/MHS/, accessed January 23, 2009; The Brown University Child and Adolescent Psychopharmacology Update, "Psychiatric Medication Doubles Among Medicaid Preschoolers," August 1, 2007, http://www.accessmylibrary.com/coms2/summary_0286-33764908_ITM, accessed January 23, 2009.

90. Chris Koyanagi, Sandra Forquer, and Elaine Alfano, "Medicaid Policies to Contain Psychiatric Drug Costs," *Health Affairs* 24 (2, 2005): 536–544.

91. Centers for Medicare and Medicaid Services, "The Mental Health Parity Act," http://www.cms.hhs.gov/healthinsreformforconsume/04_thementalhealthparityact.asp, accessed January 23, 2008.

92. Alison Flowers, "Pared Down Look at the New Mental Health Parity Act Reveals Advances and Limitations," *Medill Reports*, October 1, 2008, http://news.medill.northwestern.edu/chicago/news.aspx?id=99527, accessed January 23, 2009.

93. NCHS Data Brief, "Use of Mental Health Services for the Past 12 Months by Children Aged 4–17 Years," http://www.cdc.gov/nchs/data/databriefs/db08.htm, accessed January 23, 2009.

94. California Department of Mental Health, "The Mental Health Services Act Expenditure Report," January 2009, http://www.dmh.ca.gov/prop_63/MHSA/Publications/docs/Revised_Leg_Report_Format_FINAL_1–7_%20v11.pdf, accessed January 23, 2009.

95. Starr, *The Social Transformation of American Medicine,* 235–289; Almgren, *Health Care Politics, Policy and Services,* 39–62.

96. Paul Starr, *The Social Transformation of American Medicine,* 289.

97. Almgren, *Health Care Politics, Policy and Services,* 66–68, 309; Quadagno, *One Nation Uninsured,* 186–194.

98. Paul Torrens, "Understanding Health Policy," in Stephen Williams and Paul Torrens, eds., *Introduction to Health Services* (Clifton Park, NY: Thomson, 2008), 298; David Mechanic, "The Rise and Fall of Managed Care," in Charlene Harrington and Carroll Estes, eds., *Health Policy: Crisis and Reform in the U.S. Health Care Delivery System* (Sudbury, MA: Jones and Bartlett, 2008).

99. David Mechanic, "The Rise and Fall of Managed Care," in Charlene Harrington and Carroll Estes, *Health Policy: Crisis and Reform in the U.S. Health Care Delivery System* (Sudbury, MA: Jones and Bartlett, 2008), 345–352.

100. Mechanic, "The Rise and Fall of Managed Care," in Harrington and Estes, *Health Policy,* 349.

101. Marcia Angell, "The Truth About Drug Companies," *New York Review of Books,* July 15, 2004; Emily Berry, "Health Plans Say They'll Risk Losing Members to Maintain Profit Margins," *Truth Out,* May 19, 2008, http://www.truthout.org/article/health-plans-put-profit-margins-before-members, accessed June 27, 2008.

102. John Geyman, "Myths as Barriers to Health Care Reform in the United States," in Charlene Harrington and Carroll Estes, *Health Policy: Crisis and Reform in the U.S. Health Care Delivery System* (Sudbury, MA: Jones and Bartlett, 2008), 407–413.

103. Geyman, "Myths as Barriers to Health Care Reform in the United States," 410.

104. National Coalition on Health Care, "Facts on Health Insurance Costs," 2007, http://www.nchc.org/facts/coverage.shtml, accessed June 24, 2008.

105. Gerald Kominski, Jeanne Black, and Thomas Rice, "Medicare Reform," in Ronald Andersen, Thomas Rice, and Gerald Kominski, eds., *Changing the U.S. Health Care System* (New York: Wiley, 2007), 569–590.

106. Kominski et al., "Medicare Reform," 586.

107. Kotlikoff, *The Healthcare Fix,* 76–89.

108. Quadagno, *One Nation Uninsured,* 207–210.

109. Judith Feder, "Crowd Out and the Politics of Health Reform," in Charlene Harrington and Carroll Estes, *Health Policy: Crisis and Reform in the U.S. Health Care Delivery System* (Sudbury, MA: Jones and Bartlett, 2008), 427–433.

110. Ibid.

111. Stuart Glascock, "In Oregon, Healthcare for the Lucky," *Los Angeles Times,* March 10, 2008, A10.

112. Pam Belluck, "Universal Health Care Faces Hurdles in Massachusetts: The Massachusetts Model," *New York Times,* June 16, 2008, A20.

113. Daniel Light, "Improving Medical Practice and the Economy Through Universal Health Insurance," in Charlene Harrington and Carroll Estes, eds., *Health Policy: Crisis and Reform in the U.S. Health Care Delivery System* (Sudbury, MA: Jones and Bartlett, 2008), 433–436.

114. Light, "Improving Medical Practice and the Economy Through Universal Health Insurance," 434.

115. Kotlikoff, *The Healthcare Fix,* 85; Le Bow, *Health Care Meltdown.*

116. Le Bow, *Health Care Meltdown,* 35.

117. Kominski et al., "Medicare Reform," 569–590.

118. Light, "Improving Medical Practice and the Economy Through Universal Health Insurance," 434.

119. Raisa Berlin Deber, "Health Care Reform: Lessons From Canada," *American Journal of Public Health* 93 (January 2003): 20–24; Ken Terry, *RX for Health Care Reform* (Nashville, TN: Vanderbilt University Press, 2007), 161–163.

120. Le Bow, *Health Care Meltdown,* 26–30.

CHAPTER

10

Housing Policy

CHAPTER QUESTIONS

1. What are the major causes of homelessness in the United States?

2. Why have few social policies been developed that address the problem of homelessness?

3. Why does the United States have a shortage of affordable housing?

4. What is the role of the market economy in the provision of affordable housing?

5. How is discrimination a factor in housing availability and housing policy?

6. What are the current federal policies that provide housing for low-income persons?

7. How do middle-class and wealthy taxpayers benefit from tax policies related to housing?

8. What is the mortgage crisis, and how did it contribute to widespread economic problems in the United States?

● ● ●

THE PROBLEM OF HOMELESSNESS ●

The United States is without question the wealthiest country in the world, yet more than half a million people sleep on the streets, in shelters, or in their cars every night. These are homeless persons; their numbers wax and wane with economic circumstances and depending on who is counting, but they are a seemingly permanent fixture of American society. Along with these dramatic cases of persons lacking housing, homeless persons include families who live in motels, those who are staying temporarily with family or friends, and those whose housing situation is so unstable that they do not know where they will sleep tomorrow. Homelessness is clearly a fluid problem, but because there is a widely shared expectation in this country that everyone ought to have a place to call home, it is one of our most dramatic social issues. This is not the case in all societies; in India families camp out on public streets in urban areas, claiming their spots to sleep, cook, and eat. In the United States, living in this way is considered problematic; most Americans would recognize that having persons, much less families, make their home on the streets is undesirable. For some this situation would inspire reflection on the profound inequalities in the United States. In a country with plentiful resources, most would probably agree that no one should have to live without some form of shelter. Homelessness thus rebukes our sense of ourselves as a fair country, which is one reason that we largely ignore it.

The existence of pervasive homelessness demonstrates the failure of social policy to separate market factors from the provision of the necessities of life, just as the lack of health insurance discussed in the previous chapter does. The anomalous nature of homelessness in a country of abundance is suggested by those who seek to blame homeless persons rather than broader structural factors for their condition. Mental disorder, substance abuse, and other personal problems provide a convenient list of problems experienced by many persons who are homeless, but they mask the structural causes of lack of permanent shelter. The interaction of the *market economy* combined with *historical values that emphasize individualism, self-reliance, and a distrust of government interference in market forces* leads to our failure to ensure affordable shelter to many persons living in the United States. Forces of discrimination increase the housing burden for oppressed ethnic groups, who are disproportionately numbered among the homeless and those lacking affordable housing.

The Face of Homelessness

The first question to ask about homelessness is, What is it? Is it living on the streets most nights? Does living in one's car constitute homelessness? What about staying with friends or relatives on a temporary basis? Do persons housed in shelters for homeless constitute part of the current homeless population? Policymakers differ on the exact definition of homelessness, but they do agree that it is characterized by transience of place and instability and flux in terms of shelter.[1] Persons without shelter one day may be in a motel the next, only to return to the streets the day after. Others may be able to stay with friends a few days a week and be forced to go to a homeless shelter on the other days. The federal government attempts to bring clarity to the ambiguous nature of homelessness by defining a homeless person as an individual who

Homeless persons in an urban area

SOURCE: © iStockphoto.

lacks a fixed, regular, and adequate nighttime residence and who also has a primary nighttime residence that is a supervised publicly or privately operated shelter designed to provide temporary living accommodations, an institution that provides a temporary residence for individuals intended to be institutionalized, or a public or private place not designed for, or ordinarily used as, a regular sleeping accommodation for human beings, such as streets, under bridges, or in cars.[2] This official definition is important because it drives eligibility for government programs serving homeless persons.[3] This is clearly a narrow definition of homelessness that limits the number of people eligible for benefits; for example, someone who had a place to sleep the night before he or she appeared at a homeless shelter may not receive help, even if he or she has no place to sleep on the night he or she applies. Natural disasters can leave people without a home, but most people have the means to recover from a temporary crisis and do not become homeless. This is one reason why the effects of Hurricane Katrina in New Orleans were so striking. Many of the economically marginalized persons affected by the hurricane had no ability to pay for substitute housing and so became officially homeless, whether living in FEMA-sponsored trailers or homeless shelters. The lack of shelter becomes a social problem when poverty limits the ability of individuals to locate alternative resources.

During the past 2 decades more families have experienced homelessness than in previous years. Families tend to spend a shorter time homeless than individuals, but families finding shelter are continually replaced by other families experiencing temporary loss of housing. According to a survey conducted by the Department of Housing and Urban Development, on a single night in January 2007, there were 671,888 sheltered and unsheltered homeless persons nationwide. On this night nearly two thirds of the nation's homeless population (63% or 423,400 persons) were individuals, and more than one third (37% or 248,500 persons) were persons in families. Among all homeless persons, almost 6 in 10 persons (or 58%) were sleeping in an emergency shelter or in a transitional housing facility; the rest were sleeping on the streets or in other places not meant for human habitation. Homeless persons in families were much more likely to be sleeping in an emergency shelter or a transitional housing facility than in places not meant for human habitation. About 72% of homeless persons in families were sheltered, and 28% were unsheltered.[4] (See Table 10.1.)

TABLE 10.1   **Homeless Individuals and Persons in Families by Sheltered Status, January 2007**

Household Type	Number of Persons in 2007	Percentage of Individuals and Persons in Families in 2007
Total		
Sheltered	391,401	58.3
Unsheltered	280,487	41.7
Total	671,888	100
Individuals		
Sheltered	213,073	50.3
Unsheltered	210,304	49.7
Total	423,377	100
Persons in Families		
Sheltered	178,328	71.8
Unsheltered	70,183	28.2
Total	248,511	100

SOURCE: 2006 and 2007 Continuum of Care Application: Exhibit 1, CoC Point-in-Time Homeless Population and Subpopulations Charts. Retrieved from http://www.hudhre.info/documents/3rdHomelessAssessmentReport.pdf

Of course the number of homeless persons on any one night is not a clear indication of the number of persons experiencing homelessness over the course of a year. The federal estimate of the number of homeless persons living in homeless shelters sometime between 2006 and 2007 was 1,588,545 persons. Of these, 356,899 were adults in families, and approximately 340,000 were children under age 17. The night before entry into a homeless shelter that year, 116,770 persons had stayed in places not meant for human habitation. Of those staying at least one night in a homeless shelter, approximately 558,000 were African Americans, 513,00 were Whites, and 314,000 were Latinos. African American families tended to stay in emergency housing longer than other families. During the period between 2006 and 2007, African Americans constituted 90% of persons who spent more than 180 days in emergency shelters. Families in emergency housing are also younger than families in transitional housing; more than half of the adults in emergency shelters were between ages 18 and 30; more than half of homeless children living in emergency shelters were under age 6.[5] (See Table 10.2.)

TABLE 10.2   **Estimate of Sheltered Homeless Individuals and Persons in Families During a 1-Year Period, October 2006– September 2007**

	Total Number	Percentage of Sheltered Homeless Population
Total Number of Sheltered Persons	1,588,545	100.0
Individuals	1,115,054	70.2
Adults in Families	356,899	22.5
Children Under 17	340,000	21.4

SOURCE: Homeless Management Information System data, October 2006–September 2007. Retrieved from http://www.hudhre.info/documents/3rdHomelessAssessmentReport.pdf

This picture of homelessness in the United States is necessarily incomplete. What is clear is that families constitute a large proportion of homeless persons and that African Americans are disproportionately represented among those who are homeless. (See Figure 10.1.)

Transitional housing programs are designed to provide a period of stabilization and intensive services to help a family succeed in obtaining and retaining permanent housing; transitional housing relies on the assumption that residential programs can ease the transition from more impersonal institutions, like homeless shelters, to regular housing. The idea of transitional housing emerged in the mental health and corrections fields as a way of enabling former prisoners or mental hospital residents with an intermediate level of supervision that would facilitate adjustment to

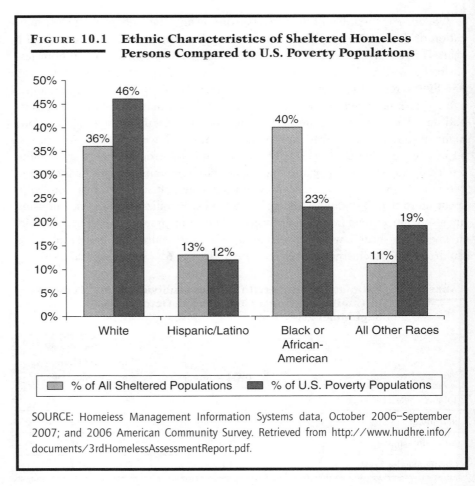

FIGURE 10.1   **Ethnic Characteristics of Sheltered Homeless Persons Compared to U.S. Poverty Populations**

SOURCE: Homeless Management Information Systems data, October 2006–September 2007; and 2006 American Community Survey. Retrieved from http://www.hudhre.info/documents/3rdHomelessAssessmentReport.pdf.

independent living in the community. Families are more likely to use transitional housing than individuals; 31% of families who were homeless spent some time in transitional housing in 2007. The average length of stay in emergency housing for families in 2007 was 15 days; for transitional housing, it was 150 days.

Based on 2007 inventory data, an estimated 19,069 homeless residential programs operate nationwide, including 6,140 emergency shelters (33%), 7,275 transitional housing programs (39%), and 5,654 permanent supportive housing programs (28%). The national inventory of homeless residential programs includes an estimated 611,292 beds distributed in the following manner: 211,451 beds in emergency shelters (35%), 211,205 beds in transitional housing (35%), and 188,636 beds in permanent housing (30%).[6] (See Figure 10.2.)

Homelessness is compounded by other problems—lack of health insurance for most homeless means they receive necessary medical care late, if at all, and

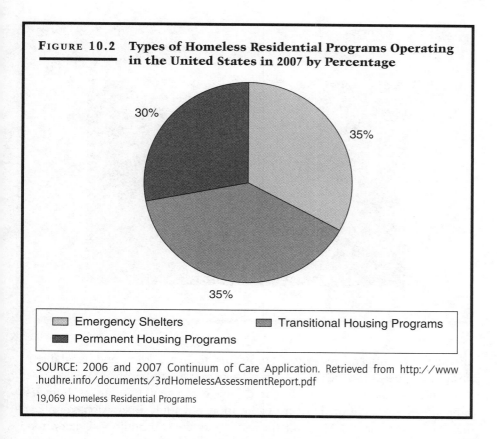

FIGURE 10.2   **Types of Homeless Residential Programs Operating in the United States in 2007 by Percentage**

Emergency Shelters   Transitional Housing Programs
Permanent Housing Programs

SOURCE: 2006 and 2007 Continuum of Care Application. Retrieved from http://www .hudhre.info/documents/3rdHomelessAssessmentReport.pdf

19,069 Homeless Residential Programs

often in emergency rooms. Once hospitalized, homeless persons tend to stay far longer than persons with homes. Their mortality rate is higher, and their life expectancy is shorter than that of persons with homes by 45 years. Estimates are that about half of homeless women are fleeing domestic violence.[7]

Homeless Youth

Youth who are homeless on their own, without an accompanying parent, experience even more challenges than those who are with their parents. Few of these unattached youth show up at adult homeless shelters, finding other ways of surviving on the street. Drugs, sexual assault and exploitation, sexually transmitted diseases, emotional and mental health problems, and food scarcity are problems commonly faced by homeless youth. Called "unaccompanied youth" in federal statistics, the number of homeless and runaway youth was estimated to be approximately 1,682,000 in 2002, the last year for which statistics are available. Approximately 6% of these youth are estimated to be gay, lesbian,

Homeless adolescent in Hollywood, California

SOURCE: © iStockphoto.

bisexual, or transgendered. Family problems, financial crises, and instability of foster placements are the three main reasons that youth become homeless.[8]

Homeless youth have similar needs for permanent housing as homeless adults, with the additional factor of education and adult supervision complicating the policy picture. Many of the services offered to adults—shelters, food banks, and job counseling—are inadequate for homeless youth, who must meet their developmental and educational needs as well. Until the reauthorization of the McKinney-Vento Homeless Assistance Act in 2001, states were allowed to operate special schools for homeless children; the reauthorized act prohibited such arrangements. The act further mandated that schools provide transportation to homeless children whose parents requested it.[9]

● HISTORY OF HOMELESSNESS IN THE UNITED STATES

Homeless children and their mothers were eligible for local charitable assistance under the Poor Laws adopted in the colonial period. As discussed in Chapter 7, in the 19th century the form of this local relief changed from outdoor relief, where families might be boarded with neighbors at town expense, to indoor relief, where families would be housed in local poorhouses or almshouses in gender-segregated arrangements. In these poorhouses regular work and religious worship were mandated. Poorhouses were thought to be less expensive than outdoor relief and enjoyed great popularity with local officials responsible for aiding the worthy poor. Vagrancy laws were passed by cities and towns in the late 19th century to warn out beggars and idle poor from public areas, forcing persons who were homeless to move from town to town in a permanent state of transience.[10]

It is impossible to estimate the number of homeless persons or families during this period, as these statistics were not routinely kept. State and local officials turned away from indoor relief in the early 20th century and reverted again to outdoor relief and the parsimonious aid that characterized it. When the effects of the Great Depression threw many families out of their homes and into parks and temporary encampments in the countryside, homelessness became a national problem. More families and individuals took to the road, some riding trains, others walking or driving, to try their fortunes outside their hometowns. Individuals who were homeless were subject to the vagrancy laws of the previous century. When they appeared in towns and rural communities, they were often met with hostility and pressure to leave. This was especially true of the African American sharecroppers from the South who migrated to urban areas in the North.[11]

The number of homeless persons, especially of homeless families, declined in the 1940s with the effects of the New Deal policies and, more important, the economic growth that occurred as a result of World War II. The deinstitutionalization of the mentally disordered in the late 1960s, absent the establishment of the necessary outpatient services for the deinstitutionalized population, led to a large increase in persons who were homeless and mentally ill in the late 1970s. The number of homeless persons grew again in the 1980s, as housing and social service cuts increased under the policies of the Reagan administration.

Homelessness then and now represents a threat to the social order in small-town America. When homelessness was first recognized as a social problem in the 19th century, the issue of blame emerged as Americans sought to understand the causes of homelessness. These same issues of blame are evident in popular attitudes toward homelessness; the question of whether persons who are homeless are "worthy" to receive help has been an unfortunate theme in the social response to homelessness. Many people believe that virtually all homeless persons are alcoholics, drug addicts, mentally ill, or some combination of the three.[12] While some long-term homeless persons inevitably suffer from these conditions, the vast majority of homeless families are homeless because they cannot afford a place to live. Homeless children in particular are likely to suffer from serious health, psychological, and developmental problems associated with their homeless status.[13] While most Americans understand that homeless children should not be blamed for their condition, the same is not true of their parents.[14]

The first major federal initiative to address homelessness was the Stewart B. McKinney Homeless Assistance Act, passed by Congress in 1987 and renamed the McKinney-Vento Act by President Clinton in 2000. This act made federal monies available to communities that wished to offer emergency shelter, transitional housing, and permanent supportive housing for homeless persons. Under this act Congress authorized a total of 20 possible programs that offered a multitude of services, including education, job training, mental health care, primary health care services, substance abuse treatment, and veterans' assistance services. Funding was through block grants or a competitive process by states and localities. There is strong consensus that the act has not kept pace with the need for funding and programs that result from an increase in the number of homeless persons. The fact that some of the funding was available through a competitive process limits the universality of the policy. Its supporters viewed the act as the first step in a full-scale effort to end homelessness, but more substantial efforts have not materialized.[15]

In 2001 Congress passed the McKinney-Vento Homeless Education Assistance Improvements Act as part of No Child Left Behind. The act sought to extend federal policy on homelessness to children in homeless families in order to ensure their access to public education. The act prohibited segregation of homeless children in separate schools or separate classrooms.

In a largely rhetorical pronouncement, the Department of Housing and Urban Development, along with President Bush in his federal budget initiative of 2003, adopted the goal of ending chronic homelessness, defined as being homeless for 1 year or four times in 3 years, in 10 years. Over 200 communities have followed this federal lead and adopted 10-year plans to end chronic homelessness. However, federal policy is inadequate to support these efforts. The funding for the McKinney-Vento Act has been cut recently, with a 36% funding decrease by 2010 proposed by the Bush administration.[16] Second, there is no federal policy offering a comprehensive approach to solving the problem of homelessness. Instead the McKinney-Vento Act focuses solely on emergency measures, not on the causes of homelessness. Real efforts to solve the problem of homelessness would include the creation of jobs that pay a living wage; adequate unemployment benefits for all workers, including those in the secondary labor market; provision of affordable housing; and creation of national health insurance. (See Table 10.3.)

● THE PROBLEM OF AFFORDABLE HOUSING

More pervasive than the problem of homelessness is the problem of affordable housing. A number of Americans are housed in marginal conditions, struggling to meet the increasingly high cost of even substandard housing. On its own, the *market economy* will not produce low-cost housing, because the return on investment to builders is too low. In other words, low rent or very inexpensive home prices would not be profitable. As a consequence economically marginalized families

TABLE 10.3   **Summary of Federal Policies for Homeless Persons and Their Families Outlining Provisions and Impact on Problem**

Federal Policies	Time Frame	Provisions	Impact on Problem
Stewart B. McKinney Homeless Assistance Act renamed the McKinney-Vento Act in 2000	Passed by Congress in 1987 and renamed by Clinton in 2000	• Provided federal monies to communities that wished to offer emergency shelter, transitional housing, and permanent supportive housing for homeless persons • Authorized a total of 20 possible programs that included a multitude of services, including education, job training, mental health care, primary health care services, substance abuse treatment, and veterans' assistance services • Funding was through block grants or a competitive process by states and localities	• Act has not kept pace with the need for funding and programs and the increase in the number of homeless persons • Funding was available through a competitive process, which limited the universality of the policy • Act was the first step in a full-scale effort to end homelessness, but more substantial efforts have not materialized
McKinney-Vento Homeless Education Assistance Improvements Act	2001	• Part of No Child Left Behind • Act sought to extend federal policy on homelessness to children in homeless families in order to ensure their access to public education • Prohibited segregation of homeless children in separate schools or separate classrooms	• Funding for the McKinney-Vento Act has been cut with a 36% funding decrease by 2010 proposed by the Bush administration • No federal policy offering a comprehensive approach to solving the problem of homelessness as the McKinney-Vento Act focuses solely on emergency measures, not on the causes of homelessness
Department of Housing and Urban Development and President Bush in his Federal Budget Initiative adopted a goal of ending homelessness	2003	• Adopted the goal of ending chronic homelessness, defined as being homeless for 1 year or four times in 3 years, in 10 years • Over 200 communities have followed this federal lead and adopted 10-year plans to end chronic homelessness	• Federal policy has been inadequate to support these efforts with funding cuts

often live in substandard housing, sometimes with many more people in a housing unit than is safe or sanitary. Some live in garages where fire hazards and inadequate sanitation threaten health and safety; others pay far more in rent and housing costs than their budgets allow, forcing them to scrimp on food, utilities, clothing, and other necessities.

Affordable housing is defined as housing that does not cost more than 30% of a household's gross income. Housing costs in this measure include taxes, insurance, and utility costs. When housing costs are more than 30% of household income, housing is considered unaffordable. Families who pay more than 30% of their income for housing may have difficulty affording necessities such as food, clothing, transportation, and medical care. In 2006, the number of severely burdened households—paying more than half their income for housing— surged by almost 4 million to 17.7 million households. Fully 47% of households in the bottom-income quartile were severely burdened in 2006, compared to 11% of lower middle-income households and just 4% of upper middle-income households.[17] Shockingly, approximately 14 million households in 2007 paid more than 50% of their annual incomes on housing. The lack of affordable housing constitutes a hardship for low-income households, preventing them from meeting their other basic needs, such as nutrition and health care, or saving for their future and that of their families. There are only about 6 million rentals affordable to the nearly 9 million households with the lowest incomes, and nearly half of these are either inhabited by higher-income households or left vacant by their owners.[18]

One third of Americans, or more than 36 million households, live in rental housing.[19] The number of renter households increased by more than 2 million from 2004 to 2007, which lowered the national homeownership rate to 68.1% in 2007. Homeowners and renters differ in several important ways: Homeowners are more affluent than renters, are more likely to live in single rather than multiple families, are more likely to live in the suburbs than in urban areas, are more likely to reside in places with physical deficiencies, are more likely to be White, and are more likely to be single. Renters are more likely to be "shelter poor" than homeowners; that is, they spend more than they can afford on housing.[20] In spite of the demand for inexpensive rental units, it is estimated that the number of low-income renters exceeds the number of available rental units by at least 2 million. Not only is the supply of rental units available for low-income persons inadequate; rents have increased much faster than the income level of renters. Families with one full-time worker earning only the minimum wage cannot afford rent for a two-bedroom apartment anywhere in the United States. One study found that in 60 large metropolitan areas of the United States, persons receiving the mean wage in five occupations—janitor, retail salesperson, elementary school teacher, licensed practical nurse, and political office—are unable to afford to rent a two-bedroom or, in some cases, a one-bedroom apartment. Homeownership is similarly out of reach for many Americans. Police officers and teachers are priced out of the homeowners' market in almost half of these urban areas, and janitors and salespersons are unable to buy a home in any of these areas. Half of low-income renters who purchase housing in the *market economy* without any public subsidies pay more than 50% of their income on rent, a percentage that severely squeezes their remaining income to an inadequate amount for other necessary living costs.[21]

The inadequate supply of rental units and the high cost of rent combine to demonstrate the failure of the *market economy* to deliver and sustain low-income housing to low-income persons absent public subsidy. The profit incentive, central to all market transactions, deters the movement of capital into low-income housing. Low rents mean less profit and also fewer resources available for maintenance and upkeep of housing units. One response of landlords to this downward economic pressure has been to raise rents above the level affordable for low-income persons in an effort to attract higher-paying renters. This move toward gentrification of previously low-income areas has driven low-income renters from the rental market in some urban areas.

PROFILES IN LEADERSHIP

Jesse Jackson, 1941–

Jesse Jackson was born to a teenage unwed mother in 1941 in Greenville, South Carolina. He grew up at a time of extreme social segregation in the South, which restricted him from most areas of civic and social life that White people take for granted. Despite his being raised in this hostile environment, Jackson was determined that nothing would hold him back from realizing his dreams. He was intelligent and determined and believed that he would succeed despite the obstacles imposed by White society on Black people.

Jesse Jackson

SOURCE: From the Library of Congress, U.S. News & World Report Magazine Photograph Collection, photographed by Thomas J. O'Halloran.

(Continued)

(Continued)

Beginning in the late 1950s, he completed high school and entered the University of Illinois. In 1963 he became a leader of civil rights demonstrations and was arrested for disturbing the peace. In 1964 he graduated from North Carolina A&T and later that year entered the Chicago Theological Seminary. An important event came in 1965, when Jackson met Dr. Martin Luther King, Jr., in Selma, Alabama. The two men agreed to work together to protest segregation and to fight for civil rights. Soon after, Jackson became the head of the Chicago chapter of the Southern Christian Leadership Conference (SCLC). One of Jackson's major achievements would be to provide the leadership for a program created by Dr. Martin Luther King, Jr., in 1966 called "Operation Breadbasket." This program focused on increasing the number of jobs for low-income Black Americans with the threat of economic boycotts for businesses that refused to cooperate with the program. This program achieved great success and eventually spread across the country.

After the assassination of Dr. King in 1968, Jackson became more prominent as a national civil rights leader, and many saw him as the heir to Dr. King. After the assassination of King, riots erupted in many U.S. cities. Jackson was often in the middle of these events, trying to broker agreements or arguing for changes in local laws and regulations related to urban housing discrimination. In all of these activities he worked closely with the SCLC and other civil rights leaders. In 1971, Jackson resigned from the SCLC and decided to strike out on his own. Angry and bitter over the deteriorating relationship with the leadership of the organization that was founded by Dr. King, he would devote his efforts to a new organization, "People United to Serve Humanity" (PUSH). It would be a national organization with many similarities to Operation Breadbasket and would focus on economic empowerment. His focus on improving education and especially housing for the poor enlisted widespread support and admiration. He developed connections with many supporters in government, foundations, and the corporate sector.

Despite the success of these programs, Jackson realized that his message had to be heard by a much wider audience, and he concluded that he could be more effective in his work if he became involved in politics. In 1984, at the Democratic National Convention in San Francisco, Jackson was introduced as a candidate for President of the United States. He was the first Black candidate to mount a serious run for the presidency. In spite of his efforts, Walter Mondale became the nominee of the Democratic Party. Mondale eventually lost to Reagan, who went on to his second term as president.

Yet Reverend Jackson had a major impact on the Democratic convention when he assailed the Reagan administration for ignoring the needs of the poor while courting the wealthy and major corporations. He called for nothing less than the changing of America's priorities with an emphasis on social justice and equality. Supporters of Jesse Jackson came to be known as the "rainbow coalition," reflecting the wide diversity of ethnic groups and including people from many backgrounds and cultures. This new force in America became the symbol of hope for millions of people who felt left out of the political process and left behind in a land of plenty. Jackson's message included calls for assistance for the poor and elderly and other vulnerable populations, a reduction in the nuclear arms race, and other benefits for Americans, especially improved housing for low-income Americans.

Throughout the 1990s, Jackson was asked often to intervene in labor issues in the United States and other issues in foreign countries. His life has been devoted to seeking social justice and fighting for those most vulnerable in our society. He has been tireless in his effort to build a more equitable and just society in this country and focused the nation's attention on the need for affordable housing for economically marginalized persons of all ethnicities.

FEDERAL HOUSING POLICIES ●

What should be the role of government in housing policy? One of the most important policy initiatives is to ensure that all Americans have affordable housing and permanent shelter. Other roles include ensuring nondiscrimination in housing and promoting balanced metropolitan growth. Housing is central to the economy of the United States, accounting for one fifth of the gross domestic product. Housing construction generates employment and consumption of other goods, including building materials, household items, and other home-related goods. Housing generates property taxes for local governments, along with other revenues for building permits and other fees.

Beginning with the wave of Southern and Eastern European immigrants at the end of the 19th century, the housing conditions in low-income urban areas have ranged from below standard to grossly inferior. The introduction of public sanitation in urban areas in the early 20th century improved some of the health hazards associated with slum dwellings, but conditions had improved so little by Franklin Roosevelt's second inauguration in 1936 that he could argue that a third of the nation was "ill housed." In 1940, 45% of all American households—and up to 80% in some Southern states—did not have indoor plumbing. Things improved rapidly after World War II; the percentage of homes without indoor plumbing decreased to 17% in 1960 and to 3% in 1980.[22]

The first federal legislation related to housing in 1937 created public housing projects as a response to the housing crisis caused by the Great Depression. Public housing is an example of supply side housing policy, where government provides living units at affordable prices. Housing vouchers are another federal strategy to stimulate housing demand in the private rental market. Vouchers encourage landlords to rent to economically marginalized persons by subsidizing the difference between their income and a maximum allowable rent. Other federal strategies include block grants to states to encourage states and local governments to support low-income housing. The Community Development Block Grant is the largest block grant program. The Low-Income Housing Tax Credit program offers tax incentives to private enterprise to participate in developing low-income rental units. The Fair Housing Act of 1968 made discrimination on the basis of ethnicity in the housing market illegal. All these policies will be discussed below.

The U.S. Department of Housing and Urban Development (HUD), founded in 1965, was designed to oversee public housing and other subsidy programs. HUD directs the FHA (Federal Housing Administration) insurance program. The Federal Housing Administration was established under the Roosevelt administration in 1934 as a way of stimulating new housing construction and reducing unemployment in the construction industry. Through the FHA the federal government offered government-insured mortgages for qualified lenders. This federal backup encouraged the private mortgage industry to offer more funds at lower interest rates. By setting standards for home construction, the FHA also reassured lenders about the soundness of the properties they were underwriting and encouraged more lending. Combined with the Veterans' Administration program for home loans instituted after World War II (the GI Bill), the FHA encouraged widespread homeownership among White working-class persons in the United States in the 1950s and 1960s. The FHA promoted ownership in White communities, not African American or ethnically mixed communities, because it was reluctant to give mortgage insurance to properties in these neighborhoods. Under criteria for assessing the value of property in determining the amount of the loan, the FHA in 1935 declared that residential neighborhoods dominated by ethnic minorities were poor investments, due to "adverse influences" of "inharmonious racial or national groups." Largely as a result of these federal policies, urban neighborhoods received much less help from the FHA than suburban neighborhoods. Until the late 1970s, the vast majority of homes purchased with mortgages underwritten by FHA insurance were in suburban areas. Construction for single-family homes was favored over that for multiple-family dwellings or rehabilitation of existing housing stock, further disadvantaging lower-income urban residents who often could not afford to purchase single-family homes. In this way the federal government fostered segregation and inequality.[23] The FHA changed these practices in the 1980s and began underwriting mortgages in urban minority neighborhoods. These loans allow for lower down payments than conventional mortgages, but they also involve higher interest rates and higher fees. As discussed below, ethnic minorities tend to receive specialized mortgages with higher interest rates and more risk of foreclosure.

HUD also administers public housing, rental voucher programs, housing and community development block grants, and housing programs serving the elderly, the homeless, and other special needs populations. It also supervised Fannie Mae, Freddie Mac, and Ginnie Mae, the three major institutions in the secondary mortgage market. The Federal National Mortgage Association, known as Fannie Mae, and the Federal Home Loan Mortgage Corporation, known as Freddie Mac, are two private institutions created and monitored by the federal government that provide a secondary market for home mortgages. Fannie Mae was created during the Roosevelt administration as a public agency, but in 1968 Congress changed it to a "government-sponsored enterprise," another example of the interconnection between the private *market economy* and the government. When banks and other local institutions loan money for mortgages, Fannie Mae, Freddie Mac, and Ginnie Mae buy these mortgages, providing a steady source of funds to banks for future mortgages. Thus Fannie Mae and Freddie Mac encourage banks to lend money to potential homeowners and contribute to lower interest rates.[24] The interest rate for home mortgages reflects the prime interest rate set by the Federal Reserve Board, the oversight board appointed by the president designed to regulate the banking industry and monetary policy in the United States.

Beginning in 2000, demand for home purchases and relatively low interest rates, encouraged the banking and other allied industries offering home mortgages to offer home loans at initially low variable interest rates, often with no down payments required. Home equity loans based on variable interest rates also became increasingly popular and encouraged homebuyers to leverage the value of their property. Variable rates, while initially low, are likely to increase over time. An added problem with home equity loans was the fact that these loans were based on the value of the property, not the income of the borrower. Proceeds from home equity loans were used to purchase other goods and took on the illusion of savings for some families. When mortgage interest rates rose, many families could no longer afford to pay their mortgages and home equity loans, resulting in a wave of mortgage foreclosures. Banks took back the foreclosed properties and sold them to others at reduced costs, thus increasing the housing inventory and further depressing the housing market. In a cascading series of consequences, the wave of foreclosures meant that revenue from property taxes was reduced in many cities, reducing public services at a time when the number of persons who are homeless increased.[25] The concept of the "housing bubble," with its artificially inflated housing prices, emerged to parallel the stock market bubble of the 1990s. Both bubbles were deflated when stock prices and housing prices fell dramatically.[26]

While instrumental in making home loans more available, Fannie Mae and Freddie Mac were implicated in the foreclosure crisis because these secondary mortgage banks protected banks offering consumer loans from the risk of unpaid loans and in turn encouraged them to issue more risky loans to consumers. As the value of the mortgages held by these secondary mortgage institutions fell with mortgage foreclosures, the Treasury Department in 2008 declared that the federal government would bail them out, if necessary. In the meantime the government placed Fannie Mae and Freddie Mac under federal control and guaranteed their outstanding debts. This bailout, which began a series of federal interventions, into the financial markets, could cost taxpayers $100 billion or more.[27]

Housing Mortgages and Government Intervention in the Market Economy

In October 2008 the Bush administration proposed a $700 billion rescue of the financial institutions that control the market for credit in the United States, most of which are intimately tied to the stock market. The mortgage meltdown had

Home foreclosure during mortgage crisis

SOURCE: © iStockphoto.

implicated financial firms who had created and then invested in mortgage-backed securities, known as mortgage derivatives. Holding these securities had become a huge liability when the U.S. mortgage market collapsed as homeowners defaulted on their loans. The guarantees to commercial banks offered by Freddie Mac and Fannie Mae had created a virtually risk-free investment with an artificially high return. This caused two problems. First, guaranteed low risk and artificially inflated reward caused money to flow into housing that otherwise would have been more effectively invested in other segments of the economy. As housing prices fell, homeowners saw their equity decline. As mortgages flipped "upside down," properties were worth less than their mortgages. Holders of mortgage-backed securities, absent a true market, had no means to price their investments, making them virtually worthless and unable to be sold. The result was a drying up of liquidity in the credit market as these debts held by financial institutions could not be sold or retired.

At the same time as the value of the mortgage derivatives held by investment firms exceeded their original worth, trading and speculation on Wall Street had pushed the paper value of these securities far beyond their real value. The actual value of these mortgage securities was unknown at the time of the government proposal to buy these securities from investors and rescue the firms from debt. As word of the problems of these investment banks spread, confidence dropped, and a large stock sell-off caused a loss of the paper profits associated with the housing bubble. Eventually, the housing bubble and the financial markets that created mortgage derivatives and traded in them had to burst—an unsupported money expansion can't go on indefinitely.

Initially a government bailout of firms holding mortgage security debt was proposed in order to reestablish the credit markets, the lifeblood of market capitalism, which had frozen due to these debts and lack of liquidity in financial markets. The hope was that these measures would return the stock market to equilibrium. Congress would not pass the rescue legislation until it included several projects that appealed to individual members (known as "pork") and finally agreed to a $820 billion bailout or "rescue" package, funded by federal borrowing through the sale of treasury bonds, adding to the federal deficit and the huge taxpayer burden. At the same time as Congress debated the bailout plan, the failure of the largest U.S. insurance company, AIG, led the federal government to offer the company $150 billion, technically a loan, in rescue funds. The Bush administration abandoned its original strategy of bailing out financial firms with mortgage derivative debt and decided to use at least some of the funds to invest money in banks to encourage them to unfreeze lending to consumers. The Treasury Department, which oversaw the funds, gave $125 billion to the country's nine largest banks and an additional $125 billion to regional banks, but an easing of the credit market did not accompany the infusion of federal resources.[28] The federal government also stepped in to guarantee $1.5 trillion in new debt held by the banking industry and ensure $500 billion in business deposits, making the total cost of the bailout package $2.25 trillion, more than the money spent on the wars in Iraq and Afghanistan. The Treasury Department hoped its investment in the banking industry would be at least partially repaid or even profitable in future years, when government would sell its equity shares in a rising economy as banks returned to financial health.[29] Meanwhile, unemployment rates were rising as consumer confidence was falling; the country was in a recession and possibly heading toward a depression.[30]

This government bailout is unprecedented and constitutes the biggest government intervention in the *market economy* since the New Deal. The Bush administration described the rescue plan as essential in order to stabilize the stock market, protect individual and corporate investments from disappearing further, and return liquidity to the credit markets, freeing up money for business and consumer loans.[31] Underlying the urgency of the Bush administration request for congressional approval of these funds was the implicit realization that an unregulated market economy cannot be sustained. The social construction of the "free market economy" was exposed as an elaborate fiction. The era of deregulation of banks and other financial firms that began under the Clinton and Bush administrations will have long-term negative consequences for taxpayers who have met their own debts in good faith or who have lost homes and savings due to the financial crisis. Although the call for emergency government intervention stood Adam Smith on his head, it did not include a specific provision to allow restructuring of existing high-interest mortgages by financial institutions to make them more affordable; nor did it help any homeowners who had already lost their homes. Estimates were that 6 million people would default on their mortgages in 2008 and 2009, putting them in jeopardy of losing their homes, but no federal action to aid these homeowners was planned.[32] The moral problems inherent in this rescue by taxpayers are obvious: If people taking unnecessary risks are ultimately rewarded, then what is to prevent anyone from taking excessive risks in the future? This crisis in the *market economy* has been called an "earthshaking blow to the most basic principle of our economic system," our belief in the superiority of "free markets," by one economist.[33] If viewed in this light, this government intervention could have the effect of overturning decades of distaste and fear of the regulation of market capitalism.

Discrimination in Housing

One goal of housing policy is to eliminate discrimination in the buying, occupying, and selling of houses. The federal policy passed in 1968 and strengthened in 1988, known as the Fair Housing Act, prohibits racial discrimination by real estate agents and others operating in the housing market. How are people discriminated against in the housing market? They may be told no housing is available in certain areas where housing stock exists or shown fewer rentals or homes for sale than are available. Prospective renters may be offered disadvantaged leases or have their rental applications denied solely on account of their ethnicity. Persons in the market for homeownership may find discrimination in the kind of housing they are shown; for example, they may not be shown housing in White neighborhoods, or they may be discriminated against in the amount and kind of mortgage financing they are offered. For example, they may not be offered the best interest rates, or they may be offered mortgages with higher fees or be asked for higher down payments (see discussion of subprime loans below). Lenders may be more likely to foreclose when mortgage payments are delinquent with ethnic minorities than they would with White borrowers.[34] One of the most infamous forms of discrimination in housing transactions is known as "redlining," when lenders refuse to give loans to persons in specific geographic areas or impose heavy restrictions on borrowers living in areas with high concentrations of ethnic groups, especially African Americans and Latinos. As discussed above, the FHA encouraged redlining in its mortgage policies for decades. Redlining is now illegal, but more informal and equally detrimental discriminatory practices such as those described above still exist in the housing market.

HUD has carried out nationwide audits of discrimination and bias in the housing market since 1977. The most recent audit, in 2000, matched paired auditors, one White and one African American or Latino, in 23 metropolitan areas. The results indicated that African American and Latino renters and homebuyers experienced discrimination in their housing transactions. African Americans most often encountered discrimination in their ability to inspect homes they were interested in purchasing and in the availability of rental housing. Latinos were more likely to encounter discrimination in the availability of rental units as well as in opportunities to inspect homes they wished to purchase. The study found that geographic steering, where clients are shown housing only in areas where their ethnic group predominates, is prevalent.[35]

The growth in the secondary mortgage market discussed above made it easier for African Americans and Latinos to negotiate loans, since more loans were available to consumers. Some of this increase in the amount of credit available was due to the growth of subprime mortgages. Because they are offered to lower-income households with less stable credit histories, subprime mortgages are considered riskier. As a result they have higher costs, including higher interest rates and higher fees. Some purveyors of subprime mortgages utilized predatory lending practices, wherein high-cost loans and high-pressure tactics are marketed to lower-income persons, some of them from ethnic minority groups. As with the home equity loans discussed earlier, subprime loans are often given without respect to the ability of the consumer to pay; instead they are based solely on the value of the property.

Discrimination pervades the subprime mortgage market. A disproportionate rate of subprime loans has been found in minority communities. Many of these households, up to 50%, would have qualified for prime mortgages, which are less costly with lower interest rates and fees, but buyers were not offered prime mortgages by predatory lenders. Homes bought with subprime mortgages are more susceptible to foreclosure, harming minority neighborhoods with abandoned properties and reduced home values. Subprime mortgages are offered for refinancing existing mortgages as well as purchasing new homes. The market for mortgages is bifurcated, with Whites more likely to be offered prime mortgages and African Americans and Latinos more likely to be offered subprime mortgages and suffer a higher rate of foreclosure.[36]

Federal efforts to end discrimination in housing practices began in earnest with the passage of the Fair Housing Act in 1968, which prohibited racial discrimination in sale or rental of housing. The provisions of this act barred landlords and real estate agents from refusing to rent or sell to persons because of their race, outlawed racial discrimination in real estate advertising, barred real estate agents from lying about the availability of housing in order to block sale to ethnic minorities, and forbade agents from discussing the current or potential ethnic composition of a neighborhood in order to "promote panic selling."[37] The Fair Housing Act was a significant shift away from the domination of the free market economy, with its implicit toleration of discriminatory practices. With this policy, as with the Civil Rights Act of 1964 and the Voting Rights Act of 1965, the federal government adopted a social policy that barred ethnic discrimination in areas where longstanding tradition and practices had enshrined it. Of course, passing a law does not automatically eliminate discrimination in housing or elsewhere. The recourse for persons discriminated against focused on civil, not criminal, remedies and depended on actions taken by injured parties. In 1988 Congress strengthened the Fair Housing Act by giving HUD some authority over the enforcement of the law, which now includes laws against discrimination against children and handicapped persons.[38]

Federal efforts to stop banks and other financial institutions from the practice of redlining center on the Community Reinvestment Act, passed in 1977, which requires banks and other financial institutions to serve the credit needs of the communities from which they receive deposits. In other words, if a low-income minority community funds the bank with its deposits, then this bank must also lend to members of the community. Federal bank regulators evaluate the lending practices of banks periodically; those who do not meet the lending needs of their communities to the satisfaction of bank regulators may be denied the right to acquire or merge with other financial institutions, to open other branches, and to engage in other regulated bank practices. Community advocacy groups have the right to challenge proposed bank mergers based on lending practices of institutions. Enforcement of these regulations is left largely in the hands of local and state officials and nonprofit community-based organizations. Nonprofit organizations are also involved in bringing complaints to HUD about violations of the Fair Housing Act. In spite of efforts to toughen these two laws designed to prevent discrimination in housing, their enforcement has fallen far short of what is required to finally eliminate discrimination from the housing market.[39]

Tax Expenditures

The federal government subsidizes a small amount of housing for low-income persons (see below), but the majority of housing subsidy is given to middle-class and wealthy persons through tax expenditures. Tax expenditures are tax revenue not collected due to deductions, credits, and exemptions. Unlike direct subsidies for housing for lower-income persons, tax expenditures are rarely subject to public discussion or debate, yet their impact far exceeds that of direct subsidies. In 2005 the federal government spent $39 billion on public housing, rental vouchers, and other direct housing subsidies, but it provided $121 billion to homeowners through tax expenditures. By far the largest proportion of tax expenditures is the tax deductions given to homeowners who are paying interest on a home mortgage. Other tax benefits enjoyed by homeowners include the deduction of property tax payments and the exclusion of capital gains taxes from the sale of principal residences. Homeowners with high incomes benefit from these tax expenditures much more than do lower-income homeowners, first because lower-income taxpayers are less likely to itemize deductions, which eliminates the use of mortgage interest write-offs, and second because the value of the deduction depends on the tax rate. A $1 deduction for families taxed at the 33% rate is worth $0.33 off of that family's income tax liability, whereas a family taxed at 15% receives only $0.15 off its income tax bill for the same $1 deduction. Thus tax expenditures for housing are more valuable to families with higher incomes.[40] For this reason taxpayers with incomes of $100,000 or more account for more than 54% of the mortgage interest tax deductions, although they only account for 11% of all tax returns; taxpayers earning under $30,000 account for 45% of all taxpayers but receive only 2% of the mortgage interest tax deductions. Taxpayers earning $30,000 to $50,000 make up 20% of all returns but receive only 8% percent of mortgage interest deductions. In sum very few low-income people receive these tax deductions because they are less likely to itemize, less likely to own a home, and in a lower tax bracket that makes their value negligible.[41] The net effect of the homeowner tax deduction is to promote inequality. Renters, who tend to have lower incomes than homeowners, do not receive this tax deduction. The mortgage interest deduction is essentially a reward for high-income families, who are less likely to need such a tax break to purchase and maintain a home in the first place. In fact the mortgage interest deduction is really an incentive to borrow money, rather than merely an incentive to buy a home, because it rewards upper-income persons who pay interest on mortgage loans. The mortgage and banking industries therefore defend this tax expenditure fiercely because it encourages borrowing, one reason that this policy has been resistant to change.[42]

Federal Housing Subsidies

The Department of Housing and Urban Development is the federal agency responsible for administering housing policy for low-income persons. When HUD was first established in 1965, it had a large budget commensurate with its ability to make multiyear grants. In the 1980s the Reagan administration cut the HUD budget by 70%. Currently HUD accounts for only 1% to 2% of the federal budget. The expansion of the supply of affordable housing for low-income families is central to HUD's mission.[43]

In 2005, the federal government spent approximately $39 billion on housing assistance for low-income Americans. This figure is expected to be 19% lower in 2011, if plans to trim housing assistance are fully implemented. As we have seen, the federal government also spent $121 billion in tax expenditures in 2005—more than three times the amount spent on housing assistance for low-income persons. When both housing assistance and tax benefits were taken into account, the poorest fifth of American households—those earning less than $19,000 per year—received approximately $34 billion in housing subsidies in 2006. By way of contrast, the richest fifth of American households (those earning over $92,000) received approximately $94 billion in subsidies, nearly three times more than the poorest fifth and accounting for roughly half of all housing subsidies distributed in 2006.[44]

Public Housing

When the public housing program was first established in 1937, it was seen as a way to generate employment for persons in the construction industry, as much as it was viewed as a means of housing low-income families. The Housing Act of 1949 committed taxpayer funds to the construction of new public housing, which was to be supported largely through tenant rents. Between 1949 and 2004, public housing units increased from approximately 170,000 to over 1,200,000. The peak period was 1994, when 1.4 million units were available. After that date, federal money went into preservation and redevelopment of public housing, rather than construction of new housing. Since the 1990s, the federally supported public housing inventory has declined by more than 150,000 units, due to a policy decision to stop funding construction of public housing in favor of demolition or investment in mixed-use neighborhoods as discussed below. Currently there are about 1.16 million housing units, located in close to 14,000 public housing developments across the country, the majority of which were built before 1985. More than 2.3 million Americans lived in public housing in 2008; 35% of these were families with children, and 65% were disabled or elderly persons. A larger proportion of families living in public housing in 2008 were working than were on welfare.[45]

Support for public housing has declined dramatically, largely because of its negative image and compromised reputation. Public housing has become associated with deep poverty, crime, lack of care, and neglect, even though a large part of the public housing program shelters the elderly and disabled. Large, urban projects housing low-income families have undermined general confidence in public housing, even as few high-rise units remain in public housing stock—most have been torn down. Most public housing developments are more than 30 years old and will need a serious infusion of federal resources over the next few years to maintain livability standards, but this money has not been available since 2000. Approximately $32 billion will be required to renovate some units, demolish others, and construct new ones.[46]

In order to forestall opposition by the real estate industry and its lobbyists when public housing was created in 1937, advocates for public housing agreed that it would not compete with the private housing market. Public housing was mandated to serve the poorest of the poor, those who could not afford private rental housing. This fact, along with the low level of resources that have been committed to public housing over the past 50 years, has seriously hampered the program's flexibility and quality. Strict income requirements are applied before any family is considered eligible, and the vast majority of public housing residents have an annual income of less than $15,000, with an average income of approximately $10,000 per household, including welfare, Social Security, Supplemental Security Income, wages, and other income sources. In 2007 approximately one half of the residents of public housing were White, and 46% were African American. From its inception public housing depended on the desire of local communities to partner with the federal government to establish housing projects. Localities that did not want to have a public housing project in their communities were under no obligation to do so. As a result public housing was confined to low-income urban areas where local governments generally desire to offer housing to low-income persons and excluded from wealthy, middle-class areas. The majority of public housing is located in central urban areas, with far fewer housing projects in suburbs. Residential segregation in public housing was promoted by local authorities. Communities that opposed the establishment of public housing with ethnically mixed or predominantly minority residents were free to exclude them. Housing projects in low-income White communities served predominantly White residents. The segregation of public housing evident today is due to these early local decisions about who could live in which communities.[47]

Public housing looks different from other rental housing, another factor in stigma associated with it. The main reason for this difference in construction standards, landscaping, and so forth is the budgetary constraints on construction of public housing established by the federal government in 1937 and again in the Housing Act of 1949. Additional factors include the desire not to compete with private rental housing, which reduced the number of amenities and conveniences, leading to apartments having cinderblock walls; few common spaces and elevators, even in high-rise buildings; and open lobbies. Much of the public housing stock has been improved with renovation or even demolition and rebuilding. Most public housing now serves seniors and people with disabilities or provides homes to families with children in small or medium-sized developments outside of high-poverty areas.[48]

Recognizing the difficulties associated with having only very low-income families living in public housing, Congress in 1974 and again in 1998 attempted to reduce the percentage of low-income persons residing in public housing by increasing the number of rental vouchers offered to these families in order to encourage them to look for housing outside public housing. Some policymakers have argued that public housing should be eliminated altogether and housing help for lower-income persons should be limited to vouchers. Yet vouchers have limitations: The majority of households in public housing include an elderly person or an individual with a disability; both groups often have difficulty finding units to rent with vouchers. Many public housing developments are arranged to accommodate residents' mobility impairments; private housing usually is not. Many private landlords are unwilling to accept vouchers; the vacancy rate may be low, and some elderly or disabled consumers may have difficulty using vouchers. Finally, renting in the private market does not offer the support services available for elderly and disabled persons through some housing projects.[49]

HOPE VI Program

Under HUD's HOPE VI program, launched in 1992, the federal government offered grants to local housing agencies to redevelop and redesign public housing. HOPE VI awarded local housing authorities grants on a competitive basis to demolish public housing units and replace them with refurbished apartments featuring amenities found in private market rentals. The goal was to offer mixed-income housing to the local community and at the same time offer former tenants vouchers to rent apartments in the private market.[50] Since HOPE VI began, many distressed public housing projects formerly filled with low-income families have been redesigned to encourage mixed-income occupancy and reconstitute the projects as multiuse residences. Local housing authorities have been given HUD grants to demolish and redevelop dilapidated public housing units. HOPE VI's goal of building economically diverse but integrated communities and giving former residents more purchasing power in the private rental market has had mixed success. Many former residents of public housing projects have moved to much safer neighborhoods since 2000, but some remain in their original neighborhoods, living with drug trafficking and violent crime. Of those remaining in public housing, half reported serious problems with crime and drug trafficking.[51] Partly as a result of these problems, support for Hope VI has waned, and the Bush administration cut monies to support it. Congress finally reauthorized funding for HOPE VI and other funds for public housing in 2008, although at a much reduced level.

HOPE VI also offers funds for supportive services for residents of public housing, such as job training and day care. One study looked at five developments where residents were given the opportunity to move out of housing projects in 2000. Close to half of the residents moved to market-based rental housing, utilizing housing vouchers. Children in families who moved out of public housing did better in school than children whose families stayed. Yet poor health and health access problems were reported to be severe in both groups 5 years later.[52] A recurring complaint about the impact of HOPE VI on former housing project residents is that one set of miseries was exchanged for another, as former public housing tenants moved to equally poor, racially segregated neighborhoods, the only places they could afford rental housing with their vouchers. Relocating the housing project tenants to adjacent areas imported more poverty to those areas, according to some critics.[53] Moving low-income persons around without changing their underlying circumstances can accomplish little.

Low-Income Housing Tax Credit (LIHTC)

Another far more indirect source of funding for public housing is the Low-Income Housing Tax Credit (LIHTC), established in 1986, a federal program giving tax credits to states that in turn give the credits to developers of low-income housing, who then sell the tax credits to investors who are incentivized to invest in low-income housing. These tax credits can be used against any income, so they are attractive to investors. LIHTC thus draws capital to low-income housing that would not otherwise be available because of the low return on investment discussed earlier in this chapter. By stimulating private investment, this indirect federal subsidy effectively sidesteps the question of whether to support outright federal grants for low-income housing.

Housing Vouchers—Section 8 Housing

The second major way the federal government supports low-income housing is the voucher program discussed above. Originally established in Section 8 of the Housing Act of 1974, vouchers are issued to low-income families to purchase housing on the private rental market. The voucher program is administered by HUD and by local housing authorities. Vouchers constitute the largest housing subsidy offered by the federal government. Vouchers are less expensive than public housing since they utilize preexisting housing stock and they offer greater freedom of location to consumers using the vouchers. However, there are fundamental problems with vouchers, all of which can be summed up under the fact that receiving a voucher does not guarantee that housing will be available. Some of the difficulties inherent in using HUD vouchers include the fact that a rental unit approved under the voucher program must meet federal housing standards, the rental unit must charge below the maximum allowable rent, and the landlord must be willing to accept federal vouchers. Section 8 vouchers depend for implementation on a network of over 2,000 local, state, and regional housing organizations. Low-income families with children, elderly, and persons with disabilities are eligible for vouchers. Families with children receive approximately 60% of Section 8 vouchers; the rest are divided between elderly persons and persons with disabilities. There is a waiting list in many areas of the country to receive vouchers; many more persons are eligible for them than receive them. In 2006 over 40% of local housing agencies had closed their waiting lists due to excess demand for vouchers.

When families or individuals receive a voucher, they have 60 days to find a qualifying apartment and a landlord willing to accept it. If they do not find housing in this period, they lose the voucher. About 30% of households receiving vouchers were unable to utilize them in 2000. Elderly persons have a lower rate of success in terms of utilization of vouchers than other groups. To qualify for the voucher program, households are required to contribute

30% of their income for rent and utilities. Local agencies are awarded a set number of vouchers to allocate each year, based on the number awarded the previous year. Federal funding of vouchers is thus tied closely to previous years' funding, limiting the responsiveness of the program to current needs. Funding for new vouchers can occur in case of emergencies, such as Hurricanes Katrina and Rita.

Used extensively, vouchers can reduce homelessness and housing instability and assist families in moving out of high-poverty neighborhoods. Vouchers have been shown to reduce food insecurity in families receiving them by freeing more family income from housing costs. Under the voucher program, rents charged to families rise as family income rises, leading some to fear that vouchers discourage work. Recent research has found that receiving a voucher had no significant impact on work or unemployment, refuting this theory.[54] One effect of vouchers is to encourage residential segregation, since because of discrimination African Americans and Latinos who hold vouchers are likely to be unable to rent in predominantly White neighborhoods. This result is in direct opposition to the stated federal goals of poverty deconcentration and racial integration associated with the voucher program.[55] Another factor increasing poverty concentration and segregation in the use of vouchers is the rising costs of rents in many urban areas. Vouchers are limited in how much rent they will subsidize, and landlords in competitive rental markets may not be interested in participating in the voucher program, with its rent limitations and administrative requirements.

Housing for Elderly Persons

Elderly persons have distinct housing needs, and many elderly persons have experienced difficulties in accessing housing using Section 8 vouchers. The federal government recognized the lack of fit between vouchers and some elderly persons, especially the frail elderly, who may have difficulty locating adequate housing on the private market. Many seniors need more than housing; they need social services or special housing with access for wheelchairs and walkers. This issue will continue to grow as baby boomers age. The largest federal program designed to meet the needs of elderly persons is Section 202, designed to empower nonprofit organizations to build and operate housing for low-income elderly. This program provides grants for capital necessary to construct or rehabilitate housing suitable for seniors, as well as assistance with rental costs for seniors living in these housing units.

Administered by HUD, the program has produced more than 6,000 housing facilities that include over 250,000 units since its inception in 1959. Some of these housing facilities employ a HUD service coordinator to assist elderly persons with their needs and to perform case management tasks. Since most elderly would prefer to stay in their own homes when possible, those seniors who choose to live in Section 202–supported housing are older and frailer, with the average age in the high 70s.[56]

Housing Opportunities for Persons With AIDS (HOPWA)

Established by the Affordable Housing Act of 1990, HOPWA funds housing for low-income persons with HIV/AIDS and their families. States and metropolitan areas are allocated these funds based on their eligible population; 90% of the funds are designated for 83 metropolitan areas and 34 states with populations of at least 500,000 and with at least 1,500 cases of AIDS. The funds can be used by local governments and nonprofit agencies to offer supportive services to persons who wish to remain in their homes, enable homeless persons to secure affordable housing, and provide other services such as health care, mental health treatment, treatment for chemical dependency, nutritional and case management services, and assistance with activities of daily living. Housing costs, including construction or rehabilitation of new housing and rental assistance, are also funded through this program.[57]

Community Development Block Grants

Replacing programs for urban renewal and Model Cities, the Community Development Block Grants (CDBG) were established in 1974 under HUD with the goal of developing decent housing and expanded economic opportunities for low-income persons. Included in the funding guidelines are the acquisition or retention of real property, the rehabilitation of residential and nonresidential buildings, social services, and economic developments. Public works and government maintenance cannot be funded, but otherwise the block grants give localities a great deal of leeway. HUD gives annual grants to larger cities and urban communities to encourage the development of viable communities in low- and moderate-income areas. The program offers local communities more flexibility than other HUD programs. In 2005 the CDBG budget was $4.7 billion, a reduction from previous years.[58]

The Housing Trust Fund

In 2008 Congress passed the Housing and Economic Recovery Act and established a Housing Trust Fund, a permanent program with a dedicated source of funding. At least 90% of the funds in the Housing Trust Fund must be used for the production, preservation, rehabilitation, or operation of rental housing. Up to 10% can be used for the following: homeownership activities for first-time homebuyers; production, preservation, and rehabilitation of housing stock; down payment assistance; closing cost assistance; and assistance for interest rate buy-downs. At least 75% of the funds for rental housing must benefit extremely low-income (30% or less of area median income) households, and all funds must benefit very low-income households (50% or less of area median income).[59] The designers of the program clearly recognized the need for an ongoing government structure to fund and oversee affordable housing construction. See Table 10.4 for a summary of federal housing policies.

RECOMMENDATIONS FOR NEW HOUSING POLICIES ●

Tax Expenditures for Homeowners

Eliminating tax expenditures for homeowners is essential for the promotion of social justice and equity in housing policy. Housing credit should be given to all taxpayers and be refundable for low-income persons paying little or no taxes. Earned Income Tax Credits could be used to return housing credits to these taxpayers, in which case the tax refunds should be tied to the median housing costs in metropolitan areas, which would dramatically improve access to existing housing by low-income families. If childless couples were included in this Earned Income Tax Credit increase, housing cost burdens could be relieved for an additional 500,000 families.[60] Utilizing the Earned Income Tax Credit policy would supplement the existing federal policies supporting low-income housing and cover more people with housing needs. Universal policies administered through the tax system are ultimately preferable to piecemeal legislative programs, which can be cut or disappear according to political contingencies.

Housing Vouchers and Public Housing

The federal budget has cut monies for Section 8 housing and other housing programs for homeless persons since 2005. While many policymakers would

TABLE 10.4   **Summary of Federal Housing Policies Outlining Provisions and Impact on Problem**

Federal Policies	Time Frame	Provisions	Impact on Problem
Federal Housing Administration (FHA)	Established under Roosevelt administration in 1934	• Established to stimulate new housing construction and reduce unemployment in the construction industry • Federal government offered government-insured mortgages for qualified lenders to encourage the private mortgage industry to offer more funds at lower interest rates	• By setting standards for home construction, the FHA also reassured lenders about the soundness of the properties they were underwriting and encouraged more lending • Encouraged widespread homeownership among White working-class persons in the suburban areas in the 1950s and 1960s but not in ethnic minority groups and mixed neighborhoods • Federal government fostered segregation and inequality with this practice • FHA changed these practices in the 1980s and began underwriting mortgages in urban minority neighborhoods
Legislation that created public housing and Housing Act of 1937	1937	• Supply side housing policy, where the government provides living units at affordable prices OR • Housing Act of 1937 committed taxpayer funds to the construction of new public housing, which was to be supported largely through tenant rents • Public housing was mandated to serve the poorest of the poor, those who could not afford private rental housing	• Public housing units increased from approximately 170,000 to over 1,200,000 between 1949 and 2004 • Since the 1990s, the federally supported public housing inventory has declined by more than 150,000 units, due to a policy decision to stop funding construction of public housing in favor of demolition or investment in mixed-use neighborhoods discussed below • Support for public housing has greatly declined

Federal Policies	Time Frame	Provisions	Impact on Problem
Department of Housing and Urban Development (HUD)	Founded in 1965	• Designed to oversee public housing and other subsidy programs • Administers public housing, rental voucher programs, housing and community development block grants, and housing programs serving the elderly, the homeless, and other special-needs populations • HUD directs the FHA insurance program and supervises Fannie Mae, Freddie Mac, and Ginnie Mae, the three major institutions in the secondary mortgage market	• Fannie Mae, Freddie Mac, and Ginnie Mae bought mortgages, providing a steady source of funds to banks for future mortgages and encouraging banks to lend money to potential homeowners and contribute to lower interest rates • In 2000, demand for home purchases and relatively low interest rates encouraged the banking and other allied industries offering home mortgages to offer home loans at initially low variable interest rates, often with no down payments required, and made home loans more available, which led to a housing bubble and mortgage meltdown • Federal government placed Fannie Mae and Freddie Mac under federal control to guarantee their outstanding debts
Housing Voucher Section 8 of Housing Act	1974	• Vouchers are issued to low-income families to purchase housing in the private rental market • Largest government housing subsidy	• Vouchers are less expensive than public housing since they utilize preexisting housing stock and they offer greater freedom of location to consumers using the vouchers • Receiving a voucher does not guarantee that housing will be available
Fair Housing Act	Passed in 1975 and strengthened in 1988	• Prohibits racial discrimination by real estate agents and others operating in the housing market • Barred landlords and real estate agents from refusing to rent or sell to persons because of their race	• Disproportionate rate of subprime loans has been found in minority communities

(Continued)

TABLE 10.4 (Continued)

Federal Policies	Time Frame	Provisions	Impact on Problem
		• Outlawed racial discrimination in real estate advertising • Barred real estate agents from lying about the availability of housing in order to block sale to ethnic minorities • Forbade agents from discussing the current or potential ethnic composition of a neighborhood in order to promote panic selling • Congress strengthened the Fair Housing Act by giving HUD some authority over the enforcement of the law, which now includes laws against discrimination against children and handicapped persons	
Community Reinvestment Act	1977	• Required banks and other financial institutions to serve the credit needs of the communities from which they receive deposits	• Helped stop "redlining," when lenders refuse to give loans to persons in specific geographic areas or impose heavy restrictions on borrowers living in areas with high concentrations of ethnic groups, especially African Americans and Latinos
Low-Income Housing Tax Credit (LIHTC)	1986	• A federal program giving tax credits to states, which in turn give the credits to developers of low-income housing, who then sell the tax credits to investors who are incentivized to invest in low-income housing	• By stimulating private investment, this indirect federal subsidy effectively sidesteps the question of whether to support outright federal grants for low-income housing

Federal Policies	Time Frame	Provisions	Impact on Problem
Housing Opportunities for Persons With AIDS (HOPWA)	1990	• Funds housing for low-income persons with HIV/AIDS and their families	• Funds can be used by local governments and nonprofit agencies to offer supportive services to persons who wish to remain in their homes, enable homeless persons to secure affordable housing, and provide other services such as health care, mental health treatment, treatment for chemical dependency, nutritional and case management services, and assistance with activities of daily living
HOPE VI Program	1992	• Federal government offered grants to local housing agencies to redevelop and redesign public housing • Goal was to offer mixed-income housing to the local community and at the same time offer former tenants vouchers to rent apartments in the private market • Also offers funds for supportive services for residents of public housing, such as job training and day care	• Many distressed public housing projects have been redesigned to encourage mixed-income occupancy and reconstitute the projects as multiuse residences • Goal of building economically diverse but integrated communities and giving former residents more purchasing power in the private rental market has had mixed success • Bush administration cut monies to support it. Congress finally reauthorized funding and other funds for public housing in 2008, although at a much reduced level
Housing and Economic Recovery Act	2008	• Established a Housing Trust Fund where 90% of the funds in the trust fund must be used for the production, preservation, rehabilitation, or operation of rental housing	• At least 75% of the funds for rental housing must benefit extremely low-income (30% or less of area median income) households, and all funds must benefit very low-income households (50% or less of area median income)

(Continued)

TABLE 10.4 (Continued)

Federal Policies	Time Frame	Provisions	Impact on Problem
		• Up to 10% can be used for the following: homeownership activities for first-time home buyers; production, preservation, and rehabilitation of housing stock; down payment assistance; closing cost assistance; and assistance for interest rate buy-downs	• This creates an ongoing government structure to fund and oversee affordable housing construction
Government Intervention in Housing Market	2008	• Congress passed an $820 billion bailout or "rescue" package, funded by federal government borrowing through the sale of treasury bonds, adding to the federal deficit and the huge taxpayer burden	• This government bailout is unprecedented and constitutes the biggest government intervention in the market economy since the New Deal

like to replace public housing with tenant-based vouchers, the two programs are not completely interchangeable. Many public housing developments provide benefits that housing vouchers do not, especially for elderly and disabled persons. As discussed above, not all neighborhoods have landlords willing to accept vouchers or housing that meets federal standards, forcing elderly persons to move out of these neighborhoods. Combining the demolition of public housing with a voucher program for former residents will limit access of millions of low-income families to housing assistance. According to the National Low Income Housing Coalition, not *all* public housing merits preservation; a small proportion of remaining units are located in areas where preservation may be ineffective or counterproductive.[61]

As we have seen, there are many federal policies currently in place to increase the access of low-income persons to adequate housing, but the availability of federal and state support to ensure their ongoing viability is problematic. Public housing needs federal resources for ongoing operation, as well as for future rehabilitation and conversion to mixed use, where feasible. HUD should combine the voucher program and public housing in one program, to ensure that both programs work together to meet community needs in an integrated manner. Both programs are essential for low-income persons who cannot purchase housing in the private housing market. Over 150,000 vouchers have been lost in budget cuts since 2005; these should be restored. The LIHTC can be utilized as an important supplemental resource for public housing redevelopment, as long as states commit the limited amount of such credits they receive to public housing. Congress should consider measures to further support use of LIHTCs at public housing developments.

HUD should discourage local housing agencies from retaining or establishing large non-mixed-income housing projects in low-opportunity areas with high poverty rates or high crime rates, low-quality schools, and low access to public transportation and other services, in light of research that demonstrates adverse effects on public housing tenants living in large developments in these areas. Instead these developments should be converted to mixed-income projects or should be relocated in higher-opportunity neighborhoods. This would eliminate extreme concentrations of poor families in neighborhoods with public housing, which research has linked to harmful effects on residents, especially children.[62] Restoring funding for HOPE VI to its level in 2003, before the sharp funding cuts of recent years, would enable these changes in the location and configuration of public housing. Requiring mixed-income development would provide upward pressure on quality by attracting people paying market rates for rentals.[63]

CONCLUSION

From its beginning in the New Deal, housing policy for low-income people in the United States has been inextricably tied to the needs of the *market economy,* especially the homebuilding and financial sectors that had collapsed during the Great Depression. Key business leaders were involved in the development of the Housing Act of 1937. Leaders of the real estate, insurance, and banking industries all testified in favor of the legislation. Their hope was that federal funding would revitalize their sectors of the economy and provide a needed infusion of government monies to solve their economic problems.[64] In this respect little has changed. The housing market and federal housing problems are intimately connected to the larger market forces and have less to do with the needs of low-income and marginalized groups than with the resolution of economic downturns. Profits made in housing construction, sales, and loans have been the driving force in the shifting housing policies and regulations sponsored by the federal government.

The *historical ideologies* that assume that everyone who works hard has equal opportunity to move up the economic ladder presume that securing housing is an automatic result of personal qualities of self-reliance, individualism, and hard work. Unfortunately, separating the reality from these historically based assumptions has been particularly difficult in the creation of housing policy. The reluctance to provide extensive housing support disproportionately affects members of oppressed ethnic groups, who also have to face *discrimination* in the housing market when they do attempt to access housing in the private market. As long as housing policy remains the handmaiden of the *market economy*, the real needs of disadvantaged Americans will be an afterthought. The separation of housing policy from the vagaries of the market economy through the public provision and guarantee of affordable housing should be the first priority for those seeking to promote social justice in access to housing in the United States.

Policy Analysis Example: Public Housing Policy

Implications of the Policy

1. Changes in the distribution of material resources. Are there any changes to the distribution of material resources, including income and other tangible benefits, as a result of the policy for direct or indirect target groups?

Persons living in public housing receive shelter at low cost subsidized by taxpayers. They are eligible for housing without time restrictions. Depending on their continuing eligibility, they can stay in this housing for many years, thereby achieving housing security. Indirect targets of the housing program include housing providers on the private market who may lose renters, although the program is geared to those who cannot afford to purchase housing in the private market.

Another resource many public housing units provide to residents is accommodations and services provided to elderly or disabled persons. Indirect targets of the public housing policy include families who do not have to share accommodations with family members who do not have stable housing, homeless shelters, and transitional housing facilities that have more space available for others with housing needs due to the provision of public housing for some. Some persons living in public housing have had direct experience with drug trafficking and crime; others living in mixed housing developments sponsored by federal programs like Hope VI have found the quality of life improved as a result of living in mixed public housing.

2. Changes in distribution of services, rights, and statuses. Are there any changes in the services, rights, or statuses as a result of the policy?

Under Hope VI services such as job training and day care—services unavailable or unaffordable outside of public housing—may be offered to residents. Public housing may carry a stigma for some of its residents, giving them a separate and reduced status in their communities. Public housing has tended to increase discrimination and segregation, as most public housing units are segregated by practice and found in residentially segregated communities. The right to live in diverse communities is limited by public housing. Children living in public housing tend to do poorly in school compared to those living in private housing. Health indicators are lower for families in public housing, suggesting that economic and other conditions there do not foster health. Fear of crime and risk of drug use are psychological stressors that may be increased among public housing residents. Thus the likelihood of incurring the unwanted status of crime victim or drug abuser may be increased among those living in public housing, while the status of homeless person may be reduced.

DISCUSSION QUESTIONS

1. What are the limitations of the McKinney-Vento Homeless Assistance Act?

2. What are the causes of the affordable housing crisis? Which new policies do you think would make a positive difference in the amount of affordable housing available to low-income persons?

3. Why are tax expenditures given to home buyers and not renters? Should tax expenditures be continued? If so, in what form?

4. How have factors related to discrimination influenced housing policies and the availability of affordable housing for certain ethnic groups?

5. What are the strengths and limitations of public housing and Section 8 vouchers?

6. What are the limitations of the market economy in providing access to housing?

7. How did declining housing prices trigger a crisis in the broader economy?

8. How would you change housing policy to ensure more equitable access to all forms of housing, including homeownership?

NOTES

1. Martha Burt, Laudan Aron, and Edgar Lee, *Helping America's Homeless* (Washington, DC: The Urban Institute Press, 2001), 2.

2. U.S. Department of Housing and Urban Development, "Federal Definition of Homeless," http://www.hud.gov/homeless/definition.cfm, accessed August 20, 2007.

3. Burt et al., *Helping America's Homeless*, 6.

4. U.S. Department of Housing and Urban Development, "The Third Annual Homeless Assessment Report to Congress," July 2008, http://www.hudhre.info/documents/3rdHomelessAssessmentReport.pdf, accessed August 20, 2007.

5. Ibid.

6. Ibid.

7. Martin Donohoe, "Homelessness in the United States," *MedScape: Ob/Gyn & Women's Health*, July 7, 2004, http://www.medscape.com/viewarticle/481800, accessed August 23, 2008.

8. National Coalition for the Homeless, "Homeless Youth," June 2008, http://www.nationalhomeless.org/publications/facts/youth.pdf, accessed August 22, 2008.

9. U.S. Department of Education, "Education for Homeless Children and Youth Program," July 2004, http://www.ed.gov/programs/homeless/guidance.pdf, accessed August 22, 2008.

10. Michael Katz, *In the Shadow of the Poorhouse* (New York: Basic Books, 1996), 85–113.

11. Allen Tullos, "The Black Belt," *Southern Spaces*, April 2004, http://www.southernspaces.org/contents/2004/tullos/4a.htm, accessed August 23, 2008.

12. Burt et al., *Helping America's Homeless*, 98–99.

13. Debra Hernandez Jozefowicz-Simbeni and Nathaniel Israel, "Services to Homeless Students and Families: The McKinney-Vento Act and Its Implications for Social Work Practice," *Children and School* 28 (January 2006): 37–44.

14. Burt et al., *Helping America's Homeless*, 149.

15. National Coalition for the Homeless, "McKinney-Vento Act," June 2008, http://www.nationalhomeless.org/publications/facts/McKinney.pdf, accessed August 23, 2008.

16. Martha R. Burt, "Strategies for Reducing Chronic Street Homelessness," Urban Institute, March 2004, http://ww.urban.org/url.cfm? ID=1000775, accessed August 24, 2008; Martha Burt, "Reauthorization of the McKinney-Vento Homeless Assistance Act," October 16, 2007, Urban Institute, http://www.urban.org/publications/901120.html, accessed April 12, 2009.

17. Joint Center for Housing Studies of Harvard University, "State of the Nation's Housing," June 23, 2008, http://www.jchs.harvard.edu/media/son2008_fact_sheet.pdf, accessed September 4, 2008.

18. U.S. Department of Housing and Urban Development, "Affordable Housing," http://www.hud.gov/offices/cpd/affordablehousing/index.cfm, accessed August 25, 2008.

19. National Low Income Housing Coalition, "Out of Reach 2007–2008," http://www.nlihc.org/oor/oor2008/, accessed September 4, 2008.

20. Alex Schwartz, *Housing Policy in the United States* (New York: Routledge, 2006), 28.

21. Schwartz, *Housing Policy in the United States*, 31–32.

22. Schwartz, *Housing Policy in the United States*, 5.

23. Schwartz, *Housing Policy in the United States*, 51; Kenneth Jackson, *Crabgrass Frontier: The Suburbanization of the United States* (New York: Oxford University Press, 1985), 191–210.

24. William Rohe and Harry Watson, "Homeownership in American Culture and Public Policy," in William Rohe and Harry Watson, eds., *Chasing the American Dream: New Perspectives on Affordable Home Ownership* (Ithaca, NY: Cornell University Press, 2007), 1–13; Schwartz, *Housing Policy in the United States*, 57.

25. National League of Cities, "Housing Finance and Foreclosures Crisis: Local Impact and Responses," April 2008, http://www.nlc.org/ASSETS/580A9E2DD 59E42809E3C4FBBD6AC1A99/PARHousingRB2008.pdf, accessed September 13, 2008.

26. Joel Blau with Mimi Abramovitz, *The Dynamics of Social Welfare Policy* (New York: Oxford University Press, 2007), 360–361.

27. Stephen Labaton and Andrew Sorkin, "U.S. Rescue Seen at Hand for Two Mortgage Giants," *New York Times,* September 6, 2008, A1; Stephen Labaton, "All Grown Up and, Some Say, Unneeded," *New York Times,* September 15, 2008, 4, wk.

28. Edmund Andrews, "U.S. Shifts Focus in Credit Bailout to Consumer," *New York Times,* November 13, 2008, A1.

29. Mark Landler and Eric Dash, "Drama Behind a Banking Deal," *New York Times,* October 15, 2008, A1; Floyd Norris, "A Winner for Treasury? Time Will Tell," *New York Times,* October 15, 2008, B1.

30. Paul Krugman, "Depression Economics Returns," *New York Times,* November 14, 2008, A29.

31. Julie Creswell and Ben White, "Wall Street, RIP," *New York Times,* September 28, 2008, A1; Peter Bernstein," What's Free About Free Enterprise?" *New York Times,* September 28, 2008, BU1.

32. *New York Times,* "Show Us the Hope," A30, October 2, 2008.

33. Bernstein, "What's Free About Free Enterprise?" BU8.

34. Daniel Immergluck, *Credit to the Community: Community Reinvestment and Fair Lending Policy in the United States* (Armonk, NY: M. E. Sharpe, 2004), 2–17.

35. U.S. Department of Housing and Urban Development, "Discrimination in Metropolitan Housing Markets: National Results from Phase I of HDS2000: Executive Summary," http://www.huduser.org/Publications/pdf/Phase1_Executive_Summary.pdf, accessed September 23, 2008; Schwartz, *Housing Policy in the United States,* 218–227.

36. Schwartz, *Housing Policy in the United States,* 233–237.

37. Douglas Massey and Nancy Denton, *American Apartheid* (Cambridge, MA: Harvard University Press, 1993), 195.

38. U.S. Department of Housing and Urban Development, "Fair Housing and Equal Opportunity," April 30, 2008, http://www.hud.gov/offices/fheo/, accessed September 26, 2008.

39. Schwartz, *Housing Policy in the United States,* 242–246.

40. J. Michael Collins, "Federal Policies Promoting Home Ownership," in William Rohe and Harry Watson, eds., *Chasing the American Dream: New Perspectives on Affordable Home Ownership* (Ithaca, NY: Cornell University Press, 2007), 67–93.

41. Adam Carasso, "Who Receives Homeownership Tax Deductions and How Much?" Urban Institute, August 1, 2005, http://www.urban.org/publications/1000804 .html, accessed September 14, 2008.

42. Collins, "Federal Policies Promoting Home Ownership," 79, 83.

43. U.S. Department of Housing and Urban Development, "Affordable Housing."

44. Schwartz, *Housing Policy in the United States,* 69–73.

45. U.S. Department of Housing and Urban Development, "HUD's Public Housing Program," November 28, 2007, http://www.hud.gov/renting/phprog.cfm, accessed September 17, 2008.

46. Barbara Sard and Will Fischer, "Preserving Safe, High Quality Public Housing Should Be a Priority of Federal Housing Policy," Center on Budget and Policy

Priorities, revised October 8, 2008, http://www.cbpp.org/cms/?fa=view&id=655, accessed October 2008.

47. Schwartz, *Housing Policy in the United States,* 106–111.

48. Sard and Fischer, "Preserving Safe, High Quality Public Housing Should Be a Priority of Federal Housing Policy."

49. Sard and Fischer, "Preserving Safe, High Quality Public Housing Should Be a Priority of Federal Housing Policy."

50. Schwartz, *Housing Policy in the United States,* 117–121.

51. Susan Popkin, Bruce Katz, Mary Cunningham, Karen Brown, Jeremy Gustafson, and Margery Austin Turner, "A Decade of HOPE VI," Urban Institute, May 18, 2004, http://www.urban.org/publications/411002.html, accessed September 19, 2008.

52. The Urban Institute, "Many From Nation's Most Beleaguered Public Housing Projects Moved to Safer Neighborhoods but Challenges Remain," June 26, 2007, http://www.urban.org/publications/901091.html, accessed September 25, 2008.

53. Sudhir Venkatesh, "To Fight Poverty, Tear Down HUD," *Los Angeles Times,* July 25, 2008, A19.

54. Center on Budget and Policy Priorities, "Policy Basics: Introduction to the Housing Voucher Program," July 6, 2007, http://www.centeronbudget.org/cms/index.cfm?fa=view&id=279, accessed September 26, 2008.

55. Schwartz, *Housing Policy in the United States,* 166.

56. U.S. Department of Housing and Urban Development, "Section 202 Supportive Housing for the Elderly Program," November 8, 2007, http://www.hud.gov/offices/hsg/mfh/progdesc/eld202.cfm, accessed September 28, 2008; Schwartz, *Housing Policy in the United States,* 206–208.

57. U.S. Department of Housing and Urban Development, "Housing Opportunities for Persons With AIDS (HOPWA) Program," June 19, 2008, http://www.hud.gov/offices/cpd/aidshousing/programs/, accessed September 28, 2008.

58. U.S. Department of Housing and Urban Development, "Community Development Block Grant Program," September 23, 2008, http://www.hud.gov/offices/cpd/communitydevelopment/programs/, accessed September 26, 2008; Schwartz, *Housing Policy in the United States,* 180–182.

59. National Low Income Housing Coalition, "National Housing Trust Fund," http://www.nlihc.org/template/page.cfm?id=40, accessed April 12, 2009.

60. Michael Stegman, Walter Davis, and Roberto Quercia, "Tax Policy as Housing Policy: The EITC's Potential to Make Housing More Affordable for Working Families. Urban Institute," October, 2003, http://.www.urban.org/url.cfrm?ID=1000973.

61. National Low Income Housing Coalition, "National Housing Trust Fund," http://www.nlihc.org/template/page.cfm?id=40, accessed April 12, 2009.

62. Sard and Fischer, "Preserving Safe, High Quality Public Housing Should Be a Priority of Federal Housing Policy."

63. National Low Income Housing Coalition, "National Housing Trust Fund."

64. Frank Gotham, "Racialization and the State: The Housing Act of 1934 and the Creation of the Federal Housing Administration," *Sociological Perspectives* 43 (2, 2000): 291–317.

11

The Impact of Globalization and the Post-9/11 United States

CHAPTER QUESTIONS

1. What is globalization? What has been its impact on the U.S. economy and on the economies of developing countries?

2. How has globalization impacted human migration and trafficking?

3. What are the implications for human rights across the globe under globalization?

4. What has been the impact of 9/11 on social policy in the United States?

5. What is the impact of the wars in Iraq and Afghanistan on social policy in the United States?

6. What does the election of Barack Obama signify in terms of future openings for social justice and social change?

● ● ●

INTRODUCTION ●

What is globalization, and why should social workers care about it? According to a leading economist and expert on globalization, it involves the "closer integration of the countries and peoples of the world . . . brought about by the enormous reduction of costs of transportation and communication and the breaking down of artificial barriers to the flows of goods, services, capital, knowledge . . . across borders."[1] In other words globalization begins with the lowering of tariffs ("artificial barriers") between countries, which protect domestic manufacture from competition from foreign goods. Globalization encourages free movement of capital, goods, and services through reduction of trade barriers, but it does not formally encourage migration of people from one country to another. While social workers in the industrialized world may have given little thought to the impact of globalization on their clients and their practice, in less developed countries globalization has been a routine part of daily economic, political, and social life. These transnational corporations have brought both the benefits of market capitalism and its accompanying social costs or externalities. Social workers in industrialized nations may notice the impact of globalization in the contraction of jobs at home, as corporations increasingly choose to operate in developing countries where labor is cheaper and regulations affecting corporations and corporate profits are fewer. They may experience the impact of globalization through the increased migration of workers, both voluntary and involuntary, to their countries. They may experience the environmental impact of the global economic network as pollution brought by transnational corporations to developing countries spread to their own borders. They and their clients may be affected by global diseases such as HIV/AIDS or avian flu, which transcend national boundaries. Finally they may experience the perils of unstable global financial markets jeopardizing the economic stability of their home countries. Yet globalization itself has the potential for many positive outcomes, including an increased awareness of multicultural connections among people all over the world. One social work scholar defined globalization as a "process of global integration in which diverse peoples, economics, cultures and political processes are increasingly subjected to international influences." At its best, the process of globalization could lead to an "inclusive worldwide culture, a global economy and above all, a shared awareness of the world as a single place."[2]

The term *international social work* has often been added to textbooks and social work courses as a means of acknowledging that social workers operate in an interconnected world, but the discussion of international social work has often been focused on international organizations, rather than on social problems resulting from the operation of multinational corporations in less developed countries. Globalization is not the same as international social work, which some argue has been based on a Western model of social work endeavoring to influence the rest of the world (especially underdeveloped countries) through "postcolonial cultural hegemony."[3] Although European colonial rule ended in the mid-20th century when previously colonized countries threw off their former rulers, Western political and economic control of developing countries continued their cultural domination. The West claimed superiority over other less developed countries through its assumption that economic and technological progress made Western countries inevitably superior. In the Western hemisphere, for example, the United States attempted to maintain its cultural and economic influence over Central and South America. Western cultural models, including social work education and practice, were exported to other countries under the conviction that they were universally applicable. Insofar as proponents of international social work have attempted to export Western social work models to other countries without incorporating other cultural worldviews and practices, they have participated in a postcolonial agenda. Some question whether globalization is essentially the same as postcolonialism, where the industrial Global Northern countries dominate the world.[4]

Unquestionably, globalization has had positive results for some people in countries in the Global South, a term some writers prefer to *developing*, which implies that development is a desirable end goal.[5] Many people in the Global South live better and longer lives as a result of their countries' interaction with the global economy; some of these countries have had their debt forgiven by the countries in the Global North, foreign aid to the Global South has increased, and some goods are cheaper in local economies.[6] But globalization has some profound downsides, including increased poverty and inequality, environmental pollution, increased migration and dislocation, the rise of immigration and refugees, and human trafficking, all of which will be discussed in this chapter. Since there is no world-governing body committed to looking at social policy solutions to these negative consequences of globalization, there are no policies to mitigate them. In spite of an undeniable increase in the standard of living in some countries, the overall divide between the haves and have-nots has increased under globalization.[7]

Another reason that millions of people may be disadvantaged by globalization is that the Global South has no power over the economic decisions made by the Global North; policies favoring the latter nations have been imposed on the Global South. Yet all countries need a voice in the global economy. When the North recommends and designs infrastructure or agricultural products, these projects may fail in countries in the South, yet countries still must pay back the loans they incurred to build the recommended projects. The impact on the global environment, especially in the countries in the South, has been largely negative. These are some of the factors that explain why there have been so many protests against globalization.[8]

IMF AND WORLD BANK ●

The World Bank and the International Monetary Fund (IMF) were created after World War II to aid in the reconstruction of postwar Europe, ensure global stability, and prevent another worldwide depression. Both institutions are funded by taxpayers from several countries, with the United States having the greatest authority among the industrialized nations that fund and control these institutions. Since the 1980s, the IMF and the World Bank have promoted a strict, free market ideology, insisting that debtor countries demonstrate a commitment to the free market if they want to receive loans. Debtor countries have been ordered to cut deficits and raise taxes and interest rates. Some of these policies have hurt the populations within debtor nations by reducing government spending and squeezing limited private income for increased taxes. These policies continue because both the IMF and the World Bank answer to corporate and financial interests in the Global North, not to the governments in the Global South they are designed to aid economically.

Transnational corporations are not always welcome in countries of the Global South, in the same way that Wal-Mart is not always welcome in communities in the United States.[9] Clearly, interests of industrialized countries, including the United States, are different from the interests of countries in the Global South. As countries in the Global South struggle to pay off debts to the IMF, economically marginalized persons in these countries may suffer terrible burdens, including cuts in fuel or food subsidies and rising prices of goods that threaten their survival. Government health care and public education expenditures may be cut at IMF direction. The IMF can and does dictate internal economic policy for debtor countries; assistance is suspended when these countries are viewed as not living up to IMF standards of low inflation and balanced budgets. IMF officials assume that markets function perfectly; thus when unemployment grows in debtor countries, the problems are seen as tied to other nonmarket factors, such as corrupt unions, politicians, or excessively high wages.[10] On the other hand, the IMF is acutely responsive to global financial markets and seeks to stabilize them and to ensure the flow of credit. In October 2008 it announced that it would deploy some of the $200 billion in loanable funds at its disposal to emerging markets for short-term financing to ease global credit problems.[11]

● ECONOMIC IMPACT OF GLOBALIZATION IN THE UNITED STATES

NAFTA (the North American Free Trade Agreement) went into effect on January 1, 1994, creating a regional "free trade" area among the United States, Canada, and Mexico. Proponents of NAFTA claimed it would create jobs, eliminate barriers to trade, and raise living standards. While importing goods from overseas may result in lower consumer prices in some cases, multinational corporations laid off hundreds of thousands of workers in the United States as they exported their manufacturing and services to other countries in the Global South, where labor is cheaper. In the United States half a million U.S. jobs were lost as corporations moved production to Mexico to utilize or exploit cheaper labor, depending on your point of view. From 1992 to 2002 approximately 1 million jobs were lost in the United States due to the rise of imports from Mexico and, to a lesser extent, Canada, which replaced domestically made goods. As U.S. manufacturers like General Electric moved part of their operation to Mexico, job losses in the United States were accelerated. Even the threat of moving to Mexico gave U.S.-based companies leverage in labor negotiations.[12]

Trade Deficit

When more goods are imported into the United States from other countries than we export outside the country, the United States is said to be in a *trade deficit*. One effect of NAFTA and other trade agreements under globalization has been to increase the trade deficit. While jobs are created in businesses that export goods to other countries, they are lost in sectors where imported goods replace goods made domestically. Since *trade deficits* have risen over the past 10 years, more jobs have been displaced by imports than created by exports under global trade agreements, including NAFTA. Globalization has led to a net loss of jobs in the United States. While job loss caused by rising trade deficits is the most acknowledged problem associated with globalization, its impact on wages is a problem for an even larger number of workers. According to the Economic Policy Institute: "Even if trade flows begin to balance and there is less job loss in the future, the integration of the U.S. economy with those of its low-wage trading partners will pull down wages for many American workers, and will contribute to the ever rising inequality of incomes in the U.S. economy."[13] The effects of globalization on the U.S. labor market are also felt by other workers similar to those who are displaced by imports or the loss of manufacturing jobs. These workers resembling displaced workers in terms of education and experience are forced to compete with greater numbers of the newly unemployed displaced workers, driving down wages due to the increased supply of labor.

Tax Breaks for Multinational Corporations

One of the most important aspects of globalization in the United States is the tax code allowing U.S.-based corporations overseas (known as multinational corporations) to delay paying taxes on any profits made overseas until the money is returned to the United States. While the corporate tax rate on profits of companies operating solely in the United States is 35%, when profits are earned overseas taxes can be postponed for years, a policy known as deferral. Additionally, corporations operating in the Global South pay much less in taxes on profits to the host countries. Corporations defend the tax breaks by arguing that if they had to pay U.S. tax rates, they would not be competitive with countries with much lower taxes on corporations.[14] Yet it is clear that such tax breaks offer deep incentives to corporations to move their businesses to the Global South, thereby maximizing their profits and increasing unemployment in the United States as these jobs move elsewhere. Estimates are that such tax expenditures will cost $90 billion over the next 5 years. Many companies saw their overall U.S. tax rate drop to 18% (from 35%) due to these tax breaks over the past 5 years, paying lower taxes overseas and deferring other taxes. U.S.-based companies have billions of dollars in overseas accounts that are untaxed.[15]

● ECONOMIC IMPACT OF GLOBALIZATION ON THE GLOBAL SOUTH

In spite of the widespread belief that globalization helps less economically advantaged countries like Mexico by creating new jobs, when U.S.-based corporations moved into Mexico after NAFTA in the 1990s, tens of thousands of small Mexican businesses were forced to close because they could not compete with transnational corporations. The competition from U.S. imports undermined the Mexican economy and led to 8 million Mexican families dropping out of the middle class and into poverty between 1994 and 2000, with the number of Mexicans working for less than minimum wage increasing by over a million during this period.[16]

One of the major problems with globalization is that in spite of the rhetoric about free trade and economic cooperation, the United States has not allowed countries in the Global South to export their agricultural products to the United States or elsewhere in order to protect the prices of farmers in the United States. This deprives farmers in these countries of export income yet forces them to open themselves to competition from imported subsidized farm goods. In combination these policies have helped push farmers from the Global South out of business and created widespread unemployment. One consequence of this trade imbalance in agriculture is that globalization has helped industrialized countries far more than it has countries in the Global South. Tariffs generally favor countries in the Global North at the expense of countries in the Global South. For example, tariffs on goods manufactured by countries in the Organisation for Economic Co-operation and Development (OECD), primarily countries in the

Global North, are one quarter of those on goods manufactured by countries outside the OECD, primarily in the Global South. This discrepancy makes it virtually impossible for countries in the Global South to compete with OECD countries in the world market, since their goods are more expensive.[17]

Of course, the global economy encompasses more than factors in non-Western countries. Many forms of work have been shifted to these countries, including telephone call centers. Western countries take raw materials out of non-Western countries and utilize them in their own manufacturing processes. U.S. financial markets are deeply entwined with financial markets in emerging economies such as Brazil and Korea. The financial crash of October 2008 affected markets across the global economy, as financial institutions in these countries were left holding massive foreign debts that could not be paid off.[18]

While globalization in the form of transnational corporations (TNCs) may bring low-wage employment to non-Western countries, it also negatively affects local producers, who must compete with large corporations where economies of scale reduce the cost of production and result in lower-priced goods than those offered by local producers. To compete, local producers may reduce the price of goods by cutting wages or employment, thereby hurting local workers. Some observers conclude that poverty and inequality are the inescapable consequences of globalization in many countries in the Global South hosting TNCs.

NONGOVERNMENTAL ORGANIZATIONS ●

Alongside agencies of the United Nations, in the Global South private or nongovernmental organizations (NGOs) carry on much of the work of social welfare within countries affected by poverty, famine, and disease. Their work includes relief and development, advocacy for human rights, education, youth services, and HIV/AIDS work. Some examples of NGOs include the International Committee of the Red Cross, Catholic Relief Services, and the Christian Children's Fund, all of which have annual budgets of over $100 million. Some U.S. foreign aid is channeled through NGOs (see below). Smaller, more flexible NGOs include the American Friends Service Committee, Oxfam, and other nonsectarian agencies that sponsor aid programs to countries not part of the official U.S. foreign aid commitment. NGOs are less bureaucratic than official agencies and are more likely to work through grassroots organizing than governmental organizations. Examples of developmental activities undertaken by NGOs include forming local cooperatives for food sharing, teaching and sponsoring improved farming techniques, sponsoring preventive health care techniques, and local sanitation improvements.[19]

● **U.S. FOREIGN AID**

The United States gives a limited amount of foreign aid to countries perceived to be geopolitically important to its strategic interests. Additionally, the United States distributes surplus food in order to support farm prices in this country. Foreign aid is therefore used to benefit the domestic economy and to further geopolitical interests, rather than for humanitarian reasons. Israel and Egypt received half of the foreign aid budget, while the poorest countries received about a quarter of U.S. foreign aid.[20] Most of the foreign aid given by the United States is given by private foundations, not the federal government. Of the $122.8 billion of foreign aid provided by Americans in 2005 (the most current data available), $95.5 billion, or 79%, came from private foundations, corporations, voluntary organizations, universities, religious organizations, and individuals, says the annual *Index of Global Philanthropy*.[21]

● **PROTESTS AGAINST GLOBALIZATION**

In the ideal world envisioned by advocates of globalization, nations in the Global South compete with each other to offer social and political environments most hospitable to foreign investment, which include favorable tax structures for corporations and investors and low expectations for environmental regulations or social welfare policies.[22] Yet the contours of globalization are influenced not just by international organizations and corporations, as this scenario suggests, but by social protest on the ground. Because globalization brings with it inequality, loss of income for local producers within the Global South, and loss of control over national political and economic development through the power of transnational corporations, many have protested its power and reach. Struggles over globalization have taken place in both the Global North and the Global South to regulate and oppose strategies of globalization. These actions have been taken by organized groups at the local, regional, and international level and have been strenuously opposed by government forces. Protests have focused on an insistence that international corporations and organizations adopt socially responsible and environmentally responsible economic policies.[23] Some decry the failure of transnational corporations and other forces of globalization to develop a social policy infrastructure in the Global South parallel to those that exist in the Global North. Some object to the increasing inequality between countries in the Global North and those in the Global South.[24] Others object to the loss of national autonomy in the face of externally imposed criteria for economic development. Protests include those by international labor movements focusing on issues related to health and safety, women and child workers, and other labor-related issues. Many of these transnational labor movements were inspired by NAFTA, which was viewed as exploitive of workers in Mexico. Other struggles against the unmitigated power of transnational corporations in globalization include international campaigns by consumer groups to improve standards for workers within particular industries, such as the successful campaign targeting workers' conditions in the textile industries in Guatemala working for Gap, Inc. When protestors urged consumers to redirect their spending away from international corporations that exploit workers, they were relatively successful insofar as they received media support.[25]

In the Global North protests have focused on meetings of the World Trade Organization, the IMF, and the World Bank, where the so-called G8 (the wealthiest industrial countries: the United States, the United Kingdom, Canada, Japan, France, Russia, Italy, and Germany) gathered to plan their global economic strategy. The most famous protest, known as the "Battle of Seattle 2000," was a large and well-organized protest (with an estimated 30,000 participants) against a meeting of the then G7. The organizers of the protest adopted the following motto: "May our resistance be as transnational as capital."[26] The protests effectively disrupted the talks, which resumed the following year with smaller but still notable protests.

The purposes of these G7 and G8 meetings of leading industrialized countries in the Global North were to develop trade agreements, including agreements over intellectual property rights, and to agree on debt management for nations of the Global South. Insisting on intellectual property rights of industrialized countries backfired in 2001, when the G7 meeting strengthened the rights of U.S. pharmaceutical companies to keep nations in the Global South from selling drugs at lower prices. International outrage forced pharmaceutical companies to sell AIDS drugs at low cost to certain countries in Africa, but other lifesaving drugs continue to be out of reach for individuals in the Global South. Even with more pharmaceutical companies cooperating, only 1 in 5 of the estimated 25 million infected persons in Africa are receiving retroviral drugs.[27]

As a result of these protests, efforts to encourage socially responsible corporate behavior in transnational corporations emerged through voluntary codes of conduct regarding unjust labor practices and environmental pollution. These voluntary efforts have largely failed because of the lack of implementation and enforcement standards. Such codes may be seen as ways to avoid public regulation of transnational corporations, just as voluntary agreements among businesses in the Progressive Era and the New Deal were efforts to stave off federal regulation.[28]

● SOCIAL POLICY AND GLOBALIZATION

As Roth pointed out, for Western countries the externalities caused by market capitalism are ameliorated by a comprehensive set of policies adopted by the political system, including Social Security, some form of financial help for children and families, unemployment and disability insurance, and health care. Notably the United States does not offer a policy for health care, as we have seen in Chapter 9. However, in non-Western countries, none of these policies exist. Neither citizens of these countries nor international corporations pay any taxes for these or other social policies. The low tax rate is an important reason why U.S. corporations desire to relocate their operations to the Global South.[29] Some argue that globalization also undercuts support for the welfare state in the United States, as companies are less concerned with ensuring the well-being of workers in this country through tax-supported welfare programs the more they rely on workers from other countries.[30]

In order to build social policy infrastructure in the Global South to mitigate the worst effects of transnational corporations operating within their borders, increased taxation of citizens in these countries may appear to be a fair solution. However, higher taxes will increase the economic burden of globalization in less developed countries, thereby promoting more inequality.[31] Instead of expecting less developed nations to bear the costs and burdens of creating new social welfare infrastructures to ameliorate the worst effects of globalization, the Western countries should develop global structures, which would guarantee a minimum standard of living in the countries that host TNCs, to be financed by the global corporations themselves. The World Trade Organization, the World Bank, and the International Monetary Fund are not equipped or designed to develop or deliver social policies that parallel the social policies that exist in industrialized countries.

As the above suggests, the consequences of globalization are mixed. Globalization means the market economy drives social policy in the Global South, and social welfare policies are usually undercut by the exigencies of the market economy. This is especially true of countries that receive loans from the International Monetary Fund and the World Bank. These loans usually include stipulations that countries receiving them in the Global South bring their economic policies in line with the unrestricted market economy, as discussed above. In other words, little or no inference with the operations of transnational corporations or the domestic market economy is allowed for debtor nations.[32] Yet the fact is that in the Global South, as well as the Global North, capitalism depends on the state for regulation of social relations through laws to enforce contracts, provide a trained labor force, and guarantee social stability.[33] The state must maintain conditions hospitable to the market economy, so some state regulation is necessary. The interests of foreign governments in protecting transnational corporations and globalization are evident in government reactions to protests against globalization.

POLICIES TO PROTECT AGAINST ●
THE SOCIAL COSTS OF THE GLOBAL ECONOMY

The first step in righting the injustices caused by globalization should be debt forgiveness. Without forgiveness of debt, countries in the Global South cannot meet the needs of their citizens, much less grow economically. These countries currently must commit large proportions of the money made on exports to debt reduction. Widespread international support for debt forgiveness has been evident since the Jubilee movement of 2000, a global social movement that pressured countries in the Global North to commit to debt forgiveness in 24 countries in the Global South. Additionally, the IMF and the World Bank need to loosen their restrictions on loans and grants to countries in the Global South in order to maximize their political autonomy and their control over economic development.[34] Within countries in the Global South, democratic structures to guide development must be established so that these countries can control their own economic fate. Finally a world body must establish labor policies, environmental policies, and a minimum social welfare structure to protect citizens currently suffering some of the worst effects of the inequality exacerbated by globalizations. Transnational corporations must be forced to comply with these international standards, as well as provide the economic support for the emerging social welfare infrastructure and enforcement of environmental standards. All governments trading with the United States should encourage, not forbid, unionization of their workers. Tax breaks for these TNCs operating overseas must be ended. Many persons in the Global South are in the agricultural sector. Farmers need to be able to compete on the world markets with some guarantee of price stability. Tariffs must be equal between countries in the Global North and Global South to stop the disadvantage the latter countries experience in the world market. Finally the IMF should return to its original function, providing funds to restore demand in countries experiencing economic recession. Just as federal spending, including deficit spending, has been used to bring the U.S. economy out of recessions and depressions, so too large-scale spending on infrastructures and public works programs by the IMF can provide jobs, increase aggregate demand and restore economic stability, and encourage economic structures that promote social justice.[35] The World Bank itself recognized in 2006 that "inequality of opportunity, both within and among nations, sustains extreme deprivation, results in wasted human potential and often weakens prospects for overall prosperity and economic growth."[36]

PROFILES IN LEADERSHIP

Nelson Mandela, 1918–

Nelson Mandela

SOURCE: Corbis.

Nelson Mandela was born in South Africa in 1918. His father was a relatively wealthy man, rich enough to maintain four wives and 13 children. Mandela was the youngest child in the family. He attended a mission school as a child where his education was influenced by standard British textbooks. As he matured, he realized that most textbooks he had studied recognized only White leaders, whereas Africans were described as savages and thieves. This awareness of the negative depiction in the literature of Africans fueled his commitment to fight for social justice and social change.

He attended educational institutions at University College of Fort Hare and the University of the Witwatersrand, receiving a degree in law in 1942. His education as well as his earlier Methodist teaching greatly influenced his spiritual values.

As a young man, Mandela developed a reputation as a radical, joining the African National Congress (ANC) in 1944. By the late 1940s, Mandela had become a significant public figure occupying key positions in the main African political movement of the period. During the late 1940s, White Afrikaner nationalism had emerged, emphasizing racial separation and segregation and instituting other racist policies such as restricting the movement of Africans into city areas, putting African schools under state control, banning interracial marriage, limiting voting rights for Africans, and requiring African women to carry passes to travel to urban areas. This evoked massive civil disobedience, and Mandela himself was arrested several times. Riots and strikes by workers also followed.

By this time, Mandela was heavily involved with the ANC as a leader and strategist. At this time Mandela was committed to nonviolence as the most effective protest strategy. In 1956 Mandela was put on trial for treason for engaging in acts of resistance against the apartheid policies of the South African ruling party. He was acquitted in 1961.

In 1960 in Sharpeville, 30 policemen fired into a crowd of 5,000 people, killing 69 people and wounding nearly 200 others. Mandela and others organized protest activities. Warrants were issued for his arrest, leading him to flee the country. At this time the South African government banned the African National Congress, and Mandela decided armed resistance would be necessary for the success of the movement. Eventually he was arrested and convicted of plotting to overthrow the government by violent means. From August 1964 to 1989, Mandela was in prison and isolated on Robben Island, off Cape Town, for 17 of those 25 years. In spite of his isolation in a prison cell, Mandela had many visitors and much written communication from the outside world. During his imprisonment Mandela's reputation grew steadily. He became the symbol of resistance to apartheid in South Africa. During his prison time, Mandela was deprived of both daylight and music, at great cost to him. He never wavered from his political beliefs during the long dark years of his imprisonment.

By the 1980s, the government began to institute a series of reforms abolishing most of the most repressive policies and laws. Calls came from political leaders of other countries to release Mandela. He was moved to more comfortable quarters and was able to receive visitors. He also began a series of discussions with government leaders regarding reforms and was eventually released from prison in 1990.

In 1991 Mandela was elected president of the African National Congress, the opposition party in South Africa. In 1993, Mandela received the Nobel Prize for Peace. In 1994 he was elected president of South Africa. His administration addressed poverty and health problems in the country, especially among the long oppressed African population. Nelson Mandela became an international hero for fighting racial and social injustice. His stoicism and courage during his long years of imprisonment continue to be inspirational to a new generation of activists across the globe.

MIGRATION AND IMMIGRATION ●

One of the arguments used by the Clinton administration to support NAFTA was that it would deter illegal immigration from Mexico to the United States because jobs would be more plentiful in Mexico if the treaty were ratified. The Mexican president, Carlos Salinas, also used this argument to persuade his union leaders in the United States to ratify the treaty, saying, "We want to export goods, not people to your country."[37] Ironically, over 100,000 Mexicans demonstrated against NAFTA in 2002 in Mexico City, protesting against the bankruptcy of farmers and dairy producers who could not compete with the subsidized produce of U.S. and Canadian agriculture. The collapse of

Immigrant farm workers

SOURCE: Associated Press.

the Mexican agricultural industry led to increased migration to the United States, since jobs did not materialize in Mexico in anywhere near the numbers that had been promised. The vast majority of jobs gained in Mexico were in the assembly plants near the U.S. border; in the rest of Mexico, job losses predominated. Exploitation and mistreatment of Mexican workers at these plants were widespread. The Mexican government has not allowed its workers in border assembly plants (known as *maquiladoras*) to organize unions. Similarly environmental pollution in Mexico and on the U.S.-Mexican border increased dramatically in the first 10 years of NAFTA's existence.[38] The collapse of Mexican agriculture after NAFTA was instrumental in sending millions of Mexicans north into the United States to look for work. Competition from U.S.-based stores like Wal-Mart has forced closure of stores selling Mexican-made goods. Wages along the Mexican border have actually been driven down by about 25% since NAFTA, due to an oversupply of workers and government resistance to unionization. The result is sweatshop pay of $0.60 to $1 an hour in these U.S.-owned plants.[39]

NAFTA did not decrease immigration from Mexico but contributed to its increase from 1994 to 2005. Mexicans who immigrated to the United States sent $17 billion home in 2002, constituting the country's second largest source of earnings. Such ambitious Mexicans leave their homeland bereft of their energy and initiative; through their migration Mexico is subsidizing the secondary labor market in the United States.[40] This stream of migration became one of the most lasting, if unintended, effects of NAFTA.

HUMAN RIGHTS AND GLOBALIZATION ●

In general the human migration associated with the effects of globalization has been toward countries in the Global North, as discussed in the example of migration from Mexico to the United States. There have been other forms of involuntary migration since the emergence of globalization, including human trafficking, large-scale movements of refugees, and other forms of human displacement. Forced labor exists throughout the world but is more prevalent in South Asia and Brazil, where economic deprivation forces some into cruel situations of debt bondage and forced domestic labor. The United Nations, which defines forced labor as "all work or service which is exacted from any person under the menace of any penalty and for which said person has not offered himself voluntarily," estimates that at least 12 million people are exploited through forced labor, the majority of them women and girls.[41] Other estimates are closer to 27 million people.[42] Girls and women who are sexually exploited account for approximately 11% of forced labor victims; many of them have been victims of sexual trafficking.

Trafficking is distinct from forced labor in that the added elements of movement of a person or migration are involved, along with deception or coercion about the migration and a high risk for sexual exploitation or prostitution. The United States and other industrialized countries in the Global North are the main destinations for those trafficking in human beings; as demand for forced labor is highest in the United States and other countries in the Global North. Victims of sexual trafficking may be beaten into submission, their passports may be stolen, and they may be locked up when not performing sexual acts on command. Thailand is a destination for sexual trafficking for women from Cambodia and China, as well as the source of sexual trafficking to Japan and Taiwan. Women are tricked or coerced into becoming prostitutes, a situation from which they can rarely escape. Law enforcement often looks the other way, and few traffickers are brought to the attention of the police or prosecuted. Sexual trafficking is highly profitable; its victims are likely to be forced to work as prostitutes or in the sex industry, including in pornography.[43]

Sexual trafficking occurs in the United States as well. In 2004 the U.S. State Department estimated that approximately 17,500 persons were trafficked into the United States annually. The exact numbers are difficult to determine because much such trafficking is not reported to authorities. The United Nations estimates that the United States is the second most popular destination for sexual trafficking, after Italy. The United States is a center of the Internet-based pornography business, including child pornography. Sexual trafficking victims, especially children, may be forced to perform sexual acts, in spite of laws against child pornography.[44] In 2000 Congress passed the Victims of Trafficking and Violence Protection Act, which protects victims of sexual trafficking from prosecution and grants them a "T-visa," which allows them to stay in the United States while the prosecution of their traffickers takes place. Federal authorities will assist them with services during this period; after 3 years they can apply for permanent residency.

What can social workers do about forced labor and sexual trafficking? Coming forward to self-identify as a victim of sexual trafficking and claiming the rights and benefits under the Victims of Trafficking Law is not easy; most victims live in secrecy, as their traffickers keep them out of public view in order to avoid exposure. Social workers and other advocates can facilitate this process by advocating for sexual trafficking victims' rights to emergency shelter and safe houses. Once safely removed from their dangerous environments, social workers can work to help their clients access the benefits available to them under the law. Stricter enforcement of the Trafficking Law will help identify victims, and outreach by social workers working with immigrant groups is the first step in stopping this deplorable practice. Of course, all human trafficking is facilitated by the inequalities fostered in the Global South by the forces of globalization as described above. Working with groups that seek to redress the current injustices associated with globalization as it is now configured would reduce the number of women and children who are victims of sexual trafficking. Viable roles in domestic economies for women and men in the Global South would constitute a strong deterrence to the practice of sexual trafficking.

Another equally important step would be to urge Congress to ratify the United Nations Universal Declaration of Human Rights, adopted by the United Nations in 1948 (see Table 11.1). According to this accord, every human being has economic, political, and social rights, which include the affirmation that "all humans are born free and equal in dignity and rights."[45] The United States refuses to ratify the International Covenant on Economic, Social and Cultural Rights because of its statements about economic, social, and

TABLE 11.1   **Universal Declaration of Human Rights**

PREAMBLE

Whereas recognition of the inherent dignity and of the equal and inalienable rights of all members of the human family is the foundation of freedom, justice and peace in the world,

Whereas disregard and contempt for human rights have resulted in barbarous acts which have outraged the conscience of mankind, and the advent of a world in which human beings shall enjoy freedom of speech and belief and freedom from fear and want has been proclaimed as the highest aspiration of the common people,

Whereas it is essential, if man is not to be compelled to have recourse, as a last resort, to rebellion against tyranny and oppression, that human rights should be protected by the rule of law,

Whereas it is essential to promote the development of friendly relations between nations,

Whereas the peoples of the United Nations have in the Charter reaffirmed their faith in fundamental human rights, in the dignity and worth of the human person and in the equal rights of men and women and have determined to promote social progress and better standards of life in larger freedom,

Whereas Member States have pledged themselves to achieve, in cooperation with the United Nations, the promotion of universal respect for and observance of human rights and fundamental freedoms,

Whereas a common understanding of these rights and freedoms is of the greatest importance for the full realization of this pledge,

Now, therefore,

The General Assembly

proclaims

This Universal Declaration of Human Rights

as a common standard of achievement for all peoples and all nations, to the end that every individual and every organ of society, keeping this Declaration constantly in mind, shall strive by teaching and education to promote respect for these rights and freedoms and by progressive measures, national and international, to secure their universal and effective recognition and observance, both among the peoples of Member States themselves and among the peoples of territories under their jurisdiction.

Article I

All human beings are born free and equal in dignity and rights. They are endowed with reason and conscience and should act towards one another in a spirit of brotherhood.

Article 2

Everyone is entitled to all the rights and freedoms set forth in this Declaration, without distinction of any kind, such as race, colour, sex, language, religion, political or other opinion, national or social origin, property, birth or other status.

   Furthermore, no distinction shall be made on the basis of the political, jurisdictional or international status of the country or territory to which a person belongs, whether it be independent, trust, non-self-governing or under any other limitation of sovereignty.

(Continued)

TABLE 11.1 (Continued)

Article 3

Everyone has the right to life, liberty and security of person.

Article 4

No one shall be held in slavery or servitude; slavery and the slave trade shall be prohibited in all their forms.

Article 5

No one shall be subjected to torture or to cruel, inhuman or degrading treatment or punishment.

Article 6

Everyone has the right to recognition everywhere as a person before the law.

Article 7

All are equal before the law and are entitled without any discrimination to equal protection of the law. All are entitled to equal protection against any discrimination in violation of this Declaration and against any incitement to such discrimination.

Article 8

Everyone has the right to an effective remedy by the competent national tribunals for acts violating the fundamental rights granted him by the constitution or by law.

Article 9

No one shall be subjected to arbitrary arrest, detention or exile.

Article 10

Everyone is entitled in full equality to a fair and public hearing by an independent and impartial tribunal, in the determination of his rights and obligations and of any criminal charge against him.

Article 11

(1) Everyone charged with a penal offence has the right to be presumed innocent until proved guilty according to law in a public trial at which he has had all the guarantees necessary for his defense.

(2) No one shall be held guilty of any penal offence on account of any act or omission which did not constitute a penal offence, under national or international law, at the time when it was committed. Nor shall a heavier penalty be imposed than the one that was applicable at the time the penal offence was committed.

Article 12

No one shall be subjected to arbitrary interference with his privacy, family, home or correspondence, nor to attacks upon his honor and reputation. Everyone has the right to the protection of the law against such interference or attacks.

Article 13

(1) Everyone has the right to freedom of movement and residence within the borders of each State.

(2) Everyone has the right to leave any country, including his own, and to return to his country.

Article 14

(1) Everyone has the right to seek and to enjoy in other countries asylum from persecution.

(2) This right may not be invoked in the case of prosecutions genuinely arising from non-political crimes or from acts contrary to the purposes and principles of the United Nations.

Article 15

(1) Everyone has the right to a nationality.

(2) No one shall be arbitrarily deprived of his nationality nor denied the right to change his nationality.

Article 16

(1) Men and women of full age, without any limitation due to race, nationality or religion, have the right to marry and to found a family. They are entitled to equal rights as to marriage, during marriage and at its dissolution.

(2) Marriage shall be entered into only with the free and full consent of the intending spouses.

(3) The family is the natural and fundamental group unit of society and is entitled to protection by society and the State.

Article 17

(1) Everyone has the right to own property alone as well as in association with others.

(2) No one shall be arbitrarily deprived of his property.

Article 18

Everyone has the right to freedom of thought, conscience and religion; this right includes freedom to change his religion or belief, and freedom, either alone or in community with others and in public or private, to manifest his religion or belief in teaching, practice, worship and observance.

Article 19

Everyone has the right to freedom of opinion and expression; this right includes freedom to hold opinions without interference and to seek, receive and impart information and ideas through any media and regardless of frontiers.

Article 20

(1) Everyone has the right to freedom of peaceful assembly and association.

(2) No one may be compelled to belong to an association.

(Continued)

TABLE 11.1 (Continued)

Article 21

(1) Everyone has the right to take part in the government of his country, directly or through freely chosen representatives.

(2) Everyone has the right to equal access to public service in his country.

(3) The will of the people shall be the basis of the authority of government; this shall be expressed in periodic and genuine elections which shall be by universal and equal suffrage and shall be held by secret vote or by equivalent free voting procedures.

Article 22

Everyone, as a member of society, has the right to social security and is entitled to realization, through national effort and international co-operation and in accordance with the organization and resources of each State, of the economic, social and cultural rights indispensable for his dignity and the free development of his personality.

Article 23

(1) Everyone has the right to work, to free choice of employment, to just and favourable conditions of work and to protection against unemployment.

(2) Everyone, without any discrimination, has the right to equal pay for equal work.

(3) Everyone who works has the right to just and favourable remuneration ensuring for himself and his family an existence worthy of human dignity, and supplemented, if necessary, by other means of social protection.

(4) Everyone has the right to form and to join trade unions for the protection of his interests.

Article 24

Everyone has the right to rest and leisure, including reasonable limitation of working hours and periodic holidays with pay.

Article 25

(1) Everyone has the right to a standard of living adequate for the health and well-being of himself and of his family, including food, clothing, housing and medical care and necessary social services, and the right to security in the event of unemployment, sickness, disability, widowhood, old age or other lack of livelihood in circumstances beyond his control.

(2) Motherhood and childhood are entitled to special care and assistance. All children, whether born in or out of wedlock, shall enjoy the same social protection.

Article 26

(1) Everyone has the right to education. Education shall be free, at least in the elementary and fundamental stages. Elementary education shall be compulsory. Technical and professional education shall be made generally available and higher education shall be equally accessible to all on the basis of merit.

(2) Education shall be directed to the full development of the human personality and to the strengthening of respect for human rights and fundamental freedoms. It shall promote understanding, tolerance and friendship among all nations, racial or religious groups, and shall further the activities of the United Nations for the maintenance of peace.

(3) Parents have a prior right to choose the kind of education that shall be given to their children.

Article 27

(1) Everyone has the right freely to participate in the cultural life of the community, to enjoy the arts and to share in scientific advancement and its benefits.

(2) Everyone has the right to the protection of the moral and material interests resulting from any scientific, literary or artistic production of which he is the author.

Article 28

Everyone is entitled to a social and international order in which the rights and freedoms set forth in this Declaration can be fully realized.

Article 29

(1) Everyone has duties to the community in which alone the free and full development of his personality is possible.

(2) In the exercise of his rights and freedoms, everyone shall be subject only to such limitations as are determined by law solely for the purpose of securing due recognition and respect for the rights and freedoms of others and of meeting the just requirements of morality, public order and the general welfare in a democratic society.

(3) These rights and freedoms may in no case be exercised contrary to the purposes and principles of the United Nations.

Article 30

Nothing in this Declaration may be interpreted as implying for any State, group or person any right to engage in any activity or to perform any act aimed at the destruction of any of the rights and freedoms set forth herein.

cultural rights, which are not in line with the belief in individual responsibility held by many Americans.

These enumerated rights are an explication of one of the central tenets of the social work profession recognized in the National Association of Social Workers' *Code of Ethics:* the mandate for social workers to challenge social injustice, pursuing "social change, particularly with and on behalf of vulnerable and oppressed individuals and groups of people." These social change efforts must focus on issues related to "poverty, unemployment, discrimination and other forms of social injustice," according to NASW.[46] Clearly the commitment to social justice must be extended globally, along with the recognition that globalization has an impact on persons in the United States, affecting their economic well-being and their social and political rights.

● MOST AND LEAST LIVABLE COUNTRIES: UNITED NATIONS HUMAN DEVELOPMENT INDEX, 2007

The Human Development Index (HDI), published annually by the United Nations, ranks nations according to their citizens' quality of life rather than strictly by their traditional economic figures. The criteria for calculating rankings include life expectancy, educational attainment, and adjusted real income. Tables 11.2 and 11.3 show the 2007 index.

TABLE 11.2 **Most Livable Countries, 2007**

1.	Iceland	16.	United Kingdom
2.	Norway	17.	Belgium
3.	Australia	18.	Luxembourg
4.	Canada	19.	New Zealand
5.	Ireland	20.	Italy
6.	Sweden	21.	Germany
7.	Switzerland	22.	Israel
8.	Japan	23.	Greece
9.	Netherlands	24.	Singapore
10.	France	25.	Korea, Rep. of
11.	Finland	26.	Slovenia
12.	United States	27.	Cyprus
13.	Spain	28.	Portugal
14.	Denmark	29.	Brunei Darussalam
15.	Austria	30.	Barbados

TABLE 11.3   **Least Livable Countries, 2007**

1.	Sierra Leone	16.	Angola
2.	Burkina Faso	17.	Rwanda
3.	Guinea-Bissau	18.	Guinea
4.	Niger	19.	Tanzania
5.	Mali	20.	Nigeria
6.	Mozambique	21.	Eritrea
7.	Central African Republic	22.	Senegal
8.	Chad	23.	Gambia
9.	Ethiopia	24.	Uganda
10.	Congo, Dem. Rep. of the	25.	Yemen
11.	Burundi	26.	Togo
12.	Côte d'Ivoire	27.	Zimbabwe
13.	Zambia	28.	Timor-Leste
14.	Malawi	29.	Djibouti
15.	Benin	30.	Kenya

SOURCE: *Human Development Report, 2007/2008*, United Nations. Retrieved from hdr.undp.org

THE UNITED STATES POST 9/11 AND THE RISE OF PROGRESSIVISM ●

After the attacks of 9/11 on the United States, the war on terrorism became the global mission for the Bush administration, leading to the war in Afghanistan and, in 2002, the invasion of Iraq. The fiscal and ideological impact of the subsequent war in Iraq and Afghanistan swept aside progressive concerns about health care access, affordable housing, and growing inequality in income. As of October 2008, the United States had spent $864 billion on wars in Iraq and Afghanistan and other "war on terror"-related activities, according to a report prepared for Congress by the Congressional Research Service. Of this amount, $657 billion, or 76%, was spent on the war in Iraq.[47] These expenditures, combined with tax cuts initiated by the Bush administration and supported by Congress, pushed the federal deficit to record highs by the time Bush left office.

Department of Homeland Security

Domestically, the Bush administration looked to tighten security by increased enforcement of immigration policies. To that end the Department of Homeland Security (DHS) was established in 2002 as a cabinet-level department with an estimated budget of $37 billion and 169,000 employees. It was designed to oversee all matters related to immigration and naturalization formerly under the jurisdiction of the Immigration and Naturalization Service. DHS was charged with protecting the security of the American homeland, which included preventing terrorist attacks within the United States, reducing the vulnerability of the United States to terrorism, and minimizing the damage from potential attacks and natural disasters. After a major reorganization of agencies related to domestic security, DHS was put in charge of the Transportation Security Administration and the Secret Service, making it the third largest executive agency in the federal government.[48]

One of the major responsibilities of DHS is oversight of immigration policies, including efforts to "secure the border" in order to reduce the number of undocumented immigrants entering the United States. DHS apprehended 961,000 foreign nationals attempting to enter the United States in 2007; the majority of these were either deported or returned voluntarily to their home countries.[49] In its role as securer of the borders, DHS has overseen the construction of a border fence along the southwestern border of the United States. Pedestrian fencing, vehicle fencing, and a high-tech virtual fence are included in the fencing project.[50] By the beginning of the Obama administration the border fence had still not been completed, and Obama indicated uncertainty as to whether it would be continued. While more than 600 miles of the fence have been built, many doubt its effectiveness, as ways over and under the fence have already been discovered by persons smuggling undocumented persons into the United States. The cost per mile of the fence built thus far has been estimated to be over $3 million. Objections to the border fence have been mounted by human rights, animal rights, and environmental groups, who argue that the fencing is dangerous to those attempting to cross into the United States, to animals, and to the natural habitat along the border.[51]

PATRIOT Act

Shortly after the attacks of 9/11, Congress at the urging of the Bush administration passed the PATRIOT Act, which authorized the federal government to access medical records, tax records, phone records, and library records.[52] The

American Civil Liberties Union objected strongly to the act on the grounds that it allows the Federal Bureau of Investigation (FBI) as well as investigators at the Department of Homeland Security to conduct unwarranted searches and vastly expands the power of the federal government over the private life of residents of the United States.[53] In 2006 Congress renewed the PATRIOT Act, making most of its provisions permanent. Congress acted in spite of strong objections of some, after Bush called the PATRIOT Act a vital tool in the fight against terrorism. In the 2006 version of the act most libraries were exempt from the "sneak and peek" provisions of the law that allowed the FBI to look into personal records without a court order.[54] The American Bar Association has called for greater congressional oversight of the PATRIOT Act to ensure that the act does not violate the First, Fourth, and Fifth Amendments to the Constitution.[55] In 2003 former Vice President Al Gore criticized the PATRIOT Act, saying that it diminished personal freedoms and weakened U.S. security through "mass violations of civil liberties."[56] Some have questioned the potential of the PATRIOT Act to undermine dissent and destabilize progressive social movements. In short, the act can be used to investigate a wide variety of things, not just actions linked to terrorism.[57] Ironically, in the long run, dissent was not quenched, and a progressive social movement emerged out of the strictures of the post-9/11 era.

No Child Left Behind

The Bush administration launched its major domestic initiative in 2001, when Congress passed No Child Left Behind (NCLB). The stated objective of this act is to improve school performance by having states set standards for student performance measured by standardized testing and then rewarding schools that meet those standards.[58] Efforts to improve teacher competence and student performance have been made at state levels, but this is the first federal initiative to improve education in local schools. The method chosen to improve education is state-sponsored testing of all children. The Bush administration believed that testing was the best measure of school and teacher performance.

The Obama administration has not indicated whether it will push for revisions of No Child Left Behind in 2009.[59] Under the provisions of the act, children in the third through eighth grades must be tested using state-developed standardized tests every year in reading and math. The act dramatically increases the role of the federal government in education. Individual states must report their results by school district and demographic groups each year. Schools that continue to score low on these tests and not make adequate yearly progress will eventually lose federal funding.[60]

Criticisms of the act center on the necessity of teachers focusing on testing, rather than broader learning; elimination of nonacademic courses from school curriculum, such as art and music, in an effort to prepare students to pass the tests; and potential punishment of low-income schools whose students have traditionally done poorly on academic tests by ultimately withholding federal resources after low test performance. Schools in low-income areas are likely to need more, not less, funding to meet the educational needs of students living there, and No Child Left Behind does the reverse. Immediate beneficiaries of the act were companies that designed standardized tests.[61] Some research indicates that NCLB's assessment criteria are not broad enough to meet the needs of students with disabilities and that the act creates pressure on schools to exclude these students and contributes to higher dropout rates among students with disabilities. In some states, students with disabilities have not made adequate yearly progress as defined by the act and lowered overall scores for school districts. Advocates for students with disabilities applaud the inclusion of students with disabilities in the overall assessment scheme of NCLB but see unintended consequences in the pass/fail outcome measurement of the test, which they feel discriminates unfairly against students with disabilities.[62]

While NCLB had as its objective improving education for students living in poverty, children of color, new English learners, and students with disabilities, the act demands 100% proficiency of all students by 2014. Schools not meeting these goals will be sanctioned in various ways, including closing schools and combining them with other schools. Unfortunately, while implicitly promising equal opportunity through testing and accountability, the law ignores the deep educational inequalities in public school systems across the country. Schools that are well funded outspend schools with fewer resources by 3 to 1 in most states. Schools in economically marginalized areas are using out-of-date textbooks, have no science labs, and depend on untrained teachers. Many of these schools are in need of serious renovation, as their physical structures are unsound. Testing will do little to improve educational standards in these schools, and threats of sanctions will not accomplish what substantial federal investment in public education could.[63]

NCLB obscures the deeper causes of poverty and inequality by assuming that mandatory testing will force schools to make up for the economic structures and historical ideologies that promote inequality in the workplace and among families in the United States. The act has been effective in convincing many that the federal government is concerned about equal outcomes for children of color and children from economically marginalized families; yet even if NCLB were to be successful in raising test scores, that alone could not change the factors discussed in Chapters 3, 4, and 5 that push families into poverty.[64]

Hurricane Katrina

For some Americans the Bush administration reached its nadir in the initial federal reaction to Hurricane Katrina. Expectations of a swift and effective federal response were high, based on the belief that severe national disasters like Hurricanes Katrina and Rita in 2005 called for the resources of the federal government, especially the Federal Emergency Management Agency (FEMA), which had been placed under the auspices of the Department of Homeland Security. The final death toll of 1,836 people made Katrina the third deadliest hurricane in U.S. history. Damages, including the loss of homes and businesses, were estimated to be over $100 billion, making Katrina the costliest hurricane in the nation's history.[65] Media coverage of flood victims in New Orleans begging for help led people to question the willingness of local, state, and federal governments to mount effective disaster relief. The fact that many of those

Devastation caused by Hurricane Katrina

SOURCE: AP Photo/Ric Feld.

pictured in temporary shelters, trapped on rooftops, or wading through the high water were African Americans fueled the belief of many Americans that discrimination played a role in the slow and ineffective government response to the disaster.

FEMA was roundly criticized for its late response to the crisis and its overall management.[66] Many victims who lost housing were sent to neighboring states with no means of return. Other storm victims were lodged in trailers provided by FEMA; initially they were to be moved out in 2007, but after public outcry they were allowed to stay in these trailers far from their home through 2009.[67] Most have not been given assistance to relocate or return to their original neighborhoods. The economically marginalized neighborhood hardest hit by Katrina, known as the Ninth Ward, suffered almost complete devastation and has not yet been rebuilt.

Many Americans and others across the globe were shocked to see the naked inequality exposed by Katrina in the Ninth Ward of New Orleans. Discrimination seemed to be threaded through the inadequate response to the crisis; many wondered if the federal response would have been different if more of the victims had been White.[68] Yet in spite of the shocking nature of the poverty and discrimination exposed by media coverage of Katrina, one study conducted in 2006 found that Katrina did not raise awareness of poverty and inequality among Americans; respondents stated they already knew these problems existed.[69] Katrina did not lead to a sea change in the American response to injustice; its most lasting legacy may have been the disillusionment with the Bush administration's response to the crisis.

● RISE OF PROGRESSIVISM

Many factors led to a new emergence of progressivism around the time of the 2008 presidential election. As discussed earlier, the contraction of social welfare spending during the Bush administration, along with the failure of the federal government to act effectively in the aftermath of Hurricane Katrina, caused many Americans to turn away from conservative ideology about the role of the federal government. The Bush administration's massive tax cuts for the wealthiest Americans were not translated into tangible benefits for middle-class and economically marginalized Americans. Many Americans viewed the war in Iraq as a costly and ill-conceived effort that had not been a success or worth the number of American lives lost. By 2008 a majority of Americans felt that the decision to invade Iraq had been wrong.[70] In August 2008, 58% of those polled stated they wanted American troops withdrawn from Iraq within a year, and another 20% wanted troops brought home immediately.[71] These factors combined to produce an interest in an antiwar candidate and in a recommit-ment to a federal role in issues such as health care and education. Barack Obama's candidacy seemed to promise both themes critical to the new progres-sivism: an anti-Iraq war stance combined with a vision that embraced the return to a faith in a proactive government that would advance the interests of the mid-dle class and economically marginalized persons, instead of affluent persons. During the campaign many progressives were heartened by the vigorous dis-cussion of health care reform that had been absent from the Bush years, espe-cially since health care reform would benefit economically marginalized persons who had no access to health care. Health care reform became the symbol of what an empowered federal government could accomplish for Americans who had been left out of the Bush tax revolution. Under Obama's candidacy tax reform also took center stage as a way to redress the growing inequality of the Bush years. Obama proposed a tax cut on middle-income Americans, as well as on those who make so little money that they effectively owe no taxes at the end of the year (but still pay payroll taxes), who would receive a tax refund. At the same time Obama explicitly called for an end to the Bush tax cuts for the wealthy. Both of these tax measures would reduce income inequality, which had been growing under the Bush administration. These proposals galvanized pro-gressives disenchanted with the supply side economics favored by the Bush administration. Progressives read between the lines and hoped that Obama would return to a proactive liberal federal model that would engage the resources of the federal government to solve some longstanding social problems and begin to move the country toward more equality and social justice.

Obama's campaign theme was "Hope," which carried him through the Democratic nomination process. However, in the fall of 2008 the economic cri-sis derailed the train of hopeful commitments Obama had made in his Democratic acceptance speech and forced the candidate to confront the realities of an unregulated financial sector spinning out of control, wiping out the assets of many Americans in the stock market, in retirement accounts, and in the equity in their homes. For progressives the failures of the unregulated financial sector revealed the moral and intellectual bankruptcy of the conservative revo-lution and its emphasis on free market fundamentalism, the belief that unregu-lated markets will work perfectly to deliver prosperity and economic growth.[72]

Meaning of Obama Candidacy and Election

Barack Obama won the presidential election by a relatively wide electoral margin with 53% of the popular vote, a larger margin than George Herbert Walker Bush, Bill Clinton, or George W. Bush. What does the election of Barack

President Barack Obama and family

SOURCE: AP Photo/Pablo Martinez Monsivais.

Obama, an African American man, mean about racism and discrimination in the United States? Has the theory of the racial contract been overturned by his election? The racial contract theory argues that there has been an implicit assumption in this country since the first White settlement in the 17th century that Whites will subordinate all people of color. Obama's election effectively ends the automatic subordination of African Americans and other persons of color by Whites; at the least the racial contract has been renegotiated to exclude Obama. Obama represents a multiethnic background: He has an African father and a White mother (hence an African American in the literal sense of the word) and spent part of his childhood in an Asian, predominantly Muslim country. Obama has stepped out of the racial contract, claiming multiple identities as a global leader, while always acknowledging his African American culture and roots. He displays an ease with his complex ethnic background that will increasingly characterize the 21st-century American. Would his chances have been slimmer if he were the descendant of slaves in the narrative trajectory most dominant in African American life? It may be that Obama slipped the bonds of the tragic history of racial domination born out of slavery and Jim Crow, two narratives that have entwined so many other African Americans seeking political and economic power.

How has the meaning of Whiteness changed as a result of the election? While Whiteness still carries privilege in many of the same ways it did before, there has been a clear decline in the cultural presumption of White dominance in political affairs that may or may not resonate to other areas of social life.[73] Economic justice will not automatically follow the Obama election. Yet there is no question that something shifted in the tectonic plates that have held ethnic relationships in dominant and subordinate places from the 18th century onward, in spite of the successes of the civil rights movement and the ascendancy of the African American middle class from which Obama and his wife come. Whiteness means less than it did, and being African American means something ineluctably different as a result of Obama's election. Whether this will translate into broader social gains is yet to be seen. The coercive arm of the state continues to operate against men of color in law enforcement and prisons, jobless rates are higher in urban areas of color, and homeless rates are higher. Racism continues to oppress economically marginalized persons of color, but the narratives attached to ethnicity have shifted. Other successful African Americans have transcended racial boundaries—Tiger Woods, Oprah Winfrey, and Colin Powell, for example—by not emphasizing their ethnic differences and by allowing Whites to admire them without having to fundamentally change their stereotypes about African Americans.[74] Is Barack Obama one of these non-ethnically identified celebrities? Or is he a transformational figure who can reshape our image of ourselves and each other? The fact that he won overwhelmingly among those who were voting for the first time, most of them under 30, suggests that Obama represents the future face of American political and cultural possibilities. We are not yet a postracial nation, though we aspire to be. We still live within the categories of domination and privilege that we have inherited from previous generations. Rather than turning our backs on ethnic differences, we have crossed a bridge to a future where ethnicity matters less.

Barack Obama and Social Movements

The Obama campaign was similar to a social movement in that it drew from a groundswell of protest against the war in Iraq, embraced a positive message of social change and social justice outside the bounds of traditional political campaign, and was led by a charismatic leader who established ongoing political and communication structures that can potentially carry on the work of the movement. Its use of technology and Internet social networking during the campaign, aided by the large fundraising effort of the progressive Internet-based political operation MoveOn.org, can be a vehicle for summoning popular support for other social policy changes during the next 4 years. Obama has access to millions of people through his use of social networking, a tool that he can continue to use throughout his administration.[75] In this way he has created an institutional structure critical to an ongoing social movement. A governing Obama will not hold the same sway over the public imagination as a candidate Obama did, as he begins to act politically rather than rhetorically. Yet the possibility of significant policy change remains, something that was not anticipated by progressive scholars a few years ago.[76]

Economic Recession, 2008–2009

By the beginning of Obama's presidency, a global recession had slowed economic growth in the United States as well as in China, South Korea, Japan, and Europe.[77] In February 2009 the unemployment rate had climbed to 7.6% in the United States, with some states such as California suffering over a 9% unemployment rate. Over 500,000 jobs a month were lost between November 2008 and January 2009. The highest increases in unemployment occurred among African Americans, Latinos, and persons considered disabled.[78] Nationwide businesses announced closings and bankruptcies, throwing more workers into unemployment. What caused the dramatic job losses and business closures? In many ways the processes that contributed to the recession were similar to contributing factors to the Great Depression. In Chapter 7 we learned how the collapse of the stock market caused a crisis in confidence and a collapse of the credit market. In 2008 these factors were again intertwined as stock market losses were accompanied by a contraction of the credit market following the collapse of the housing bubble (see Chapter 10). As in the 1930s, a dramatic decline in consumer confidence due to these stock losses, housing foreclosures, and tightening of the credit market meant that sales of consumer goods dropped, and businesses began trying to reduce their losses by laying off workers. The rising unemployment further reduced consumer confidence and the demand for goods. The recession of 2008 can be described as the biggest downturn in the U.S. economy since the Great Depression. Some economists have predicted a long period of deflation, where prices, wage investment, and credit continue to decline and unemployment rates rise into double digits.[79] The Congressional Budget Office estimates that the current recession, which began in December 2007, will last until mid-2009, making it the longest recession since World War II.[80]

Economic Stimulus Bill

The Obama administration introduced a major economic stimulus bill to Congress in January 2009. The idea behind the stimulus package, according to Obama, was to create or save 2 million to 3 million jobs between 2009 and 2011. Some of the money was to go to rebuilding the nation's infrastructure: bridges, roads, refurbishing public schools, and so forth. These are the measures that were directly related to job creation and clearly echoed the public works programs of the New Deal. The final bill passed by Congress on February 13, 2009, included $500 billion in spending programs and $287 in tax relief.[81] The Obama administration strategy is to substitute government demand for private sector demand (as in the New Deal); to increase oversight of financial and credit markets, especially for institutions that have received monetary transfers from the federal government; and to provide an increase in the amount of benefits for unemployed persons and economically marginalized persons. The legislation included $87 billion to states to help them with increasing Medicaid costs. Unemployment insurance benefits were extended and increased by $100 a month. Over $100 billion was targeted to public schools, universities, and child care centers to avert teacher layoffs and modernize school buildings, as well as provide new funds for Head Start, Early Head Start, and other prekindergarten programs. Food stamp appropriations were increased by $20 billion. Also included were tax cuts to low-income and middle-class families, as well as small businesses.[82]

Many conservatives objected to the spending on social programs. Direct aid to lower-income families (as in increased food stamp spending) was seen as not useful by conservatives, who demanded more tax cuts as the method to stimulate the economy. For many conservatives in Congress, the faith that tax cuts would restart the economy had survived the failed supply side economics experiments of the Bush era.[83] Liberals saw increases in unemployment insurance and food stamps as ways to stimulate demand, as well as to alleviate economic distress. They pointed out that for each dollar spent on food stamps by the federal government, $1.73 is spent by recipients, making it one of the best stimulus measures. Each dollar spent on unemployment benefits puts $1.64 back into the economy.[84]

The stimulus package represents the largest increase in spending on social programs for low-income Americans since the Great Society of Lyndon Johnson in decades, in which the War on Poverty, Medicare, and Medicaid were passed. Food stamps, expanded child care for low-income families, services for the homeless, increases in education spending for low-income students, and refundable tax credits for low-income workers all represent a sea change in federal priorities and the biggest increase in social spending since the 1960s. While spending on these social programs is temporary and designed to stimulate the economy by putting money in the hands of those most likely to spend it, thereby increasing consumer demand, some think the benefits will be hard to roll back after the 2-year package expires.[85] One area that may need additional funding is welfare. In spite of the worsening economic situation in the United States, the welfare rolls were reduced in most states in 2008, raising the question of how well the new welfare policy is meeting the needs of families during the deep recession. The federal government only pays for a limited period on welfare; any more must be paid for solely by states. By contrast the federal government pays for all the costs of food stamps, and the use of food stamps increased dramatically by 12% percent in 2008, suggesting that the need for economic assistance is there but the resources to provide the assistance are not.[86]

Conservatives also were concerned about driving up the federal deficit with the stimulus package, although it had already risen to record levels under the Bush administration. Obama inherited a deficit of $1.2 trillion, which is likely to rise to $1.5 trillion as a result of the stimulus package and other expenditures by October 1, 2009.[87] Conservatives had said little when the Bush administration drove up the budget deficit to finance the Iraq war; nor had they objected to the bailout of the financial industries under the $700 billion Troubled Assets Relief Program requested by Bush in 2008. In 2009 they complained that the deficit would increase as a result of the Obama stimulus package.[88] Ironically, the stimulus package of $787 billion was substantially less than the $2 trillion in tax cuts granted during the Bush administration.[89] On top of the economic stimulus bill, Obama announced a $75 billion antiforeclosure plan to help lenders and borrowers renegotiate loans and keep consumers from defaulting on their mortgages. The funds will come from the money set aside for the bank bailout fund.[90]

Progressive Possibilities of the Obama Administration

What can be expected of the Obama administration? The economic crisis contributed strongly to Obama's election and trumped political obstacles associated with his ethnic background. Great challenges and opportunities now face Obama, the most important of which is to accomplish what no other president has been able to do: oversee the development and adoption of a comprehensive health policy that would cover all Americans. Increased unemployment will cause more people to lose health insurance; the cost of health insurance and health care will emerge as salient issues during the first year of his administration. Obama signed an expansion of the State Children's Health Insurance Program (SCHIP), the federal state low-cost insurance program for low-income families, into law early in his administration. Congressional Democrats had struggled for 2 years to pass an expansion of the program, only to have it vetoed twice by President Bush. The bill signed by Obama preserves low-cost insurance for 7 million children and adds 4 million more children. Obama stated that this bill was a "down payment" on his commitment to provide health care coverage for every American. During his campaign he asserted that health care was a "right," indicating his strong commitment to passage of a health care policy.[91]

While some argue that the costs of a major health care policy would be prohibitive when added to the costs of the federal stimulus package, other health policy advocates have argued that a comprehensive national health insurance policy building on current programs such as SCHIP and Medicare may cost up to $15 billion the first year but would eventually save more than $1.6 trillion in national health care costs.[92] No estimates for the cost of universal coverage reach the level of the stimulus package requested by Obama and already passed by Congress of $787 billion. One way to think about the opportunities for a national health care policy during the Obama administration is to consider the fact that defining moments in the history of social policy innovation have always occurred at times of crisis.[93] The New Deal is the paradigmatic example of how a serious economic crisis allowed political leaders and the general population to think in new ways about issues they had ignored. A permanent system of social insurance provided by the Social Security Act could not have been passed in 1935 without the impetus of the Great Depression, just as the social upheavals of the 1960s were critical to the passage of Medicare and Medicaid. Many have compared the potential of the Obama presidency to Franklin Roosevelt's New Deal, when a proactive federal government in a period of severe economic crisis reshaped the economic and political landscape. Crisis makes people see things in new ways; the Obama administration could take advantage of this opportunity in several ways. Social justice demands that the federal bailout of the financial institutions be accompanied by federal commitment to the creation of social policies that seek to address injustice, including meeting the housing needs of low-income persons and those threatened by the mortgage foreclosure crisis. The most important of these policies is the creation of a national health care system to bring the United States in line with all other industrialized nations and to provide health care as a right to all Americans.

In spite of his efforts to craft a universal appeal, Obama has recognized the need for action to restore the rights of oppressed minority groups. The first bill

Obama signed was the Lilly Ledbetter Fair Pay Act, which extends the statute of limitations allowing victims of pay discrimination on the basis of gender and other grounds to seek federal relief under Title VII of the Civil Rights Act of 1964.[94] He has stated that he will ask Congress to change the "Don't Ask, Don't Tell" policy prohibiting lesbian, gay, bisexual, and transgendered persons from serving openly in the military. According to a poll in late 2008, 81% of Americans want gays and lesbians to be able to serve openly in the military.[95] Obama announced that a major push for immigration reform would take place in late 2009, with the anticipated support of two national labor unions. Progressive reform of immigration policies would inevitably lead to legalization of millions of undocumented workers, a prospect the Obama administration has indicated it will embrace.[96] On the whole, Obama has charted a new direction for a progressive agenda not dependent on identity politics. As the first African American president, he is well positioned to advance a progressive economic agenda. Obama can move the country toward a discussion of economic inequality that would put aside the older divisions pitting one ethnic group's rights over another's. In this way Obama offers a unique opportunity to unite ethnic groups behind an agenda of more progressive taxes, health care, support for public education, and affordable housing. Recent research suggests that the decline in the quality of and investment in public education over the past 30 years, especially in urban areas, has paralleled the increase in inequality and decline of economic growth in the United States.[97] The economic crisis may have the paradoxical effect of emphasizing what diverse groups necessarily share: economic pain and the need to write a new economic future for the country.

As noted above, Obama wants to reverse the tax policies of the Bush administration by raising taxes on the affluent. These tax cuts will end in 2010 automatically unless renewed (called "sunset provisions"). Bush wanted to renew these tax cuts, which would reduce federal revenue by $1.7 trillion by 2014.[98] Obama has stated he will not renew them and campaigned to end them when he took office; however, once he took office the depth of the economic recession and the need for a stimulus package postponed his tax cuts initiative, over the objections of some Democratic congressional leaders.[99] Before his election he stated that taxes on the affluent should be raised to pre-Clinton era levels and said he wanted to make the Social Security wage tax more progressive, taxing those who make over $102,000 (the current top taxable income) to pay for Social Security benefits. In these ways he ran for office as a classic redistributionist, who wants to use the federal government to redistribute income downward, as opposed to upward, as in the Bush years.[100] As president, Obama has submitted a budget that proposes further tax increases on the affluent by letting the Bush tax cuts expire in 2010 in order to help pay for his health care program and has called for stricter limits on itemization of deductions taken by affluent families.[101] Obama's $3.55 trillion budget for fiscal year 2010 redistributes income downward and spends more on social programs than on defense, a sharp change in course from the past 30 years. At the same time Obama pledged to cut the federal deficit in half by 2014.[102] Obama recognized that the economic interests of the United States were linked to those of the global economy and, along with other leaders of the Global North, pledged $1.1 trillion in funds to increase the capital reserves of the International Monetary Fund at the G20 (an expanded version of original G8, which includes countries in the Global South) meetings in London in April 2009.[103]

Using the tax system to achieve equality has been part of the progressive agenda since 1913, when the Sixteenth Amendment to the Constitution made income taxes possible. The original progressive reformers in the beginning of the 20th century included Jane Addams and Theodore Roosevelt, who believed that human action could shape a more socially just society. This idea was radical for its time as the 19th century had seen an unfettered unfurling of the market economy absent any government protections of workers or families. Progressives turned this laissez-faire approach to government involvement on its head by insisting that social policies at the state and federal level could result in a transformation in the lives of economically marginalized Americans. The Obama administration has pledged to return to this original vision of progressive reform by imposing stricter regulations on the financial markets, using the tax system to redistribute income downward, ensuring affordable health care for all Americans, and increasing access to quality education.

Obama is thus a real progressive who may be captive to the limitations of the recession and federal deficit but who is likely to seize opportunities that come his way to advance the tax, health care, energy, and education policies to which he is committed. Progressive expectations may outstrip Obama's ability to make deep social policy change of the kind he has promised. While time will tell whether the moment will be seized by Obama and his administration, for the first time in decades, social policy changes that will advance social justice are more than possible; they are likely.

DISCUSSION QUESTIONS

1. What do you see as the greatest benefits to the United States of globalization? The greatest drawbacks?

2. How does globalization affect the Global South? Are the reduction of trade barriers and other measures central to economic globalization helpful or damaging to these countries?

3. What policies should the United States adopt with respect to immigration from the Global South?

4. What policies should be adopted to stop human trafficking by the United States or by global financial bodies such as the IMF?

5. What kind of policy infrastructure should be developed by countries in the Global North to ensure a minimum standard of living in countries in the Global South hosting transnational corporations? Who should oversee and enforce these policies?

6. How did the policies of the Bush administration lead to the rise of progressivism?

7. What factors made the election of Barack Obama possible?

8. What are your expectations for the next 4 years in terms of social policy change? Which factors will encourage the adoption of social policies promoting social justice, and which may discourage them?

9. In your opinion has the United States entered a period of sustained progressive social change? Why or why not?

NOTES

1. Joseph Stiglitz, *Globalization and Its Discontents* (New York: Norton, 2003), 9.

2. James Midgley, *Social Work in a Global Context* (Thousand Oaks, CA: Sage, 1997), xi, 21.

3. Malcolm Payne and Gurid Askeland, *Globalization and International Social Work* (Hampshire, England: Ashgate Publishing, 2008), 1.

4. Payne and Askeland, *Globalization and International Social Work*, 17.

5. Payne and Askeland, *Globalization and International Social Work*, 1.

6. Stiglitz, *Globalization and Its Discontents*, 4–5.

7. Stiglitz, *Globalization and Its Discontents*, 5; William Roth, *The Assault on Social Policy* (New York: Columbia University Press, 2002), 24–26.

8. Stiglitz, *Globalization and Its Discontents*, 6–25.

9. Stiglitz, *Globalization and Its Discontents*, 67–69.

10. Stiglitz, *Globalization and Its Discontents*, 19–22.

11. Tom Bawden, "New IMF Fund for Emerging Markets," *Times Online*, October 30, 2008, http://business.timesonline.co.uk/tol/business/economics/article5043590 .ece, accessed October 30, 2008.

12. Jeff Faux, *Global Class War* (New York: Wiley, 2006), 129–139.

13. Josh Bivens, "Trade, Jobs and Wages," Economic Policy Institute, May 6, 2008, http://www.epi.org/content.cfm/ib244, accessed November 12, 2008.

14. Roth, *The Assault on Social Policy*, 29; Elizabeth Auster, "Business: Corporate Tax Breaks," *The Plain Dealer*, October 29, 2008, http://blogs.cleveland.com/business/ 2008/10.html, accessed November 12, 2008.

15. Ryan Donmoyer, "Democrats Consider Rolling Back Overseas Tax Breaks for Major U.S. Corporations," *Bloomberg News,* February 17, 2007, http://www.iht.com/articles/2007/02/12/bloomberg/bxtax.php accessed November 12, 2008.

16. Jessica Maxwell, "Corporate Globalization," Peace Council, http://www.peacecouncil.net/pnl/03/723/Globalization.htm, accessed November 11, 2008.

17. Susan Mapp, *Human Rights and Social Justice in a Global Perspective* (New York: Oxford University Press, 2008), 14.

18. Paul Krugman, "The Widening Gyre," *The New York Times,* Monday, October 27, 2008, A23.

19. Lynne Healy, *International Social Work* (New York: Oxford University Press, 2001), 143.

20. Healy, *International Social Work,* 138.

21. Jaroslaw Anders, "United States Is Largest Donor of Foreign Aid," America.gov, May 24, 2007, http://www.america.gov/st/washfile-english/2007/May/20070524165115zjsredna0.2997553.html, accessed November 16, 2008.

22. Nicola Yeates, "Globalization and Social Policy: From Global Neoliberal Hegemony to Global Political Pluralism," *Global Social Policy* 2 (1, 2002): 70.

23. Yeates, "Globalization and Social Policy," 69–89.

24. Roth, *The Assault on Social Policy,* 23–45; Ellen Meiksins Wood, "Modernity, Postmodernity or Capitalism?" *Review of International Political Economy* 4 (3, 1997): 539–560.

25. Yeates, "Globalization and Social Policy," 79.

26. Quoted in Yeates, "Globalization and Social Policy," 81.

27. Stiglitz, *Globalization and Its Discontents,* 245–246; Avert, "HIV and AIDS in Africa," http://www.avert.org/aafrica.htm, accessed November 8, 2008.

28. Stiglitz, *Globalization and Its Discontents,* 233–236.

29. Roth, *The Assault on Social Policy,* 24–27.

30. Yeates, "Globalization and Social Policy," 72–74; Roth, *The Assault on Social Policy,* 33–34.

31. Payne and Askeland, *Globalization and International Social Work,* 12.

32. Stiglitz, *Globalization and Its Discontents,* 5–9; Yeates, "Globalization and Social Policy," 72.

33. Payne and Askeland, *Globalization and International Social Work,* 11–15; Yeates, "Globalization and Social Policy," 73–74.

34. Stiglitz, *Globalization and Its Discontents,* 244–250.

35. Stiglitz, *Globalization and Its Discontents,* 240.

36. The World Bank, "World Development Report 2006: Equity and Development," http://go.worldbank.org/UWYLBR43C0, accessed November 18, 2008.

37. Quoted in Faux, *Global Class War,* 37.

38. Faux, *Global Class War,* 143.

39. Roger Bybee and Carolyn Winter, "Immigration Flood Unleashed by NAFTA's Disastrous Impact on the Mexican Economy," Common Dreams.org, April 25, 2006, http://www.commondreams.org/views06/0425–30.htm, accessed November 15, 2008.

40. Faux, *Global Class War,* 142.

41. Quoted in Mapp, *Human Rights and Social Justice in a Global Perspective,* 29.

42. Kevin Bales, *Disposable People: New Slavery in the Global Economy* (Los Angeles: University of California Press, 2004), 5.

43. Mapp, *Human Rights and Social Justice in a Global Perspective,* 32.

44. David Hodge, "Sexual Trafficking in the United States: A Domestic Problem With Transnational Dimensions," *Social Work* 53 (2, 2008): 143–151.

45. Mapp, *Human Rights and Social Justice in a Global Perspective,* 18.

46. National Association of Social Workers, *Code of Ethics* (Washington, DC: Author, 2006).

47. Congressional Research Service, "The Cost of Iraq, Afghanistan, and Other Global War on Terror Operations Since 9/11," http://assets.opencrs.com/rpts/RL33110_20060614.pdf, accessed October 15, 2008.

48. U.S. Department of Homeland Security, "About the Department," http://www.dhs.gov/index.shtm, accessed February 7, 2009.

49. U.S. Department of Homeland Security, "Immigration Enforcement Actions: 2007," December 2008, http://www.dhs.gov/xlibrary/assets/statistics/publications/enforcement_ar_07.pdf, accessed February 7, 2009.

50. U.S. Department of Homeland Security, "DHS Moves Forward on Border Fencing and Technology Improvements," December 7, 2007, http://www.dhs.gov/xnews/releases/pr_1197058374853.shtm, accessed February 7, 2009.

51. Stephanie Simon, "Border Fence Project Hits a Snag," *Wall Street Journal,* February 4, 2009, http://online.wsj.com/article/SB123370523066745559.html?mod=googlenews_wsj, accessed February 7, 2009.

52. U.S. Congress, "H.R. 3162" (The USA PATRIOT Act), October 24, 2001, http://epic.org/privacy/terrorism/hr3162.html, accessed February 7, 2009.

53. American Civil Liberties Union, "Safe and Free: USA PATRIOT Act," November 14, 2003, http://www.aclu.org/safefree/resources/17343res20031114.html, accessed February 7, 2009.

54. CNN.com, "House Approves PATRIOT Act Renewal," March 7, 2006, http://www.cnn.com/2006/POLITICS/03/07/patriot.act/, accessed February 7, 2009.

55. American Bar Association, "Resolution on the PATRIOT Act," February 10, 2003, http://epic.org/privacy/terrorism/fisa/aba_res_021003.html, accessed February 7, 2009.

56. Quoted in Ronald Brownstein, "Gore Urges Repeal of PATRIOT Act," *Los Angeles Times,* November 10, 2003, http://www.commondreams.org/headlines03/1110–01.htm, accessed February 7, 2009.

57. Patrice Le Clerc and Kenneth Gould, "The U.S. PATRIOT Act and the Future of Social Movements," Paper Presented at the Annual Meeting of the American Sociological Association, Montreal, Quebec, Canada, August 11, 2006, http://www.allacademic.com/meta/p_mla_apa_research_citation/0/9/5/8/1/p95818_index.html, accessed February 7, 2009.

58. U.S. Congress, "P.L. 107–110" (No Child Left Behind Act of 2001), http://www.ed.gov/policy/elsec/leg/esea02/index.html, accessed February 8, 2009.

59. Eddy Ramirez and Kim Clark, "What Arne Duncan Thinks of No Child Left Behind," *U.S. News and World Report,* February 8, 2009, http://www.usnews.com/articles/education/2009/02/05/what-arne-duncan-thinks-of-no-child-left-behind.html, accessed February 8, 2009.

60. U.S. Department of Education, "Questions and Answers on No Child Left Behind," September 9, 2003, http://www.ed.gov/nclb/methods/whatworks/doing.html, accessed February 8, 2009.

61. Stephen Metcalf, "Reading Between the Lines," *The Nation,* January 10, 2002, http://www.thenation.com/doc/20020128/metcalf, accessed February 8, 2009.

62. Center for Evaluation and Education Policy, Indiana University, "Report: No Child Left Behind Is Out of Step With Special Education," November 15, 2006, http://newsinfo.iu.edu/news/page/normal/4379.html, accessed February 8, 2009.

63. Linda Darling-Hammond, "Evaluating 'No Child Left Behind,'" *The Nation*, May 21, 2007, http://www.thenation.com/doc/20070521/darling-hammond, accessed February 8, 2009.

64. David Hursh, "Exacerbating Inequality: The Failed Promise of NCLB," *Race, Ethnicity and Education* 10 (September 2007): 295–308

65. Martin Wolk, "How Hurricane Katrina's Costs Are Adding Up," MSNBC, September 13, 2005, http://www.msnbc.msn.com/id/9329293/, accessed February 8, 2009.

66. U.S. Government Accountability Office, "Hurricane Katrina: Ineffective FEMA Oversight of Housing Maintenance Contracts in Mississippi Resulted in Millions of Dollars of Waste and Potential Fraud," November 2007, http://www.gao.gov/new.items/d08106.pdf, accessed February 8, 2009.

67. Ibid.

68. David Dante Troutt, ed., *After the Storm: Black Intellectuals Explore the Meaning of Katrina* (New York: New Press, 2006).

69. Lisa Trei, "Katrina Did Not Raise Awareness of Poverty, Study Finds," *Stanford News Service*, March 8, 2006, http://news-service.stanford.edu/news/2006/march8/katrina-030806.html, accessed February 8, 2009.

70. Pew Charitable Trusts, "Public Attitudes Toward the War in Iraq: 2003–2008," March 19, 2008, http://www.pewtrusts.org/our_work_report_detail.aspx?id=36716, accessed February 13, 2009.

71. Rasmussen Reports, "Iraq Troop Withdrawal," August 5, 2008, http://www.rasmussenreports.com/public_content/politics/current_events/the_war_in_iraq/iraq_troop_withdrawal, accessed February 13, 2009.

72. Stiglitz, *Globalization and Its Discontents*, 84–85.

73. Hua Hsu, "The End of White America?" *Atlantic Monthly* 303 (January/February 2009): 46–56.

74. Marc Ambinder, "Race Over?" *The Atlantic* 303 (January/February, 2009): 62–66.

75. Lynn Sweet, "Obama Team Stimulus Sell: Bully Pulpit, Social Networking, Phone Banks," *Chicago Sun Times*, February 9, 2009, http://blogs.suntimes.com/sweet/2009/02/obama_team_stimulus_sell_bully.html, accessed February 14, 2009.

76. Charles Noble, *The Collapse of Liberalism* (Lanham, MD: Rowman, 2004), 170.

77. Edmund Andrews, "With Grim Job Loss Figures, No Sign That the Worst Is Over," *New York Times*, Saturday, February 7, 2009, B1.

78. Bureau of Labor Statistics, "Employment Situation Summary," February 6, 2009, http://www.bls.gov/news.release/empsit.nr0.htm, accessed February 6, 2009.

79. Paul Krugman, "On the Edge," *New York Times*, February 6, 2009, A23.

80. Congressional Budget Office, Monthly Budget Review, Fiscal Year 2009, http://www.cbo.gov/ftpdocs/100xx/doc10069/04–2009-MBR.pdf, accessed February 7, 2009; Congressional Budget Office, "The Budget and Economic Outlook: Fiscal Years 2009–2019," January 2009, http://www.cbo.gov/doc.cfm?index=9957, accessed April 15, 2009.

81. David Herszenhorn and Carl Hulse, "House and Senate in Deal for $787 Billion Stimulus," *New York Times*, February 12, 2009, A1.

82. Robert Pear, "More Money for Medicaid and the Jobless," *New York Times,* February 14, 2009, A11; Jason DeParle, "For the Needy, a Variety of Help," *New York Times,* February 14, 2009, A11; Sam Dillon, "Schools Get Large Infusion of Money," *New York Times,* February 14, 2009, A11.

83. Herszenhorn and Hulse, "House and Senate in Deal for $787 Stimulus," A1.

84. Mark Zandi, "Moody's Economy," Testimony before the House Committee on Small Business, July 24, 2008, http://www.economy.com/mark-zandi/documents/Small%20Business_7_24_08.pdf, accessed February 15, 2009.

85. Michael Fletcher, "For Social Programs, Long Awaited Boost," *Washington Post,* February 16, 2009, A02.

86. Jason DeParle, "Welfare System Failing to Grow as Economy Lags," *New York Times,* February 2, 2009, A1.

87. Jackie Calmes, "Obama Planning to Slash Deficit, Despite Stimulus," *New York Times,* February 22, 2009, A1.

88. David Sanger, "Reinvention or Recovery?" *New York Times,* February 1, 2009, A1.

89. Paul Krugman, "Failure to Rise," *New York Times,* February 13, 2009, A25.

90. "Mr. Obama's Foreclosure Plan," *The New York Times,* February 19, 2009, A22.

91. Kevin Freking, "Obama Views SCHIP as First Step to Covering 'Every Single American,'" February 5, 2009, http://www.cnsnews.com/public/Content/Article.aspx?rsrcid=43068, accessed February 15, 2009; Jason Linkins, "Obama: Health Care Should Be a Right" (Video), *The Huffington Post,* October 7, 2008, http://www.huffingtonpost.com/2008/10/07/obama-health-care-should_n_132831.html, accessed February 16, 2009.

92. The Commonwealth Fund, "New Plan Would Provide Health Insurance for Almost All Americans," May 2008, http://www.commonwealthfund.org/newsroom/newsroom_show.htm?doc_id=684844, accessed February 6, 2009.

93. David Sanger, "Reinvention or Recovery?" A1.

94. "Obama Signs Lilly Ledbetter Act," *Washington Post.com,* January 29, 2009, http://voices.washingtonpost.com/44/2009/01/29/obama_signs_lilly_ledbetter_ac.html, accessed February 15, 2009.

95. CNN.com, "Obama Aide: Ending 'Don't Ask, Don't Tell' Must Wait," January 15, 2009, http://www.cnn.com/2009/POLITICS/01/14/obama.gays.military/, accessed February 16, 2009.

96. "Immigration Reform and Hard Times," *New York Times,* April 14, 2009, A20.

97. Claudia Goldin and Lawrence Katz, *The Race Between Education and Technology* (Cambridge, MA: Harvard University Press, 2008), 1–11.

98. Matthew Hall and Peter Orszag, "Key Points on Making the Bush Tax Cuts Permanent," Brookings Institute, January 21, 2004, http://www.brookings.edu/opinions/2004/0121useconomics_gale.aspx, accessed February 15, 2009.

99. "Pelosi Parts With Obama Over Bush Tax Cuts," *The Huffington Post,* January 8, 2009, http://www.huffingtonpost.com/2009/01/08/pelosi-parts-with-obama-o_n_156260.html, accessed February 15, 2009.

100. David Leonhardt, "A Free Market-Loving, Big Spending, Fiscally Conservative, Wealth Redistributionist," *New York Times Magazine,* August 24, 2008, 28–52.

101. Jackie Calmes and Robert Pear, "Obama to Call for Higher Tax on Top Earners," *New York Times,* February 26, 2009, A1.

102. Janet Hook, "It's the End of an Era," *Los Angeles Times,* February 27, 2009, A1; Office of Management and Budget, "Budget of the United States Government, Fiscal Year 2010," http://www.whitehouse.gov/omb/budget/, accessed April 17, 2009.

103. Helene Cooper, "Obama Ties US to the World," *New York Times,* April 3, 2009, A1.

Index

About the Author

Jillian (Mary Ann) Jimenez has a PhD in American history and a PhD in social policy, both from Brandeis University. She received her MA in literature from the University of California–Los Angeles (UCLA) and an MSW from San Diego State University. Dr. Jimenez taught American history for 8 years at Pitzer College in Claremont, California, and the UCLA School of Public Affairs, Department of Social Welfare, before coming to California State University–Long Beach, Department of Social Work, where she is currently a professor. She teaches social policy and research in the MSW program. She is also the editor of *Reflections,* a peer-reviewed journal of narratives. She has won numerous awards, including a Graves fellowship for teaching excellence and a Silberman grant for her research on the history of African American grandmothers. Her first book, *Changing Faces of Madness,* explored treatment of the mentally disordered in the colonial period. Dr. Jimenez has published widely on the intersection of history and policy in the areas of mental health, child welfare policy, HIV and AIDS, and welfare policy. She lives and works with her husband, Dan Jimenez, PhD, who also teaches social work at California State University–Long Beach.

Supporting researchers for more than 40 years

Research methods have always been at the core of SAGE's publishing program. Founder Sara Miller McCune published SAGE's first methods book, *Public Policy Evaluation*, in 1970. Soon after, she launched the *Quantitative Applications in the Social Sciences* series—affectionately known as the "little green books."

Always at the forefront of developing and supporting new approaches in methods, SAGE published early groundbreaking texts and journals in the fields of qualitative methods and evaluation.

Today, more than 40 years and two million little green books later, SAGE continues to push the boundaries with a growing list of more than 1,200 research methods books, journals, and reference works across the social, behavioral, and health sciences. Its imprints—Pine Forge Press, home of innovative textbooks in sociology, and Corwin, publisher of PreK–12 resources for teachers and administrators—broaden SAGE's range of offerings in methods. SAGE further extended its impact in 2008 when it acquired CQ Press and its best-selling and highly respected political science research methods list.

From qualitative, quantitative, and mixed methods to evaluation, SAGE is the essential resource for academics and practitioners looking for the latest methods by leading scholars.

For more information, visit **www.sagepub.com**.